BEYOND INTELLECTUAL SEXISM
A NEW WOMAN, A NEW REALITY

Joan I. Roberts

Editor

DAVID McKAY COMPANY, INC.
New York

This book is dedicated to

Annette Harrison
Born July 31, 1941   Died January 22, 1972

Joyce Telzrow
Born September 27, 1943   Died January 13, 1974

and to those who continue their work

Mary Jo Buggs and the feminist faculty of the Wisconsin
Coordinating Council of Women in Higher Education.

Beyond Intellectual Sexism
A New Woman, A New Reality

COPYRIGHT © 1976 by

Joan I. Roberts

Design by Gloria Gentile

MANUFACTURED IN THE UNITED STATES OF AMERICA

Library of Congress Cataloging in Publication Data

Main entry under title:

Beyond intellectual sexism.

1. Women's studies—United States—Addresses, essays, lectures. 2. Feminism—Addresses, essays, lectures. I. Roberts, Joan I. II. Title.
HQ1181.U5B48   301.41'2'0973   76-4905
ISBN 0-679-50631-4   0-679-30292-1 paper

Contributors

Ruth H. Bleier, associate professor, University of Wisconsin, received her M.D. from Medical College of Pennsylvania, practiced medicine for eight years, and, after postdoctoral study, assumed a faculty position as an experimental neuroanatomist at Johns Hopkins University, School of Medicine. A specialist in brain research, she has published a cytoarchitectonic atlas, *The Hypothalamus of the Cat,* and numerous articles on the structure and functioning of the hypothalamus, such as cellular degeneration of nuclei following decortication. As a founder and co-chairwoman of the Association of Faculty Women at the University of Wisconsin, she has participated in numerous workshops and conferences on biological aspects and needs of women and has filed formal complaints on noncompliance to affirmative action and on inequities in women's sports and physical education. She is a member of the American Association of Anatomists, Society for Neuroscience, and American Women in Science.

Rae Lesser Blumberg, acting associate professor, University of California, San Diego; previously at the University of Wisconsin; received her doctorate in sociology from Northwestern University. Widely traveled, she has conducted research in Australia, Israel, and South America where she lived in Bolivia and Venezuela. In Venezuela, she served as resident research adviser to the Ministries of Education and of Health and Social Welfare. She has written a forthcoming book, *Stratification: Socioeconomic and Sexual Inequality,* and numerous articles. Most recently, these have stemmed from her research on a 1973–74 Ford Foundation Faculty Fellowship on the Role of Women in Society, and include a general cross-cultural paradigm of sexual stratification, theory-testing research on political-economic preconditions for mother-child families, and work on the interrelationship of economic factors, female status, and fertility. In other publications, she has co-authored articles on societal complexity and familial complexity in the *American Journal of Sociology,* ethnicity and extended families in the *American Sociological Review,* and has written on education, urban ecology, and political economy in developing countries. Currently, she is working on a book detailing her theory-testing research (utilizing a 61-society pilot sample) on women's relative economic power as a primary determinant of their status and life options vis-à-vis men.

iii

Germaine Brée, Kenan Professor, Wake Forest University, and Professor Emeritus and Vilas Professor, Institute for Research in the Humanities, and French Department, University of Wisconsin, received her degree from the University of Paris. Previously at Bryn Mawr College from 1936 to 1953, with the exception of two years when she served in the French Army, she then chaired the Department of Slavic and Romance Languages, New York University. Recipient of sixteen honorary degrees, awarded the Chevalier of the Legion of Honor, the Bronze Star Medal, she also has been a Fulbright Professor to Australia and England. Author of over fifty articles, she has published two books on Proust including *The World of Marcel Proust,* one on Gide, two on Camus, another, *Camus and Sartre: Crisis and Commitment, An Age of Fiction: The French Novel from Gide to Camus,* and one entitled *Women Writers in France.* On the Executive Committee of the Modern Language Association as president, she is currently writing a book on the history of French literature from 1920 to 1970.

Julia M. Brown, associate professor, University of Wisconsin, received her Ph.D. from the University of Southern California, subsequently teaching on the faculty there and at Mt. Holyoke, Wellesley, and Douglass colleges. Active in several professional organizations, she has served in various capacities to promote sports programs, particularly for women, on both the local and national levels. She has served on the national basketball committee, on several boards of women officials, and is currently on the U.S. Olympic Committee for Canoeing and Kayaking. She has published extensively on sports medicine, fundamentals of movement, recreational games, skiing, camper-counselor relations, and has developed instructional television programs in physical education. As a proponent of women's rights, she drafted the Association of Faculty Women's Guidelines for Affirmative Action on Physical Education and Athletics, chaired the Equity Action Committee, and served on the Committee on Women's Athletic Programs and Facilities.

Laura J. Burger, research director, Research Coordinating Unit, University of Minnesota, received her Ph.D. in home economics education from the University of Wisconsin where she held research assistantships in home economics. A specialist in research education and development, she has published technical reports, presented papers, and written guides and handbooks for teachers of vocational-technical subjects.

Ingrid Camerini, instructor for fifteen years at the University of Wisconsin, received her advanced degree from the University of Stockholm, Sweden, where she specialized in Scandinavian Studies. Active in the Modern Language Association and in the Society for the Advancement of Scandinavian Studies, she has published reviews on Swedish women writers and writes and lectures on topics pertaining to this subject. She is currently conducting research on an early Swedish woman novelist and is teaching a course she has originated on women in Scandinavia. As a member of the steering committee of the Association of Faculty Women, she has been consistently involved in the many actions of that organization.

Kathryn F. Clarenbach, associate professor, University of Wisconsin Extension, received her doctorate from the University of Wisconsin in political science. An early and outspoken advocate of women's rights, she chairs the Women's Education Resources Department, the Governor's Commission on the Status of Women, and sits on the National Advisory Board, National Organization for Women. Her pioneering work includes being a founder and first chairwoman of the National Organization for Women, first president of the Interstate Association of Commissions on the Status of Women, chairwoman of the national organizing conference of the National Women's Political Caucus, and convener and officer of the Association of Faculty Women. Recipient of several awards, she is listed in *Who's Who of American Women* and *Two Thousand Women of Achievement.* Her numerous publications include the *Handbook for Commissions on the Status of Women* and recent articles on sex stereotyping in the public schools, women and careers, women and law, women and athletics. Typical of her heavy lecture schedule are addresses to the National Council of Canadian Women and the National Association of Governing Boards of Higher Education.

Elizabeth Fennema, assistant professor, University of Wisconsin, received her Ph.D. in curriculum and instruction from the University of Wisconsin. Specializing in mathematics education and curriculum theory, she has taught at all levels of education, consulted with various public school systems, produced modules for teacher training in mathematics education, and published on mental imagery and the reading process, symbolic and concrete models in learning mathematical principles, and sex differences in the learning of mathematics. Research in progress with Julia Sherman focuses on mathematics learning, sex, and spatial visualization. As a member of the American Educational Research Association, she helped organize the Women's Caucus and a special interest group, Research on Women in Education. She has served as faculty adviser to Pi Lambda Theta, a national honorary society for women in education, and is active on the Equity Action Commitee and in the Women's Studies Program.

Bonnie Cook Freeman, assistant professor, University of Texas, Austin, recently received her Ph.D. in social sciences and education from the University of Wisconsin where she was awarded the Shaw and the Ford Foundation fellowships, the National Science Foundation Traineeship, and the Outstanding Teaching Assistant Award. Her dissertation on the political consciousness of academic women will be published in the near future. She has contributed to a volume on the rights of children and is currently conducting research on the political life of faculty women and on sex-role innovation with Joan Roberts. At Wisconsin, she was a founding member of the Women's Coalition and the Graduate Women's Caucus. At Texas, she teaches a new course on sexism and racism, is actively engaged in the development of women's studies, and is a member of the women's faculty organization. She is a member of the American Political Science Association.

Kay Ann Johnson, instructor, University of California, San Diego, is a Ph.D. candidate in political science at the University of Wisconsin where she received NDFL and Ford Foundation fellowships. Widely traveled in the Orient, she has lived in Hong Kong. She has presented papers, given lectures and speeches on China and Chinese women, appearing on television and radio on these topics. A member of the committee of Concerned Asian Scholars, the American Political Science Association, and the Women's Coalition, she is developing women's studies and continuing her research on Chinese women and Chinese foreign policy.

G. Kass-Simon, assistant professor, University of Rhode Island, and previously a project associate of the University of Wisconsin, received her Ph.D. from the University of Zurich, Switzerland, following an M.A. in English from Columbia University. Specializing in the neurobiology of simple organisms, her publications in articles and abstracts report research findings on such topics as the primitive coordinating mechanisms, electrical transmission and problems of regeneration in Hydra. A member of Sigma Xi, American Association of Zoologists, and American Women in Science, she was a member of the steering committee of the Association of Faculty Women, leading the development of an affirmative action program. Active with the Women's Caucus at the University of Rhode Island, she continues her strong commitment to changing the status of women.

Diane F. Kravetz, assistant professor, University of Wisconsin, received her doctorate in social work and social psychology from the University of Michigan. Co-author of *Contracts in Group,* she also has published articles on heart rate as a minimal cue for the occurrence of vicarious classical conditioning. More recently, her publications focus on sex-role stereotyping and social work education, sex-role concepts of women, and consciousness-raising groups, and she is presently involved in a nationwide survey of women's consciousness-raising groups. Also, she has participated on panels and in workshops concerning sexism in social work and in psychotherapy. A member of the Association of Faculty Women, she is actively involved in women's studies and teaches a course on sexism and social work practice. She was a member of the Chancellor's Committee on Women's Studies and is on the faculty of the Women's Studies Program at the university.

Karen Merritt, Academic Planner in Arts and Humanities, University of Wisconsin Central Administration, received her Ph.D. in English, specializing in medieval literature at Harvard University. A Phi Beta Kappa and Woodrow Wilson fellow, she held a professorial position at Occidental College before coming to Wisconsin. She has also held the position of Acting Associate Dean of the School of Fine Arts at Milwaukee. A member of the Modern Language Association and the Medieval Academy of America, she is also on the steering committee of the Association of Faculty Women and has been active in the Wisconsin Coordinating Council of Women in Higher Education.

Victoria Junco Meyer, instructor for fifteen years in Spanish language and literature, received her advanced degree in philosophy from the University of Mexico, Mexico City. After teaching in Mexico, she joined the faculty at Vassar College. Her latest publication is a book, *Gamarra ó el Eclecticismo en Méjico.* A member of Sociedad de Geografía y Estadística, Associación de Universitarias Mejicanas, Unión Feminina Ibero-Americana in Mexico, she is also a member of the steering committee of the Association of Faculty Women. As a courageous proponent of women's rights, she has been particularly concerned with discrimination in employment.

Elizabeth A. Monts, chairwoman, Department of Home Economics Education, Arizona State University, previously chairwoman of home economics education, University of Wisconsin, received her Ph.D. at Texas Woman's University. After teaching at the secondary level, she specialized in curriculum, supervision, and evaluation, producing technical surveys and several articles on applied problems and administration of home economics education. Extensively involved in consultation in community colleges and school systems, she is a member of Omicron Nu, the American Home Economics Association, and the Association of Supervision and Curriculum. Actively working to change women's status both in and out of her discipline, she has co-chaired the Association of Faculty Women at Wisconsin, is now an officer of the Faculty Women's Association at Arizona and a founder and vice president, Women in Higher Education in Arizona, a statewide coalition of women faculty. Listed in *Who's Who in the World of Women.*

Jane Allyn Piliavin, professor, School of Family Resources and Consumer Sciences University of Wisconsin, received her doctorate in social psychology from Stanford University. Previously at the University of California at Berkeley, Mills College, and the University of Pennsylvania, she is a Phi Beta Kappa, a Fellow of the American Psychological Association, a member of the Society for Experimental Social Psychology, and the Association of Women in Psychology. Co-author of *Adolescent Prejudice,* and of several articles in periodicals such as the *Journal of Personality and Social Psychology,* she has examined communication, dissonance, and equity theories. She has been involved in research on sex-role interaction in small groups: "playing dumb" and "stroking," the dynamics of "playing hard to get," the effect of the psychologically absent father, and the role of the supportive significant male in female career aspirations. Teaching a course on sex roles and society, she is presently involved in women's studies.

Annis V. Pratt, associate professor, University of Wisconsin, received her Ph.D. in English literature at Columbia University where she was a President's Fellow and a member of Phi Beta Kappa. Previously at Emory University, she has authored *Dylan Thomas' Early Prose: A Study in Creative Mythology,* co-edited *Doris Lessing: Critical Studies,* and written two books of poetry, *The Elements* and *Transparent Woman.* A prolific writer and poet, her fiction and poetry is published in major literary reviews and her scholarly articles in various academic journals. Researching three hundred years of women writers, her findings will appear in two forthcoming volumes, *Feminism and Fiction* and *Feminism and Poetry.* An outspoken women's rights advocate, she was convener and first chairwoman, Atlanta chapter of the National Organization for Women. A member of the Modern Language Association, she recently chaired a forum on the new feminist criticisms. A measure of her commitment to women's studies is her teaching load of four courses on women and literature.

Hania W. Ris, M.D., associate clinical professor of pediatrics at the University of Wisconsin, Center for Health Sciences and Medical Director, Wisconsin School for Girls, Department of Health and Social Services, received her M.D. degree from the University of Zurich, Switzerland. She was previously on the faculty of the medical schools of Johns Hopkins, Cornell University, and University of Cincinnati. Specializing in adolescent medicine, she is conducting research in venereal disease, particularly as it affects teen-age girls; presenting papers on venereal disease, sex education, birth control, and abortion within the United States and abroad. She has published articles on venereal disease, quality care for institutionalized youth, minors' consent for health care, women's rights. Dr. Ris recently returned from a journey through the People's Republic of China and has published a number of articles on medical care, social institutions, and women in China. Fellow, American Academy of Pediatrics; member, Society for Adolescent Medicine; member, Ambulatory Pediatric Association; pediatric consultant to Head Start program; member of the Governor's Health Planning Council in Wisconsin; delegate to Task Force on Legal Rights and Justice, White House Conference on Youth. She recently received the Zero Population Growth Humanitarian Award for contributions to social and medical reform in the field of health care and for advocacy of birth control and other health care measures that will improve the quality of life. A member of the Association of Faculty Women, she is an indefatigable proponent of women's rights.

Joan I. Roberts, previously assistant professor, University of Wisconsin, received her doctorate in social psychology from T.C., Columbia University, where she was a President's Scholar. Previously at Hunter College and Makerere College, East Africa, she has edited *School Children in the Urban Slum: Readings in Social Science Research*; co-edited *Educational Patterns and Cultural Configurations* and *Schooling in the Cultural Context*; and is the author of *Scene of the Battle: Group Behavior in Urban Classrooms* and a forthcoming volume, *The Ethos of Learning.* Specializing in racial, ethnic, and cultural influences on individuals and groups, her articles now focus on women's culture, racism and sexism, women's studies, and institutional noncompliance to affirmative action, and her research is on sex-role innovation. A member of the Associations of Psychology, Anthropology, and Sociology, she is a founder and first co-chairwoman of the Association of Faculty Women, a founder and first coordinator of the Wisconsin Coordinating Council of Women in Higher Education, originator of women's studies courses and conferences. Listed in *Who's Who in American Education, Leaders in Education, Who's Who of American Women, World Who's Who of Women*; she is currently unemployed, fighting a negative tenure ruling.

Ann Seidman, associate professor, University of Massachusetts; director, research project on occupational segregation of women, Wellesley College, Research Center on Women, received her Ph.D. in economics at the University of Wisconsin where she was subsequently on the faculty. A Phi Beta Kappa, she is author of *An Economics Textbook for Africa, Comparative Development Strategies in East Africa, Ghana's Development Experience, 1951–1965,* co-author of *Unity or Poverty? Economics of Pan-Africanism,* editor of *National Resources and National Welfare: The Case of Copper.* She has published numerous articles on African economic development in scholarly periodicals such as the *Journal of African Studies Review.* On the Board of Directors, African Studies Association; member of the American Economic Association; previously co-chairwoman, employment committee, Association of Faculty Women; active as a local board member, League of Women Voters; she has spoken widely on the economic status of women in America and Africa.

Julia A. Sherman, lecturer, University of Wisconsin Extension; associate scientist, Wisconsin Psychiatric Institute; consultant, Wisconsin Department of Mental Hygiene, received her Ph.D. in clinical psychology from the State University of Iowa. Listed in *American Men* (sic) *of Science* at the age of twenty-six, she is a member of Phi Beta Kappa; Diplomate, American Board of Examiners in Professional Psychology; member, American Psychological Association, American Women in Psychology. An experienced clinician, she has practiced in various clinical settings such as the Minneapolis Institute of Psychiatry and Neurology. She has published *On the Psychology of Women: A Survey of Empirical Studies* and several articles such as "Field Articulation, Sex, Spatial Visualization, Dependency, Practice, Laterality of the Brain and Birth Order," and in *Psychological Review,* "Problems of Sex Differences in Space Perception and Aspects of Intellectual Functioning." Currently researching space perception and mathematical reasoning, she is a founder of the Women's Research Institute of Wisconsin. A member of the Association of Faculty Women, she teaches a course on the psychology of women.

Preface

To the women who contributed their thinking to this book, I offer my gratitude. And to the hundreds of feminist women with whom I have worked during the last decade, I give credit for establishing the conditions that make this volume possible. With little encouragement, women across the nation have resolutely pressured for institutional and societal change. It is these women who have done the work that organizational administrators should have done. Out of a sisterhood of courage, they have forced American institutions to show the first signs of minimal compliance to laws that are supposed to "guarantee" equal status for every female person. With little initial economic support or academic approval, women at the University of Wisconsin and at other institutions have developed a new discipline, women's studies, which has only belatedly received even token recognition. Experiencing difficult changes in their personal lives, they have nevertheless confronted male-controlled institutions, some risking careers for the hope of a new dignity for girls and women.

The women scholars whose achievements are described in the list of contributors may seem to invalidate the conclusion in *The Academic Marketplace* that women scholars cannot look forward to normal professional careers. However, a redefinition of the successful, of the "elite" woman is needed. The costs of "making it" in a "man's world" are not enumerated in the usual descriptions of academic women. Therefore, let me recount the costs born by some of the "elite" women in the academic world. The case histories of these Ph.D. women are typical of many others I have known whose experiences would fill an anthology of horror stories:

—Twenty years as a peripheral member of her department, finally promoted to an assistant professor.

—Earned two Ph.D.s relevant to field, praised by students, tenure denied.

—Published five books during year, merit pay denied since only "scholarly articles" were being considered that year.

—Job application rejected; one reason discovered: ethnicity of family member.

—Doctorate in social science, recently received professorship after fifteen years in nonprofessorial position.

—Her "woman's" program denied equal funding, making it impossible for her to offer proper instruction in her specialization.

—New Ph.D. in French, not reappointed, male member with M.A. retained; now working on M.S. in Library Science.

—Denied tenure, terminated one week before receiving Ph.D.; five others in her department did not even have M.A.s; only chairman had Ph.D.

—Accepted a part-time, nontenured position in order to have time for children, later offered a nonprofessorial position with tenure and no chance for promotion if she would not "push" for position she deserved.

—Laboratory research endeavors not given due credit for publication record, was refused professorial appointment.

—In department where there was no female Ph.D. candidate for past ten years, she passed two parts of preliminary doctoral exam, termed "deficient" in third, retook all three parts twice more, was accepted by woman faculty member in another department, passed fourth exam, completed degree, accepted position in a leading institution.

—At time of death, an assistant professor emeritus.

Such are the careers of "elite" women in academe.

In this book, academic women analyze the scholarly work in their own disciplines, documenting the distortions and omissions which foster an "intellectual" rationalization of female inferiority and sex discrimination. As a collective effort, it is a survey of knowledge, not a set of theoretical discourses on limited topics. In my chapter on the ramifications of the study of women, the genesis of the volume, the implications of women's studies, and an orienting framework are provided. At the request of my editor at David McKay, I include a personal synthesis of the pictures of power and powerlessness to which I reacted in the chapters of others. When referring to specific facts from their work, I have stayed as close to their own words as possible and, without literary redundancy, attributed these facts to them. However, through the processes of selection and interpretation, I have reworked their ideas into my own conception of cultural and political alternatives. Therefore, the synthesis, written in a style distinctively different from the remainder of the book, is totally my own responsibility. It cannot and should not be read to obtain a simple summary of facts in the works of others.

Some of the contributors will not entirely agree with the theoretical frameworks I have developed or with specific implications I have derived from their own work. Each woman in this book is at a different level of consciousness of the female predicament. Each is at a different point in her history of intellectual inquiry about women. In some instances, I as the editor do not feel that the presentations and interpretations fully reflect my own position. But a collective effort should represent the full diversity of women's thinking. It should not be tailor-made to fit the needs of the editor.

This book is the most time-consuming effort of my scholarly career since it represents five years of laborious work that started with the involvement of scholars, most of whom had not previously applied their training to the study of women, moved at a hectic pace through their involvement in my women's studies course, and concluded with their published efforts in the new field of women's studies. To trace the genesis and development of this volume is to trace the growing consciousness of each contributor and to document the development of women's studies and the history of the women's movement at one institution. The working title of this volume was *Women Scholars on Woman: Changing Perceptions of Reality*, which has been used extensively in bibliographies and women's studies programs.

For the work of all women who have given so generously of their time to other women, to all those who worked with me in my women's studies courses, to those who have contributed to this volume, and to the hundreds across the nation who rallied to my support in my own legal action against the University of Wisconsin, I say thank you very much. And to my editors, Tren Anderson and Nicki Benevento, who, under the trying circumstances of my public hearings, remained consistently supportive, I express my appreciation for their commitment to me and to this book.

J.I.R.
Syracuse, New York

Contents

1

WOMEN IN THE NONCONTINGENT CULTURE

1

The Ramifications
of the Study of
Women
Joan I. Roberts

At a meeting of the chancellors of the University of Wisconsin, one chancellor asked me, "How do you see women's studies—as errata?" My immediate thought was that he must have facetiously said *erotica*. Checking this initial reaction, I realized that he quite seriously considered the study of women to be two or three pages of corrections to the book of knowledge already written by men.

In *this* book, a group of faculty women answer his question with a decisive No. Their work, brought together here, represents not only the personal ideas of several women, but the *process* of collective action so critical to the new thinking of women about their relation to one another and to the competitive system of authority prevailing in male-dominated institutions. Both as process and product, this book is a very special collaboration by women at one university. I believe it is a symbol of new forms of being for women who refuse, by their identification with one another, the "inferiority" assigned to them.

THE GENESIS OF THE BOOK

The conception and growth of the book attests to the newly formed bonds of cooperation among women. In 1970 I initiated a women's studies course that was designed to be a collective effort of faculty women from many disciplines.* At the

* For a complete description, see my article from which the next few paragraphs are taken, "A

3

same time, many of these women had joined together in December 1970, forming the Association of Faculty Women. I was able, from this base of support, to know of the existence of other women academicians. With roughly 170 women on a faculty of 2300 in the university, the statistical probability of finding women without a formalized political and professional group was low. Thus, the first political nut to crack was the age-old isolation of women. But a second, equally hard-shelled problem emerged: their highly restricted occupational roles. Two-thirds of the small group I found were in traditional "women's" professions: nursing, women's physical education, and home economics. How does one create an interdisciplinary course when most disciplines are not represented? What followed was an exhaustive search for the one woman in physiology, the one woman in psychology, the one woman in law, and on and on through each of more than one hundred departments in the university.

Why not, in this situation, turn to men? The answer is simple. Few, if any, were knowledgeable. Fewer still had any consciousness of the feminist perspective. Even finding the exceptional man did not solve a second problem, which was to raise the consciousness of women and to engage them, both politically and intellectually, in the control of their *own* lives.

When I began my search in 1970, many of the women were just beginning to understand their oppression, just starting to speak up for themselves. Nevertheless, only one of the twenty-nine women refused to be involved in the new class, and this was because of travel problems. *Many*, however, said they had no specialized knowledge of women from their own intellectual perspectives. To these women I would respond, "Who else does?" To determine this, one woman in mathematics education sent a questionnaire to the male faculty (no other women were in that departmental area) and received replies that showed not only ignorance but, in some instances, antagonism as well.

In most cases, the women faculty had to hew out the rough outlines of their problems from scant material. Many began work with only a cursory knowledge of the enormity of the problem. Only five women had either extensive political or intellectual knowledge that prepared them for their involvement. Nevertheless, they came to the course from history, political science, English, economics, sociology, Afro-American studies, textiles and clothing, home economics education, social psychology, neurophysiology, psychology, pediatrics, gynecology, social work, early child development, psychiatry, behavioral disabilities, anthropology, nursing, library science, curriculum and instruction, physical education, and administration. Twenty-four different disciplines were represented: The women were there and they came—an interdisciplinary joining of minds from every place where women could be found in the university.

Throughout the last five years, I have hoped that women faculty would publish their thinking from the course. This idea, originally agreed upon by the women, was a concurrent objective along with all the others. Eventually, women students in the first courses were also asked to contribute. Slowly, with hard work and revisions, an anthology has evolved with a final group of twenty-one contributors—all originally from or currently at the University of Wisconsin at Madison. I shall integrate their

Multi-Faceted Approach to a Women's Studies Course," in *Female Studies*, vol. 8, ed. Sarah Slavin Schramm and published by K.N.O.W., Inc., 1975.

ideas in the next chapter, but in this chapter my purpose is to indicate the possibilities inherent in their work, and my objective is to detail some of the ramifications of the study of women. This framework, in which the facts and questions of the contributors can be expressed, may provide meaning for a future in which women's thinking is central to the restructuring of society.

THE MEANING OF WOMEN'S STUDIES

The meaning of our work in women's studies has, for at least some of us, changed substantially over the last few years. When I first commenced my work in this area, I conceived of the study of women as essentially concerned with role reinterpretation and role expansion based on the documentation of, and subsequent change in, social inequities. The basic task was to discover and present the full facts of sex discrimination, to add new knowledge to that which already existed, and to formulate new directions that would reduce inequities by a redefinition and an expansion of roles for men and women.

I soon began to realize that the task was going to be considerably more difficult than that proposed in this original definition of the problem. It was going to be, eventually, a daring and difficult reassessment of social reality, bringing us inevitably into intellectual confrontation with many major paradigms current in the literature of several disciplines. After beginning the search for relevant facts and concepts, some of us came to realize that neither facts nor concepts about females existed in critical scholarly areas. In still other areas, ideas, presumed to pertain to both sexes, were in actuality based on the study of males and extended to females. When females were studied, the paucity of fact and prevalence of opinion were painfully apparent. Thus, the challenging and arduous task before us was to rethink the concepts inherited from men—about them, about us, and, therefore, about humanity.

Some women have mistakenly assumed that we can study existing models and theories in each of our disciplines and modify them without questioning their origins. One social psychologist, speaking to women at a research conference, attempted to make female "passivity," as detailed in the psychological literature, the basis for heightened reflectiveness which could lead to greater creativity.[1] Such logic can stand only if the basic concept stands, and "passivity" is a concept that is riddled with masculist biases.[2] Clearly, then, we must begin our investigation of the concepts themselves. The study of women will engage us in a reassessment of the nature of knowledge, first, through reconceptualization, and then through the construction of new explanatory systems.

Even the modes of inquiry are being subjected to careful scrutiny. In our search for knowledge of ourselves, we find repeatedly that the "scientific" methods are essentially reasserting, with new terminological "weightiness," the same biases against women. Strangely, the "objectivity" of science has sustained a subjective bias that maintains, against the woman's experience of her own life, the myths of female inferiority. Thus, some of us have begun to question the propriety of a social science that remains several steps removed from the "subjects" studied. We have begun to question the findings from natural science that are propounded far from the field of the natural habitats of each species. And we question the humanities where the criticism of intellectual work is too often more important than the creation of that which is to be critiqued. Many of us wonder why institutions look backward, constantly reiterating the glories of previous male thinkers whose ideas have sustained grossly distorted theories of female existence.

If the masculist God of religious belief is dead, as publicly proclaimed, why are women subjected to a new masculist God of science from whom they obtain no greater justice? The male-defined essence of existence remains thoroughly alive. In fact, the old male cosmogony is clearly reflected in a recent pronouncement by a leading religious official: "Satan and his cohorts are using scientific arguments and nefarious propaganda to lure women away from their primary responsibilities as wives, mothers and homemakers. . . . Satan is determined to destroy you. You cannot compromise with him." [3] Despite such pronouncements, Satan is not leading women astray; women are leading one another away from a cosmogony that assumes male leadership in religion or in science. As women *themselves* change the nature of both religious *and* scientific knowledge, our understanding of social reality will change, too. In this way, some of us have come to see that the creation of new social being is the ultimate objective of the study of women.

For those of us who teach courses in this area, the new reality is constantly being created in the students with whom we work. The women, and those few men who dare to face women honestly, are daily engaging in the creation of a social reality that, for many of them, goes far beyond simple role innovation. They face the historical and current facts of sexism with shock, and out of that shock an initial impetus to achieve equality emerges. But as this occurs, a more important transformation engages them in a new sense of self and a new feeling for future possibilities. Listen to three older women, of the more than four hundred students I have known in my courses, as they reflect on these new possibilities:

> For a while I thought that what I was doing was totally nihilistic. I was the one who was crazy enough or foolhardy enough to say shit to the whole thing: I won't accommodate the paternalistic system. But I have begun to see that it isn't nihilism. Maybe there's a reality to what I'm doing that is totally positive. In opting out entirely, or as entirely as I dare, I'm reaching a new plane of validity or honesty or clarity.

> Clarity isn't the word I'm seeking. It's a new integration—an intuitive integration. If I try to pull it together logically right now, it isn't going to work.

> We're returning to the same thing. It's called intuitive because women haven't expressed, in words, their own reality. We call it intuitive because we've no language to clarify it.

The problem for women thinkers now is to conceptualize that new reality. The women students who come to us feeling inauthentic, uncertain, even crazy, are afraid but exhilarated with a fuzzy but sharp sense of new being. Our problem is not only to help them create and live that new being, but also to clarify and conceptualize it intellectually.

To do this, some of us have to begin with the historical development of knowledge in each discipline in order to grasp the existential and social factors that invade basic concepts and distort explanations about women and, therefore, about humanity. Underlying knowledge in all disciplines is an ontological set of assumptions about the nature of being or existence. These ontologies, whether derived from religion or science, are subject to the cultural conditions of the particular historical period in which they arose. Basic to our own cultural ontology is the sexual caste system, ordained by religion and in part sustained by science. Essentially, as de Beauvoir stated it, we are "the other" whose meaning for existence is defined as nonbeing or, at best, as peripheral or contingent being.[4]

As women openly reject this idea, we become self-determined ontological exiles who are confronting and changing the symbols and values basic to the thought systems of our culture. Our exclusion from decision-making parallels our exclusion from the creation of explanatory schemata. Those of us whom Germaine Greer labels "intellectual escapees" have too often denied our own experience and accepted only the ideas and procedures defined by the men's thought systems. As Mary Daly suggests, those of us who have perceived the reality of sexual oppression have exhausted ourselves in breaking through the barriers surrounding us, leaving little time or space or energy for our own interpretation of existence. But this interpretation is exactly what is necessary: "What is required of women at this point in history is a radical refusal to limit our perspectives, our questioning, our creativity to any of the preconceived patterns of male-dominated culture."[5] As Daly puts it, we have had the power of naming stolen from us. We must reclaim the right to speak—to name the self, the world, the meaning of our own existence.

As we destroy the images that maintain unequal social arrangements and sustain a façade of change through tokenism, we find ourselves living in a new space, centered in the lives of women, located in the interstices between institutions. As Daly expresses it, "The new space has a kind of invisibility to those who have not entered it . . . it is experienced both as power of presence and power of absence . . . it is participation in the power of being . . . an experience of becoming whole."[6] Women studies courses, although seen by many men as trivial, are the core of these experiences. The possibility of experiencing, even vicariously, both the absence and presence of women in their new space may come as a threatening shock to some men.[7]

It may be even more surprising that women are also entering a new time dimension, rejecting linear time and, in particular, refusing to be caught in the past.[8] Women feel acutely the complex problem of living in the presently felt experience of being a woman while dealing with the demands of a masculist past. Speaking about one major theorist in sociology, a graduate student put it succinctly: "He slammed the door in my face fifty years ago. Why should I bother with him now? He said nothing to women then and he has nothing to say to me about me now." The serious study of women brings us into abrupt confrontation with institutions that live in the historical past. For women living on the boundaries of new time, few adequate models from the past may exist. In fact, we are now reversing the academician's usual approach based on the slow accretion of new knowledge built on previous models. Instead, women break the models that repeatedly demean their existence or degrade their being.

THE SOCIOLOGY OF KNOWLEDGE

As women define their own ontological meaning within new dimensions of time and space, we will probably use only those segments of explanatory systems that can be adapted to our problems. One useful set of ideas is embodied in the sociology of knowledge first suggested by Karl Marx and later articulated by Karl Mannheim.[9] For Marx human consciousness is determined by social being. Because he avoided the sexual caste system as the precursor of social class, Marx conceived of ideology as false consciousness abstracted from material conditions and used to mask social-class differences. Mannheim extended the idea by including a variety of social groups—occupational, geographical, national—that shape human consciousness. Like Marx, he overlooked the most basic social grouping by sex.

Nevertheless, Mannheim's basic assumptions about the sociology of knowledge are useful since he showed that any system of thought is in part a product of the social conditions in which it is produced. Systems of thought so blatantly distort women that in consciousness-raising groups today they return to their daily lives and earliest experiences to begin the difficult reevaluation of the nature of their existence. Similarly women scholars, when faced with concepts that either exclude or distort women, often begin our analyses at the fundamental level of cultural and existential intrusions into the perceptions of female, and thus, human reality.

The ideology about women consists of either intentional or unintentional deceptions or distortions that present females in accordance with the socially accepted power distribution by sex in our society. These sexual politics are so accepted as the "natural order" that distortions about women are often not open to the thinker's own conscious intent. The perspective of the thinker, the whole mode of conceiving of women, is in large part determined by the historical and social setting, only a portion of which may appear in conscious thought. In this way, sexist assumptions come to pervade "empirical" theories of women.

Social factors penetrate not only the content but also the forms of knowledge about women. Ideas about women cannot, therefore, be understood on the level of ideas. Every formulation is possible only in relation to previous experience with women; every choice of problem is a selection from many possible options; every analysis will be completed within the context of a sexual caste system. For these reasons, as Mannheim states, the genesis, form, content, scope, and intensity of expression will all be influenced by social conditions.

The social position of the thinker is first established in the earliest social groups—girls or boys—with which children identify. If male, identification with a presumed "masculine" superiority creates a pervasive and subtle perspective which, although unknown at times to the person, will influence the way he views women, what he perceives in them, and how he construes them in his thinking. The sexist perspective can be observed in the total absence of certain concepts about women, in the refusal to deal with selected life problems of women, in the exaggerated presence of concepts about women in highly limited areas, in the dichotomized nature of the structure of categories used, and in the simplistic level of abstractions developed.

The dominant modes of thought used to order experience about and with women intrudes, not only into thought systems, but even into the model of how fruitful thinking can be carried out. Historically, the most obvious bias is that fruitful thinking cannot be undertaken by women at all. In recent versions, women are relegated to limited spheres of productive thought. Less obvious are the intrusions related to early and largely artificial dichotomization and polarization of the world learned by male children which come to be associated with a pseudo sense of superiority. How polarization and dichotomization affect thought systems is still open to much consideration. The "we and they," the "foe and friend," the "reward and punishment"—the ubiquitous and fallacious paired opposites are obvious. What is unclear is the extent to which social sex polarization provides the basis for such dualistic thinking.

Without careful scrutiny of the underlying assumptions that form the social perspective of the thinker, attempts to change the conditions of women and men will probably fail. As both sexes try to equalize their different social groups, agreements and disagreements will focus more on opinions than differences in the total outlooks underlying these opinions. Witness, for example, the recent debate on quotas. But it is the social perspectives, the matrices of assumptions, that we must look at if we are to determine the sources of differences.

Increasingly, a detached perspective, to use Mannheim's term, is occurring among women as we leave traditional social positions, as large groups of us shift away from historically accepted norms and institutions, and as we clash with men's interpretations of us. But out of these conflicts, critical analysis may make the underlying assumptions that intrude into knowledge visible to both groups.

To sum up, in women studies we are beginning to make clearly visible the social factors that condition every product of thought about women. To do this, we will eventually take as our problem the total mental structure underlying the assertions—the perspective of the thinker, her or his whole mode of conceiving of women as determined by the historical and social setting.

ROLES, SYMBOLS, AND BELIEF SYSTEMS

Knowledge is obviously both a social product and a producer of social change. The next critical question for thinkers in women's studies is: what is the process by which a body of knowledge comes to be socially established as reality? If reality is socially constructed, then the relationship between "objective" reality as defined by male-dominated institutions and "subjective" reality as experienced by the individual woman in her own awareness becomes the important issue.

If objective reality is constructed by people's characterization of themselves in social roles, as Luckmann and Berger believe, then these roles must be the mediating links between the social order and beliefs about it.[10] The problem with this formulation is that most social roles are allotted to men, and few to women. Thus the beliefs about the social order must be primarily determined by men who occupy most of the roles in which definitions of the situation, of social positions, and of the actual behaviors of people are determined. Normative cultural patterns arise as a result of the men's belief that both they and women will behave according to their role expectations.

Although categorization schemes of role sets will necessarily narrow choices and habitualize behavior, they are presumably fluid, being reallocated throughout the system. The question is, reallocated to whom and in whose system? If the social order and beliefs about it are determined primarily by role expectations of men in their roles, then the categorization schemes do not narrow expectations for women since they are excluded from most of them from the beginning. Thus, if social roles mediate between knowledge and social change, the new knowledge about women may have little impact. Furthermore, role expansion and reinterpretation will not necessarily lead to changes in the underlying perspectives or even in various social beliefs. Since few women will only gradually move into the traditional roles of men, and even fewer men will move into the traditional roles of women, it is likely that women will be forced to take on the only slightly modified social beliefs of the men with whom they interact.

For women, roles that presumably interconnect to form the male-dominated social order are not the critical mediators between knowledge and social change. Social structure does not exist apart from people's beliefs about it—and it is the beliefs that legitimize it. The legitimization of social beliefs about female inferiority is reinforced by a distribution of "knowledge" that leads men to perceive they have legitimate power. This perception can continue only as long as *women* think men have legitimate power. With increasing divergence in knowledge valued by women and by men, the diverse criteria for facts become increasingly irreducible. In this situation, the key aspect of social reality must involve perceptions of political power and, more precisely, the underlying perspective that legitimizes the domination by men of most social roles.

If women conceive of roles as clusters of symbols organized into patterns of meaning, then the translation of knowledge into a new reality can occur only when symbols of legitimization are destroyed. George Herbert Mead believed the emergence of the self was possible only because common symbols, images, and meanings were shared through empathic communication.[11] In the process of symbolization, we can imagine ideas, create images, and constitute objects that could not exist outside the symbolization inherent in social relations. In this sense, a woman can take on a role, make a role, or even reject the conception of roles, particularly if a new perspective redefines the situation. Consensus on the legitimacy of roles depends on agreement on symbols and meanings.

THE ORGANIZATION OF IDEAL CULTURAL IMAGES

If we are to translate women's new reality into knowledge and then into social reality for both women and men, we must change critical symbols, those images central to cultural patternings of belief systems that legitimize the right of men to name and control the existence of women. In this effort, duality in thinking—the subject-object split—serves no useful function. If imagery is the target, then the images must involve not merely feeling but perceiving and thinking as well. In agreement with Arnheim, we must state that "thinking involves images and images contain thought." [12]

The most powerful images are those represented by figures of speech since they intensify some perceptions while screening out others. Metaphoric assertions about women provide images that may organize behavior around roles as symbolic clusters of meaning. Metaphors,* as sets of organizing analogies, may even form the

* I will use metaphor here in its broadest sense as one form of cultural imagery while being aware that some of the figures cited are technically metonymies and synecdoches.

central images of belief systems. Since metaphors link domains of social experience, metaphoric assertions translate experience from one domain to another by virtue of a common factor which can be generalized between experiences in two or more domains.[13] In fact, Fernandez believes that metaphors perform a locating function that establishes people in relation to one another, leading to a hierarchy of role relationships. To him the logic is derivative; imagery is primary, with metaphors conceived as strategies taken in respect to feeling. If we avoid his dichotomy and accept Suzanne Langer's formulation of feeling as all that is felt, then metaphors about women will entail image and thought simultaneously.

Culture may be conceived of as an indefinite possible combination of metaphorical continua that organize social identity by linking domains of imagery. The strategic use of metaphors to place a person in more or less desirable positions on several metaphorical domains serves to organize shared expectations into plans for behaviors. Roles then are predicated on metaphorical connection of domains of experience.

In our culture, metaphors for bodily parts as well as for persons are essential to the organization of belief systems about female inferiority. Metaphoric strategies consistently used by men make assertions that, by analogy, place women in nonhuman or animal categories, becoming human or child categories, or subhuman categories. Thus, woman is, as metaphorical body part, a piece of ass. Woman as nonhuman or animal is pussy. Woman as becoming human is a child, unable to control emotions. Woman as subhuman is, as Aquinas put it, a misbegotten male. In each case, the metaphoric assertion sustains political disparity: the moral of the metaphor sanctions negatively the woman's existence.

Fernandez suggests some initial metaphorical dimensions, the most important of which involves assertions that place a person either up or down, or under or over, along dimensions. In our culture, the man is literally and figuratively on top with the woman positioned below. Whether these and other continua are themselves indirect assertions of the basic sex polarization remains unexamined. As Suzanne Langer says, "in studying the history of words it is impossible to judge whether the physical or the material or some other meaning is the oldest. . . . The root metaphor is the image conveyed by the word and this image may mean a feeling, an act, an object, even a personality or place." [14]

Although the task is difficult, the most important metaphors come from repeated everyday experience. And if we examine another salient dimension, the hard-soft continuum, the speculation that critical organizing metaphorical schemes are indirect derivatives of sex polarization seems possible. The hard, unfeeling "he-man," the man who has "a hard on," and the tough guy with the soft heart are just a few of many common phrases. The invidious distinction between "hard" and "soft" data carries metaphorical derogation. The scorn for Adlai Stevenson when he disagreed with the Kennedy policy on Vietnam was expressed in terms of his softness, or in other words, his womanliness. The strategic use of these particular metaphors to place women in undesirable positions has obvious implications for female inferiority in the social order. Moreover, the possibility that critical metaphorical continua that form key cultural images are *themselves* linked with sex polarization is highly possible.

Boulding said that the fall of ideal images leads to societal collapse. If the metaphoric cross-referencing of domains gives culture a sense of wholeness, and if key images are associated with sex polarization, then the study of women can substantially express not only women's own sense of reality, but also potentially restructure the meaning of the social order. The sexual caste system basic to male-defined existence will not stand if cultural integration is broken because women and men cannot agree on the aptness of each other's images. Societal collapse is not imminent; cultural reintegration is.

POLITICAL IMAGERY: RETHINKING THE MIGHTY WARRIOR, THE JUST JUDGE, AND THE GOOD SHEPHERD

Reintegration will focus initially on the political system in which myth and metaphor create a male-manipulated reality. The metaphors, necessary to the self-conceptions and self-justifications of men who seek dominance to the exclusion of women, depend on terms that create a soothing world in which women believe they are "protected" from real or imagined enemies. Ambiguous terms used to glorify women's exclusion have led them to believe that threatening situations can be avoided. To believe this, painful and inconvenient facts are excluded and self-serving courses of action justified.[15] Once the male metaphorical view is accepted, information is rearranged to fit it. Even the language style, with fake concern for "the ladies," with the careful control of language to exclude commonly used male obscenity, with the prop line of seemingly well-bred, properly dressed wives—all these are used to sustain the political metaphors that mask female exclusion. Despite these "valiant" efforts to maintain a façade, the study of women unmasks the evocation of an out-group, the manufactured tigers of which Elaine Morgan speaks, that increase dependence on militaristic men.[16] For those women who have worked for women's rights, the image of the benevolent leader wisely leading his flock to safety is already dead. The further belief in the "just" man leading an obedient and industrious nation to victory is equally stale.

The erosion of key political metaphors simply signals the more complex task of examining metaphors established as ideal images. Basic to this endeavor is the job of investigating the sex polarization inherent in common metaphorical continua. Perhaps in this way we can determine the critical foci around which symbols cluster to form roles. These, we may assume, will form the basis of legitimization of unequal power relations. When this system of symbolically expressed social beliefs is made clearly visible, then the intrusion of social factors into knowledge about women will become patently obvious. Simultaneously, the real lives of women, as they experience a new ontology, may come to be expressed in a social order restructured to represent the whole of humanity, not the projections of one half onto the other. This book is only a beginning. Each woman has taken only the first steps toward a new social reality. Describing some of the fallacious assumptions and raising some of the initial questions, each woman, from her own discipline, has begun a work that will move us inexorably closer to a new social reality.

NOTES

1. Elizabeth Douvan, "Higher Education and Feminine Socialization" (Wingspread Conference on Women's Higher Education convened by the National Coalition for Research on Women's Higher Education and Development, March 1972).

2. Julia Sherman, *On the Psychology of Women: A Survey of Empirical Studies* (Springfield, Ill.: Charles C Thomas, 1971).

3. "Mormons Warned: Satan at Work in Women's Lib," *Capital Times*, 1973.

4. Simone de Beauvoir, *The Second Sex* (New York: Alfred A. Knopf, 1952).

5. Mary Daly, "Theology after the Demise of God the Father: A Call for Castration of Sexist Religion," in *Women and Religion: 1972. Proceedings of the Working Group of Women and Religion*, ed. Judith Plaskow Goldenberg (Waterloo, Ontario: American Academy of Religion, CRS Executive Office, Waterloo Lutheran University, 1973), p. 10. I am indebted to Dr. Daly for her excellent theoretical discourse.

6. Ibid., pp. 11–13.

7. George Gilder, *The Suicide of the Sexes* (New York: Quadrangle Press, 1973).

8. Dorothy Lee, "Autonomous Motivation," in *Anthropology and Education* (Philadelphia: University of Pennsylvania Press, 1961), pp. 103–21.

9. Karl Mannheim, *Ideology and Utopia*, trans. Louis Wirth and Edward Shils (New York: Harvest Books, 1936), pp. 264–90.

10. Peter L. Berger and Thomas Luckmann, *The Social Construction of Reality* (Garden City, N.Y.: Doubleday, 1966).

11. George Herbert Mead, *Mind, Self and Society* (Chicago: University of Chicago Press, 1934).

12. Rudolph Arnheim, *Visual Thinking* (Berkeley: University of California Press, 1969).

13. James W. Fernandez, "Persuasions and Performances: Of the Beast in Every Body and the Metaphors of Everyman," *Daedalus*, Winter 1972.

14. Suzanne Langer, *Philosophical Sketches* (Baltimore: Johns Hopkins Press, 1962).

15. Murray Edelman, *Politics as Symbolic Action* (Chicago: Markham, 1971).

16. Elaine Morgan, *The Descent of Women* (New York: Stein & Day, 1972).

Pictures of Power and Powerlessness: A Personal Synthesis
Joan I. Roberts

Cooperation among women is the force that sustains civilization.[1] When all the wars are over, when the strategies and tactics of each are finally analyzed and "eulogized," when the last strut is strutted, what will remain is the unity of women, giving life and cherishing it as they have cherished it even through the barbed-wire world of Auschwitz and the mushroom-clouded air of Hiroshima.

In this century, women have learned that the barbarism of men in power must be stopped if life is to be sustained. The age-old bonds among women, quietly expressed in the confines of home, family, and neighborhood, covertly exercised in auxiliaries formed out of subordinate status, are now stretched tight and taut with overt demands for full, public personhood. Complete individuality within a noncontingent[2] women's culture rejects, by its nature, the booted march to power. Women do not wish to kill that which they have borne. In the emerging women's culture, the old concern for cooperation now mingles with a new respect for strong individuality, openly and directly expressed.

Although this book is a collective effort, an outspoken product of the age-old silent support of women for one another, it is also a public statement of personal strength. Out of respect for the individual autonomy of each woman, this chapter presents only my own personal reactions to the ideas of each of them. It cannot and should not be read as a simple summary of the evidence presented in each chapter.

MUSCLE, THE MEASURE OF MORALITY

To create new cultural images of women is to form new images of power. To rethink the male-female bond is to restructure the meaning of force in all human endeavors. The inequity between women and men ultimately resides in one fact, differential physical strength. This difference, exaggerated by socialization for strength in men and weakness in women, is the basic source of social inequality in all human relationships, the prototype of all subsequent forms of humiliation. It is muscle rather than mind that has too often governed the fate of women and their children. This fact is one that men and women try to avoid. However, the central and unavoidable issue is the capacity and willingness to exert physical force in order to impose one's will over another. A change in the relation of women to men will require a radical reassessment of force and realignment of power.

Physical strength is often translated into the capacity to accumulate resources, which, as substitutes for personal prowess, serve the same purpose: to impose the primacy of one's desires and to obtain special privilege. In this translation, women themselves have become a form of property. A lucky combination of genes or a sheer accident of birth has allowed a few women a brief but false sense of control. For the many, their condition as chattel has been the concrete historical reality. It is money and not morality that has too often determined the lives of women and their children. As in the past, men now control most institutional sources of money. The ability and desire to exert economic force as a substitute for brawn is the crucial issue. Since conflicting political theories are largely based on forms of economic control, a change in the status of women, who are one form of money, will necessitate a dramatic reordering of social priorities and a drastic redefinition of authority.

Stripped of niceties, the political system depends on the raw use of physical and economic power as configurated in territorial terms. To obtain special privilege and maintain a stigmatized group over which power is exerted, the movement of the "inferior" person through time and space must be controlled. Freedom is the right, however illusory, to conceive of time and space as belonging to the self and to experience a sense of being able to control and direct one's own movement through the short span of human life. Death, final motionlessness, can be exacted of an "inferior" who refuses inferiority. Although witchhunts and wars have taken their toll of women, the "other" is needed to bear the sons who carry the father's name to another generation of men who will continue the exertion of power over one another.

More commonly, incarceration in institutions, isolation of the recalcitrant, and severe restriction to the "proper" sphere are controls imposed on subjugated women. In a "man's world" force is the ultimate threat (whether or not it is used) that backs woman into her "rightful" domain. Economic muscle in the marketplace keeps her at home where she "belongs" or conversely pushes her, as a member of a poorly paid reserve labor pool, into dead-end jobs whenever she is needed to bolster men's power on the occasions when it is threatened by other men.

To coexist as unequals within circumstances of the greatest intimacy, women must come to believe the physical, economic, and political inequities are just and justifiable. The whole of culture must, of necessity, be organized around images which sustain disparity. Intellectual life, as institutionally organized, must transmit patterns of inequality so that people will believe that the subordinate position of women is only "natural," that their shrunken time and space are not only proper but even protective.

Trained to believe that obedience to male authority brings protection, women soon learn that an unattached female is free game; as no man's property, she is every man's prey. Few women realize that men protect *themselves* from other *men* who threaten their power. Women and children, if property of the few males at the top, may indirectly receive full protection. This fact, however, masks an even more elementary truth: Men protect their power from *women*. A woman who exerts full individuality in economic or political spheres is, with few exceptions, seen as a threat to be handled promptly and, if necessary, forcibly.

Of course, it is easier if the stigmatized themselves sustain the invidious distinctions that perpetuate their subjugation. Women are particularly vulnerable to this strategy. Species survival demands intimacy with those claiming superiority and requires a prolonged period of child care for the products of that intimacy. These basic physiological facts, although changing with recent medical innovations, still provide the special circumstances that impel women to incorporate and to sanction their subjugation. In a culture entirely controlled by men, even a woman's unique strengths confirm her "inferiority."

THROUGH THE MASCULIST SCREEN

Every culture develops a distinctive perspective, a screen through which everything is filtered and interpreted. When men dominate all phases of societal life, that screen constitutes a masculist world view, a system of thought and feeling which "explains" women's peripheral place in the operation of the universe, the meaning of her existence as the "other," the origin and destiny of her life, the rationale for her success or failure as an appendage to men, even her tragedy and joy as a member of the second sex. This screen through which all aspects of human life are identified and integrated may retard or accelerate an understanding of natural processes. An obvious example is the medieval world view of the Catholic church which stopped the discovery and application of new ideas basic to the well-being of the human species. During much of recorded history, the world views of Western cultures have impeded progress toward an accurate and complete comprehension of human reality because the cultural screens have sustained an invidious distinction against half of humanity.

Without a culturally induced perspective, experience is meaningless; *with* the masculist perspective, women's experience is still essentially meaningless. A world view represents an integration of separate bits of experience into a logically consistent framework, the patterned meaning of life. Without logical interconnections, the purpose and plan of life crumble; thus, it is imperative that the screen meshes to form an integrated whole. If women are ontologically inferior, then that inferiority must extend to all areas of human existence. If there are any in which women, for biological reasons, must exhibit superior capability, then that aspect of life must be seen as separate, isolated, different from all others. And to be consistent, even it must be under male domination; thus, childbearing is controlled by male gynecologists, childrearing by male school administrators and psychologists, and both functions by the "head of the household" within the family.

When cultural images fallaciously categorize half of humanity as subhuman, there will inevitably arise a set of illogicalities which must be explained away. The ideal images must appear congruent if metaphorical assertions are to hook hierarchically the separate domains of existence. When half of a culture's members are stigmatized and the other half glorified, then any attack on inconsistencies will ultimately lead to an assault on the false rationalizations of all power configurations. If one questions the legitimacy of authority in the basic social unit, logic inevitably leads one to examine the bases of all societal conceptions of power, both achieved and ascribed.

The world view provides not only the categories, the content of culture, but also the premises which order complex thought. As a species, we are aware of being aware; we possess intentionality. As a species, we are also exceptional in our complex internal patterning of external stimuli. We map our world around our intentions. Ideal images come to represent in condensed form critical cultural categories; metaphoric assertions represent the logic of image manipulation. When women deny their caste status, they refuse to accept the images, the categories, *and* the structural logic that connects them together. Because we are not dealing with a small segment of the human race, the explication of the cultural premises which order thought and feeling will force a restructuring of masculist logic.

RITUALS THROUGH THE MASCULIST SCREEN

The logic of male chauvinism is most sharply expressed in the images associated with universal life crises—birth, puberty, mating, and death. None of these ritualized events is possible without sexual intercourse, and all of them are culturally infused with ceremonial sex typing. At birth, the neural system provides the capacity to cope with a limited variety of sensory experiences; the higher nervous centers are not yet fully developed. To survive, the child must adjust to a particular set of stimuli and to the distinctive cultural pattern they represent. For the species to survive, adults must carry culture to the young; they do this by regularizing a predictive pattern that marks the flow of time, denoting the biological changes of life. Ceremonial organization of life crises typically catches the female in a net of humiliation. Consider the options available to women in different cultures: Is it better to be born as a "second-best" child or to be born in a society that practices female infanticide? Is it better to feel compelled to marry instead of following a career or to be sold as property in a prearranged business deal? Is it better to be without status at the death of a husband or to be thrown on the funeral pyre to die as the devoted wife of a dead man?

To debate the content of rites of passage, *past* or *present*, is futile; it is the logic underlying rituals that is critical: The cosmological premises of that logic deny full humanity to women even in death. That we die is, in a sense, probably more important than that we live. But even in death, woman, so central to new life, symbolized as the giver of all life, goes to God the Father, her ultimate fate a heavenly subordination to the male who presumably created all things—even the Mother who created him.

In rites of passage, three phases are identified: separation from the group one is leaving, transition between the old and new, and incorporation into the new group. For woman, life as a whole has been a separation out, never to be incorporated into the body of humanity as an equal person. Women have lived for centuries in ritualistic separation, for a few decades in uneasy transition, and never in incorporation. Beauvoir's the "other" has had nothing to become part of because humanity is defined as male. Even in the rituals themselves, women have never been able to incorporate fully the young girl who remains separated from childhood, always apart, always becoming but never fully human. To incorporate a younger woman, an adult woman can only claim her for membership in a subordinate group of "misbegotten males." Only when the adult female denies that status is she able to claim the young girl as a complete human person.[3]

From a societal point of view, the most significant transition is the initiation at puberty into community membership and adulthood. The question is, Whose community and whose adulthood in whose world? Contingent living in a male-defined culture, with status fixed by her relations to men, is a makeshift approximation for a woman. Ironically, incorporation is most difficult in those societies that deny the existence of a female culture or refuse to recognize the reality of sexism. In such "advanced" societies, the young woman faces a compounded problem. Presumably, there is no reason the older woman cannot incorporate the younger since no official subordination is overtly recognized. The sham, the lie of this pretense, is patently obvious.

Women do not become women when they are accepted into a mature body of female elders. It is marriage to a man which traditionally defines a woman. On official entrance into contingent being, the girl becomes a "woman." Those women who remain unmarried may retain adolescent status during their entire lives—the maiden aunt, the old maid—these women may never be seen as "real" adults because men have not legitimized their existence and because women could not.

As women recognize and reject inferior status, they begin to claim their own and their acts create still another power confrontation because the right to define womanhood is denied men. The significance of professional and professorial role models for younger women lies primarily in this fact and only secondarily in their value for female occupational socialization. In the enculturative process, the critical period for learning about potential work roles occurs at younger ages.

CLAIMING OUR OWN

Women are presumed to control the early enculturation of children until puberty is reached. Under the direction of husbands, clergymen, policemen, and male judges, physicians, psychologists, school principals, and superintendents, this "privilege" is quickly denied if the woman does not reinforce the masculist world view which firmly reestablishes traditional sex-role identities, which, in turn, reinstate female inferiority. After puberty, males have usually dominated what is fallaciously considered cognitive learning as opposed to the presumed affective learning erroneously thought to characterize much of earlier socialization. Stereotypically, man, the logical one, deals with "advanced" thinking; and woman, the emotional one, with feeling and elementary thought.

Tossing out this institutionalized fallacy, the truth is this: The young learn cultural categories of knowledge, canons of discrimination, and processes seen as change in the relation among the variables of existence. In fact, the whole of human life around the child, the structure of social groups, and their relation to other aspects of the environment can be conceived of as symbolic learning. As women change these social groupings, as they take control of their own lives, they consciously set out to help girls achieve the same self-direction, the same control of both psychological and physical time and space. This forces a fundamental power confrontation with men over whose world view will be transmitted to the next generation. If women's presumed control of prepubertal enculturation ever becomes a reality, the image of the compliant, long-suffering woman and of the tough, self-serving man will rapidly reach a very tardy death.

The demise of central cultural images is no easy accomplishment. The incorporation of a world view is arranged from birth onward on the basis of categories of inclusion-exclusion which derive from sex differentiation as related to age, generation, and sequence of birth order. A girl or boy will participate in only those cultural experiences deemed "proper" to her or his sex group. Training for selective stupidity is experienced by women throughout life but particularly during the postpubertal learning controlled by men. To break this dominance involves still another power confrontation, one in which thousands of university women are now actively engaged. The essence of affirmative action, bitterly fought by some men, is the collapse of male control over the symbol systems developed and promulgated in institutions of "higher" learning. Although equal pay and opportunity are important, the crucial issue is women's insistence on their inclusion in the production and dissemination of knowledge about themselves and their world.

For each sex, the masculist cultural screen, justified by "men of knowledge," provides different sets of images and associated categories, canons, and processes. The pitiful retreat to "quota" and "quality" as excuses for the continued exclusion of women from male domination of postpubertal learning is a last-minute, last-ditch stand doomed eventually to defeat. Men's words ring hollow when women know, as they now know, the full extent of their exclusion from systems of knowledge; when women realize, as many now do, the incapacity of intellectual paradigms to explain or predict female behavior; when women comprehend, as they now do, the destructive potential of total male control of human thought. Because of female exclusion from thought systems, the hardest thing for a man to know *is* what a woman thinks. But it is harder still for him to listen and to accept her thoughts because they are certain to shake the foundation of his beliefs. We turn now to women thinkers, who in this book express their ideas on the nature of human reality as seen by them as women and as scholars.

BRAIN, BODY, AND BEHAVIOR

We begin by examining masculist assumptions about the biologically inherent "inferiority" of women. To justify the destruction or domination of other creatures, the traditional theological version of *Homo sapiens* leads us to believe that humans, as possessors of souls, are different from all other forms of life. The "lords" of creation are above all animals. Curiously, the "lordess" continues to be seen as animalistic, enticing the fully human male into carnal acts, bleeding monthly in a repetitive reminder of our origins, birthing babies while grunting with the work of it and screaming with the pain of it. All these life-producing acts remind men that they are a living part of animal life, just one more species.

Ironically, the death-producing acts, murder and war and even rape, become glorified, with history a recounting of the territorial squabbles of battling males.[4] Yet these acts, the most barbaric and animalistic, are not seen as subhuman. On the contrary, they are mythologized as the noblest, most courageous acts of the human species. This peculiar reversal of logic is needed to rationalize intraspecies hostility. Those made powerless are really subhuman, incomplete copies of the victorious male; thus, it is normal to exert power over them, to beat them when necessary, to rape them when they "ask for it."

When one-half of a species sees the other half as legitimate prey, the usual inhibitory mechanisms controlling intragroup hostilities become lost in cultural configurations destructive beyond the wildest dreams of the bloodiest war lord. The decimation of women and children in twentieth-century warfare may now make the military the safest place for them.

Despite the obvious fact that male needs for power have placed us all in push-button peril dreading total annihilation, the traditional animalistic image of women still pervades the thinking of the "man on the street." At the same time, men of learning now rightly defend the Darwinian fact that we are all animals. In a final ironic twist, female inferiority is at present sustained by improper generalizations from the lives of caged female rats, wild female baboons, and other assorted creatures. After centuries of condemnation, it is *still* necessary for Ruth Bleier, a physician and neuroanatomist in brain research, to attack the cultural assumptions of female biological inferiority. Although the current thinking is often a tired, tedious variant of an ancient and repugnant theme, women must still prove that all primates have similar brains, that humans differ in a cerebral cortex characterized by a higher ratio of association to receiving areas, and that male and female human beings are *both*, therefore, capable of the *same* complex thought.

Even as research destroys the old theological version of "natural" inferiority, new scientific "proof" remains sexist. Earlier scientific thought (if it can be so labeled) held that the brains of women and of certain racial groups were smaller and therefore inferior. When this bigger-the-better thesis became embarrassingly difficult to defend, a few men presumably possessing large, superior brains turned to intelligence tests only to wade into another quagmire. The more recent laboratory research has shifted to hormonal and genetic causation. Some now postulate that brain functioning is androgen dependent, but no studies of primates show this effect. Some now propose that predominant functioning of right or left hemispheres is linked to the capacity for white male superiority in particular forms of abstract thought: White women and black men and women are supposed to exhibit a different hemispheric usage. Here we have a restatement on other more sophisticated causal grounds of the earlier brain-size argument. In both, masculist logic insists on overlooking differential enculturation as a logical cause of results. This, despite solid evidence on the ruthless exclusion of women and nonwhite races from abstract thought systems.

In cultural imagery, the brain somehow becomes connected to the possession of a penis. In fact, Bleier has to restate the obvious: The hypothalamus is the only part of the brain involved in the control of the pituitary and through it the gonads; the hypothalamus has no direct relation to the association areas of the cerebral cortex which controls the higher thought processes. Still the image of the castrated little woman with her deficient brain and the large man with his superior brain are drawn in the imaginations of people. If this little woman tries to equal the big man, if she dares to think original thoughts, psychological and even physical malfunctioning may follow such folly. If she does not lose her mind from "too much thinking," she is certain, at least, to become desexed, living out her life as an old-maid schoolteacher or librarian.

In the cultural world view, thinking is masculine. For a woman to think "serious," deep thoughts is therefore an alien act. When women in the late 1800s applied for admission to universities, they were told they would become, among other things, "hermaphroditic monstrosities" whose reproductive organs would shrivel away. Even today, women have to prove that their brains are not in their wombs. In short, they have to fight a world view that pictures them as defined by their "purpose in life" and portrays them in the only professions they have been able to wrest from men, those seen as extensions of their "natural" roles.

This complex of cultural categories, expressed in key images, rests on the premise that women and all else were created by men. To most people in Western cultures, creativity, like thinking, is masculine. For centuries, women were thought to be vessels which received the seed of men. Men implanted the human being; women provided the incubator for it. Even the woman herself originated from an extra rib of a man which a superordinate man acted upon. Ironically, as Bleier points out, the primal streak is female; in fetal life, we all begin morphologically as female.

Women, after centuries of masculist oppression, finally relearn what they originally knew: their rightful role in the act of creation. Men do not create women; men do not produce new beings to be grown in female hothouses; men do not carry and birth new life; men do not own a "natural" creative principle. The male control of thought has forced women to deny their obvious, innate creativity. With even the act of birth itself redefined, creative acts of both body and mind become a male prerogative. After biological creativity is denied it is easy to refuse intellectual originality by forcing woman into an ugly double bind: If she dares to use her small, inferior brain, she will lose her primary identity, her womanliness. Even worse, she will by her unnatural acts lose her ability to bear and rear children and thus imperil the survival of the species. Among the "enlightened" it is appropriate for a woman to think, provided that she thinks of her children and her husband first and provided she realizes her incapacity to think abstractly within most "male" fields.

After reading the history of women, one can only question the validity of the whole structure of masculist thought. To maintain the terrible lie of female inferiority, this logic relies on a hierarchy of polarized images. Much male thought seems to derive from the competitive polarization of life. But when men make dissimilar that which is essentially similar, they are stuck with the problem of how to get the poles back together again for mating purposes. Placing the "intelligent, creative" male at one pole and the "intuitive, emotional" female at the other, in short, creating the *opposite* sex, stresses the differences, not the commonalities of women and men. If men accentuate the positive, it will lead them to eliminate the negative; eventually there becomes no easy way to integrate similarities. With brains at one end and beauty at the other, men can fornicate with an object, but they cannot talk to it. This simply means that they will look to other men in male culture, reinforcing in that process the dominance of their own kind. Women, "protected" or, as translated, confined in separate domiciles, trained to see themselves as inferior, forced into economic and social dependency, are limited to a devalued culture occasionally tolerated in groups connected to and contingent upon male social organizations. Rejecting this option, some have moved to an underground culture that has been historically obliterated and only recently recognized, but with the usual sneering condescension.

It is to the masculist cultural configuration, to the male-defined social structure, that homophobia can be traced; it is based, in part, on a fear that polarized men and women will not come back out of their segregated groups, that they will not mate with each other. Excessive fear of homosexuality is more probable in a society that makes the sexes opposite, dissimilars hard to conjoin. Excessive fear of homosexuality is more probable in a society that makes one of the polarized sexes unfit for anything "serious" or "important." It is this lie that leads to the ambiguous attitudes men hold about women. Polarized into their "superior" group, they must nevertheless produce children with a subservient, inferior being—with a woman who "never had a thought in her head."

It is not surprising that Freud's concepts sustaining polarized subjugation of women were most quickly incorporated. Even Jung, who also assumed bipotentiality, ended up with the anima and animus, continued polarizations from mythology, now located within the *same* individual. According to Bleier, bisexuality may be the norm. Cultural imagery may channel people toward heterosexuality, but many human beings have asexual, bisexual, homosexual, and heterosexual experiences during their lives. In this channeling people become culture-bound, responding stereotypically to social definitions instead of biological mechanisms. Just as animals produce stereotyped responses to appropriate biological triggers without conscious selection among options, so human beings may stereotypically respond to social definitions without a realization of alternative possibilities. Gender identity is culturally determined and, as Bleier points out, studies of hermaphrodites show that gender identity comes to be congruent with *socially* assigned sex identity.

To sustain dichotomized existence, scholars must deny results from hormonal research in which both estrogens and androgens are found in *both* women and men; findings from animal research in which homosexuality and heterosexuality are *both* observed; conclusions from human investigations in which a wide variety of sexual practices are reported. Kinsey not only broke the Victorian silence on sex, he also unintentionally but irrevocably cracked the idealized duality of sex roles.

Some may wonder why feminists support lesbians in their ranks. The usual justification is based on freedom from sex-determined roles for all women and on the concomitant human right of individual choice and personal privacy without the intervention of the state. But on a much deeper level, women must support lesbian women if they are to break the sex segregation that legitimizes "femininity," the scenario for subjugation. Paradoxically, the woman-identified-woman is needed so that all women can insist that each woman and each man are both male and female. The homosexual woman, even in the humdrum activities of daily life, is a living symbol of self-sufficiency, a female who denies by her independent life style the polarized image of "feminine" dependent passivity.

These women also crack the cultural belief that a woman's identity and her ultimate reason for being are achieved when she "captures" and copulates with a man. The world view assumes that men are superior not only intellectually but also sexually. Sex, like thought and creativity, is male defined. Woman, lacking a glorious appendage, goes looking for it and the bigger-the-better motif rears its unbecoming head again. But when women say we are capable of loving one another, then the assumption of male sexual superiority shrinks to everyday proportions.

The premise of a stronger sex drive in the powerful male feeds on an image of female sexual inadequacy. To escape this fallacy, the duality of Eve, the wanton woman, and Mary, the virgin mother of men, has been espoused. It is an astounding fact that scholars in the twentieth century are still searching for the location or even the existence of an orgasm in women. In contrast, Bleier turns away from this belated and bewildered search and proposes instead that women's sexuality can be best represented by Mary Jane Sherfey's concept of satiation-insatiation. If, as Masters and Johnson found, women are capable of multiple orgasms, then the traditional conception of female sexuality is destroyed. The physical strength of the potent man who "takes" the submissive, impotent woman is the societal image; but the anatomical capacity of women, who can experience up to fifty orgasms with mechanical manipulation, is the biological reality. Bleier believes that the male incapacity to respond to this "inordinate" sexuality may have led to the myth about the innate "passivity" of the "weaker" sex. The virgin Mary as the dutiful wife is not likely to demand too much, and the wanton Eve as the local whore offers services that are only occasionally purchased. In short, female sexual assertiveness must be denied or the logic of duality becomes invalid.

This image of innate female passivity continues to pervade the cultural world view. Thus we find that the research of the day is still invaded by cultural images which anthropomorphize concepts and subsequently sustain polarized sexual politics. Bleier questions the assumption that studies of animal behavior can be used to explain human sex-role behavior. To her, such an assumption overlooks the fact that human beings are qualitatively different; because of their cerebral cortex, they are both the producers and the products of their culture. Nevertheless, to live in a female body, rat or human, invites a set of assumptions.

Studies of aggression in rats suggest that introducing additional androgen at birth "produces" more fighting behavior; thus, males are hormonally more "aggressive." The catch is that subsequent research shows that the introduction of additional estrogen at birth also "produces" more "aggressive" behavior. The choice of research topic itself, and the easy use of a complex, culturally loaded concept, aggression, for a specific behavior, fighting, can be contrasted with other research in which female rats behave in a fashion inconsistent with masculist sex stereotypes. In an open field study cited by Bleier, female rats were more likely to investigate a new environment. In human terms, these actions could be easily labeled higher curiosity or exploratory behavior. Instead, they are simply labeled by the researcher "higher activity level." To attribute greater curiosity or exploratory propensity to female rats would deny female passivity, a quality necessary to "protection" or confinement of the human female. If the woman does not need male "protection," what unique social function is left to him? Even in *Rattus*

rattus, a female who explores and subsequently controls her own space and time raises unsettling questions.

FEMALE STRATEGIES: ANIMAL ADAPTATIONS AND ADAPTIVE SIGNIFICANCE

G. Kass-Simon, a researcher in and professor of zoology, joins Ruth Bleier in an attack on methodolatry,[5] the blind acceptance of objective technique presumably existing in a cultural vacuum into which no bias intrudes. Stressing the evolutionary thesis that that which has been adaptive is distinctive and discretely so for each individual living group, Kass-Simon deplores the sexist extrapolation of human ethics from research on other primates and even nonprimates. Peeling back the layers of cultural mythology, she carves out the core of the matter, which stated succinctly is this: Throughout the "natural" world, males are "naturally" dominant, and if women are "allowed" power, they will disrupt the functioning of human society.

This "scientific" assertion is not original to science. It is a recurrent, repetitive theme, told and retold in folklore, literature, drama, and music. In varying guises, it is also found in theology and the social sciences of psychology and sociology. To diverge briefly and somewhat facetiously, the storybook tale goes something like this.

> *Once upon a time, a long time ago, a hairy man, a strong and mighty hunter, wanted a woman who evidently didn't want him because he, club in one hand, used the other to drag her, still unwilling, into his cave. (Presumably she didn't have the sense to have a cave of her own, thus explaining the origins of patrilocality.) Once in the cave, he, without any foreplay other than the previous dragging about, "subdued" her—in short, he raped her. After this display of superiority, the woman came to "accept" her proper place at home in the cave, scorching pieces of mammoth meat on the coals or lying flat on her back in the bat dung submitting gladly to her master.*
>
> *In due time, she, as the saying goes, "was with child" which she promptly begat. By now the woman, slightly bald and still bruised, "realized" that her son needed a father. Who would he emulate in a fatherless cave? From this beginning, all other females developed "feminine wiles" to catch and keep a father. After a few thousand years, she gained from these female tactics a better social position—only one man could now beat or rape her. By the beginnings of recorded history, she had achieved the status of a genuine wife—her wiliness obtaining her a legal position approximately equal to a slave.*
>
> *Over the next several centuries, she began to worship men as gods, learning the true meaning of man's morality and replacing her own wayward ways with faith, hope, and charity (which her wiliness led her to believe she sorely needed from someone). Somewhere along the time line, she and a very few others timidly insisted on looking into a few books about faith, hope, and charity. This distressed the hirsute elders, who feared she might believe the words she read. Foreseeing calamitous ruin, the men forbade her education. But the woman swore everlasting and eternal obedience. It wasn't long after this that she stopped looking obedient and then stopped being obedient and even began to act like the superior man, wearing pants, swearing, smoking, drinking—all signs of superior masculinity.*
>
> *And as the woman began to act more like the man, the man began to act more*

like the woman, coming down to her level, losing his sanctity in process. The woman has now degenerated to the point that she and others of her kind shamelessly roam the streets, leading good women astray, good men into impotence, and everyone into the suicide of the sexes and the collapse of the society. The moral of the story? Equal pay for equal work, but the man who lets a woman have power is a jerk because the "natural" world will surely go berserk.

In a succinct form, the parable of the mouse matriarchy, an interpretation of research findings from an experimentally overcrowded mouse colony, restates this folklore. Essentially, the researchers found that a number of behavioral changes occurred under conditions of extreme overcrowding. Out of all the behaviorial shifts brought on by unnatural stress, the development of a mouse matriarchy is the one singled out for attention. The decline and death of every last mouse is, in large part, attributed to those uppity mouse mothers. The parallels to crowded metropolitan centers with human matriarchies (presumably black) and shiftless young males (again presumably black) are then drawn. The moral of this interpretation of objective research is obvious: Women in power means the destruction of society.

Kass-Simon retorts with one simple truism from evolutionary theory: If conditions change too rapidly for adaptation to occur, then any population will go into decline and die. The essential problem is not the mouse matriarchy but the human patriarchy which argues from the animal kingdom to the human species without attending to the enormous variation in form, physical attributes, and behaviors specifically developed in the adaptive process for each living group. We can argue universal traits only in terms of the adaptive significance for a particular population. If this is untrue, then women would be fully justified in accepting a killer image from such species as the praying mantis in which the female bites off the head of her mate while copulating with him. Women, too, can make simplistic generalizations from isolated traits of particular species, choosing those that foster images of female power. Or they can insist on intellectual integrity by denying the validity of masculist reasoning.

Each species must perpetuate itself, and each develops particular forms of mating behavior and techniques to ensure the survival of offspring. But the human species, because of a qualitative difference—the cerebral cortex—has produced technological potentials which can change the requirement for copulation between substantial numbers of women and men. However, sperm banks may already be antiquated repositories if cloning becomes a reality. Assuming that mating will continue to mean species survival, can we accept the further assumption that exaggerated sex differences heighten its probability?

It is easy to accept the idea that bright coloration of males in particular species is an adaptation used to protect females and babies, ensuring the survival of the young. But one can hardly credit human males in distinctive military attire with fewer attacks on human females and babies. The pilot in male military garb does not look to see if a person is wearing a dress before he releases his bomb. And in the latest adventure in barbarism, foot soldiers in clearly marked military uniforms were not particularly concerned with protecting Vietnamese women and their children. To the contrary, some were even forced to walk through fields in which mined explosives were detected when the distinctively dressed women were blown into unidentifiable fragments.

Exaggerated sex differences in appearance or size can be functional in species inhabiting large territories where one sex cannot easily find the other. But accentuation of differences cannot be applied as an adaptive technique to a social species whose numbers cluster together even in masses. In large population centers, it is safer if women are *not* distinctively attired in order to protect themselves from attacks by males of their *own* species. Even the exaggeration of physical differences in size is dysfunctional for women who want to exert their own individuality. Women who wish to be liberated from male dominance can no longer afford to perpetuate it by purposely choosing males in accordance with media-manipulated images of masculinity. A six-foot-four tough guy is the last person a five-foot-four gentlewoman should look for. The adulation of masculine strength is a cultural lag based on an image useless in a society in which brains are presumably more important than brawn. Moreover, females in the human species cannot rely on biologically inherited inhibitory mechanisms that automatically halt aggression in other species. Anomic conditions in large urban conclaves further strip away the meager social sanctions that were intended to control intraspecies aggression.

The survival of offspring is not now, nor was it ever, *primarily* obtained through protective male strength. In fact, the future of new generations is squarely in the hands of women today. If women do not control birth, the world may become uninhabitable for them and their children.

THE ESSENTIAL EMANCIPATION

If powerful men, who control religions, economic and political systems in the world's nations, continue to deny the validity of birth control and abortion, our species will in all probability not survive. Given projected world population statistics, the impasse on a woman's right to control her body simply means that men are unwilling to give up their ultimate power over women even when species survival is at stake. It will not be a mouse or human matriarchy that brings about our destruction; it will be the male control over propagation which, if unchecked, will lead to overcrowding, famine, and death. Hania Ris, a pediatrician, a specialist in juvenile medicine, and an indefatigable proponent of a woman's right to her own body and a child's right to be wanted, stresses this fact as she discusses the imperative need for the essential emancipation. The complete control of time and space is gained through the ownership of the body living within these dimensions. Even more fundamental is the right to control the *internal* space and time *within* the body of another person. The ultimate in total power is the arrogant abrogation of a woman's right to say whether her own body will be inhabited by another creature. The final, complete, and total abuse of a woman's dignity is the denial of her right to control her own internal space and time.

Women have been traditionally responsible for birth control and, at the same time, have had no control over birth control. This absurd illogicality creates species behavior that is flatly, undeniably non-adaptive. Few living groups tolerate female exclusion from the behaviors that control number, spacing, and location of births. Males are certainly not excluded in particular species patterns; but in the human species, men have created cultures in which they achieve "manhood" by the impregnation of the largest number of females. The head count of children sired has too long served to define the "masculinity" of the sire, not the welfare of the woman who bears the children, nor the well-being of the children themselves.

Barefoot and pregnant in the kitchen, the woman, once having lost control of her internal space and time, now finds power to control *external* space and time sharply limited. One can hardly rebel while one is bearing a child or tending a newborn infant. One cannot move freely through self-directed time and space with a brood of four to twelve children in pursuit. Active exploration of the world is difficult when a woman's body is literally worn out from repeated births, stillbirths, and miscarriages.

"Pregnancy is the domination of one by two." This domination is perpetuated by cultural images of the self-sacrificing woman who is assumed to live for others. Woman can die because of botched abortions or difficult pregnancies, as long as the fetus lives. In short, a woman should sacrifice even her very life for others, symbolically in the daily acts of life and ultimately in the act of giving birth. Although the woman alive can birth other children, she should sacrifice her life even though the fetus is not fully human and incapable of normal existence. If such self-sacrifice were expected of men, we would hardly face today the possibility of total oblivion through acts of war.

The sacrifice of women will eventually lead to the sacrifice of the species. In 1915, 100 million Americans existed; another 100 million have since been added. Around the globe, 3.9 billion people exist; but by the year 2000 a total of 7 billion are expected to inhabit the world. As Ris points out, the course ahead is suicide, starvation, economic and social disaster; these are the prices we will pay for continued masculist domination. Men can no longer expect to live parasitically off the sacrifices of women nor can they continue to use them as property in marriage arrangements. Women pay dearly with higher maternal and infant mortality when they, as owned objects, do not control the proper number and spacing of births nor even the ages at which they give birth. Those who "belong" to poor or racially "unacceptable" men are caught in a stratification system which increases the probability of death or disability for both women and children. Excluding the wealthy woman, who is a piece of property too valuable to be kept barefoot and pregnant, all women continue to live in fear because their fundamental biological right has been stolen from them by the very men who claim to prize them.

It is an easy step from the sacrifice of an object to the exclusion of it from other rights. The "protection" of women by loving men is impossible when their own system denies "their" women the rights that require protection. It is women who must battle for the freedoms they deserve; and it was a woman, Margaret Sanger, who led the fight for a woman's right to her body. Jailed eight times for her efforts, her leadership has, until recently, remained unknown to younger women. If the work of strong feminist leaders were openly acknowledged or widely known, their lives would shatter the pictures of male "protection," revealing a portrait of lies. Thus, a woman who protects other women must be discredited; her own portrait touched up to make her appear immoral, evil, insane, or merely simple-minded. As Lionel Tiger and other learned men "know," only men "bond" together. If women do try to protect other women, and men do not, what is all the male bonding for?

At this point in history, the "nonexistent" bonding of women is backing the clergy against the wall. To reclaim the right to their own creativity is to deny the symbolism of male cosmogony. Historically, only a male god has had the right to decide who he will implant with himself. If the male god's control of creation is to be continued by male priests, they must change theology to incorporate female creativity. This is an extraordinarily difficult task because the assumption underlying theological thought is female sacrifice writ large. Women live to produce the gods of creation, the love of sons divinely sanctioned. They cannot birth the goddesses of creation because these have all been destroyed. The only remaining female link to divinity is through one woman who acted as a receptacle for the birth of a male child. So much for the love of daughters.

The fight over abortion has less to do with the life of the "unborn" than with the continuation of a male-dominated cosmogony which sanctions male-controlled social structures. Although the attacks on the Supreme Court decision continue unabated, the flock of the faithful do not follow their shepherds: 68 percent of married Catholics already use birth control not approved by the church; 56 percent of Catholic people believe the choice to bear a child is a personal decision; even 27 percent of Catholic male physicians favor the high court ruling.

Hania Ris provides equally compelling statistics about poor women, particularly those of racial minorities, who suffer most under the male cosmogony of creation. Contrary to the earlier power polemics of some black men, the majority of black women approve of birth control and abortion, provided their control excludes the possibility of genocide. In one study cited by Ris, seven of ten black women wanted three or fewer children and eight out of ten believed in family planning. About 75 percent were *already* using birth-control techniques, unfortunately of *low* reliability. Yet some white men in power say women on welfare want more babies. And some black men in power say the white men want black genocide. The critical image of women held by both groups is the picture of a silent woman who sits respectfully listening to "*the* man" or "*her* man" as each tells others what the woman thinks and feels. The silence of both black and white women in public situations is assumed.

Men still believe they have the right to speak for women. Their official voices echo down the centuries, drowning out the voices of foremothers who attempted to control births intelligently. Obliterated from most history books, women have had, with or without the cooperation of men, no choice. If pregnant, the Scarlet Letter was branded on *their* foreheads. When men *have* been involved in birth control, their experiments, including the current use of the "pill," have been conducted on *women's* bodies. One study cited by Ris shows that 39 of 42 medicinal plants used for birth control were for female ingestion. According to Ris, the earliest record of oral contraception was 2736 B.C. in China; of the diaphragm and douche, 1850 B.C. in Egypt and 1500 B.C. in India; of coitus interruptus, by Jews in antiquity; and of the condom (used historically for protection of the male from disease) in cave paintings.

In more recent history, men pompously continue to legislate the lives of women. Adapting Aristotle's ideas, Aquinas believed the male fetus to be a person forty days and the female eighty days after conception. In the 1200s the Catholic male clergy considered abortion acceptable before the fetus moved. In 1588, by male papal decree, all abortions were murder. Three years later, another male papal decree reversed this position, establishing a forty-day limitation. That ruling lasted until 1869 when male clerics again prohibited abortion. It is this "logical," "humane" tradition, traced by Ris, which is now being fought by women all over the world. If women cannot control the caprice of male celibates, what can they control? If not their own biology, how then their own psychology?

SOME PSYCHOLOGICAL "FACTS" ABOUT WOMEN: WILL THE REAL MS. PLEASE STAND UP?

Theologically, female psychology is, at best, schizophrenic and, at worst, paranoiac. From the pedestal to the pit, the cosmological imagery is devoid of almost everything but delusion. Scientifically, the old duality dawdles along, dangling old myths in bright new polysyllables which remain disgustingly familiar when stripped of pseudo profundity. Julia A. Sherman, clinical psychologist, practitioner, and researcher, reviews the extant psychological literature for facts about women and, after finding these "facts," she ironically asks, "Will the real Ms. please stand up?" With great restraint, she reaffirms her belief in empiricism but disclaims an objective science that is too often subjective.

In contrast to Sherman, some women believe that the real problem is not the *use* of scientific method but the assumed *split* between objectivity and subjectivity underlying the use of it. Already proved erroneous in physics by Einstein, this false dichotomy continues in the social sciences with disastrous consequences when applied to the study of human life. To the new religion of the day, devotees pay homage to a methodology that continues to deny the reality of women's lives. Sherman, although skeptical, leaves the methodological structure intact, uses the established criteria to assess the quality of results, and finds them dismally lacking, too often an incoherent statement of an ancient folklore.

The thread holding together the torn pieces of women's psychology is the continuity of male power. Theories of female development, such as Freud's explanation of identity formation, are inadequate and incorrect, more usefully read as justification of sexual politics than a treatise on the female psyche. Although insufficient, a few studies of sex socialization do show early learning of power differentials: By six, boys enact the roles of policeman and President, flexing small muscles which will later enforce masculist law. Little girls are trained to inhibit anger and aggression. Later, the "admirable restraint of men" will be triggered by disdain for women who are programmed never to provoke, always to placate—the costs of "protection." As an adult woman, she will be so tamed that she shrinks from even a muscle substitute, any weapon that logically could be used to reduce physical inequity in strength. In short, she has fully learned that "femininity" equals weakness and "masculinity," strength.

This cultural imagery influences the choice of research topics that reflect the recurrent rationalization of female subordinate status; thus, when hormonal differences are researched, the studies focus on the effects of androgen on behavioral aggression, implicitly justifying the quiet withdrawal of women from public affairs. How hormones affect gentleness or sensitive responsiveness to others remains unquestioned and never analyzed. After considering the available research, Sherman recognizes the replacement of a biological myth with a chemical one, saying, "Hormones are destiny no more than anatomy is destiny."

Strangely, undeniable differences in weight, height, and muscle mass, although sharply subject to cultural constraints, are seldom analyzed in terms of their obvious power implications in the child's development or in the adult's life. It almost seems as if the researchers avoid the obvious, but try to justify it indirectly through anatomical images or, more currently, hormonal symbols. Perhaps the image of "rational" man, of "civilized" life itself, cannot stand the direct examination of the female predicament.

The power theme also threads its way through studies of intelligence. Paradoxically, researchers look for differences, not similarities. One of the few studies of commonalities demonstrates an average correlation of .90 between female and male thinking. Yet psychologists trudge along in search of differences, discovering en route "superior" male analytical reasoning. But careful factor analysis of their research reveals that most of the sex variance can be attributed to a difference in *spatial* reasoning. Certainly this thought process is one which is severely negated by cultural constrictions on female space and time, by societal restrictions on objects available to females, and by the actuality of their entire lives.

Despite these facts, the psychologist, Sherman, like the neuroanatomist, Bleier, must continue to fight the battle against female "inferior" intellect. Behind the academic façade is an implicit vindication of male control; without "superior" intellect, how can men in authority explain their continued exclusion of "the little woman"? According to Sherman, the studies used to support this power trip are replete with methodological and sexist errors; notions that fit the popular bias are accepted without question, even without statistical test. Under Sherman's scrutiny, the general structure of psychological knowledge comes under severe attack. For example, trait psychology when studied from the woman's perspective simply cannot survive the assault. The women's critique uncovers the flimsy structure of masculist thought; Sherman as sleuth even discovers the case of the disappearing sex difference when she compares studies from different time periods.

If artificial sex differences are disappearing, their absence has yet to be noticed by most researchers. This is hardly surprising. Exaggerated incongruities are essential to any rationalization of inequity. If "the same" cannot also be "less than," then the same cannot be recognized. Dissonance must be emphasized in *all* cultural images if the masculist screen is to mesh together: If women are intellectually different and "less than," then they must also be emotionally different and "less than." It is possible to speak of emotion as separate from intellect only because of the subject-object split; yet, with supreme irony, the assumption of male rationality and female irrationality is the base on which is founded the images of women's emotional lives.

Caught on an unhappy merry-go-round, the woman is irrational because she is emotional; she is emotional because she is not fully rational. Whether up or down, the wooden steed is stationary while the calliope wheezes out the same old tune as the carousel goes round and round. To keep this carnival atmosphere, people must and do overlook one simple fact: Acts of aggression contain emotion. Evidently, researchers assume that male aggression is also rational. Female "maladjustment" exonerates exclusion of women from the "important" arenas of male debate. To sustain this inequality, we must all disregard the facts: More men are alcoholics, more are drug addicts, more commit suicide, and more commit homicide. It is clearly time for women to walk away from the midway and to leave the sideshow.

The concept of aggression, as Sherman details it, is a sponge term, soaking up any and all meanings. There is no agreed upon nomenclature. Is it fantasy, verbal, or physical? Is it directed to a person or an object? With or without intention to harm? Is it dominance aggression to "extend" the life space or attack aggression to engage another creature? Out of confusion comes one initial finding: Males engage in attack aggression more than females. Psychologist Kenneth Clark recently suggested that men in power should receive regular doses of anti-aggression drugs. His recommendation was received with polite smiles. But the cross-cultural dominance of half a species more inclined toward attack aggression is no laughing matter in the global village. The exclusion of "maladjusted" women can no longer be justified. In fact, their inclusion might bring some sanity to an imbalanced world which can no longer withstand *male* maladjustment.

"Make love, not war," the slogan of the peace generation, assumes that sensual and sexual responsiveness are distributed evenly throughout the entire species. But again Sherman must join Bleier in an attack on the mythology of female sexuality. Leaving untouched the male origins of most experiments, she notes that males seem to have an earlier interest and a higher involvement in sex, including pornographic presentations of it. Because men are trained to be voyeurs and women, exhibitionists, these findings are hardly surprising. If half the population is to exhibit sexuality while admitting no interest in it, these results scarcely reveal anything important. In a culture that prohibits exploration of women's own internal space and time through negative sanctions on masturbation, the more complex and less obvious bodies of women will never be examined or known by them. Furthermore, pornography often combines male power fantasies with sadistic domination of females; it is therefore unclear why female subjects should be titillated by experimental versions of the old imagery. Research findings that detail the obvious and ignore complex causation add little to a knowledge of women. Until the thread of male domination is cut, the study of the human psyche will not be achieved. As Sherman puts it: "In the past psychology has constructed the female; now females must reconstruct psychology."

ON FEMININE SELF-PRESENTATION IN GROUPS

Jane Allyn Piliavin, a social psychologist, sets out to look for information on perceptions of "appropriate sex roles," finding remarkably little in the social psychological or sociological literature. She asks, What *really* is expected of women and men? How do women and men perceive their own personalities and their ideal selves? How do members of the opposite (*sic*) sex want to live their lives? What do women and men *actually* do? And how do others behave toward those who do not conform to their expectations? She concludes with W. I. Thomas, "If men [*sic*] define situations as real, they are real in their consequences." And asks, Are we acting on assumed or actual biases? If assumed, women may behave according to the expectations of men even if they do not actually hold them.

We return in Piliavin's questions to an explication of the unstated premises of implicit culture. The most significant premises are often so deep in the cultural matrix of beliefs that they are considered the "natural" state of affairs. So natural that to study them is to study the "obvious." The absence of research on the questions Piliavin asks of the literature is the first step in explication. One does not study the trivial; the powerless position of women, the "frilly" nature of their lives has made the study of them the study of triviality.

From the sparse research available, one study of sex socialization is found by Piliavin who reports the researcher's conclusion that there is a high cross-cultural consistency in sex-role socialization. To explicate the cultural biases in this conclusion, it is necessary to reconsider the research at some length. Unfortunately, this comparative study of isolated traits taken out of social context suffers from the usual problems of this type of research, i.e., unbalanced sample of cultures, simplistic rating procedures, differences in ethnographic methods and reports of the same phenomena. More importantly, the use of culturally bound terms from one society are used to subsume the beliefs and behaviors of other groups, which as separately configurated may create a Gestalt that carries quite different meanings for the same terms. When men study women using the reports of predominantly male researchers, they will find it hard to avoid adding a second source of bias.

The researchers themselves, in their early work, note this fact saying that the ethnographers could have been biased in favor of seeing the same kind of sex differences in our culture and that the judges who rated each cultural group could have been expected to find in other cultures the sex roles familiar in their own, inferring them from the ethnographic materials. Although these biases are subsequently denied, there seems no other possible mode of interpretation because there is so little explication of sex roles in our own culture. Bias is most likely when prejudice is not believed to exist.

Examples of explanatory assumptions from their own work might help to clarify the sexist error. First explanation: Men go out hunting; hunting requires a high degree of skill. Their unstated assumption? Presumably, it takes no highly developed skills or complex knowledge to bear and raise children, to make vegetables, fruits, and small animals grow, or to minister to the needs of others. Yet it is reliably estimated that over 60 percent of the diets of most cultural groups are provided by women and their children, meat from large animals being an uncertain source of food.

Second explanation: Men go out killing other men and their kin; warfare requires a high degree of skill necessitated by life or death situations. The unstated premise? Presumably, the bearing and raising of children in societies in which infant and maternal mortality are extremely high takes no greater order of skills even though women, too, face life-and-death conditions.

Assuming that these sexist biases do not affect categories and concepts, the findings indicate that females are expected to be more nurturant, responsible, and somewhat more obedient, while males are to be more achieving and self-reliant. "Nurturant" is roughly defined as being more helpful to younger siblings and other dependent people; "responsibility," as the performance of chores in domestic economy, the "drudge" work of society; and "obedience" is never clearly defined at all. For boys, "self-reliance" also lacks definitional clarity while "achievement" is defined in terms of training toward excellence in standards of performance.

The family in which children learn these sex-typed roles is never questioned as a structural means of control over female adults and children. Nor are the socialized characteristics, when defined, analyzed for cultural bias. For example, a category such as "achievement," even in choice of word, is loaded with American cultural values. In fact, the concept of motivation itself, in American social science, is often limited to achievement motivation, a form of striving for dominance over persons and processes often founded on presumed deprivation of particular biological needs. In contrast, a female anthropologist, Dorothy Lee, posits autonomous motivation, denoting a more generalized urge generated by social needs to reach out to the full possibilities of human capacity.

Even if we accept uniform cross-cultural socialization, temporarily overlooking biased concepts, we can only conclude that the "superior" strength of men has too often been used to create castelike status for women everywhere. In the trilogy of female characteristics, obedience is the most interesting concept. To whom is this obedience extended and how is it enforced? How did the nurturance of others and the responsibility for their social welfare come to be denigrated? When and by what means did the killing of animals and humans achieve such prestige? If obedience is demanded, how has it been enforced? If the results are accurate, this sad commentary on the "progress" of "civilization" needs no further comment.

Turning from anthropological data on other societies, Piliavin analyzes the interaction of women and men in American cultural groups. As in Sherman's critique, the characteristics inculcated through social expectations form a litany of subjugation. The "small" girl is expected to inhibit verbal and physical aggression, to be submissive, passive, dependent, and conforming, and to learn restraint of sexual needs. The "large" boy is expected to exhibit aggressiveness, inhibit dependency, and is prepared to make sexual "conquests" and to acquire money and power.

Some researchers assume that more negative sanctions are directed toward boys who violate their role expectations. Although this tentative generalization cannot be supported by historical facts, whether economic, legal, or social, it does seem plausible if limited to one particular condition. Erving Goffman, in his earlier theoretical work on role theory, believed that people stage their roles in life, using backstage and front-stage areas. What happens backstage must remain hidden from those watching the show. In daily life, one doesn't expect the dishwasher to saunter in and out of the dining room; this behavior would violate the social setting, lending little grace to "elegant" dining.

Similarly, in life as a whole, men play the starring roles on front stage in a theater constructed by them. Women are usually relegated to support functions backstage. To maintain this peculiarly one-sided performance, everyone has to believe that the woman should be excluded. If a male begins to exhibit "female" characteristics, he is equivalent to the unwanted dishwasher, violating male domination of front stage. Thus, a little boy who is a "sissy" or a man who acts like a woman will be severely sanctioned because each has "given the act away." No man should want to behave like a woman, a member of an inferior caste. If he does, the "rightness" of the caste system will be questioned and the starring roles will have to be shared.

When comparing men's and women's perceptions of each other, Piliavin finds that men may have less restrictive expectations than women think they do. It may well be that some women "cherish their chains," holding firmly to sex discrimination, fearing the loss of female "virtue" and male "protection." But Piliavin also concludes that stereotyped sex roles are more likely in public situations. If we then ask who controls most public situations, we return full circle to male domination. This does not diminish the irresponsibility of some women who continue to support prejudice, who repudiate identification with strong women struggling in their behalf, and who claim young girls for subordinate status and contingent life. Even these acquiescent women, despite their disclaimers, do not control the ultimate sources of *public* sanction; this fact should serve as a reminder to them and their male counterparts that it is illogical and unethical to blame the victim and not the victimizer.

When women and men interact in groups, their stylized roles produce predictable patterns, with males tending to engage in task behaviors and females in socioemotional acts. If either sex refuses to enact these calculated performances, social sanctions can be severe. Lesbian women, who refuse to play the game, avoid the performance even before it begins. They pay for their strength with a lifetime of closeted secrecy. Career women who seek success in high-status roles may also pay a high price for their sex-inappropriate behavior. Women who were experimentally induced to express influence in Piliavin's own careful research were objects of mixed reactions. Even the female experimenters were not taken seriously. Women in Matina Horner's research, who responded to identical descriptions of outstanding male and female medical students, expressed fear of social rejection, doubts about femininity, and distortion and denial of facts. One fearful reaction to the female student's success: "Her fellow classmates are so disgusted with her behavior that they jump on her in a body and beat her. She is maimed for life." Piliavin, in her small-group research, finds this reaction unfounded and sums up her own to the work in her field: "[we] seem to be up against a self-fulfilling prophecy based on a myth, rather than a conspiracy backed up by social ostracism. Perhaps we have nothing to fear but fear itself." Although optimism is always welcome, it alone will not recover our lost history nor rip off the façade behind which women are forced to live. It is real *intellectual work* and active political *involvement* that *together* will change the lives of women around the world who are, indeed, symbolically and sometimes actually maimed by a system of female exclusion and male domination.

WOMEN SOCIAL WORKERS AND CLIENTS: COMMON VICTIMS OF SEXISM

In American culture, poor women, particularly those on welfare, *do* have more to fear than fear itself. Most of them are literally or figuratively beaten down; and many of them and their children are indeed physically, mentally, and emotionally maimed for life. The woman at the bottom of the heap, who lives without a man or with an "unsuccessful" man, is a casualty of the patriarchal system that trains her to be dependent and penalizes her for dependency. In masculist society, poverty *is* a *woman's* problem. Families headed by women constitute only 14 percent of the population, but make up 44 percent of the poverty population. All women share in different degrees a common economic discrimination. Women workers earn about half the median salary of men, and black women average about one-third less than their white sisters. This discrimination most assuredly creates fear; but it is not the fear itself women must fight but the masculist system that creates it.

To Diane Kravetz, a professor of social work, both women social workers and clients are common victims of sexism—all share powerlessness. Once a "women's profession," the field of social work is now male dominated. When men were recruited to raise the profession's status, they simply assumed most of the power positions, leaving the women bereft. Even the professionals have become segregated into outer-oriented male community organizers and inner-oriented female caseworkers.

Along with other female professions, social work has the prime objective of making cohesive that which is fragmentary and disintegrating. However, the traditional role of synthesizer is valued only when the social fabric starts to rip apart. Essentially, the social worker's job is to patch together the masculist system so that the ragged holes will not be seen. Ironically, women in social work stitch back together the torn fragments of a system that pulls the lives of women apart. Caught· in the compassion trap, they enforce masculist rules and regulations, sustaining in the process the oppression of themselves and other women.

According to one welfare mother the welfare woman trades in *a* man for *the* man. What does this unholy state of matrimony produce? An exaggeration of all the negative imagery of woman. The welfare mother is seen as lazy, immoral, incompetent. Unlike other women, she is expected to work and to make ends meet, even when full-time employment at women's wages makes this impossible. All women are caught in the sexist trap, but for the woman on welfare the jaws are sprung and the painful jagged world is unescapable.

The image of the childlike irrational woman is fostered by bureaucratic infantilizing. In a doll's house without dolls, the state dictates the woman's relation to men, controls every dollar she spends, and reserves the right to enter the home without notice. Extending these husbandly prerogatives with their own wives to poor women, male bureaucrats strip "their" women of every semblance of dignity. Poor mothers with children are simply illegitimate, not part of the "deserving" poor.

Kravetz points directly to the ultimate reason for female acquiescence. Women feel they have no outlet for resentment and anger; anger is then turned inward, with depression the unhappy, even tragic result. Confrontation between women and men must be avoided, even if it costs the woman her sanity. Held in her unclenched hand is the deep rage of every woman. The elaborated social structure keeps that hand from becoming a fist, using the woman herself to maintain her closed-in resentment of a vulnerability enhanced by masculist social conventions. Slack-handed, the woman is then used to take on all the failures of family and others, a passive receptacle for the sins of all. Kravetz claims that therapy and marriage, two socially approved institutions for women, serve to *diffuse* anger, providing isolated, individual solutions to the *collective* problems of women as a caste.

In large numbers, women can protect *themselves*, according to *their* own perceptions of their *own* needs. As individuals, when threatened with the ultimate sanction of physical force, their last recourse and only option is to maim or kill. A man does not fight bare-fisted a three-hundred-pound bear with the intent to damage it moderately. The intent is to remove it. The initial inequity in strength allows no other course of action. Similarly, if women are to express their anger outward, they must, as individuals, face the reality of the ultimate sanction that can be and has been used against them. Until a woman's basic fear of retaliation is faced, and until the terrible reality of her final recourse is acknowledged, the cultural image of female passivity will continue. And condescension toward the "fragile" woman who "needs" protection will accompany it.

Kravetz cites a study by Broverman in which clinicians' choice of adjectives to describe the healthy, mature adult were found to be the same as those used to characterize a healthy, mature male. Those used for the "healthy, mature" female differed significantly with the familiar caste characteristics indicated, i.e., more submissive, less independent, and less objective. According to these findings from therapists, a woman who wants to be a "healthy" adult will have to become a man. If she adapts to the female version of maturity, she is automatically maladjusted. This double bind, historically derived from the ultimate sanction of force, will collapse when women and men face honestly their physical disparity and the kind of society it has produced; one hopes that the dialogue engendered will produce a culture in which gentleness is the mark of maturity for all.

THE NEW FEMINIST CRITICISMS: EXPLORING THE HISTORY OF THE NEW SPACE

Values of the women's world remain within it. Muted and subdued, still they survive, yet to be uncovered. Women pay for the "chivalrous" gift of male "protection" with the self-sacrifice of their own noncontingent culture. What gift is this with strings attached? Protection swapped for obedience, submission, and conformity. Even worse, "security" is bartered for exclusion, for eventual oblivion. Removed "for her own good" from the men's competitive world, a woman's destruction is justified by a final resort to muscle, again used as the measure of morality. Behind the stately rhetoric and the parliamentary maneuvers, when the chips are down, when a man has to fight another man, a woman is a "liability." Yet that "liability" is the historical affirmation of life, the denial of the ultimate use of force.

The rejection of the creative force of women is not the criminal act of a few uncouth ruffians. The real villains can be found in the ivory tower where "refined" men of "learning" ponder *their* universe, proclaiming the meaning of *their* world. When Annis Pratt walks into *their* observatory and peers through *their* telescopes at the literary heavens, she looks for her own star and finds a black hole where it should be. As a professor of English, Pratt's painful realization of her own oblivion sends her on a search through two hundred years of women's literature, focusing her own lens on the history of the new space now being created by women for themselves. As Pratt explores deeper into women's inner space, she struggles toward the explication of women's culture, the underground values kept alive by women who would not accept their exclusion, who braved the loss of male "protection," suffered the ready absence of "chivalry" for "their kind of women," to write the words they felt to be their own.

Moving through the strata of feminist criticisms, Pratt digs down to the bottom layer and finds herself explicating the imagery of the new space. Searching for theorists among the male thinkers on whose thought she has been trained, she turns to Frye but finds him saying that the poet is not father of his poem; he is at best a midwife, the work of mother nature herself, "her privates, he so to speak." To accept his imagery, Pratt would have to speak from the phallus of father nature, his privates, she, so to speak. With absurdity piling on absurdity, she turns to social theorists, choosing Jung, whose archetypes provide constructs for analysis of the emergent imagery. But once again she is frustrated; caught in the masculist trap, she finds Jung saying that man locates woman just where man's shadow falls, only too liable to confuse her with it. Despite his sympathy, she is stuck with his dichotomized categories, the anima and animus, continued dualities of the masculist world view. Finally, with theoretical variations, she develops her own version of archetypal criticism which she uses to cut through the masculist screen. Stepping through the sheared edges she finds underlying patterns, configurations that other scholars have not seen. To them women's literature is comprised of a few books which are abnormalities in a space devoid of organized coherence.

But when Pratt looks at the female literary galaxy, she finds a uniformity of concerns underlying the words written by women. From even the most nonfeminist sources, a theme of rebellion emerges. One pattern, the theme of marital rebellion, recurrently depicts the female suffering under the chauvinist husband, who is eventually killed off. After his death, the woman finds a more sensitive man. This smothered anger arises in the works of the most unlikely writers.

Somewhat startled, Pratt finds a second wave, one she calls the fatal effects of matrimony in which the destruction of any creativity of the mind leads to insanity or suicide. This theme is epitomized by one female character who is denied the use of her creative talent by her husband who sends her off to "rest" in the country. Once there she slowly goes insane, eventually ripping off the yellow scroll wallpaper in her room so she can let the woman out. The husband comes to visit, finding her bloody and covered with wallpaper. The female hero says, "I don't know why that man should faint dead away."

From the tragic or comic plots, Pratt identifies one genre of writing in which the light, witty, intelligent woman, critical of society and marriage, succumbs to it, refuses to play out the traditional role, and dies. Death for the woman who dares to be different, who says, "I will not take your 'gift.' " A second genre is the fallen woman whose slightest wiggle of sexuality, of erotic initiative, leads to heavy punishment. A third is the drowning effect in which women drown out what they are saying about feminism, hiding their anger from even themselves.

To be published or to be socially "acceptable" after appearing in print, women have been forced to deny explicitly or implicitly their own personal integrity. Early in the struggle to escape oblivion, women writers so frequently used male pseudonyms that the literary guessing game, is he really a he or just a she, became a parlor pastime. Yet the new images of a noncontingent culture draw power from the flow of women's determination, which was sustained throughout the most trying circumstances. Through the intense literary images of their work, the patterns of covert resistance provide a historical base for the overt rebellion of women today.

FRENCH WOMEN WRITERS: A PROBLEMATIC PERSPECTIVE

The extraordinary idea that women are the talkative sex is a peculiarity of masculist logic that transcends national boundaries. If women are, in fact, more verbally proficient, their continued exclusion from public speech, either spoken or written, seems a flagrant misuse of a superior talent. To get out of this illogicality, women's talk is seen as gossip, men's, as discourse. When women first publicly broke their angry silence, the shock was not only that they spoke, but that they had anything to say. That "silly chatterboxes" could not only think but also write their thoughts down page after page in a logical manner was a funny joke, an absurdity barely tolerable and hardly acceptable. The shock welled up from violations in the cross referencing of metaphorical images. In historical reality, the female sex is best characterized *not* by talk but by a silence born out of subjugation.

In the New Testament when Paul admonished women to be silent, his words, on which other men stacked their own, set the "sacred" standard for hundreds of years of quiet submission. As scripture, all these words justified centuries of silence. To break that intolerable stillness was the great battle and astonishing achievement of nineteenth-century women writers and political activists. The courage to crack two thousand years of public withdrawal, previously broken by only a few exceptional women, was shared across national boundaries and so was the opprobrium that ensued. Germaine Brée, a professor of French literature and internationally known scholar, examines the forms of that opprobrium as they continue in this century.

Unlike Pratt, Brée does not grapple with the explication of women's culture in the literary works of French women. Although she questions whether there are real differences in female and male use of language, she leaves the answers to linguistic analyses as yet undone. She asks if we can distinguish natural from cultural differences between the sexes and concludes that the answers are, at this point, unclear. The cultural study of French women writers dates back to the thirteenth century, and for this reason, the analytical problems created by a dearth of previous analyses are difficult. Further, the rapidity of social change in this century makes cultural analyses even more problematic. In contrast to Pratt, Brée appears to conceive of masculist culture as *the* culture. Yet she draws a clear picture of the mythic Frenchwoman, innately superior, sophisticated, and self-possessed: the lady as fashion plate, objet d'art with elegance, bon goût, and a narcissistic chic which "at least does not sentimentalize sexual relations."

But it is not this "feminine" adaptation, real or imagined, from which outstanding female authors have emerged. As Brée notes, the foremost French women writers are outsiders, from the provinces, rural origins, lower social classes, peripheral or foreign groups, and lesbian subcultures (the last a group omitted in her chapter). The rejection of the mythological Frenchwoman, the personification of slick sophistication, is inherent in the situations of their lives.

Turning to the characters found in earlier women's writing, where, it is asked, are the lost images of the awesome women; the queenlike figures of advanced years, the earth mothers, the pioneer mothers, the superbly aging whores and opera singers with young lovers? Intuiting the essence of women's culture, Brée turns to the masculist world and considers its reception of female writers who produced these images of women. She discovers the usual sexual politics: French male critics seem to display no greater gallantry to female "intruders" than the men of other cultures. Configured in different terms, they nevertheless use discouragingly familiar tactics: They ignore, omit, exclude, leaving women almost entirely outside their own evaluative system. In anthologies, the ratio of four to twelve token women to three hundred men is consistent. The literary efforts of women in this century continue to carry the clear connotation of inferiority. Brée finds the analysis of female literature strangely related to the erotic attraction, moral proclivities, and emotional life of the author. Commenting on one important author, a male critic claimed that no woman writer showed less intelligence and none in contrast so much sensibility; having no invention, no creative imagination, only complete truth of heart with love as the foundation of her life.

Nowhere is the usurpation of all creativity more succinctly expressed than in another critic's uncritical reliance on this generalization: "From the point of view of intelligence, she has perceptions, memory, imagination. What is lacking is the capacity to produce seeds, that is to say, ideas, what the Latins call genius." This seems more an exercise in semenology than an analysis upon which to base a literary judgment. Perhaps the real "genius" of academic life is the capacity to produce an overweening masculist arrogance.

In the critical writings of feminist women, one theme repeats itself over and over again: Women are not taken seriously. Leaving aside the obvious sexual connotations of the verb, the word "serious" requires examination. The imposed state of "nonseriousness" (there is no word for this peculiarly female condition) when combined with a physical state of vulnerability together form the existential theme of female life from birth onward. Vulnerability allows the arrogant imposition of "nonseriousness" to go unchecked.

Perhaps we can better understand the "seriousness" of this problem if we turn it upside down. If one-half of the population is not "taken seriously," then the other half must compensate for this fallacy by taking itself *too* seriously. The consequences of an exaggerated sense of one's own worth is plain old-fashioned pomposity, which can only be pricked by the lilting laughter of a little woman who no longer stands in awe of the big man, who no longer sits quietly listening to his pious pronouncements ballooning out of an overly inflated sense of importance. It really is about time for women to have the belly laugh they have waited for after centuries of crushing, crashing boredom. But for many women, laughter will not soon come.

IMAGES OF WOMEN IN CONTEMPORARY MEXICAN LITERATURE

Life seems to hold little laughter for Mexican women, if we accept the images of them in the writing of Mexican men whose works have received critical acclaim in this century. From their words, Victoria Junco Meyer, a faculty woman specializing in Spanish literature and language, forms a mosaic, a composite image of suffering and sorrow. The combined forces of Spanish and Indian cultures create the Madonna-like creature, whose modesty is the repository for the reputations of husband and father, blended with a fatalistic earth mother, stoic, resigned, impassive, whose maltreatment is the single constant in her life.

The masks carved by men cover the women's faces and their most intimate feelings. When the masquerade stops, when the males take off their own masks, their faces show that they love, fear, despise women. In cultural mythology, goddesses of creation are also goddesses of destruction: "Does she hide life within herself or death? What does she think? Or does she think? Does she truly have feelings? Is she the same as we men are?"

There can be no answers to these questions from a muted creature who is passive, forcibly opened, violated, deceived, her children the offspring of *ma-chismo,* the violent affirmation of masculist physical domination. Never asked to consent, woman participates passively. Open, offering no resistance, she loses her identity, her name; "she is no one; she disappears into nothingness; she is Nothingness." Annihilation is then turned into a virtue; long-suffering, indifferent to pain, the virgin mother is pure receptivity, the one who consoles, quiets, calms. The one who weeps.

From the men's image of upper-class woman, there is no solace for this earthy, virgin mother. There are only different masks, masks of emptiness worn by women whose shallow love affairs become grostesque with age. An upper-class woman during the revolutionary period says: "Offering me so little of life, he had refused to give me death too; he would have done better to give me something whole, one or the other." But the exchange of servitude for protection leaves the man nothing whole to offer, only the deceit of his own social conventions. From the cult of feminine spiritual superiority, the semidivine woman can offer nothing in return, only the mask, the façade he requires her to wear. If she takes off the mask of spirituality and engages in premarital intercourse or other "sins," nothing is complete, "everything [is] by halves—pride, sin, love, shame." Trapped in the incongruities of the masculist world view, women express their anger in hostile silence, withdrawal of emotional commitment: "I am a weak woman—all I want is a life of peace. . . ."

Analyzing the anguish of modern "man," another male writer describes the woman's dilemma in one character who was so good that everyone took advantage of her. She did not want to offend them or quarrel with them. Instead she committed suicide. There was nothing else she could do because she was so good. Premature death is a woman's only means of ending a life of suffering under the masculist yoke. The only thing God gave her was "a long, weary life." Born with a weakness to overcome, she is open and therefore passive; the only female free from the curse is the virgin mother. Short of divine intercourse, the woman has one other way out; she can become a hard, closed person who uses others. The majority do not escape. The masculist screen filters through an image of peasant woman who should and eventually does quietly suffer anguish and desperation; disillusioned with life, even death holds no peace: It is "not the summing up of all, but merely an agonized continuation of life." To make a life is to create something out of suffering the injustices men have inflicted.

Nowhere in this book does the basic dilemma of woman become so visible. From Meyer's analysis of the women, who as secondary characters people the books of men, comes forth the sorrow of woman subjugated by masculist force. Through the Latin cultural screen, the blows, although muffled by the cloaked virgin imagery, are at least acknowledged. What remains to be openly recognized is the retaliatory strength of feminist women who refuse to accept the *macho* meaning of their own existence; who attack the religious, economic, and legal systems which institutionalize their own suffering; who give a name to their nothingness—as they proudly and defiantly speak the word, woman.

WOMEN IN LEGAL PERSPECTIVE

The intense and painful images of women in literature are reflected in laws that codify the masculist values, attitudes, and practices of a sexist society. As the final arbiter of social conduct, the system of jurisprudence through which men hand down rulings on women is one of the staunchest supporters of inequitable treatment of women. To Kathryn Clarenbach, political scientist, professor, and a founder of the National Organization for Women, the challenge for women is to force the law to lead in changing social practices and beliefs.

What are the ancient origins of the "legal" suppression of women? How did the idea of woman as irresponsible permeate thousands of statutes? How does one-half of humanity justify their right to exclude the other half from the formation, application, and enforcement of laws? How have men presumed to decide on the imprisonment or death of women who have had no part in determining the laws by which they are judged?

Clarenbach traces female disenfranchisement to the "golden" age of Western civilization, to the "rational" Greek culture in which men philosophized on Utopia while their slaves and women were legal property. Most women were slaves and most slaves were women. Male slaves were in a better situation than women. After buying their freedom, they were released from bondage; but women remained chattel and property. When a woman "gave" her hand in marriage it literally signified the passing of chattel from father to husband. In the ceremonial rite of passage today, the father of the bride "gives" her away, symbolically renewing the husband's right to claim his property and denying in his act women's right to claim their own.

The idea that women never reach maturity, that they are forever children in need of "protection" passed through canon law to English common law and from there to the American system. The con game of "protection" has lasted a very, very long time. Having "won" the battle of the sexes,the masculist tautology is complete. *Male:* You need my protection. *Female:* From whom do I need protection? *Male:* From other men and animals. *Female:* But with other women I can protect myself from animals. And *you* are a man. *Male:* I'm not like other men. *Female:* I don't think I need or want your protection. *Male:* Take my protection or else. *Female:* I "need" your "protection" from other men who are "not" like you.

The human race will never grow up until the children's hour is over, until little girls are no longer expected to play by the rules of the game without being able to set the rules, until the neighborhood bully is no longer able to enforce the rules of "his side" when the little girls refuse to play by them. The best way to deal with uppity girls and women is to toss them out of the game entirely, "allowing" them to sit as observers on the sidelines.

Essentially, Blackstone did just that in his sixteenth-century ruling: In marriage the man and woman become one, and that one, in law, is the man. The disappearance of the rivulet into the river Thames, his watery metaphor, is the image that is still the reality. To exclude women completely, they are simply made to disappear into the image of man. And woman then does, indeed, lose her identity, her name; she is indeed then no one; she is nothingness; she is nothing. The trouble is that she still *is* something; her body keeps on breathing and her mind (however badly stunted) goes on thinking. The problem is simply this: She did not cease to exist.

With these evidences of corporality before them, our "wise founding fathers" wrote in the Declaration of Independence that all men were created equal, but they meant quite literally all *men.* The Supreme Court has previously ruled that the

Fourteenth Amendment, which guarantees equal protection, did not intend to include nor did it include women. Although recent rulings on women are more hopeful, Clarenbach can conclude only that the laws of this nation solidly freeze the idea of male supremacy. In fact, Blackstone's principle of coverture still inheres in forty-two states. Even in community property states the husband is often in control of the marital community. As nonentities, women still have no legal right in some states to enter into business contracts, or to obtain loans without the consent of husbands.

To the thousands of laws that limit women are added a few that are presumed to "protect" them. "Protective" laws frequently treat women as irresponsible children, and despite the good intentions of *some* of their original proponents, have often been used to protect *men*, not women *or* their children. Laws that equalize, such as the Equal Rights Amendment, are a primary route of escape from complete masculist entrapment. Litigation on one law after another combined with the pressure for changes in administrative rulings are two other roads to freedom. But emancipation will never be achieved as long as the structure of masculist institutions remains intact. Built on concepts of power accumulation and competitive fighting, the institutions themselves are the ultimate targets of change. As long as the "tooth and claw" mentality prevails, a women's culture *cannot* be accommodated to masculist systems no matter how much they are altered. Even when men grudgingly admit that women are equal, and glowering move over to sit by them in councils of power, women will not yet be free. Freedom to be a male impersonator is no freedom at all.

No one should have power who has not looked into the abyss. Women have seen it in the terror of the sick and dying they have tended through the tumultuous upheavals of history. They have seen it in the bewildered or bright eyes of their children. They have not only looked into the abyss through the eyes of those dependent on them, but they have also lived inside the eternal vacuum of nothingness imposed on them by men. Yet women, and the few sensitive men who have faced themselves and women honestly, are not often those in power. The men in power, and the token women who too often impersonate them, have achieved their "heights" by manipulating the appearances of life and by avoiding the essence of existence. It is as though the eternal wisdom of the universe has become "inoperative."

POWER, PATRIARCHY, AND "POLITICAL PRIMITIVES"

To accumulate power or to distribute it, that is the question. For the men who govern, the ultimate problem is whom to exclude. Who is in the in-group that will extend one's own power base and who is in the out-group that will threaten it. Some people are carefully excluded without appearing to have been omitted, others are excluded with open contempt; but only *one* group is consistently, constantly excluded with little or no thought at all. Particular racial or ethnic groups have suffered painful, humiliating exclusion in different places and times; but women have been eliminated so long that their disappearance seems only "natural."

Political science, the study of politics and government, certainly has an intellectual interest in democracy as one form of rule *presumably* based on the participation of all. Strangely, the double standard in American political life seems of little consequence. After all, one doesn't think too hard about studying one's own shadow. Besides, it disappears into the self with fair regularity at noon every day. But behind the long procession of black-robed judges, gray-suited senators, and uniformed generals, shadowy images of a constant ghost, a consistent specter, flit in and out. Woman, although nothing, is still something; that damnable woman who did not vanish decently in one whole piece keeps flittering through the pictures. This indecent display of a ghost who should remain properly invisible has to be dealt with occasionally. How to deal with her? Trivialize her.

Bonnie Freeman, a specialist in political socialization and a professor of social science and education, examines that trivialization in the research conclusions and interpretations which implicitly exonerate the eradication of females, as "political primitives." After reviewing the political science literature, Freeman concludes that male researchers simply see politics as beyond a woman's concern and her absence as beyond their own. When studied, she is found to be less politically knowledgeable and active, and more conservative and more responsive to candidate personality. She is also unable to conceptualize issues or to deal with conflict and contention. According to Freeman, greater responsiveness to issues with "moral overtones" is coughed at in a gentlemanly way, while the scholar comments on her naiveté which is seen as slightly embarrassing, if not potentially dangerous. The hard, realistic approach does not evidently encompass "moral" issues.

Freeman rethinks the findings: From voting records, women appear to be somewhat more humanitarian, less supportive of violence, of the use of military force or of government policies of war. They are more often opposed to universal military training, to harsh, punitive treatment of criminal offenders, and more often favor gun control and consumer and conservation issues. If this is a picture of a "political primitive," then perhaps we need fewer "political sophisticates."

Presumably, female emotionality crops up in a number of political places. Their responsiveness to the physical appeal of candidates, as an example, is an interesting finding. How women could vote more frequently for the sexiness of Eisenhower, Kennedy, *and* Johnson seems a difficult problem in aesthetics. Presumably, women are more gullible about engineered political images while men respond to charisma. One can only wonder at the immaturity of conceptualization in these statements, all of which require a greater gullibility among women than many can now muster.

Freeman points to a study of educated couples in which the husbands believed their wives held the same conservative attitudes as their own. When the wives were interviewed separately, they tended to be more liberal in their views. When women break their silence to express their own world view, there may be some interesting surprises for both sexes.

But what if the sparse research is correct as it now stands? What if women, who have been excluded from the smoke-filled rooms, *are* unknowledgeable about cigars and macro-power ploys? If the women's movement has done nothing else, it has helped women to find out a *great deal* about the male power brokers. What will happen when the female populace, in general, finds out how many mediocre men rule their destinies? What will happen when masses of women realize just how badly some men need power and how badly they exercise it? What will happen when a majority of women discover how threatened men are to share their power with women?

Women *and* men are stuck with the historical results of generations of "warriors." We all face the abominable possibility of annihilation. We have lived through two world wars, innumerable "states of emergency," and countless "limited interventions." Women have watched male leaders muddle tearfully or defiantly through the quagmire of Watergate where the *real* use of masculist power by the *real* chauvinists in power became obvious to all of us. Perhaps it is time for the shadows, the "political primitives," to reconsider their peripheral existence.

Too often, men have overlooked the micro-power situations, considering them too unimportant to research. But the macro levels of power will change when women snap apart the masculist world view, when they no longer restrain their use of space and time because of fears of masculist violence—molestation, rape, or death. When the fundamental basis of power as expressed in the family is uncovered, then the process of "interior colonialization," the heart of subjugation, will be stripped bare. Perhaps then the macro political system from which it is derived will be known as a rudimentary adaptation, the evolutionary vestige of cave men who have yet to leave the cave.

The global village belongs to *all* of us. Women can sit in their living rooms and watch the rejection of raped Bangladesh women. They can observe the greedy manipulation of power on the 18-inch diagonal screen. They can hear the stupidity of masculist rulers, whose mangled language and muttered platitudes float into even the kitchen. To all this, many women now say: "Consciousness-raising groups and to hell with bridal showers!" For thousands of employed women, there is even a greater sense of urgency.

WOMEN WHO WORK

In countries throughout the world, women come together in small groups to engage in thoughtful dialogue, deeply questioning present societal structures and seriously considering future cultural patterns more appropriate to them and their children. From an examination of their own lives, they clarify the elements of the con game and identify the fundamentals of familial power, the prototype for all subsequent forms of masculist authority. In this process, sexist images of religious, legal, and social institutions collapse into puffs of dust, and as the stale air of centuries of oppression blows away, attacks on the legitimacy of economic systems gather strength.

Walled in on one side by masculist creeds, on another by sexist laws, on a third by social conventions, the fourth wall of economic discrimination, when nailed into place, has boxed in women completely. Battering down the house that Jack built, women now pound on the most rigid barrier of all, the wall barring economic equality. Although they still face great disparities in income, their increasing economic independence loosens the masculist grip that has historically squeezed out the self-determination of a woman and left her with fear for herself and her children. There are those who say that women are their own "worst enemies," that they have "let this happen" to them. What *does* a woman with children do when faced with absolute masculist tyranny? With no economic means of support available to her, will she consciously choose penury, starvation, and death for her children? For the first time in two millennia, women can now see options for self-sufficiency. The choice of wife, nun, governess, prostitute, or wife, fieldhand, domestic servant, prostitute are viewed as nonchoices from a previous time. And, although respected as legitimate choices, the options of teacher, nurse, librarian, home economist, and social worker are seen as insufficient.

Although women know their salaries average only about half those of men and even though they realize women are restricted to the most boring and least prestigious tasks, they have continued to enter the labor force until over 40 percent of it is now female. As Ann Seidman, professor of economics, states, women have, during this century, begun to move into the complete spectrum of the economy.

The question for women now is, What form of economy? Seidman cites statistics which show that 23 percent of all manufacturing profits can be attributed to lower salaries of women. If this estimate is correct, capitalism is substantially underwritten by the cheap labor of women. In the capitalistic world view, women work for "pin money"; they are "temporarily" employed and "unreliably" engaged in jobs to which they show no "real" commitment. Given the jobs women are "allowed," it is surprising that they have so much commitment.

The masculist mythology of working women is interesting only as an additional story in an anthology by Father Goose. Two-thirds of working women have *no* choice but to work. These include widows, divorced women, single women, and wives of men whose incomes are insufficient to sustain families above poverty levels. Other married women consistently state that financial need is their main reason for employment. Inequitable salaries, limited in-service training, inadequate fringe benefits, nonexistent promotion to positions of authority, and boredom with tedious tasks—all these are insufficient deterrents to women who need or want to work outside the home.

The mixed "blessings" of capitalism are becoming increasingly obvious to women whose lives are used to support a social-class system to which they are hooked as appendages. The capitalistic belief system maintains economic practices which ultimately deny the well-being of half of the population. As Engels pointed out, capitalism heavily relies on the family as the unit of control by which women are subjugated. How cultural imagery interconnects with the material base through the mediation of family groups is an urgent question for women. It is already clear that any "pure" form of capitalism deserves a hasty and not very elaborate funeral. Although socialism seems more congenial to women, it too has alien shapes, shadows of still another form of masculist control.

All cultures must deal with four imperatives. First, species survival demands reproduction which requires sexual relations and necessitates patterns of childbearing and rearing. Second, physical survival of living members forces them to seek food and shelter, which leads to the development of economic systems. Third, as a social species, members must develop techniques of communal survival from which grow political and legal systems. Finally, a species characterized by self-consciousness must explain the unknown in order to survive psychologically while surrounded with uncertainty. This leads to belief systems in which a cosmogony of causation is established which legitimizes the actions in *all* spheres of life.

Unfortunately, Marx, a nineteenth-century man, chose to emphasize only one of these—the economic system historically controlled by men, upon whose production was built their *own* social stratification system. But, women ask, what of the reproductive system which produces the workers who produce the goods? Is not this system more "fundamental"? From it, the *earliest* division of labor, which is sexual in nature, must flow. And if this is so, the social-class system must be primarily derived from the initial subjugation, not of male workers, but of female persons.

All of these questions and assertions assume a model of linear causation. But what if the masculist world view, which has depended on a logic of time lines, is also erroneous? What if the most fundamental error is the search for mono-causation? What if the world is really a field of interconnecting events, arranged in patterns of multiple meaning? What if the search for a simplistic "orderliness" is, itself, the common problem of both capitalism and socialism?

Marx's analysis of ideology must also come under attack. Again, females are essentially excluded from the belief system primarily thought to mask social-class differences. But what of the sex-caste differences from which the ideology of stratification must have arisen? For women, the basic difficulty with socialist theorists is that they *assumed* the "other" could be conveniently *subsumed*. The masculist ideology underlying the socialist ideology is the problem for women thinkers.

Without substantial revisions, socialism in its variant forms is an insufficient model for the liberation of women. As Simone de Beauvoir discovered, after a lifetime of communist affiliation in France, the problem is to develop a noncontingent women's culture to guard the rights of the female populace. Without this strength, there is no assurance of equality in any economic-political system devised by men. It may be instructive to look at societies in which different economic systems have been adopted to find out what happens to the women of different countries.

WOMEN IN SWEDEN

What is happening to women in a society that has espoused a modified form of socialism? Ingrid Camerini, a professor of Scandinavian languages and literature, examines the status of women in the economy and in the educational and political systems of Sweden, a nation experimenting with a compromise between Adam Smith and Karl Marx. All socialist countries proclaim the principle of sex equality, and the Swedish government is no exception. While American women expend precious time and energy in the battle for a constitutional amendment, women in socialist countries live under governments that have already proclaimed sex equality as a basic legal right of female citizens. However, the success of these policies seems to depend more on the strength of feminist women than on the "liberated" actions of men in power. A male proclamation backed up with wavering indecision and inaction does not create new images of women. The current debate in Sweden emerges out of women's rejection of the image of woman in two roles, mother and worker. To some Swedish women, *both* women and men have the *same* role—to be human beings. This "radical" reconception is yet to be implemented in reforms of existing social practices. The vast majority of boys continue to enter technical-industrial lines, while most girls enter clerical, commercial, home economics, and social studies. At universities, women continue in the humanities and social sciences. As in the United States, sex-segregated preparation for economic roles continues. Unlike the American experience, a new cultural pattern seems evident: Females represent 19 percent of those in medicine, 30 percent in dentistry, 33 percent in pharmacy, and 27 percent in the natural sciences. In comparison to the United States, these figures represent a startling contrast. Still, Camerini concludes that traditional patterns predominate; the schools have essentially failed to produce new egalitarian belief systems upon which social changes in adult choices are predicated.

Because the industrial revolution came late to Sweden, one could expect, given the socialist analysis, that the brief history of change in material culture would retard the struggle for female equality. But there is little difference in the full employment rates of women and men. Facing an earlier shortage of male workers, Swedish employers had to attract female labor. With a subsequent recession, this trend has slowed down. As in all countries, whether Sweden, the United States, or China, the same process occurs: When men need the labor of women they are "allowed" into the work force; when men do not, women are excluded or "accepted" on the peripheries. What is common to all economic and political systems is the primacy of men.

In this century, women are not graciously accepting their exclusion. The increase of married women in the labor force in the United States is paralleled in Sweden with 10 percent in 1930, 55 percent in 1970, and a projected 67 percent in 1985. Yet sex-segregated work roles flourish, growing with the increase of women workers. Camerini cites one study in which 75 percent of working Swedish women are found in 25 of 300 occupations. With larger numbers of women, whole departments of certain industries employ females exclusively.

In time it is likely that these new roles will be denigrated. Denied equivalent prestige, the earnings will reflect lower status and eventually the sex segregation will produce the predictable cycle of sex discrimination. Equal pay in Sweden, as in the United States, is still a myth: 41 percent of full-time working women and only 9 percent of men earn less than $4,000; in contrast, only 4 percent of working women earn more than $8,000 compared with 23 percent of men.

Unless a society purposely and systematically integrates *all* occupations to achieve equal proportions of women and men, the increase in female workers will simply sustain invidious distinctions. The other alternative is to recognize and create separate sex cultures with equal veto power over each other. In this case, sex segregation in jobs would be consciously created with insistence on equal prestige and remuneration. In either alternative, a noncontingent woman's culture is needed to offset the culture of men that has become *the* culture of all. Changes in masculist economic systems based on male theories of economic and political power will not achieve female autonomy. Even if androgyny is the final goal, it will be reached only when women in independent association have sufficient strength to insist on their own definition of the female component of the unified human psyche. Without their own input into a new imagery, the male version is likely to reform women to act like modified men.

This assumes that men will attempt androgyny. If Camerini's analysis of the political system holds, even the liberal Swedish male is unlikely to give up easily male imagery. Women's names on lists of candidates are still placed at the bottom of the ballot. This act symbolizes their "inclusion" in Swedish political life. The government's own investigating committees, even those looking into the status of women, are overwhelmingly male. Trade unions, even those which have supported women's equality, continue female exclusion; one union with a female membership of 30 percent had no females on the board.

The substratum for this power structure is composed of thousands of families in which women duplicate ad infinitum the work of other women. Recently, women's work in the home has been termed an essential to the community, subject to cash reimbursement. Nevertheless, new marriages over the last three decades are down 35 percent, and recent marriage and divorce laws ease the legal stranglehold on women and men who choose to couple with the blessings of the state.

According to Camerini, child-care facilities, although on the increase, are grossly inadequate to meet the needs of women and men who both work. When compared to the United States, however, the Swedish attempts seem awesomely prodigious. Any effort at all would be better than the record of male legislators in the American culture, who still debate with the image of a nineteenth-century family which did not exist even in the nineteenth century.

Camerini cites statistics produced by male economists who have acknowledged that the Swedish gross national product would rise 25 percent if the unused labor potential of women were tapped, and another 25 percent if sex discrimination and other barriers were totally abolished. In contrast, Seidman must quote a little-known statistic to prove that the American economy gains almost a quarter of its profits from sexism. What statistics are probable in a nation that has interwoven economic, political, and social life into a single fabric of total socialism?

WOMEN IN CHINA: PROBLEMS OF SEX INEQUALITY AND SOCIOECONOMIC CHANGE

After a recent visit to China, Kay Ann Johnson, a political scientist specializing in Eastern political systems, depicts massive attempts to alter images of women and family in China. Despite substantial improvements in women's status, Johnson concludes that female demands have been shelved when they did not coincide with male priorities. To assume that sex equality will be automatically achieved as workers' conditions improve is to believe in the latest masculist myth.

Yet much credit is due to those women and men who have overthrown, in an astonishingly brief time, some six thousand years of overt female slavery. Traditional marriage, as a contract between two families, entailed a body price for the female who was transferred to the male's family for breeding sons and performing menial work. On the death of a husband, in-laws retained control over the widow, who, with no money to buy her freedom, could accept celibate servitude, wait for a man to buy her, or commit suicide.

Johnson sums up the subhuman image of woman in one Chinese proverb, which says that a wife is like a horse a man has bought—he can ride it or flog it as he likes. To keep this "animal" under control, space and time must be sharply circumscribed. Confined within the man's home or his adjacent lands, the Chinese woman was further hobbled by foot binding, a practice that maimed and crippled millions. As one woman expressed it, women were regarded as dogs who came to despise themselves.

In various forms, this system of bondage in the family was closely tied to economic and political structures which had existed for thousands of years. If these were to collapse with the communist revolution, the role of woman must change. Thus, the revolutionaries abolished buying and selling in marriage; prohibited child betrothal, concubinage, and polygamy; outlawed interference in remarriage of widows; provided the right to sue for divorce; and granted formal rights in sharing household property and in land reform. With some economic independence, a Chinese woman could say that when her husband told her to get out of his house, she could now reply, "Get out of my house *yourself*."

The changes documented by Johnson seem to parallel those in some Western countries beginning a century earlier. The remaining and real question to be asked is, How has female involvement in political and economic life changed? According to Johnson, women's organizations were formed to fight deference, fear, and fatalism. Collective effort was used to counteract the threats and beatings women experienced as they exerted independence. Forcible action by these groups was used to deal with the most offensive and abusive husbands who were publicly beaten. The silent submission of centuries was sliced apart in decades.

But by 1948 a directive was issued that the women's organizations were to be carefully managed by the party so that land reform would not be endangered. The *ultimate* revolution affected the prerogatives of all men of all classes, hindering the solidarity of male peasants. Johnson states that sex warfare occurred in the 1950s with an increase in suicide, torture, and murder of women, particularly those active in the fight for women's rights. Even the courts could not be relied upon by women and they, weary and wary, began to withdraw.

In the first five-year plan, equality was to be achieved by a socialist transition of the entire society. But sex-segregated patterns and full employment of men took precedence over the liberation of women. Mirroring the American back-to-the-house propaganda of the same decade, the patriotic female was pictured in her traditional role. During the Great Leap, sex inequality would again be swept away by changes in the socioeconomic sphere. Sex-typed division of labor "shielded" women from competition with men. The "natural" jobs for women looked strangely similar to those described as "natural" by male imperialistic capitalists. A reemergence of traditional kinship obligations hit hardest the feminists, who were labeled selfish daughters who disrupted female socialist duties. As Johnson says, women's liberation was deferred to economic gain, leaving the political question unresolved.

During the cultural revolution, mass political organizations attacked even the editorial policy of women's state-directed journals as "intoxicated with the small heaven of motherhood." Small numbers of women began to be included in leadership positions and the women's organizations were disbanded. Presumably, women had by then no further need for special representation. Johnson notes, however, a resurgence of concern in the 1970s. But without their *own* noncontingent culture, women are likely to be included only at the demands of men in power.

Fundamental to the exclusion of Chinese women is a theoretical base which overemphasizes production and the economic system while it understates the political importance of reproduction. Eventually, all four basic cultural imperatives must be intermeshed into any explanatory system which purports to free women.

From his analysis, Marx could predict class warfare but he could not predict sex warfare. The battle of the sexes is, however, no light topic of bantering conversationalists; it is the oldest rebellion of the most consistently subjugated group of human beings. The longest revolution is still unfinished business in any national system controlled by any group of men.

THE EROSION OF SEXUAL EQUALITY IN THE KIBBUTZ

If women in whole nation-states have not achieved equality, how have those in experimental communes within a new nation fared? In the Israeli kibbutzim, collective control of production is again the key cultural assumption. Because the economy is the ultimate explanatory principle, maximal status is given over to capital creation, the area traditionally controlled by men, rather than service activities often performed by women. This theoretical lopsidedness appears to reemphasize the original disparity in prestige.

Although founded on the principle of sex equality, the reversion to stereotypic roles is explained by female aversion to physical labor, by their "natural" proclivities, by their "pathological" overidentification with male activities. Rae Blumberg, a professor of sociology, rejects psychological explanations that blame the victims. Staying firmly within the material cultural matrix, she claims that the most important source of change is technological shifts in systemic variables. Tracing the stages of economic development, Blumberg shows that increase in service activities was accompanied by increasing age of original founders, by larger numbers of children, and by a rise in the standard of living. As the kibbutz changed from a preindustrial, subsistence economy to a period of economic growth to a stage of surplus capital, the nature of work and the division of labor were altered.

Over time, women gave up their new identities while men made no attempts to take on the full range of female functions. The original male founders were never assigned to infant care, and male immigrants, who came during the stage of economic growth, were not interested in pots and pans. The image of a pioneer blazing new trails over a kitchen sink was not very appealing. With no seniority principle applied to women and men, both sets of men took over production. Women with children were unlikely to leave and they gradually gave up their capital-producing activities. As they gave up these roles, they lost their voice in decision making on economic issues and the men came to control production and managerial positions. More recently, women have moved, during the period of capital surplus, to subsidiary industries and, with increasing emphasis on education, to technical and professional roles.

This highly condensed and oversimplified account of Blumberg's theoretical ideas does not do justice to her complex theory, but it does suggest the extent of her commitment to an analysis derived from the productive base of social life. A Marxist axiom is that all work is equal. No person's job is less important than another's because all contribute equally to the well-being of society. Without a concomitant analysis of the belief system, we are still left with the unresolved issue of inequitable allotment of prestige in sex-segregated economic roles. There is no logical reason why tending a child should be less glamorous or important than digging a ditch. The unanswered question is why the cultural imagery of sexual roles never successfully changed throughout the stages of economic development. As long as the prestige system is male originated and controlled, the allocation of importance in decision making will remain unchanged. If the reproductive base were given equal status with the productive in the explanatory system, perhaps the socialist theory would not reinforce the primacy of traditional male roles.

Even with total involvement in economic activities, women will not achieve sexual equality if prestige allocation is controlled by men who reinforce it by muscle. Margaret Mead's cross-cultural analysis of sex roles suggests one generalization. Regardless of the specific task, male control of prestige defines male tasks as more important. If basket weaving is "women's" work in one society, it is likely to be less prestigious. If men weave baskets in another society, it is likely that it is considered highly prestigious. Any activity can be construed to be of marginal importance to any group. If the socialist belief system relies heavily on the primacy of production, the traditional domain of men, rather than reproduction, the sphere of women, the prestige allocation is predictable. Ironically, reproduction produces the only valid reason for production. No economy need exist if no babies exist to inherit it. Only a noncontingent women's culture can insist on the primacy of children.

We turn now to the inculcation of the capitalistic ideology in the education of the young in American culture, which also stresses the ultimate importance of production, again controlled by men but without the common consent of all male workers.

WOMEN AND GIRLS IN THE PUBLIC SCHOOLS: DEFEAT OR LIBERATION?

How does a belief system come to be expressed in the cultural imagery? How does the culture of men come to be the culture of all? How does prestige allocation come to be controlled by men? How do females come to "accept" subjugation? Enculturation of the young into a masculist world view needs the full cooperation of educational systems. Elizabeth Fennema, a professor of mathematics education in curriculum and instruction, examines sexism in the public schools, which are thought to be the province of women. Female predominance in elementary schools is even believed to "feminize" boys, "causing" their reading and behavior problems.

Who *does* control education? Fennema finds that the cultural imagery of education as a female domain is inaccurate. Education is not a "woman's profession"; it is controlled by men. Although roughly 85 percent of elementary and 50 percent of secondary teachers are women, only 1 percent of school superintendents are female and almost all boards of education are predominantly male. Depending on the state, 66 to 75 percent of all school principals are men. The recent increase of male elementary principals produces a ratio of five men to one woman. All these educators are trained in schools of education at colleges and universities in which the faculty are, again, predominantly male. The prestige allocation system *of* men gives over control of child rearing *to* men.

Fennema asks, Is this because women perform more poorly in positions of power? From her review of the research, she answers, No. In fact, *higher* pupil learning occurred in schools headed by *female* principals. The masculist world view pictures women in power as incompetent; the research proves otherwise. Hooked to the imagery of incompetent administrator is another of female incapacity to be a full "professional." The word "professional" in this context is simply an adjective used to describe the old boys' club. Entrance of females as substandard "professionals" into education has presumably "damaged" the profession.

Another interpretation is possible. Consider the alternative that males in power, in an effort to look "objective," have borrowed assembly-line models from industry and bureaucratic procedures from business, making women nonprofessional workers on a production line and children raw products to be shaped according to manufacturing specifications. If educational systems were really controlled by women, their organizational model would have been derived from their *own* experience with children in the mother's role in the family. In fact, the one-room schoolhouse with older children helping younger under the tutelage of a mothering teacher is the more appropriate version of a female organizational model. Instead we live in the most age-graded culture in the world with children sharply segregated on the questionable criterion of chronological age.

What happens to children in this system? Fennema, as Bleier and Sherman, must deal with intelligence by sorting out the sex differences presumed to exist. Working on the problem of female intellectual "inferiority," she cannot use IQ tests because these are purposely neutered. Females tend to score higher than males so items showing this difference are simply dropped. Fennema turns to achievement tests and finds that girls in kindergarten through fourth grade do better than boys when they are tested on the entire set of skills. But at puberty, boys begin to show higher achievement scores on particular tests. The price of sexism is heavy; at adolescence girls show undeniable patterns of underachievement, conforming to societal expectations of selective stupidity. The beginnings of this pattern can be traced to the fourth grade so that the presumed negative influence from predominantly female elementary faculties cannot be proved to exist. Nor can the "innate" sexual competencies of children be substantiated: American boys do more poorly in reading, but English and Nigerian boys do better than girls in reading.

Clearly cultural preparation for adult sex roles creates a cognitive deficit which matches expectations in the masculist world view. What happens to the emotional lives of female children? Fennema says that by puberty the girls' self-concepts decrease markedly. By the beginning of young womanhood, girls have learned that females are emotionally inferior beings. Earlier in this chapter, vulnerability and an imposed state of nonseriousness were postulated as existential themes of female life. To these can be added a third theme—the essential unworthiness, the badness, even the dirtiness of being female. Through explicit and implicit learning, the metaphorical imagery pictures an unworthy being. Even female body parts and processes carry connotations of shameful dirtiness. Behind every clean little girl in a perky pinafore is a dirty, menstruating woman, a potential Sadie Thompson opening the beaded curtain. The most insidious discrimination is the devaluation of a person as unclean, as a profanation of the fully "human" state. What little girls incorporate are the existential themes of vulnerability, nonseriousness, and unworthiness or uncleanliness.

These themes are so deeply embedded in the cultural matrix that they are not believed to exist. They are glossed over in public schools by the neuter mentality.

Why, of course we treat boys and girls exactly alike! From the very limited research available, Fennema points to a study which shows that boys have more blame contacts with teachers. But they also have more *praise* contacts. In short, they simply get more attention. Subsequent research will probably show that the only place the neuter mentality exists is in the minds of adults who cannot see sexism because it ·is ingrained in every inch of the masculist screen through which they view the world.

WOMEN AND HIGHER EDUCATION: VOICES FROM THE SEXUAL SIBERIA

In public schools, women are conspicuously present as teachers of young children; in colleges and universities, women are conspicuously absent in every discipline except those three or four allotted to women. Women are entirely out of the prestige system, and as outsiders, they are of no use to men in their own power network. This conclusion by two men in their sociological study *The Academic Marketplace* is the starting point for Karen Merritt's analysis of women in higher education.

As a result of current pressure from women students and faculty, a few women have entered university administration; and Merritt, as a newly appointed administrator, examines female exclusion in colleges and universities by men who have refused "to take seriously" women's right to knowledge. According to Merritt, the current denial of female rights has a long history: Female minds were too "fragile" to withstand the rigors of "masculine" studies; female bodies were too "weak"—the childbearing apparatus would be irreparably damaged by the strain of thinking; female morals were too unsteady—the presence of women would create a corruptive atmosphere that would destroy the purity of the ivory tower.

Ridicule, a favorite masculist weapon, was and still is used to trivialize the legitimate rights of women. "Chemistry enough to keep the pot boiling and geography enough to know the rooms in her house is sufficient education for a woman." A knowledge of the dimensions of captivity is insufficient for women who walk out of their "protected" cages. Stepping out of confined time and space, women who wanted knowledge became the "enemies of the race" whose "unladylike" behavior threatened propagation. In the previous century, threats of withdrawal of "protection" were thinly veiled. Emma Willard, on proposing her plan for a female seminary to the men in the New York State legislature, felt obliged to promise continued *obedience* in return for the "protection" of men. Oberlin, the first college to admit women, allowed them to attend classes if they did not break the traditional female silence. In public assemblages, they were to remain respectfully silent. At Vassar, statistics rolled out every year showing that female graduates did, indeed, marry—proof that their ovarian fluids had not drained away to the brain and that their learning in no way incapacitated them for subservience in marital bliss.

When M. Carrie Thomas of Bryn Mawr decried the fact that their women faculty had only an elementary school preparation, she was told that there is an intuitive something in ladies of birth that enabled them to do without college training and to make better teachers for women college students. Maria Mitchell, professor of astronomy at Vassar, protested several decades ago the *same* pattern of discrimination women decry *today:* preferential hiring of men, inequitable salaries, exclusion of women from committee appointments and from positions of authority, total control by male presidents and male boards of trustees.

Merritt's review of the history of women in higher education is a painting of a battlefield in which every female victory was fought at high cost to the "enemies of the race." Their tenacity has *not* produced the results they envisioned. Merritt shows a statistical decline, only now beginning to reverse, in the numbers of female graduate students receiving advanced degrees and in the pitifully low proportions of female faculty. Jessie Bernard's important study of women in higher education today began with the statement that she had never been discriminated against although she was chased out of the sacred precincts of the Faculty Club when she crossed "the invisible line." To her great credit, Bernard now recognizes in her subsequent distinguished work the *many* invisible lines which interconnect to form the web of discrimination. Bernard's statistical profile of faculty women, reinforced by Helen Astin's later work, portrays a pattern of lower rank, pay, and status. Exploding the myth that educated women do not use their education, Astin found that 91 percent of the women doctorates she studied were employed, with an average of 11 to 15 months taken off for childbearing during their careers. The process by which these women survived, as Merritt stresses, was a severe test of endurance: Only about one percent received the Ph.D. compared to 10 percent of male candidates in the same period. The women took, on the average, 12 years to finish their degrees and were about 4.5 years older than their male counterparts at the time the doctorate was awarded. Merritt emphasizes a critical finding: The *greatest* number of complaints of sex discrimination came from the *most productive* women (as measured by the shaky standard of number of publications). The *closer* a woman gets to masculist *power,* the *more intense* the discrimination.

The severe testing continues throughout the woman's career. Merritt cites a recent study in which identical résumés of males and females were sent to department chairmen, whose decisions were found to be based on the sex rather than the qualifications of applicants. A second study using identical credentials, while varying only the sex of applicants to graduate study, produced similar results. While teaching, the same results were found when two identical lectures, one attributed to a man and the other to a woman, elicited more favorable evaluations of the male instructor.

All this evidence is insufficient to force a substantial number of male administrators and faculty to give much credence to affirmative action programs which have been used to create a façade of change. Again the masculist economy takes precedence over the liberation of women. When female demands threaten the power base, collusion between men in government and in education slows the implementation to a snaillike pace. The lack of enforcement of Title VII by the Department of Health, Education, and Welfare has forced several women's organizations to file suit against the federal government itself. And the recent watered-down guidelines for Title IX are the newest evidence of masculist refusal to give economic and political priority to the liberation of girls and women in American educational institutions. One of the most hotly debated issues is the elimination of discrimination in physical education.

WOMEN IN PHYSICAL EDUCATION: THE
DRIBBLE INDEX OF LIBERATION

Ironically, physical education, the maligned stepchild of the academic world, is the arena of the most difficult intellectual debate on sexist imagery. It is on the playing fields and in the locker rooms that the mythology is most complexly configurated. Inequitable facilities, finances, and programs *do* represent unfair treatment; unequal physical strength *is* partially caused by purposeful training for female weakness; uneven distribution of prestige based on the glorification of male muscle *does* promote a cultural configuration of power in which women are excluded. *But* what is ultimately at stake are the rites of passage into "masculine" and "feminine" polarized identities. The fundamental issue is the conception of self.

With a few subcultural exceptions, American society is thought to have *no* formalized puberty rituals, no organized ceremonies of separation. But *are* there institutionalized rites of passage? From research Bonnie Freeman and I are conducting, the earliest and most lasting memories of female separation and exclusion are those associated with physical education in schools. At first, we considered this to be an artifact of the masculist screen; only the most blatant occurrence of sexism would be remembered and the hundreds of less obvious reminders of inferiority would be blurred. Although this blurring does occur, the blatancy began to emerge as important in and of itself. It now appears that games in the upper grades in elementary schools and gym classes in junior high schools are the situations in which girls and boys go through the American version of puberty rites.

Because of the double and contradictory cues for females, the ritual is simultaneously accepted and rejected. For most boys, the rituals are consistent and the ceremonial segregation becomes a mark of prestige. Separated from one another, boys and girls learn images of male dominance and female submission: The football hero and the head cheerleader are the pictures incorporated in overevaluation of large muscle in competitive, brute force and underevaluation of smaller muscles in spectator antics. The current outcry about "integration" of athletics has less to do with "chastity" or "protection" than with the collapse of critical organizing metaphors.

Women educators in physical education have had to contend with all the illogicalities of woman's inferiority in their worst form. As adults officiating at ceremonial transition without any formal recognition of this function, they are asked to create women in a new role while the society continues to reward the old one. Their job is even more difficult because of conflicting conceptions of social class. Acting on the idea of "equality," American public school systems nevertheless reflect the socioeconomic structure. Fighting the historical image of the upper-class lady, delicate, fragile, and physically inept, the alternative is the poor woman, "toughened" with work, capable of the hardest physical labor. In athletics, the compromise struck between these images is represented in the respectable picture of a graceful performer—the ballerina, swimmer, ice skater, gymnast—the woman whose performance appears effortless even though she is exerting severe muscular energy. Heaven help the woman who sweats and grunts!

Supporting these female images in class society is the elimination of competition, of any expression of dominance which could crack female confinement and shatter masculist control of space and time. Thus, team sports are less "ladylike" than individual sports; the female is pictured as never in body contact with a male except for sexual purposes and never with a female for any purpose. To be "protected," woman must never test her own capacity to protect herself, never know the upper limits of her own strength. She must engage in no aggressive act so that she will never be the recipient of one. If she has the misfortune to be a "recipient," she remains almost totally defenseless because pushing, pulling, or even *thinking* of doubling up her fist are all alien acts.

In American culture, the way to handle disparities in strength is to withdraw all capacity for female self-defense, relying instead on male "gallantry." But what happens when the occasional man does not feel particularly "gallant" or when armies of men lose their collective "chivalry"? To defenseless woman, the threat of physical domination never completely disappears.

The most difficult image for women in physical education is the portrayal of the "mannish," "masculine" female athlete—the woman with muscles who knows how to use them. The girl or woman who actively uses her own body has been equated often with a lesbian in the popular imagery. Homophobia has successfully squelched the development of competent female athletes and reduced involvement in active team sports requiring energetic, assertive contact between groups of women. Moreover, it has reinforced the "impropriety" of female bonding. If women are teammates, comrades together, how long would they continue to accept subjugation? Guilty until proven innocent, women athletes have labored under the fallacious presumption of a life style which should *never* have carried any shameful connotation for *any* woman. At the same time, professionals in physical education have had to counteract the worst elements of masculist culture.

As Julia Brown, a professor of physical education, points out, the struggle for female control of women's athletics involved confrontations over the win-at-any-cost mentality, the belief that defeat is unspeakable. Fighting the commercialism and exploitation of athletes, they have denounced the competitive conception of sports, preferring a female emphasis on the cooperative participation of all women. In their uncomfortable position as the repository of all the cross-currents of an illogical mythology, they have created some dysfunctional results in their efforts to protect women. Avoiding the development of "stars," they trained generalists, not specialists, overlooking the highly skilled female athlete. Shunning the glorification of one player at the expense of others, they even refused Olympic competition until female participation from other cultures forced a reevaluation. Unable to set their own values in a noncontingent culture, separate from the masculist version of "femininity," women in physical education have been forced too often to react against rather than act on.

Brown traces all these elements in the changes of rules in basketball. Over time, this game mirrors in miniature the status of women in society. With a strong women's movement, there was freedom to play full court and unlimited physical movement. In decades in which the fight for women's rights was subdued, restrictions on time and space were imposed. Although the parallels are not exact, the number of dribbles allowed is, indeed, an interesting index of changing attitudes toward liberation. In the future, women's autonomy in a noncontingent culture may free women to experience their bodies fully and let loose the self-directed determination of professionals to direct, not reflect, the social changes in women's roles in society. As the surprised high priestesses of ceremonial coming of age, women in physical education have a particularly heavy responsibility to help sort out the cultural mythology that limits the lives of all.

THE STATUS OF HOME ECONOMICS AND THE STATUS OF WOMEN

If specialists in physical education face the violation of cultural myths, home economists must look directly at the picture of continued subjugation in the ideological version of their profession. Although experts in nutrition, dietetics, textiles and other technical fields, home economists live with the stereotyped picture of a teacher, hair neatly encased in a net, who tells "sweet, young things" how to cook eggs, sew aprons, and make centerpieces. The study of all things pertaining to the home must, by the nature of the subject, require "little" intellectual effort. To live within the accepted center of a fallacious mythology is to enter into the state of imposed nonseriousness with its concomitant trivialization of the mind. Inferiority is inherent in a woman's acceptance of the traditional images of women.

As Elizabeth Monts, professor of home economics, notes, the discipline did not begin with a limited vision. Founded by a woman sanitary chemist from Massachusetts Institute of Technology, home economics was to be the study of laws and principles concerned with the immediate environment in relation to the human being as a social person. Only in a narrow sense was it to pertain to housework. This sweeping synthesis of several disciplines rested on the integrating theme of the family which served as the organizing rationale for the existence of a new discipline.

To fulfill the original intent of this innovative conception requires a deep and difficult analysis of sex roles within familial structures. Unfortunately, Monts finds no special recognition of women as women until the advent of curricular changes in the 1960s. To her and to many feminist women today, few courses in home economics can be considered appropriate to a women's studies program. Yet the emphasis in all aspects of the family—housing, foods and nutrition, child development, human relationships, clothing and textiles, health and safety, consumer economics—*ought* to make sense to liberated women and men who want to create better conditions for ordinary people.

But this very emphasis on the family is the critical problem. As long as the traditional family and a modified version of the traditional female form the core of home economics education, no forward movement toward a noncontingent woman's culture can be made. A radical redefinition of sex roles and of the family itself must be undertaken. Without redefinition, the field will lose its synthesizing base, becoming a collection of disciplines with loose affiliations. To educate women and men to new realities of the "immediate environment," the old mythology must be thoroughly examined and substantially rejected.

As Monts points out, home economists have been active in the areas of child protection and in consumer legislation, but they have not historically thrust themselves into the center of the conflict over the status of women. Very recently, support for the Equal Rights Amendment and the elimination of sexist economic and legal barriers have been publicly proclaimed by the National Association of Home Economists. But to lead, they must go beyond legal changes to a deeper reconsideration of female mythology upon which the discipline is, in part, based.

CREATING A NONCONTINGENT CULTURE

For many women, the old symbols of masculist culture are already dead. For them, the original sin is lifted from Eve's maligned head; the passivity of pure receptivity is taken from Mary's bowed shoulders; the stigma of insanity is removed from Joan of Arc's ashes and handed to her persecutors; the eccentricity of Mary Wollstonecraft is correctly renamed courage; the scarlet letter on Hester's imagined face is smoothed away with quiet hands; and the ridicule heaped on Susan Anthony's "awkward" figure is transformed into praise for a tall woman of incredible strength.

Still, the task ahead of all women today is formidable: to rethink and to reconstruct a new culture in which female autonomy and dignity are ensured. Altering sexist laws and conventions is one step toward the future. Changing existing sex roles is another. Restructuring the meaning and nature of families is still another. Reworking the child-rearing processes is yet another. Reorganizing the structure of institutional life is one more gigantic step ahead. From these determined steps forward, the final stride will be taken when women alter the essence of human life, the cultural configurations of existence.

One woman walking alone cannot stride into a new humanity. Thousands together can. While attacking institutional practices, the end goal must be clear: the creation of a noncontingent culture. There will be no split in the ranks of women over "legalists" and "culturalists" if all women understand that every action moves them toward their *own* conception of human life. This will not be achieved through mere trust in the existing political or economic structures. It *will* be achieved when women understand that only an autonomous women's culture can insure the incorporation of their *own* values into any system *jointly* devised by women and men.

Perhaps the early Quaker system begun by Margaret Fell with George Fox and other Friends is one model to consider. In Quaker meetings, women and men used to sit separately on each side of a dividing wall. After separate *consensual* decisions were reached, neither group could take action without the *independent* agreement of the other. Clearly this system cannot work if the culture *outside* the meeting house is controlled by men who hold all positions of power. But if *all* institutional life were similarly modeled, then this image becomes worthy of consideration— *within* a culture in which the *fundamental* value is *peace*. A peace predicated on purposeful withdrawal of violent alternatives for *both* men and women whether *together* or *alone*. The future of this alternative depends on men's capacity to break away from their historical proclivity for violence and on women's capacity to assert their preference for peace.

Another alternative is the sharp demarcation of cultures into separate sex roles with equal valuation of each backed up by the threat of total female retaliation if excluded or if attacked; this is the only way for women to equalize physical differences in strength in a culture in which the *fundamental* value is *force* based on power. In this unfortunate situation, equality could *only* be achieved through equalizing the *threat* of violence.

The third alternative postulates complete integration through the incorporation of women into roles occupied by men in institutions controlled by them. This assumes an eventual goal of androgyny. Androgyny, if construed to mean that women and men are more intellectually, emotionally, and biologically alike than unlike, is an acceptable assumption in any model discussed. However, one difference remains. Disparity in physical strength can be minimized but it is unlikely it will ever be equalized. This simply means that a power differential also remains. Brain power will partially offset physical disparity, but, given a culture in which the ultimate recourse is to force, androgyny can be approximated but never fully attained.

Furthermore, androgyny based on assimilation of women into *male*-controlled culture will probably produce women who simply act like men. Not women and men who both come to act like each other. The probability of women taking on men's values in a society dominated by men is extremely high because they will only slowly allow "their" kind of women into power under the pressure of "other" women who wear out their lives to achieve token changes for Aunt Tomasinas, who will continue to treat women as men in power have always treated them.

If the hope for a new humanity rests with women, it will not be achieved by those who shrink from the steps ahead, by those who say, "But *my* man isn't like that." After hearing many women, even those who fully recognize systemic discrimination, exclude their own males, we can conclude only that individual acts of particular men when collected together indicate *no* systemic discrimination or that these acts must be separated from an analysis of a system for which even the most decent men are ultimately responsible.

Individual acts of love, honor, and decency are not uncommon between women and men. In my life and in the life of *every* woman, there are men we like or love or cherish. But the problem is to create a society in which these acts are built into the processes and structures and into the idealized imagery, the belief systems created by both women and men. This is possible only when women assert the strength of their own values and their own beliefs through collective action in a noncontingent culture.

NOTES

1. This assumes that current trends in recent historical research on women will continue to indicate extensive cooperative bonds and that initial findings from social scientific research will further demonstrate greater cooperation among women. It is probable that their cooperative behavior derives historically from the nurturant relationship they have had with children and from the conditional relationship they have had with men stronger than themselves. These imposed states necessitated female bonding for survival.

2. A noncontingent women's culture is a female-controlled system in which women map information developed by themselves from an environment over which they have control. Information is carried in conceptual patterns held in common with other women and involves them in mutual patterns of social interaction and shared patterns for

making a living. It is assumed that interaction with men will continue but this interaction will proceed in *both* an independent and an interdependent manner. The nature of this interdependence excludes dependence on males for definitions of female identity and on masculist groups, organizations, and institutions for organized social life; it includes independence from male-determined and -dominated life options and from masculist cultural interpretations of reality. This tentative definition does not include the points of articulation between the two groups. Alternative possibilities will be briefly considered at the conclusion of this chapter.

3. The success of female rites of passage will vary in different cultures in relation to the status accorded women.

4. In contrast to other species, human territoriality extends beyond the need to ensure an adequate food supply; more commonly, it involves the imposition of a belief system to achieve dominance.

5. Methodolatry, in its broadest definition, refers not only to bias within scientific methods, but to the adulation of the procedures themselves.

WOMEN:
BIOLOGICAL
INFERENCES
AND INTERVENTIONS

Brain, Body, and Behavior
Ruth H. Bleier

In a sense, the brain serves as the link among all the topics in this book; it is,
after all, the organ of our consciousness. With it we perceive the external
world, store our perceptions in the form of memory, which we call experience and
learning, and then use this body of experiences to determine our unique responses
to our perceptions of the external world. The brain thus becomes the single most
potent force in our development, our self-conception, our self-expression; and it is
also the instrument for the construction and transmission of the body of ideas and
practices that constitute our culture.

The basic structure and organization as well as mechanisms of functioning are
the same for brains of all vertebrate species, though certain areas subserving
particular functions are more highly developed in certain species: touch in
raccoons, vision-flight coordination in birds, and so forth.

The part of the brain that, in its organizational development and volume,
distinguishes human beings from other species is the cortex, the outer surface
layers. In all animals, the cortex receives and transforms into conscious perceptions
the various modalities of stimuli from the external world—visual, auditory, tactile,
olfactory, gustatory. In an animal with a smooth-surfaced brain, such as the rabbit,
almost the entire cortex is involved in receiving such stimuli; thus, most of the
cortex constitutes *primary receiving areas*. The intricately and deeply folded
pattern of the human cortex provides a larger volume and area of cortex relative to
the rest of the brain than that of other animals, and the primary receiving areas
constitute considerably less than half of the total cortex. The rest of the cortex is

involved in a further processing of the primary information it receives—storing perceptions and experiences (memory and learning) and associating them with other previous and ongoing perceptions and experiences. All of these together determine one's intellectual, emotional, and motor responses to a stimulus.

These *association areas* provide the substrate for the infinite variety of responses of humans (and, to a lesser degree, other primates) to a particular stimulus as contrasted with the relatively stereotypic nature of responses of animals with a less complex cortex. This presents an important paradox. Humanity in general manifests a variety of responses to a given stimulus. But as individuals, with the cortical capacity for creative, novel, variegated responses, we become bound and imprisoned by stereotypic responses to certain sets of stimuli (our culture) even while our creativity is responsible for the very existence of a culture. Personal liberation and creativity require freeing oneself from stereotyped responses, which are in any case unworthy of our cerebral cortex.

THE HYPOTHALAMUS AND CYCLES

The hypothalamus, a part of the brain that particularly concerns us here, does not participate in higher intellectual functions. It is, however, concerned with functions essential to the survival of the individual and the species: feeding and drinking behavior, body-temperature regulation, blood pressure and heart rate, mating behavior and reproduction. There is another important difference between the hypothalamus and the rest of the brain: It functions in part like an endocrine gland. Its nerve cells (neurons) are influenced not only by impulses from other nerve cells like the rest of the brain but also directly by hormones in the body—ovarian, testicular, thyroid, adrenal, and pituitary. This fact is of significance in the influence of the hypothalamus on certain behavioral and physiological sex differences. In addition, neurons of the hypothalamus manufacture hormones that regulate the hormonal output of the "master" endocrine gland, the pituitary.

The hypothalamus thus regulates the various functions of the pituitary gland, which is attached to the hypothalamus and, through it, the ovaries as well as other endocrine glands. The pituitary secretes two hormones that regulate cyclic activity of the ovaries: follicle stimulating hormone (FSH) and luteinizing hormone (LH). The hypothalamus secretes an FSH-releasing factor (FSH-RF) and an LH-releasing factor (LH-RF). At a particular point near the beginning of the normal human female's 28-day menstrual cycle, the hypothalamus begins to increase its production of FSH-RF, causing the pituitary to release increasing amounts of FSH, which in turn results in the growth and maturation of one ovarian egg and its envelope, the follicle. The follicle produces the hormone estrogen, which has two important effects on the hypothalamus. As the blood level of estrogen rises, it *suppresses* hypothalamic production of FSH-RF (negative feedback) and *stimulates* hypothalamic production of LH-RF (positive feedback). The surge of LH-RF on approximately the fourteenth day of the cycle causes the mature egg to erupt from its follicle (ovulation). The follicle then begins to produce the hormone progesterone, which *suppresses* hypothalamic production of LH-RF and of FSH-RF. The interplay of these opposing effects at different phases of the 28-day period results in menstrual cyclicity in females.

The purpose and effect of the "pill," a combination of estrogen and progesterone, is precisely to disrupt this delicately balanced mechanism in order to prevent ovulation. What the long-term effects may be of such hormonal manipulation of neuronal function are unknown. This and other unknown as well as known hazards require greater caution than is now generally exercised in the prescribing and taking of contraceptive pills.

THE HYPOTHALAMUS AND SEXUAL DIFFERENTIATION

In contrast to females, in males there is a fairly constant level of pituitary production of LH having a continual effect on the testicular cells that produce the male androgenic hormone testosterone, although there is evidence in several species to suggest cyclic fluctuations of sex hormone levels in males also (Kihlstrom 1971). Studies have shown that cyclicity of sex hormone production is regulated by the hypothalamus. Studies in rats have suggested to some investigators that the differentiation of hypothalamic mechanisms regulating cyclicity appears to be determined by the presence or absence of androgens in the fetus or newborn. They have concluded that in the absence of androgens, a cycling type of hypothalamus develops; if androgen is present, a noncycling type results (Levine 1971). Thus, if a male rat is castrated at birth, his pattern of pituitary release of FSH-LH at maturity is cyclic. Ovarian transplants into such a male undergo cyclic ovulation (Harris 1964). If a newborn female rat is given a single injection of testosterone in the newborn period, she will not have cyclic ovulation at maturity (Harris and Levine 1965). Control studies have been done to eliminate both the pituitary and the gonads (ovaries and testes) as the organs responsible for regulation of cyclicity. It is clear, however, as Johnson (1972) emphasizes, that this scheme of androgen-dependent sexual differentiation of the brain is oversimplified and that much critical data have yet to be acquired before an adequate theory can be developed. Furthermore, recent work indicates that results in rodents may not apply to primates since all attempts thus far to demonstrate such an organizing or developmental effect of androgens on the primate hypothalamus have been unsuccessful (Karsch et al. 1973).

THE HYPOTHALAMUS AND MATING BEHAVIOR

Experiments have also been interpreted as demonstrating that the presence or absence of androgenic effect on the hypothalamus of the newborn or fetal rat (and monkey) determines the predominant pattern of mating behavior at maturity. (For a review of this complex field of research, hormonal effects on brain development and behavior, see Davidson and Levine 1972.)

The female rat comes into heat or estrus at the phase of her five-day cycle when estrogen and progesterone are in a particular balance. At this time her sterotyped behavior pattern is to assume the lordotic posture (elevation of the rump) in the presence of mature males. The male, being acyclic, is stimulated by the presence of the estrous female (her odor and her presentation) to his stereotyped mating behavior which is to mount and attempt intromission. Neither will perform these behaviors in the absence of their own or administered sex hormones. Both sexes will, however, normally also exhibit some sexual activity which is characteristic of that of the opposite sex; i.e., females sometimes mount and males are sometimes mounted. Early experiments produced some expected results. They showed that a male rat, castrated *in adulthood* and given estrogen, will not exhibit lordosis. The sexual behavior of a male rat castrated *at birth* and given estrogen as an adult is, however, indistinguishable from that of a normal female; indistinguishable not only to the human observer but to other male rats who respond to him as to an estrous female (Levine 1971). If a newborn uncastrated female rat is given an injection of testosterone, her female pattern of sexual behavior ("receptivity") as an adult is abolished, even following injections of estrogen and progesterone. Her behavior following injections of androgens as an adult resembles that of a male with increased mounting and attempts at intromission (Harris and Levine 1965).

Results of other studies, however, exploring unanticipated (i.e., heterotypical or unstereotyped) hormonal effects, confound this simple scheme. Beach (1942) found that the lordosis response was enhanced in females castrated and given *testosterone* prepuberally. Other workers have demonstrated that estrogen given to newborn female rats abolishes the lordosis response in the mature animal (Levine and Mullins 1964) and increases her mounting activity with estrous females (Sodersten 1972).

The literature on animal studies is vast and has been recently reviewed by Money and Ehrhardt (1971, 1972), who summarize their conclusions concerning animal data thus:

> *Experimental animal studies of the influence of prenatally or neonatally administered sex hormones on the subsequent manifestations of sexual behavior implicate an organizing action of sex hormones and related substances on the brain, probably the region of the hypothalamus. The rule would appear to be that female-male bipotentiality applies initially prior to the influence of any sex hormone in the course of brain development. Bipotentiality would appear to persist when the early hormonal environment is feminine, so that either the feminine or the masculine component of mating behavior can be elicited in adulthood, dependent, among other things, on whether the eliciting hormone is estrogen or androgen. Bipotentiality is resolved in favor of unipolar masculinity of mating behavior if the early hormonal influence at the critical differentiating period is androgenic. The feminine component is then inhibited. Once this is accomplished, the feminine component will, in many, though perhaps not in all species, be elicited only under special conditions, for example, direct brain stimulation, or not at all. In the course of normal differentiation, the initial completeness of inhibition of feminine potential varies across species. Thus it is more complete in the rat than the hamster. In man it is probably not very complete, and is perhaps individually variable, as well. (Money and Ehrhardt 1971).*

IMPLICATIONS OF ANIMAL STUDIES FOR HUMAN BEHAVIOR

What might be the implications of these studies for humans and their patterns of sexual activity and sex identity? A number of problems make any generalizations about animal and especially human behavior based on hormone studies risky at this time: First, this field of research is new and many critical experiments have not been done. Second, the action of a given hormone may vary with the species of animal used, the dosage, and the timing of administration or withdrawal. Third, ovaries produce *androgens* in addition to estrogens and testes produce *estrogens* in addition to androgens, and the adrenal cortex of both sexes produces both hormones during fetal and postnatal life. In addition, fetuses of both sexes are exposed throughout pregnancy to estrogens and high levels of progesterone from the maternal ovaries and placenta. Thus, what physiological levels of any of these compounds may be present at various stages of development are quite unknown. Fourth, there is a *family* of androgens and a *family* of estrogens being produced. All the forms are closely related structurally or chemically both within and between the two families and are easily transformed metabolically one into the other in both sexes. To what degree this is constantly occurring is also unknown. Fifth, a recent significant finding in all species thus far studied, including primates, is that the brain *itself* converts androgens to estrogens (Ryan et al. 1972). For other reasons also, such as the fact that estrogen rather than androgen is localized in the nucleus of the cell, this finding raises the possibility that estrogen is the metabolic form in which these compounds act at their target sites, such as the brain.

There are obvious and clear-cut physical differences between the sexes that are related to different levels of estrogens and androgens. It is nonetheless interesting to speculate about the possibility that there are in the course of development relative and shifting rather than absolute blood levels of both types of hormones and that physical development and some aspects of sexual behavior may be to some degree influenced not only by genetic and cultural factors, but also by relative levels of hormones in the developing individual.

The examination of human behavior is further complicated by the absence of known stereotyped patterns of sexual activity which can be used as a measure of female- or male-type, such as lordosis and mounting frequency in animals.

Sexual expression and sex identity for humans occur within an individual and cultural as well as a biologically defined context. In the adult of both sexes, either estrogen or androgen may increase libido. But people are not dependent on sex hormones as are animals since, following removal of the ovaries or testes, most men and women continue the same pattern of sexual activity as that prior to removal. Furthermore, it is clear that women are not tied to their cycle phase as are other mammalian species.

Of overriding importance is the presence of an adequate stimulus. A multitude of cultural, experiential, and perceptual factors will determine at any moment whether a woman wishes to and does indeed engage in sexual activity. Similarly such factors will determine the object of sexual interest—which person and which sex. It goes without saying that all our social and legal institutions, mores, and ideologies approve and support only monogamous heterosexual relationships. And this cultural conditioning to one's sex role and sex identity begins within months after birth.

It is also probable that most deviations from the expected norm are themselves the result of a complex of cultural and experiential factors that are unique for each individual. Observations of animals in which cultural influences play an insignificant role make one wonder how humans might behave were cultural restraints removed. Is it possible that bisexuality is a biologic norm and heterosexuality an anatomic convenience that is, to be sure, enhanced as the dominant pattern by certain stimuli—odors or colors in certain species and by cultural conditioning in humans?

The power of one's immediate cultural environment or social interactions is demonstrated by studies of hermaphrodites (Money 1970). These indicate that psychosexual differentiation and sex identity are independent of genetic and hormonal sex (and also, therefore, of appearance of external genitalia). Gender identity is, rather, congruent with sex assignment; i.e., the person sees her/himself as belonging to the sex of assignment (usually by parents) and rearing.

RELATIONSHIP BETWEEN BIOLOGY AND BEHAVIOR: CONCEPTUAL AND METHODOLOGICAL PROBLEMS

It is clearly necessary for women to begin to examine every field of knowledge for its set of assumptions and premises since every field has been developed and dominated by men. Problems and issues are thus often defined from a particular perspective with a particular set of biases or blindnesses.

The question, for example, of the relationship between biology and behavior is a most difficult one because too little is known and too much emotion is invested. There are, of course, measurable biological and measurable psychological and behavioral differences (viewed statistically) between men and women. The serious logical fallacy often made, however, is to assume that there is a necessary *causal* relationship between these differences; for example between androgen and "aggressiveness." For this assumption there is no convincing evidence whatsoever in humans, and to use animal data as evidence that particular psychological or behavioral sex differences in humans are caused by particular *biological* sex differences is to ignore a fact that in other contexts is recognized to be of supreme importance: that humans are *qualitatively* different from all other animals. They are different precisely because of their brain and their culture which is the unique product of that brain. Individual social behavior is, in turn, formed by and expressed within the context of that individual's culture and is, in fact, nonexistent without it.

As described earlier, while neuronal structures and mechanisms in the hypothalamus and the rest of the brain of rats, cats, and so on, are retained in primates, the critical development in the latter, especially in humans, is in the growth and organization of the cerebral cortex. Cortical mechanisms, specifically as they are manifested in their most dramatic products—learning and culture—come to be dominant as determinants of human behavior, as contrasted with the biologically based stereotyped behavior of most other animals.

One cannot, for example, talk about "maternal instinct" as a biological fact or product as long as every baby girl is given a baby doll before she can walk or talk, as long as every little girl has to read books about what *girls* do and what *boys* do, as long as little girls see their mothers and other women being only mothers. In short, one cannot begin to assess the existence of such an "instinct" until society ceases to prescribe the maternal or the familial as the sole valid, useful, acceptable, and normal role for women.

Or take the matter of intelligence. Any aspect of human behavior, whether a pathological complex such as schizophrenia or tuberculosis, or a normal variant such as intelligence, manual dexterity, athletic ability, or mathematical skill, is determined by the interaction between that individual's biological state (prenatally and throughout postnatal life) and her environment, including her unique history of accumulated experiences. Of overriding importance as determinants of specific behavioral reactions of individuals are, however, the latter—her culture or tradition, her socialization, her experiences. That this is true is implicit in the fact that it is precisely culture or the accumulated effect of individual and social experience that sets human behavior apart from that of every other species.

There is no evidence whatsoever that women are not as intelligent or as creative as men, given the fact that they are (although in tiny numbers) in fields for which they have been allowed to be educated only during the last fifty to a hundred years. Women have not only made it but have been outstanding in every field once considered exclusively male—mathematics, physics (including Nobel laureates), business, banking, economics, mechanical and electrical and electronic engineering, philosophy, and so on. That is, there are women who excel in abstract thinking, mathematical thinking, hard-headed business; women who are aggressive, independent, and creative. As with blacks and the periodic controversy over their intelligence as compared with whites, so long as there are women or blacks who can and do accomplish all the things that men or whites do, then it is clear that these characteristics are not outside the biological capabilities of the group. Therefore, one must look to the effects of culture on characteristics that are peculiarly human and peculiarly cultural. Intelligence, aggressiveness, and the like, are, after all, developed and manifested only within a social and cultural context.

Psychological tests showing sex differences in children in certain concepts, e.g., those involving spatial perception, should be used not as reflections of *innate* characteristics but as indices of the *plasticity* of the human mind as it is affected and molded by social attitudes and practices.

A basic scientific principle is involved here. The effect of one variable cannot be measured when other variables are uncontrolled and even undefined. To what degree biology determines behavior can never be known until clearly existing cultural determinants are controlled.

Another serious methodological error obstructs some scientific approaches to truth. Concepts and terms that embody certain social biases, stereotypes, and assumptions are used to interpret data observed, for example, by experimental psychologists or by psychiatrists. These interpretations and conclusions are then used as evidence to support and "prove" those very stereotypes and assumptions.

Biases, incorrect assumptions, faulty interpretations, erroneous conclusions are not unknown in any field or science, even one so seemingly objective as anatomy. These may even approach fad proportions; but sooner or later the truth will emerge and, generally, little except time has been lost and little damage done. This is because in the biological or physical sciences, the behavior or structure or function of the object of study is not changed one whit by all the scientific nonsense that might be said about them. Einstein's theory, whether right or wrong, would have no effect whatsoever upon the movement of celestial bodies. In the behavioral sciences, however, theories and pronouncements by "experts" have potentially a very real effect upon the phenomena observed. Here the objects studied—people—

are conscious and aware, and theories interpreting their character and behavior affect that behavior often in destructive and self-fulfilling ways.

Women are "shown" (either directly or by extrapolation from animal studies) to be passive or instinctively maternal or incapable of abstract thought or lacking in libido. These characteristics then constitute the stamp of approval for feminine normality. The pressure is there, subtle or blatant, unremitting and nearly inescapable except for those who dare to be viewed as deviant: Either behave in the way (pseudo)science has described as normal and healthy for your sex; or be suspect and, consequently, guilty, insecure, and unable to acknowledge your own needs, goals, or abilities.

Thus, having a female body invites a set of assumptions—about one's mind, intelligence, capabilities, skills, motives, intentions, emotions, and goals—and worst of all, a set of behavior patterns: The woman graduate student is asked, "What's a good-looking girl like you doing in physics?" The woman student wanting to go into botany and ecological research is told she ought to be a journalist instead. Nursing is recommended to the woman premed since it is "less arduous" and she'll get married anyhow. Untold numbers of women are daily being channeled from fields of their choice to those that men traditionally have reserved for them.

AGGRESSIVENESS AS CONCEPTUAL PROBLEM

One example of such a biased concept is *aggressiveness*, a word charged with value—a different value for men and for women—and applied anthropomorphically to the interpretation of animal behavior. In our culture aggressiveness in men is desirable; it is rewarded and encouraged in business, sports, and war, and is considered a male characteristic. Agressiveness in women is, however, a social liability; it is considered unattractive, undesirable, embarrassing, and downright unfeminine. Passivity is thus a feminine characteristic. What is perhaps even more insidious is an implication that aggressiveness includes such characteristics as independence of mind, decisiveness, imagination—all, therefore, masculine qualities.

The observation is made that male rats in a cage fight; females do not. When given an electric shock, the male rats fight more; the females do not. Aha! Now we have more proof that males *are* naturally aggressive. What about the equally obvious (or ridiculous?) conclusion that females must be more intelligent since fighting each other is clearly an inappropriate response to being shocked by some human being?

Starting, presumably, with the assumption that "aggressiveness" is an androgen-linked male characteristic, early studies demonstrated that male rats castrated at birth were less "aggressive" (i.e., fought less) as adults (Conner and Levine 1969) and that female mice given androgen at birth were more "aggressive" following androgen injections as adults (Edwards 1969). The fact seems to be little known that a subsequent study (Edwards and Herndon 1970) showed that newborn female mice given *estrogen* at birth also fought more as adults.

Strangely enough, the same freedom and ease with which the generalization is made linking aggressiveness with masculinity are not exercised in interpreting data that have possible implications for feminine characteristics that do not fit the stereotype. In open-field tests, female rats exhibit greater exploratory activity and less defecation. I have yet to see the conclusion that females, then, are more curious, inquisitive, adventuresome, and since they defecate less, less anxious.

Nor, of course, should such conclusions be drawn any more than those concerning aggressiveness. One of the problems is conceptual. *Aggressiveness* is clearly a behavioral complex, not a sex-linked gene. The behavioral response of *fighting* or *attack* is not synonymous with *aggressiveness*. Fighting behavior can and will be elicited in any species or sex given the appropriate stimulus. A female rabbit may be ferocious in defense of her young. Female hamsters, *which are larger than males*, fight more. Odors, especially those of the estrous female, will elicit fighting in male rats. The fact that androgen may prove to be an important element in activating the olfactory (smelling) mechanisms of male rats in response to an estrous female (resulting in their fighting each other) will have obvious implications for species survival mechanisms rather than for a universal masculine characteristic of aggressiveness.

FEMALE SEXUALITY

The other side of "masculine aggressiveness" is, of course, "feminine passivity and receptivity" and the associated social and psychiatric myths that have become established concerning women's sexuality. It is interesting that the concept of feminine sexual passivity should have arisen at all with so little evidence. Among animals, it is the male who is passive until an estrous female displays her presence by odor, color, posture, and so on. Serious studies of human behavior indicate what women have long known or suspected—that their libido starts as young as, and lasts longer than, that of men. Furthermore, women are capable of (and probably usually prefer) several orgasms, particularly if they have escaped the legislated nonsense of the compulsory vaginal orgasm (Sherfey 1966).

Sherfey (1966) develops a convincing hypothesis about the suppression of female sexuality. "In every culture studied, the crucial transition from the nomadic, hunting, and food-gathering economy to a settled, agricultural existence was the beginning of family life, modern civilization, and civilized man. . . . With the domestication of animals and the agricultural revolution, for the first time in all time, the survival of species lay in the extended family with its private property, kinship lineages, inheritance laws, social ordinances, and, most significantly, many surviving children. . . . Many factors have been advanced to explain the rise of the patriarchal, usually polygynous, system and its concomitant ruthless subjugation of female sexuality (which necessarily subjugated her entire emotional and intellectual life). However, if the conclusions reached here are true, it is conceivable that the *forceful* suppression of women's inordinate sexual demands was a prerequisite to the dawn of every modern civilization and almost every living culture."

The suggestion is made by Sherfey that women for physiological reasons are and always have been sexually insatiable, unlike men. With the accumulation of private property, she implies, it was necessary for men, who became the producers in settled agricultural economies, to ensure that their wealth be passed on only to their own sons. For this reason, the man had to suppress the ebullient sexuality of the bearer of his children lest she present him with the sons of other men. The protection of lineages for the inheritance of private property was considered by Engels (1970) also to be a crucial factor in the origin of the family (i.e., institutionalized monogamy) and state.

Recent studies (at this writing, still in press; see Kolata 1974) of the !Kung people provide important evidence that the transition from a food gathering–hunting economy to a settled agricultural mode was critical to the change in women's status from one of equality. Nomadic hunters and gatherers for the past 11,000 years in the Kalahari Desert, the !Kung have begun in the last decade to settle in agrarian villages near the Bantus; less than 5 percent are still nomads.

Formerly the women provided at least half of the food consumed, and child care and food preparation were shared by men and women. Since settling into agrarian villages, the men clear the fields and tend the cattle while the women perform domestic chores. The channeling of skills is further accentuated by the fact that the men, since they tend the cattle of the Bantus, learn their language; consequently, the men are the ones who conduct business with the Bantus. Along with the loss of economic status by women, presumed biological effects of dietary changes are reinforcing their domestication through a marked increase in their fertility and consequent frequency of pregnancy.

While it may indeed be the case that the accumulation of private property and the establishment (by men) of institutions and suppressive mores to protect their property were, as Sherfey states, "a prerequisite to the dawn of every modern civilization," it is important to acknowledge that they are only modern civilizations as we know them to be, capitalist and imperialist, based upon the oppression by one class of all other classes. The implication is clear from the analyses of both Engels and Sherfey that sexual oppression, with men ruling women, may well have been the original form of class oppression and a model and training ground for all subsequent forms.

That "civilization" may indeed have evolved in that way hardly precludes all other possible forms nor justifies the continuation of ideologies and institutions that limit potential and destroy the lives of one group in the interests of another.

Society, aided by some psychiatric theories and practice, has established passivity and receptivity as the norm for feminine sexual and other behavior. If she deviates sexually, she is called promiscuous or a nymphomaniac; if she deviates socially, she is called aggressive and castrating. A norm is set which is social, *not* biological; and the woman who deviates is stigmatized. Stereotypes are thus constructed which serve the purpose of maintaining the status quo in our homes and professions.

The myths of female passivity have served well to keep the little woman back at the ranch and busy at the range and, until recently, quietly guilty about the restiveness she feels under a variety of restraints imposed upon her being. The findings of Masters and Johnson (1966) ought to explode the myths about female sexuality; the assertive self-determination of women themselves will explode the remaining myths of biological inferiority.

REFERENCES

Beach, F. S. "Male and Female Mating Behavior in Prepuberally Castrated Female Rats Treated with Androgen." *Endocrinology* 31 (1942): 672–78.

CONNER, R. L., AND LEVINE, S. "Hormonal Influences on Aggressive Behaviour." In *Aggressive Behaviour*, edited by S. Garattini and E. B. Sigg. Amsterdam: Excerpta Med., 1969. Pp. 150–63.

DAVIDSON, J. M., AND LEVINE, S. "Endocrine Regulation of Behavior." *Annual Review of Physiology* 34 (1972): 375–408.

EDWARDS, D. A. "Early Androgen Stimulation and Aggressive Behavior in Male and Female Mice." *Physiology and Behavior* 4 (1969): 333–38.

EDWARDS, D. A., AND HERNDON, J. "Neonatal Estrogen Stimulation and Aggressive Behavior in Female Mice." *Physiology and Behavior* 5 (1970): 993–95.

ENGELS, F. *The Origin of the Family, Private Property and the State* (1891). New York: International Publishers, 1970.

HARRIS, G. W. "Sex Hormones, Brain Development and Brain Function." *Endocrinology* 75 (1964): 627–48.

HARRIS, G. W., AND LEVINE, S. "Sexual Differentiation of the Brain and Its Experimental Control." *Journal of Physiology* 181 (1965): 379–400.

JOHNSON, D. C. "Sexual Differentiation of Gonadotropic Patterns." *American Zoologist* 12 (1972): 193–205.

KARSCH, F. J.; DIERSCHKE, D. J.; AND KNOBIL, E. "Sexual Differentiation of Pituitary Function: Apparent Difference between Primates and Rodents." *Science* 179 (1973): 484–86.

KIHLSTROM, J. E. "A Male Sexual Cycle." In *Current Problems in Fertility*, edited by A. Ingleman-Sundberg and N. O. Lunell. New York: Plenum Press, 1971. Pp. 50–54.

KOLATA, G. B. "!Kung Hunter-Gatherers: Feminism, Diet, and Birth Control." *Science* 185 (1974): 932–34.

LEVINE, S. "Sexual Differentiation: The Development of Maleness and Femaleness." *California Medicine* 114 (1971): 12–17.

LEVINE, S., AND MULLINS, R. "Estrogen Administered Neonatally Affects Adult Sexual Behavior in Male and Female Rats." *Science* 144 (1964): 185–87.

MASTERS, W. H., AND JOHNSON, V. E. *Human Sexual Response*. Boston: Little, Brown, 1966.

MONEY, J. "Sexual Dimorphism and Homosexual Gender Identity. *Psychological Bulletin* 74 (1970): 425–40.

MONEY, J., AND EHRHARDT, A. A. "Fetal Hormones and the Brain: Effect on Sexual Dimorphism of Behavior—A Review." *Archives of Sexual Behavior* 1 (1971): 241–62.

MONEY, J., AND EHRHARDT, A. A. *Man and Woman, Boy and Girl*. Baltimore, Md.: Johns Hopkins Press, 1972.

RYAN, K. J.; NAFTOLIN, F.; REDDY, V.; FLORES, F.; AND PETRO, Z. "Estrogen Formation in the Brain." *American Journal of Obstetrics and Gynecology* 114 (1972): 454–60.

SHERFEY, M. J. *The Nature and Evolution of Female Sexuality*. New York: Random House, 1966.

SODERSTEN, P. "Mounting Behavior in the Female Rat during the Estrous Cycle, after Ovariectomy, and after Estrogen or Testosterone Administration." *Hormones and Behavior* 3 (1972): 307–20.

4

Female Strategies:
Animal Adaptations
and Adaptive
Significance
G. Kass-Simon

A great deal of publicity has recently been given to a study on the disastrous effects of overcrowding on a population of mice. The study, conducted by John B. Calhoun of the National Institutes of Mental Health, has become well known largely because of the ease with which the popular imagination has been able to find parallels between mouse society and human societies. Thus, a recent newspaper account of the study was entitled: "Of Mice and Men: 'Heavenly' Welfare State: Every Last Mouse dies." [1]

In Calhoun's study a population of mice was raised in the laboratory in a controlled environment that provided all of the necessities and none of the adversities of a natural habitat. The mouse population began with two females and two males, increased to over 2200 individuals within two and a half years, but then rapidly declined until every mouse died.

As space in the cage became scarce, the female mice forced their older offspring out of the nests. These juveniles, who could not find space to establish a territory of their own, wandered about the cage and never became part of the social structure of the rest of the population. Despite the continued abundance of food and the apparent good health of the individuals, all breeding virtually stopped after the population reached its peak. This, of course, resulted in the ultimate death of the population.

Ordinarily, this sort of information would be of little use to those of us concerned with the attitudes of our society toward women. But the article makes the repeated point that among the deleterious changes that took place in the

74

disintegrating mouse society was a shift from a male-dominated to a female-dominated social structure. Although Calhoun describes the development of a whole series of socially destructive behaviors in both males and females,[2] which cannot reasonably be described in the language of social hierarchy, it is the fact of female dominance that has drawn the reporter's attention. That the displaced juvenile males become totally inactive, save for the minimal movement required to obtain food, or that they become exceedingly aggressive and intolerant of the least physical disturbance, is quietly overlooked. Nor is any mention made of the fact that virtually all adults, with the exception of the few aggressive females, no longer sought to maintain their territories and ceased to display any territorial defense behavior. What is mentioned and what is emphasized is the change in female status that took place as the population became overcrowded. "Adult males lost their traditional dominant position" and "the older female mice not only had 'lib,' they had clout." The following parallel between mouse society and human society is drawn with reference to the displaced juveniles:

And as many adult males in the inner cities are overwhelmed by the multitude, humiliated by a poor self-image based on their lack of prestige-building skills and rendered less relevant by the welfare check, is it not logical that they should often become nonentities, drifting from woman to woman, and that the matriarchy of unmarried or loosely married women should take over? [3]

And there is no question that the writer of the article, if not Dr. Calhoun as well, considers the shift from patriarchy to matriarchy a symptom of the deterioration of a once healthy society, if not precisely the sole cause of the society's demise. To quote Calhoun: "For an animal as complex as man, there is no reason why a comparable sequence of events should not also lead to species extinction."

Is one surprised, then, if we conclude from this, that even a small change in male and female roles, or far worse, a shift toward a female-dominated social order, represents nothing less than a steppingstone toward the inevitable extinction of human society?

The writings of Harry and Margaret Harlow carry a similar message.[4] This time, the lesson to be learned is that women who are mothers had better stay home and minister to their children lest these grow up to be unsocial, unloving, and perhaps even autistic adults. The Harlows and their coworkers have demonstrated in innumerable studies, which they extensively reviewed in *Behavior of Nonhuman Primates*, that rhesus monkeys deprived of social interaction with other animals at given times during their development display certain behavioral traits not found in monkeys not so deprived. Among the most famous of their findings is the one in which they describe how an infant monkey will cling to a cloth dummy and treat it as though it were another animal, even preferring it to a strange live monkey and using it to find security when it is frightened by unknown animate or inanimate objects.

The Harlows and every other psychologist, educator, sociologist, and ethologist who has ever quoted the study refer to this cloth dummy as a "surrogate mother." The implied suggestion is that infants, be they humans or monkeys, have an innate need for mother love, so much so that they will create a substitute inanimate mother if a live one is unavailable. This inference, that children must have their mothers, is inevitable because of the term "surrogate mother" rather than "surrogate animal." The fact that it has been shown by the Harlows and their coworkers that motherless monkeys raised simply in peer groups of two or four animals grow, albeit more slowly, into normal, heterosexual adults is almost entirely ignored.

In the same way, the Harlows and everyone else persistently refer to animals raised in physical isolation during their first year, without either contact with a live mother or with any other live animals, as "motherless monkeys." [5] Here one cannot help but conclude that it is their motherlessness and not their isolation which is the cause of the subsequent development of the females into brutal or at best indifferent mothers. The take-home lesson is obvious: if a society wishes to ensure that its children grow up to be well-adjusted, loving adults, it must ensure that they be reared by their mothers.

But the real question, in both the mouse and the monkey studies, is not whether because of a previously established frame of reference or some unintentional prejudice we seriously misinterpret the observations. Rather, the question is whether it is in any way possible to learn from these or any other animal studies what is inherently natural or unnatural, and therefore what is inherently good or bad, and therefore what must or must not be done, in human society? Or to put it in terms of women and their social and biological roles: is it possible to argue from examples in the animal kingdom about what is and what is not appropriate to the nature of something called the "female animal"?

Zoologists come into contact, at least indirectly, with many kinds of animals; and if biology has but one thing to teach, it is this: that which is, is that which has been successful. An enormous variety of form, physiology, and behavior exists among animal groups. This is so because every peculiarity and every unusual trait represents, in some way, an adaptation that has not only permitted the group's survival but has often been the very thing which has ensured that survival. It might be instructive for us to look at some of these adaptations and see just how they contribute to species survival; in this way, perhaps we can decide whether or not it is possible to argue from one group of animals to the next about the universality or naturalness of any given trait. Let us look first at a particular pattern of behavior and see whether we can distinguish something called "adaptive significance."

One of the more fascinating behavioral sequences is the series of events that occurs during courtship and mating of the praying mantis. The praying mantis is a rather large insect closely related to locusts and grasshoppers; the female has the rather extraordinary habit of biting off her mate's head at the moment of mating. This happens because mantises, which are usually very quiet, have a tendency to strike out at any moving object in their path; even when that object is the female's future mate. When a mating sequence begins, the male will often fly toward the female in a single flying leap that usually causes it to land facing her, head on. The male's body curves toward the female's and his antennae begin to brush the female's head. This causes her to strike out at him. As soon as she has devoured his head, the male's abdomen begins intense and continuous copulatory movements accompanied by a lateral-rotary movement which carries the abdomen onto the female's back, out of reach of her jaws. Although not all males lose their heads during mating, the abdomens of those that have been beheaded not only perform copulatory movements that are far more intense than those of the intact male, but also display the lateral-rotary movement that is lacking in the intact male.[6]

Now the physiological explanation for this extraordinary phenomenon is actually quite simple: the phallic nerve that is responsible for the copulatory movement of the abdomen and that originates in the last segment of the abdomen is inhibited by another nerve whose origin lies in the head of the mantis. As soon as the female severs this inhibitory nerve by biting off her mate's head, the normally suppressed phallic ganglion in the abdomen begins to fire at an enormously increased frequency that causes the abdomen to perform intense copulatory movements.

The adaptive significance here is obvious: the likelihood of fertilization and therefore the production of progeny is vastly enhanced by the female's cannibalistic behavior toward the male's head. But this, it must be pointed out, can only be so in those animals where a nerve in the head inhibits copulation, while one in the body engenders it.

There are other ways that species have developed to ensure the survival of their kind. Such adaptations are as often as not physical as well as behavioral. As a rule, one is accustomed to assuming that except for small differences, the male and female of a species tend to look very much alike. Thus, except for plumage differences, it is often impossible to tell a male bird from a female of the same species; or, without reference to the genitals, a male dog or cat from a female dog or cat. Even among humans, if it were not for the secondary sexual characteristics of beard and breasts, dressed women and men would be virtually indistinguishable from one another.

Now this arrangement whereby the physical characteristics of a group are essentially the same for all its members is very useful. It becomes a simple matter for the members of a group to recognize one another and so ensure continued group cohesion, as well as the avoidance of mistaken attacks on one's friends. Similarly, small differences in appearance allow the individual members of the group not only to distinguish one another but also to recognize at a glance such socially important traits as age and sex.

Under some circumstances, say, if the number of individuals in a group is very small, or if the territory they occupy is very large, or if the behavior is lethargic and inactive,[7] it becomes difficult for members of a species to find one another. Under these circumstances, special mechanisms must develop that will make certain that mating can continue or, at least, that offspring will continue to be produced.

In some cases this has led to the development of parthenogenic or nonsexual reproduction. In other instances, the necessity of guaranteeing that male and female make contact for mating has so overwhelmed all other considerations that it has caused the most unexpected and wide-ranging changes in the appearance, physiology, and behavior of one of the sexes.

One way of making absolutely certain that male and female will be together when they release their eggs and sperm is to arrange things so that the two partners are permanently attached to one another. This is exactly what happens when one of the partners becomes a parasite on the other. The angler fish, which lives in very deep sea waters, is more or less an inactive, lethargic sort of animal. Rather than hunt its prey, it normally lurks in the dark without moving anything except its strangely modified dorsal fin, which it flicks to and fro periodically in front of its face. The dorsal fin, which arises at the back of the fish's head, has evolved into a long, thin filamentous outgrowth that is thickened at the end. The whole arrangement looks very much like a fishing line with a bit of bait on a hook, and the angler fish uses this to catch unsuspecting prey that are foolish enough to approach the bait.

Now this sedentary behavior on the part of the angler fish is not very conducive to seeking or finding a mate. Nor does this stealthy method of catching prey permit the congregation of a school of angler fish in one spot. So, in order to ensure that fertilization will take place and to sidestep the problem of a necessarily scattered population, the female angler has become the host of her parasitic mate. The male angler, which is about one-fourth the size of the female, becomes attached to the female's body in so intimate a fashion that the bloodstreams of the two animals flow through a joined circulatory system.[8] A similar parasitism exists in the marine worm, *Bonellia,* where the male has become reduced to a small ciliated organism living within the genital tract of the female.[9]

Although there is a parasitic worm that represents at least one well-known instance in which the female is the parasite and the male the host, it is somewhat easier for us to imagine why it might be the female and not the male that has retained its free-living, nonparasitic features. As a working hypothesis, we might suppose that it is likely to be exceedingly important that the rate at which eggs are produced and/or the time of their release need to be absolutely responsive to the exigencies of the environment; it will be the fertilized egg and not the fertilized sperm that will develop into the growing embryo. Such external control over egg production might easily be mediated through the female's nervous and hormonal systems, which are likely to be sufficiently sensitive to environmental changes to be able to regulate egg production and release.

Specializations to secure species success are not by any means limited to problems of mating and encounter. The subsequent survival of the offspring is certainly of equal importance. And it is a rule of thumb that the fewer the offspring produced, the more active and protracted is the care of the offspring. But despite the fact that we are accustomed to associating child care with physical motherhood, it is not to be assumed that brood care always automatically falls to the bearer of the offspring. Many instances exist among fish and birds where it is the father and not the mother who tends the young. Male seahorses, sticklebacks, and Siamese fighting fish all are responsible for brood care. The male stickleback not only builds the nest but also tends both eggs and offspring when they are hatched. Once the brood is hatched the male keeps his young close together in a school. Should one somehow manage to swim away a short distance, the male picks it up in its mouth and spits it back into its proper place in the school. During this time the male is very careful to keep all potential predators away from his brood, including the mother of the brood. Should a female happen to pick up one of the offspring in her mouth, she would not spit it out, but would simply devour it.[10]

Now we may be extremely hard put to find a reasonable explanation for the female's peculiar behavior. One might well wonder what the adaptive significance could possibly be in having a mother devour her own offspring. It is very likely that this is entirely the wrong question to ask. By way of looking for the right question, let us consider what happens to female and male sticklebacks after the female has produced her eggs.

After spawning, the female is free to wander off; if she meets another male, she can mate with him and produce another clutch of eggs and then go off again until the end of the mating season. At the same time, the male who has been left tending the nest will mate with several other females who might swim by, within two or three days, before beginning to hatch out his eggs. In this way, since all the eggs hatch more or less at the same time, the resulting school of fish consists only of half-brothers and sisters rather than absolute siblings. Later, when the individuals of this school mate, they have already been somewhat protected from the genetically disastrous effects of absolute inbreeding. Here the factor that seems to be important to the success of the species is the genetic dispersal that results from the female's leaving the nest.

But to get back to our original problem: why are female sticklebacks capable of devouring their young? The answer to this seems to lie in the fact that females don't stay around long enough to rear their offspring and therefore require no specific inhibition to the normal gulping-swallowing response seen in fish. The male stickleback, on the other hand, must tend the young, and so some sort of mechanism has evolved that inhibits his swallowing response. This inhibition is probably triggered by the young themselves.

That this kind of inhibition exists in some animals is well documented. Experiments have shown that were it not for such inhibitive mechanisms,[11] some mother birds would surely peck their offspring to death. Thus the turkey hen, which tends to attack any furry or hairy object near her nest, is prevented from attacking her own chicks by the peeps they emit. A hen that has been made deaf surgically does not hesitate to peck her offspring to death. This acoustically caused inhibition is an effective and efficient mechanism. As Konrad Lorenz points out, a hen cannot know all her potential predators and so it is safest to strike out indiscriminately.[12] To protect her own chicks, it is only necessary for an additional mechanism to have evolved: that is, the recognition of the sound of her own offspring to inhibit her nest-defense response.

So far we have been looking at individual traits to see what role they have played in keeping the species in question alive. In fact, animals do not simply differ from one another in isolated traits, but rather in a whole array of attributes. It is this unique complex, distinct for each group, that represents all the ways in which a given group has managed to survive in its particular niche.

At the beginning of this chapter we talked about Calhoun's study of the expired mouse society. We saw that among the several characteristics that became manifest as the society declined was the development of a social structure that might be described as a female-dominated matriarchy. Whether such a matriarchy was in fact instrumental in causing the ultimate demise of the mouse colony is, as we have seen, unclear, since so many other socially harmful traits also emerged. But even if it were true that a causal connection existed between the extinction of the mouse colony and the emergence of the matriarchy, the fact of matriarchy in itself can in no way be associated with declining societies in general. Among mammals, the African wild dog and the hyena are famous for successful matriarchal social orders. Perhaps the most famous and most fascinating example of a supremely successful matriarchy, and one that is female dominated in the extreme, is to be found in the common honeybee.[13] As we have just pointed out, animal adaptation represents an entire complex of special traits, and so we might find it useful to look more closely at a honeybee society and observe some of the physical, reproductive, physiological, and behavioral specializations that have made these societies such highly integrated, finely tuned machines.

Honeybee society is divided into classes of individuals according to the job each member of the class performs in the life cycle of the hive; members of each class differ from one another not only in their status-determined behavior but also in their appearance and physiology. There is but one female in the hive capable of breeding, and that is the queen bee. She is larger and lives ten or twelve times longer than anyone else in the hive. The queen can produce viable eggs whether they are fertilized or not. However, unfertilized eggs develop only into male bees and in order to produce female offspring it is necessary for the queen to mate with a male.

This mating occurs only once in her entire life: soon after she has emerged from the brood cell, where she has been feeding and growing since birth. After mating, the sperm are stored inside her body in a sperm sack where they are maintained for the remainder of her life, which spans some four or five years. The queen can then produce male or female eggs at will, simply by releasing sperm from the sack. Since the male's only job in the hive is to mate with a queen, male bees are allowed to survive only for the duration of the breeding season when young queens are being produced for new colonies. After that, they are no longer tolerated in the hive and, because they are not fed, ultimately starve to death. This arrangement reduces the number of individuals that must be fed during the winter when food is less abundant. And at the same time it ensures the colony of the continual production of fertilized eggs.

Although it is the duty of the queen bee to lay eggs, and although it is she who is the final determinant of whether a male or female egg will be produced, all the other jobs in the hive fall to the worker bees. These too are females, but unlike the queen they are incapable of producing eggs. Their inability to produce eggs results from the fact that, as larvae, they were given less nourishing food than the prospective queens. Nonetheless, except for reproduction itself, every other facet of the hive's activity is controlled by these nonreproductive females. Even here, they actually determine whether or not the queen is to release the sperm from her sack to produce fertilized eggs. If the worker bees build small cells, the queen fills them with the fertilized eggs of potential workers. If the cells are somewhat larger, the queen fills these cells with unfertilized eggs for potential males. If the cells are larger still, fertilized eggs are laid that then become prospective queen larvae. This is a very efficient mechanism, for it is far easier for the workers, who are scurrying about the hive, to be responsive to what sort of individual the society ought to produce in order to maintain its numerical status quo, than it is for the queen, who goes from cell to cell, laying eggs almost incessantly, like a chess king going from square to square.

The division of labor in the hive corresponds both to the age of the individual and to her particular physiology. Thus, when a worker bee emerges, her first job is to prepare and clean the cells for the next brood. Next, while she is still young, her salivary glands grow and develop and begin to produce a highly enriched secretion that is fed to the young larvae. After her nursemaid stage, the bee's glands begin to atrophy and her wax glands develop; this class of workers now becomes the builders of cells and the defenders of the hive. (It is this class that determines what sort of egg the queen will lay.) Finally, in her last stage of life, the bee's wax glands atrophy and she becomes a forager. Now she leaves the hive daily to bring back nectar and pollen for the other members of the hive and for the newly produced brood.

One may well wonder about the adaptive significance of having the various jobs performed by different individuals in the hive. One answer is simply that at some time in the past, before bees became social, an individual female is thought to have been able to perform all the various tasks herself. That is, she was able not only to produce the young, but also to build cells, care for the brood, defend her home, and gather food without help. But as populations grew, it became increasingly more difficult for a single individual or even a pair of individuals to do all the work for the growing number of offspring. And so the job was simply divided up among various types of females. But the next question that immediately comes to mind is, Why is the work divided along age rather than sexual lines? Why are the various categories of workers all females of different ages?

In a series of experiments, Karl von Frisch and his colleagues were able to produce hives that lacked one or another class of worker bees. First they produced a hive in which the foragers were removed. The bees at first continued on in their normal fashion, simply drawing on the reserves in the hive. But then, as stores were depleted and the population was in danger of perishing, very young workers, those who were still nursemaids and builders, began to leave the hive to gather food. But this, which seems not to have required any profound physiological changes on the part of the young workers, is not nearly so surprising as what happened when first nursemaid bees were removed from the hive and then builders.

If nursemaids, bees whose salivary glands are large and who secrete food for the young, were removed, builder bees, whose salivary glands should long since have atrophied, took over the job. And much like human wetnurses, they were able to produce food for the young long after they no longer had young of their own to rear. Similarly, when builder bees were removed, foragers whose wax glands had already atrophied formed new glands in response to the hive's need for builders.

So now it looks as though the reason for having all the workers of different ages but of the same sex is that it is vitally important for a population, whose members must perform different jobs, to be composed of individuals who are able to change both their behavioral roles and their physiological attributes in response to the requirements of the population. And it is a far easier genetic maneuver to program one type of individual for the entire physiological repertoire, and simply to turn each portion of the program on and off as necessary, than it is to institute an entirely new program in the genome of a different sort of individual. In other words, it is easier to allow the female, who presumably already had all these capabilities, to run each one off in sequence, or turn them on as necessary, than to introduce some of these capabilities into the males' genetic repertoire.

By this time it ought to be abundantly clear that adaptations and specializations are defined specifically and differently for each and every group according to the pressures that group encounters in its peculiar socioecological niche. (This is no less true for the special situations of human populations than it is for other animal groups.) As we have already said, it is universally true that that which exists is that which has been adaptive. And now we should add: that which is adaptive is distinctly and discretely so for each individual group. To argue that the contingencies faced by one species are likely also to be faced by even a closely related species is to ignore completely the special anatomical, physiological, and environmental features that delineate one group from another. Honeybee or mouse societies are no more analogues for human societies than is the mating behavior of the praying mantis a prototype of human sexual responses. And it cannot be possible, therefore, to allow monkey behavior toward cloth dummies to predicate our children's upbringing any more than it is possible to insist that stickleback brood care necessitates human fathers to stay home to tend their babies while mothers go off to seek other mates. Such ethical judgments based on examples from "nature" are simply not possible.

But having said that, it must also be said that inherent in the concept of continued survival or continuing adaptiveness is the absolute requirement for the retension of one kind of flexibility or another. This holds true, a priori, for all living things. In the final analysis, when conditions change, unless populations reproduce very quickly so that they can produce different types of individuals in short periods of time, or unless the change is so slow that new genetic adaptations can arise, a wide spectrum of behavioral and physiological responses provides the only way in which a group can remain adaptive to the contingencies of a new situation. When conditions change abruptly, if a population cannot acclimate to its new circumstances, it perishes. Calhoun's mice, who were indeed able to overcome some of the stresses of overcrowding, could not respond adaptively enough to permit the population to maintain its numbers; their physiology and behavior simply had not been designed to cope with a sudden lack of space. And in the end what finally did them in was, very likely, that same mechanism which had evolved in the first place to prevent overpopulation in the wild. In nature space is virtually unlimited; when a population grows too large for its territory, it might simply stop breeding until its juveniles were old enough to leave and find territories of their own. In the wild, this is a very efficient way to keep the numbers in a population constant. But in captivity, since space became permanently scarce, breeding permanently stopped, and the population disappeared.

One might note, as an aside, that the problem of overpopulation is handled very differently in a honeybee population: By limiting reproduction to only one female in the society, overproduction of offspring is automatically limited by the number of eggs she can produce in a given period of time. But here, too, this adaptive mechanism can suddenly become maladaptive; should the queen unexpectedly die, or be removed by some overzealous experimenter, in the absence of other presumptive queens, the whole bee population would die off very quickly.

So what we are left with is the fact that, although it is not possible to reason that a lack of space for human populations will inevitably result in the development of a matriarchy followed by extinction, or to argue that the death of, say, the queen of England will result in the extinction of the British populace, it is important to know that no matter what trait or adaptation we are talking about, for whatever group of organisms, that trait is successful only as long as the conditions that produced that trait remain unchanged. New circumstances produce new traits. This being true, we had better be warned, before we are tempted to erect a system of ethics on the basis of the success of past characteristics and adaptations, that such a system would only be as good as, and could last only as long as, the world that fashioned it.

In his book *The Mountain People*, Colin Turnbull describes the rather radical and unexpected changes that have taken place in the social structure and behavior patterns of a people who have suddenly been deprived of all their hunting lands.[14] These people, the Ik of Uganda, are constantly on the verge of death by starvation. Food is so scarce that individuals who cannot forage for themselves are not fed and therefore die. The old, the weak, and the useless, that is, people of about thirty-five years of age, die of starvation because no one will give them food.

Children are not fed or cared for by either parent. After the age of three, when the mother no longer nurses her child, children are cast out of their parents' compounds to form roving bands who go about in search of food. If a child makes the mistake of thinking that its parents will feed and care for it after it is three years old, and if it therefore lingers about the parents' compound, it is simply abandoned and left to die of starvation. Turnbull describes one instance where a mother rejoiced because her nursing infant, which had been left on the ground, was captured by a leopard and devoured.

This lack of parental love and care, which is reminiscent of the behavior of the Harlow monkeys and which we think of as not only inhuman but maladaptive in our society, is, as Turnbull points out, the only way in which the Ik can survive. After all, it is always possible to make more babies; the important thing is to ensure that the reproductive members remain alive and that they will be succeeded by new reproductive members. And this, apparently, is what the Ik society does: children are fed until the strongest can care for themselves.

This behavior, which is so different from our own, is simply an illustration of behavioral flexibility within the human species. It is one of the possible ways in which the survival of the species under changing circumstances can be ensured. It ought to make us think twice about making assertions about what is natural and unnatural and what is the nature of the human female or, for that matter, the nature of children or adults in general. To quote Turnbull:

The Ik teach us that our much vaunted human values are not inherent in humanity at all, but are associated only with a particular form of survival called society, and all, even society itself, are luxuries that can be dispensed with.[15]

NOTES

1. J. L. JONES, "Of Mice and Men: 'Heavenly' Welfare State: Every Last Mouse Dies," *Wisconsin State Journal*, 18 March 1973.

2. J. B. CALHOUN, "Control of Population: Numbers," *Annals of the New York Academy of Science* 184 (1971): 148–55.

3. JONES, "Of Mice and Men."

4. H. F. HARLOW and M. K. HARLOW, "The Affectional Systems," in *Behavior of Nonhuman Primates*, vol. 2, ed. Schrier, Harlow, and Stollnitz (New York: Academic Press, 1965).

5. Ibid.

6. K. D. ROEDER, *Nerve Cells and Insect Behavior* (Cambridge, Mass.: Harvard University Press, 1967).

7. LESLIE REID, *The Sociology of Nature* (Baltimore: Penquin Books, 1962).

8. Ibid.

9. L. A. Borradaile, F. A. Potts, L. E. S. Eastham, and J. T. Saunders, *The Invertebrata* (Cambridge, England: Cambridge University Press, 1961).

10. K. Z. Lorenz, *King Solomon's Ring* (New York: Thomas Y. Crowell, 1952). See also N. Tinbergen, *Social Behavior in Animals* (London: Methuen, 1953).

11. K. Lorenz, *On Aggression* (New York: Bantam, 1967).

12. Ibid.

13. K. von Frisch, *The Dancing Bees*, trans. Dora Ilse (New York: Harcourt, Brace, 1953).

14. C. Turnbull, *The Mountain People* (New York: Simon & Schuster, 1972).

15. Ibid., p. 294.

The Essential Emancipation: The Control of Reproduction
Hania W. Ris

Every woman should be able to control her own reproduction. This is essential not only for her emancipation but also for her welfare and the welfare of any children she may choose to have. Every child should have the right to be born into the security of an unbroken home, to be wanted and loved, not neglected and rejected. Our concern should be not just with life, but with quality of life for all women, children, and men.

POPULATION CRISIS

The concern for population growth and its sequelae dates back to antiquity. Han Fei-Tau (Chou Dynasty *ca.* 500 B.C.) states that "the life of a nation depends upon having enough food, not upon the number of people." [1] Tertullian, the Latin church father (*ca.* 160–*ca.* 230, from *De Anima*) writes that "the scourges of pestilence, famine, wars and earthquake have come to be regarded as a blessing to overcrowded nations, since they serve to prune away the luxuriant growth of the human race." [2]

It is often difficult to appreciate the compounded increase in population growth even at a modest yearly growth. For instance, a doubling of a certain population would occur in 6930 years with a rate of a yearly increase of 0.01 percent as compared to a doubling in 693 years at a yearly increase of 0.1 percent. [3]

Let us take a look at the growth of population in the United States. We had 100 million people in 1915, and we have added another 100 million since. At the present rate of increase, we shall add another 100 million in the next thirty years. Although we constitute only 6 percent of the world's population and occupy 6 percent of the land area, we consume from 35 to 50 percent of the world's different mineral resources.[4] This poses great ethical and social problems.

The world population of 3.9 billion will reach 7 billion in the year 2000. Although it took ten past generations to double the world population, we will double it again in less than two generations.[5] Seventy-five million human beings are being added annually to the earth's population, many of them hungry. Indignity and tragedy are the inevitable result of this involuntary propagation.

In contrast, the animal kingdom, through built-in physiological and behavioral mechanisms, controls the number of its young when the environment is unfavorable. It was observed in western Uganda that when food is scarce and crowding exists, the onset of fertility in the female elephant is postponed from age eleven to eighteen, and the spacing of calves is extended from four years to nine. On Iowa marshland, if the number of muskrats rises too high, the mother muskrat produces fewer embryos or reabsorbs them. The English scientist Bruce found recently that the common house mouse, if mounted by a strange male, aborts within four days after conception. She also aborts if she only sees him or smells him if there are too many mice. An Arctic rodent, the lemming, the snowshoe hare, and man lack such controls and resort to suicide or death by starvation.[6]

In the *New York Times* of September 26, 1971 there appeared a two-page advertisement signed by, among others, Dr. Paul R. Ehrlich, Dr. John Rock, and representatives of industry pleading for population control, reminding us that every seven and one-half seconds a new American baby is born. "He is a disarming little thing, but he begins to scream loudly in a voice that can be heard for seventy years. He is screaming for 26 million tons of water, 21,000 gallons of gasoline, 10,150 pounds of meat, 28,000 pounds of milk and cream, 9000 pounds of wheat and a great storehouse of all other foods, drinks and tobaccos. These are the lifetime demands of his country and its economy." [7]

Benefits of Birth Control

The benefits of birth control to the family are manifold: It promotes responsible parenthood; wanted and loved children; a decrease in morbidity and mortality of mother and child; an increase in economic stability; an increase in family stability; a decrease in illegitimacy, criminal and legal abortions; a decrease in mental retardation; and an increase in mental and physical health.

These benefits were documented explicitly in a study conducted by Dr. Joseph D. Beasley in Louisiana. It is well established that prematurity is a major factor contributing to infant mortality and may be associated with mental retardation. If the spacing period between pregnancies is more than 23 months, the chances of prematurity are 8 percent; when the spacing period between pregnancies is 12–23 months, the prematurity rate increases to 10 percent; and if the spacing period is less than 12 months, it increases to 18 percent. Age of the mother is another high-risk factor. Infant mortality in the first 28 days of life is 20 percent greater than the national average in mothers under 20 years and 100 percent greater than the national average in mothers over 35 years of age. High parity, which means the high number of children that the woman has born, is another risk factor. Stillbirths and deaths before 28 days of life increase as the birth order increases. It rises from 3 percent among the first four children born to 6 percent in the seventh child. In addition, maternal mortality rates for mothers aged 30–39 is twice that of mothers aged 20–29. Maternal mortality in women pregnant out of wedlock was four times as high as in married women. Fetal death, prematurity, and infant mortality were twice as high as for offspring of married women. Infant mortality is 50 percent higher in the lower socioeconomic class than in the upper- and middle-income class.[8]

In summary, proper spacing of children, appropriate age for motherhood, marital and economic status assuring adequate income not only promote the welfare of infant, mother, and family, but also decrease the infant and maternal mortality.

Unavailability of birth-control measures not only puts the mother and child at risk, but also results in tremendous costs to society while promoting dependency and poverty. For instance, an inquiry of the Wisconsin Department of Health and Social Services yielded an estimate of over $2 million for one month (June 1972) spent in Wisconsin specifically for out-of-wedlock mothers and their children.

Birth-control Legislation

In December 1970 the Family Planning Services and Population Research Act was passed, the purpose of which is to "assist in making comprehensive voluntary services readily available to all persons desiring such services" and in addition "to establish an Office of Population Affairs in the Department of Health, Education and Welfare as a primary focus within the Federal Government on matters pertaining to population research and family planning, through which the secretary of Health, Education and Welfare . . . shall carry out the purposes of this Act." There was overwhelming endorsement of government support of family planning as evidenced by a vote of 298 to 32 in the House. Fifty-seven out of 94 Catholic representatives present voted for the bill. The Senate voted unanimously in favor of the bill. The voluntary nature of the proposed government-sponsored services was stressed throughout the bill's history.[9]

If birth-control programs are to be effective in preventing unwanted children among married and unmarried women, they have to be easily accessible to the married and unmarried, irrespective of income. There is mounting evidence that such programs are effective in reducing the rate of illegitimacy, according to Beasley's[10] report from Louisiana, Sarrel's[11] report from Connecticut, and Tyler's[12] report from Georgia.

On the legislative level, California was the first state in the nation requiring that family-planning information be issued with each marriage license (Bill AB 2255, which became effective in November 1970). This information consists of a list of family planning and birth-control clinics located in the county in which the marriage license was issued. In addition, California sponsors through its Health and Social Services Department, a toll-free telephone line, which anybody can call for contraception and abortion referrals.

In contrast to the California law, Wisconsin still refers to birth-control devices as "indecent articles" and prohibits their distribution and sale to the unmarried.

This law was established in 1933, forty years ago, and even at that time was denounced as a backward step. Margaret Sanger, world-famous birth-control advocate, stated in 1933, "Wisconsin is not keeping up with accepted usage and modern attitudes in the dissemination of scientific birth control information." Many bills to liberalize this archaic birth-control law have been introduced in the past years, but all of them were defeated by the representatives, who consider the issue political dynamite.

Recently (March 1972) the U.S. Supreme Court, in the Baird case in Massachusetts, ruled that it is unconstitutional to deny birth-control services to the unmarried: "Whatever the rights of the individual to access to contraceptives may be, the rights must be the same for the unmarried and the married alike." Said Justice William Brennan in the majority opinion, "If the right to privacy means anything, it is the right of the individual married or single, to be free from unwarranted government intrusion into matters so fundamentally affecting a person as the decision whether to bear or beget a child." As a result of the Supreme Court decision, several clinics in Wisconsin, on the advice of their attorneys, have started to serve the unmarried. But the laws in Wisconsin are still to the contrary.

THE PREGNANT ADOLESCENT GIRL

The pregnant adolescent girl is at high risk not only medically but also emotionally and socially. She is also at a high suicidal risk. Dr. J. E. Jekel of the Yale University College of Medicine reported that among 530 pregnant unmarried adolescent girls between the ages of 11 and 17, 68 of them made one or more suicidal attempts. The youngest was a girl of 13.[13]

There are more pregnancies among girls aged 15 and younger than there are suicides at all ages annually,[14] but there have not been comparable efforts at prevention, despite the relative ease of preventing premature pregnancies.

The tragedy of the young girl who is pregnant out of wedlock has been well described by Arthur Campbell: "She suddenly has 90 percent of her life's script written for her. . . . Her life choices are few and most of them are bad." [15]

Many people have suggested that the out-of-wedlock problem is not now so acute since most of these infants can find homes. The facts are to the contrary. Only a small percentage of infants born out of wedlock ever are released to social agencies for adoption, and some of those who are given up are never adopted because of racial background or physical defect. For example, in 1971 in Wisconsin, only 21 percent of the infants born out of wedlock were released for adoption.

The younger the mother, the less likely she is to give up a baby for adoption. Since so many of these young women are ill equipped to support themselves, let alone children, they necessarily become welfare recipients.

In addition to out-of-wedlock births, there is legitimatization of out-of-wedlock teen-age pregnancies. Nationwide, 48 percent of teen-age marriages involve a premarital pregnancy; approximately one-half of these marriages ends in divorce within the first four years, four times more frequently than other marriages.

It is well established that many girls who have had illegitimate pregnancies are going to keep on having them unless they are given the knowledge and opportunity to avoid them. A well-documented study from Yale University Medical Center[16] reported the following. One hundred girls, age 12 to 17 and pregnant out of wedlock, were studied without guidance for five years. In the five-year period, the 100 girls produced 340 more babies; nine of the girls married, 60 percent were on state welfare.

In contrast to the above is a study from Upstate Medical Center in Syracuse, New York.[17] One hundred and eighty unwed adolescent mothers were given comprehensive guidance and birth-control information. In the subsequent two years, there were only 17 second pregnancies, 8 of which occurred to girls who had married.

The increase of illegitimacy rates in the age groups 15 to 19 and under 15, along with the documented knowledge of the serious health, social, emotional, educational, and economic hazards facing a teen-ager who becomes pregnant and her child born out of wedlock, dictate the necessity of birth-control education and services.

Professional medical groups recognize this necessity. In the past few years there has been a change in attitude among physicians about prescribing contraceptives for the sexually active minor. This is exemplified in the new policies adopted by several prestigious medical organizations. The American Medical Association (AMA), the American College of Obstetricians and Gynecologists, the American Academy of Family Physicians, and the American Academy of Pediatrics went on record endorsing birth-control services for the teen-ager who needs them. Specifically, the recommendation of the American Academy of Pediatrics is: "The teen-age girl whose sexual behavior exposes her to possible conception should have access to medical consultation and the most effective contraceptive advice of methods consistent with her physical and emotional needs."

Public support is exemplified by the recommendation of the President's Commission on Population Growth and the American Future (March 1972) that "states adopt affirmative legislation which will permit minors to receive contraceptive and prophylactic information and services in appropriate settings sensitive to their needs and concerns." [18]

In a recent survey, a Gallup poll of June 1972, 73 percent of those surveyed agreed that birth-control information services and counseling should be made available to unmarried teen-agers who need and want them. There was no significant difference in the response in relation to race, sex, age, education, religion, political affiliation, income, and region. In fact, 68 percent of the Catholics surveyed were in agreement with this recommendation as compared to 73 percent of Protestants.[19]

One does not presume to pass ethical judgment on premarital sexual relationships. If a minor makes such a decision, however, the individual and society should be protected against unwanted pregnancies resulting in compromised, neglected, and rejected infants.

A common argument used by those opposed to the availability of birth-control services is that it would put a stamp of approval on premarital sexual relations and promote promiscuity. Yet a recent national survey reporting that 14 percent of unmarried girls have had intercourse at age 15, and 37 percent at age 18, also established the fact that a majority of these girls never used contraceptives or used them irregularly. Approximately 50 percent had not used contraception the last time they had intercourse. Of the 50 percent who used contraceptives, only 10 percent used methods most effective in preventing pregnancy.[20] This study indicates that sexual intercourse is common among teen-agers and cannot be attributed to easy access to contraception.

The health risks of pregnancy, though greater, are not limited to the very young and out of wedlock. Dr. Herbert Sandmire, writing in the *Wisconsin Medical Journal* of April 1972, reviewed 48 consecutive deaths reported by the Wisconsin Maternal Mortality Study Committee. He found that 32 of the 48 deaths in the three-year period 1969–71 inclusive could have been avoided, that 32 of these women had serious and medically important reasons not to be pregnant. Five of the 32 deaths followed illegal abortions performed by nonphysicians.

One tragic case was that of a woman in her seventh pregnancy, with five living children, who had chronic hypertension of several years' duration. Her request for abortion was denied. She later was admitted near term in a comatose state. One day prior to her death, the patient delivered a macerated, stillborn infant. As Dr. Sandmire has said, "One might logically conclude that the five motherless children and the decedent's surviving spouse might have preferred to preserve their family unit even if it meant sacrificing of an early embryo."

RESTRICTIVE LAWS

The attitudes of legislators toward birth control is a reflection of the history of restrictive birth-control laws in this country. Following the Civil War and the economic depression of 1873, the Puritan values in the United States became strong and were expressed through the Temperance Movement, the Young Peoples Christian Endeavor, and other organizations whose major purpose was to clean up vice. In 1872 Anthony Comstock was appointed as leader of the YMCA's new Committee for the Suppression of Vice. After diligent effort on Comstock's part, including intimidation practices, the United States Congress on July 3, 1873, passed a law barring mailing, distribution, and advertisement of obscene literature and indecent articles, which referred to birth-control devices as: "every article or thing designed or intended for the prevention of conception or procuring of abortion, and every article or thing intended or adapted for any indecent or immoral use." Congress further provided that these articles "shall not be conveyed in the mails." Violation of the law was considered a misdemeanor and carried with it a fine of up to $5000 or imprisonment at hard labor of up to ten years, or both, at the discretion of the courts.[21] This bill is commonly referred to as the Comstock Act. In order to enforce the new law, Comstock was appointed as a special agent to the Post Office Department, a position he held for thirty-three years. He also prevented importation of birth-control devices, especially the condom, which was popular and was produced at that time in England. Comstock also promoted the passage of at least half a dozen "Little Comstocks" at the state legislative level. He considered prevention of conception as the greatest crime and instigated prosecution of persons known as preventionists and abortionists.

THE ROLE OF MARGARET SANGER

At the beginning of the century Margaret Sanger, a nurse working in the slums of the lower East Side of New York City, was moved by the plight of poor immigrant women who were denied knowledge of and access to contraception. She challenged the restrictive federal law with her publication *The Woman Rebel*. Under federal indictment and facing a possible sentence of forty-five years in prison, she fled to England in 1914 where she obtained great support from Aldous and Julian Huxley, Havelock Ellis, and Bertrand Russell. She traveled to the Netherlands where she visited the world's first and only birth-control clinic, which made a great impact on her. In 1916 she opened the first birth-control clinic in the United States in the slums of Brooklyn and was promptly arrested. She was jailed eight times but continued her fight for the rights of women to birth control—a term she coined. In the year 1917 she was sentenced to thirty days in jail, only a light sentence because of public outrage resulting from her arrest. The New York Court of Appeals had confirmed her conviction, but Judge Crane broadened the interpretation of the New York penal law, which permitted contraception "for the cure or prevention of diseases," to mean *not only* venereal diseases but "an alteration in the state of the body or some of its organs interrupting or disturbing the performance of the vital functions." As a result of this interpretation, she founded the New York Birth Control League and its publication, the *Birth Control Review* (1916). She organized the first Birth Control Conference on November 13, 1921. The meeting was raided by one hundred New York policemen on Archbishop Hayes' orders. Margaret Sanger was taken in a police van to the station house with a crowd following that was so large that reserves were called to maintain order.

In the early 1920s, Margaret Sanger organized an international conference that recommended to the League of Nations that their members limit their population not only according to individual needs, but also with consideration of the countries' resources. Thus the birth-control movement acquired a broader scope. After the Second World War Margaret Sanger founded the International Planned Parenthood Association.

In 1921 she formally established the American Birth Control League of which she was president from 1921 to 1928. At the beginning of 1923, the League established a birth-control clinic. The clinic prescribed birth control for "health reasons" only in order to operate within Judge Crane's interpretation of the law. Margaret Sanger had difficulty gaining the support of the medical profession, which solidly and strongly disapproved of birth control on social grounds, although a significant number approved of it on strictly medical grounds.

An exception was Dr. Robert L. Dickenson, a New York gynecologist who, in 1925, motivated the New York Obstetrical Society, the New York Academy of Medicine, and the American Medical Society to endorse birth control. When in 1929 the police raided the clinic and arrested two physicians and two nurses, and confiscated medical records of patients, the medical community vigorously objected and the judge dismissed the case. In 1937, the Committee on Birth Control of the American Medical Association gave endorsement to "voluntary family limitation."

It is not commonly known that Eleanor Roosevelt persuaded the federal government to become actively involved in the birth-control movement. In 1940 she publicly declared her approval of birth control and, at her invitation, representatives of three federal agencies and the National Birth Control Federation met at the White House. In October 1940 the Surgeon General's Office announced that the United States Public Health Service would approve state requests for funds for "a child spacing program," but would not be part of propagandizing such a program.[22]

Margaret Sanger, who virtually founded the birth-control movement in the United States, retired to Arizona in 1942 and died in 1966.

Margaret Sanger was jailed eight times in the course of her activities; this occurred more than fifty years ago. Can it happen today? As unbelievable as it may sound, the *New York Times* on September 21, 1971, reported that William Baird, Jr., the birth-control advocate, was arrested together with a Suffolk County housewife, Mrs. Manfredonia, and charged with impairing the morals of a minor, Mrs. Manfredonia's fourteen-month-old daughter, by subjecting her to a public lecture on contraceptives. Mrs. Manfredonia stated that her daughter had a four-word vocabulary. The case was dismissed in the county district court on the basis that it is not illegal to dispense birth-control information in New York State.

The 1873 Comstock Act was finally repealed by Congress on January 8, 1971, after nearly one hundred years. The states have also modified their "Little Comstocks," so that contraception is legal for adults in all states except Wisconsin. However, about twenty-three states prohibit display and advertisement of contraceptives except in medical and pharmaceutical journals. At least twenty-seven states prohibit the sale of contraceptives through vending machines. In several states the courts have modified or nullified the restrictive laws.

The Commission on Population Growth and the American Future recommended that: "(1) states eliminate existing legal inhibitions and restrictions on access to contraceptive information, procedures, and supplies; and (2) states develop statutes affirming the desirability that all persons have ready and practicable access to contraceptive information, procedures and supplies." [23]

METHODS OF CONTRACEPTION

Methods of contraception presently used in the United States include the following: hormonal steroids, commonly referred to as the pill; intrauterine devices (IUD); diaphragm; chemical contraceptives (foams, creams, jellies); condoms; coitus interruptus; and rhythm or the "safe period" technique.

In order for any method to be effective, it has to be acceptable to its user, woman and man alike. The best method may fail if the person dislikes it for one reason or another and therefore is not using it consistently. Not only physical side effects of a given method have to be considered, but also the convenience of its use, the presence of hidden fears such as the loss of the diaphragm or condom within the body, and the availability of privacy and sanitary facilities. The level of education and attitudes about sexual practices play a role in success and failure of all methods. Women and men should share the responsibility for contraception. They should choose a method in consultation with a physician or a counselor who is sympathetic to their needs and is knowledgeable in available contraceptives and their use. They should be free to choose a method, to change it, or to use more than one method. At least one follow-up regarding proper usage of the method prescribed by the physician or counselor is of utmost importance.

Oral Contraceptives

Oral contraceptives were discovered in 1955 and licensed for use in 1960. Since that time they have affected the lives of millions of women and their families, who for reasons of health, family planning, or poverty wished to avoid another pregnancy.

"The pill" is composed of two hormones produced normally by the ovary: progesterone and estrogen. The presently available oral contraceptives in the United States combine a synthetic progestin with a small amount of estrogen. The dosage schedule is constantly being adjusted as more experience is gathered. One variation is the sequential therapy—estrogen alone is given for 15 or 16 days, followed by a combination of progestin and estrogen for the remaining 5 days of the 20- or 21-day schedule. Most other preparations contain the combination of both hormones, estrogen and progesterone.

It is of paramount importance to take the pill regularly at the same hour of the day. Variation of as little as six hours may result in pregnancy, especially with the low-dosage pills.

The most common side effects consist of nausea, weight gain, headache, bloating, breast tenderness, and breakthrough bleeding (bleeding between menstrual periods). These side effects (except for breakthrough bleeding) have been reduced considerably with the lower dosage of hormones now available, and they usually disappear after the fourth cycle. However, the pill is definitely contraindicated in women with diseases of the liver, cancer, varicose veins, and abnormal blood clotting.

There has been a great deal of publicity connected with a major but very rare complication of the pill, namely, the thromboembolism or blood-clotting disorder; for the user of oral contraceptives it is estimated to be 4.4 times that of nonusers. The mortality from thromboembolic disorders attributable to oral contraception is about 3 per 100,000 women per year, much less than the mortality from planned or unplanned pregnancy, which is over 20 per 100,000.[24]

There is no doubt that the pill interferes with the natural hormone cycle. For this reason physicians wonder about its long-term effect over a period of several decades. So far, some women have been taking it over a period of ten years without evidence of ill effects, other than those previously indicated.

The effectiveness of the pill according to a report of the Advisory Committee on Obstetrics and Gynecology to the FDA on August 1, 1969, is almost 100 percent for the combined pill if taken according to instructions. This is reflected in a pregnancy rate of about 0.1 per 100 women per year. The effectiveness of the sequential pill is somewhat lower—0.5 pregnancies per 100 women per year. The pregnancy rate of IUD users is three to four times higher, and those using diaphragms with contraceptive creams is ten to twenty times higher.[25]

Data from the 1970 National Fertility Study revealed that nearly 6 million married women of reproductive age were using the pill. The pill is the most popular method of contraception, and it accounted for 34.2 percent of all current contraceptive practices in 1970. In 1965 this percentage was 23.9. In 1970 about half of all younger women who were using contraception were using the pill as compared with 21 percent of older women. Among young black women its usage increased between 1965 and 1970 from 30.8 percent to 54.1 percent of all current practices.[26]

The search for an oral contraceptive dates back to antiquity. Written record of the search for control of fertility dates back to 2736 B.C. The Chinese *Book of Changes* recommends the ingestion of quicksilver (mercury) on an empty stomach: "The taker will never become pregnant." [27]

In the Middle Ages, lead was a popular contraceptive agent; it also produced many cases of lead poisoning.[28] A variety of herbs and plants were used at all times in various parts of the world in the hope of controlling fertility. Out of 42 plants reported by Finch and derived from folklore of primitive people, from so-called "popular medicine" of Western civilization, and from nineteenth-century books on medieval botany and materia medica, 39 were recommended to be taken by women, two by women and men, and only one by men.[29]

Intrauterine Devices

Intrauterine devices (IUDs) are designed in various forms and made of different substances, such as plastic and metal. They are made in the shape of a loop, bow, spiral, "T," and in various other forms. Recently a new IUD—the copper seven—which has been used successfully in a number of other countries, was approved for use in the USA. According to the data published so far, it is easier to insert than other types and has a lower incidence of side effects, and a lower expulsion rate. It possibly has a lower failure rate and seems to be well tolerated by women who have never been pregnant. Most IUDs measure about one inch in diameter. They are introduced into the uterus through a small tube the size of a soda straw into which the device is compressed. After introduction into the uterus the device expands and assumes its original shape. It is still unclear how the IUD works to prevent pregnancy. Many investigators believe that several mechanisms are involved.[30] The IUD provokes a nonbacterial change in the lining (endometrium) of the uterus resulting in production of a substance yet unidentified that has either spermicidal or blastocidal action. This substance may travel from the uterus into the tubes. There is also evidence of increased tubal motility associated with IUDs, which permit more rapid transport of ova through the tubes. The egg, even if fertilized, may be too immature for nidation (implantation), or the uterus may not be ready to accept a fertilized egg. Another suggestion is based on a study that demonstrated that the Lippes loop attracts a large number of cells (macrophages), the function of which is to destroy foreign tissue. These cells recognize the fertilized egg as foreign in contrast to the nonfertilized egg and destroy it. In the copper seven device, the copper may have direct action on the sperm and also may interfere with implantation.

Side effects of the IUD consist of irregular bleeding and occasional uterine cramps lasting for only two to three months after insertion. More serious complications are infection and perforation. The occurrence of pelvic inflammatory disease (PID) has been reported to be 2.5 percent in the first year and 1.5 percent in the second year. A recent recommendation for usage of sterile prepackaged devices is likely to reduce the percentage of infections. Perforation of the uterus following insertion is extremely rare and its incidence varies between 1 and 4 per 10,000 insertions and may be the result of trauma inflicted during insertion. The failure rate, or pregnancy rate, varies between 1.5 and 3.0 per 100 women during the first year of use, depending on the type of IUD. These rates tend to decline during successive years. Some pregnancies occurred because the device was expelled without the patient noticing it; other pregnancies occurred while the device was in place. Pregnancy may proceed to full term with the IUD remaining in the uterus without interfering with the development of the fetus. Tubal pregnancies may occur with the IUD in place.[31]

In clinic patients the IUDs have proved more reliable than the traditional methods of contraception and somewhat less reliable than the oral contraceptives. Among women in the lowest socioeconomic group the rates of continuation are higher with the IUD than with oral contraception; it does not require daily medication or manipulation before intercourse, or sustained motivation. The IUD can be removed at any time when pregnancy is desired and does not interfere with future conception.

The early intrauterine device was introduced by Graefenberg, a German physician, in the 1920s.[32] It consisted of a silver ring that was introduced into the uterus. In spite of successful reports the ring fell into disrepute because of fear of infection. Modern IUDs have been in use only a little over a decade (1959). As of 1969, from 6 to 8 million intrauterine devices were in use, about 1 million in the United States, and the number has been increasing. Its popularity has increased from 1.2 percent of all married women who were practicing contraception in 1965 to 7.4 percent in 1970.[33]

The concept of an IUD is not new; it has been known for centuries to the inhabitants of North Africa who have placed pebbles into the uterus of their female camels to prevent pregnancies during the long trip across the desert.

Chemical Contraceptives and the Diaphragm

The spermicidal chemical contraceptives contain a chemical that kills the sperm and a nonreactive base that blocks the opening of the cervix mechanically. Vaginal foams, jellies, and creams are introduced into the vagina with an applicator. This may be done within an hour prior to coitus. If a longer period has elapsed or coitus is repeated, another application is required. The vaginal foam is associated with fewer complaints as to aesthetics and appears to be more effective than creams and jellies. Douching is forbidden until six hours after the last coitus. The chemical contraceptives are a high-risk method unless used in conjunction with a diaphragm or a condom.

The diaphragm together with spermicidal jelly or cream has been found to be an effective method in highly motivated women. Occasional failure may result from improper placement or displacement during intercourse. This failure accounts for about 2–3 pregnancies per 100 women per year.[34]

The diaphragm is a shallow rubber cup designed to cover the cervix (neck of the uterus). It is made of rubber or synthetic rubber and built around a flexible metal ring that keeps it in place. It comes in different sizes and has to be fitted by a physician. The size of the diaphragm required may change after initial intercourse, following delivery, pelvic surgery, or excessive weight gain or loss. The woman has to be instructed as to its proper insertion. It is inserted prior to coitus and it must remain in the vagina for six hours; it may remain for twenty-four hours without causing discomfort. A douche may be used after removal, but it is not required. A douche should not be used prior to six hours after intercourse.

The diaphragm was invented by the German physician Frederick Adolphe Wilde in 1838. He used a rubber cap to produce a barrier. Another German physician, Mensiga, popularized this method.[35] Modern science and technology perfected the method by adding the spermicidal cream to it.

One of the earliest references to mechanical occlusion of the womb for the purpose of contraception is in Petri Papyrus, 1850 B.C., which recommends the dung of crocodile with honey, and in Ebers Papyrus, 1500 B.C., which describes a tampon made of lint and soaked with acacia and honey with instructions to introduce it in the vagina prior to intercourse.[36] Honey has a physical clogging capacity, and acacia contains gum arabic, which under fermentation liberates lactic acid anhydride and when dissolved in water forms lactic acid. The motility of the spermatazoa is arrested at pH of 6.0 or below. (A neutral solution such as water has a pH of 7.0; a figure above 7.0 indicates alkalinity, below 7.0, acidity.) As testimony to the validity of some of the ancient practices, gum arabic, or gum acacia, is being used in modern contraceptive jellies.

Pliny the Elder in A.D. 79 recommended wool tampons. Similarly, in the sixth century, Aetius of Amida recommended a cup made out of the shell of pomegranate to be introduced into the vagina. A Jewish physician, Avicenna, who lived in Baghdad (978–1037) recommended the pulp of pomegranate to be inserted before coitus to serve as a mechanical protection. Pomegranate pulp and rind are acid; therefore, in addition to occlusion, they will reduce the motility of the spermatozoa. In the eighteenth century Casanova tried gold balls as a mechanical barrier. The ancient Talmudists advised a sponge for this purpose. As late as 1962 the International Planned Parenthood Federation was advising that a sponge with a thread attached to it for easy withdrawal could be used as an improvised birth-control device.[37] The plugging of the vagina with small balls or wads of feathers was common practice in ancient India and Asia. In Sumatra a ball made of opium molded in the shape of a cup was introduced into the vagina. In Japan and China a small disc of very silky oiled paper was used against the cervix to prevent the penis from touching the uterus. Slovak women used clean linen rags. Hungarian women used melted beeswax as a mechanical device for prevention of conception.[38]

Compared to the use of a physical barrier, all authorities agree that the douche is a useless method of contraception because the sperm enters the cervical canal within seconds after ejaculation. Despite its unsatisfactory record, it is used widely. Havemann stated, "About the best that can be said about the douche is that it is better than nothing at all. But it is not much better than nothing at all." [39] The only value of a douche is in an emergency, when a condom breaks or slips. Two tablespoons of vinegar in a quart of lukewarm water is as good as any chemical; it has some spermicidal action by virtue of its acidity.

Throughout the ages douching preceded by fumigation of the vagina was a popular method of contraception. The first account of it dates to Petri Papyrus, 1850 B.C.: "Fumigate her in her vulva with minnis [a drug], then she will not receive his seed." This was recommended to take place prior to coitus, to be followed by a douche of wine and garlic. Special vessels for fumigation were used. For douching, a tube made out of the horn of various animals was made. The most common was the bill of the ibis, which is directly related to the stork. Its failure at contraception may provide the origin of the stork story. Special women, licensed by the state, were employed to administer the douche.[40]

Once it was realized that ejaculated fluid is the cause of conception, many methods of evacuation of the fluid were devised. The Hindu in the Sacred Vedas written about 1500 B.C. devised a tube for this purpose made out of wood and ivory and covered with a bladder of a buffalo to supply the force for withdrawing the fluid. The Hebrews also recommended douching through a pipe (Leviticus 16: 16–18).[41]

In the first century B.C. an Indian physician describes in detail the method of fumigation prior to coitus and states that a woman who treats her vagina with the smoke of neem wood will not conceive. Two thousand years later, the foaming tablet was substituted for fumigation for its spermicidal effect.

The Condom and Coitus Interruptus

The condom, frequently referred to as a "rubber" or "prophylactic," is a synthetic rubber sheath worn over the erect penis. It is shaped like a finger of a glove. It prevents the sperm from entering the vagina and also protects both partners from contracting venereal diseases. It is a highly effective contraceptive. However, additional use of spermicidal jelly, cream, or foam by the woman is recommended for the purpose of lubricating the vagina and for additional protection in case of breakage or slippage of the condom.

Data from the National Fertility Study indicate that only 14.2 percent of couples using contraception relied on the condom in 1970 as compared to 21.9 percent in 1965. The condom is used in combination with spermicidal foam, cream, or jelly.[42]

How far back can the condom be traced? In a cave at Combarelles dating from prehistoric times, a scene of a man and woman engaged in sexual intercourse is depicted on the wall. The man wears a sheath over his penis. Legend has it that Minos, king of Crete, used a sheath made out of the bladder of a goat to protect his sexual partner from his scorpion-bearing semen. In ancient and Imperial Rome bladders of animals were used to receive the semen during coitus. The early Egyptians also used them. They were mainly used for protection from disease; their effectiveness as contraceptives had not been realized at the time. The Chinese at an early period in history were making sheaths out of oiled silk paper, while the Japanese were making them out of tortoise shell or leather. The Djukas, a primitive tribe of New Guinea, used a *female* sheath made of a plant. It was about six inches long, made in the form of a seed pod, closed on one end and open on the other. It was introduced before intercourse into the vagina, closed-end first.[43]

Gabriello Falloppio, the Italian anatomist, in his book *De Morbo Gallico* (published posthumously in 1564), recommends a linen sheath that fits over the penis as protection against syphilis. The next mention of the sheath in the literature is in the seventeenth and eighteenth centuries in France and England. It is the first time the name *condom* appears, which is supposed to derive from Dr. Condom, its inventor in the Court of Charles II (1660–85). This, however, could not be verified. In 1717, Daniel Turner, a physician, mentioned the word condom and from then on it appeared in all textbooks on venereal diseases. By the end of the nineteenth century condoms became so popular that they started to be sold wholesale; these were made out of animal intestines. Casanova (1725–98), the Venetian adventurer and author, used them not only for prevention of infection but also to prevent impregnating his partners. He refers to condoms as the "English riding coat" (*redinggote anglaise*), "the English vestment which puts one's mind at rest," "the assurance caps." With their use Casanova was satisfied. His only objection: "I do not care to shut myself up in a piece of dead skin in order to prove that I am perfectly alive." [44]

In withdrawal or coitus interruptus, the male withdraws to permit ejaculation outside the vagina and away from the external genitalia. Coitus interruptus was known in antiquity. There is reference to it in the Old Testament, Genesis 38, in the books of Hippocratic writers, and in records of other civilizations. While coitus interruptus has been responsible for many contraception failures when ejaculation begins before withdrawal, it is reputedly responsible for the decline in Western European population from the eighteenth century onward. A survey conducted several years ago in Great Britain showed that 44 percent of the couples interviewed practiced withdrawal at times and around one-fifth to one-third of them practiced it at all times. By contrast, in the United States only 18 percent of couples practice it at times and fewer than 5 percent use it as an only method of contraception.[45] A more recent survey in the United States indicates that only 2.1 percent of married couples relied on coitus interruptus in 1970 as compared to 4 percent in 1965.[46] Apparently, American couples prefer it only when other methods of contraception are not available.

Rhythm Method

The rhythm method, also referred to as "temporary abstinence," is the only method of contraception accepted by the Roman Catholic church. Yet a recent survey conducted by Dr. Charles F. Westoff of Princeton University and Dr. Larry Bumpass of the University of Wisconsin revealed that 68 percent of white married Catholic women used birth-control methods disapproved of by their church; 53 percent of those using such methods were receiving communion at least once a month, a measure of their commitment to their church.[47]

The rhythm method is based on calculation of the "safe period" with consideration of the time of ovulation and the time of survival of the sperm and ovum. In young women, in whom the menstrual cycle is irregular, the safe period is difficult to predict. In others, the safe period should be calculated on the basis of a written record of menstrual cycles for a period of at least one year in consultation with a physician or a chart, such as "The Safe Period" published by the Planned Parenthood World Population. The measurement of basal body temperature adds to accuracy of the determination of the time of ovulation. A drop of temperature, followed by a rise (usually around 0.7 degrees F.) indicates that ovulation has occurred. The pregnancy rate for women using the calendar method only is 14–40 per 100 woman-years; for women using the calendar method and basal temperature the rate is 3.2–8.0.[48] It is clear that the lowest rate is obtained by intelligent, highly motivated women and men.

In women who menstruate regularly at twenty-eight-day intervals, intercourse from the tenth to the seventeenth day of the cycle is likely to result in pregnancy. Furthermore, pregnancies are documented when the only intercourse occurred immediately prior to, following, or even during a menstrual period.

The theoretical period of sperm survival after release is forty-eight hours. There is evidence, however, that they may remain viable in the Fallopian tubes as long as one week. The ovum may survive for longer than twenty-four hours.[49]

VOLUNTARY STERILIZATION

Voluntary sterilization has become increasingly popular in recent years with the rising concern over social and environmental problems resulting from population growth. In 1965, eight percent of married couples with wives under forty-five years of age had been sterilized; by 1970 this percentage increased to 11 percent, which represents over 2.75 million couples of reproductive age who have chosen sterilization as a contraceptive method. Almost one-half of these sterilizations represent vasectomies. While in 1965 tubal ligation and vasectomies were equal in prevalence, in 1970 there were more vasectomies than tubal ligations. In 1970 voluntary sterilization was the most popular method of contraception used by older couples in which the wife was 30–44 years of age. However, vasectomies are extremely rare among blacks; they represent 1 percent of the risk population as compared to 9 percent among whites. Tubal ligations are twice as common among black women as compared to white; a greater preference has *apparently* been found among blacks for the female than for the male operation.[50]

Presently no state prohibits voluntary sterilization. The last legal barrier was removed in May 1973 in Utah (*Parker* v. *Rampton*). The decision resulted from a suit brought by women who have been denied voluntary sterilization by their physicians. Although most legal obstacles to voluntary sterilization have fallen, many women still are being denied sterilization because of arbitrary hospital actions, ranging from refusal to admit any patient for sterilization to requiring husband's consent.

The Association for Voluntary Sterilization Inc., 14 West 40 Street, New York, N.Y. 10018, will provide literature and the names of clinics and physicians who perform sterilizations in individual communities.

The male sterilization, or vasectomy, is a very simple procedure, which can be performed under local anesthesia in the physician's office. It consists of cutting the vas deferens, or sperm duct, through which sperm travels from the testicles to the genital passages. Thus the sperm cannot move up the duct and be ejaculated during sexual intercourse, and the seminal fluid will not contain sperm. Sterilization does not have any effect on production of male sex hormones, libido (sexual desire), potency, or orgasm. Occasional emotional side effects of the male following vasectomy are largely related to preexisting doubts about sexual adequacy and mistaken equation of sterility with impotence.

Female sterilization is more complicated and older methods require hospitalization of three to five days. The operation, which is done under general anesthesia, is referred to as tubal ligation. It involves tying, cutting, or cauterization of the fallopian tubes through which the egg travels from the ovary to the uterus. It can be done through an abdominal incision or through the vagina. It is best performed shortly after delivery as the tubes at that time are much more easily accessible.

New and simplified techniques of female sterilization have been introduced. In laparascopy a small incision is made in the lower abdomen; the tubes are visualized with the aid of an instrument and cauterized. The procedure is not regarded as major surgery and only a few hours or at most an overnight hospital stay is required.

Couples who consider their families complete or, who by reason of inherited diseases may wish to have complete protection from further pregnancy, frequently choose sterilization. When the decision for sterilization is made, it should be kept in mind that the effects of the operation should be regarded as permanent and that reversibility cannot be guaranteed. New techniques are being developed to increase the reversibility rate.

In ancient times, male sterility was produced by castration to render slaves safe guardians of a harem. These slaves became known as *eunuchs*. The word derives from the Greek and it means *bed* and *guarding*. The Assyrians, Babylonians, and Chinese (the Chinese as early as 1100 B.C.) used eunuchs as servants in imperial palaces. Castration also played a part in the Greek priesthood of Cybele, the goddess of nature. Indibulation, or putting a ring or a clasp on the penis as a means of contraception and abstinence, was practiced by the Romans.[51] A nineteenth-century report refers to an Australian tribe that performs a mutilating operation on the urethra of the young, indolent, or weak males that prevents deposition of semen in the vagina.[52]

Female sterilization by removal of the ovaries was practiced by ancient Egyptians. The kings of Lydia castrated the women of their harem. The motives of the mutilating operation were clearly stated to be to avoid pregnancy. A painful method of reversible sterilization was practiced by certain primitive tribes in the Dutch East Indies and by the native women of Java; it consisted of manual backward bending of the uterus in such a fashion that it would occlude the opening of the cervix and prevent the sperm from entering the uterus. Another device, for prevention of adultery, was the girdle of chastity made of metal and placed in such a position that it guarded the opening of the vagina. It was known to be used in biblical times, and it was introduced into France during the Crusades in the twelfth century.[53]

The quest for control of fertility by women and men is nothing new; it has been universal in virtually every culture and it has existed for several thousand years. Some of the contraceptive techniques used in the past were ineffective and detrimental. Others were ingenious and effective, such as vaginal plugs, impregnated with gummy substances, which not only acted as mechanical barriers, but also affected the motility of the sperm; and lemon juice and vinegar, which act as spermicidals.

ABORTION

The Supreme Court Decision

In a historical decision on January 22, 1973, the Supreme Court ruled 7–2 that the criminal abortion laws in almost every state violated a constitutional right of privacy. Justice Harry Blackmun wrote in the majority opinion that the right of personal privacy under the Ninth and Fourteenth amendments permits a woman and her doctor to decide whether she will have an abortion. Seven Justices upheld this decision, three of them considered conservative appointees and one a Catholic, Justice Brennan.

The ruling addresses itself to the three stages of pregnancy. This is important to note. The daily press with headlines such as *Abortion Legal in First Three Months* perpetuates an erroneous interpretation of the decision: that abortion is only legal in the first three months and that the Justices defined what constitutes life (which they clearly abstained from doing).

According to the Supreme Court decision, abortion is totally legal for any woman in the first trimester (three months) of pregnancy. The only restriction is that a licensed physician should perform the abortion.

In the second trimester of pregnancy a state may regulate, if it chooses, the facility in which abortions are performed, but "only in ways that are reasonably related to maternal health." The Court emphasized that these regulations must be based only on a state's interest in protecting the health of the woman.

In the third trimester the state may, again if it chooses, "regulate, and even proscribe, abortion except where it is necessary in appropriate medical judgment, for the preservation of the life or health of the mother."

In no way did the Justices deal with a difference in the value of fetal existence in the first and second trimester. Indeed, they specifically abstained from such a judgment. They said: "The unborn have never been recognized in the law as persons in the whole sense," and again, "When those trained in the respective disciplines of medicine, philosophy and theology are unable to arrive at a consensus (on the beginning of life), the judiciary, at this point in the development of man's knowledge, is not in a position to speculate on the answer."

The Supreme Court decision has had an international impact (*New York Times*, February 11, 1973). In France, until recently, it was a crime to facilitate, perform, or undergo an abortion. The penalties were particularly severe for doctors, who were subject to up to ten years in prison, high fines, and the threat of permanent loss of license to practice. A woman submitting to an abortion risked a fine of up to $1000. In spite of these penalties, 345 French physicians, encouraged by the U.S. Supreme Court decision, issued a manifesto stating that they had been performing illegal abortions for several months.[54]

Since the issuance of the manifesto in February 1973, the French National Assembly voted (on November 29, 1974) by a wide margin to legalize abortion, on request, during the first ten weeks of pregnancy (*New York Times*, November 30, 1974). This became law on January 18, 1975, overturning an anti-abortion law adopted in 1920. This is an historic precedent for a Roman Catholic country. The moving force behind this legislation was a woman, Simone Veil, the minister of health appointed by President Valéry Giscard d'Estaing.

This event was preceded by a law that became effective in November 1974, which authorized general distribution of contraceptives, to be subsidized by the social security system. This new law also provides contraceptives to girls under eighteen without parental consent (*New York Times*, November 28, 1974).

Although the Catholic church around the world continues to oppose abortion, in this country one Catholic group, the National Association of Laity's Human Life

Committee, with about 4000 members nationwide, applauded the judicial decision. Their spokesman stated that the decision in no way impedes the right of the Catholic church to limit or prohibit abortion for its members. However, the Catholic hierarchy and many Catholic groups (which also oppose modern methods of birth control and sterilization) are pressing for a constitutional amendment that would invalidate the Supreme Court's decision on abortion.

Since the Supreme Court decision does not compel any woman to have an abortion nor any physician to perform one, the organized and often irrational reaction of abortion opponents is unjustified. Nothing in this decision should offend those who for religious or other reasons oppose abortions. They can continue to adhere to their principles as long as they do not try to interfere with the freedom of choice of those who have other views. What it implies is that no woman may be denied an abortion because of the religious or moral beliefs of *other* people. This is in keeping with the law of the land—separation of church and state. Members of churches should be protected in their rights to hold and practice particular religious beliefs, but they should not be allowed to impose those beliefs by law on other people.

There has been a rising public acceptance of abortion. A 1972 Gallup poll revealed that 64 percent of the public (including 56 percent of Roman Catholics) believe that the decision to have an abortion should be left solely to the woman and her physician. This is a 24 percent increase in public approval since 1969.[55]

The Court's ruling does not suggest that abortion is a preferred method of birth control; both professionals and lay people consider it a subsidiary method to be used when the primary method of contraception fails or is not available. Even the most effective birth-control method has a failure rate of 1 percent. In the United States this rate would mean one-quarter of a million compulsory pregnancies per year, terminating in the births of one-quarter of a million unwanted children, unless abortions were available.

Abortion is also an important procedure in serious hereditary and congenital diseases that can be diagnosed by amniocentesis between twelve and fourteen weeks of gestation, allowing an additional three weeks for growth of cells in vitro. Amniocentesis is a voluntary procedure for high-risk families, and it has a high degree of safety for the woman and the fetus. Currently, most chromosomal abnormalities and up to thirty-four inborn errors of metabolism can be diagnosed by this technique.[56] German measles in a pregnant woman can produce serious congenital anomalies in her offspring and therefore is also an indication for an abortion.

A nationwide survey conducted by *Modern Medicine* magazine a month after the Supreme Court decision on abortion revealed that nearly two-thirds of 33,000 physicians favored the decision. Younger physicians supported the decision in greater numbers than older physicians. Seventy-five percent of those under 35 years of age favored the decision as compared to 59 percent of those 65 and older. Along religious lines, 92 percent of Jewish physicians, 69 percent of Protestants, and 27 percent of Roman Catholics favored the Supreme Court decision.[57]

New York's Experience with Legalized Abortion

In March 1970 New York State passed one of the most liberal abortion laws in the Western world, permitting abortion for any woman who seeks it, with no restriction as to marital status, consent of spouse, or place of residence, providing she is less than twenty-four weeks pregnant and the procedure is carried out by a licensed physician in a proper facility.

The impact of the first two years of the liberalized abortion law in New York City, especially its effect on maternal mortality and morbidity, infant mortality, and illegitimacy, has been striking.[58]

First, there has been a dramatic decline in maternal mortality, which is not surprising since criminal abortions had been the main cause of maternal death. It dropped from 52.2 per 100,000 live births for the two years preceding the new abortion law to 37.7 for the two-year period under the new abortion law (July 1970 to July 1972), a statistically significant decline of 28 percent.

Second, there has been a substantial decline in maternal morbidity caused by incomplete or "septic" abortions, performed in the past by back-street abortionists.

Third, there has been a decline of 11.8 percent in out-of-wedlock births, which previously showed a yearly rise. It marked the first decline since 1954, when records were first kept.

Fourth, there has been a decline in infant mortality from 24.4 per 1000 live births in 1969 to 20.3 for the first six months of 1972 (a decline of 16.8 percent), through reduction of high-risk pregnancies, proper spacing of births, and reduction of unwanted pregnancies. This was achieved not only through abortions, but also through increased availability of birth control as part of the aftercare of abortion.

Fifth, the New York City experience shows that women of all ethnic and racial groups avail themselves of the opportunity to prevent unwanted births, and in many cases at little or no cost. Statistics show that 44.7 percent of New York City abortions were performed on nonwhite women, whose minority group constitutes 18 percent of New York City's population, and 4 percent on Puerto Rican women, whose group forms 8 percent of the city's population.

The safety of legal abortion can be demonstrated on the basis of 402,059 abortions performed in New York City during the first two years of liberalized abortion.[59] For the first trimester abortion the death rate dropped from 2.1 per 100,000 abortions in the first year to 0.5 in the second year. The 0.5 rate constitutes one case, and there is some question about the gestation time reported in this case. The overall abortion death rate up to 24 weeks of gestation dropped from 4.6 per 100,000 in the first year to 3.5 in the second year. It is well to keep in mind that the U.S. maternal mortality rate is over 20.0 per 100,000 births.

Complication rate is another measure of safety. For first trimester abortions the complication rate was 3.0 per 1000 abortions during the second year of New York City's experience. For the first and second trimester abortions, it rose to 7.2 per 1000. For the second trimester alone, complication rose to 28.6 per 1000. For her own safety, a woman wishing to have an abortion should be able to secure it as early as possible in the first trimester. With the availability of abortion clinics in New York City there was an increase of first trimester abortion for New York City residents from 73 percent in the first year of the liberalized law to 81 percent in the second year.

An easy access to reliable pregnancy tests with assurance of confidentiality should be available at a nominal charge without necessitating a visit to a physician. This should ensure earlier diagnosis of pregnancy. In Switzerland and Sweden, for instance, such tests can be obtained easily through a pharmacy or other facilities.

The idea that the poor and minorities are not interested in birth control is a myth. According to Bogue,[60] blacks who are poor favor control of their fertility but are unable to achieve the two- and three-child family they desire. A sampling of 1010 black women aged 18 to 44, conducted in 1967, showed that 67.2 percent of them thought that three or fewer children made an ideal family. Eight out of 10 approved of family planning, 1 out of 10 was neutral, and 1 out of 10 opposed it. Although 75 percent of the women were practicing birth control, a large proportion were using methods of low reliability.

Beasley et al.[61] conducted a similar study in 1965 among black women in New Orleans: Three-fourths of the women interviewed did not want to become pregnant again, two-thirds of them wanted more information on how to prevent future pregnancies, nine-tenths thought that they should have the right to control the size of their families and that family planning clinics should be available for the indigent. Nine-tenths wanted their children to be informed about birth-control techniques. Although motivation for effective birth control in this group of women was high, it was frustrated by lack of information and services.

According to the report of the Commission on Population Growth and the American Future, college-educated black couples have by choice fewer children on the average than their white counterparts.[62] The above data are eloquent testimony to the desire of members of minority groups to limit their family size to improve the quality of life for themselves and their children.

As a result of availability of abortion and other birth-control services in New York City, the birthrate among the city's women on welfare dropped by 33 percent as compared with 1970. The birthrate for the entire New York City population dropped by 12.4 percent.[63] This is testimony not only to women's acceptance of abortion and to their desire to control their family size, but it is a direct contradiction of the myth that women on welfare want babies in order to increase their income. It is also testimony to the fact that control of family size avoids financial dependency and alleviates poverty.

MODERN WOMEN AND ANCIENT PRACTICE

It is unfortunate that the modern woman has had to use primitive methods to produce abortion. Because of our archaic abortion laws, women had no access to sophisticated methods of modern medicine. Given the current debates, it is instructive to examine the history of abortion customs and laws.

Plato (427–347 B.C.) recommended abortions for pregnant women over forty and those whose pregnancy was the result of incest. Plato believed that human life began at birth. Aristotle (448–380 B.C.) advocated that a woman who had a sufficient number of children should have the benefit of an abortion.[64] In contrast to Plato, Aristotle believed that life began for the male fetus forty days after conception and for the female fetus eighty days after conception, and that abortions be performed prior to the beginning of life.[65]

Reference to medical recommendation for abortion dates to the second century A.D. Soramus of Ephesos recommended it for complications of delivery, such as a narrow pelvis. In 1772 an English surgeon, William Cooper, wrote, "In such cases where it is certainly known that a mature child can not possibly be delivered in the ordinary way alive, would it not be consistent with reason and conscience for the preservation of the mother, as soon as it conveniently can be done, by artificial modus to attempt to produce an abortion." [66]

The New Testament is silent on the subject of abortion. According to Thomas Aquinas's views (1225–74) presented in the *Summa Theologica*, the soul unites with the "boy" fetus at forty days after conception and with the "girl" fetus eighty days after conception, an idea borrowed from Aristotle. Papal as well as theological opinion oscillated with the times. Pope Gregory IX (1227–41) declared that abortion was acceptable before the fetus had moved. More than three hundred years later, in 1588, Pope Sixtus V proclaimed all abortions to be murder. Only three years later, a new pope, Gregory XIV, revoked all penalties for abortions, except when performed after forty days of gestation. This law lasted until 1869 when Pope Pius IX prohibited abortion at any time. In 1930 Pope Pius XI stated "The life of each [woman and fetus] is equally sacred and no one has the power, not even the public authority, to destroy it." It is well to remember that the prohibition of abortion by the Catholic church is only one hundred years old. Today, the Catholic church is actively and strongly opposing all abortion reforms and the recent Supreme Court decision.[67] However, a 1971 meeting of Catholic bishops of the Scandinavian countries, although supporting the right of the unborn, came out with a plea to counsel and support any woman in her wish for an abortion.[68]

Neither the Jewish nor the Protestant religion sets the time at which the fetus acquires a soul. According to Jewish theologians, a fetus is not a person until it is born. The Japanese Shinto religion shares the same concept.

Abortion Laws in the United States
Prior to the Supreme Court Decision

It is not generally appreciated that our country's restrictive abortion laws were not introduced for religious or moral reasons, nor for concern for the embryo. The stated reason was a concern for the life of the woman, who at that time, before the era of antiseptic surgery, had fifteen times as great a chance of surviving childbirth as surviving an abortion. The first abortion law in the United States was enacted in Connecticut in 1821. This law presumably was passed to protect the health and the life of the pregnant woman, since abortion, as any other surgical procedure at that time, was associated with serious complications and even death. Abortion was outlawed except when necessary to save the life of the woman. Other states adopted their abortion laws on the same basis.[69]

Prior to introduction of abortion reforms, an estimated one million criminal abortions were performed each year, a ratio of 300 for 1000 live births.[70] About 350,000 women were admitted to U.S. hospitals each year as a result of complications from self-induced abortion or those performed by unskilled abortionists. Deaths from illegal abortions were estimated at 1000 annually.

Until recently all states had restrictive laws, prohibiting abortions except when it was necessary to save the life of the mother. The courts have challenged the vagueness of this part of the law.

Colorado in 1967 was the first state to liberalize its abortion law, and prior to the Supreme Court decision, twelve other states changed their laws following the Colorado pattern (proposed by the American Law Institute in the late 1950s).

However, liberalization, with many restrictions still present, did not bring women the necessary reform needed, and back-street abortions with tragic sequelae and discrimination against the poor continued.

In 1970 Hawaii became the first state to permit abortion without restrictions, except for residence requirement; Alaska passed a similar law shortly thereafter. In March 1970 New York passed one of the most liberal laws in the world. In Washington State, in November 1970, as a result of a statewide referendum (56 percent in favor, 44 percent against), a law was passed permitting abortions up to sixteen weeks of pregnancy.

The District of Columbia law permitted abortions only to save the life or protect the health of the woman. On appeal to the U.S. Supreme Court, a challenge produced two forward-looking definitions of "health" in 1970, which permitted the establishment of six abortion clinics. First, the Supreme Court defined health in the broadest terms, saying it includes physical as well as mental health. The physician performing the abortion can make a judgment as to the total health of the patient, without consultation with a psychiatrist. Second, the Court stated that when an abortion is claimed to be illegal, the burden is on the prosecution to prove beyond reasonable doubt that the abortion was not necessary for mental or physical health. This, indeed, is difficult to prove.

Abortion and Public Opinion

In April 1971 President Nixon ordered military hospitals to abandon liberalized abortion policies. Abortion, he said, is "an unacceptable method of population control." In spite of the presidential order, the President's Commission on Population growth and the American Future (established by Congress in March 1970, appointed by the President, and chaired by John D. Rockefeller III)[71] formally recommended on March 17, 1972, that all states, following New York's example, greatly liberalize abortion laws and permit a physician to perform an abortion at the patient's request under conditions of medical safety. Further, the commission recommended that federal, state, and local governments make funds available to support abortion services and that abortion be included in comprehensive health insurance, both public and private.

The commission based its decision not on grounds of population control, but on the right of women to make their own moral choices, to control their own fertility, and to avoid the burdens of unwanted childbearing. Four Roman Catholic members of the twenty-four-man commission expressed varying degrees of dissent to the abortion recommendations.

It has been well documented that Catholic women avail themselves of abortions. For example, out of 1400 referrals for abortion by the Clergy Consultation Service in Milwaukee in 1972, 70 percent of the women were Catholic.[72]

On the national level, the 224-member House of Delegates, the policy-making arm of the conservative AMA, in June 1970 passed a resolution that permits the decision for abortion to be made by the woman and her physician with consultation with two other physicians.

Increasingly during recent years many lay, religious, and professional organizations have publicly advocated sensible liberalization of abortion laws. Among the many women's groups supporting abortion-law repeal are the American Medical

Women's Association, the National Organization for Women (NOW), the Interstate Association of Commissions on the Status of Women, the Young Women's Christian Association of the USA, Church Women United, Catholic Women for Abortion Law Repeal, Episcopal Churchwomen of the USA, the National Council of Jewish Women, the National Home Economics Association, and many others.

Probably the most prestigious and informed support came from the President's own commission, whose published report was the result of two years of research at a cost of over a million dollars. It is ironic and unprecedented that not only did President Nixon disapprove of his commission's recommendation, but in his zeal, through a letter made public, he endorsed and supported Cardinal Cooke and the archdiocese of New York in their attempt to repeal the liberalized New York State abortion law.[73] The commission was fearful that its report might be suppressed because of controversial recommendations not in line with administration policy. Therefore, members of the commission formed a company, Population Education Inc., and decided to make a filmed version of the report. The result was a privately funded film that was judged to be "good and balanced" by the Office of Population Affairs and the General Service Administration of Health, Education and Welfare (HEW), who agreed to purchase a hundred copies and distribute them upon request to schools.

Commercial networks refused to sell Population Education Inc. prime television time to show the film because of its controversial content. On November 29, 1972, the film was shown over many public broadcast stations and the controversy started anew. Although the mail received by HEW was five to one in favor of the film, the former chief of HEW, Elliot Richardson, halted the purchase of the film because of its sensitive nature. The opposition came mainly from the Catholic church and its organizations. Dr. Louis Hellman, HEW's deputy assistant secretary for population affairs, defended the right of the public to know what the commission recommended. Dr. Allan Guttmacher, president of Planned Parenthood, said he deplored the Nixon administration's courtship of the Catholic vote and the political nature of the decision.

Despite the Supreme Court's decision, the antiabortion groups, in an organized effort, are trying through a constitutional amendment to overturn the Court decision, which they have dubbed the "Black Monday" decision.

What Remains to Be Done

For the wealthiest country in the world, which prides itself on reaching the moon, we occupy the fifteenth position in the world in our infant mortality rate for both white and nonwhite population combined. Fourteen other nations have lower infant mortality. The infant mortality rate for the nonwhite population puts us in twenty-sixth position.[74] Among those deprived infants who survive, there is mounting evidence that inadequate feeding during critical periods of pregnancy and early life reduces the number of brain cells, thus compromising the intellectual development of the child for life.

If the tragedy of unwanted births and illegitimacy is to disappear, if infant mortality and morbidity are to be reduced, if we respond to the plight of the adolescent girl who is a child herself as she gives birth to children, if we have compassion for the women and men who are unable to provide for the children they already have, then we must protect the Supreme Court decision from the efforts of antiabortion groups, which are attempting to destroy it through a constitutional amendment. Furthermore, we must extend abortion services at nominal fees to all women throughout the country who desire them. And, finally, we must launch a massive birth-control program that will reach every woman and man, irrespective of race, income, age, or marital status, so that fewer women will become pregnant involuntarily. It is with the quality of life that we must be concerned.

NOTES

1. GARRETT HARDIN, *Population, Evolution and Birth Control* (San Francisco: W. H. Freeman, 1964), p. 18.

2. Ibid., p. 18.

3. Ibid., p. 17.

4. *Men and Molecules: The Closing Circle*. Transcript 551, 1972 (American Chemical Society News Service, 1155 16 St., N.W., Washington, D.C. 20036).

5. Ibid.

6. ROBERT ARDREY, *The Social Contract, A Personal Inquiry into the Evolutionary Sources of Order and Disorder* (New York: Atheneum, 1970), pp. 202–7, 208, 216–18, 228–30.

7. ROBERT RIENOW and LEONA TRAIN RIENOW, *Moment in the Sun* (New York: Ballantine Books, 1967).

8. Testimony by DR. J. D. BEASLEY, *Family Planning Services. Hearing before the Subcommittee on Public Health and Welfare of the Committee on Interstate and Foreign Commerce, House of Representatives of the United States* (Washington, D.C., 3–7 August 1970, Serial No. 91–70; Washington, D.C.: U.S. Government Printing Office, 1970), pp. 329–44.

9. "Milestone U.S. Family Planning Legislation Signed into Law," Literature and Comment Section P.L. 91–572, *Family Planning Perspectives* 1, no. 1 (January 1971): 2–3.

10. JOSEPH D. BEASLEY, RALPH F. FRANKOWSKI, and C. MORTON HAWKINS IV, "Louisiana Family Planning," *American Journal of Public Health* 61 (1971): 1812–25.

11. P. SARREL and C. DAVIS, "The Young Unwed Primipara: A Study of 100 Cases with a 5-Year Follow-up," *American Journal of Obstetrics and Gynecology* 95 (1966): 722–25.

12. CARL W. TYLER, WERNER S. TILLACK, JACK C. SMITH, and ROBERT A. HATCHER, "Assessment of a Family Planning Program: Contraceptive Services and Fertility in Atlanta, Georgia," *Family Planning Perspectives* 2, no. 2 (March 1970): 25–29.

13. J. E. JEKEL, "Suicide Among Pregnant Teenagers," *Medical Aspects of Human Sexuality* 7, no. 2 (February 1973): 209–12.

14. L. J. REDMAN and E. J. LIEBERMAN, "Abortion, Contraception and Child Mental Health," *Family Planning Perspectives* 5, no. 2 (Spring 1973): 71–73.

15. A. A. CAMPBELL, "The Role of Family Planning in the Reduction of Poverty," *Journal of Marriage and the Family* 30 (1968): 236–45.

16. SARREL and DAVIS, "Young Unwed Primipara."

17. HOWARD J. OSOFSKY, *The Pregnant Teenager* (Springfield, Ill.: Charles C Thomas, 1968), pp. 22–35.

18. *Population and the American Future: The Report of the Commission on Population Growth and the American Future* (New York: New American Library, 1972), pp. 188–90.

19. R. POMEROY and L. C. LANDMAN, "Public Opinion Trends: Elective Abortion and Birth Control Services to Teenagers," *Family Planning Perspective* 4, no. 4 (October 1972): 44–55.

20. J. F. KANTNER, "Sexual Experience of Young Unmarried Women in the United States," *Family Planning Perspectives* 4, no. 4 (October 1972): 9–18.

21. *United States Statutes at Large*, 44th Cong., 1875–77, vol. 19, p. 90.

22. DAVID M. KENNEDY, *Birth Control in America: The Career of Margaret Sanger* (New Haven: Yale University Press, 1970); EMILY TAFT DOUGLAS, *Margaret Sanger: Pioneer of the Future* (New York: Holt, Rinehart, 1970); MARGARET SANGER, *My Fight for Birth Control* (New York: Farrar & Rinehart, 1931).

23. The Report of the Commission, pp. 167–68.

24. *Methods of Contraception in the United States.* A publication of the Medical Committee of Planned Parenthood–World Population (New York: Planned Parenthood Federation of America, 1965), p. 5.

25. Ibid., p. 4.

26. CHARLES F. WESTOFF, "The Modernization of U.S. Contraceptive Practice," *Family Planning Perspectives* 4, no. 3 (July 1972): 9–12.

27. B. E. FINCH, *Contraception through the Ages* (London: Peter Owen, 1963), p. 98.

28. Ibid., p. 99.

29. Ibid., pp. 104–9.

30. "How IUD's Prevent Pregnancy in Humans," Literature and Comment Section, *Family Planning Perspectives* 2, no. 3 (June 1970): 213.

31. *Methods of Contraception in the U.S.*, pp. 5–8.

32. FINCH, *Contraception*, pp. 42–43.

33. WESTOFF, "Modernization of Contraceptive Practice," p. 12.

34. *Methods of Contraception in the U.S.*, pp. 8–11.

35. FINCH, *Contraception*, p. 43.

36. NORMAN E. HIMES, *Medical History of Contraception* (New York: Schocken, 1970; first published in 1936 by Williams and Wilkins Co., Baltimore), pp. 59–66.

37. FINCH, *Contraception*, pp. 38–41.

38. Ibid., p. 42.

39. ERNEST HAVEMANN, *Birth Control* (New York: Time Inc., 1967), pp. 36–37.

40. FINCH, *Contraception*, pp. 29–30.

41. Ibid., p. 30.

42. WESTOFF, "Modernization of Contraceptive Practice."

43. FINCH, *Contraception*, pp. 46–48.

44. Ibid., pp. 48–50.

45. HAVEMANN, *Birth Control*, pp. 35–36.

46. WESTOFF, "Modernization of Contraceptive Practice."

47. CHARLES F. WESTOFF and LARRY BUMPASS, *Science* 179 (January 1973): 41–44.

48. *Methods of Contraception in the U.S.*, p. 11.

49. *The Student Guide to Sex on Campus*, Student Committee on Human Sexuality, Yale University; medical consultant, Dr. Philip Sarrel (New York: New American Library, 1971).

50. LARRY L. BUMPASS and HOMER B. PRESSER, "Contraceptive Sterilization in the U.S.: 1965 and 1970," *Demography* 9 (1972): 531–48.

51. FINCH, *Contraception*, pp. 66–67, 71.

52. Ibid., p. 70.

53. Ibid., pp. 76–80.

54. *New York Times*, 11 February 1973.

55. POMEROY and LANDMAN, "Public Opinion Trends," p. 44.

56. MAUREEN HARRIS, ed., *Early Diagnosis of Human Genetic Defects: Scientific and Ethical Considerations*, A Symposium sponsored by the John E. Fogarty International Center for Advanced Study in the Health Sciences, National Institutes of Health, Bethesda, Md., 18–19 May 1970. (Washington, D.C.: U.S. Government Printing Office, 1970. Stock No. 1753-0004).

57. "33,000 Doctors Speak on Abortion," *Modern Medicine* 41 (14 May 1973): 31–35.

58. *New York City Abortion Report: The First Two Years* (October 1972). Reported by Gordon Chase, Health Services Administration, City of New York.

59. *Chase Report on Two-Year Data from NYC Abortion Experience: Cites Favorable Trends in Safety and Public Health Benefit* (1972). Health Services Administration, the City of New York, Gordon Chase, Administrator.

60. DONALD J. BOGUE, "Family Planning in the Negro Ghetto of Chicago," *Miemauk Memorial Fund Quarterly* 48 (1970): 2, pt. 2.

61. JOSEPH D. BEASLEY, CARL L. HARTER, and ANN FISHER, "Attitudes and Knowledge Relevant to Family Planning Among New Orleans Negro Women," *American Journal of Public Health* 56 (1966): 1847–57.

62. *The Report of the Commission*, p. 109.

63. New York State Department of Social Services, Office of Research, *Trends in Births in Family Public Assistance Cases in New York City 1961–1972* (Albany, N.Y.: March 1973), Program Brief No. 1.

64. LESLIE ALDRIDGE WESTOFF and CHARLES F. WESTOFF, *From Now to Zero: Fertility, Contraception and Abortion in America* (Boston: Little, Brown, 1968, 1971), p. 126.

65. VON C. MULLER, "Zur Geschichte des artefiziellen Aborts," *Geburtshilfe und Frauenheilkunde* 26 (1966): 223–31.

66. Ibid., p. 226.

67. WESTOFF and WESTOFF, *From Now to Zero*, pp. 127–28.

68. *Wiener Zeitung*, 2 September 1971.

69. "Abortion and the Unwanted Child: An Interview with ALAN F. GUTTMACHER, M.D., and HARRIET E. PILPEL," *Family Planning Perspectives* 2, no. 2 (March 1970): 16–24.

70. WESTOFF and WESTOFF, *From Now to Zero*, pp. 117–18.

71. The Report of the Commission, pp. 175–78, 264.

72. *Milwaukee Journal*, 16 February 1973.

73. *New York Times*, 7 May 1972.

74. MYRON E. WEGMAN, "Annual Summary of Vital Statistics, 1971," *Pediatrics* 50 (1972): 456–59.

3

WOMEN:
THE SELF AND
SOCIAL INTERACTION

Some Psychological "Facts" About Women: Will the Real Ms. Please Stand Up?
Julia A. Sherman

In the present state of our knowledge, nothing is more difficult than evaluating the psychological facts about women. Issues are so intensely emotional that a researcher with an unpopular view expresses it in an aside during private conversation. Many scientists avoid the topic altogether as "too controversial to work with at this time." Other, less sensitive individuals barge into print with sloppy, biased speculations posing as fearless champions of "objective truth."

"FACTS" AND THE SOCIOLOGY OF KNOWLEDGE

It has become increasingly apparent (Myrdal 1972, Bernard 1972) that social science facts are often "facts." "Facts" must be evaluated in the light of the values and motivations of the writer. What then are mine? I want to understand the factors affecting the psychological development of women through the life cycle. Knowing these factors, their timing, and their relationship to one another will make it possible for individuals and society to make more intelligent choices. However, well-informed decisions derive neither from a sexist bias that suggests females are weak in mind and body nor from a bias that denies any biological basis for behavior and/or denies all nonanatomical differences between the sexes. The welfare of women is better served by an identity based on reality rather than ideology, and the scientific method is one of the most effective ways of apprehending reality.

113

However, at this time, many basic questions regarding the nature of women's reality remain unanswered in the scientific literature.

Are there premenstrual depressions? If so, are they attributable to physical causes or to cultural suggestions of sickness, or both? If there are premenstrual depressions, of what practical significance are they? Can most women expect to enjoy a love 'em and leave 'em sexuality? Is breast feeding psychologically better for a child? Can a single woman rear a child just as successfully as a couple? Are women more emotional than men? Can women expect to do as well as men in the study of advanced mathematics? Do tiny children require the full-time attention of their mothers to ensure healthy development? Could women be as physically strong as men if they worked at it?

Seeking the answers to questions such as these, in 1965 I began systematically reading the available research literature. The results of that inquiry were published in 1971 in *On the Psychology of Women: A Survey of Empirical Studies*. There has been increasing recognition of the need for more knowledge about the psychology of women; but some object to the very phrase "psychology of women," thinking this implies difference, and *difference*, given the terms of sexual politics, will be made to mean *inferior*. This is clearly a real problem, but the way to attack it is to attack the *use* of knowledge, not knowledge itself.

A major obstacle to the pursuit of knowledge about women is the fact that there are only a handful of women in the major research institutions of our country. Very few women have access to research funds and facilities. As Helen Astin commented at the December 1972 AAAS meeting, a "critical mass" of women is needed in order to effect a breakthrough. Otherwise, from the social psychological point of view of reference group and identity group, the few females are isolated and placed under severe pressure to conform to the androcentric ethos. Only when many more high-status females are in our research institutions will females be free to develop an alternate reference group. Until then, departments of psychology are likely to regard the psychology of women as "too narrow" a specialty while being highly impressed with the potential significance of research on conditioning penile erections. Until then, those interested in humans will study monkeys (Tarvis 1973).

The amount of research on the psychology of women has increased vastly since I began my studies in 1965, but massive gaps remain in the research literature. The situation is the same as with any submerged group: Women's problems and interests are rarely recognized and certainly not considered important enough to research. This situation will remain until women unite to see to it that funds, resources, and personnel are made available.

What follows is a brief summary of some important psychological issues and their implications. I will cover some theories of female development and material about sex differences. The question of the extent of biological influence in producing these differences seems an interesting and important one and will be emphasized.

THEORIES OF FEMALE DEVELOPMENT

Women are born female, but how do they become "feminine"? Theorizing derived from Freud supposed that girls identify with their mothers, taking unto themselves the characteristics of their mothers. A review of the evidence, however, does not show that girls are any more similar to their mothers than to women in general (Sherman 1971). Furthermore, the evidence shows that parents of both sexes influence their children of both sexes. In general, Freud's theory of sexual identification has been found to be inadequate and incorrect. (The evidence for and against Freud's theory of female psychosexual development is dealt with by Sherman 1971.)

It has also been supposed that females become "feminine" because of the influence of the culture. It is well known that considerable variation exists in what a given culture considers desirable for women. Jerome Kagan (1964) has summarized what women are supposed to be like in our culture. They are to inhibit aggression and open display of sexual urges; to be passive with men; to be nurturant to others; to cultivate attractiveness; and to maintain an affective, socially poised, friendly posture with others. Males are to be aggressive in the face of attack; independent in problem situations; sexually aggressive; in control of regressive urges; and suppressive of strong emotions, especially anxiety. It should be noted that Kagan does not appear to consider "aggressiveness" a strong emotion. This would seem to be an example of sex bias creeping into a scientific description. If one believes that men are not emotional, then expressions of aggression would by definition not be emotional. My favorite example of this intellectual sleight of hand is the enraged husband yelling at his tearful wife, "Why do you have to be so damned emotional?"

Sociologist Talcott Parsons (1955) has characterized the female role as expressive and the male role as instrumental. The feminine expressive role is characterized by giving rewarding responses in order to receive rewarding responses. A woman is supposed to be oriented to people, to the self and others. By being solicitous, appealing, and understanding, a woman seeks to get a pleasurable response by giving pleasure. The masculine, instrumental role is defined by a behavioral orientation toward goals that transcend the immediate interactional situation. The interaction is viewed as a means to an end, and there is little concern about the immediate emotional responses of others to him. Rather than soliciting positive responses, instrumental role playing requires the ability to tolerate the hostility it will very likely elicit. As applied to the family, the instrumental role player, the father, presumably takes the lead in relations *outside* the family, while the mother is more active *within* the family (Johnson 1963). This summary of Parsons' theory provides some idea of what he is talking about, but his actual theory is much more complex. Empirical data offers Parsons' theory only limited support (Sherman 1971).

But how would these cultural ideals actually affect the development of girls? It is not possible to give a precise answer to this question, but cognitive psychologist Lawrence Kohlberg (1966) has found that four- to five-year-old children are aware that only males play the extrafamilial roles involving violence and danger. Examples of such roles are policeman, soldier, fireman, robber. By ages six to seven, nearly all of a small sample of American children were aware that the high-power roles—President, policeman, general—are male roles.

Kohlberg thinks that children do not need to be taught this, but that they figure it out by observing the world about them. According to Kohlberg, some time between the ages of three and seven, a girl reaches sufficient intellectual development to realize that she is female and will always be female. At that point she begins to value the female because it is like herself, and she wishes to act the way females are supposed to act. How females are supposed to be and act she figures out from what she observes around her. If Kohlberg is correct, the emphasis the women's movement has placed on the manner in which females are portrayed in the media is very much to the point.

If theories of female socialization are this imprecise, a summary of empirical findings of what influences girls to be more "feminine" or more "masculine" may provide greater clarity. Incidentally, the idea of a girl becoming "masculine" seems very negative to many people; but when one realizes that stereotyped "masculinity" is associated with strength, and stereotyped "femininity" is associated with weakness, it becomes apparent that becoming more "masculine" could mean becoming stronger. The evidence, in fact, does not clearly show that "masculinity" in women is associated with maladjustment (Sherman 1971). Returning to the influences which make girls more "masculine" or more "feminine," we find, in brief summary, that a warm relationship with the father tends to "masculinize" girls. On the other hand, girls whose fathers directly encouraged "feminine" activities were more "feminine." An upbringing that was restrictive of sensual and aggressive gratifications was associated with "femininity." Girls whose older siblings were brothers were found to be more "masculine" (Sherman 1971).

NATURE-NURTURE PROBLEM

Any attempt to understand how women came to be as they are is apt to run into the question of nature vs. nurture. In the 1930s this controversy took the form of an either/or proposition. The question was posed, "Is nature more important in determining human development or is nurture more important?" In recent years it has been recognized that both nature and nurture are important and that their influences are intertwined. In fact, it has become abundantly clear that any given end result of human development will have not just one cause, but typically a chain of interconnected causes. Furthermore, the same apparent end effect can often be arrived at by different routes. It is also important to remember that evidence of innate causal factors in a particular behavior does not mean that it cannot be modified. We inherit predispositions, which are then shaped by our interaction with the environment.

SOME PHYSICAL SEX DIFFERENCES

As a background for the discussion, I would like to sketch briefly some of the physical differences between the sexes. Of the twenty-three pairs of chromosomes that determine human inheritance, one pair controls sexual development. In the case of females, the two chromosomes are similar to each other and by scientific convention are designated XX. The corresponding male pair are called XY. Y contains about 5 percent less genetic material than X, and the genes of X and Y do not seem to be parallel to each other. Males are not females because of genes on the Y chromosome that guide male development (Childs 1965). It is important to note that the differences between the sexes are not simply a difference of protrusions in different places. Every cell in the entire body of a female is different from those of any chromosomal male.

We also know that while both sexes have both "male" and "female" hormones, that is, both androgens and estrogens, the proportion of each is different in the two sexes. Sex-typical hormones tend to have more effect on an individual of the appropriate sex. In other words, a given amount of estrogen would have more effect on a chromosomal female than on a chromosomal male. The female cell is so constructed as to respond more to estrogens. Androgens and estrogens are differing, but not opposite hormonal families. In fact, the two groups of hormones have sometimes similar, sometimes opposing effects (Money and Ehrhardt 1972; also see Bleier, chap. 1 in this volume).

The idea that hormones determine behavior is simplistic and misleading. Hormones rather appear to facilitate certain behaviors or lower the threshold of stimulation required for a certain response. There are two main points of dimorphic hormone influence—one occurs during very early development and the other during adolescence and continuing throughout most of adulthood. The evidence from animal and human studies suggests that excess hormones, either "male" or "female," during a critical period of very early development result in an increased likelihood of certain characteristics, many commonly associated with males. The evidence for the effects on humans rests largely upon the studies of individuals with various incongruities of chromosome, prenatal hormone influence, and sex of rearing (Money and Ehrhardt 1972). The essential behavioral effects appear to indicate that such individuals will be less likely to prefer sedentary rather than vigorous, especially outdoor, activity; be more likely to show greater self-assertiveness in competition for position in a dominance hierarchy; be more interested in careers and less interested in self-adornment and maternalism; and possibly have a higher IQ. Moreover, they tend to desire people seen in sexually stimulating pictures rather than fantasize they *are* these people or that they are creating desire in others. The latter reactions are considered feminine responses. It is difficult to be sure of the primary vs. the secondary effects in cases such as these. For example, it seems likely that the career vs. maternal interests would be influenced by the girls' early knowledge that they are different. Being smart, they might prefer to emphasize an option where they are advantaged rather than disadvantaged.

In adolescence and adulthood, the essential behavioral effects of exogenous androgens appear to be that they increase impetus to sexual behavior in females and only in males who have insufficient androgens. In males, depending on life history, lack of androgens is reported to lead to a diminution of assertiveness which is restored when the androgen level is restored (Money and Ehrhardt 1972). Little systematic evidence is available regarding effects of androgens on assertiveness in females. Judging from the effects on animals, on males, on the sexual impetus of females, and on females at the prenatal level, one would expect that androgens would be associated with increased assertiveness. The tentative nature of these conclusions should be emphasized.

Behavioral effects of estrogens are even less clear. In adult males they decrease impetus to sexuality. In females estrogen decrease does not appear to affect libido while decrease of androgens does (Sherman 1971). Some believe that estrogen may sometimes enhance female libido (Kennedy 1973), and the phase of the menstrual cycle dominated by estrogen appears to be one of greater initiative sexually and otherwise (Money and Ehrhardt 1972), though female sexual cycle changes are more complex than this generalization might suggest (Sherman 1971). Progesterone, the pregnancy hormone that dominates the ovulatory phase of the cycle, appears to have sedative qualities (Sherman 1971).

On the basis of this evidence, what can one conclude about women? In the first place, it must be recognized that many details and complexities are quite unsettled and that it is difficult for investigators to view data uninfluenced by sexual stereotypes (see Bleier, chap. 1 in this volume, Davidson and Levine 1972, Ramey 1973). It must also be recognized that humans, when compared to animals, are much less determined by biological factors and that hormonal influences, while discernible, are vastly modified by cognitive intention, personal and social experience. This truth is nowhere more vividly illustrated than in the account of a genetic male being reared as a female (Money and Ehrhardt 1972). Hormones are destiny no more than anatomy is destiny.

Other physical sex differences include the fact that boys are muscularly about 10 percent stronger than girls at age seven, and about 50–60 percent stronger by age eighteen. Concerted effort could probably decrease but not eliminate these differences. The male forearm is proportionately longer than that of the female and influences the manner in which boys and girls throw a ball. On the average, girls weigh 5 percent less at birth and 20 percent less at age twenty. They are 1–2 percent shorter as children and 10 percent shorter by age twenty. The homeostatic mechanism works somewhat differently in the two sexes. Females show a more marked physiological reaction to stress and a more rapid recovery. While more male than female children are born with vision defects, male infants seem to prefer visual stimulation while female infants prefer auditory stimulation. The maturation rate of the two sexes is quite different. Females mature, at least in some respects, more rapidly than males. Females appear to be born after a shorter gestation period; their permanent teeth come in earlier; and they reach their final physical growth earlier. Progress to skeletal maturity can be gauged by measures of bone ossification. By this measure, at age five, girls are a year ahead of boys. At age thirteen, they are two years ahead of boys in skeletal maturity. Girls stop growing earlier. They reach 98 percent of their height at $16\frac{1}{2}$; boys reach 98 percent of their adult height by $17\frac{3}{4}$. There is evidence that in some intellectual and emotional ways girls also mature more rapidly than boys; but the extent, nature, and implications of this more precocious maturation is not currently agreed upon by scholars (Sherman 1971).

PSYCHOLOGICAL SEX DIFFERENCES AND SIMILARITIES

The only study I have found that explicitly considered the question of the psychological similarities as well as the differences between the sexes concluded that there is extreme similarity between male and female thinking, the average correlation being .90 (Bennett and Cohen 1959). Discussion of sex differences must be considered within this context. In fact, Kogan (1972) questions the emphasis on sex differences and suggests it may be related to temperamental factors within scientists.

One basic scientific task is classification that proceeds by cataloging differences and observing the regularities of their occurrence. From a physical point of view, it was easy for scientists to divide humans into male and female, though details of the factors influencing this physical differentiation are still far from being understood. From a psychological point of view, the differences between the sexes have been variously cataloged. Only in the last few years have scientists in any number seriously attempted to study the regularity of sex differences and the factors influencing their development. One result of this new emphasis is the case of the disappearing sex difference. Increased research, improved conceptual models, and cultural change have revealed many sex differences to be more apparent than real.

One conceptual improvement lies in the area of the critique of trait psychology. The psychological literature has long been dominated by this viewpoint. It is a simplification with a certain amount of validity, but one that needs to be replaced by more sophisticated concepts (Mischel 1968). Much of the existing research has been structured within the context of the trait assumptions, including much of what is known about sex differences. Ironically, discussion of sex differences has traditionally belonged in the specialty called, "individual differences." What is actually discussed, however, is not individual differences but average differences between the group called male and the group called female.

Much of the research on sex differences is replete with methodological and sexist errors. Conclusions often attribute differences to sex when no effort has been made to control other relevant factors. Notions that fit popular bias are accepted without question and often without statistical test. Results pass through an interpretive process that ends with platitudes that could have been pronounced before the research began (Sherman 1971). It is most revealing that when the subjects were rats, it was immediately obvious to investigators that performance on spatial tasks is no general index of ability (Dawson 1972). When the subjects have been human females, however, there has been no similar insistence on conceptual accuracy. Investigators have been only too willing to generalize from spatial tasks to analytic ability (Sherman 1967, 1971). However, these scientific inaccuracies are not surprising since the study of sex differences is an intellectual garbage heap with many a banana peel for the unwary to slip on.

Passive Dependency

A case in point is the question of sex differences in passive dependency. There seemed to be a great deal of evidence that women are more passive-dependent than men. Judith Bardwick (1971) stated that "the American girl rarely achieves an independent sense of self and self esteem." For some time it has been clear that dependency is neither a unitary nor a bipolar trait (Hartup 1963, Maccoby and Masters 1970) and that any such sex difference develops after about age six and is largely cultural in origin. However, new evidence and conceptualization make untenable the conclusion that, on the whole, females are more dependent and passive than males, at least among the white middle class (Sherman 1971). The conclusion is too broad and lends itself to stereotypic interpretations. My research did not even show a sex difference in trait measures of dependency. College females ($N=25$) scored no higher on the Kessler-Passive Dependency Scale than males ($N=25$), nor did females show higher scores on the Succorance Scale of the

Edwards Personal Preference Schedule. This finding is not in keeping with previous studies (Edwards 1959, Spangler and Thomas 1962, Brim et al. 1962). Perhaps in the past the sex difference was more affected by sex stereotypes that required males to seem independent and females to seem dependent. Changing attitudes toward sexual stereotypes may have resulted in a case of disappearing sex difference. Apparently it was mostly the females who changed since they admitted to fewer items on the Need for Succorance Scale. The mean score was at the 27th percentile for college women while the mean of the college males was at the 54th percentile, according to Edwards (1959) norms.

Maccoby and Jacklin (1972) have analyzed the different meanings of the term passive dependency and examined the evidence for sex differences related to various meanings. They found that observation studies show different results from rating studies, raising questions about bias. For this reason they prefer to rely for their conclusions on studies that minimize global ratings.

The dependent child they define as "one who is especially likely to remain near his mother or other adults, ask for help when it is not really needed, seek attention and be upset over separation from the attachment object" (Maccoby and Jacklin 1972:3). They conclude that there is no initial difference between the sexes in this sort of behavior.

But can the Maccoby and Jacklin conclusion be extended to the adult years? Would adult men and women matched in relevant characteristics and circumstances score differently in *behavioral ratings* of dependency behavior? It seems unlikely. Dependency behavior among adults is probably sex typed, at least in traditional settings, with males expressing inability to find the salt in the kitchen and females declining to take responsibility for car repair.

In fact, a general stroke deficit has been noted among women (Wyckoff 1971); that is, women are expected to do considerable nurturing without reciprocation. Thus, because of caste expectations (Freeman 1971), many women find themselves expected to give while not receiving. This situation could create the appearance of women being more "dependent" than men since the male dependency needs would be met while the female needs would not. This state of affairs would be revealed by behavioral ratings of discrete behaviors, but not by questionnaires such as Need for Succorance. Ironically, the Women's Movement has placed upon its leaders a burden equal if not exceeding the expectations of the disciples of Christ. They are to receive neither fame, nor profit, nor even a fair wage from the movement while giving their all—a perfect prescription for a stroke deficit. This attitude results from a lack of recognition of its relationship with sexual caste expectations.

Another aspect of the term passive dependency is passivity or its converse, activity. Contrary to earlier conclusions (Sherman 1971), Maccoby and Jacklin (1972) conclude that male children are not in general more active than female children. Greater activity in the male is limited to "aggression"-producing stimuli—a birthday party of all boys, for example.

In regard to the assertion that boys are more likely to initiate interactions between the sexes, they cite little data but conclude that the patterning of interaction between the sexes is such that females often give cues to indicate their willingness for an encounter. Is the resultant male response evidence of initiative?

This leads to the one generalization that they think is entirely valid: Females are more passive than males in the sense of being more nonaggressive. The terms "aggressive" and "nonaggressive" also have many meanings, but in this case they mean that "the male does have a greater tendency to attack or retaliate in certain interpersonal situations" (Maccoby and Jacklin 1972:11). Note that they add: "we do not know whether this generalizes into any sort of aggressive style of problem-solving in other kinds of situations" (Maccoby and Jacklin 1972:11–12). If I understand them correctly, they wish to differentiate an attack aggressiveness, which they conclude has a biological basis, from an "aggressiveness" in problem solving, which may be a different sort of behavior with different antecedents and consequences. For Maccoby and Jacklin, it would appear that the crucial difference between the sexes lies not in what has been called passive dependency, but in the area of attack aggressiveness. They suggest that this male characteristic may sometimes interfere with close relations with others. Bardwick (1971) comments that boys' "out-of-bounds" behavior forces them to develop independence from adult opinions. Possibly a corollary of the greater attack aggressiveness of males is some greater psychic distance from others, but let us consider this question of aggressiveness in more detail.

Aggressiveness

"Aggressiveness" has multiple meanings and connotations. The term is used to mean self-assertion, describing individuals able to speak up for themselves, able to say no to unreasonable requests. It is used to mean dominance assertion, attempting to be the ruler or the prevailing force. Attack aggression is something different. It refers to a willingness to attack or retaliate in certain interpersonal situations (Maccoby and Jacklin 1972). Aggression may also vary as to whether it is verbal or nonverbal, whether it is expressed using the large muscles or small (e.g., pummeling vs. pinching), and whether it is directed toward an object or a person. If directed toward a person, it will also vary if it does or does not involve physical contact and if the intent is to injure. The term "physical aggression" (Sherman 1971) has been used to refer to body contact emphasizing brusque movements of the large muscles, though not necessarily with the intent to injure. Behaviors like tattling have been called pro-social aggression (Sears, Rau, and Alpert 1965). These different types of aggressiveness might be measured in terms of latency, frequency, amplitude of response, and ease of arousal in the presence of aggressive stimuli.

There is no agreed-upon nomenclature of aggressive behavior, and it is difficult to compare the work and conclusions of various authors. What do the various meanings and usages of "aggressiveness" have in common? Perhaps they are related to the defense and extension of life space. An aggressive act is behavior given as a signal that one's life space has been trespassed or threatened psychologically, symbolically, or physically.* Dominance assertion represents an attempt to extend life space. Life space refers to the physical space and psychological attitudes and behaviors closely attached to the self. The following are types of aggression behaviors which, though not exhaustive, may help clarify discussion.

* In some instances aggressive behavior may be evoked not as a result of actual trespass or threat to life space, but as the outcome of internal cognitive processes that arrive at this conclusion. Moreover, aggressive acts may also occur as a result of abnormal conditions in which rage centers of the brain are stimulated.

A. Verbal (verbal aggression, assertiveness)

B. Involving body contact

    1. Emphasizing large muscles and brusque movements

      a. With intent to produce harm (attack aggression)
      b. Without malicious intent (rough-and-tumble play)

    2. Other sorts of body-contact aggression, e.g., pinching, poisoning, giving an electric shock

C. Involving high-amplitude physical contact with objects closely associated with the opposing life space, e.g., property destruction

D. Arrangement of circumstances to induce harm

    1. Self-righteous acts (pro-social aggression, e.g., tattling)
    2. All manner of subtle destructive acts

E. Fantasy aggression (daydreams, dreams)

It is hypothesized that matched male and female groups will differ in frequency, latency, amplitude of response, or threshold of arousal of response on some of these behaviors and not others. Furthermore, sex differences will be expected in life-space perceptions. Let me briefly indicate the state of evidence relating to these tentative formulations.

A. The sexes are quite similar in verbal aggression as children (Oetzel 1966).

B and C. From the earliest ages of measurement, males make more brusque, large-muscle physical contact with persons and objects whether for sport or malice (Maccoby 1966, Sherman 1971, Maccoby and Jacklin 1972). There is also some evidence that aggression-eliciting stimuli have different effects on men and women (Fischer, Kelm, and Rose 1969). Crimes, especially crimes of personal violence, are much more commonly committed by males than females, though that ratio is decreasing. Still in 1970 the male/female ratio of adult arrests for violent crimes was about 10 to 1 and 4 to 1 for property crimes (Noblit and Burcart 1972).

B (2). Females have not differed from males when directly or indirectly given permission to aggress, especially when the aggression is not an extreme motoric sort (Mallick and McCandless 1966, Leventhal and Shemberg 1969).

D. Evidence suggests that there is less difference between the sexes when the measures of aggression include more indirect forms (Feshbach 1969). Bennett and Cohen (1959) found greater controlled rage, less *overt* aggression, and more covert hostility among large samples of American women than men. Little girls have been described as showing more pro-social aggression than boys (Sears, Rau, and Alpert 1965).

E. There are not many studies of sex differences in fantasy aggression. I know of no studies of daydream differences and the few projective studies in the Oetzel (1966) bibliography split with four results showing more male aggression, one more female aggression, and one no difference. Studies of dreams show no overall sex difference in dream aggression before age twelve, though males show significantly greater "physical" aggression. After age twelve there is a sex difference in overall aggression as well (Hall and Domhoff 1963, Siñán Dominguez Laws 1965).

Money and Ehrhardt (1972) think that dominance assertion may be the crucial variable that differentiates the sexes, rather than "attack aggressiveness." The suggestion is that males more than females attempt to rule, to prevail in situations. Insofar as the dominant authority in society is concerned, Margaret Mead points out that no known society exists in which women have not been subject to the authority of some male, whether it be a father, husband, or brother. She concludes that matriarchy is a pure myth, that it has never existed, though many cultures trace lineage through the mother only (Mead 1958). A study of women aged forty to sixty-five suggests that dominance in women is age related. Older women saw themselves as more dominant than younger women, whom they pictured as sweet, bland, and passive. Men agreed with this general picture (Neugarten 1956). Domination by men is of course the theme of Kate Millet's book *Sexual Politics*.

Money and Ehrhardt (1972) apparently reject the view that males have a greater tendency for attack aggression, on the grounds that human females masculinized prenatally did not show an increase in fighting compared to normal girls. These females, however, have neither a Y chromosome nor the continuing influence of male hormones. Furthermore, those reared as girls would be subject to the cultural proscription of physical aggression common to their sex (Sherman 1971). Money and Ehrhardt (1972) also describe the primary defect of the XYY individual as one of excessive impulsiveness, not attack aggression. The impulsiveness, however, appears to be linked with acts of aggressive violence (Jarvik et al. 1973). More careful study and observation of differences in types of aggressive behavior may help to clarify this question.

What might account for a greater male tendency toward dominance assertion and physical aggressions? Several lines of evidence suggest a biological basis: (1) the association of impulsiveness and/or violence with the Y chromosome; (2) the early appearance of the sex difference in physical aggressiveness; (3) the apparent association between testosterone and dominance assertion in males, and (4) the cross-cultural universality of male dominance.

The third point is based largely on clinical observation rather than systematic studies and may be somewhat shaky in a number of respects. The implication is that because males have more testosterone, they are more dominant. But what if estrogen were to play a similar role among females? Fighting behavior was increased in female mice given estrogens during the neonatal period (Edwards and Herndon 1970). For example, perhaps girls with their ovaries removed before puberty would also grow up more docile and less assertive, as has been reported of their male counterparts. The fact that individuals with Turner's syndrome are thus described suggests that this might be true (Money and Ehrhardt 1972). These individuals have only one X chromosome rather than two, and because their external genitalia look female, they are reared female. They do not have fully functional gonads of either sex, however, and experience a deficit of sex hormones. It could be argued that these individuals are part of a continuum of strength of hormone influence depending upon chromosomes, type and levels of hormones.

Further complexities are introduced by the fact that the relationship between hormones and behavior is a two-way street; attitudes and emotions readily alter hormone functioning (Sherman 1971). Thus, for example, some hormone differences between the sexes may be influenced by sex-stereotypic attitudes, differences in status roles and expectations, and indirect effects of physical differences in size and anatomy.

It is clear that some of the behavioral sex differences stem not from central nervous system effects but from the average greater size and muscular strength of males. Maccoby and Jacklin (1972) include this factor as one of three biologically based factors underlying the traditional status differences between the sexes. The other two factors are greater male dominance assertion and attack aggression, and female childbearing and nursing. It can be appreciated that many biological bases of sex status no longer operate as inexorably or as cogently as in times past, so that the female caste status is increasingly dysfunctional.

So far there has been no discussion of cultural influences in the development of sex differences in attack aggression and dominance assertion. Such influences clearly exist and are strong (Sherman 1971, Joreen n.d.). In general the influence of cultural factors on the development of aggression is considered decisive (Berkowitz 1962). We can safely assume that, biological influences notwithstanding, humans need not be destined to violence; and, in particular, females need not be destined to submission.

What then does one say to the personnel director who hesitates to hire women for management positions because they won't be "aggressive" enough. First of all the director will need to think about the individual woman and man. Second, the director will need to consider what kinds of aggression are necessary to fulfill the job requirements. Careful examination of stereotyped images of job requirements often reveals misconceptions. For example, it might well be that a cooperative individual would be more effective than an "aggressive" one, not to speak of one prone to attack aggression.

Sexuality

Questions regarding sex differences in sexuality have become more acute during this period of rapid change. In recent years a sexual revolution is said to have taken place in this country. Who won the revolution? In spite of the fact that the sexual revolution was highly touted as the sexual emancipation of women, some evidence suggests that it has not been as beneficial to women as some would have us believe. For example, Judith Bardwick (1971) found that almost none of the 150 young women she interviewed reported reaching coital orgasm. This figure is sharply discrepant both with Kinsey figures (Kinsey et al. 1965) and with the figures of the *Playboy* survey (Hunt 1973). In the *Playboy* survey, three-fourths of young women engaging in premarital intercourse had orgasms at least part of the time. Seymour Halleck (1967), however, found that a disproportionate number of the girls coming for psychiatric help were having premarital relations. Another investigator found that a sample of 25 women students in therapy had significantly less social activity but significantly more sexual experience compared to a matched sample of 25 other women (Swenson 1967).

In general the *Playboy* survey found that premarital sex has become both acceptable and widespread and that the change is especially noteworthy in females. People, especially younger ones, are having more sex and more varied sex. Nevertheless, most sexually liberated single girls still feel liberated only within the context of an affectionate or loving relationship. Barbara Seaman (1973) suggests that those who benefit from the social change are those who are able to be highly selective. The girl who is too insecure to refuse what does not appeal to her may be more bewildered and pressured than in the days of greater social and institutional sanctions against sexuality. The easy sex propaganda of the sexual revolution can be twisted into a tool for sexual exploitation of women, with a fun morality substituted for a sin morality. The end effect may also be coercive.

The evidence suggests that female sexuality has been somewhat different from male sexuality in at least three ways (Sherman 1971): (1) the patterning of the development of female sexuality has been different in that sexuality has not become important to women until a later stage; (2) sexual appetite has rarely been as imperative in women as in men; (3) *potential* capacity for orgasm is greater in women than in men. Let us briefly examine each of these propositions.

Perhaps partly because the male genitals are more obvious and accessible than the female genitals, and perhaps partly because of chromosomal, hormonal, anatomical, and cultural factors, boys become strongly interested in sexuality much earlier than girls. Males tend to move from privatized sex to sociosexuality while females have done the reverse and at a later stage of life (Simon and Gagnon 1969). Two independent studies have shown that during adolescence, girls are not especially interested in sex while adolescent boys are consumed with sexual interest (Ehrmann 1959, Douvan and Adelson 1966). During adolescence, girls engage in heterosexual activities primarily for social and not sexual reasons, but this is not true of boys. The Kinsey investigators (1965) found, for example, that petting activity in males and females was very much parallel but that measures of the cumulative incidence of orgasm peaked at ages 16–18 for males, but not until the thirties for females. It remains to be seen how much the greater freedom of young women will change this picture.

Now to the proposition that the male sexual appetite is generally more imperative. If androgens underlie pressure to sexuality for both sexes, and males have more androgens, then males would be expected to have more sex drive. Although logical, this is best regarded as a tentative conclusion for some of the reasons already discussed. By this line of reasoning, part of the greater sex interest of women in later years would be accounted for by the increase of androgens compared to estrogens and progesterone.

Massive amounts of evidence testify that males are more interested in sex than are females. The Kinsey group (1965) described this as a difference in response to "psychological factors." They found a whole host of factors that stimulated women less than men, although the difference between men and women was not absolute. Two to 3 percent of women were more responsive than men; 30 percent were about the same, and the rest were less sexually stimulated by psychological factors than were men. It would appear that men have a lower threshold of sexual arousal; that is, it takes less to arouse men sexually. Again, it will be necessary to check the effect of the sexual revolution on these factors. For example, the *Playboy* survey (Hunt 1973) found a great increase in female response to erotica. Money and Ehrhardt (1972) think that romantic stories are the pornography of females just as visual materials are the pornography of males. It is not clear whether they mean to imply that actual genital-pelvic arousal occurs as frequently for females as males under these conditions. There is again a hint here of female verbal, ear preference compared to male visual preference.

The point has also been made that males' sexual responses are more easily conditioned than are those of females. That is, each sexual experience affects subsequent sexual behavior more for males than is the case for females (Udry 1968). We know that learning generally is more firmly established by reward. Gebhard (1965) explained the fact that many more males than females have sexual "perversions" on the basis that the very high male sex drive more frequently results in one-shot conditioning to the extraneous stimulus properties of the sexual situation, thus setting up the "perversion" habit.

With the exception of Bardwick (1971), there has been general acceptance of the view that women have more orgastic capacity than men (Masters and Johnson 1966). That is, after an orgasm, women can again immediately engage in sexual activity leading to another orgasm while men usually cannot. This finding has generated the speculation that sexuality in women might be insatiable (Sherfey 1966). Some fear and concern has even been expressed in this regard. Such fears are groundless. The big change in women's acceptance of sexuality came at an earlier time, and the rate of change has slowed in recent years. Comparative data is not available on many points, but in 1929 (Davis 1929) 67 percent of a sample of married women indicated that they preferred less frequent sex; in 1953, only 16 percent of a sample of married women preferred less sex (Burgess and Wallin 1953) while the figure was only 6 percent in 1966 (Bell, 1966). The big change, over 2 percent a year, occurred from 1929 to 1953, while the rate of change was only half that during the years from 1953 to 1966. Admittedly, data on how many wives want more sex would be more to the point. It will be interesting to see the comparisons of the Kinsey and *Playboy* survey data.

As far as orgasm is concerned, the Kinsey group (1965) estimated that the average woman has an orgasm in 70 to 77 percent of marital coitus, increasing from 63 percent the first year to 85 percent the twentieth year of marriage. The *Playboy* survey found the great majority of married women always or almost always have coital orgasms (Hunt 1973). Johnson and Masters (1964) stress fatigue and preoccupation as the most frequent reasons for absence of female coital orgasm. Gebhard (1966) estimated that neurophysiologic and unconscious psychological factors account for only five to ten percentage points' variation in orgasm capacity. The importance of duration of foreplay and coitus was accentuated by his finding that the likelihood of coital orgasm greatly increased with the duration of foreplay (over 20 minutes) and the duration of intercourse (over 16 minutes).

Emotionality

The question of sex differences in emotionality has often been invidiously used against women. Generally, when we refer to someone as emotional, we mean that their emotions are excessive for the situation, or that their emotions change drastically without obvious reason. Emotionality also tends to imply maladjustment. Are women more maladjusted than men? The answer is no, according to the conclusion of an extensive mental health survey in midtown Manhattan. The survey concluded that there is no difference in the overall psychological adjustment of the two sexes (Srole et al. 1962). There are, however, differences in the styles of maladjustment. Many more men than women commit suicide; more men are alcoholics; more men are drug addicts; more men commit crimes (Howard and

Howard 1974). Men have been found to score higher than women on a measure of psychoticism (Eysenck and Eysenck 1969). I cite these facts about men in order to cast this matter in its proper perspective. Not long ago, a political official suggested that women were not fit for high office because they are subject to "emotional storms." Men, too, have their emotional weaknesses. It would be a valid generalization to say that the male style of maladjustment shows more attack aggression and acts against other people, while the female style shows more fear and personal discontent. Emotionality, however, has come to be defined by measures of fear and personal discontent. This appears to be an example of sex bias; surely rage is just as much an emotion as fear.

Massive amounts of data indicate that women are more fearful and anxious (Sherman 1971). These data, however, are based largely on interviews or questionnaires that have little control for the individual's willingness to reveal. In other words, the data are basically derived from asking people either in person or on paper whether or not they are "nervous." The apparently greater fearfulness of females is partly the result of boys learning that they are not supposed to admit fear or anxiety. Direct observation and study of infants and children from the age of one month to eight years failed to show any sex difference in average fearfulness (Bronson 1969). Moreover, in answering questionnaires about fears and anxiety, no difference was found between the sexes in the first grade; but in later years, the difference between the sexes widened along with a measurable increase in defensiveness among the boys (Hill and Sarason 1966). Other studies show that the apparent sex difference in fearfulness does not appear when more subtle measures are used (Bendig 1959, D'Andrade 1966, Wilson 1966). It was also found that the proportion of men to women willing to admit to a particular fear was significantly related to its social acceptability (Wilson 1967). In other words, the most accurate way to describe the sex difference in fearfulness and anxiety is to say that after age seven, females are more willing than males to *admit* and display fear and anxiety.

It has been argued that women are innately more emotionally unstable since they go through more hormonal changes than do men (Terman and Tyler 1954). It has been shown that females respond to stress with more physiological reaction in the autonomic nervous system and that they show a quicker physiological recovery from stress (Sontag 1947, Berry and Martin 1957). It cannot be assumed that there is a one-to-one relationship between a particular physiological state and a particular emotional state. Schachter (1964), in a now famous experiment, has shown that the same underlying physiological state may be labeled in different ways depending upon cognitive and contextual factors. That is, the emotions and individual experiences are not simply determined by physiological state, but are highly influenced by what the person is thinking and how the person perceives the situation. This finding points up exciting new possibilities for women to gain more control over their bodies. Women who are more knowledgeable about the physiological changes of their bodies will be in a far better position to make accurate cognitive interpretations of these changes. For example, if a woman knows she feels lousy because her menstrual period is coming next week, she is less likely to think that she feels lousy because her children are misbehaving and hence she is less likely to overreact to them. There is some evidence that extreme reactions *are* lessened when women are aware of their cyclic bodily changes (Tonks et al. 1968).

Am I suggesting that women are indeed subject to "emotional storms"? Let us again be sure that this question is viewed in light of the fact that there is no overall difference in the emotional adjustment of the sexes. The next point that should be made clear is that "emotional storms" is much too strong a phrase. There is evidence of discernible changes in emotional state that accompany the menstrual cycle, pregnancy, childbirth, and menopause. There is no good evidence that these events have any important adverse effects on women's performance level. For example, there is no consistent effect of menstruation either on absenteeism or industrial efficiency (Smith 1950a, b), and there is no evidence of general impairment in intellectual functioning (Seward 1946, Wickham 1958). An extensive review is given elsewhere (Sherman 1971). For an illustration of either sex bias, poor scholarship, or both in connection with this question, see Tiger and Fox (1971).

At this point it might be well to describe in more detail the emotional changes under discussion. During the menstrual cycle there is evidence of increased tension during the premenstrual week, during the first day or two of menstruation, and at mid-cycle, at the time of ovulation (Sherman 1971). The best known of these tension periods is called premenstrual tension. This has been defined as irritability, depression, and swelling of the body, and it is estimated to occur in 39 percent of women (Sutherland and Steward 1965).

The causes of cyclic changes are a matter of controversy. Psychoanalysts have attributed them variously to inability to accept one's femininity, fear of pregnancy, frustration of pregnancy wishes, and the like. Several studies show a relationship between unwholesome attitudes toward menstruation and menstrual symptoms, but the evidence does not permit the conclusion that the attitudes *caused* the menstrual symptoms (Sherman 1971). In recent years there seems to have been a switch away from the psychogenic view of premenstrual tension, and emphasis has been placed on physiological causes of the cyclic symptoms. These have been summarized by Katharina Dalton (1964) as water retention, allergic phenomena, hypoglycemia or low blood sugar, and capillary fragility. A hypoglycemic attack is characterized by trembling, weakness, faintness, irritability; it may be mistaken for an attack of anxiety. It is interesting to note that a well-controlled study showed significant improvement in 79 percent of women given a high-protein diet to counteract the hypoglycemia and diuretic pills to counteract the tendency to retain water (Morton et al. 1953). This evidence has led me to conclude that while some women's attitudes may have adverse effects on their menstrual functioning, many discomforts of the menstrual cycle are physiologically based.

Even less is definitively known about emotional changes accompanying other biological events of a woman's lifetime. One expert has characterized pregnancy as a time of "vegetative calm" (Benedek 1959), but more careful observation shows that at least the last six weeks of pregnancy are a time of increased tension (Grimm 1961). After childbirth, it is estimated that 30 percent of normal women have some emotional upset (Gordon and Gordon 1959), popularly known as the "baby blues." A husband-and-wife team, Katharine and Richard Gordon, found such factors as insufficient help and rest, change of residence, and absence of the husband were significantly associated with emotional disturbance following childbirth. Based on their findings, the Gordons provided advice and guidance to a group of new mothers and found that only 2 percent of them had emotional problems at the half-year mark, compared to 28 percent of a group of control mothers (Gordon and

Gordon 1960). The babies of the instructed mothers were significantly less irritable, and had fewer feeding and sleeping problems. The beneficial results could still be statistically shown four to six years later in both the mother and child. This is an example of what can be done for women and an example of the kind of precise knowledge and caring that makes a difference.

There also is surprisingly little good information about the effects of menopause. The existing evidence, however, suggests that menopause is not *the big event* in the lives of most women during their middle years (Neugarten 1968). As far as emotional symptoms during menopause are concerned, menopausal women experience more irritability, nervousness, and depression than nonmenopausal women of the same age (Neugarten and Kraines 1965). On the other hand, emotional symptoms were fewer at menopause than at adolescence, for example. In other words, emotional symptoms were not conclusively more common at menopause than at other age periods. Moreover, women aged 55–64 reported unusual tranquility.

An English study found that 90 percent of women were never incapacitated by symptoms they attributed to menopause; 14 percent of them reported no symptoms at all, and 21 percent had only hot flushes. Thirty-one percent reported nervous instability (Barrett et al. 1933). Hormone-replacement treatment for postmenopause has received considerable attention in recent years, but insufficient data are available to draw definite conclusions about the indications and advisability of such treatment. Once again, a glaring need for more research is apparent.

Is there then anything to be done about hormonally related emotional changes in women? Because such questions are so prone to misinterpretation, let me indicate once more that these emotional changes in women should be considered as a nuisance, not as a misfortune or disaster. Nonetheless, it is well to keep nuisances under control. There is a need for more education among women about their bodily functioning. As I have indicated, women who are aware of emotional changes related to biological events will be in a much better position to cope with them. Additionally, some information is already available regarding how best to cope with the effects of menstuation and childbirth. This kind of information could be much more widely disseminated.

Analytical Ability

The belief that women have inadequate analytical ability has been used to justify women's exclusion from important positions in society. This belief appears to underlie the thinking of many who accept women only reluctantly into research-oriented academic departments. This belief often underlies objections to Women's Studies programs, which are seen as nonacademic and lacking in "solid" intellectual content. Women are considered intellectually inadequate, unproductive, and uncreative until they decisively prove otherwise. In some instances this has meant that their acceptance as regular members of an academic department has been delayed until they have acquired international reputations. In most instances, women have not even had the opportunity to prove themselves. Scientists and liberals are often not scientific, liberal, or even merely fair.

Most people are aware that the consensus among scientists is that, in general, no difference exists between the sexes in intellectual ability. *In general* this is true.

When it comes to specifics, however, agreement is not so apparent. A 1968 review of the scientific literature has concluded that males are superior in abstract and logical thinking (Garai and Scheinfeld 1968). In my opinion, the evidence does not support a broad conclusion that includes either abstraction or analysis in the verbal area. Almost all the evidence that males are superior in analytical ability rests on tasks involving analysis of spatial problems. There is consensual agreement among scholars that, on the average, women perform more poorly than men on spatial tasks, though some think there is only a "true" difference on the spatial task of visualization, the ability to imagine relationships as they change in space. It should be remembered that while women on the average do not perform as well on spatial tasks as do men, individual women may perform very well, better than most men. Also, spatial skill and verbal skill are not much related, and it is the latter that predicts general intellectual achievement. Moreover, the difference between the sexes in spatial skill cannot begin to account for the exclusion of women from whole areas of study (Kogan 1972).

During the preschool years, girls appear to be superior to boys in space perception, with a shift in favor of males occurring about age six (Coates 1973) and commonly found by age eight; during adolescence, the difference between the sexes in space perception apparently widens (Sherman 1971). On the average, males show a superior performance in aspects of geometry, mathematical problem solving, engineering, architecture, and the mathematical and physical sciences (Sherman 1971). There is some evidence that one of the reasons for an average male superior performance in these areas is the matter of superior skill in spatial analysis. However, these activities are sex typed for men. Performance in mathematical problem solving can be improved by a pep talk to the effect that it is all right for women to excel in mathematical problem solving (Carey 1955). On the other hand, changing a test of spatial skill to make it more appealing to females did not improve their scores (Castore and Stafford 1970). Recent data collected by myself and Elizabeth Fennema suggest that sex differences in spatial visualization and mathematics achievement are another example of disappearing sex differences. Our data also showed the importance of socio-cultural factors in producing apparent intellectual sex differences.

The greater "passivity" and "dependency" of women might incline them to take a less analytical approach (Maccoby 1966). As previously indicated, it is no longer apparent that women are indeed more "passive" and "dependent." The same sample of Wisconsin undergraduates who failed to show a sex difference in "passive dependency" also did not differ on measures of analytical cognitive approach, the Rod-and-Frame test, the Embedded Figures test, or the Draw-A-Person test, though they did differ on the Spatial test of the Differential Aptitude test. The former tests have been thought to be more influenced by personality factors, though only one of six possible correlations between these measures and the dependency measures was significant. For females, this correlation occurred between the Succorance Scale of the Edwards Personal Preference Schedule and the Rod-and-Frame test. The latter test is very disquieting to some people who dislike dark rooms and find themselves not knowing up from down in the blackness of the experimental conditions. Neville (1972) demonstrated a relationship between dependency arousal and decrement in Rod-and-Frame performance among females, but not males. Curiously the effect of manifest anxiety on RFT performance does not appear to have been studied, though many studies contrast various psychiatric diagnostic groups.

Perhaps part of the reason women do more poorly on spatial tasks is that they are less experienced in making spatial judgments (Sherman 1967, 1971). Although the fact that females appear to be equal or ahead of males until about age six (Coates 1973) would seem to contradict this hypothesis, it may be that the effects of differential sex-typed activities must accumulate to have their effect. Many possibly relevant games and activities occupy males more than females: blocks, aiming games, construction toys, model construction, working with machines, direction finding, map reading, courses in mechanical drawing, analytical geometry, science and mathematics generally. There is evidence (Sherman 1967, 1971, 1974) that practice improves performance on spatial tasks, though the evidence has not been sufficient to convince scholars generally that this is true. For example, in one study, even though the women performed better with training, the investigator decided that they had not really learned because even when they made the correct response, they said it seemed wrong (Witkin 1948). While part of this disagreement is a philosophical one related to the differences between learning theory and Gestalt theory, more research should establish the point that individuals can significantly improve their performance on spatial tasks. In fact, contrary to earlier conclusions, my samples of Wisconsin undergradutes showed significant improvement with simple practice on the Rod-and-Frame test (Sherman 1974).

Aside from the dependency and practice hypotheses of this sex difference in spatial analysis, there are several others. It has been proposed that boys become more "analytical" because they must figure out their sex-role requirements while girls need only copy their mothers who do simpler things and are more often around as a model (Lynn 1969a, b). The idea is that boys develop an early edge in problem solving because they have more of a problem in learning their sex role. However, there is some direct evidence contradicting this hypothesis (Kohlberg and Zigler 1967). Another explanation, sharply criticized by Parlee (1972), rests on the idea that estrogens are more potent activating agents than are androgens (Broverman et al. 1968).

Other explanations include the possibility that more men than women inherit at least one form of spatial ability (Stafford 1961, Hartlage 1970, Bock and Kolakowski 1973). The hypothesis is that a recessive gene (for superior spatial ability) is carried on the X chromosome. Thus, individuals with only one X chromosome (Turner's syndrome) should be more likely to show superior space perception. Instead the opposite is true (Garron 1970). Bock and Kolakowski (1973) offer an explanation to reconcile these apparently contradictory findings. Sex differences in the development of cerebral dominance for verbal and spatial functions have also been hypothesized, but none of at least three different competing hypotheses has clear empirical support. (Buffery and Gray 1972, Maccoby and Jacklin 1972, Sherman 1974). In much of the literature on lateralization of cerebral function, it has been assumed that what is true for one sex is true for the other. Furthermore, sex of subjects is often not reported and data are not analyzed separately by sex. Researchers in this area need to be more alert to the factor of sex as well as handedness.

If it is true that verbal skill is sex preferred for females and space perception is the sex-preferred male skill, then the history of education is really the history of how to educate males (Sherman 1971). We have been willing to go to great lengths to teach boys to speak correctly, read, and spell. One cannot but wonder what the effect would be if the same amount of effort were spent on intensive training in spatial skills and problem solving for girls. What I am suggesting is that the whole structure of the educational system may be much more directed toward maximal male achievement than has been realized.

In summary, I have tried to present briefly an examination of some characteristics thought to be important in the differences between the sexes. It seems, however, that progress is outrunning research. Many apparent sex differences now appear illusory. It might be well to take the bull by the horns and attempt to establish some commonly valued characteristics for both sexes. These would be characteristics of what one could call simply the "mature" personality, though a better name may be found. Broverman and her colleagues (1972) found that the positively valued masculine traits entail competence, rationality, and assertion while the positively valued feminine traits form a cluster reflecting warmth and expressiveness. Perhaps this can point the way, for both sexes, to a new ideal personality having the capacities of both strength, rationality, and emotional resonance. Rather than focusing on which is better, male "traits" or female "traits," or proving that women are just as good as men, we may do better by deciding what we value in people and how these values can be developed. Rather than focus on traits we may do better to focus on what behaviors are effective for what tasks. For example, questions have arisen about the desirability of women being analytical. There are those who say that, given a chance, women can analyze as well as men. There are others who contend that women think differently from men. They believe that women are more intuitive and perceptive, and that this is good. Most anyone would agree that it is undesirable to think in a concrete and illogical manner, but if the words and phrases are turned in a different way, they would not be so sure that it is well for women to be abstract and analytical. The ideal goal for both sexes may be the ability to be both analytical and intuitive. Some problems can be solved best in one way, some in another. Intuition is a poor guide in constructing a bridge, and logic a useless tool in understanding a dream. The ability to go back and forth between these two approaches often marks the most fruitful intellectual activity.

The tasks for women scholars are many: redefine the past, cope with the present, and soar into the future. In the past psychology has constructed the female; now females must reconstruct psychology.

REFERENCES

BARDWICK, JUDITH M. *Psychology of Women: A Study of Biocultural Conflicts.* New York: Harper & Row, 1971.

BARRETT, L.; CULLIS, W.; FAIRFIELD, L.; AND NICHOLSON, R. "Investigations of the Menopause in 1000 Women." *Lancet* 1 (1933): 106–8.

BELL, R. R. *Premarital Sex in a Changing Society.* Englewood Cliffs, N.J.: Prentice-Hall, 1966.

BENDIG, A. W. "College Norms for and Concurrent Validity of Cattell's IPAT Anxiety Scale." *Psychological Newsletter of New York University* 10 (1959): 263–67.

BENEDEK, THERESE. "Sexual Function in Women and Their Disturbance." In *American Handbook of Psychiatry*, edited by Silvano Arieti. New York: Basic Books, 1959. Pp. 726–48.

BENNETT, E. M., AND COHEN, L. R. "Men and Women: Personality Patterns and Contrasts." *Genetic Psychology Monographs* 59 (1959): 101–55.

BERKOWITZ, LEONARD. *Aggression: A Social Psychological Analysis.* New York: McGraw-Hill, 1962.

BERNARD, JESSIE. "Sex Differences: An Overview." Paper presented at the meeting of the American Association for the Advancement of Science, December 1972.

BERRY, J. L., AND MARTIN, B. "GSR Reactivity as a Function of Anxiety, Instructions, and Sex." *Journal of Abnormal and Social Psychology* 54 (1957): 9–12.

BOCK, R. D., AND KOLAKOWSKI, D. "Further Evidence of Sex-linked Major-gene Influence on Human Spatial Visualization Ability." *American Journal of Human Genetics* 25 (1973): 1–14.

BRIM, O. G.; GLASS, D. C.; LAVIN, D. E.; AND GOODMAN, N. *Personality and Decision Processes.* Stanford: Stanford University Press, 1962.

BRONSON, GORDON. "Fear of Visual Novelty: Developmental Patterns in Males and Females." *Developmental Psychology* 2 (1969): 33–40.

BROVERMAN, D. M.; KLAIBER, E. L.; KOBAYASHI, Y.; AND VOGEL, W. "Roles of Activation and Inhibition in Sex Differences in Cognitive Abilities." *Psychological Review* 75 (1968): 23–50.

BROVERMAN, INGE K.; VOGEL, SUSAN R.; BROVERMAN, DONALD; CLARKSON, FRANK; AND ROSENKRANTZ, PAUL. "Sex-role Stereotypes: A Current Appraisal." *Journal of Social Issues* 28 (1972): 59–78.

BUFFERY, A. W. H., AND GRAY, J. A. "Sex Differences in the Development of Spatial and Linguistic Skills." In *Gender Differences, Their Ontogeny and Significance*, edited by C. Ounsted and D. C. Taylor. London: Churchill, 1972.

BURGESS, ERNEST W., AND WALLIN, PAUL. *Engagement and Marriage.* Philadelphia: Lippincott, 1953.

CAREY, G. L. "Reduction of Sex Difference in Problem Solving by Improvement of Attitude through Group Discussion." Ph.D. dissertation, Stanford University, 1955.

CASTORE, C. H., AND STAFFORD, R. "Effect of Sex Role on Performance." *Journal of Psychology* 74 (1970): 175–80.

CHILDS, B. "Genetic Origins of Some Sex Differences among Human Beings." *Pediatrics* 35 (1965): 798–812.

COATES, SUSAN. "Sex Differences in Field Independence among Pre-school Children." In *The Psychology of Sex Differences*, edited by R. Friedman et al. New York: Wiley, 1974.

DALTON, KATHARINA. *The Premenstrual Syndrome.* London: Heineman, 1964.

D'ANDRADE, ROY. "Sex Differences and Cultural Institutions." In *The Development of Sex Differences*, edited by Eleanor E. Maccoby. Stanford: Stanford University Press, 1966.

DAVID, KATHARINE B. *Factors in the Sex Life of Twenty-two Hundred Women.* New York: Harper, 1929.

DAVIDSON, JULIAN M., AND LEVINE, SEYMOUR. "Endocrine Regulation of Behavior." *Annual Review of Physiology* 34 (1972): 375–409.

DAWSON, JOHN. "Effects of Sex Hormones in Cognitive Style in Rats and Men." *Behavior Genetics* 2 (1972): 21–42.

DOUVAN, ELIZABETH, AND ADELSON, JOSEPH. *The Adolescent Experience*. New York: Wiley, 1966.

EDWARDS, ALLEN L. *Edwards Personal Preference Schedule*. New York: Psychological Corporation, 1959.

EDWARDS, DAVID A., AND HERNDON, JAMES. "Neonatal Estrogen Stimulation and Aggressive Behavior in Female Mice." *Physiology and Behavior* 5 (1970): 993–95.

EHRMANN, WINSTON. *Premarital Dating Behavior*. New York: Henry Holt, 1959.

EYSENCK, S. B., AND EYSENCK, H. J. "Scores of Three Personality Variables as a Function of Age, Sex, and Social Class." *British Journal of Social and Clinical Psychology* 8 (1969): 69–76.

FESHBACH, NORMA. "Sex Differences in Children's Aggressive Responses toward Outsiders." *Merrill-Palmer Quarterly* 15 (1969): 249–58.

FISCHER, D. G.; KELM, H.; AND ROSE, A. "Knives as Aggression-eliciting Stimuli." *Psychological Reports* 24 (1969): 755–60.

FREEMAN, J. "The Legal Basis of the Sexual Caste System." *Valparaiso University Law Review* 5 (1971): 203–36.

GARAI, JOSEF E., AND SCHEINFELD, AMRAM. "Sex Differences in Mental and Behavioral Traits." *Genetic Psychology Monographs* 77 (1968): 169–299.

GARRON, DAVID. "Sex-linked, Recessive Inheritance of Spatial and Numerical Abilities, and Turner's Syndrome." *Psychological Review* 77 (1970): 147–52.

GEBHARD, PAUL. "Factors in Marital Orgasm." *Journal of Social Issues* 22 (1966): 88–95.

GEBHARD, PAUL. "Situational Factors Affecting Human Sexual Behavior." In *Sex and Behavior*, edited by Frank A. Beach. New York: Wiley, 1965.

GORDON, R. E., AND GORDON, K. K. *The Split-Level Trap*. New York: Bernard Geis, 1960.

GORDON, R. E., AND GORDON, K. K. "Social Factors in the Prediction and Treatment of Emotional Disorders of Pregnancy." *American Journal of Obstetrics and Gynecology* 77 (1959): 1074–83.

GRIMM, ELAINE. "Psychologic Tension in Pregnancy." *Psychosomatic Medicine* 23 (1961): 520–27.

HALL, CALVIN, AND DOMHOFF, BILL. "Aggression in Dreams." *International Journal of Social Psychiatry* 9 (1963): 259–67.

HALLECK, SEYMOUR. "Sex and Mental Health on the Campus." *Journal of the American Medical Association* 200 (1967): 648–90.

HARTLAGE, L. D. "Sex-linked Inheritance of Spatial Ability." *Perceptual Motor Skills* 31 (1970): 610.

HARTUP, W. W. "Dependence and Independence." In *Child Psychology*, edited by H. W. Stevenson. Chicago: University of Chicago Press, 1963.

HILL, K. T., AND SARASON, S. B. "The Relation of Text Anxiety and Defensiveness to Test and School Performance over the Elementary-school Years: A Further Longitudinal Study." *Monographs of the Society for Research in Child Development* 31 (1966).

HOWARD, E. M., AND HOWARD, J. L. "Women in Institutions: Treatment in Prisons and Mental Hospitals." In *Women in Therapy: New Psychotherapies for a Changing Society*, edited by V. Franks and V. Burttle. New York: Bruner/Mazel, 1974. Pp. 357–82.

HUNT, MORTON. "Sexual Behavior in the 1970s." *Playboy*, October 1973.

JARVIK, L. F.; KLODIN, V.; AND MATSUYAMA, S. S. "Human Aggression and the Extra Y Chromosome: Fact or Fantasy?" *American Psychologist* (1973): 674–82.

JOHNSON, M. M. "Sex Role Learning in the Nuclear Family." *Child Development* 23 (1963): 319–34.

JOHNSON, VIRGINIA, AND MASTERS, WILLIAM. "Sexual Incompatibility: Diagnosis and Treatment." In *Human Reproduction and Sexual Behavior*, edited by Charles W. Lloyd. Philadelphia: Lea & Febiger, 1964.

JOREEN. "The Bitch Manifesto." Distributed by Know, n.d.

KAGAN, J. "Acquisition and Significance of Sex Typing and Sex Role Identity." In *Review of Child Development Research*, edited by M. L. Hoffman and Lois W. Hoffman. New York: Russell Sage Foundation, 1964. Pp. 137–67.

KENNEDY, B. J. "Effect of Massive Doses of Sex Hormones on Libido." *Medical Aspects of Human Sexuality* 7 (1973): 66.

KINSEY, A.; POMEROY, W. B.; MARTIN, C. E.; AND GEBHARD, P. *Sexual Behavior in the Human Female.* New York: Pocket Books, 1965.

KOGAN, NATHAN. "Sex Differences in Creativity and Cognitive Styles." Paper presented at the meeting of the Invitational Conference on Cognitive Styles and Creativity in Higher Education sponsored by the Graduate Record Examinations Board, November 1972.

KOHLBERG, L. "A Cognitive-developmental Analysis of Children's Sex-role Concepts and Attitudes." In *The Development of Sex Differences*, edited by Eleanor Maccoby. Stanford: Stanford University Press, 1966. Pp. 82–173.

KOHLBERG, L., AND ZIGLER, E. "The Impact of Cognitive Maturity on the Development of Sex-role Attitudes in the Years 4 to 8." *Genetic Psychology Monographs* 75 (1967): 89–165.

LEVANTHAL, D. B., AND SHEMBERG, K. M. "Sex Role Adjustment and Nonsanctioned Aggression." *Journal of Experimental Research in Personality* 3 (1969): 283–86.

LYNN, DAVID. "Curvilinear Relation between Cognitive Functioning and Distance of Child from Parent of Same Sex." *Psychological Review* 76 (1969a): 236–40.

LYNN, DAVID. *Parental and Sex Role Identification: A Theoretical Formulation.* Berkeley: McCutchen, 1969b.

MACCOBY, ELEANOR, ed. *The Development of Sex Differences.* Stanford: Stanford University Press, 1966.

MACCOBY, ELEANOR E., AND JACKLIN, CAROL NAGY. "Sex Differences in Intellectual Functioning." Paper presented at the meeting of the Educational Testing Service Invitational Conference on Testing Problems, October 1972.

MACCOBY, ELEANOR, AND MASTERS, JOHN. "Attachment and Dependency." In *Carmichael's Manual of Child Psychology*, edited by Paul Mussen. New York: Wiley, 1970.

MALLICK, SHAHBAZ, AND McCANDLESS, B. "A Study of Catharsis of Aggression." *Journal of Personality and Social Psychology* 4 (1966): 591–96.

MASTERS, WILLIAM, AND JOHNSON, VIRGINIA. *Human Sexual Response.* Boston: Little, Brown, 1966.

MEAD, MARGARET. In *Discussions on Child Development*, edited by J. M. Tanner and Barbel Inhelder. New York: International Universities Press, 1958.

MISCHEL, W. *Personality and Assessment.* New York: Wiley, 1968.

MONEY, JOHN, AND EHRHARDT, ANKE. *Man & Woman: Boy & Girl.* Baltimore, Md.: Johns Hopkins Press, 1972.

MORTON, J. H.; ADDITION, H.; ADDISON, R. G.; HUNT, L.; AND SULLIVAN, J. J. "A Clinical

Study of Premenstrual Tension." *American Journal of Obstetrics and Gynecology* 65 (1953): 1182–91.

MYRDAL, GUNNAR. "How Scientific Are the Social Sciences?" *Journal of Social Issues* 28 (1972): 151–70.

NEUGARTEN, BERNICE, AND GUTTMAN, DAVID. "Age-Sex Roles and Personality in Middle Age: A Thematic Apperception Study." In *Middle Age and Aging*, edited by B. L. Neugarten. Chicago: University of Chicago Press, 1968. Pp. 58–71.

NEUGARTEN, B. "Adult Personality: Toward a Psychology of the Life Cycle." In *Middle Age and Aging*, edited by Bernice L. Neugarten. Chicago: University of Chicago Press, 1968. Pp. 137–47.

NEUGARTEN, B. AND KRAINES, RUTH. "Menopausal Symptoms in Women of Various Ages." *Psychosomatic Medicine* 27 (1965): 266–73.

NEVILL, D. D. "Experimental Manipulation of Dependency Motivation and Its Effects on Eye Contact and Measures of Field Dependency." Ph.D. dissertation, University of Florida, 1971. Ann Arbor, Mich.: University Microfilms, 1971. No. 72-16-639.

NOBLIT, GEORGE, AND BURCART, JANIE. "Crime and Women in America: Some Preliminary Trends of a Decade (1960–70)." Paper presented at the meeting of the Pacific Sociological Association, Spring 1973.

OETZEL, ROBERTA. "Annotated Bibliography." In *The Development of Sex Differences*, edited by Eleanor E. Maccoby. Stanford: Stanford University Press, 1966.

PARLEE, MARY. Comments on "Roles of Activation and Inhibition in Sex Differences in Cognitive Abilities" by D. M. Broverman, E. L. Klaiber, Y. Kobayshi, and W. Vogel. *Psychological Review* 79 (1972): 180–84.

PARSONS, TALCOTT, AND BALES, R. *Family Socialization and Interaction Process.* Glencoe, Ill.: Free Press, 1955.

RAMEY, ESTELLE. "Sex Hormones and Executive Ability." *Annals of the New York Academy of Sciences* 208 (1973): 237–45.

SCHACHTER, S. In *Psychobiological Approaches to Social Behavior*, edited by P. H. Leiderman and D. Shapiro. Stanford: Stanford University Press, 1964.

SCHEINFELD, AMRAM. *Women and Men.* New York: Harcourt Brace, 1944.

SEAMAN, BARBARA. *Free and Female.* Greenwich, Conn.: Fawcett, 1973.

SEARS, R.; RAU, L.; AND ALPERT, R. *Identification and Child Rearing.* Stanford: Stanford University Press, 1965.

SEWARD, GEORGENE. *Sex and the Social Order.* New York: McGraw-Hill, 1946.

SHERFEY, MARY JANE. "The Evolution and Nature of Female Sexuality in Relation to Psychoanalytic Theory." *Journal of the American Psychoanalytic Association* 14 (1966): 28–128.

SHERMAN, JULIA. "Field Articulation, Sex, Spatial Visualization, Dependency, Practice, Laterality of the Brain and Birth Order." *Perceptual and Motor Skills* 38 (1974): 1223–35.

SHERMAN, JULIA. *On the Psychology of Women: A Survey of Empirical Studies.* Springfield, Ill.: Charles C Thomas, 1971.

SHERMAN, JULIA. "Problem of Sex Differences in Space Perception and Aspects of Intellectual Functioning." *Psychological Review* 74 (1967): 290–99.

SIMON, W., AND GAGNON, J. "On Psychosexual Development." In *Handbook of Socialization Theory and Research*, edited by David A. Goslin. Chicago: Rand McNally, 1969. Pp. 733–52.

Siñán Dominguez Laws, Ruth. "Estudio psicológico de la agresión, desgracias, actos amistosos y buena suerte, en los sueños de un grupo de niños mexicanos." (Psychological study of aggression, misfortunes, friendly acts, and good luck in the dreams of a group of Mexican children.) *Archivos Panameños de Psicologia* 1 (1965): 281–351. Abstract in *Psychological Abstracts.*

Smith, Anthony. "Menstruation and Industrial Efficiency: I, Absenteeism and Activity Level." *Journal of Applied Psychology* 34 (1950a): 145.

Smith, Anthony. "Menstruation and Industrial Efficiency: II, Quality and Quantity of Production." *Journal of Applied Psychology* 34 (1950b): 148–52.

Sontag, L. W. "Physiological Factors and Personality in Children." *Child Development* 18 (1957): 185–89.

Spangler, D. P., and Thomas, C. W. "The Effects of Age, Sex, and Physical Disability upon Manifest Needs." *Journal of Counseling Psychology* 9 (1962): 313–19.

Srole, Leo; Langer, T.; Michael, S.; Opler, M.; and Rennie, T. *Mental Health in the Metropolis.* New York: McGraw-Hill, 1962.

Stein, Aletha Huston, and Smithells, Jancis. "Age and Sex Differences in Children's Sex-Role Standards about Achievement." *Developmental Psychology* 1 (1969): 252–59.

Sutherland, H., and Stewart, I. "A Critical Analysis of the Premenstrual Syndrome." *Lancet* 1 (1965): 1180–83.

Swenson, C. "Sexual Behavior and Psychopathology: A Test of Mowrer's Hypothesis." *Journal of Clinical Psychology* 18 (1967): 406–9.

Tavris, Carol. " 'Harry, you are going to go down in history as the father of the cloth mother': A Conversation by Way of Collision," with Harry F. Harlow. *Psychology Today*, April 1973, p. 65.

Terman, L., and Tyler, Leona. "Psychological Sex Differences." In *Manual of Child Psychology*, edited by L. Carmichael. 2nd ed. New York: Wiley, 1954.

Tiger, L., and Fox, R. *The Imperial Animal.* New York: Holt, Rinehart & Winston, 1971.

Tonks, C. M.; Rack, P. H.; and Rose, M. J. "Attempted Suicide and the Menstrual Cycle." *Journal of Psychosomatic Research* 11 (1968): 319–23.

Udry, J. R., and Morris, N. M. "Distribution of Coitus in the Menstrual Cycle." *Nature* 220 (1968): 593–96.

Wickham, M. "The Effects of the Menstrual Cycle on Test Performance." *British Journal of Psychology* 49 (1958): 34–41.

Wilson, G. D. "Social Desirability and Sex Differences in Expressed Fear." *Behavior Research and Therapy* 5 (1967): 136–37.

Witkin, H. A. "The Effect of Training and of Structural Aids on Performance in Three Tests of Space Orientation." Report No. 80, Division of Research, Civil Aeronautics Association, Washington, D.C., 1948.

Wyckoff, Hogie. "The Stroke Economy in Women's Scripts." *Transactional Analysis Journal* 1 (1971): 16–20.

7

On Feminine Self-Presentation in Groups*
Jane Allyn Piliavin

A great deal is being written lately about the changing social roles of men and women. This is only to be expected. During the course of any social change, members of those groups affected by it generally become self-conscious about their behavior and the behavior of other groups toward them. Nevertheless, although most writers on this topic seem to be confident that they know the ingredients of woman's "traditional role" and our culture's expectations concerning male and female social interactions, this confidence may be ill-founded. Of course we do at times find blatant examples of clear role violations, for example, when a group of liberationists went to a construction site for the purpose of whistling at the well-muscled, attractive, shirtless construction workers to make them uncomfortable and to make a point. And men sometimes find it fun to comment on little specific behaviors we all see as sex-typed, for example, to ask in mock confusion "Am I still supposed to light your cigarettes now that you're liberated?"

In fact, when one sets out to look for information on perceptions of "appropriate sex roles," it is remarkable how little there is. What *is* expected of men and women in our society? How do men and women perceive their own personalities and their ideal selves? What do they perceive that members of the

* This paper is indebted to the work of Rachel R. Martin, who performed a literature search, acted as experimenter, and helped with data analyses. Thanks are also due to Irving Piliavin for his very helpful comments on rewriting. The research was supported by National Science Foundation Grant #GS-27053.

138

opposite sex would want them to be like? What do men and women actually *do?* And how do others behave toward those who do not conform to their expectations? This chapter addresses a number of these questions, presenting what data I could find from the work of others and some preliminary data of my own. Although the research itself is basically atheoretical, one framework into which I would like to fit the discussion is W. I. Thomas's famous statement, quoted by Merton in his discussion of the self-fulfilling prophecy, that "if men define situations as real, they are real in their consequences." The general point is that if women believe that certain behaviors are expected of them (due to early socialization experiences), they will be likely to engage in those behaviors. The evidence for this effect in other contexts is quite compelling (see, e.g., Rosenthal 1966, 1968; Berscheid and Walster, 1974). This effect should be found even when those with whom they are interacting do not hold those expectations. The *assumed* reward contingencies can, under these circumstances, be more powerful determinants of behavior than the *actual* reinforcements present.

In organization, this chapter moves from the global to the specific, and from the inside out. That is, I first discuss some evidence concerning expectations for male and female behavior cross-culturally, and then move to expectations held by adults in the United States who have been surveyed. Next I discuss studies of what individuals expect of themselves, how they view their own personalities, and what they personally hold as ideals for the opposite sex and for themselves. The next step is to look at what evidence exists concerning the actual behavior of men and women in social interactions and at research on expectations concerning the consequences of role violations. Finally, I report on preliminary findings from my own research into behavior in two-sex discussion groups and the reactions of men and women to female role-violating behavior in such groups.

I do not purport to be an expert on cultural differences in role expectations, or on cultural differences in anything, for that matter. I do know that societies exist in which men have little to say about what goes on, just as societies exist in which women are expected to be seen and not heard. The general trend, however, is for different behaviors to be expected of men and women in any given society; moreover, there is a good deal of consistency across societies in what is expected of the members of each sex. One index of this can be found in Barry, Bacon, and Child (1957), a study that employed the cross-cultural files. This index is the percentage of cultures in which there is evidence of a sex difference in socialization pressures on a variety of behavioral-personality characteristics (see table 7.1).

These data are from varying numbers of societies and are based on the reports of a wide range of anthropologists frequently using unknown methods; nevertheless, the difference in the expectations held for members of the two sexes in the cultures sampled is quite striking. Pressures are clearly put on girls to be more nurturant and responsible while boys are pushed to be more achieving and self-reliant.

In a summary article published in 1964, Kagan lists a large number of expectations that the members of our culture hold concerning desirable characteristics and appropriate role behaviors for males and females.[*] The studies tend on the

[*] The definition of role employed in this paper is taken from Nye (1970) and is as follows: "role becomes a set of behaviors believed by the group to be the *right* behavior for one occupying a

TABLE 7.1 Differential Socialization Pressures by Sex
on Five Behavioral-Personality Characteristics

		Percent of Cultures Showing Greater Socialization Pressures		
Characteristic	*Number of Cultures*	*Toward Male*	*Toward Neither*	*Toward Female*
Nurturant	33	0	18	82
Responsible	84	11	28	61
Obedient	69	3	62	35
Achieving	31	87	10	3
Self-reliant	82	85	15	0

SOURCE: H. Barry III, M. K. Bacon, and I. L. Child, "A Cross-cultural Survey of Some Sex Differences in Socialization," *Journal of Abnormal and Social Psychology* 55 (1957): 328. Copyright 1957 by The American Psychological Association. Reprinted by permission.

whole to be methodologically poor, using only college samples or samples drawn in unspecified ways from broader populations; but their numbers lend a certain credence to the overall conclusions. People think girls and women should be small and pretty, while boys and men should be large and strong. Men should be aggressive if attacked or dominated; women should inhibit both verbal and physical aggression. Females should be nurturant, passive, dependent, and conforming; males should inhibit dependency and cultivate self-reliance. Women should be submissive with men, should inhibit overt sexual desire, and should cultivate domestic skills; men should be interpersonally dominant, should make sexual conquests, and should acquire money and power.

As an aside, I would like to add that the sanctions specifically for sex-role violation by little boys are more severe than for little girls. A tomboy is of much less concern to her parents than is a "sissy," and a girl who wants to be a doctor is thought less strange than a boy who wants to be a hairdresser. As far as I know, no data bear directly on this contention, although Hartley (1959) has an interesting discursive article on the conflicting pressures that are applied to male children in our society.

SELF-IMAGE

Studies of the attitudes of individuals toward their own personalities: self-images, relationship of real to ideal self, etc., are of limited worth due to sampling limitations, procedural errors, and concept ambiguity. Bennett and Cohen (1959), for example, have reported on a study whose sample is essentially unknown because the method used in obtaining it is not reported. In their study, for whatever it is worth, they found that women as compared to men feel greater inadequacy of functioning, greater fear and weakness, less maturity, more controlled rage, but also

position—such as mother, husband, or child. . . . We take the position that roles are normatively defined by the group and the presence of such normative definition *can be determined by the operations of sanctions to enforce the norms* (p. 4)."

greater social empathy and greater happiness. Men feel greater competence, more egocentrism, more control over the environment, more need to achieve, and more imagination. They conclude, "Masculine thinking is associated more with a desire for personal achievement . . . while feminine thinking is associated more with a desire for social love and friendship (p. 153)."

In a second study, McKee and Sherriffs (1960), using a college sample, asked men and women to describe themselves and also to say how they think the opposite sex would like them to be and how *they* would like the opposite sex to be. Men apparently perceived correctly that women would like them to be less sex-typedly masculine than they perceived themselves to be; women wanted greater warmth, empathy, etc., and men knew it. On the other hand, "man's ideal woman" as the women saw her was more sex-typedly female than was the ideal woman actually reported by the men.

Steinman (1963) obtained similar results in a study of college females and their parents. The girls saw their own role as more "liberated" than the role they perceived their fathers preferring for them, and they had an even stronger discrepancy between their view of themselves and their estimated "man's ideal woman." Again, the fathers had a good deal more liberated view of their own ideal woman than the daughters had. Steinman and Fox (1966), in a methodologically sound national sample across class lines, show again that it seems to be the women who are most rigid about the female role. Responding to the same Fand Inventory of Feminine Values employed in the previous Steinman study, women saw themselves as about half and half self- and other-oriented, and saw their own ideal self as more self-oriented but man's ideal woman as more other-oriented. The responses of men, however, showed that their ideal woman was less other-oriented than the women's guess at the men's ideal and was actually very close to the real selves described by the women!

The three studies described in sequence above appear to add up to a conclusion that women are suffering from a myth of their own making. But, as W. I. Thomas (rephrased) might say, a myth is as good as a mile in these cases. Before we accept this conclusion uncritically and exonerate society, men, and the establishment from all responsibility, let us pause to consider that these data are all based on verbal responses to rather transparent inventory questions. The men's money may not actually be where their mouths are. There is even some sneaking suggestion that this may be the case in the data reported by Steinman and Fox. When they divide their items into "global" and "specific" items, they discover that the men tend to be more liberal in their attitudes on the global than on the specific questions. When it gets close to home and down to earth, does it begin to pinch a bit?

BEHAVIOR IN GROUPS

Given the differential expectations for male and female behavior, the extent to which these expectations seem to have been internalized into people's self-images, and the presumed sanctions on inappropriate role performance, we would certainly predict that studies of group interaction would show differences in the behavior of males and females. That is, one's suspicions would be that the internalized expectations of significant others, backed up by negative sanctions for role-violating behavior, would direct men's and women's behavior in the "sex appropriate" direction. Male behavior would thus be expected to be more aggressive, more achieving, more self-reliant; female behavior should be more passive, more supportive nurturant, more dependent. In relationship to the world of work these expectations are unquestionably confirmed. Are there also observable differences in interpersonal "styles" in face-to-face groups?

Zelditch (1955) suggested a framework for the study of the family that incorporates these differential role behaviors. Earlier small-group research with all-male groups (Bales and Slater 1955) had demonstrated that one person in a group generally emerged as the one who led in the solution of problems directly related to the group's job (the task leader) while another individual (the best-liked man) tended to specialize in tension-reducing, "socioemotional" activities. Since these two behaviors fall so neatly into a "male" and a "female" category, Zelditch predicted that in the family, task leadership would be the province of the father while socioemotional leadership would be the job of the mother.

There has been little support for this prediction in studies of actual families. Leik (1963), in a cleverly designed but rather small study of nine families, found that when family members (mother, father, and college-age daughter) interacted in their natural family group, there was little evidence for such sex-typed behaviors; only the daughter's difference from her father in supportive behaviors exceeded chance levels. When the same individuals interacted in artificial families (unrelated mother, father, and daughter) or in same-category, three-person groups (all mothers, all daughters, etc.), their behavior was significantly more sex-typed along the lines of Zelditch's predictions. One major problem of interpretation is that the same-category groups were run first, then the artificial families, and finally the real families. The decreasing stereotypic behavior could thus be due to an adaptation effect of some kind. Leik had in fact hypothesized that it was public surveillance that made for stereotypic sex-role behavior. Decreasing sensitivity to surveillance over time could account for the results. The overall consensus concerning family role divisions, however, remains that it is an individual family matter in many cases based on skill rather than stereotyped sex-role considerations.

The only published study of any scope to investigate the behavior of men and women in task-oriented groups (as opposed to therapy or encounter groups, with which I will not attempt to deal) was done by Strodtbeck and Mann in 1956. This was a very realistic study, really a model of the field experiment. Subjects were selected from jury pools in Chicago and Saint Louis. The investigators had them listen in groups of twelve to a tape recording of a trial and then deliberate under the watchful eye of bailiffs as if it were all real. Observers were present in the room, recording, hopefully unobtrusively, the groups' interaction using Bales' twelve categories. Twelve groups were run. In the three "positive emotional" categories of the Bales system: "shows solidarity," "shows tension release," and "agrees," women were overrepresented compared to men at a probability of less than .001. In two of the task-orientation categories, "gives opinion" and "gives orientation," men were overrepresented with chance probabilities of .01 and .05 respectively. Interestingly, women were more active (were scored as contributing more acts). These data rather strongly support the presupposition that there will be a division of labor along sex lines in two-sexed groups.

There now exists one other study, as yet unpublished, which confirms

Strodtbeck and Mann's basic findings. Martin (1972), using Bales' revised category analysis (Bales 1970), scored sixty-four ten-minute tape-recorded four-person group discussions taken from a larger study to be discussed in greater detail later. Her intent was not only to provide a replication, sixteen years later, in a very different setting, and with very different subjects (college students), of the Strodtbeck and Mann study, but also to add a parallel analysis of same-sex groups using the same case to discuss. Using an event-recorder, she coded sixteen all-male, sixteen all-female, and thirty-two mixed-sex (two males, two females) groups, having practiced on sixteen other mixed-sex groups. One-sex groups were scored as a unit; in mixed-sex groups, the sexes were scored separately. Her reliabilities, calculated against sample scorings by a male, were acceptably high. The changes made by Bales in his scoring system are relatively minor and do not obviate the opportunity for replicating the earlier study, since it is still possible to contrive a "task-behavior" set of categories (by adding "gives opinion" and "gives orientation") and a "socioemotional" set of categories (by adding "friendly," "dramatizes," "shows temper," and "agrees"). Although Martin had predicted both some differences due to type of group (same sex as against mixed sex) and some differences due to sex of actor, she obtained only effects due to sex. As in the Strodtbeck and Mann study, males have a significantly greater proportion of task behaviors and females a very highly significantly greater proportion of socioemotional behaviors. There was no difference in activity between the sexes, with males accounting on the average for 50.3 percent of the total acts scored in the mixed-sex groups. The finding of greater female activity in the jury study is thus not generalizable; it must be attributable to one of the many differences between the studies.

ON THE MANAGEMENT OF IMPRESSIONS

Role behavior that conforms to expectations is seldom questioned—only deviance is scrutinized. Yet conformity is worth consideration—why does a person act as he or she is expected to (or as they think they are expected to)? Obviously, there is the expectation that interpersonal rewards will follow appropriate behavior, and that punishment, rejection, etc., may follow inappropriate behavior. These negative outcomes are the sanctions referred to by Nye (1970) as basic to his definition of role expectations. But does the "performer" play out his or her role consciously or unconsciously? Goffman suggests:

> . . . when an individual appears before others . . . [s]ometimes the individual will act in a thoroughly calculating manner. . . . Sometimes he will intentionally and consciously express himself in a particular way, but chiefly because the tradition of his group . . . require [sic] this kind of expression. . . . Sometimes the traditions of an individual's role will lead him to give a well-designed impression . . . yet he may be neither consciously nor unconsciously disposed to create such an impression. (1959:6)

In the area of sex-role behavior, it has been suggested that a good deal of "performance"—on both sides—is carefully calculated. Goffman states, citing Komarovsky (1946:186), that:

> American college girls did, and no doubt do, play down their intelligence, skills, and determinativeness when in the presence of datable boys. . . . These performers are

reported to allow their boyfriends to explain things to them tediously that they already know; they conceal proficiency in mathematics from their less able consorts; they lose ping-pong games just before the ending. "One of the nicest techniques is to spell long words incorrectly once in a while. My boyfriend seems to get a great kick out of it and writes back, 'Honey you certainly don't know how to spell.' " (Goffman 1959:39)

This calculated behavior has its costs, as reported again by a respondent of Komarovsky's, "I sometimes play dumb on dates, but it leaves a bad taste (p. 188)." Many intelligent and self-directing women are unable to play this charade. What can they expect to be the consequences? Goffman suggests that behavior that violates expected role performance is very uncomfortable for all participants:

Some of the assumptions upon which the responses of the participants had been predicated become untenable and the participants find themselves lodged in an interaction for which the situation has been wrongly defined and is now no longer defined. At such moments the individual whose presentation has been discredited may feel ashamed while others present may feel hostile, and all the participants may come to feel ill at ease. (1959:12)

Goffman further states that if a performer does slip out of an expected role, the audience will help that person "maintain face" by either ignoring the slip or helping the performer to reinstate the expected role. Data from the old group dynamics literature suggest that a deviant who maintains a position far from that of a group on matters important to the group will first become the target of communications from the other group members attempting to "bring him around." If these efforts to influence behavior fail, the person will be psychologically excluded from the group and communications to him or her will decrease (Schachter 1951). Putting these data together with Goffman's hypotheses, we would have to conclude that there is every reason for men and women to adhere to expected sex-role behavior. The consequences of continual violation of the expectations of others would be social ostracism. Are there data on the response of men and women to nonconformers in this area?

Before citing the formal data that exist on response to female nonconformers, I would like to point out that society also places sanctions on the male for nonconformity to certain sex-role expectations. Transvestism in the male is frequently a crime; in many communities a man caught wearing a dress on the street is subject to arrest. There are no such crimes for women. Indecent exposure is a serious crime only for men; women are quite free in our society to flaunt their bodies openly. Men are prosecuted for desertion and nonsupport of their families; women are not. Whether the effeminate adult male is more socially rejected than the masculine, "butchy" female or the "castrating bitch" is probably a moot point; actual overt male and female homosexuals, however, are treated differently by the law. It is almost unheard of for lesbians to be arrested or harassed; the treatment male homosexuals are subjected to is an entirely different matter. The most severe sanctions applied to males are for "unmasculine" behavior or for sexually "perverted" behavior. Hypermasculine sexual behavior (e.g., rape) seems to receive less severe sanctioning than indecent exposure, judging by the difficulty of obtaining convictions in rape cases (Lear 1972).

WOMEN'S FEAR OF SUCCESS AND
ROLE-VIOLATING BEHAVIOR

If social rejection is likely to follow from a female behaving in sex-inappropriate ways, there are clear implications for her achievement motivation and her performance in competitive situations involving men. Since success in such areas is a prerequisite for taking on most of the high-status roles in our society, having problems with achievement could effectively block women from high-status occupations even in the absence of overt discrimination. That the achievement behavior of women is different from that of men has consistently been found by scores of confused investigators. Matina Horner (1969, 1970) has hypothesized fear of success as a major factor attenuating the expected relationship between measured achievement motivation and achieving behavior in women. Her basic method has been to give the following beginning of a story to females (for males, the words in parentheses are substituted) and ask them to complete it:

> *After first-term finals Anne (John) finds herself (himself) at the top of her (his) medical school class.*

In response to their cue, men in her Michigan sample tended to write almost entirely positive stories predicting financial success, happy marriage, and the attainment of renown in the profession. Only 8 percent of men wrote stories in which anxiety was evident. Sixty-five percent of the women, on the other hand, wrote stories full of fear of social rejection, doubts about femininity, or distortion and denial of the facts. Probably the most extreme fear of social rejection story Horner received was the following, written by an honor student:

> *Anne starts proclaiming her surprise and joy. Her fellow classmates are so disgusted with her behavior that they jump on her in a body and beat her. She is maimed for life.*

Two of the more interesting denial stories were the following:

> *Anne is really happy she's on top, though Tom is higher than she—though that's as it should be . . . Anne doesn't mind Tom winning.*

> *Anne is talking to her counselor. Counselor says she will make a fine nurse.*

A good proportion of the stories explicitly mention the conflict between success in the career and success in marriage, for example:

> *Anne has a boyfriend, Carl, in the same class and they are quite serious. . . . She wants him to be scholastically higher than she is. Anne will deliberately lower her academic standing the next term . . . and . . . soon drops out of medical school. They marry and . . . she raises their family.*

Horner performs some other rather revealing analyses, among them an investigation of the relationship between her projective measure and performance in competitive vs. noncompetitive situations. Of 17 women high in fear of success, 13 did better when working alone; while of 13 women low in fear, 12 did better in competition.

More than two-thirds of the men did significantly better in the competitive situation. Finally, she related the fear of success measure to characteristics of the women, such as academic record and ability and future plans. Most women with fear of success had high intellectual ability and histories of academic success; nevertheless, they aspired to "traditional" female careers such as housewife, nurse, teacher.

These later analyses certainly suggest that the measure that Horner calls fear of success is indeed a personality characteristic, since it relates to other intrapersonal measures. Nonetheless, a couple of flaws in her design leave the major finding of greater fear of success among women open to an alternative explanation. First, no men responded to Anne, and no women responded to John. Perhaps the responses of the women are largely a reflection of their knowledge of the world, in which rejection *is* likely to befall the "Annes." If so, men should respond in the same way to Anne as women do, indicating that Horner does not really have a measure of personal anxiety about success. In 1970 I took the same stories and randomly handed them out to a class of beginning psychology students at the University of Pennsylvania, thus assuring that both sexes would respond to both stems. My scoring of their stories was rather crude. I used three categories: anxiety or conflict, mixed reactions including denial, and basically positive reactions that could include some reference to a struggle. The data are presented in table 7.2.

TABLE 7.2   Responses to Anne and John by Male and Female Subjects: University of Pennsylvania Study

Response Category	Male Subjects			Female Subjects		
	John	*Anne*	*Total*	*John*	*Anne*	*Total*
Anxiety or conflict	4	3	7	3	10	13
Mixed—includes denial	4	5	9	5	5	10
Positive—can include some struggle	5	9	14	7	2	9
	13	17	30	15	17	32

X^2 for John vs. Anne among female subjects = 6.50, $p < .05$
X^2 for male vs. female subjects responding to Anne = 8.22, $p < .02$

Although it was hardly a polished study, the above data do support Horner's contention that the greater anxiety shown by her women reflects a personal fear of success rather than a perception of the reality of the situation. A further replication of Horner found in our data is that again it is the women with the best academic records, as indexed by their reported grade-point averages, who are most likely to write Anne stories that show anxiety or conflict. Among the 10 women responding with anxiety to the Anne stem, 8 had GPAs of 3.3 or higher. Among those 7 in the other two categories, *all* had GPAs below 3.3.* Fisher's exact probabilities test yields a two-tailed *p* value of .004 for this difference. GPA was unrelated to anxiety

* The mean GPA for the anxious group was 3.38; the mean for the mixed and nonanxious group was 2.87.

in the other three samples. In our small sample, there did not appear to be support for the idea that the more anxious women were going into "feminine" occupations in greater numbers. Almost all of our women were going into teaching, social work, or the like. It should be noted as we move on to the discussion of the Alper (1971) study that the levels of anxiety in stories about John and in male stories about Anne is a good deal higher than that found by Horner. Some 53 percent of girls' stories about John and of all male stories are anxious or mixed, and 22 percent of these stories fall in the anxiety category alone.

Alper (1971) attempts to qualify Horner's conclusions further by asking whether college women do not want to be achievers at anything, or "is it that they do not want to achieve what Horner's 'Anne' has achieved; namely, the top grade in her medical school class? (p. 1)." She reports data of her own from Wellesley College females. Given the "Anne" stimulus, she reports that 89 percent told avoidance stories; given the "John" form, 50 percent told avoidance stories (these proportions are much like my own). Then she deleted the words "medical school" from the Anne stem and obtained a significant drop in the percentage of avoidance stories. These data support exactly the point I have been trying to make; namely, it is sex-inappropriate behavior that is anxiety producing, not success per se. Alper goes on to suggest that "rewording the stimulus to read 'after first term finals, Anne finds herself at the top of her class in a school of nursing,' should result in a further *decrease* in the percentage of avoidance stories in women (p. 2)." She adds that on the "John" form with men one might expect an *increase* in anxiety if John is tops in nursing!

A further refinement introduced by Alper is the Wellesley Role-Orientation Scale (WROS), tapping three aspects of sex-role orientation. Also, she uses several TAT-type pictures designed to get a more reliable and thorough measure of imagery related to fear of success and related matters. On the basis of the WROS, she divides her subjects into High and Low feminines, and on the basis of response to some of the pictures she further divides them into Ambivalent and Unambivalent Highs and Lows. It is the Ambivalent among both Highs and Lows that she sees as the anxious ones in Horner's study.

Additional recent findings from Horner (1972) indicate that: (1) fear of success is increasing in white men and (2) fear of success is almost as high in black men as in white women, and almost as low in black women as in white men. A partial confirmation of this latter finding is provided by Weston and Mednick (1972), using a sample of 85 black and white females in two southern colleges. Class had no effect within the heterogeneous black sample, but black and white middle-class women differed with the whites being significantly more anxious. The results are consistent both in response to the typical "Anne" cue and to the cue, "Jennifer has just been informed that her three-act play will be produced in New York this coming season."

Weston and Mednick conclude:

> Horner (1968) has suggested that the high fear of success found in white Ss is probably due to the aggressive overtones of intellectual competition needed for success in these areas, since aggression has been socially linked to a lack of femininity and its display is seen as leading to negative consequences (i.e., social rejection). The present findings suggest that success in intellectually competitive

situations does not elicit [similar] fear in the black college woman [as in whites]. This may be related to . . . different sex role patterns. . . . A successful woman is an economic asset and attractive rather than threatening to a black man. Hence, success as here projected is not to be feared. (p. 71)

One provocative finding in all the research since Horner's original study is that a significant proportion of men appear to be writing fear of success stories. None of the current researchers in this area have concerned themselves with this fact, but it would seem to bear examination. What might be the sources of fear of success in general—rather than just among women? Might there be a more general phenomenon to be addressed than the one being attended to? Might it, for example, merely be the case that women—traditionally more interpersonally sensitive—were a bit advanced in displaying a now prevalent reaction to "material success" among today's people-oriented undergraduates? The question cannot be answered, of course. I raise it only to emphasize both the complexities of the issues being confronted and the inadequacy of the current data to handle those complexities.

THE CONSEQUENCES OF SUCCESS AND THE WOMEN'S RESPONSE

Horner (1972) also investigated some career choices and reasons for changing given by high and low fear of success women by means of an intensive interview study. She states, "The attitude of male peers toward the appropriate role of women, which they apparently do not hesitate to express, appears to be the most significant factor in arousing the motive to avoid success in these girls (p. 65)." The evidence is very strong in this interview study that most young women receive little or no encouragement in their aspirations for careers from their boy friends. "When asked, for instance, how the boys in their lives feel about their aspirations, even the less ambitious goals, a frequent response—in fact, the most common response—was: 'They laugh' (pp. 65–66)." She also reports that she has data on the actual sex-role attitudes of some of the boy friends, and that it is these attitudes that "proved to be the most significant factor accounting for the presence or absence of fear of success in the girls (p. 66)."

Komarovsky (1946), also in an interview study, found many of the same type of reported conflicts. She notes, however, that while 40 percent of her subjects reported such conflicts with dates, 60 percent did not. On the basis of her earlier work and this more recent interview study, Horner concludes:

In light of the high and if anything increasing incidence of the motive to avoid success in our data it seems apparent that most otherwise achievement-motivated young white women when faced with a conflict between their feminine image and expressing their competences . . . adjust their behaviors to their internalized sex role stereotypes. (1972:67)

These women apparently choose to withdraw from competition. In Goffman's terms, they do not wish to see their performances discredited, so they avoid putting on the performances in the first place.

Some additional data may be pertinent here, although they were collected without any intent to investigate sex-role behavior in achievement-related situations. In the summer of 1969 I carried out a large-scale study of interpersonal attraction in competitive situations. Male and female subjects competed in same-sex pairs in a contest involving problem solving. Half of the Ss thought their partner was like them in personality; half, different. One interesting finding was that men tended to rate themselves as more competent than their partner, while females tended to rate themselves as less competent than their partner (the basic difference was that men rated themselves as more competent than women rated themselves, at $p < .001$, while the two sexes rated their partners at about equal levels of competence). Both men and women rated the similar partner as more competent, more likable, and all-around nicer than the different partner. The really fascinating part of the data is yet to come. If Horner's speculations are correct, the reason women fear success is that they believe that social rejection may follow too-successful behavior. It occurred to me in looking at the data just described that there was one group of subjects of the four groups I have just mentioned (men and women with similar or different partners) in which we might predict that subjects would perform less well in the competition on the basis of Horner's ideas: the women with partners similar to them. Why? Volumes of research (e.g., Byrne 1972) demonstrate that we like those who are similar to us, and expect them to like us. We should therefore expect female subjects with a similar other to want to avoid being rejected by this potential friend, and to consequently suppress their performance. Performance data are presented in table 7.3 in terms of the number of problems correctly solved of the total of 30.

TABLE 7.3   Number of Problems Correctly Solved by Male and Female Ss Paired with a Partner Similar or Different in Personality

	Similar	(N)	Different	(N)	Difference
Male subjects	19.044	(45)	18.380	(50)	n.s.
Female subjects	17.435	(46)	18.920	(50)	$t = 2.10, p < .05$
DIFFERENCE	$t = 2.22, p < .05$		n.s.		

Since subjects were randomly assigned to the similar and different conditions, it is hard to attribute these differences to a process much different from the one suggested.

The general conclusion we can draw from the above in reference to Goffman's hypotheses is that yes, the woman who has accepted and internalized society's expectations for her, or the woman who simply is aware of these norms without internalization, does tend to show anxiety about achievement. The source of this anxiety appears to be a fear of social rejection by liked others, particularly, but not exclusively, males, and this anxiety (or intentional action) can suppress achievement. But is all this a myth? Men do not write anxiety stories about Anne to any greater degree than they do about John. Might it not be the case that men do *not* reject the intellectually achieving woman and Horner's and Komarovsky's interview subjects are oversensitive or exaggerating? Does this type of behavior make others uncomfortable, as it should if it is perceived as in violation of a norm? And do the observers of such "inappropriate" role behavior try to "put her back in her place," as seemingly shown in some of Horner's "denial" stories? *

RESEARCH ON SEX-ROLE BEHAVIOR IN MIXED-SEX GROUPS

Schwartz (1970) made the initial attempt to test Goffman's hypotheses experimentally in regard to the consequences of violating the role expectations of others; specifically, she tested responses of other group members to a female in a mixed-sex group who was induced to increase markedly the amount of her participation in the group. The assumption underlying the research was that "overparticipation" in such a discussion group would be perceived as a violation of appropriate sex-role behavior. Briefly, her basic design (derived from Bavelas, Hastorf, Gross, and Kite, 1965) was as follows. Subjects from the introductory psychology subject pool were invited to participate in a group-discussion experiment. Each group of four discussed one case study for ten minutes, during which time the assistant to the experimenter was recording the amount of time each participant talked. On the basis of these data, a "target person" was selected, usually the quietest person in the group. During the second discussion, an operant-conditioning procedure involving the use of red and green lights to provide "feedback" to group members was employed to try to induce the "target person" to increase the amount of his or her participation. What was done was to present a green light to the target person whenever he or she said *anything* (and occasional red lights for silence) while simultaneously doing the reverse to the most talkative members of the group. This discussion lasted twenty minutes. Finally, there was a third discussion with no feedback, again lasting ten minutes. After each discussion, each member of the group rated each other member and himself or herself on four scales: amount of participation, quality of ideas, effectiveness in leading the discussion, and general leadership ability. Each group member also rated each of the three others on how much they would like to continue the discussion with them outside the experiment and how much they thought they could come to like them.

Four types of groups were subjected to this procedure: all male groups, all female groups, mixed-sex groups in which a quiet male was the "target person," and mixed-sex groups in which a female was the "target person." Seven groups of each type were run. We had several hypotheses, generally based on Goffman, concerning differences that would be found between the first three types of groups, all of which are control groups, and the last group, which is essentially the experimental group.

1. The manipulation would be less successful for the female target person in the mixed-sex group, since it would be an attempt to make her perform in an inappropriate sex-role fashion.

* An amusing aside, in this case in regard to the male role, is cited by Alper. One of her stimuli, the Father-Baby picture, showing a man in a bathrobe at 2:00 A.M. giving a baby a bottle, was uniformly perceived as female by a sample of male Columbia students, while only one of 78 female Wellesleyans made that error.

2. This same target person would "backslide" more in talking time during discussion three as compared to the other three target people.

3. Others' leadership ratings of the experimental group target person would show less increase from the first discussion to the second than would the ratings of the other three target people (Increases are to be expected on the basis of the Bavelas et al. 1965 study).

4. The experimental group target person would be liked less after her "inappropriate" behavior during discussion two, as compared to the other target people.

5. Everybody in the experimental group would enjoy discussion two less than the other two discussions, whereas no differences were systematically to be expected between discussions for the other three groups.

No predictions were made for differences between male and female group members in their response to the target individuals, but analyses to discover any such differences were planned.

Results of the Schwartz Study

The first and most obvious question that needed to be answered was whether the initial assumption—on which the entire study was predicated—was correct; namely, that men would do more talking in a mixed-sex group of strangers than would women. If this were not the case, it would be hard to argue that there is a norm against females "overparticipating."

The data are quite clear in this regard. In the fourteen mixed-sex groups, the two men talked, on the average, 65 percent of the time during the first discussion. In the fourteen groups there were only three in which the person who talked the most (the definition of "the leader" in the Bavelas et al. study) was female. These differences from chance expectations of 50 percent talking time and seven leaders for each sex were significant.

In regard to the five experimental hypotheses, however, the data are not so cooperative. The only "target person" who did not show significant increases in talking time was the *male* in the mixed-sex group. All others, including our "critical" target female in the mixed-sex group showed highly significant change as a result of our manipulations, and maintained some of that change into discussion three. Hypotheses 1 and 2 are clearly wrong. There is in the data some hint that hypothesis 3 may be partially correct, however. The other woman in the mixed group in which we made a female talk more seemed not to notice the increased participation of her "co-female," either in comparison to the men in the same group or in comparison to women in an all-female group responding to their "target person." The results were not significant statistically, but were suggestive of the kind of denial of female achievement behavior found in some of Horner's stories. Perhaps the "other woman" was trying to help the target female to "maintain face" as Goffman suggests is generally done under circumstances in which a person engages in inappropriate role behavior.

The final two hypotheses in the study were that group members would dislike the female target person in the mixed-sex group after her "improper" behavior and that everyone, target person included, would be uncomfortable. The data suggest that at least the men, this time, seemed to dislike the overly loquacious target female, as compared to how they felt about a male under similar circumstances, and that the effect remained to some degree into the third discussion. There is very little support for the last idea, and, in fact, it is clear that *all* the target individuals, including the "critical" target female in the mixed-sex group, enjoyed very much being the recipient of our operant-technique reinforcements and being the center of the discussion. This finding is completely consistent with the discovery that it was not difficult to get the target female to talk more in the first place, and the fact that she did not backslide more than the other target individuals. Whatever sanctions may be operating against this kind of behavior in this group setting, they do not seem to be very powerful.

Replication and Extension of the
Group-discussion Study

Undaunted by the rather meager results of the Schwartz (1970) study, we carried out a larger experiment in the spring of 1971. The same basic design was used, with sixteen groups in each of the control conditions (all male, all female, and mixed groups with a male target person) and thirty-two in the mixed group with a female target person. A further addition in this study was that half of the groups were run with a female experimenter and half with a male experimenter.*

The first distressing discovery, on analyzing the data from this study, was that the men in the forty-eight mixed groups did not talk a significantly greater proportion of the time during the first discussion than did the women. The two males talked only 51.7 percent of the time overall, and there was no difference attributable to the sex of the experimenter that could bring these results into harmony with those obtained by Schwartz. There is a clear indication that the one person who talked the most ("the leader") was more likely to be male than female; in thirty-one of the forty-eight mixed-sex groups the "leader" was male, and this number is significantly different from the twenty-four to be expected by chance ($p < .05$). Nonetheless, the effect is far from overwhelming, to put it mildly, and this failure to find much heavier participation by males than females casts doubt on our basic assumption that women "are not supposed to" contribute as much as men to such discussions. The difference between the two studies is uninterpretable and baffling.

Consistency with the Schwartz study is better from this point on. We again found no difficulty in getting the female target person to increase her participation during the second discussion, replicating the Schwartz finding although once again disconfirming our original hypothesis! In these data, the individual who seems to be hard to budge is the male target person in an all male group who has a female experimenter (more will be said about this in the last section). Furthermore, there are no significant differences between types of target individuals in the amount of maintained change during discussion three. Hypotheses 1 and 2 are now unequivocally invalidated.

* Gene Cranston Anderson was mainly responsible for organizing the "team" that was required to collect the data that are partially presented here, and served, with Rachel Martin, as an experimenter. We are greatly in her debt for the smoothness with which the very complex task of collecting the data was carried out.

There is some confirmation of the tentative finding of the Schwartz study that the other female in the mixed-sex group is ignoring, denying, or in some way distorting the increased contributions of the female target person, while the males are not (see table 7.4). The pattern of the data from the two studies is the same, although as can be seen the changes are all smaller in the larger Wisconsin study. Due to the larger sample, however, the effect shown is by discussion three significant. We can conclude with some certainty that males are more sensitive to changes in the contribution of the female target person than is the other female in the mixed-sex group; it also looks more like denial on the part of the female than like hypersensitivity on the part of the males. The target person *has* changed her behavior, after all, and it is only the other female in her group who seems not to have noticed it!

There is also some indication of an effect on the liking measure, although the effect is somewhat different from that found in the Schwartz study (some of the problem in comparing the two studies adequately may be due to the failure of the male target person in Schwartz's mixed-sex groups to increase his participation). The general conclusion to be drawn—somewhat more tentatively than that concerning perception of participation—is that males and females differ in their affective reaction to the female target person in the mixed-sex group. The other female appears to like her more (a lot more in the current data, slightly more in the Schwartz data) while the two men like her a bit less in both studies. The effect is, again, significant in the larger study. It seems interesting that the effect of the target female's behavior on her being liked dissipates somewhat when her talking decreases at the third discussion, although the effect on the leadership ratings becomes greater over time. One further odd fact is that the two measures are not correlated; that is, it is not those who perceive the changes in her behavior who consequently like her less. The two effects seem to be independent.

A SERENDIPITOUS PROBLEM

Before drawing any conclusions, we will return to the provocative data on the resistance apparently shown by some male subjects to being "manipulated" by a female experimenter. The effect is shown in table 7.5. Interesting as the apparent difference is in the effectiveness of male and female experimenters in getting the man to increase his talking time, it is unfortunately not statistically significant. Because of its interest, however, we carried out an "efficiency" analysis, in which we looked at the amount of change obtained by male and female experimenters divided by the number of lights they gave the target person in these all male groups. A borderline difference appeared ($p = .082$, two-tailed, using a Mann-Whitney U-test). Female experimenters get much less effect for the same amount of effort expended in an attempt to change the men's behavior (it should be emphasized here that it is really always the same person—a female—who is manipulating the lights; the subjects just *think* that it is a male in the "male experimenter" condition. Thus the results cannot be due to some difference in style of manipulation). Finally, although the differences in actual change in talking time did not reach statistical significance, the perceptions of the other group members of the contributions of the target individuals *do* differ significantly. The last line of

TABLE 7.4 Changes in Leadership Index and Measure of "First Impression" Liking, from Discussion 1 to 2, and from Discussion 1 to 3, for Both Schwartz Data and Larger Replication Study (*sex of target person in parentheses for clarity*)

SCHWARTZ DATA

Leadership Index:

	Mixed: Female TP		Mixed: Male TP		One-sex Groups	
	2–1	3–1	2–1	3–1	2–1	3–1
Male ratings	(F) 8.714	7.071	(M) 4.429	3.714	(M) 6.971	3.243
Female ratings	(F) 6.143	2.714	(M) 4.786	3.714	(F) 9.029	5.986
DIFFERENCE (M-F)	2.571	4.357	− .357	.000	−2.058	−2.743

First Impression Liking:

	Mixed: Female TP		Mixed: Male TP		One-sex Groups	
	2–1	3–1	2–1	3–1	2–1	3–1
Male ratings	(F)− .571	− .429	(M)+ .857	+2.143	(M)+ .414	− .100
Female ratings	(F)+ .571	0.000	(M) 0.000	0.000	(F) + .500°	+1.100°
DIFFERENCE (M-F)	−1.142	− .429	+ .857	+2.143	− .086	−1.200

WISCONSIN REPLICATION

Leadership Index:

	Mixed: Female TP		Mixed: Male TP		One-sex Groups	
	2–1	3–1	2–1	3–1	2–1	3–1
Male ratings	(F) 2.292	1.562	(M) 1.917	1.125	(M) 2.728	3.896
Female ratings	(F) 1.292	−1.406	(M) 2.458	− .156	(F) 3.728	3.354
DIFFERENCE (M-F)	1.000	3.968	− .541	1.281	−1.000	.542

First Impression Liking:

	Mixed: Female TP		Mixed: Male TP		One-sex Groups	
	2–1	3–1	2–1	3–1	2–1	3–1
Male ratings	(F)− .226	− .047	(M)− .187	− .375	(M)+ .271	+ .208
Female ratings	(F)+1.156	+ .688	(M)+ .312	+ .219	(F) + .250	+ .417
DIFFERENCE (M-F)	−1.422	− .734	− .499	− .594	+ .021	− .209

°N for this cell is only 6 because of missing data.

table 7.5 presents these data. Most interestingly, these data show that the male in the mixed-sex group is also not perceived as changing his behavior for the female experimenter. This is interesting because it is the male target person in the mixed-sex groups who was hard to change in the Schwartz study, in which there was, of course, a female experimenter. One further anecdotal fact from her study is that on two of her data sheets from *all-male* groups she has written "did not take seriously"—although in both those groups she obtained change in amount of participation from the target person. Taken together, these data are consistent, if not always statistically significant. The male target individual seems inclined either not to respond to the attempted manipulations of a female experimenter or to respond in a way that is not perceived as increased contributions, or to respond "nonseriously." This is not exactly news. Men have a reputation for not taking women seriously (see Horner, 1972) and for resenting having women in positions of authority over them. On those bases, these results are not unexpected.

The analysis of the data from the larger study is far from complete. In particular, we would like to compare responses of males and females to the female who *does not* talk more in the second discussion and contrast those results with those cited above. We also want to look at the relationship between our personality measures and both response to the female who "steps out of line" and the target person's own response to attempted manipulation. Are the males who wouldn't budge for the female experimenter higher on the Traditional Family Ideology scale, for example? Are the women who wouldn't change for anybody in the mixed-sex groups more traditional? Many further questions may arise as data analysis proceeds. At the present time, we can draw the following conclusion tentatively: a female experimenter will have less effect in manipulating the verbal output of a male target person in all-male groups (and to some degree in mixed-sex groups) than will a male experimenter, and the differences in the behavior of target individuals under these circumstances will be perceived by the other members of the group. Also with some certainty, we can conclude that males are more sensitive to and aware of increases in the verbal output of female target individuals in mixed groups than are females. Whether this is due to "vigilance" on the part of the males or denial on the part of females cannot at present be determined, but it looks more like the latter. One other suggestive finding is that females seem to increase their liking for another female who increases her participation in a mixed-sex group (even though they claim not to have noticed it!) while males decrease their liking for her slightly.

In terms of the larger questions to which this research is addressed, we cannot, of course, make any sweeping generalizations. In our studies to date, the negative consequences of the type of "female role-inappropriate" behavior we have been looking at certainly do not appear to be too severe. Men don't like her any better, but they certainly don't hate her, and "the other woman" likes her more. Certainly there is no evidence that "her classmates jump on her in a body and beat her," which Horner's subjects seem to be so afraid of. The major conclusion to be drawn from this research to date is therefore that, as was suspected from reading the Steinman, Steinman and Fox, and McKee and Sherriffs studies cited earlier, one of the major deterrents to female active participation is the myth that men prefer women who do not do so. The intimation from these data, furthermore, is that it is the women who do not recognize the behavior as an increased contribution when it

TABLE 7.5 Comparability of TP's Talking Times, Manipulation of Lights, and Perceived Change in Behavior as a Function of Group Type and Experimenter Sex, Wisconsin Study, 1971

Group Type:	Female Experimenter				Male Experimenter			
	Male	Female	Mixed: M	Mixed: F	Male	Female	Mixed: M	Mixed: F
Number of groups;	8	8	8	16	8	8	8	16
TP percentage talking time, discussion 1:	15.75	17.75	18.87	15.63	13.50	15.63	19.75	22.50
Change, discussion 1 to 2	3.75	14.12	9.12	9.12	12.12	12.75	14.75	9.62
Change, discussion 1 to 3	3.50	9.00	4.38	5.56	7.38	7.62	7.00	3.25
Manipulation effects: TP red lights, discussion 2	7.75	6.62	7.38	10.21°	9.00	6.12	7.25	6.19
Change in leadership index: others (2–1)	+ .563	+ 3.875	.000	+ 2.938	+ 4.917	+ 3.583	+ 3.417	+ 1.708

°*N* for this cell = 14 due to malfunctioning of recording apparatus.

occurs. Along these lines, Goldberg (1968) has reported that women subjects evaluated the same essay more favorably when it was presented as having been written by a woman as compared to a man. I would be the last person to suggest that prejudice and discrimination against women is not rampant in this as in most societies. But in terms of what sanctions may exist against simple self-expression and active participation in an intellectual discussion, we seem to be up against a self-fulfilling prophecy based on a myth, rather than a conspiracy backed up by social ostracism. Perhaps we have nothing to fear but fear itself.

One caution must be inserted into this generally optimistic conclusion. The Martin (1972) analyses of the discussions of these same groups show that the *type* of contribution made by males and females to the group discussion is different, with males contributing more task behavior and females providing more socioemotional input. The results of her analysis should perhaps give us pause as to what kinds of contributions we may be reinforcing in target individuals of the two sexes. When a female increases her participation, it may actually be a very different type of event than when a male increases his participation. In fact, the lack of rejection we have basically found in the initial study may well be due to the fact that the increase in talking done by the female TP may be of the "socioemotional" sort, and *may thus not be perceived as sex-inappropriate.*

A second qualification might stem from the data from Horner (1972) and illustrative material from Komarovsky (1946) that seems to indicate that once one gets into a "serious" relationship with a man—as opposed to a passing casual intellectual interchange—the rules may change. Remember the intimation from Steinman and Fox (1966) that men tend to be less liberal on specific items than on global ones? It begins to sound like the interracial liberal faced with the busing of his own child or, in the words of Tom Lehrer, the Christian Scientist with appendicitis. It was the statement that "no wife of mine is going to graduate school" that led the present author to break off an engagement and do that very thing. Most women are better socialized to the requirements of the female role than I was; most, according to the above authors, would not have gone to graduate school. What I am suggesting is that men may indeed react positively, or at least not negatively, to a woman acquaintance who behaves in an intellectually aggressive manner. They may even enjoy the company of intelligent, vivacious, self-directing women and want them for wives. The question is whether this desire is likely to be translated into the actual behavioral sacrifices that a husband of a *full-fledged* female professional must make: compromises concerning job opportunities, sharing family responsibilities, less attention and ego building, and, perhaps, even living with the knowledge that his wife is more capable than he is at many things. With the present state of our knowledge, as represented by the research reported in this paper, this must remain an unanswered question.

REFERENCES

ALPER, T. G. "Achievement Motivation in College Women." Paper presented at the meetings of the Eastern Psychological Association, New York, 16 April 1971.

BALES, R. F. *Personality and Interpersonal Behavior.* New York: Holt, Rinehart, & Winston, 1970.

BALES, R. F., AND SLATER, P. E. "Role Differentiation in Small Decision-making Groups." In *Family Socialization and Interaction Process*, edited by Talcott Parsons and R. F. Bales. Glencoe: Free Press, 1955.

BARRY, H., III; BACON, M. K.; AND CHILD, I. I. "A Cross-cultural Survey of Some Sex Differences in Socialization." *Journal of Abnormal and Social Psychology* 55 (1957): 327–32.

BAVELAS, A.; HASTORF, A. H.; GROSS, A. E.; AND KITE, W. R. "Experiments on the Alteration of Group Structure." *Journal of Experimental Social Psychology* 1 (1965): 55–70.

BENNETT, E. M., AND COHEN, L. R. "Men and Women: Personality Patterns and Contrasts." *Genetic Psychology Monographs* 67 (1963): 275–352.

BERSCHEID, E., AND WALSTER, E. "Physical Attractiveness." *Advances in Experimental Social Psychology*, vol. 7, edited by L. Berkowitz. New York: Academic Press, 1974.

BREHM, J. W. *A Theory of Psychological Reactance*. New York: Academic Press, 1966.

BYRNE, D. *The Attraction Paradigm*. New York: Academic Press, 1972.

GOFFMAN, E. *The Presentation of Self in Everyday Life*. Garden City, N.Y.: Anchor, 1959.

GOLDBERG, P. "Are Women Prejudiced Against Women?" *Trans-Action* 5 (1968): 28–30.

HARTLEY, R. E. "Sex-role Pressures and the Socialization of the Male Child." *Psychological Reports* 5 (1959): 457–68.

HORNER, M. "Fail, Bright Women." *Psychology Today* 62 (November 1969): 36–38.

HORNER, M. "Femininity and Successful Achievement: A Basic Inconsistency." In *Feminine Personality and Conflict*, edited by J. Bardwick et al. Belmont, Calif.: Brooks, Cole, 1970.

HORNER, M. "The Motive to Avoid Success and Changing Aspirations of College Women." In *Readings on the Psychology of Women*, edited by J. Bardwick. New York: Harper & Row, 1972.

KAGAN, J. "Sex Typing and Sex Role Identity." *Review of Child Development Research* 1 (1964): 137–66.

KOMAROVSKY, M. "Cultural Contradictions and Sex Roles." *American Journal of Sociology* 52 (1946): 184–89.

LEAR, MARTHA WEINMAN. "Q. If you rape a woman and steal her TV, what can they get you for in New York? A. Stealing her TV." *New York Times Magazine* 19 January 1972.

LEIK, R. K. "Instrumentality and Emotionality in Family Interaction." *Sociometry* 26 (1963): 422–35.

McKEE, J. P., AND SHERRIFFS, A. C. "Men's and Women's Beliefs, Ideals, and Self-concepts." In *The Adolescent: A Book of Readings*, edited by M. Seidman. 1960.

MARTIN, R. R. "Sex Role Differentiation in Small Group Discussion." Unpublished manuscript, University of Wisconsin, 1972.

MERTON, R. "The Self-fulfilling Prophecy." In R. K. Merton, *Social Theory and Social Structure*. Revised ed. Glencoe: Free Press, 1957.

NYE, F. I. "The Delineation of Substantive Family Roles." Paper read before the National Council on Family Relations, Chicago, Ill., October 1970.

PILIAVIN, J. A. Unpublished research, University of Pennsylvania, 1970.

ROSENTHAL, R. *Experimenter Effects in Behavioral Research*. New York: Appleton-Century-Crofts, 1966.

ROSENTHAL, R. *Pygmalion in the Classroom: Teacher Expectations and Pupil Intellectual Development.* New York: Holt, Rinehart, & Winston, 1968.

SCHACHTER, S. "Deviation, Rejection, and Communication." *Journal of Abnormal and Social Psychology* 46 (1951): 190–207.

SCHWARTZ, E. "Sex Roles and Leadership Dynamics: A Study of Attitudes Towards the Female Sex Role." Senior Honors thesis, University of Pennsylvania, 1970.

STEINMAN, A. "A Study of the Concept of the Female Role." *Genetic Psychology Monographs* 67 (1963): 275–352.

STEINMAN, A., AND FOX, D. J. "Male-Female Perceptions of the Female Role in the United States." *Journal of Psychology* 64 (1966): 265–76.

STRODTBECK, F. L., AND MANN, R. D. "Sex Role Differentiation in Jury Deliberation." *Sociometry* 19 (1956): 3–11.

WESTON, P. J., AND MEDNICK, M. T. "Race, Social Class, and the Motive to Avoid Success in Women." In *Readings on the Psychology of Women*, edited by J. Bardwick. New York: Harper & Row, 1972.

ZELDITCH, M., JR. "Role Differentiation in the Nuclear Family: A Comparative study." In *Family Socialization and Interaction Process*, edited by T. Parsons and R. F. Bales. Glencoe: Free Press, 1955.

8

Women Social Workers and Clients: Common Victims of Sexism

Diane F. Kravetz

Social work is generally identified as a woman's profession. Women constitute a majority in the National Association of Social Workers; correspondingly, social work has traditionally assumed those nurturant and supportive functions consistent with stereotypic definitions of the female role. These factors have protected social work from feminist criticism and obscured issues of women's liberation in the field. Nevertheless, social work discriminates against women and works to maintain the status quo concerning the "proper" role of women in this society. This is evident in the practices toward women in the profession and in the policies and treatments that the profession sanctions for its clients, most of whom are women. Women social workers share a common experience with women clients as victims of discrimination based on sex.

The present constraints on women stand in striking contrast to the historical origins of social work. Guided by a commitment to help the disadvantaged of society, women provided the intellectual and philosophical foundations for this emerging profession. They also provided the major impetus for its growth and development.

Social casework began with the volunteer charity work of women in the nineteenth century. These women visited the poor, sick, and handicapped; they offered spiritual guidance, moral rehabilitation, and some material assistance. By the 1890s, their activities had evolved into the Charity Organization Societies, which were established to organize, coordinate, and provide services to the needy.

160

Women such as Josephine Lowell, Zilpha Smith, and Mary Richmond held significant leadership positions in these organizations and provided the foundations for the development of professional casework.

In contrast to casework's emphasis on individual adjustment, group work began within a social reform movement. As leaders in the settlement houses from the 1880s to the early 1900s, Florence Kelley, Lillian Wald, Grace and Edith Abbott, and Julia Lathrop were committed to changing the social and economic conditions that oppressed immigrants in American cities. They worked to organize and improve community services and to involve immigrant groups in political reform. The best known of these women was Jane Addams who was the founder of Hull House, a settlement located in an impoverished neighborhood in Chicago. She was acclaimed both nationally and in Europe for her intellectual excellence, her substantial political influence, and her writings on education, democracy, and the problems of women in urban life. Jane Addams was a leader in many national reform organizations, including the Women's International Peace Congress, later known as the Women's International League for Peace and Freedom.[1]

Workers in the settlement movement were involved with many social reforms of particular concern to women. They fought for the abolition of child labor and were primarily responsible for the bill establishing the Children's Bureau in the Department of Labor. Settlement workers also struggled to achieve better working conditions for women and helped organize women's labor unions.[2] "It was this first generation of social reformers who established the remarkable tradition of effort and achievement that gave social work its 'golden age.' Social reformers included an amazingly energetic group of men and women, but certainly the women—the 'social feminists'—played a dominant role in nearly every important reform of the period. The outstanding characteristic of the social feminists was the tremendous diversity of skill, concern, and achievement that they displayed over a period of about 25 years."[3]

Although the philosophies underlying early group work retain some influence today, social reform is no longer a primary function of social work. This became clear in the 1920s as group workers such as Grace Coyle, Clara Kaiser, Gertrude Wilson, and Gladys Ryland moved to middle-class leisure-time agencies, adopting the more conservative goals of socializing youth for responsible participation in democracy. At the same time, casework moved toward the development of practice theory, with a greater emphasis on expertise and training, and adopted Freud as its mentor. Mary Jarrett, Virginia Robinson, and Jesse Taft became proponents of this new psychiatric perspective in casework. Although the focus and politics of social work had shifted, women remained the standard bearers of social work theory and practice.[4]

The 1950s marked the rise of discrimination toward women in social work. By this time, social work had become preoccupied with professionalism, which meant developing a theoretical knowledge base, encouraging advanced training, and seeking public recognition and support. Since 70 percent of all social workers were women, however, social work could at best attain marginal professional status. As explained by Kadushin in 1958: ". . . the prevalent feeling is that women ought not to compete with men for occupational status. This expresses itself in a tendency to resist free entrance of women into occupations dominated and controlled by males and to derogate occupations dominated by women. The prestige of social work is, therefore, adversely affected because it is identified as a woman's profession." [5]

The caretaker nature of social work also contributed to its low status among the professions. As described by Adams, the role of the social worker mirrors in many ways the role of the housewife: "Both have a broad mandate that is not clearly defined or specially visible to outsiders; neither on first sight appears to require skills recognizable as unique and essential to its successful operation; for both, the primary objective is to facilitate the growth and adjustment of others and help to make cohesive what is often fragmentary or disintegrating. The functions and skills of both social workers and home-based women are invariably seen as valuable only when their temporary absence results in disruption and malfunction, in either the small family or larger society." [6]

To counter the negative effects of being a "woman's profession," social work moved to reduce the influence of women. Chafetz describes this process as "an effort to defeminize social work, i.e., make it more intellectual, rational, scientific, and administrative." [7] Men were recruited into the field, and in the 1950s, the proportion of men significantly increased. "They were welcomed not as a source of competition but as a means of overcoming the female image and of raising the profession's status." [8]

Developments in the social work methods in the 1950s and '60s illustrate the effects of the influx of men. Casework, the most developed and tradition bound, continued to be defined as supportive, nurturant, and oriented toward individual "cases"; women continued as casework's major theorists and practitioners. However, although women continued to write about and practice group work, many of the approaches that evolved in the 1950s and '60s were developed by men, notably Robert Vinter and William Schwartz. Community organization emerged as a social work method during the late 1940s and '50s. Viewed as the organizational, action-oriented method, community organization was and is overwhelmingly male. The push toward professionalism and male dominance of social work theory appear to be highly interrelated phenomena.

A rigid and pervasive division of function, based on sex-role stereotypes, emerged and persisted. At present, the social work profession does not prepare, encourage, or reward women for challenging their traditional roles; further, women are often discouraged from seeking advancement due to accurate perceptions of limited opportunities.

Two-thirds of the members of the National Association of Social Workers are women. Yet men are twice as likely as women to hold administrative positions. Community organization and administration, predominantly male, are the high-status social work methods and draw the highest salaries. In 1968, the median salary for men was $12,000, for women, $10,500. Also, salaries increase differentially according to sex, with increases for men being greater than for women.[9] The dominance of men is also apparent in the 1971–72 directory of nationally elected and appointed personnel of NASW; only one-third of the available positions were filled by women.[10] As stated by Scotch, "It is true that women may be out of circulation during their childbearing years or because of male-dominated households or individual preferences may be less job-oriented than males. Whether either of these biological or cultural factors should be the economic determinants of an occupational reward system is open to question." [11]

Many of the present problems of women in social work are common to all working women. Studies have shown that women value masculine traits more than feminine traits; women also fear that being intelligent, assertive, and competent will make them less desirable.[12] Their fears are often confirmed; working women are criticized by family and friends for abandoning their traditional roles as wives and mothers. The lack of adequate child-care facilities in most communities makes these problems even more difficult to resolve. When child care is available, it is costly, and tax relief has only recently been available to moderate-income women.

Obligations and rewards for women center around their being wives and mothers. Occupational roles are secondary in importance and often incompatible with family demands.[13] There is clear evidence that the requirements of marriage and family life conflict with the careers of social work women. In a 1968 survey of NASW members, 86 percent of the men were married whereas only 52 percent of the women were married. One-third of the women had never been married; less than one-tenth of the men had never been married.

Further, significantly more men than women are able to be parents and full-time employees. Ninety-seven percent of the male members of NASW are full-time workers. Of the female members, 75 percent are employed full time, 15 percent work part time, and 9 percent are not employed. For married female workers without children, 80 percent are employed full time. Of women with children between the ages of six and ten, 40 percent are employed full time, 44 percent work part time, and 16 percent are unemployed. For women with preschoolers, 27 percent work full time, 42 percent part time, and 31 percent do not work at all.[14]

Tropman's study of the high attrition rate among married female social workers found that being married was not a primary problem for women; rather, the crucial variable was having children before attending graduate school. The presence of children under six years of age after the M.S.W. determined whether women chose to work, and if so, if they chose to work full or part time.[15] Herberg obtained similar results in her study. Being married before entering graduate school and having fewer children were related to higher work participation by social work women. Lack of substitute child care and household help were frequently identified as the factors inhibiting women from continuing their careers.[16] Until the social and economic circumstances of working mothers are significantly altered, women in social work will not be able to weigh the extent of their family and career involvement freely.

Social work education promotes the differential treatment of men and women. A study by Brager and Michael indicates the extent to which sex-role stereotypes affect recruitment and training: "Casework and group work are person-oriented, concerned with behavior, focused inward, and related to feelings. Community organization is interested in people primarily as members of community collectives; it is more system-oriented and its focus is outward. . . . The service and treatment roles of the caseworker and group worker are more clearly delineated and structured than the organizer's, and caseworkers and group workers are less often required to be the initiators of interaction and activity with clients. On a scale of passivity-activity, or submissiveness-aggression, community organization practice requires more activism and aggression than do the other social work methods. . . . Male-female differences coincide with the differences among the social work methods." [17]

This description reflects a very narrow and unsubstantiated view of all three social work approaches and is rooted in stereotypic notions of male-female behavior. The discussion strongly implies that division of labor based on sex is a realistic approach to personal and professional demands. It does not deal with the obvious stereotyping and the detrimental effects of institutionalized sexism on the perceived and real choices of students, both male and female.

A survey of social work doctorates, 1920–68, shows that the ratio of males to females among doctoral recipients is much greater than the male-female ratio in the profession as a whole. Of all social work doctorates, 61 percent were awarded to men, 39 percent to women. "In the early periods of the doctoral programs women accounted for 85 percent of the recipients. With each succeeding decade, however, the difference decreased steadily, so that in the 1960–68 period 65.5 percent of all social work doctorates were earned by men." [18] These patterns may result from traditionally based conflicts for women, but they may also result from tracking and general attitudes toward women who pursue higher degrees. Women have few role models at the doctorate level and are likely to receive little active support for the pursuit of their doctorate.

The social work educational process fosters myths and prejudices about women. Distortions and false statements are notable in the theories taught in human growth and behavior and psychopathology courses. Stereotypic views of female development and anti-woman bias by personality theorists such as Freud and Erikson are often uncritically taught.[19] Courses in marriage and the family often ignore the assumptions underlying traditional roles and norms, thereby reinforcing the status quo. Ehrlich examined the stereotypes of women in six recent marriage and family texts and found that "so-called value-free social science is full of myths and folklore about the female, which are presented as factual and are used to justify her subordinate status." [20] Course content should prepare students to understand different family forms and marriage styles and to deal with the issues and problems which confront both traditional and nontraditional families.

In other areas, the unbalanced influence of men is also evident. For example, in 1968–69, only 11 percent of the deans and directors of accredited graduate schools in the United States and Canada were women.[21] Further, a study of five professional social work publications, 1964–68, found that two-thirds of the books reviewed in these journals were authored by men, 65 percent of the books were reviewed by men, and 60 percent of the journal articles were written by men.[22]

The above patterns strongly indicate the presence of discrimination based on sex in both social work education and in employment practices. Although substantial research is necessary in order to make any definitive statements, tracking at the M.S.W. level, differential recruitment for the doctorate, and salary and promotion standards in the field reflect institutionalized sexism.

In addition to the discrimination encountered by women social workers, sexism is also evident in social work policies and practices with women clients. As observed by Wilson: "Women social workers are still seeing themselves as a group distinct from their clients; and yet women social workers are probably the only group who share a similar oppression with many of their clients." [23] Social workers must recognize that reduction of options and exclusion from formal authority structures, both in the home and in the community, are common problems for all women, workers as well as clients. Consequently, given societal attitudes and discriminatory practices toward women, it is not surprising that the majority of social work clients are women.

The Aid to Families with Dependent Children program is a clear example of the effects of anti-woman values on social welfare policy and practices; it embodies the condescension and discrimination that all women face. As stated by Johnnie Tillman, the first chairwoman of the National Welfare Rights Organization, "The truth is the AFDC is like a super-sexist marriage. You trade in a man for the man." [24] When women fail to get a man to pay expenses for them and their children, they are defined by this society as lazy, immoral, and incompetent; unlike other women, they are expected to work. In recent years, there have been increasing efforts to get AFDC mothers to obtain employment. Most mothers on AFDC have children under twelve, about two-thirds have children under six, and the average number of children in the family is three. Most mothers on AFDC cannot earn enough money to pay for child care; few can earn more than $3000–$4000 per year. Also, at this time, communities are not prepared nor equipped to provide the kind of child-care and enrichment programs needed by low-income children. [25]

Since they have not succeeded in the traditional manner, welfare women are infantalized by the system. Like possessive, jealous husbands, welfare departments dictate the extent of relationships with other men, control expenditures of every dollar, and by their attitude and behavior remove every semblance of independence and dignity for "their women." As noted by Tillman, all women, even poor women, should be able to choose whether to work and how to care for their own children. Further, the welfare problem would be greatly solved if "woman's work" was considered work. "I'd start paying women a living wage for doing the work we are already doing—childraising and housekeeping." [26] Women's traditional functions should be recognized for the important and essential role they play in society.

The National Welfare Rights Organization has suggested that to eliminate sexism from welfare, there should be no categories based on sex or marital status; the only determinant should be need and family size. This would remove distinctions between women and the "deserving poor," i.e., the aged, blind, and disabled. As of January 1, 1974, however, administration of the so-called adult categories has become the responsibility of the Social Security Administration. This further separates AFDC recipients from the aged, blind, disabled, and recipients of earned social security benefits. The AFDC program is totally under the control of state and local authorities, and women remain at the mercy of local attitudes and prejudices.

Psychological problems also become a woman's issue because women are the majority of clients in therapy. Data based on admissions to mental hospitals, psychiatric admissions to general hospitals, psychiatric outpatient care, private psychiatric care, treatment by general physicians, and community surveys clearly show that more women than men are being treated for psychological problems. [27] The kinds of problems that women bring to therapy are often indicative of women's inability to cope with powerlessness and role difficulties. Guilt, conflict over aggressive fantasies and behavior, and low self-esteem are common problems for women. These symptoms also reflect the values society has imposed and women have internalized: (1) that women do not have abilities and personal styles that are important, and (2) that women are responsible for all failures of others in their families.

When individual needs and societal demands do not coincide, psychological disturbances may result. For example, a study by Gove found that married women have significantly higher rates of psychological distress than married men; single, divorced, and widowed women do not have rates higher than their male counterparts. Gove suggests that the differences between the sexes may be due to the fact that the role of the married woman has become increasingly problematic and thereby promotes psychological difficulties.[28] Women are expected to be passive and dependent in a society that rewards aggression and independence. Women are expected to feel satisfied and fulfilled within the limitations of a domestic role. Any problem is defined as their own personal failure to adjust, not as a problem caused by external role constraints and contradictions.

Depression is a good example of the relationship between psychological distress and societal constraints. Depression is predominantly a female symptom and is traditionally defined as anger directed inward. Placed in a subordinate role, with corresponding lack of power, women are very vulnerable. Dependent on the continuing goodwill and approval of others, women are unlikely to express hostility or dissatisfaction toward those in power. Therefore, anger can only be turned inward, often in the form of helplessness and confusion. A therapeutic goal of adjustment to the situation only reaffirms for women that it is not wise to express dissatisfaction with one's destiny.

Conformity and repression can no longer be the only acceptable indicators of successful therapy. Social workers must redefine the psychological problems of women.[29] This will not occur until workers recognize how their own attitudes contribute to the problems of women in therapy: "Insofar as a therapist accepts society's role prescription for women, he [sic] is implicitly accepting the value judgement that underlies it: that women are basically inferior to men. Thus, even when no specific role conflicts are at issue, in therapy—when 'women's issues' are never mentioned—the therapist's unconscious attitude toward patients is to some extent antitherapeutic."[30] The imposition of values may take the form of the worker discouraging women from developing those aspects of their personality and abilities that are considered "unfeminine." It might also be communicated that women should define themselves in terms of their relationships with men and children.

Chesler analyzed the similarities between marriage and therapy as two major socially approved institutions for women. Both institutions isolate women from one another and emphasize individual rather than collective solutions to problems. Both institutions are based on definitions of women as helpless and dependent on men for their survival in everyday life. Both are mechanisms for social control.[31] Therapy supports the marriage relationship and the status quo by allowing women to express their anger in a "safe" environment and thereby not disrupt the marriage.

It has been demonstrated that clinicians have different standards of mental health for men and for women. Broverman et al. asked a group of psychiatrists, psychologists, and social workers to describe a healthy mature man, a healthy mature woman, and a healthy mature adult. They found that clinicians have different concepts of health for men and women and that these differences correspond to sex-role stereotypes. The descriptions of a healthy man paralleled descriptions of a healthy adult. Descriptions of a healthy woman significantly differed from those of a healthy adult, with woman described as more submissive, less independent, more emotional, and less objective. Characteristics judged as healthy for adults and for men were also those that are considered more socially desirable. The study concludes that normal behavior for women is perceived as less healthy than normal behavior for men. "Thus, for a woman to be healthy, from an adjustment viewpoint, she must adjust to and accept the behavioral norms for her sex, even though these behaviors are generally less socially desirable and considered to be less healthy for the generalized competent mature adult." [32] These findings suggest that clinicians accept stereotypic role definitions of women and in practice are likely to guide their clients toward acceptance of these "normal" female attributes, whether or not they are defined as desirable by women themselves and regardless of the price women must pay for "adjustment" and "normality."

Social workers should be aware of their own sexist assumptions and the resulting limitations they impose upon their clients. A worker must be receptive to those women who do not wish to conform to traditional role definitions or to stereotypic female behaviors. Also, the range of alternatives offered to women who are confused, ambivalent, or simply unhappy must be increased. Within the traditional roles of wife and mother, a large number of significant structural and interpersonal changes can be made. Women should be able to have dignity and be valued for nurturant, child-caring behaviors and for other work in the home; these behaviors should not be taken for granted. Finally, women clients must be encouraged to be aware of environmental constraints and to use that awareness to discover new solutions for redefined problems. This is not a radical statement; it is an accepted social work function, i.e., to increase options and opportunities of clients.

Regardless of the extent of change that is appropriate in treatment, it is essential that women social workers recognize their unity with women clients. Problems must be discussed in terms of institutionalized oppression and discrimination, not only as the personal problem of any individual woman. Many workers legitimize their resistance to this approach by quoting the social work maxim "start where the client is." This argument is best countered by Wilson: "The correct revolutionary procedure is apparently to raise the consciousness of the worker, the black, the unemployed, but not that of the unsupported mother, the depressive, the shoplifter, the teenage drug addict or the prostitute—these typically 'women's' problems are seen as individual hang-ups. Unlike children and adult men, toward whom the attitudes of some social workers have greatly changed, these women, along with mental patients and the old, are considered as groups for whom collective political action is thought inappropriate." [33]

The legitimate functions of social workers include establishing linkages between people and societal resource systems and contributing to the development and modification of public policy and legislation. [34] As advocates and organizers, social workers should use their expertise to modify the social conditions that affect women detrimentally. These skills should be applied to three problematic areas: (1) discrimination in social work education; (2) discrimination in personnel practices within the profession; and (3) discrimination in policies and practices toward clients.

In social work education, there should be no tracking of women students into casework and group work and away from community organization and administration; women must be encouraged to develop the skills required for the entire range of social work functions. Investigations into distribution of financial aid and faculty advising at both the masters and doctoral levels are necessary to discover what processes and factors are involved in the disproportionately low number of women who pursue and complete a doctorate. Also, each course in a social work curriculum must be examined in order to identify and challenge the myths and biases that perpetuate discrimination.

In social work agencies, discriminatory practices must be halted. Women should be given equal access to the decision-making structures and be represented at every administrative level. All cases of discrimination should be publicly challenged whenever they cannot be resolved through established channels. Communication between women in all agencies within a community should be maintained around these issues, and collective action should be utilized when necessary.

Two assumptions have contributed to the development and maintenance of the existing power structure: (1) that facilitating, supportive, and nurturant functions are secondary in importance and female in nature; and (2) that objectivity, rationality, and aggressiveness are the appropriate norms. These two assumptions must be challenged before any significant reversal of existing practices can occur. Those tasks that have traditionally been identified as female are essential for the maintenance of all social systems, i.e. groups, families, communities, and organizations, and their value must be acknowledged. The persons who fulfill these functions must be chosen on the basis of individual preference and skill, not arbitrarily on the basis of sex. Social work, in its attempt to improve its image and expertise, must cease to work under the same sexist assumptions that permeate other professions. Upgrading in terms of purpose, method, training, and salaries is necessary and appropriate, but not at the expense of women.

In addition to eliminating discrimination within the profession, social workers must also involve themselves in eliminating the sexism that limits the options of clients. Workers must identify the norms and policies that promote anti-woman attitudes and behaviors in agencies and in the community. Insight and behavioral adjustment assume individual responsibility for individual problems; social workers must take an advocacy, change-oriented stance toward social structures that reduce women's dignity and limit their potential for growth.

The welfare system should be examined to determine how cultural conceptions of women influence its operations.[35] Mental health agencies should take into account the social, economic, and political circumstances of women. Placing women in groups where they can share personal experiences enables women to realize that their problems are not unique and to identify the changes needed in their personal lives, in their interpersonal relationships, and in their communities. Agency policies should reflect an understanding that social conditions are a major contributing factor to the psychological problems of women and should define cultural norms and social institutions as the appropriate targets for change.

Legislation concerning abortion, the availability of birth-control information and devices, adoption, child care, homosexuality, promiscuity ("uncontrollability"), divorce, and employment must be carefully examined and challenged when based primarily on sexist attitudes and assumptions. Finally, institutional settings in which workers play an important role, such as girls' training schools, women's prisons, public schools, and mental hospitals, must be investigated; women should not be trained for "women's work" only nor rewarded for "feminine" behaviors only. Socialization and treatment of women should not be based on sex-role stereotypes.

Social work has the responsibility to rid itself of discrimination at all levels and to use its professional expertise to overcome the sexism that limits the options of its clients. As community organizers and social planners, social workers must assume the role of advocate and develop the necessary resources to eliminate economic, legal, and social discrimination. Women social workers have the opportunity to work with women clients, sharing knowledge, skill, and experience. Recognition of common bonds, shared goals, and mutual support will strengthen women workers and clients in their efforts to change the social conditions that oppress all women.

NOTES

1. For a sensitive portrayal of Jane Addams, see JILL CONWAY, "Jane Addams: An American Heroine," in *The Woman in America*, ed. Robert J. Lifton (Boston: Beacon Press, 1964), pp. 247–66.

2. ALLEN F. DAVIS, "Settlements: History," in *Encyclopedia of Social Work*, ed. Robert Morris (New York: National Association of Social Workers, 1971), 2: 1175–80.

3. WINIFRED D. W. BOLIN, *Feminism, Reform, and Social Service: A History of Women in Social Work* (Minneapolis: Minnesota Resource Center for Social Work Education, 1973), p. 8.

4. A brief overview of the history of casework and group work can be found in SCOTT BRIAR, "Social Casework and Social Group Work: Historical and Social Science Foundations," in *Encyclopedia of Social Work*, pp. 1237–45.

5. ALFRED KADUSHIN, "The Prestige of Social Work—Facts and Factors," *Social Work* 3, no. 2 (1958): 40.

6. MARGARET ADAMS, "The Compassion Trap," in *Woman in Sexist Society: Studies in Power and Powerlessness*, ed. Vivian Gornick and Barbara K. Moran (New York: Basic Books, 1971), pp. 559–60.

7. JANET S. CHAFETZ, "Women in Social Work," *Social Work* 17, no. 5 (1972): 18.

8. BERNARD C. SCOTCH, "Sex Status in Social Work: Grist for Women's Liberation," *Social Work* 16, no. 3 (1971): 6.

9. ALFRED M. STAMM, "NASW Membership: Characteristics, Deployment, and Salaries," *Personnel Information* 12, no. 34 (1969): 34–45.

10. *National Association of Social Workers Directory of Elected and Appointed Personnel— 1972.*

11. SCOTCH, "Sex Status in Social Work," p. 9.

12. See MATINA S. HORNER, "Femininity and Successful Achievement: A Basic Inconsistency," in *Feminine Personality and Conflict*, ed. J. M. Bardwick (New York: Brooks/ Cole, 1970), pp. 45–76; PHILIP GOLDBERG, "Are Women Prejudiced Against Women?" *Trans-Action* 5, no. 5 (1968): 28–30; and PAUL ROSENKRANTZ, SUSAN VOGEL, HELEN BEE, INGE BROVERMAN, and DONALD M. BROVERMAN, "Sex-Role Stereotypes and Self-Concepts in College Students," *Journal of Consulting and Clinical Psychology* 32 (1968): 287–95.

13. For an excellent discussion of the social factors which determine the role of women in American society, see CYNTHIA F. EPSTEIN, *Woman's Place* (Berkeley: University of California Press, 1971).

14. STAMM, "NASW Membership."

15. JOHN E. TROPMAN, "The Married Professional Social Worker," *Journal of Marriage and the Family* 30, no. 4 (1968): 661–65.

16. DOROTHY C. HERBERG, "A Study of Work Participation by Graduate Female Social Workers: Some Implications for Professional Social Work Training," *Journal of Education for Social Work* 9, no. 3 (1973): 16–23.

17. GEORGE BRAGER and JOHN A. MICHAEL, "The Sex Distribution in Social Work: Causes and Consequences," *Social Casework* 50, no. 10 (1969): 597.

18. JOHN J. BALDI, "Doctorates in Social Work, 1920–1968," *Journal of Education for Social Work* 7, no. 1 (1971): 12.

19. For discussion of the anti-woman bias in personality theory, see PHYLLIS CHESLER, *Women and Madness* (Garden City, N.Y.: Doubleday, 1972); MARY A. DOHERTY, "Sexual Bias in Personality Theory," *Counseling Psychologist* 4, no. 1 (1973): 67–74; and NAOMI WEISSTEIN, "Psychology Constructs the Female," in *Woman in Sexist Society*, pp. 207–24. Also, see MARY C. SCHWARTZ, "Sexism in the Social Work Curriculum," *Journal of Education for Social Work* 9, no. 3 (1973): 65–70.

20. CAROL EHRLICH, "The Male Sociologists Burden: The Place of Women in Marriage and Family Texts," *Journal of Marriage and the Family* 33, no. 3 (1971): 421–30. Additional articles concerning marriage and the family may be found in *Journal of Marriage and the Family* 33, nos. 3 and 4 (1971); JESSIE BERNARD, *The Future of Marriage* (New York: Bantam, 1972); and HERBERT A. OTTO, *The Family in Search of A Future* (New York: Appleton-Century-Crofts, 1970).

21. *Graduate Professional Schools of Social Work in Canada and the U.S.A.* (New York: Council on Social Work Education, 1968), pp. 2–12.

22. AARON ROSENBLATT, EILEEN M. TURNER, ADALENE R. PATTERSON, and CLARE K. ROLLESSON, "Predominance of Male Authors in Social Work Publications," *Social Casework* 51, no. 7 (1970): 421–30.

23. ELIZABETH WILSON, "Women Together," *New Society*, September 1972, p. 504.

24. JOHNNIE TILLMAN, "Welfare Is a Women's Issue," *MS*, Spring 1972, p. 111.

25. BETTY E. COGSWELL and MARVIN B. SUSSMAN, "Changing Family and Marriage Forms: Complications for Human Service Systems," *Family Coordinator* 21 (1972): 505–16.

26. TILLMAN, "Welfare Is a Women's Issue," pp. 111–16.

27. PHYLLIS CHESLER, "Patient and Patriarch: Women in the Psychotherapeutic Relationship," in *Woman in Sexist Society*, pp. 362–92; and WALTER R. GOVE, "The Relationship Between Sex Roles, Marital Status, and Mental Illness," *Social Forces* 51, no. 1 (1972): 34–44.

28. GOVE, "The Relationship Between Sex Roles, Marital Status, and Mental Illness."

29. For discussion of the psychological problems and treatment of women, see CHESLER, *Women and Madness*; PAULINE B. BART, "Depression in Middle-Aged Women," in *Woman in Sexist Society*, pp. 163–86; and VIOLET FRANKS and VASANTI BURTLE, *Women in Therapy* (New York: Brunner Mazel, 1974).

30. BARBARA STEVENS, "The Psychotherapist and Women's Liberation," *Social Work* 16, no. 3 (1971): 14–15.

31. CHESLER, *Woman in Sexist Society*.

32. INGE K. BROVERMAN, DONALD M. BROVERMAN, FRANK E. CLARKSON, PAUL S. ROSENKRANTZ, and SUSAN R. VOGEL, "Sex-Role Stereotypes and Clinical Judgments of Mental Health," *Journal of Consulting and Clinical Psychology* 34, no. 1 (1970): 1–7.

33. WILSON, "Women Together," p. 504.

34. ALLEN PINCUS and ANNE MINAHAN, *Social Work Practice: Model and Method* (Itasca, Ill.: F. E. Peacock, 1973), chap. 1, "The Nature of Social Work Practice," pp. 3–36.

35. For additional information, see CAROL GLASSMAN, "Women and the Welfare System," in *Sisterhood Is Powerful*, ed. Robin Morgan (New York: Random House, 1970), pp. 103–14; JUDITH LEVIN and PATRICIA VERGATA, "Welfare Laws and Women—An Analysis of Federal Sexism," *Rutgers Law School*, May 1971.

WOMEN
AND LITERATURE:
PORTRAYER
AND PORTRAYED

9

The New Feminist Criticisms: Exploring the History of the New Space

Annis V. Pratt

The new space, then, has a kind of invisibility to those who have not entered it. It is therefore inviolable. At the same time it communicates power which, paradoxically, is experienced both as power of presence and power of absence. It is not political power in the usual sense but rather a flow of healing energy which is participation in the power of being. . . . The burst of anger and creativity made possible in the presence of one's sisters is an experience of becoming whole, of overcoming the division within the self that makes nothingness block the dynamism of being. Instead of settling for being a warped half of a person, which is equivalent to a self-destructive non-person, the emerging woman is casting off role definitions and moving toward androgynous being.—Mary Daly, *Beyond God the Father*

When I started thinking about writing feminist criticism in 1970, I did not realize that by 1974 I would find myself in an uncharted country whose landscape was nonetheless home. Scholarship, and the solitary pursuit of the literary history of women, has turned into an adventure on a frontier of my mind that I never knew was there. Feminist criticism leads the literary scholar through the history of the novel, poem, and play into the healing waters of her innermost being.

As it is now practiced by literary scholars in the United States, feminist criticism uses the term "feminism" in a broad rather than a narrow sense. Although many of us are political feminist activists in the contemporary women's movement, we are not using the term in a strictly political sense in our research endeavors. Rather, to us feminism connotes a broad concern with the way the status of women has been and continues to be reflected in literature. When I say "we" I am speaking at the moment specifically of feminist critics in the Midwest Modern Language Association, who, after two years of discussion and debate, in 1973 reached a consensus that there is room for a multiplicity of methodological approaches. (See table 9.1, New Feminist Criticisms.) Barbara Desmarais put it this way: "Feminist criticism may not be a single, new, and specific scholarly technique, but rather a variety of critical approaches which . . . serve as correctives unmasking the omissions and distortions of the past—the errors of a literary critical tradition that arise from and reflect a culture created, perpetuated, and dominated by men." [1] In this chapter I want to consider these criticisms and comment on my own perspective in the research I have been conducting.

Among the first techniques used at the beginning of the feminist criticism movement in 1970 and 1971 were two related methods: (1) stereotypical criticism, in which the image of woman in both male and female literature is examined for sexist bias;[2] and (2) phallic criticism, a term coined by Mary Ellmann to describe the biases found within critical works. As an example of phallic criticism, consider the fact that Louis Bredvolt in 1962 wrote a book called *The Natural History of Sensibility* in which he treats the entire gothic novel tradition without mentioning one woman gothic novelist and the entire sentimental novel tradition without a significant analysis of a woman sentimental novelist. This makes his book a natural history of *male* sensibility, a rather peculiar achievement when we remember that the term is usually applied to women writers and their characters in eighteenth-century parlance. Phallic criticism, moreover, not only *neglects* our tradition but also *abuses* it. Consider, for example, British author and critic Anthony Burgess's declaration that Austen's fiction leaves only "an impression of high-waisted dresses and genteel parsonage flirtation," that George Eliot's is at best a "male impersonation" not "wholly successful," and that Ivy Compton-Burnett's is the work of "a big sexless nemesis force." [3]

More subtle but no less destructive is the tendency of criticism to elide feminist themes within the works of woman writers, particularly the great ones: Katherine Anne Porter's detailed satires on sexual politics are evidence of her "theme of evil," or Virginia Woolf's lifelong treatment of the status of women is unimportant in relation to her imagery and her stylistic innovations. Between deletion, elision, and derision, male (and not infrequently female) critics and literature professors have kept the rich and revolutionary tradition of the woman's novel well under wraps.

For this reason, the techniques of spadework criticism, involving the discovery and revival of "forgotten" woman authors, and of bibliographical research, have become very important to the new feminist criticisms.[4] Many woman authors were not haphazardly "forgotten" but deliberately buried, their works far too critical of contemporary sexual norms for them to survive such censors as William Dean Howells and Walter Page. Thus Charlotte Perkins Gilman's masterpiece *The Yellow Wallpaper* remained buried until the Feminist Press recently reissued it, and the career of Kate Chopin was snuffed out when her realism went too far for timid reviewers. Librarians, bibliographers, and scholars will find the morgues of their university libraries filled with whole canons of work by women authors, put there to molder because a critical taste chiefly characterized by conservative concepts of "male" and "female" declared them worthless.

In order to determine whether a given work by a woman author is minor or

TABLE 9.1   The New Feminist Criticisms

Criticism	Examples of the Mode
I. Stereotypical—Images of women in literature	Kate Millett on Lawrence, Miller, etc., in *Sexual Politics*; Dolores Barracano Schmidt, "The Great American Bitch"; Judith H. Montgomery, "The American Galatea," *College English*, May 1971
II. Archetypal—The psycho-mythological development of the female hero as reflected in patterns of symbol and myth found in women's literature	Annis Pratt, "Archetypal Approaches to the New Feminist Criticism," *Bucknell Review*: "Mrs. Ramsay's Erection" ("Sexual Imagery in *To the Lighthouse*," *Modern Fiction Studies*, Fall 1972)
III. Textual	
A. Explication and Generic	Nancy Jo Hoffman, "Reading Women's Poetry," *College English*, Fall 1972
B. The Question of a Female Style Is there a distinct "Male" and "Female" style reflecting distinct sexual sensibilities?	Josephine Donovan, "Feminist Style Criticism," in *Images of Women in Fiction*; Mary Ellmann, *Thinking About Women*
IV. Contextual	
A. Historical—The survey of trends in women's literature as related to historical forces	Annis Pratt, Chapters II-V, *Feminism and Fiction* (ms. in progress); Susan Gorsky, "The Gentle Doubters, Images of Women in Englishwomen's Novels, 1840–1920"
B. Sociological—Literature in the context of attitudes toward the family, culture, etc.; literature as document	Nan Maglin, unpublished work on Sinclair Lewis
V. Ideological—Analysis of literature from a set approach, from a nonliterary body of theory, such as Marxism, Zen, etc.	A. Marxist: Lillian S. Robinson, "Dwelling in Decencies," *College English*, May 1971; and (with Lise Vogel) "Modernism and History," in *Images of Women in Fiction*; Fraya Katz-Stoker, "The Other Criticism: Feminism Vs. Formalism," in *Images of Women in Fiction* B. Existentialist: the body of theory implicit in Simone de Beauvoir's *The Second Sex*; Ellen Morgan in *Contemporary Literature*, Fall 1973
VI. Bibliographical	See the work of S. Barbara Kanner (in *Suffer and Be Still*) and of Maureen Fries, *The Sense and Sensibility Collective Bibliography*

TABLE 9.1   The New Feminist Criticisms

Criticism	Examples of the Mode
VII. Spadework Criticism—Reviving forgotten women authors and determining why they were forgotten	Feminist Press editions of Gilman's *The Yellow Wallpaper*, Phelps' *Life in the Iron Mills*, Smedley's *Daughter of Earth*, with afterwords; Edwards and Diamond edition of *American Voices, American Women*
VIII. Phallic Criticism—Exposing sexism in male critics	Mary Ellman, *Thinking About Women*; Carol Ohmann, "Emily Brontë in the Hands of Male Critics," *College English*, May 1971 (NCTE *A Case for Equity* pamphlet)

major, the techniques of textual criticism—of explication and of generic analysis—must be brought to bear upon it. Immediately, the critic comes up against the fact that standards of style over the last thirty years have been set by a very small cadre of academic aestheticians, believers in the autonomy of the art world, to whom the word "sociological" is pejorative. Distaste for considering the context in which a novel is written as relevant is not always a metaphysical phenomenon; often it springs from a political situation that, as documented by radical critics, is an attempt to forget the social criticism of the 1930s after the McCarthy purges of university faculties in the 1950s.[5] Textual criticism depends upon contextual factors, in the sense that an author's choice of point of view, characterization, plotting, and imagery often derive from the dictates of the publishing market.

Although there is room in the new feminist criticisms for a variety of methodologies, this pluralism does not preclude the application of an ideology or set approach or world view to a work of art. Thus, a Marxist analysis is helpful in understanding both the nineteenth-century novel and the work of a socially conscious writer such as Doris Lessing. Existentialist feminism as developed by Simone de Beauvoir in *The Second Sex* similarly helps us to clarify the struggle of many female heroes between a desire for authenticity and those masks and roles that society expects her to wear in defiance of her true selfhood.[6] When the feminist critic ranges over a wide variety of literary works she may find herself arriving at theoretical propositions, categories, and descriptive patterns that she does not impose upon the material deductively but that spring from a careful inductive examination of her field. Some of these may conform to patterns that archetypal critics have already described as characteristic of both literature and the collective unconscious of the entire human race. As we shall see, however, those archetypal patterns have rarely been taken as typical of the female psyche; rather, they are seen as characteristics of a soul that is implicitly accepted as male.

I have found the textual, contextual, and archetypal methods most important for my research. In this chapter I provide an account of how I came to look at literature from a feminist perspective; and then I survey some of the tentative results of my explorations.

First, I came to the realization that, as Barbara Desmarais put it, there have been such distortions in the interpretation of literature that *my* culture, Western literature as seen through the works of woman writers, has been largely invisible.

Let me use a metaphor for this: If we take the world of literature as the heavens and the stars, critics can be seen as focusing different kinds of telescopes and instruments upon that space. What I found, in studying and emulating the critics available to me as models in college and graduate school, was that although their instruments were highly refined, when they came to my star they either quickly shifted focus or proclaimed a "black hole" in space. I trained myself, for example, as a Jungian literary critic, ferreting out patterns in the collective unconscious as they influenced the writing of poetry. This worked very well as long as I focused on male writers; my initial work was on the poetic prose of Dylan Thomas. I found, however, that Jung himself, toward the end of his life, admitted that one of the chief problems he and his followers had was a tendency to locate women "just where man's shadow falls. So that he is only too liable to confuse her with his own shadow. Then, when he wishes to repair this misunderstanding, he tends to overvalue the woman and believe in her desiderata." [7] I had to realize that the foremost practitioner of my research method didn't see women when he looked at them; as Joan Roberts put it during her tenure hearing, in which a panel of men refused to promote her, to many male thinkers we are, as women, invisible. When women become visible, in Jungian theory, it is not as existents, not as adult, choice-making selves; they become auxiliaries to the psychic universe of the male—as satellites, never as planets. There are, however, insights about the growth and development of the human psyche that Jung pioneered and that I found useful in understanding the psyche of the female hero in literature, particularly Jung's descriptions of the quest of the young hero for adulthood and of the older hero for rebirth and full individuation. As a feminist critic, however, I had to postulate woman as human; to Jung, she had not quite made the grade.

Another critic important to my early literary training was Northrop Frye. But what does Frye say about the typical poet? "The poet," Frye asserts, "who writes creatively rather than deliberately, is not the father of his poem. He is at best a midwife, or more accurately still, the womb of Mother Nature herself. Her privates he, so to speak." [8] Here, it seemed, the critic had got his telescope backward, or, at least, that he was not looking at it through my end. Do I, then, as a woman poet, write from the phallus of Father Nature, his privates I, "so to speak."? Frye's approach to literature, that of taking the pragmatic existent field of material and examining it inductively for patterns and archetypes, is central to my own methodology. To him, however, literature is male: He recognizes the existence of woman writers but does not describe the patterns within their works as analytically significant in a way different from that of male writers. Similarly, Joseph Campbell, another critic I have tried to emulate, has written a four-volume series of literary anthropology called *The Masks of God*, in which women turn up as goddesses, witches, objects of pursuit, and shadows to the male; but only in one instance are they heroes of their own adventures.

I took as a mandate for myself, after spending the first nine years of my career as a critic and teacher of male literature, to take textual, contextual, and archetypal instruments and focus them on my own field. I took as this field the last two hundred years of the woman's novel, and I am nearing the completion of this part of my research, which will be published under the title *Feminism and Fiction*. My intention, after finishing the first volume, is to write a second volume on women as poets since medieval times and then to entitle the two works *Feminism and the*

Literary Mind. This has taken four years so far, and I expect it will take at least five years more. Three things have come to my mind from reading all this material, three different discoveries or theoretical propositions. The first I call the "wave theory." Mary Ellen Chase, a woman novelist, literary critic, and Smith College professor, once remarked that there are three kinds of literature: "majah, minah, and mediocah" (she was from Maine). There is, as my field, this vast body of fiction since Aphra Behn published *Oroonoko* in 1688. Some of it is popular—not very good from the aesthetic point of view; a great deal of it is minor—interesting but not masterworks; and a certain amount is above minor and almost major, but forgotten. Then, at the crest of this wave of material, are the major works. What we tend to think as we study women's literature is that there are no waves underneath these great works. We see *Middlemarch*, we see *To the Lighthouse*, we see *The Golden Notebook*, we see *Sense and Sensibility*—they seem to be out there by themselves, to extend our metaphor, in space. What we find is that not only are they not isolated, but each of these major works has underneath it a galaxy of other novels by women dealing with much the same subjects in much the same way.

Consider, for example, *Middlemarch*, a very important novel by George Eliot. What do we have? We have among many other themes two marriages. The first is Dorothea's (the hero) to Casaubon, an old minister who is working on the "key to all mythologies." Dorothea marries him because she admires his mind; she wants to serve it. It's a miserable marriage. They marry for all the wrong reasons, as Eliot points out over and over again, showing how ironic it is that while it is ghastly to be married to Casaubon, he thinks, and everybody in Middlemarch thinks, that he is a perfectly acceptable husband. Dorothea, by not giving in to his tyrannical demands, overexcites him and he has a fatal heart attack. After he dies Dorothea marries a more suitable, more equal, person.

When we look at this plot after reading a number of other novels in which the hero marries first a chauvinist and then a more equal partner, in which the female hero suffers under the first while the author points out how dreadful to her this socially acceptable normal behavior is, we arrive at the wave underlying *Middlemarch*, which I have called the "double-marriage novel" as a subcategory of the "novel of marital rebellion." We notice that in *Middlemarch* there are two marital rebellion plots, but only one double marriage. In the second, Lydgate, a prominent and brilliant young doctor, has his career destroyed by the idiocies of his typical, normally female wife. By this I mean that she fully lives up to the expectations of female role behavior in the period and by so doing destroys her marriage: She is charming, she's beautiful, she's a leech; she uses money thoughtlessly; and she makes herself into an ornament. In so doing, she drags her husband into poverty. In this second plot, however, the man is ruined by excessive sexual politics and remains stuck in the mire, married to the woman.

Middlemarch has never, except by recent feminist critics, been considered a feminist book, nor have those instances throughout nineteenth-century novels in which marriage is held up to a detailed, probing, and often satiric criticism. Anne Brontë's *The Tenant of Wildfell Hall*, for example, is a double-marriage novel in which the horrors of one's husband becoming an alcoholic are illustrated before the female hero is allowed, after his death, to escape to a more suitable mate. Even Mrs. Oliphant, an overtly antifeminist author, commented on how pleasant it can be if (1) a disagreeable husband would only die but (2) since that doesn't happen often enough in life, one should enjoy it in fiction.

Two other examples, so devastating that I find it hard to read them, illustrate another subcategory of the novel of marital rebellion, "the fatal effects of matrimony." Elizabeth Stewart Phelps' *The Story of Avis*, written in 1877, shows a female hero who is an artist and whose husband-to-be assures her that marriage will not take her away from her work. They get married, and Phelps details in excruciating vignettes the deterioration of her life as first her artwork, and then her very psyche, wither away. Another example is Gilman's *The Yellow Wallpaper*. Here the narrator's husband, John, is a doctor and he says (these are my paraphrasings), "Really, my little goose, it is a strain on you to write, you must get out in the country and get a complete rest from such distractions." So he takes her to a house in the country and puts her in a nursery in which there is yellow wallpaper, bars, and a nailed-down gnawed bed. "Now, don't write, just rest," he says, and leaves her alone to sneak occasional entries into her diary. She goes insane from lack of significant occupation; the form her insanity takes is a preoccupation with the yellow wallpaper. Behind its scrolls, which she sometimes perceives as bars, she senses a woman trying to get out, and she decides her mission is to get that woman out. She drags off the wallpaper with her bare hands. Her husband breaks down the door and finds her creeping around. The last comment is her declaration that "I don't know why that man should faint dead away." This was written in 1892. So when you read in the *New York Times Book Review* that *The Diary of a Mad Housewife* is the first feminist novel, don't believe it. There is more in common between *The Golden Notebook* by Doris Lessing and *Middlemarch* than there is between *The Golden Notebook* and the works of Anthony Burgess or Samuel Beckett or almost any male novelist of the same period.

The "wave theory" leaves us with the conclusion that there is a considerable degree of continuity in the woman's novel, a uniformity of concern and an abundance of analogues that indicate the possibility that fiction by women is a body of material that can be described as a self-contained universe following its own organic principles. Describing that universe is, of course, an impossible job for a single individual. One aspect of women's studies and its subcategory of feminist criticism that I have found most heartening is that it is cooperative rather than competitive: Any number of colleagues have been willing to argue my premises with me; two graduate students coauthored chapters with me; and a helpful group of other students read widely in the woman's novel and developed synopses for my use.

The second theoretical discovery I have made has to do with genres in the novel. In my historical survey I noticed two basic plots in the novel since the eighteenth century: In the first, found very frequently, we have the bright, witty young woman setting forth into the world—Evelina, Emma, Dorothea (Dorothea gets remarried, but she is at the outset this type of woman)—but succumbing to a childlike marriage in the end. That is, there are feminist signs and portents—the hero is critical of what she sees in society, is able to be witty about marital norms, but in the end she gets married and lives happily ever after, round and round the mulberry bush. In the second plot, tragic genre, a hero is also a witty, intelligent young person who desires autonomy and self-dependence more strongly than the hero of the comic novel; and for this she must die. She is critical of capitalistic and chauvinistic mores, she is critical of the idea that she should sell herself in marriage by providing herself and her dowry as an asset to somebody else. Jane Austen's novels, although they end comically, are full of this money consciousness among women and men: "He is worth £3000 a year." In the tragic genre the hero is not going to subordinate herself to this; she declares her *non serviam*, I will not serve, and she dies. Examples of this are Maggie Tulliver in *The Mill on the Floss* by George Eliot, Rachel Vinrace in Virginia Woolf's *The Voyage Out* (her first novel), Esther Greenwood in Sylvia Plath's *The Bell Jar,* and to cite a male example, Clarissa in Richardson's *Clarissa Harlowe.* You can perceive Clarissa saying (although in all these novels the revolt is subtle, muted) *"non serviam,* I will not serve. I will not marry the old man my parents and brother tell me to marry. I will, if you insist on this marriage, run away with Lovelace the seducer, but he is not going to get away with seducing me except by drugging me and once he does that, I refuse to live." Clarissa's virginity here is the will for liberation, the only way she can protect herself from the culture. But death is dealt out by that culture for her rebellion.

Death is also dealt out at the end of novels in a genre that I call the "fallen woman" novel. Up to about 1900, if a hero shows the least wiggle of sexuality she is likely to die, usually in childbirth, as a punishment. That is, any woman who shows erotic initiative, choice making, or activism in love, such as Jane Eyre's love for Rochester, is going to be punished. Charlotte Brontë shocked the critics of her time by letting Jane Eyre propose to Rochester; they called her a sexual revolutionary, unwomanly. An exception who survives and gets her man is rare in the woman's novel; finding her gave me a sense of exhilaration, leading me to trace the history of erotic initiative in women's literature from Eleanor of Aquitaine to Victoria Woodhull. Another exception is Elizabeth Gaskell's *Ruth* (1853). Gaskell permits her hero to go on and become a useful member of the community even after she has "fallen," been seduced and borne an illegitimate baby. Gaskell allows her, in spite of the protest of the villagers, to die a very useful death, having nursed everybody, including her former seducer, during a typhoid epidemic. Elizabeth Gaskell was severely criticized for the book, which was publicly burned. She said that when this happened she knew how Saint Sebastian felt (he was the one shot full of arrows). She was tortured socially for that book.

The third critical proposition, perhaps my most startling discovery, has to do with what I call the "drowning theory." It derives from my study of plots in which sexist norms are criticized in the middle of the action but the critical hero gets it in the end; comic plots in which patriarchal misbehavior on the part of unsuitable suitors is mocked and then the hero marries somebody less ridiculous in the end. The point is that we have in both genres a pattern in which feminist consciousness is raised but society has its way in the end. Two other feminist theoreticians and I disagree on this matter: Germaine Greer and Kate Millett both feel that the happily-ever-after or drown-the-hero denouements are copouts. Greer says that sexual religion is the opiate of the supermenial, that is, that women's going in for romantic love is a way of keeping them tied to men. Millett feels that these denouements conform to the way our society is put together, and that it is pointless to raise consciousness only to snuff it out.

I hope that my "drowning theory" isn't just a pollyannish way of getting around this. I don't think it is. It comes from a phenomenon in black culture: You have a little black church back in the marsh and you're going to sing "Go Down Moses." Well, it's all right to sing "Go Down Moses" because the white folks will think you're being religious when you're really singing "get me out of here." Every now and then, though, the members of the congregation want to break loose and sing "Oh Freedom," with its chorus of "Before I'll be a slave/I'll be buried in my grave/and go home to my lord/and be free." Whenever they sing that, they've got this big old black pot in the vestibule, and as they sing they pound the pot. That way, no white folks are going to hear. The drowning effect, this banging on the pot to drown out what they are actually saying about feminism, came in with the first woman's novel and hasn't gone out yet. Many women novelists have even succeeded in hiding the covert or implicit feminism in their books from themselves, as well as from the white man who holds the publishing purse strings. As a result we get explicit cultural norms superimposed upon an authentic creative mind in the form of all kinds of feints, ploys, masks, and disguises embedded in the plot structure and characterization. This way, the woman novelist gets away with the unacceptable portrayal of women as human beings.

We must read women's fiction carefully and not be too judgmental from an ideological feminist point of view because those women are in just as bad a place as that little black church in the marsh. The women writers themselves denied that they were feminist. The strangest example is Charlotte Brontë, who even tried to hide the fact that she wrote *Jane Eyre* from her best friend. In a letter she said, in effect: "You know, of course, I didn't write *Jane Eyre*. Currer Bell wrote it, and anyway, you know my feeling that no woman should permit herself to be in love with her husband until five years after the marriage, and then only moderately." That is an example of not letting your left hand know what your right hand is doing, because the remarkable thing about Jane Eyre is her determination to get Rochester on her terms and in bed. Charlotte Brontë's work bristles with sexual repression, the heroes caught in it but struggling against it with all their might. And then we have George Eliot's favorite public posture: "I am a woman, I *am* a woman, I am a *woman*, I really am." Eliot had a lot to fight, living out of wedlock, so she bent over backward to project an image of herself as a homebody. Doris Lessing is a recent case in point; until recently she denied being a feminist. The truth is, at the time she wrote *The Golden Notebook* she was not a feminist; nevertheless, she wrote the most implicitly feminist book to come out in thirty years.

The result of my survey is an exhilarating sense of rediscovering a tradition, a culture, a whole body of material whose heroes are my heroes and whose landscape is recognizable as the landscape of my mind—as it is of everywoman's. I want to go on, to think more deeply about the relationship between patterns of character development and of literary symbols that express this development, on the one hand, and the archetypal patterns described hitherto as implicitly male. While engaged in the task of bibliographical, textual, and contextual criticism, I notice that the heroes in women's novels manifest interestingly parallel stages in their psychic development, and that these parallels between women do not mimic patterns in male literature. It was startling to postulate that volumes had been written about the development of the male psyche as if it defined the human soul. If a "myth of the hero" existed, delineating his quest for life's meaning, one could also describe a myth of the heroine, a female as well as a male quest pattern.

This is what happens when one starts looking at quest patterns and literary symbols without standard Jungian archetypal preconceptions. Jung wrote that the male in literature often has to come to terms with his "anima," the feminine other-half dormant at the bottom of his psyche. Jung described the pathologies that resulted from a male's not coming to terms with this figure, but when he described a woman trying to come to terms with her "animus," her male underside, he tended to be negative and to see her experience as neurotic.[9] Jung was delighted, for example, with Molly Bloom as Leopold Bloom's "anima" in Joyce's *Ulysses*, proclaiming the work as a perfect description of the human psyche. What he failed to document was that when a woman went down to the bottom of her psyche she found not Molly Bloom but, far more likely, Rochester. Thus we have Willa Cather's Corn God as a central figure in the rebirth experience of Alexandra in *O Pioneers*, and the God of Death coming to Emily Dickinson in his chariot. The woman writer tends to develop the figure of a frightening, seductive male: the king of her dark chamber is not Cleopatra.

I have had to ask myself whether in describing these "female" archetypal figures, I was not just getting into a reversal of figures, as stereotypical as Jungian criticism. If the work of art depends upon stereotypically "male" or "female" figures, I have described it as it is there; but an interesting fact about the modern novel, both male and female, is that it tends toward androgyny (see the outline at end of this chapter). Let me give an example of the kinds of archetypal patterns that emerge out of a close textual analysis. I set off in the fall of 1971 to do a textual analysis of Woolf's *To the Lighthouse*, word by word. Before I knew what had happened, I had come upon Mrs. Ramsay, the hero, having an erection. This was the genesis of an article, "Mrs. Ramsay's Erection," to which I applied the drowning effect and titled, for publication and promotion purposes, "Sexual Imagery in *To the Lighthouse*." [10] Here is the text in question:

> Mrs. Ramsay, who had been sitting loosely, folding her son in her arm, braced herself, and, half turning, seemed to raise herself with an effort, and at once to pour erect into the air a rain of energy, a column of spray, looking at the same time animated and alive as if all her energies were being fused into force, burning and illuminating (quietly though she sat, taking up her stocking again), and into this delicious fecundity, this fountain and spray of life, the fatal sterility of the male plunged itself, like a beak of brass, barren and bare. He wanted sympathy . . . to be taken within the circle of life, warmed and soothed, to have his senses restored to him, his barrenness made fertile, and all the rooms of the house made full of life." [11]

Those of you who are aware of male and female patterns in imagery recognize some standard female imagery here, but who is pouring what into whom? She has the erection; he's got the beak of brass, and one does not get any fluid out of a beak of brass. She has to be both male and female to him. She must perform this function for Mr. Ramsay because he is one of those academic males who have developed their brains at the expense of their psyches, and he leeches off her like a child of six.

Having discovered that Mrs. Ramsay has an erection, I had to think very sad thoughts about penis envy and to worry about whether Freud was right. Actually, it seemed to me that what was happening was that Mrs. Ramsay simply assimilated her animus; having found no appropriate person to project it upon she had taken it back to herself, as it were. She has to do this because she is not able to get anything from her emotional intercourse with the tyrannical, childish Mr. Ramsay; and he, in turn, is demanding a kind of psychological impregnation from her. The only way that she can get renewal is to go off alone and sit and look at the lighthouse, feel its strokes of light. This is an inner journey, taking her away from life:

> . . . *pausing there she looked out to meet that stroke of the Lighthouse, the long steady stroke, the last of the three, which was her stroke . . . [she] felt an irrational tenderness thus (she looked at that long steady light) as for oneself. There rose, and she looked and looked with her needles suspended, there curled off the floor of the mind, rose from the lake of one's being, a mist, a bride to meet her lover. . . .*
>
> *It silvered the rough waves a little more brightly, as daylight faded, and the blue went out of the sea and it rolled in pure lemon which curved and swelled and broke upon the beach and the ecstasy burst in her eyes and waves of pure delight raced over the floor of her mind and she felt, It is enough! It is enough!* [12]

The ecstasy is in Mrs. Ramsay's mind; it remains within the interior of her psyche, nonprojected, not realized in an actual relationship with another human being. Although Woolf does not imply this, it seems to me that this inwardness contributes to Mrs. Ramsay's death soon after. The person, Jung says, who goes down to the bottom of his psyche and falls in love with only his inner anima, entranced with an inner femininity, does not return to life; he goes mad, or dies. You can imagine what was said to me by other feminist critics after I came inadvertently on Mrs. Ramsay's erection; and this is one of the risks of objectivity, of inductive research. If the patterns are there, we must come to terms with them.

Northrop Frye, in his description of literary archetypes, also pointed out that literature as a whole falls into patterns during its development from period to period; and it is interesting to note that women's literature in and of itself also follows similar, even parallel patterns. Both Doris Lessing and Virginia Woolf, in their total work, start out with a green world of innocence and move through experience, going through a period of renewed sexuality and coming, at the end, to face some kind of cosmic resolution—an end-of-the-world event, a masque, a dance, the suggestion of a new cycle. The whole body of women's literature, in turn, seems at present to be moving toward a new kind of vision, a collective possibility, a new humanism, even while it describes inhumanities and dissensions that characterize the present society.

I have surveyed some of these patterns in the outline I present at the conclusion of this chapter as a chart for my continuing research. They are complicated, but striking in their suggestion that perhaps male and female literature is coming together, out of necessity, to transcend its historical categories in the evolution of a more androgynous possibility. For the moment, however, it seems important to conclude with a few political questions left hanging at the close of a literary project. What is the relationship between the persistence of the woman's novel at the present time and the lack of consistency in political feminism during the century? That is, does women's fiction, for all its implicit feminism, contribute anything to reform, or does it, in some way, hamper real changes in society? In a pessimistic mood one might come to the conclusion that the woman's novel performs a cathartic function of bringing into consciousness the tragic enslavement of one half of the human race only to drain off the pity and fear accompanying that consciousness through the experience of reading. In this formula the ladies of misrule are allowed to question and argue with male norms but are sent back to their proper sphere at the denouements as inevitably as the servants dressed as lords and ladies in the medieval mardi gras had to return to servitude in the hierarchy that permitted them their moment of play. Some feminists feel that if the novel only drains off indignation, it becomes a weapon in the hands of the enemy.

I take the position that, in spite of its tendency to destroy its best and marry off its brightest, the awareness created by the woman's novel is an ineradicable awareness, a cry for liberation that once heard will not go forever unregarded. In spite of setbacks in the world of politics, the woman's novel has remained an underground force throughout history, resurfacing in the 1970s to effect a new era of political feminism. Under my argument all reforms, no matter how tiny, are revolutionary: Consciousness, once raised, remains raised; and each modification makes the victims of patriarchal repression increasingly impatient with the status quo that represents a set of values not only dehumanizing but dysfunctional. There is no place left in an overpopulated world for the perpetuation of either traditional "female" functions (childbirth without check, obedience to authority) or traditional "male" prerogatives (competition rather than cooperation, a Darwinian scramble of the fittest rather than a collective endeavor to survive).

For women, history has not moved in the same phases as the textbooks declare: The bio-patriarchal lag responsible for archaic sexual practices closes down on us like a dank canopy while the beneficiaries of an outmoded power system wave their missiles in the fresh air outside. The woman's novel continues as a tenacious art and social form, holding our mirror up to the sexual politics of difficult times that have known little remedy since its inception. It continues to provide for both its authors and its audience a solace, a goad, a look at the worst in order to dream of the better, a report from the battlefields and an accounting of our wounded. But it also provides a message from the frontiers of a more fully human space than we have yet to comprehend.

NOTES

1. BARBARA DESMARAIS, in *Women's Caucus of the Midwest Modern Language Association Newsletter*, 8 October 1973.

2. See KATE MILLETT on Lawrence, Miller, etc., in *Sexual Politics*; DOLORES BARRACANO SCHMIDT, "The Great American Bitch," and JUDITH MONTGOMERY, "The American Galatea," *College English*, May 1971.

3. MARY ELLMANN, *Thinking about Women* (New York: Harcourt Brace, 1968), pp. 35, 40. See also CAROL OHMANN, "Emily Brontë in the Hands of Male Critics," *College English*, May 1971; and BARBARA WHITE, "A Bell Jar for Critics" (Ph.D. dissertation, University of Wisconsin, 1974).

4. See the work of S. BARBARA KANNER, "The Women in England in a Century of Social Change, 1815 to 1914: A Selective Bibliography," in *Suffer and Be Still*; ed. Martha

Vicinus, *Women in the Victorian Age* (Bloomington: Indiana University Press, 1972); also the Sense and Sensibility Collective Bibliography, *Women and Literature* (Cambridge: Sense & Sensibility Collective, 1973), and Maureen Fries and Anne M. Daunis, eds., "A Bibliography of Writings by and about Women Authors, British and American, 1957–1969" (Women's Caucus for the Modern Languages, 1971).

5. See LOUIS KAMPF AND PAUL LAUTER, eds., *The Politics of Literature: Dissenting Essays on the Teaching of English* (New York: Random House, 1970).

6. For a consideration of ideological approaches to literature as they differ from formalism, see LILLIAN S. ROBINSON, "Dwelling in Decencies," *College English*, May 1971, and (with LISE VOGEL) ROBINSON's "Modernism and History," in *Images of Women in Fiction* (Bowling Green, Ohio: Bowling Green University Press, 1972). See also, in the same collection, FRAYA KATZ-STOKER's "The Other Criticism: Feminism vs. Formalism."

7. CARL JUNG, *Psychological Reflections* (New York: Bollingen, 1953), p. 97. See also ANNIS PRATT, "Archetypal Approaches to the New Feminist Criticism," *Bucknell Review*, Spring 1973.

8. NORTHROP FRYE, *Anatomy of Criticism* (Princeton, N.J.: Princeton University Press, 1957), p. 98.

9. See PRATT, "Archetypal Approaches."

10. In *Modern Fiction Studies*, Autumn 1972.

11. VIRGINIA WOOLF, *To the Lighthouse* (London: Hogarth Press, 1960), pp. 61–62.

12. Ibid., pp. 100–104.

AFTERWORD:
Some Thoughts on "Beyond Male and Female" *(Work in Progress)*

Explanation: "The New Feminist Criticism" *College English* article[1] was stage (1) exploratory, raising questions; The University of Northern Iowa speech (1973) is (2) some of the results of surveying women's literature with these questions in mind; and what I am summarizing here for you for the Madison Feminist Criticism Collective is stage (3) having to do with some tentative conclusions as I near the end of the historical survey.

I. "OVERCOMING METHODOLATRY"

This is implicit in my suggestion at the MMLA forum in October 1973, that Feminist Criticism = Feminist Criticisms, as listed on the chart attached. However, in an interchange in South Bend, Indiana, with a male faculty member who was puzzled because he had come to hear my "methodology" to report back to the boys in the bar (where the male faculty lurked while I conducted a faculty seminar on NFC) and after coming across the following in Mary Daly's *Beyond God the Father*, I realized that the insistence upon a single method is not only disfunctional but an attribute of the patriarchy:

One of the false gods of theologians, philosophers, and other academics is called Method. It commonly happens that the choice of a problem is determined by method, instead of method being determined by the problem. . . .

It should be noted that the god Method is in fact a subordinate deity, serving Higher Powers. These are social and cultural institutions whose survival depends upon the classification of disruptive and disturbing information as nondata. Under patriarchy, Method has wiped out women's questions so totally that even women have not been able to hear and formulate our own questions to meet our own experiences. Women have been unable even to experience our own experience.[2]

II. BEYOND MALE AND FEMALE

During the University of Wisconsin English Departmental Seminar on New Feminist Criticism last year, Audrey Roberts (as Lillian Robinson previously, in "Dwelling in Decencies," *College English*, May 1971) called attention to the fact that my quest for a female archetypal theory as a parallel quest to the male mythos of romance might be defined as sex stereotyping. After some months of further reading in the woman's novel the hypothesis occurred to me that the archetypal pattern in the woman's novel reflects a movement *beyond* male and female categories and *toward* a more androgynous norm. (See Carolyn Heilbrun, *Towards a Recognition of Androgyny.*[3])

A. The novel moves beyond "male" and "female" by satirizing excessively "male" and excessively "female" behaviors, those characters manifesting these behaviors being satirized and those characters manifesting a blend of traditional "male" and "female" characteristics being held up as norms.

  1. satiric targets—Mary McCarthy's various *roman à clef* portraits of Edmund Wilson;[4] Dr. Pederson and his wife in Oates' *Wonderland*;[5] Jonathan, the husband in Kaufman's *Diary of a Mad Housewife*;[6] Mrs. Bennett, so female as to be ineffective, in *Pride and Prejudice*;[7] the homemaker in Canfield's novel of that title who is such a good housewife that she nearly destroys her family; and, as a nonfictional example, the sweet tender little girl (ladies first, ladies first) on the Marlo Thomas record, *Free to be You and Me*, who gets eaten by the tiger.

  2. norms—Dorothea with her community interests, in *Middlemarch*;[8] Jane Eyre daring to initiate love for Rochester; Jane in Drabble's *The Waterfall*;[9] Margaret Culkin Banning's male characters struggling to realize that their wives' careers will not destroy their manhood; Catherine Carter in Pamela Hansford Johnson's novel of that name wanting to play the part of Cleopatra with her actor-lover-husband who doesn't want anyone to equal him; the reconciliation of two talented people passionately in love with each other and their careers.[10]

B. The novel moves beyond "male" and "female" by depicting a rebirth journey in which the hero must incorporate characteristics traditionally allocated to males while suffering from conformity to expectations of femininity. Since such a breakthrough is like skinning your skin off, many fall by the wayside; few survive.

The beginning of a breakthrough means a realization that there is an existential conflict between the self and structures that have given such crippling security. This requires confronting the shock of nonbeing with the courage to be. It means facing the nameless anxieties of fate, which become concretized in loss of jobs, friends, social approval, health, and even life itself. Also involved is anxiety of guilt over refusing to do what society demands, a guilt which can hold one in its grip long after it has been recognized as false—Mary Daly, Beyond God the Father, p. 24.

1. The Wounded, The Dead, and the Mad

   (a) Novelists of Manners survive by mocking and laughing at "male" and "female" behaviors. Edith Wharton, Angela Thirkell, Nancy Mitford, Mary McCarthy, Katherine Anne Porter. The Family as Monster novel (Suckow, Oates), Growing up Grotesque (McCullers, Oates), most novelists of female adolescence in Barbara White's sample, UW dissertation, *Novels of Female Adolescence*.[11]
   Query: Is this a "things as they are" genre, in which the author plays the blues upon her blue guitar, "that's the way it is, baby," "play it as it lays?" Or does Doris Grumbach's analysis of McCarthy's satire suggest something more revolutionary:

   "Perhaps the most damaging accusation is that, in contradiction to Louis Auchincloss' view that Mary McCarthy is related to Sarah Orne Jewett and Edith Wharton in her efforts to 'preserve traditions in her own century,' her real aim is to be not a caretaker of what is still of value in her era but a wrecker of it all. Her satirical powers are directed toward total destruction of what she has found hateful." *The Company She Kept*, p. 15.[12] (Don't underestimate Wharton and Jewett, sister.)

   (b) Truncated quests, or bodies in the battle. The woman's novel as report from the battlefield, a cautionary map?
   —criticism and accommodation, where pointed criticism of sexual norms are followed by the heroes' return to their efforts to render men and matrimony more human: Kaufman's *Diary of a Mad Housewife*, heroes in Zona Gayle, Josephine Herbst, Ruth Suckow who give it another try.

   (c) The Fatal Effects of Matrimony, or, maley male drives woman crazy. "What we consider 'madness,' whether it appears in women or in men, is either the acting out of the devalued female role or the total or partial rejection of one's sex-role stereotype." Chesler, *Women and Madness*.[13]
   Atwood's *The Edible Woman*,[14] Plath's *Bell Jar*,[15] Gilman's *The Yellow Wallpaper*,[16] Boyd's *Nerves*,[17] Schaeffer's *Falling*,[18] Rhys' *The Wide Saragasso Sea*[19] (about the first Mrs. Rochester and how she got that way); experiences with breakdown of Anna Wulf and Martha Quest; incarceration of Mary Leon in Fanny Fern's *Ruth*[20] and of hero of *Play It As It Lays* by Joan Didion[21].
   Suicides—Eve in Porter's "Old Mortality," [22] hero of McCarthy's *The Group*,[23] attempts in *Bell Jar*; witherings away in Woolf's *The Voyage Out*,[24] Phelps' *The Story of Avis*;[25] suicides, in real life, of Sylvia Plath, Virginia Woolf, etc., etc.

   Oh, mother, I am tired and sick.
   One sister, new to this pain called feminist consciousness
   For want of a scream to name it, asked me last week
   "But how do you stop from going crazy?"
   No way, my sister,
   No Way.
       —Robin Morgan, "Monster"

2. Survivors

   (a) Rebirth novels—Oates' *Do With Me What You Will*,[26] *To the Lighthouse*,[27] (except that Mrs. Ramsay dies), perhaps Richardson's *Pilgrim-*

age,[28] Sharon Spencer's *The Space Between*,[29] Banning's *The Spellbinders*,[30] Atherton's *Immortal Marriage*,[31] Lessing's *The Golden Notebook*[32] (to the extent that the Anna-Saul androgyny becomes internalized, bringing Anna to new vision), Atwood's *Surfacing*.[33]

(b) The "Odd woman" novel, dealing with single women, widows, divorcees, women who are having affairs outside of matrimony, and lesbians, is likely to be a mere mirror of matrimony but more frequently produces a hero who is more "together" than the marriage novel.

   (1) mere mirrors, or "The Golden Egg" novel (after Herbst's story in which the free woman is assailed by her married friend's husband): Rosamund Lehmann's *The Weather in the Streets*, *The Echoing Grove*;[34] Anna and Molly's affairs in *The Golden Notebook*.

   (2) spinsters creative in their own space—Louisa in Freeman's *The New England Nun*; many characters in Alice Wood, Sarah Orne Jewett, and other "regional" writers; Sylvia Townsend Warner's *Lolly Willowes* who becomes a witch.[35]

   (3) women who survive their affairs intact: Jane, in Drabble's *The Waterfall*; Elena, at the very end of *Do With Me What You Will* (Oates). (But then consider Spark's *The Prime of Miss Jean Brodie*.[36])

   (4) Single parents making it on their own—Drabble's *The Milestone*,[37] Lynne Banks, *The L-Shaped Room*.[38]

°as far as I have gotten in actual readings, September 1, 1974

   (5) "Chloe liked Olivia perhaps for the first time in literature." Virginia Woolf. Actually, not the first time: women as friends in the woman's novel are a constant, often supporting each other against the onslaughts of one tyrannical male after another.
   a. a tracing of these sisterhood, women-friends theme.
   b. the lesbian novel proper—a sample of about 20.

   Query: Do lesbian couples mirror married ones or are there strong alternatives to marriage? Sample includes Stein, Sarton, Rita Brown.

(c) Is sexuality and eroticism, Romantic Love either in the heterosexual or homosexual form, a positive or negative element in women's liberation? (The Greer/vs. Eleanor of Aquitaine argument about *Erotic Initiative* carried over from Chapter III, *Feminism and Fiction* here to Chapter V.)

Theory: Jameson, in *Marxism and Form*, mentions the process of creating utopian worlds, as in Rousseau, as sneered at by intellectuals because it requires a return to the primitive, which is a return to the source, Eros, Libido (see also Rollo May, *Love and Will*). Feminist theoreticians have been rightly suspicious of this "return," which characterizes fascism and patriarchalism as in Hughes, Dickey, Lawrence, etc. However, consider: ". . . the process can be seen precisely as that return to the common source of both poetry and politics, of the erotic and the political impulses, which marks a reintegration of consciousness fragmented in the modern world." [39]

Hypothesis: In the twentieth century woman's novel, as in the earlier genre, the woman hero seeks erotic initiative, seeks a depth of sexual love, not in order to submit herself as object but in order to exercise her full range of faculties as subject; to become whole, to act as a *gestalt* of intellect, body, and heart: the human form divine includes, in its androgynous totality, the experience of love and of eroticism.

C. Black and proletarian fiction intensifies the theme of woman's oppression and includes further critiques of industrial capitalism and of racism as contributory to woman's alienation.

Hypothesis taken from Barbara White's sample of 85 adolescent novels, middle-class, white, black, and proletarian: 1. "To the heroine who is poor, adolescence generally means being old enough to help support the family. It is initiation into hard work and portends a future of hard work. . . . But this does not mean that the poor protagonist is unaware of her sex; if anything, she seems to be more disturbed by her approaching womanhood than other heroines because she fears her sex will doom her to a life of continued poverty." 2. "Black female adolescents have it worst of all, [they] are in a particularly vulnerable position because they are barred even from the traditional compensation of womanhood, that is, from being a *valued* sex object." 48 ms.

Proletarian sample includes Olsen, Smedley, Arnow, Herbst;[40] black sample Morrison, Brooks, Meriwether, Petry, Fausset, Hurston, Marshall.[41]

D. Woman aestheticians and mythologists create imagery worlds for realistic struggles. Hypothesis: That the fictional dreams of H. D., Nin, Austin, Bryher parallel as archetypal constructs the quest of the female hero for a Four-Gated City in more standardly narrative fiction. Science Fiction? Joanna Russ?

E. As in the last phase of the archetypal pattern described by Frye, *many women's novels show a motion toward a collective vision*, a utopian construct based upon criticism of things-as-they-are (including industrial capitalism and racism) and of standard sex roles. However, the fiction of the collective feminist vision contains the shadow of itself, the opposite of what is most to be desired.

1. Collective possibilities: civil war women's farm in May Sarton's *Kinds of Love*[42] and in some World War II novels; the island-commune at the end of *The Four-Gated City*;[43] perhaps collective dorm in Spark's *The Girls of Slender Means*;[44] the woman's house and dance collective in *Small Changes*;[45] the six persons in friendship in *The Waves* and elements of *The Years, Between the Acts*.[46]

2. The dialecticity of the collective vision

Two cities in *Martha Quest*;[47] the refugee camps vs. the dream in *The Four-Gated City*;
The historical vs. present world in *Kinds of Love*
The burning of the dorm in *The Girls of Slender Means*
The nuclear marriage of Miriam in *Small Changes* and the male collective from which the women escape
The negative imagery of *The Years* and *The Waves*—creation and destruction, Heraclitan flux

Possible theoretical foundation for the dialectic: from Frederic Jameson's *Marxism and Form*

(a) He has pointed out that Schiller *believed* in his utopian visions; the world of imagination having reality to the Romantic. Intellectual history has denied the "romantic desire for a concrete future utopia" as *real*. (But see Roszak, new romantic theorist of the counterculture.)

(b) T. W. Adorno, however, postulates a Negative Dialektik between an idea and reality: ". . . the practice of negative dialectics involves a constant movement away from the official content of an an idea—as, for example, the 'real' nature of freedom [(or, Annis, feminism)] . . . and toward the various determinate and contradictory forms which such ideas have taken, whose conceptual limits and inadequacies stand as immediate figures or symptoms of the limits of the concrete social situation itself." 55

(c) The dialectic between the "real" social situation and the perennial human desire for freedom is played out within the figures of art. Hence, Lukács' interest in narrative, in structure: "Lukács' particular interest is on narrative structure. The effect of the environment upon the form itself: . . . what is more important is the influence of a given social raw material, not only on the content, but on the very form of the works themselves."

(d) THEREFORE, IN THE DIALECTIC BETWEEN HISTORICITY AND THE IMAGINARY WORLD OF THE ARTIST the novel has its foundations, and, following the Marxist aesthetics of Lukács et al., a FORMALIST ANTI-formalism is made possible.

III. Which leads, in turn, to a THEORY OF THE FUNCTION OF FICTION, specifically of women's fiction within its given socioeconomic, historical, psychological context.

A. "For the notion of a realization of freedom in art becomes concrete only when, in *On Naive and Sentimental Poetry*, Schiller descends into the detail of the work of art itself, there teaching us to see the very technical construction of the work as a *figure* of the struggle for psychic integration in general, to see in images, a quality of language, type of plot construction the very figures of freedom itself." Jameson.

"Indeed most art and poetry in our culture expresses patriarchal feelings (look at the flabby, unathletic bodies of Renaissance Madonnas; read the diarrheic outpourings of misogynism in Milton, Kipling, Claudel). By contrast, the new sounds of silence, sparking forth a network of boundary communication, is the dawning of communal New Being. This is neither 'public' nor 'private,' neither 'objective' nor 'subjective.' It is intersubjective silence, the vibrations of which are too high for the patriarchal hearing mechanism. It is, then, ultrasonic." Mary Daly, p. 152. See also Joan Roberts, "The Ramifications of the Study of Women," and Bea Cameron, "Language as a Feminine Mode of Action."

B. Fiction, like poetry, is a quasi-playful construction, a fiction or faction or a making of a new thing by putting elements from the world together, following the same principles of construction as the dream and bringing about the same effect: another, not only compensatory but perhaps more real world for the sleeper, a bringing together of her experience in a coherent, structured form, to be delighted in over/and/against the apparent chaos and patriarchal tyranny of the "real" world.

The tension between the "real" world and a more humane possibility, a tension which stretches to the breaking point in the psyche of the victims of modern patriarchal industrialism, is particularly tightly strung within the woman's novel, so tightly that it resonates, that it frequently breaks and the music is lost altogether.

C. *Women's fiction is structured upon a dialectic* between the desired and the actual. The world of woman's art is not the aesthetic other-world of the new critics, self-existent, with no reference to historical and cultural context. (See Lauter et al., *The Politics of Literature*,[48] for white critics' denial of historicity; Addison Gaylord's *Black Expression*[49] for the results of apolitical literature departments on black literature.)

D. *Women's fiction is, rather, a report from the battlefield* of sexual politics; sometimes a dream of a better world; a critique of the enemy, his flaws and weaknesses, the flaws and weaknesses of the "womenly women" who are his allies; sometimes it is a cry from the prison or a shout from the barred windows of the insane asylum which is (following Chesler) a concentration camp for interning those women who protest too loudly, who are too radical in their dreams and recommendations.

E. *Women's fiction represents, sometimes, a report from women's consciousness, a delineation of that new place from its explorers,* encoded by necessity for publication in an alien world; a secret code, the work of an underground which has passed on its traditions from Aphra Behn (who was a spy) to Mrs. Opie to Jane Austen to George Eliot to Kate Chopin to Gertrude Atherton to Doris Lessing to Virginia Woolf to Joyce Carol Oates. In and of itself, like the Songs of Indians, it contains the texture of a world that is passing and a hoped-for world to come, coming itself from a new space occupied only by the most intrepid of adventurers and explored only at the risk of one's own skin.[50]

> Weave real connections, create real nodes,
>   build real houses.
> Live a life you can endure: make love that is loving.
> Keep tangling and interweaving and
>   taking more in,
> A thicket and bramble wilderness to the outside but
>   to us
> interconnected with rabbit runs and burrows and
>   lairs.
> Live as if you liked yourself and it may
>   happen:
> reach out, keep reaching out, keep bringing in.
> This is how we are going to live for a long time:
>   not always
> for every gardener knows that after the
>   digging, after the planting,
> after the long season of tending and growth,
>   the harvest comes.
>   —Marge Piercy, *To Be Of Use*

NOTES

1. ANNIS PRATT, "The New Feminist Criticism," *College English* (May 1971): 872–78.

2. MARY DALY, *Beyond God the Father* (Boston: Beacon Press, 1973), pp. 11–12.

3. CAROLYN HEILBRUN, *Towards a Recognition of Androgyny* (New York: Knopf, 1973).

4. MARY McCARTHY, *The Groves of Academe* (New York: Harcourt, Brace, 1951) and *A Charmed Life* (New York: Harcourt, Brace, 1954).

5. JOYCE CAROL OATES, *Wonderland* (New York: Vanguard Press, 1971).

6. SUE KAUFMAN, *Diary of a Mad Housewife* (New York: Bantam Books, 1967).

7. JANE AUSTEN, *Pride and Prejudice* (Cleveland, Ohio: World, 1946).

8. GEORGE ELIOT, *Middlemarch* (Baltimore: Penguin Books, 1968).

9. MARGARET DRABBLE, *The Waterfall* (New York: New American Library, 1969).

10. PAMELA HANSFORD JOHNSON, *Catherine Carter* (New York: Knopf, 1952).

11. BARBARA WHITE, "Growing up Female: Adolescent Girlhood in American Literature," Ph.D. dissertation, University of Wisconsin, 1974.

12. DORIS GRUMBACH, *The Company She Kept* (New York: Coward McCann, 1967), p. 15.

13. PHYLLIS CHESLER, *Women and Madness* (New York: Avon Books, 1973), p. 75.

14. MARGARET ATWOOD, *The Edible Woman* (Boston: Little, Brown, 1970).

15. SYLVIA PLATH, *The Bell Jar* (New York: Bantam, 1970).

16. CHARLOTTE PERKINS GILMAN, *The Yellow Wallpaper* (Old Westbury, N.Y.: Feminist Press, 1973).

17. BLANCHE M. BOYD, *Nerves* (Boston: Daughters, Inc., 1973).

18. SUSAN FROMBERG SCHAEFFER, *Falling* (New York: Signet, 1973).

19. JEAN RHYS, *The Wide Sargasso Sea* (New York: Norton, 1966).

20. FANNY FERN, *Ruth Hall* (London: Dent, 1967).

21. JOAN DIDION, *Play It As It Lays* (New York: Bantam, 1963).

22. KATHERINE ANNE PORTER, "Old Mortality," in *Pale Horse, Pale Rider* (New York: New American Library, 1962).

23. MARY MCCARTHY, *The Group* (New York: Harcourt, Brace & World, 1963).

24. VIRGINIA WOOLF, *The Voyage Out* (New York: Harcourt Brace Jovanovich, 1968).

25. ELIZABETH STUART PHELPS, *The Story of Avis* (Boston: Osgood, 1877).

26. JOYCE CAROL OATES, *Do With Me What You Will* (Greenwich, Conn.: Fawcett Crest, 1973).

27. VIRGINIA WOOLF, *To the Lighthouse* (New York: Harcourt, Brace & World, 1927).

28. DOROTHY RICHARDSON, *Pilgrimage* (New York: Knopf, 1967).

29. SHARON SPENCER, *The Space Between* (New York: Harper & Row, 1973).

30. MARGARET CULKIN BANNING, *The Spellbinders* (New York: George H. Doran, 1922).

31. GERTRUDE ATHERTON, *Immortal Marriage* (New York: Boni & Liveright, 1927).

32. DORIS LESSING, *The Golden Notebook* (New York: Simon & Schuster, 1962).

33. MARGARET ATWOOD, *Surfacing* (New York: Popular Library, 1972).

34. ROSAMUND LEHMANN, *The Weather in the Streets* (New York: Reynal & Hitchcock, 1936) and *The Echoing Grove* (New York: Harcourt, Brace, 1953).

35. SYLVIA TOWNSEND WARNER, *Lolly Willowes* (New York: Viking, 1926).

36. MURIEL SPARK, *The Prime of Miss Jean Brodie* (New York: Dell, 1962).

37. MARGARET DRABBLE, *The Millstone* (in America, *Thank You All Very Much*) (New York: Signet, 1971).

38. LYNNE BANKS, *The L-Shaped Room* (New York: Simon & Schuster, 1961).

39. FREDERIC JAMESON, *Marxism and Form* (Princeton, N.J.: Princeton University Press, 1971).

40. Tillie Olsen, *Yonnondiao* (New York: Delacorte Press, 1974); Agnes Smedley, *Daughter of Earth* (Westbury, N.Y.: Feminist Press, 1973); Harriet Arnow, *The Dollmaker* (New York: Avon, 1954); Josephine Herbst's Trexler Trilogy: *Pity Is Not Enough* (New York: Harcourt Brace, 1939); *The Executioner Awaits* (New York: Harcourt Brace, 1934); and *Rope of Gold* (New York: Harcourt Brace, 1939).

41. Toni Morrison, *The Bluest Eye* (New York: Holt, Rinehart, & Winston, 1970) and *Sula* (New York: Knopf, 1973); Louise Meriwether, *Daddy Was a Numbers Runner* (New York: Pyramid Books, 1971); Ann Petry, *The Street* (Boston: Houghton Mifflin, 1946); and Jessie Redmon Fauset, "Plum Bun," in Lee Edwards and Arlyn Diamond, *American Voices, American Women* (New York: Avon, 1973).

42. May Sarton, *Kinds of Love* (New York: Avon, 1970).

43. Doris Lessing, *The Four-Gated City* (New York: Knopf, 1967).

44. Muriel Spark, *The Girls of Slender Means* (London: Macmillan, 1963).

45. Marge Piercy, *Small Changes* (Greenwich, Conn.: Fawcett Crest, 1972).

46. Virginia Woolf, *The Waves* (New York: Harcourt, Brace & World, 1931); *The Years* (New York: Harcourt Brace Jovanovich, 1937); *Between the Acts* (New York: Harcourt Brace Jovanovich, 1974).

47. Doris Lessing, *Martha Quest* (New York: Simon & Schuster, 1964).

48. Louis Kampf and Paul Lauter, *The Politics of Literature: Dissenting Essays on the Teaching of English* (New York: Vintage Books, 1970).

49. Addison Gayle, *Black Expression* (New York: Weybright & Talley, 1969).

50. For further bibliographies and references see *Women and Literature, An Annotated Bibliography of Women Writers* (Cambridge, Mass.: Sense & Sensibility Collective, 1971); Maureen M. Fries, Anne M. Daunis, and Elizabeth A. Rinnander, *A Bibliography of Writings By and About Women Authors* (Wisconsin: Women's Caucus for the Modern Languages, 1971); and Annis Pratt, *Feminism and Fiction* (Pittsburgh: University of Pittsburgh Press, forthcoming).

French Women
Writers: A
Problematic
Perspective
Germaine Brée

From the shadowy figure of "la belle Aude," Roland's betrothed in the *Song of Roland*, to Béa B, the baffling protagonist in J. M. G. Le Clézio's recently translated novel *War*,[1] hundreds of feminine figures people French literature, an inexhaustible and diversified host. I could not begin to delineate consistent underlying patterns in the "images" of women in French literature; the simplifications would be too drastic and the exercise rather meaningless. Only a team of critics could do the job. To a specialist's knowledge of ten centuries of literature, literary conventions, and styles, they would have to add a reasonable grasp of the changing sociocultural climate of French society throughout its history. It is a tricky undertaking to decipher the significance of literary motifs when the cultural gaps are as wide as those that separate us from past centuries.

Studies concerning women in literature have been plagued by categorizations sometimes rather rapidly framed and too widely applied out of context, such as the all too prevalent Eve—the Virgin Mary dichotomy. In any realm, including criticism, patterns too readily imposed limit the value of an investigation. We have considerable work to do if we are to prevent studies on this topic from plunging into cliché, hence triviality and boredom. In this context, I once encountered a text that was enlightening and entertaining: an account of a bourgeois club in Paris which, at the time when Pierre Corneille was projecting onstage the figures of his heroic women, met in order to debate the question of the relative place of woman and monkey in God's creation, a point of disputation that goes back to early Christian theology and was surely by then purely academic. We have only recently begun to think in terms of multiple cultural frames within a given society considered at any set period, rather than in terms of a single unified, totalitarian framework. Since, sociologists tell us, the images societies have of woman affect all social relationships, it is necessary to approach the question with care. Preconceptions could easily blur our observations, to say nothing of our identity as critics.

I shall therefore limit this essay to clusters of personal remarks concerning the situation of women writers in France today, with no thought of presenting an authoritative, exhaustive study;[2] rather, I shall attempt to see how the question of the woman writer can be approached most profitably by a critic who is herself a woman. The problem is real. In a sense, we are all trying to look from the outside at a question of which we are a part. Today, when we know a woman is the author of a book, the problem of "femaleness" intrudes as never before upon our awareness as readers. Inevitably it raises the concomitant question of "maleness" in literary art. These are unsettling questions; for they are related to other unresolved and broad issues, of which I shall formulate the two that seem to me most crucial: Are there real differences between the way men and women, as distinct from individuals, use language? Second, at a time when much scientific probing is going on concerning sex differentiation, whether in the natural or the social sciences, what, if any, are the natural (as distinct from the cultural) differences between men and women and what might their consequences be for the writer? These questions, crucial as they are, are likely to remain unanswered like so many others that concern art and literature. And they alone could provide answers to the questions we are attempting to resolve concerning women's literature: Is literature written by women to be considered and evaluated as a particular kind of literature not on a par with "literature" as such, a by-product secondary in its significance? Is there such a thing as a recognizable "femininity" in writing that, with some exceptions, has confined the woman writer to minor accomplishments in that realm? If so, is its source "natural" or cultural? Do successful women writers, as a group, show different characteristics from their male counterparts? Why, on the whole, have French women writers so often attained only a rather mediocre literary quality? At present no clear answer can be given.

In our midcentury years it was a woman writer—and a successful woman writer—Simone de Beauvoir, who, in her monumental treatise *The Second Sex*, published in 1949, arose in wrath to destroy the current notions of femininity; we know with what bitterness and eloquence she denounced signs of male resentment and superciliousness in the manner in which French male critics evaluated her books. She connected this trait to the much broader question of the image of women held—overtly or covertly—by French society, and thus launched anew in France the ageless and unresolved debate concerning women with which we have lately become all too familiar. An initial *querelle des femmes* took place in France at the dawn of the fifteenth century, 1398–1402, and has gone on, more or less heatedly, ever since, surfacing in times of social unrest—during and after the French Revolution, for example, and again in our time. Today's widespread *querelle des femmes* took on a specific coloring in the atmosphere of Paris, of French society, of the existentialist perspective in which it was formulated. It has been vigorous, but restricted in the main to Parisian circles. Some of the major exchanges at the higher level of intellectual debate being *An Open Letter to Women* by Francis Jeanson, a philosopher and friend of Simone de Beauvoir's, who disagreed with some of the latter's points; an eloquent, virulent answer, *An Open Letter to Men*, by another friend of Simone de Beauvoir's, a distinguished woman journalist and minor novelist, Françoise Parturier; and finally, a restatement of the question from a different perspective, *The Misunderstanding of the Second Sex*, by a woman lawyer, playwright and essayist, Suzanne Lilar, who starts with a thorough critique of Beauvoir's thesis and goes on to propose one of her own.[3] These are but a very few of the innumerable essays, long or short, thoughtful or passionate, that the debate has inspired, either in special issues of current reviews or under such titles as *Tomorrow Women, Woman in Search of Herself, Liberated Woman?* I shall not recapitulate the arguments; we listen to them every day. To what extent is there actually an "image" of woman operative in French society today and to what extent is it detrimental or favorable to the woman writer?

Since World War II, French society, everyone agrees, has been undergoing an uneasy and possibly a major mutation. In appearance at least, French intellectuals are critically reassessing that most nationally cherished of France's collective achievements, its culture. But traditions in France die hard. Even the most dogmatic of France's neo-Stalinist Marxists, most sharply critical of the liberal and humane so-called bourgeois culture of the past, harbor strangely traditional attitudes, if not ideas, concerning women, their function in society, and their prescribed role in the family.

If French society is in fact changing, it is changing more slowly in depth than on the surface. The First World War hardly shook a stratified class structure in which mobility, restricted to money or talent, nonetheless ensured the assimilation of an intellectual elite into its higher ranks. World War II, and more surely the post-World War II technological society, has affected France more deeply—but in certain respects it may have reinforced rather than destroyed adherence to certain traditional values. The most firmly established of French values has been respect for the family. Though family hierarchies and rituals are being modified as more and more women from the middle classes and "cadres" (the new managerial group) work—women from the lower classes always have worked—the family unit and the role assigned to wife and mother are still central. French sociologists have been exploring the correlation between the status of women and the "image" of woman in the different strata of French society. Since 1945, the date at which Frenchwomen belatedly won their civil rights, their legal status has been improving rapidly in comparison with the slow start in the interwar years. A reinvigorated postwar movement in favor of women's rights has developed in France since the end of World War II. It reached a publicity climax in November 1970 when three hundred women from all walks of life and professions convened at Versailles in a "States-General of Women." The name itself, recalling the great beginnings of the French Revolution, underscored the women's determination to secure full recognition of women's independent and equal status and their full participation in the affairs of the nation. But the movement has involved only an estimated five thousand women, among them a handful of militant writers; and, in spite of an effort to emulate the militancy of American women, it has expressed less antagonistic feeling toward men, less debate on sexual incompatibilities.

In her 1963 survey of the "image" of woman at all levels of French society,[4] Marie Jose Chombart de Lauwe noted that, with the exception of the "grande bourgeoisie" (whose men, firm in their traditional notions, are averse to such changes as having wives who work or claim "equality" with them as "heads" of the family), the majority of men and women in all other classes accept both of these as fact. But, the survey indicates, the "image" of woman, the manner in which both men and women in France depict the ideal woman, has not greatly evolved and shows a measure of consistency throughout the whole society. Within a mundane Parisian framework of wealth and "sophistication" Geneviève Dariaux's *The Men in Your Life: A Guide for Every Woman* (New York: Doubleday, 1968) reflects that image in slick outline and through unconscious caricature in its 400 pages of smug technical advice on how to charm and manipulate men, from husbands to taxi drivers. It is a rare achievement so complacently to cast oneself in the mold of the mythic innately superior "Frenchwoman," a myth deflated long since by Henry James; but the apparently indestructible pattern of man-woman relationship that Dariaux travesties[5] is prevalent, if latent, throughout France. It is tenacious and appears in many films, novels, plays, publicity and social customs. Its catch words are *élégance, bon goût,* and *chic,* and it holds more appeal for a great majority of women than Simone de Beauvoir's representation of their condition in *The Second Sex.*

Dariaux's so-called wisdom is the brittle self-centered lore of the fashion plate, dispensed by expensive women's magazines in which the woman's task is clearly defined: to embody the "beautiful image" of woman as an "objet d'art," cultivating a narcissistic "chic," carefully insulated from any of the real issues and anxieties of life. Its one advantage is that it does not sentimentalize sexual relations. It is the image that French society seems to have inherited from the rituals of court life perpetuated in the salons and always refurbished in eras of economic prosperity such as the present. It is basically, if not superficially, anti-Freudian, for it implies complete self-possession. In a sense, one of the tasks of the fashionable French woman writer today, in a culture absorbing a large dose of Freud, reinterpreted by Lacan, is to accommodate the traditional with the Freudian view of woman as generally understood: both reinforce feminine narcissism, a lethal attitude for a writer. Superficial Freudian terminology merely introduces themes of sexual urgency and a new audacity in the depiction of sexual practices, but does not rescue writing from the limitations of purely anecdotical concerns and the problems of the personal life.

Simone de Beauvoir attacked the shallowness and inhumanity of the Dariaux-type image in *Les Belles Images,* one of her later novels, and Buñuel made fun of it in his film *The Discreet Charm of the Bourgeoisie.* It is related to religion, family, conceptions of sex, love, and life style; to notions concerning French superiority, culture, and art. Only when French women writers manage to liberate themselves from that image, it seems, does their work rise above the trivial. Frenchwomen, in theory, are prized by their society, along with perfumes, wines, and art, as a particularly successful French aesthetic product; a flattering situation that requires an expenditure of time, attention, and art. At its best this ideal blends with an art of living difficult to reconcile with the serious practice of writing. Paris sets its style, and Paris is still the hub of French literary life.

However outspoken they may be in their objections to this image, many French women writers conform to it to a certain extent; it is as if, prepared to dispel the image for others, they could not discard it for themselves. The "up-to-date" smartness of Paris socioliterary life has never been incompatible with a bland misunderstanding of the more significant trends in literature and the arts. Since it dictates not only a way of life for women but also a way of being, it affects them more deeply than it does men.

One is tempted to think that this subconscious need to conform to a socially conditioned image of "the Frenchwoman" may also account for the preponderant number of "outsiders" among the outstanding woman writers. Sarraute was born in Russia of Russian parents; Duras lived the first twenty years of her life in Indochina; Simone Weil came from a Jewish Alsatian family, Cixous from North Africa, Leduc from a marginal social class. Yet one cannot easily attribute to "Parisianism" the disappointing mediocrity of some women's writing. It was from its frivolity, corruption, and narcissism that the most powerful woman writer of twentieth-century France, Colette, drew her subject matter, at least in part. But Colette came to it from outside; she was not of the milieu, born to it. Firmly rooted in her provincial past and in the values of a powerful and loved mother, Sido, she was an observer more than a participant.

In a short but suggestive comparison of Willa Cather and Colette—both of whom were born in 1873 and were celebrated in 1973, their centennial year—Ellen Moers stressed the importance, in the work of these two so different writers, of the figure of the mother: "By motherhood, I do not mean the frenzied experience that is beginning to be written about with wit and bitterness by the young feminist novelists of today . . . told 'like it is' by harassed young women tending babies under the peculiar conditions of modern urban life. Cather and Colette wrote with awe about queen-like figures of advanced years, about earth mothers and pioneer mothers, about superbly aging whores and opera singers with young lovers: women of a mysteriously persistent charm that transfixes the young of both sexes." [6] We are far from the narcissistic ideal. It would seem possible critically to investigate whether one of the many reasons the women writing in contemporary France have produced so few outstandingly talented novelists might not be connected with uncertainty concerning their self-image, their role in society, and their relationship with men and women.

Women writers of competence and some of distinction have appeared in all sections of French cultural life. They are increasingly active in many media including film, radio, and television, although still less so than men. Literary and artistic Paris is no longer a male preserve. Women own galleries, paint and exhibit their work; they compose. They own theaters and direct theatrical productions. In these days of doldrums for the French theater, one exception has been Le Théâtre du Soleil, an experimental troupe directed by a young woman, Ariane Mnouchkine, whose production 1793 caused quite a sensation. Women direct magazines; they review books in literary reviews, on radio and television; and they take an active part in all facets of publishing and the book trade. They write: mainly novels, critical or documentary essays; and, though to a lesser extent, poetry, drama, or various forms of autobiography. They are published and reviewed. I have found no statistics establishing the ratio of women writers to men writers. But, by and large, women appear to be as competent and almost as numerous in all the secondary activities—criticism, book reviewing, editing—as the bulk of their confreres. They have participated, though in smaller numbers, in the literary and philosophical debates of the time: Simone Weil and Simone de Beauvoir in the midcentury, Kristeva and Cixous at present, are the more widely known but certainly not the only ones. Without them the ideological scene in France would not be the same.

They come from all sections of French society, as a brief survey of a handful of novelists shows: Albertine Sarrazin, whose novel *The Astragal* (1965) was published here in translation by Grove Press, served several prison terms for theft; Violette Leduc (1907–72) nourished her writing on the substance of her rebellious life as an illegitimate child from a working-class milieu, an outcast involved in love affairs with men and women, and successfully engaged in black marketeering during the war. *La Bâtarde* (*The Illegitimate Child*, 1965), her slightly fictionalized autobiography prefaced by Simone de Beauvoir, brought her belated recognition. Christine Rochefort (b. 1917), who shocked her reading public and opened her way to the best-seller lists by her unabashedly sexual *Le Repos du guerrier* (1958), comes from the working-class background she depicted from within in *Les Petits Enfants du siècle* (1961; translated as *Josyane and the Welfare*, 1963). Marguerite Duras (b. 1914) comes from a "petit bourgeois" milieu. This influx of writers from the working classes has had its consequences: a frankness in substance and language that plays havoc with the more evasive bourgeois proprieties. The grande bourgeoisie, as was to be expected, has furnished the main contingent of women writers with, among others, Nathalie Sarraute (b. 1903), Celia Bertin (b. 1921), Françoise Sagan (b. 1935), and Françoise Mallet-Joris (b. 1930). Simone de Beauvoir has described the petty provincial aristocracy against which she rebelled. Marguerite Yourcenar (b. 1903), one of the more powerful and solitary contemporary writers, who lives far from Paris in the seclusion of Mount Desert Island, comes from an old aristocratic family, as did also Louise de Vilmorin, a woman whose ideas concerning women were not so distant from Dariaux's, although more sensitive. Their work is understandably diverse in tone, theme, and social area. In fact, no very clear patterns emerge for the anarchic whole. They reflect rather the same anarchistic variety as does the novel as a whole, suggesting the search for new patterns where no collective ones impose themselves upon the individual: a sure sign of a society in transition.

Of these the more outstanding have tended to be iconoclastic concerning the traditional image of woman latent in French society. Christine Rochefort's novels express an outspoken revolt against women's lot in both the bourgeois and the working classes. But an altogether too great number of these women novelists are still concerned with the Romantic conflict of passion vs. social decorum, which both Madame de Staël and George Sand dramatized in their novels from the feminine point of view. More interestingly perhaps, Nathalie Sarraute's novels do not substantially distinguish between the role of male and female "voices" in the "subconversations" through which she registers and translates the fluctuating and, most often, unvoiced reactions of people to each other. And Marguerite Duras has slowly progressed toward a conception of love that transcends the male-female couple and dichotomy, or indeed any "couple." *Love* is the title of her later and stranger novel. She is, no doubt, one of the most original French writers today.

This quick glance at the number of women writers in France today and at the diversity in their origins and work would seem to indicate a highly favorable situation. But when we turn to the more academic type of criticism, a manifest contradiction exists. Women writers have indeed appeared in ever greater numbers; but when the work of selection and traditional historical ordering begins, a curious phenomenon occurs. If we deal with panoramas of literature today which aim at being exhaustive, such as Pierre de Boisdeffre's *Panorama de la littérature contemporaine*, regularly updated in each successive edition, we encounter a great many women's names. But as we move from what is in fact a repertory to critical surveys, the names of women writers tend to disappear. In 1970, a history of *French Literature Since 1945*[7] was published. It was designed to enlighten those advanced students who might be curious to know about the present configurations of French literature, more particularly its new views on culture and the literary enterprise itself. It is a fairly sophisticated book, quite up-to-date in its perspective, a book that will be read by the young. It included eight Frenchwomen only, along with Virginia Woolf, three Canadian women writers, and some passing references to three or four others, mentioned, like Colette, as predecessors or cited as critics. Not a single woman poet is mentioned. The women included are outstanding: Simone de Beauvoir, Simone Weil, Marguerite Yourcenar, Marguerite Duras, Nathalie Sarraute, Françoise Sagan. But the stringency of the selection contrasts with the more than 350 men cited—clearly an inflationary estimate.

We are obviously not dealing here only with high literature. Then why the imbalance? A 1960 *dictionnaire anthologique et critique* of contemporary writers had done somewhat better. Out of 59 entries, 6 were women: Beauvoir, Duras, Mallet-Joris, Sagan, Sarraute, and one poet, Edith Boissonnas.[8] I do not wish to bog myself and this paper down in a statistical examination of literary anthologies, enlightening though they are.[9] But I think it is fairly safe to say that a limited roster of contemporary French women writers has been adopted, with occasional variations, as significant by current male opinion—half a dozen or so over two generations, always the same. This seems to satisfy the conscience of the critics and precludes the need for further probing. Such a closure does not exist for male writers. True, as the years go by, out of the 350 male names brought forward by *French Literature Since 1945*, perhaps a dozen only will survive, while new anthologies promote some 300 new and expendable ones. The ruthlessness of the selection in the women's case may well ensure their longevity. The imbalance may in later years be redressed. But this is cold comfort for women writing today. Nor does it help younger women develop any great sense of confidence should they feel tempted to turn to writing. The cards seem heavily stacked against them, for the figures clearly imply that on the whole women's work is largely considered to be irrelevant within the mainstream of French literature in the making. Hence, in the best of intentions, those segregated chapters on "women poets" or "women novelists" only underscore the implication they try, rather patronizingly, to improve.

And this takes us full circle back to the questions I raised at the beginning. To what extent is the alleged mediocrity of French contemporary women's writing in general real; to what extent is it due to a critical blindness brought about by the habit we have acquired of male—often academic—critical paradigms that have shaped French culture and that fail to fit original forms of women's writing? If our academic criticism is conditioned by such blindness, a woman writer of marked originality would then fail to find a place within the organizing and thereby evaluative system and so fade out of sight. Or, if so great a portion of current women's writing in France is *in fact* inferior to the men's, as its expendability suggests, is it because many women writers are themselves in a state of uncertainty in regard to those paradigms and willing to settle for a quick though passing success?

Perhaps only in such terms can the question of the woman writer be profitably examined. And it would seem that the time is ripe in France for such an inquiry. There the "new" and "new new" critics have been engaged in a sweeping, sometimes pedantic, often partial and politically slanted examination of the ideological implications of linguistic forms in order to expose the functioning of social myths. Literature is one of their happy hunting grounds. Literary "values" as established and perpetuated in schools and universities through anthologies and histories of literature are considered as part of an "elitist" cultural mythology to be dismantled entirely. This antagonism regarding their own culture may be interpreted as the attempt of a post-World War II generation to steer a formerly brilliant, now stagnating culture—as they see it—in the direction of change.

But although there are outstanding women in this group, they have carefully avoided as critics the question of female writing, which Simone de Beauvoir raised in *The Second Sex*. This is possibly because, firmly established in their own "in-group," they do not wish to countenance any form of sex segregation in literary matters, a defensible position. Possibly also they reject the subjective coloring the topic injects into criticism. They favor an objective analytic stance, dealing in linguistic models and theories of writing which preclude the notion of a distinctive author, let alone a *woman* author. Generated by the language itself, through the immense literary output that language has engendered, a "text" is examined as a permutation of elements within the total linguistic system. The disappearance of the author naturally entails the disappearance of the notion of "genius," a gain for women who, in otiose discussion concerning the inferiority of their creative capacities, have been constantly confronted with the argument by default: They have produced no Shakespeares. In the long run, this present critical stance of what is a small but no longer avant-garde group may prove favorable to a reexamination of feminist accomplishment in literature. It isolates the properly literary element—the writing—from other concerns such as the social constraints imposed on women, which have been discussed abundantly. And it may then help answer the question of a *literary* differentiation in the patterns and texture of women's writing that would be free from the "sexual" connotations inherent in the study of "images."

Recently, younger critics have started to explore literary structures in new ways, applying methods inspired by the new French critics. One of them, Tom Conley, a Renaissance scholar, notes that in regard to female literature the new approach "has particular value in French prose where literary structures can be discerned, where, in late medieval society, sources of creative energy can be pinpointed. One task," he continues, "the beginning of a greater project—is to examine a number of formal modes in novels written by women; to dissect them; to situate where the tensions inherent in feminist writings are conjoined to an exterior social situation." [10] He applies the method to an early-sixteenth-century novel by a woman, Hélisenne de Crenne, long buried in obscurity, and comes up with an extraordinary insight into the novel's significance and profound originality. "Hélisenne's *Angoysses* and the conditions of its creation suggest the advent of great novels in a unique and fecund tradition" (p. 7). It should be noted that Conley takes us from the analysis of narrative structures to the situation of the woman writing; he is not content with the purely formalist approach.[11]

Lately, new evaluations of French women's writing have come from historians of literature. They suggest that the purely formal approach may not be the only, or even the most favorable, approach to an evaluation of female writing. France has a long tradition of successful women writers, starting with Marie de France in the twelfth century, a writer about whom we know little. The first "professional" woman writer known to us is Christine de Pisan (1364–1430?). In 1972, in his authoritative literary history of the late medieval period,[12] Daniel Poirion ranks Christine among the five major "creative" figures of the period between 1300 and 1480. "For the first time in France," he writes, "the story of a literary work cannot be separated from the study of a personality. Here is . . . our first *author*, and that author is a woman. And because she is a woman, [as a writer] she avoids many shortcomings of the period" (p. 206). Similarly, to the authors of the Renaissance volume in the same series, Marguerite d'Angoulême appears today as one of the four greater writers of her time, like Christine de Pisan, an innovator in their eyes: "Beyond the fact that philosophical and religious poetry in France goes back to Marguerite, that she is the first mystical poet in our literature, we owe her something more precious and greater still: a scrupulous attention, honest and unswerving, to the movements of consciousness, the appearance of the *moi* [the self] in literature." [13]

This reiteration of originality contrasts with the generally reductive view of literature by women that has often obtained in academic studies in the past. Let me quote one sentence only, in contrast, from Lanson's *Histoire de la littérature française*, which dismisses Christine as "the insufferable blue-stocking whose indefatigable facility was evenly matched by her universal mediocrity." [14] And Lanson's, it need not be stressed, was long the single voice that shaped the study of French literature in French schools and lycées. This could of course be an isolated example of misjudgment; an important one, in any case, because highly influential. Lanson has been the source of innumerable stereotypes in literary studies.

How have critics approached women's literature in our time? Without presuming to generalize, a quick look at a book which came out in the 1920s entitled *History of Feminine Literature in France*, written by a certain Jean Larnac,[15] certainly poses some questions. In a sense, it volunteers itself and would naturally propose itself to anyone seeking a quick view of the question. He opens with a moving statement of objectivity, but nevertheless with a thesis: "I should like to show [in this book] the continuity of the literary effort of women and to reveal in their works what is specifically feminine and makes a whole that is very different from masculine literature" (p. 5), it being understood that women's writings are "foreign to the masterpieces of masculine genres." He seems to posit that there is a different form of feminine art. But the connotation is clear: it is inferior. Larnac's purpose, he notes, was to counter Joseph de Maître's answer to his daughters who, in the early nineteenth century, had petitioned their father to allow them to *study* literature with their brothers. Women, their father answered, had written no masterpieces in any genre: "they composed neither the *Iliad* nor the *Aeneid*, nor *Phèdre* nor *Tartuffe*"; consequently, he had refused their request.

Let us look at Larnac's approach. For example, when he is dealing with the lyrical Renaissance poet, the beautiful Louise Labé, whom he admires: "To classify her would be a useless effort. . . . That is because she wrote according to her heart, her flesh, her senses, her nerves. Her poems seem to be the spontaneous fruit of genius" (p. 68). And then comes Marie de Gournay, Montaigne's adopted daughter: "an ugly old spinster who had claimed to be only a brain." He compares the two women: "the former [Louise Labé] turning on all her feminine charms, the second seeing salvation only in masculinization. The public chose between the two methods: Louise Labé was celebrated as a goddess; Marie de Gournay was laughed at *à l'envi*" (pp. 68–69). This is rather a strange way to assess literature—basing one's judgment on the erotic attraction of the author. Besides, what Larnac says is not true: In her day, Marie de Gournay was a highly esteemed and successful woman. Mr. Larnac's attitude here recalls that of Gustave Lanson.

How does Larnac deal with the two well-established women writers of the Classical period, Madame de Lafayette and Madame de Sévigné? Madame de Lafayette, who as we know, developed with *La Princesse de Clèves* a new kind of novel, was, he points out, disappointed in love: "Was she so ugly? Yes, if we judge by the portraits we have of her; no, according to the Duke of Retz, who was a connoisseur in the matter. I think nonetheless that she must have had more inner charm than real beauty, which would explain her early disappointment. . . . Whatever the case . . . she abandoned the fight for love and attempted to become famous by a means other than beauty—talent" (p. 121).

Madame de Sévigné, at least, was not ugly. But "would she have desired fame if she had married someone other than the Marquis de Sévigné—unfaithful, agreeable to women, detestable to his own? One may doubt it. . . . In her case, the love of fame replaced love itself. It was a value of replacement. . . . And I wonder if these substitutions of which the seventeenth century shows us many examples did not bring more or less hidden regrets? Who knows if Madame de Lafayette, seeking happiness in fame after having vainly sought it in love, was not sorry she had thus oriented her life?" (p. 106).

Well now, surely the celebrated Madame de Staël, a century and a half later, was not deprived of love; yet "would she have oriented her life in the same way if she had possessed the beauty of Madame Récamier? I think not. . . . She lacked a specifically feminine charm . . . to obtain the happiness love refused her, she resolved to conquer fame, which was only for her, according to her famous words, *le pis-aller du bonheur*, a poor substitute for happiness" (p. 175). What characterizes her as a writer, according to Larnac, besides the obvious defect to which our compassionate critic attributes her desire to write, i.e., an unwomanly lack of charm (where men, of course, have genius)? Larnac's answer: "her incapacity to reach outside herself" (p. 181). "Whatever one may say, she did not have a creative mind. . . . As for the ideas which have been much emphasized, she did not invent them: she borrowed them from those around her" (p. 181). Just like Madame de Lafayette, whom he asserts "owed to her friends the outline [of her novel], the historical documentation, all that her lack of imagination did not allow her to put together, she owed to them the perfection of her style. . . . What remains [is] the intimate life . . . of her novel—the first novel in which a human heart is dissected" (p. 126). One understands Beauvoir's exasperated reaction against male myths in *The Second Sex*.

It is a fact that French literary historians have been particularly slow to shed the often ironically indulgent "eternal feminine" approach to women's literature. How deeply they have affected women's own ideas of what they should be writing is still an open question. Mr. Larnac's definition of a woman writer's realm is simple and clear: He has his model for the woman writer, a woman poet of the Romantic era, Marceline Desbordes-Valmore—as he sees her, of course. "No woman writer showed less intelligence; none, in contrast, showed so much sensibility. . . . No [correct] spelling in her manuscripts. . . . Did she know what assonance was? Alliteration? No invention, no creative imagination, only complete truth of the heart. . . . Love was the foundation of her life" (pp. 197–201). We are fairly warned: It is not feminine to deal with ideas or to excel intellectually. We are not surprised when, in his conclusion, this obscure paragon of intelligence traces the "limits" of the feminine "genius"; making a few illuminating remarks, on the way, that have a bearing on the general question of the reputation of women writers.

He is concerned with the acclamation won by such women writers as Delphine Gay, an immensely successful playwright, novelist and journalist, also of the Romantic era: "her beauty created the illusion [that she was great]. One doesn't forgive a blue-stocking, even if she has talent—witness Marie de Gournay. One approves everything, in contrast, in a pretty woman. . . . For thirty years Delphine Gay made of her readers and spectators, lovers. As soon as she disappeared, enthusiasm was deflated" (p. 216).

Or again, speaking of the debate concerning women's intellectual capacity that followed in the wake of the Revolution, Larnac notes that Proudhon "brought a little common sense to a subject that passion had obscured." Having examined meticulously the intellectual possibilities of "women," Proudhon, he reminds us, reached the following conclusion: "From the point of view of intelligence, she has perceptions, memory, imagination. What is lacking: the capacity to produce seeds, that is to say, ideas, what the Latins called genius" (p. 189).

The conclusion is comically self-revealing. But it also furnishes a glimpse perhaps of the nature of the issue at hand. Larnac's definition of genius is strangely restricted. The innovative value of both Christine de Pisan and Marguerite d'Angoulême as defined above was not in the realm of specific ideas, but of general outlook; and this is surely as true of Marguerite d'Angoulême, Madame de Staël, Simone Weil, or Simone de Beauvoir. This fresh outlook in turn suggested new themes and adumbrated new literary patterns, sometimes confusedly. It seems to have been, critics have suggested, because women like Christine de Pisan and Hélisenne de Crenne were not shaped in the academic mold of the hour that they were able to break away from current ideological and literary patterns, sorting out, in times of social change the literary stereotype from the fact and so opening new avenues for the writer. And that too may be why their work might appear marginal to a historian of Lanson's generation, concerned methodically to establish systematic and logically ordered developments, a first total patterning of French literary history within an ideological frame.

Here we confront another question. In no sense did these women writers' contemporaries, on the whole, judge their work inferior. Christine de Pisan was widely praised and known in her lifetime. What astonished her contemporaries was that, though a woman, she wrote and thought as well as any man. It was the fact that, although she was a young woman, and "ignorant," Marie de Gournay had such an excellent understanding of his *Essays* that fascinated Montaigne. In other words, it did not occur to the more thoughtful of their male contemporaries to deny these women's accomplishment as such, however restricted by social conventions their view of women's nature might be. When dealing with Lanson or Larnac the

206 Germaine Brée

shaping perspective may reflect in part the centuries-old "academic" and classical suspicion of women; but even more the middle-class ethics of the nineteenth century. The French Revolution was inimical to women and the Napoleonic Code made minors of them, relegating them to their household duties. The Romantic image of woman in the main compensated by developing the well-known stereotype of muse or courtesan, body or soul, but surely not mind.

Larnac's sentimental paternalistic image of woman seems on the surface of it antithetical to Geneviève Dariaux's, one a degraded image of the Romantic myth, the other an equally degraded image of the liberated woman of eighteenth-century salons—a kind of bourgeois Ninon de Lenclos, with a husband in the background. It was against just such incompatible stereotypes inherited from the past and embodied in *Le Roman de la Rose* that Christine de Pisan directed her protest launching the famous *Querelle des Femmes* at the dawn of the fifteenth century; and Simone de Beauvoir through her vast study *The Second Sex* undertook the same task for our era—for the Larnacs and the Dariaux among us. Perhaps rather than the images of women within the literature, it is the image accumulated from the critical corpus that the critic must first examine. The question then arises as to the configuration we confront when, as academic critics, we look at the present scene in France in relation to the past.

The question was indirectly raised by the poet Marcel Béalu, who in 1953 published an *Anthology of French Feminine Poetry from 1900 to the Present* because, he noted, he had come to realize how few women poets were included in current anthologies of poetry. His own selection of thirty women poets was he felt "partial and incomplete." But it compared most favorably with an anthology of poetry that had appeared the year before proceeding in the usual fashion: among the approximately three hundred poets selected, a dozen women poets were mentioned, but to only four of these did the editors grant the space of *one* poem: the proportion of three hundred to four, six, or twelve when men and women writers compete for space seems to be fairly constant. By some law of optics, no doubt, women writers acquire visibility in greater numbers when a "feminine" label precludes masculine competition. A new element appears here, connected with the contemporary commercialism of the literary enterprise and its dependency upon publicity.

This is troublesome indeed and underscores another of the problems the critic who is dealing with twentieth-century literature must consider. None of us can, in all conscience, span the entire spectrum of the literature produced in any one year, let alone in ten. In the immediate turmoil of the literary marketplace—Paris—reputations are launched and selections made by quasi-parochial though sophisticated groups; from these, in due course, a far more limited number of works will sort themselves out. But if, at the outset, the tacit frame of reference implies that a significant woman writer is an exception in what is in fact a male preserve, then it may well be that promising works are lost to us in the initial shuffle. Hence the role of "feminine" categories and anthologies like Béalu's. But when anthologies of "women" poets or "women" writers, or chapters on "women" novelists, are published, critical confusion ensues. It is implicit in Marcel Béalu's preface to his *Anthology.* He questioned the poets themselves on the problem of *la poésie féminine.* "What do I care about feminine poetry, were such a thing to exist?" Edith Boissonnas answered. "It is probably nothing but a category malevolently or lazily established" (p. 8). Another poet, Jeanne Sandelion, spoke of the difficulty of dealing with critics who tend to dismiss woman's writing as "ladies' handicrafts," like needlework for example. And yet she felt that a "feminine pen," if it is authentic, would naturally be recognizable.

What Edith Boissonnas was saying, rightly, was that in the critical evaluation of poetry as such, sex is irrelevant. What Jeanne Sandelion was saying, rightly too but in contrast, was that there is an inevitable link between the person who writes and the writing; that therefore sex is relevant; and that this involves the critic's attitude toward women. Terminology here can be insidious. When we turn to the French *Littré* we are enlightened: *"Femelle,* animal of feminine sex: the female of the monkey . . . used currently when speaking disparagingly of women." *"Mâle,* he who belongs to the sex physiologically characterized by the presence of the fecundating principle . . . a vigorous man, physically and morally." *"Féminin,* belonging to the sex physiologically characterized by the ovary in animals and plants. Distinctively characteristic of women." According to its custom, *Littré* gives several examples of the usage of the term; the first of which, culled from a literary text, is: "given the defects of the feminine creature." For the *Littré,* then, the terms "female" and "feminine" clearly suggest the connection with the vegetable or animal kingdoms, and with some form of inferiority, while "male" introduces quite different notions of fecundity (i.e., creativity) and nobility, while the link with the animal is elided. The medieval patterns with regard to sex are deeply rooted in the understanding of the words themselves.

To what extent do specious associations of this kind influence our critical reception of writing by women? Should we then allow this form of categorization to be built up and should we participate in its perpetuation? I tend to think we should not. But what is needed in France today is a vigorous prospection of the literary production, not so much from the sociological as from the literary point of view in search of promising feminist writing; and a sustained effort to integrate the woman writer into the larger frame, not to dissociate her from it.

NOTES

1. London: Jonathan Cape & Wildwood House, 1973. Translated by Simon Watson.

2. Some of the material I use was first developed in a series of lectures—the Brown and Haley lectures—given in the spring of 1973 at Puget Sound University and published by Rutgers University Press.

3. Francis Jeanson, *Lettre ouverte aux femmes* (Paris: Editions du Seuil, 1965); Françoise Parturier, *Lettre ouverte aux hommes* (Paris: Albin Michel, 1968); Suzanne Lilar, *Le Malentendu du deuxième sexe* (Paris: Presses Universitaires de France, 1972). Lilar sensibly accepts the biological differences between the sexes and some of their consequences, and draws her argument from certain biological facts. She points out that men and women belong, in the first place, to the same species; moreover, only one out of twenty-three pairs of genes that program human development determines an individual's sexual characteristics. Thence the large overlapping area of potentialities the two sexes share. She accepts the psychological observations of Jean Piaget on the nondifferentiated mechanisms of development of human intelligence, which reverse the medieval concept of "reason" as the prerogative of men. Jeanson made much of the physiological roles of men and women in the sexual act, claiming superiority for the male role. This inspired

Rabelaisian anger in Parturier, who attacked him for enshrining superiority in those few inches of flesh and bade him "put it back" where it belonged and discuss the problem rationally. Her main target was the condescending attitude of the Frenchman who refuses to talk to women as adults and for whom any feminine problems can be solved by a little lovemaking.

4. *La Femme dans la société: son image dans les différents niveaux sociaux* (Paris: CNRS, 1963).

5. Here are a couple of examples of that lore and "wit": "The first step of every civilized society is to transform the males into husbands. The word still enjoys considerable prestige and is pronounced with a capital H by almost all women, even by those who claim equality with men. Before entering into the state of bliss called matrimony, the future husband must win the object of his affections by means of his attractive appearance, his seductive phrases, or his bank account—but preferably all three" (p. 203). "If you have the choice of working for or employing men rather than women, don't deprive yourself of the men on the pretext that you are only a woman; actually men are much easier to handle. . . . Personally, I could never work for a man I didn't admire. . . . A good boss is a little like 'God the Father,' and, as everyone knows, when one is seated at His right hand it is for eternity" (p. 215).

6. ELLEN MOERS, "Willa Cather and Colette: Mothers of Us All," *World*, March 27, 1973, p. 52.

7. J. BERSANI, M. AUTRAND, J. LECARME, and B. VERCIER, *La littérature française depuis 1945* (Paris: Bordas, 1970).

8. Bernard Pingaud, ed., *Écrivains d'aujourd'hui 1940–1960* (Paris: Grasset, 1960).

9. It is perhaps worthy of note that among the twelve editors of the *Écrivains d'aujourd'hui* dictionary, there was one woman.

10. TOM CONLEY, "Feminism. *Écriture* and the Closed Room: Hélisenne de Crenne's *Angoysses douloureuses qui procedent d'amours* (1538)" (manuscript, University of Minnesota, n.d.), p. 1.

11. Despite some group studies by a "collectif," the new critics in France have not forgone their names nor indeed their place in current surveys of the literary scene, nor have they been satisfied to produce anonymous texts. The machinery of language may produce the "text" but Philippe Sollers signs it, a point to which I shall return.

12. DANIEL POIRION, *Le Moyen Age II, 1300–1480* (Paris: Arthaud, 1971).

13. YVES GIRARD et MARC RENÉ JUNG, *La Renaissance I, 1480–1548* (Paris: Arthaud, 1972), p. 242.

14. GUSTAVE LANSON, *Histoire de la littérature française* (12th ed.; Paris: Hachette, 1912), p. 167.

15. JEAN LARNAC, *Histoire de la littérature féminine en France* (Paris: Editions Kra., 1929).

The Images of Women in Contemporary Mexican Literature
Victoria Junco Meyer

In Mexico, as in other countries of Occidental cultural norms, much that is considered of cultural value has been the work of men, individually or collectively, but with consistent male predominance. Since the introduction of a patriarchal society, women have been relegated to an ancillary and submissive role, an essentially passive one. Would the Mexican culture have been different had women performed a more active role? I believe that the etiology of female passivity does not transcend biological principles in which differences are absolute and essential; instead, it challenges the vital field of human values. I do not assert that women, because of their passive role in Mexican society, have not made significant contributions to many aspects of Mexican life; in fact, those contributions are even more significant when we consider that they were made within the limitations imposed upon women.

Women have lived according to the image of them created by men. Perhaps this is why Julian Marias, contemporary Spanish philosopher, has said that

> the European woman has been invented by the male who has formed his image of her, proposed to her, and, to a large extent imposed upon her his role in life, his projection or his figure of such a woman.[1]

It could be said, too, that man has invented the Mexican woman inasmuch as he has imposed upon her certain values and behavioral norms. Woman has been the "repository" of the honor and reputation of both father and husband, with the assumption that she personify virtue and depend absolutely on father or husband "since being a woman necessarily signifies insecurity." [2] It must be admitted that she has never been asked to consent to these ends and that she participates in their realization only passively because, as Mexican writer Octavio Paz states: "In a world made in man's image, woman is only a reflection of masculine will and desire." [3] The values imposed upon Mexican women are a result of historical circumstance in which Spanish and indigenous morals were fused into what is now considered the Mexican culture. These morals are "a gamut ranging from modesty and 'decency' to stoicism, resignation and impassivity." [4] Pre-Hispanic tradition conferred a scornful, subservient role upon women, a role that complemented the inferior one inherent to those women of Spanish tradition, as brought to Mexico by the conquerors. The role of woman in society included attitudes common to both elements that integrated the Mexican nationality. During three hundred years of Spanish domination, the structure of patriarchal behavior was firmly established, and it has not changed in essence since that time. By its nature, the Mexican culture is a sexist culture. Sexism is an ideology based on the needs and values of the dominant group: aggression, intelligence, strength, and efficiency in the male; passivity, ignorance, docility, "virtue," and inefficiency in the female. An interchange that demands servitude and charitably offers "protection" has gone on for many centuries.

Mexican man appears to hold great respect for woman in quotidian relations with her; in fact, there appears to be a cult of feminine spiritual superiority which teaches that woman is semidivine, morally superior, and spiritually stronger than man. Possibly this image is used as a means of limiting her self-expression.

Perhaps she would usually prefer to be treated with less "respect" . . . and with greater freedom and truthfulness; that is, to be treated as a human being rather than as a symbol or function. But how can we [men] agree to let her express herself when our whole way of life is a mask designed to hide our intimate feelings? [5]

This quotation exemplifies a prevalent male attitude toward the Mexican woman, who has worn man-made masks for too long, masks that hide her identity and provide her with the appearance desired by the male. A probable cause of her impassivity or resignation may have rested in the sad realization of the futility of her situation; accepting the ineluctable was more a matter of intelligence than of virtue.

Changes in the position of women in contemporary Mexico are in part the result of a perceptible, gradual transformation of social mores, rather than of laws, in which women have demonstrated a proclivity to broaden their cultural horizons, synchronously gaining acceptance in fields that were previously exclusively male. Social reform has been a lengthy, at times acrimonious process, but it is making possible yesterday's impossible.

In Mexico, men do not find animadversion to female equality on an intellectual level. The universities have long been open to women, and those graduating have attained high positions in professional life. Perhaps this attitude of the Mexican male may be ascribed to the absence of threat due to the low ratio of female to male participants in intellectual spheres, or to the fact that women's liberation through culture is more subdued and still within the image of a virtuous woman.

Perhaps Mexican women do not desire complete independence; even those professional women who marry and continue their careers have a vehement commitment to their role in preserving the family stability, which continues to be an imperative factor in Mexican life:

> Society is founded on the family, and, in reciprocity, society provides marriage with its moral, religious, social and economic basis. The novelists of the XIX Century (and many of the XX Century) identify happiness with marriage. . . . In this literature, the systematic defense of marriage, its advantages and demands are increased.[6]

The Mexican woman who wants to be liberated is anxious to participate in everything that prior social or religious tradition forbade, but she refuses to parrot the male. She would consider this a desertion of her generic personality and her destiny. She wants to be a full human being, with all the tacit responsibilities; to be herself, a woman, not a symbol or an idol.

The measure of liberation is another method of maintaining the male-invented role of woman in that he allows her to become liberated, but within certain limits. Mexican intellectual men criticize women who have promulgated rapid social reform. Women should be "feminine" even as intellectuals, in accordance with the image imposed upon them.

Through a gradual process, women in Mexico have changed their lot and, to a certain extent, their traditional image. Because the liberation is being accomplished on a cultural level, however, only the intellectual woman has formed her identity as a human being; the great majority of women continue to accept a plethora of limitations. The "country woman," of laudable stoicism, close to the earth, accepts her role with a fatalistic attitude. A subconscious awareness of the inexorability of her fate may compensate for the security that is absent from her daily existence. The "poor woman" does not live according to any image because her life is rarely her own; she is often abused by others, and this maltreatment is the single constant in her life.

Another genre of Mexican female roles exists in the inauthentic woman, a masked woman who consistently attempts to be what she is not. The mask is a panacea for her superficial vagary, but behind the mask she is nothing. This woman wears a variety of masks, including an intellectual one. She has not changed her image because she lacks self-identity; she appears to be liberated, but only to the degree of enjoying the freedom to act according to the mask she wears. She suffers from a paucity of ideals, an atrophy of principles.

Such images of women in contemporary Mexican society have been described in recent decades by Mexican writers such as Octavio Paz in *The Labyrinth of Solitude*, Carlos Fuentes in *Where the Air Is Clear* and in *The Death of Artemio Cruz*, and Juan Rulfo in *Pedro Paramo*.

Because of the impossibility of reviewing all images of women in contemporary Mexican literature, I have chosen to concentrate on only a few authors. Naturally, my preferences have played an important part in the selection. Nevertheless, the writers I have selected are unanimously recognized as some of the best Mexican contemporary writers. It would be interesting, in a future work, to analyze the images of women in the works of women writers.

The Labyrinth of Solitude is a series of penetrating essays in which Octavio Paz analyzes and defines Mexican character and culture. In an attempt to explain the Mexican mystery and to comment on the plight of Mexicans today, Paz goes to the "secret root" where various Mexican attitudes originated.

In his chapter "The Sons of La Malinche," Paz presents his interpretation of the character of Mexican women. La Malinche was an Indian princess, given to the Spanish conquistador Hernando Cortes when he arrived in Mexico. She was a salient figure in the Spanish conquest because of her role as mistress-interpreter for Cortes, through which she became a symbol of treason to Mexicans.

Initially, Octavio Paz posits that the stranger encounters an ambiguous, if not contradictory image of the Mexican people. They attract and repel. One reason for this dichotomy lies in the Mexican's insecurity, a near-hermetic defense mechanism. The peasant, an ancient element of society, has produced a reaction of fascination on the part of the urban dweller because of his somewhat archaic manner of dress and speech, which places him out of the mainstream of national culture.

> For everyone but himself he embodies the occult, the hidden, that which surrenders itself only with great difficulty: a buried treasure . . . an ancient wisdom hiding among the folds of the land.[7]

Woman also lives apart, separated from the center, and thus she is an enigmatic figure; she is the Enigma. Like men of alien races or nationalities, she attracts and repels.

> She is the image of both fecundity and death. In almost every culture the goddesses of creation are also the goddesses of destruction. Woman is a living symbol of the strangeness of the universe and its radical heterogeneity. As such, does she hide life within herself, or death? What does she think? Or does she think? Does she truly have feelings? Is she the same as we men are?[8]

In order to understand the role of women in Mexican society, Octavio Paz uses a "forbidden word," which carries different connotations in each Spanish-speaking country but is used always as an aggressive verb. The verb is *chingar* and in Mexico it embodies

> a plurality of meanings which ultimately contain the idea of aggression, be it in the act of molesting, or in the violent act of wounding or killing. The verb denotes violence, an emergence from oneself to penetrate another by force. It also means to injure, to lacerate, to violate—bodies, souls, objects; and to destroy.[9]

Although this verb has sexual connotations, it is not synonymous with the sexual act because when it refers to intercourse, it implies deception and violation.

> The verb is masculine, active, cruel: it stings, wounds, gashes and stains. It provokes a bitter, resentful satisfaction. . . . The person who suffers this action is passive, inert and open, in contrast to the active, aggressive and closed person who inflicts it.[10]

This quotation explains the dichotomy between the closed and the open, the two possibilities afforded by Mexican life: either to suffer the action implied by the verb or to inflict it. This conception of social interaction inevitably divides society into two groups: the strong, the aggressive, the closed; and the weak, the passive, the open. Woman belongs to this latter group. She is "La Chingada," a mythical figure who represents "the Mother forcibly opened, violated or deceived." [11] She is

> the mother who has suffered—metaphorically or actually—the corrosive and defaming action implicit in the verb which gives her her name.[12] [Her children are] the offspring of violation, abduction or deceit.[13]

The above implies a violent affirmation of the father and a not less violent humiliation of the mother. She is open, she does not offer any resistance, and this abject passivity causes her to lose her identity.

> She loses her name; she is no one; she disappears into nothingness; she is Nothingness. And yet she is the cruel incarnation of the feminine condition.[14]

The vulnerability of woman is part of her essence because she is open, but it is also aggravated by her social situation; she is subjected to many dangers against which personal morals and even masculine protection are powerless. This essential weakness in woman becomes a virtue through compensation, and thus appears a new myth, that of the long-suffering Mexican woman who develops a stoic indifference to pain. "Thanks to suffering and to her ability to endure without protest, she transcends her condition and acquires the same attributes as men." [15] This role involves the Mexican interpretation of maternity referred to as "La Llorona," the one who weeps.

"La Llorona" differs greatly from the aggressive "La Chingada" who is active; the latter comes and goes, looks for men and then leaves them. She is as hard and independent as her male counterpart, the *macho*. In her own way she seems to "transcend her physiological weakness." [16] She acquires the depraved spirit of men and applies masculine techniques of subjugation to avenge the destruction of her virginity.

> By publicly deviating from the prescribed norm, she has divested herself of precisely those attributes considered most characteristically feminine, and in the process has become somewhat masculine.[17]

The absolute contrast to "La Chingada," or violated mother, is the Virgin Mother, the Virgin of Guadalupe, or Guadalupe Tonantzin, as many Mexican Indians still call her. There exists a strong devotion to the Virgin of Guadalupe that has historical as well as religious roots. She is the Virgin who appeared to an Indian in Tepeyac, the place where a sanctuary of an Aztec goddess, Tonantzin, used to be. The Virgin represents a refuge for the oppressed, the poor, and the weak, hence the fervor with which the Indians and the poor venerate her. She is "pure receptivity: she consoles, quiets, dries tears and calms passions." [18] Upon accepting the miracle of Tepeyac, the terms of idealization are established; the woman most worthy of reverence is the Virgin—with or without a capital V.

From the Spanish conquest of Mexico emerge two symbols: Cuauhtemoc and "La Malinche." The last Aztec emperor, Cuauhtemoc, or Falling Eagle, came to power after the arrival of the Spaniards and died in their hands. He was young, exceedingly stoic, and closed; he became the symbol of the Sacrificed Son. "La Malinche," symbol of violation, personifies "La Chingada," who gave herself voluntarily to Cortes, but was forgotten when she was no longer of use to him. She represents the open, in contrast to the closed, stoic Indian, such as Cuauhtemoc. From these three representations of maternity emerge the Mexican woman; she is no one of them exactly, albeit she embodies characteristics of each of them. Today's Mexican woman often attempts to forget her past, to deny her origins. She does not want to be the daughter of "La Malinche" or to be Indian or Spaniard, but rather to start with herself and be a human being.

Among the most widely read pieces of contemporary Mexican literature are two novels written by Carlos Fuentes: *Where the Air Is Clear* and *The Death of Artemio Cruz*. He calls the former "the biography of a city . . . a synthesis of present-day Mexico." [19] In the latter, Artemio Cruz relives his life from his deathbed, a life story that in some parts parallels the Mexican Revolution of 1910.

Carlos Fuentes is as socially committed as his fellow Mexican writers of the last two decades, with the Revolution almost a character in their novels, whether these writers extol its virtues or analyze its failures. According to Octavio Paz, the Mexican Revolution was an attempt

> to reconquer our past, to assimilate it and make it live in the present. . . . It was a return to the past, . . . a search for our own selves, and a return to the maternal womb. . . . By means of the Revolution the Mexican people found itself, located itself in its own past and substance.[20]

An analysis of the female characters in the novels of Carlos Fuentes deliberately follows the interpretations from the essays of Octavio Paz because, as explained by the critic of Mexican literature, Joseph Sommers,

> Fuentes creates individuals out of Paz's Mexican types, weaves a story out of his own generation's national preoccupations, builds dreams out of the tensions between Paz's dialectical opposites, solitude and communion.[21]

In *Where the Air Is Clear*, Fuentes gives us a panoramic view of the Mexican social atmosphere in the 1950s including a discussion of social classes from the poverty-stricken *Maceualli* (Aztec term for society's lower class) to the most opulent. Thus he creates a spate of secondary characters, with the intent of defining certain stereotypes or myths with which to evaluate his main characters or as an expression of social criticism.

> In general, Fuentes treats his characters as living embodiments of the multiple thematic crosscurrents which make up Mexican life. As a result, they emerge more as representative types than as unique individuals. Some are more convincing than others.[22]

The women who most obviously function as background characters are members of the upper middle class. Their attitudes are those of "cynicism, power, intellectual snobbery and contempt for all things Mexican," [23] which is a germane example of Fuentes' poignant denigration of the upper middle class with its lack of integrity, values, and goals. The women are portrayed as wearing masks of emptiness while engaging in ephemeral "love" affairs, only to end by aging and becoming grotesque. One such background character is Natasha, object of Fuentes' attack against those of the old regime who constantly scorn modern Mexico and the nouveaux riches.

Another secondary character, this time representative of the lower class, is the prostitute Gladys Garcia. Born in a tin hut in the slums, Gladys has a father who is a bird-trapper. Destiny forces her to inherit his low social rank, assigning her to a life of continual abuse. Fuentes, however, develops a personality depth in Gladys that does not appear in the secondary characters of the upper class. Perhaps these traits are presented not with the intention of portraying Gladys as a person but instead

> to present her as the collective conscience of the lower class. She is an extremely lonely character who projects the downtrodden, berotted, and forgotten existence of her class.[24]

Fuentes presents Gladys with his usual sympathy toward women of the lower class. They are the typical passive, suffering women who are abused and destroyed by others.

Another background character of the lower class who embodies the role of the long-suffering mother is Rosa Morales. She marries, has children, and suffers the death of her husband in a crash. On seeing him dead, she exclaims with stoic resignation, "What good would it be to punish anyone; that wouldn't bring him back to me." [25] Rosa works as a maid to support her children, but her employment forces her to be absent from home for prolonged periods, during one of which her little son dies. Rosa's character serves to deprecate the indifference of the affluent toward the suffering poor.

The primary characters are developed psychologically through the use of interior monologue and direct dialogue. They have emotions, desires, and passions that make them credible human beings.

The first of these is Rosenda, a woman who is "trying to make a life out of suffering the injustices that men have inflicted." [26] She was born into a family of comfortable means during the dictatorship of Porfirio Diaz (1876–1911) when Mexico City was not what it is now, "a deformed and scrofulous [city] humped with cement and holed with secret abscesses, but small then and pastel, a city easy to know, clearly understood." [27] Rosenda marries Gervasio Pola, a colonel during Madero's regime (1911–13), who left to fight in the Revolution when she was pregnant. Gervasio is apprehended, jailed, and executed by a firing squad. Rosenda is never certain of her husband's death until she meets Captain Zamacona, who led the firing squad. By then, Rosenda's son, Rodrigo, has been born. She resents having been alone during pregnancy and delivery and begins to think of Rodrigo as an extension of Gervasio.

> I would have known that there were three of us, three; but no, we were always only two, I and the father-son; I and Gervasio-Rodrigo, one single continuation but made now not of him but of my silence and lonely decisions.[28]

She further resents the fact that Gervasio did not call her when he knew he was going to die because "after offering me so little of life, he had refused to give me death too; he would have done better to give me something whole, one or the other." [29] Perhaps if she had seen Gervasio dead, her relation with Rodrigo would have been based on different sentiments. "This identification between father and son was a desire on her part to find herself always loved, needed and accepted." [30] To fulfill this need she becomes a possessive and overly protective mother who sees her son becoming estranged and excessively critical of her. This, added to life in the chaotic city where she has to work as a "commoner," turns her into a passive, stoic, long-suffering, open woman filled with sorrow and self-pity. Her fate is to have lost her husband through inevitable circumstance, and her son because of her intense desire to dominate him while also being dominated by him.

Mercedes Zamacona is another "open" woman who lives in an atmosphere of death and sterility, with an invalid mother and sister; "a skinny cold line with black eyes, cornered in spinsterhood at thirty and already full of self-pity and making it her only pleasure." [31] There was a God, but He was a punishing God who was resented by the mother for having made her paralytic. In this environment, young Mercedes symbolizes fertility. Despite all the religious teachings of her uncle, a priest, she succumbs to rape by the church sacristan. "After that day she had nothing completely, but everything by halves: pride and sin, love and shame." [32] Her son is born and she leaves the house "walking stiff and erect, as she would always be afterward, erect, and with the new feeling of aggressive resignation which would never leave her." [33] She corresponds to the symbol of "La Chingada," and her son is forced to bear the same curse.

Another primary character, Hortensia Chacon, is an Indian who hopes to elevate her social rank by becoming a secretary. Her mother cannot understand her ambition, thus they become alienated. She meets her future husband at the café in which she works. Her only memory of their first encounter is of his coat and necktie, signifying his higher social status. They marry and have three children; but life is different. As a married woman she has to practice the endless patience she learned as a child.

> I learned how to wait, and that is the same as saying to be a woman (it isn't a woman to ask, to beg, to cause trouble; those aren't women, they never will be)[34] . . .

But her husband does not comprehend or perhaps even realize her condition. He is a man who tries to hide his insignificance by bragging to his wife about other women, fighting, or getting drunk with his friends, "without happiness or pity and without ever reaching himself through the liquor." [35] Hortensia decides to find a job and leave her husband, a decision that he finds intolerable, not because he loves her, but because it is an insult to his masculinity. It shows him that she is "more man than he." In a violent rage, he blinds her. Hortensia later meets Federico Robles who accepts her blindness as he finds himself through her authenticity and through their common Indian origin.

> Perhaps it would be wise to conjecture why Hortensia is blind. She, in her blindness is the only one who can "see." This metaphorical vision implies that she is the only one who knows what life really is. She is not blinded by a mask of unreality.[36] What makes her a better woman is her acceptance of suffering, qualified by an insistence on achieving her own identity as a woman through this very process of suffering.[37]

The author presents three leitmotifs that influence the psychological development of Robles' wife, Norma Larragoiti: "La Chingada," the mask, and Aztec mythology. Norma, born into a poor family of northern Mexico, is sent to Mexico City to live with her well-to-do aunt and uncle. Her entire life is an attempt to escape her past by identifying herself with Mexico City's elite. With her goal set, she seeks to attain it at any cost. Marriage to a millionaire is her ultimate desire, and love is grotesquely deformed: it becomes an affair of her will, not her heart. Norma meets Federico Robles and marries him, not because she loves him, but because he is rich and can give her social prestige. During the years in which she tries to escape her meager past and to attain wealth, social class, and power, she uses anyone. She lives in a world of falseness by wearing the mask of a family destroyed by the Revolution in order to deny her origin. This juxtaposition of the person that she wants to be on her real self causes her to lose her identity. Federico realizes that "her mask had been shaped by him, imperceptibly, into a face that he had invented, or at least willed." [38] Norma takes a lover, Ixca Cienfuegos, and for the first time she feels completely powerless before a man and senses that he wants to destroy her. But she wonders whether or not she is the one who wants to be destroyed by the man. "Ixca Cienfuegos, half real, half spirit, partly witness, partly active character," [39] personifies the desire to revive a consciousness of Mexico's pre-Hispanic cultural roots. Ixca represents Norma's origins and their destinies are united. Ixca tries to convince Norma to accept her Indian origin and offer herself to be sacrificed. She does not know what attracted her to him but she fears him:

My world is finished and done. To get where I am now wasn't easy, and all I want to do is enjoy it . . . and this man wants to say words, words that make me want him more and more.[40]

As the moment of the sacrifice draws near, Norma becomes increasingly atavistic. She has an insatiable desire to bite Ixca, to draw blood. When she tells him that she loves him more than herself, she shows her willingness to die for him in sacrifice. In the story, during a moment of fear, Norma's only thought is the thought of her salvation. She has denied her origins for the last time and she is doomed to an Aztec-like sacrification in fire. Another Aztec symbol lies in Norma's refusal to donate her jewels after her husband's financial ruin. In Aztec mythology, the human soul is often symbolized by a precious stone; hence, with the denial of her jewels she actually refuses to give her husband her authentic, unmasked self. By denying her origin she refuses to be herself, so she dies in a "sacrifice to the gods," as her home is set afire. Norma's determination to accomplish her goals is not an indication of self-searching but rather an affirmation of her desired, and at times imposed, mask. She is not the open, passive woman, but the closed, active, hard, and cruel woman who uses others to achieve her goals.

The Death of Artemio Cruz projects a direct accusation of the revolutionary process that appears in the novel in observations and judgments expressed by the characters. The hero, Artemio Cruz, shows himself to us "on the apex of external triumph, over a pyramid of failures, despoliations, abuses, cruelties, deceit, corpses, injustices and disillusions." [41]

The Death of Artemio Cruz *stressed one individual psychology, one destiny, traced out against the kaleidoscopic changes of twentieth-century Mexico.*[42]

Several women in *The Death of Artemio Cruz* are parallels of those in *Where the Air Is Clear*. Regina is a young girl who finds true love in Artemio, and he returns love in the same idyllic way. She is innocence, illusion, and nature. Regina and Artemio meet at the beach by noticing each other's reflections in the sea. They love each other and promise eternal love. "In looking at Regina he looked at himself. . . . All that existed, all his love, was buried in her flesh, and it contained both of them." [43] The myth vanishes as the reader learns the truth about their relationship.

> *He would go back: where? To that make-believe beach that never existed anywhere? To her child's lie? To their sea fiction that she had conjured up that he might feel clean and innocent and sure of love?* [44]

The truth is that Regina was raped by Artemio, but her "noble soul" forgave him.

Regina has the potential of representing the virgin stereotype, but Artemio converts her into "La Chingada," the violated woman. For Artemio this relationship is an encounter with himself; in her he finds his origin. But there is a conflict between Regina and the Revolution, which could also be an inner conflict in Artemio between genuineness and inauthenticity. Since he cannot discover and accept his true self, he will live the life of a mask. Regina dies, a death of dedication to Artemio Cruz.

Artemio's other wife, Catalina, is a woman who wants to be loved and dominated, but

> *her marriage to Artemio Cruz begins with feelings of hatred (for the death of her brother, for which she blames Artemio, and for the loss of her true love, Ramon) and passion (a sexual, almost animal attraction that draws her to him).* [45]

A desire for revenge was instilled in her by her father.

> *She could avenge her brother's death . . . only by embracing this stranger, embracing him but denying him the tenderness he would like to find in her. She would murder him alive, distilling bitterness until he would be poisoned.* [46]

Almost at the same time she admits her interest in him, because

> *no longer did she have to admit the memory of the rough, crude foot that had sought hers during the dinner and had filled her breast with an unknown feeling that could not be suppressed.* [47]

At twenty Catalina does not have a strong feeling of self-worth or identity. She submits to what she considers her destiny.

After her marriage, Catalina remains dichotomized by her dual forces of motivation: that of revenge, which she carries out during the day with silence and a complete lack of emotion, and by her passion, at night when she gives herself to him. Only Artemio can save her by opening himself to her, but he is incapable of providing her with any explanation.

> *He didn't dare. He asked himself why: why did not she demand it from him, the truth he was incapable of revealing . . . aware that this cowardice separated them further and made him also responsible for the shattering of their love; why didn't she insist,*

so that they might cleanse themselves of the guilt that he wanted to share in order to be redeemed? [48]

Artemio's inability to communicate and Catalina's sense of duty to her father and dead brother emphasize the aggressiveness of Catalina and her destructive hatred. She herself cannot accept her own guilt because she is insecure and lacks identity. She cannot forgive either herself or Artemio. She makes a final unsuccessful attempt to be dominated by Artemio when she tells him, "I am a weak woman. All I want is a life of peace, one in which others will make my choices for me." [49] Since he does not respond, her revenge is to deny Artemio her love and remind him of his cowardice. In the process of destroying Artemio, she also destroys herself.

Another woman in Artemio Cruz's life, Laura, is an intelligent member of high society, not a complex person, but refined and with a strong will. She represents Artemio's final chance to recover the love he lost with Regina's death. He has a choice between Laura's true love and the appearances of his social situation. Artemio has lost his capability to commit himself to a sincere love relationship. He is not strong enough to deny the mask he has built over the years. He turns away from his last chance of finding his identity through Laura's love. She refuses to see him again.

Lilia, although of higher social status than Gladys the prostitute, could be the counterpart of Gladys. Lilia gets paid to accompany Artemio Cruz to Acapulco, but "their tacit agreement did not call for love, not even for a semblance of real interest. He wanted a girl for his vacation." [50] She is young and attractive, but she is only a sex object who represents ephemeral youth to Artemio Cruz; "her sleek wet body, that tight body of full thighs, also carried hidden in it the minuscule cell of time's cancer." [51] She also is the love he wants to have and feels he could buy; but he realizes that "she was paid for, but she was escaping him. He could not hold her longer." [52] She leaves him to go to Xavier Adame, symbol of youth and virility. Artemio forgives her, a sign of his decadence. Lilia stays with Artemio knowing that they represent only a convenience to each other. She has all the money she wishes, and he has a woman to accompany him. Lilia is the final humiliation in the life of Artemio Cruz. She has sold and compromised herself, and he has prostituted his dignity.

Artemio Cruz's experiences with women are

a plural campaign of failures more than triumphs or affirmation. . . . These women appear in Artemio's days in a meaningful gamut of levels: compare the meaning (and the symbolism of the name) of Regina, brutally snatched from the protagonist in the midst of revolutionary fervor with Lilia, a tardy and disappointing reversal of what Regina is in Cruz's memory; one is associated with the days of youth and illusions which have not yet been directed through the pragmatic and acquisitive path, the other is associated with the beginning of an old age which is void of true meaning, full of solitude and boredom.[53]

Another novelist is Juan Rulfo, who brings to Mexican prose the anguish of modern man,

the agony of the solitary, faithless man, surrounded by mute symbols. . . . However, Rulfo's characters follow a notable and characteristic Mexican literary tendency in that they are country people, burdened with the failure of the Revolution, and with the centuries of a history which is useless to them.[54]

To some critics, Rulfo's short novel *Pedro Paramo* is the best Mexican novel.

Pedro Paramo *offers the collective drama of man's struggle and failure to achieve success in life. It is an archetypal representation of man's repeated fall from hope to abandonment.*[55]

The main character, who gives his name to the novel, is a typical small-town cacique: cruel, powerful, and primitive in action. He is the omnipotent god of his village universe. He does not hesitate to have his opponents liquidated, putting the lives and property of the region's people at his mercy. His role is depicted in retrospect through the narration of those characters whose lives he has affected. The novel is set in Comala, a desolate and primitive village, "the hottest place in the world." The story is narrated by Juan Preciado, son of the cacique, who comes to Comala to meet the father that he never knew, only because he had promised this meeting to his mother on her deathbed, saying that he would make his father pay for the way that he had forgotten them. But it could very well be that the true goal of Juan's pilgrimage is to find the live image of his mother, who promised to be near him in Comala, instead of being a search for the abstract image of his father. The story juxtaposes reality and fantasy while suspending time sequences to take the reader into a world that is deathless because it is already dead. In this dead world, the characters lived and later relive the drama of their existence.

When the wandering son arrives in Comala, he first meets Eduviges Dyada, a former friend of his mother. Eduviges tells Juan Preciado that she was expecting him because his mother had told her that he was coming that day. Upon learning of the death of Juan's mother, Dolores, Eduviges discovers the explanation for Dolores' distant-sounding voice and remembers that she and Dolores had promised to die together, to help each other on the final voyage. Eduviges assures Juan that she will catch up with his mother, saying, "I know the shortcuts. You just die, God willing, when you want to, not when He arranges it. Or if you want to, you can make Him arrange it earlier." [56] Juan looks at Eduviges and realizes that she must have suffered much in her life because this suffering can be seen all over her. Later, the village priest, Father Renteria, remembers his betrayal of those who loved him out of fear of offending the wealthy, but "prayers don't feed your stomach." The priest remembers Maria Dyada's plea to save her sister Eduviges,

Everybody took advantage of her, just because she was so good and didn't want to offend them or to quarrel with them. . . . But she committed suicide. That's against the will of God. . . . There was nothing she could do . . . because she was so good.[57]

Eduviges is like many of the country women in Mexico who live their pathetic existences totally dependent upon the soil. She has many children because these are her sole possessions. When life becomes unbearable, she helps God arrange her premature death, as this is the only solution available, the only means of ending her life of suffering.

Another female character, Chona, refuses her boyfriend's proposal to elope because she senses a moral duty to care for her ailing father. Chona decides to stay at home even after the boyfriend arranges the elopement, including the rental of two mules. Because of Chona's decision, her boyfriend spites her by visiting another woman. Chona is another woman trapped by her circumstantial role as she denies herself the single opportunity for happiness in life by conforming to social norms in a miserable, hopeless life. Hers is also an inescapable destiny.

Later, the wandering Juan Preciado arrives at a house that has half the roof fallen in; it is where a brother and sister live as husband and wife. Despite their abject poverty, they welcome Juan for the night and share with him what little they have. When the brother leaves in search of a strayed calf, the woman confesses her sins to Juan, explaining that she never goes out because of the ugliness of her sins, which appear as purple stains on her face. She tells Juan,

> Inside I'm a sea of mud. . . . We're too full of sin. Not one of us living here is in the grace of God. We can't even raise our eyes without feeling them burn with shame. And shame doesn't cure a thing.[58]

She had told this to the bishop during his visit to Comala to administer confirmation, but the bishop refused to forgive her. The woman goes on to explain, "I wanted to tell him that life has brought us together, has captured us and tied us to each other. . . . And the village had to be populated somehow." [59] This incestuous existence is partially due to the lonely condition in which they find themselves. The brother returns but only to say that he must depart for the night to find his calf, and he invites Juan to remain in his home. The woman suspects that her brother will never return and that he has left Juan to take care of her. At nightfall, she goes to bed, and Juan goes to the corner where he slept previously; but before dawn, the woman invites Juan to join her in bed to escape from the ticks on the floor. He gets in bed but the heat awakens him with the sensation that "her body was made of earth and covered with crusts of earth . . . melting into a pool of mud." [60] As a telluric woman, the sister is made of earth, used as the soil is used and abused as the soil is abused.

In his doctoral dissertation, Freeman interprets *Pedro Paramo* as the story of the fall from an ideal condition to death and disintegration, with the incestuous couple as an excellent elaboration of the fall-from-grace archetype. He includes much detail to prove his assertion, including an analysis of the bishop's visit.

> This God figure, unforgiving and resolute in the application of divine judgement, condemns the woman for her offense. . . . The divine judgement assumes the form of a curse of sterility, which accounts for the physical condition of Comala, the couple's house and even the woman's bareness.[61]

This same interpretation is found in an article by the Mexican literary critic José de la Colina,

> There is that couple who . . . Juan Preciado finds naked, as if they were the first human couple, Adam and Eve in a wrecked Earthly Paradise.[62]

Freeman comments that

> In essence, man is placed on earth to obey a moral code, but also to procreate, an act that, given the couple's aloneness, involves disregard for the moral issue.[63]

According to this interpretation, the woman would be the tempting Eve who seduces Juan and then simply dissolves into mud. It would seem unjust to blame the unnamed incestuous sister for her sins, as even she recognizes that she must conform to a role that is imposed upon her.

When Juan Preciado finally realizes that he is dead, he finds himself in the same coffin with Dorotea la Curraca, the woman who used to procure women for one of Pedro Paramo's illegitimate sons and who was also condemned to sterility. She tells Juan that her soul wanted her to keep on living, perhaps hoping for a miracle that would cleanse away her sins. Dorotea's wish for a redeeming miracle is a problem familiar to other female characters. Within the limits of her education she describes this problem by stating that

> Illusions are bad. It was an illusion that made me live longer than I should have. That's how I paid for trying to find my son, who was only another illusion. I never had a son. Now that I'm dead I've had time to think everything over and I understand.[64]

She realizes that God did not even give her a home in which to raise a son. The only thing He gave her was "a long, weary life." Juan remembers what his mother had told him about the beautiful Comala sky, which he has never seen, and asks Dorotea if it is as his mother had described it. Dorotea answers that she had lost interest in the sky since Father Renteria told her that her sins would keep her out of heaven.

> But he shouldn't have told me so. The only thing that gives life any meaning is the hope that when you die you'll go to a better place, and when they close that door to you and the only one that's left open is the door to Hell, then it's better not to have been born. For me . . . Heaven is right where I am.[65]

In Dorotea we see some of the religious beliefs of the Mexican peasant, including that of the wandering souls. This peasant stoically accepts life on earth and all its ineluctable suffering with a belief in a forgiving and merciful God who will grant him a halcyon life after death. When that illusion is destroyed, it would be better "not to have been born."

Through the memories of Juan Preciado and other characters in the novel, we learn about Dolores, his mother. When she married Pedro Paramo, she seemed very much in love with him, but she encountered increasing disappointment. She asked her husband about visiting her sister in another town and he gladly consented, not to please her, but because it provided an opportunity to get rid of her. Dolores displayed a sense of pride in deciding never to return until her husband would send for her which, of course, he never did. She lived in the past, reminiscing about the Comala that she glorified in her memories as a paradisaical place. Juan's love for his mother seems to satisfy his self-identity because he feels that she gave him her eyes to see Comala the way that she saw it. Dolores represents the typical long-suffering Mexican peasant mother, used to satisfy Pedro Paramo's zeal for power.

The only different woman is Susana San Juan, "a woman who isn't of this world . . . a strange girl, a sort of Ophelia, brittle and sensual, always on the dim edge of sanity." [66] Because of her insanity she is the only character who transcends the world of brutality. We first meet Susana through Pedro Paramo's childhood memories in which his thoughts of her are expressed in lyrical passages,

I was thinking of you, Susana. In the green hills. When we flew kites in the windy season. . . . When you were there looking at me with your sea-green eyes.[67]

There are several traumatic experiences in the life of Susana San Juan. She always appears to be surrounded by a tragic atmosphere that isolates her from others. After the loss of her mother when she was yet a child, her father makes her go down into a well to find what he thought to be a gold treasure, but instead she finds only a skull. Susana emerges so frightened from the well that she becomes ill. Her father, Bartolomé, takes her to another town in order to save her from Pedro Paramo. Still young, Susana falls in love with Florencio, experiences a short-lived happiness until one day he does not return home. Upon learning of his death, Susana never suspects the involvement of Pedro Paramo. She is crushed with desperation and exclaims: "You don't exist, God! I begged You to protect him. To take care of him. But You don't care about anything except our souls. And what I want is his body." [68] Pedro Paramo continuously sends messengers to persuade Bartolomé to return to Comala. When poverty finally forces Susana's father to accept the pleading. Pedro Paramo says,

I've waited thirty years for you to come back, Susana . . . I felt as if Heaven had opened. I wanted to run to you. To surround you with happiness. To cry. And I did cry, Susana, when I knew you were coming back.[69]

There is no way for Susana to avoid marrying Pedro Paramo, but he is not happy even when Susana is living in his home because she spends most of her time in her room, either sleeping or feigning sleep. She is always restless and seems tortured in her dreams. Pedro spends many worried nights at her side, contemplating her, incapable of helping her. He recognizes that something is destroying her from within, but he cannot understand the world she is living in, and that is the most important thing in his life. The reader knows that Susana never got over her love for Florencio as her dreams are about him. Even when near death, she opens her eyes and says that she had a lovely time with Florencio. Her world is built around the memory of an ephemeral encounter with love. Pedro and Susana had both built their worlds around love; but these worlds were separate and incommunicable. The cacique desperately wanted to possess his childhood love in body and soul: "His passion is the terrible destructive passion of romantic love." [70] Paramo's entire life was an attempt to reach the unattainable woman, a search for the impossible love that weakened his will.

When Pedro elevates Susana to his level and loves her not with a violent physical love, it is in that instant that Susana San Juan divests herself of any definable characteristic, she becomes a delirious mystical project, an erotic abandonment which yearns for eternity." [71]

When Susana dies, Pedro arranges to have the church bells toll for three days. This only creates a festive atmosphere in the area. Not only the people from Comala celebrate, but others come from neighboring towns to join in the festivities.

This makes Pedro angry and he swears to take revenge: "I'll fold my arms and Comala will starve to death." Pedro Paramo neglects himself, rarely sleeping but continuously thinking. He lacks a reason to live. He knows that death is not far away as he sits by the gate of his estate remembering how weak and cold the light was when Susana left him and how he had watched her climb the path to Heaven. Heaven opened up and light streamed out. She had left the shadows of this world behind her. With Susana died Pedro's will, and with it died Comala.

As Pedro dies of a wound that one of his illegitimate sons had inflicted upon him, he still thinks of her: "Susana . . . I begged you to come back." [72]

Pedro Paramo, lecherous, cruel, and destructive, affects the lives of all the characters in the novel. The only life that he cannot touch is that of Susana, his only real love. In her are the memories of his lost innocence and the dreams of an impossible love.

Susana San Juan resists the fantasies of her father and the love of Pedro by becoming insane. Insanity becomes her single worldly freedom that cannot be corrupted by men.

All the women in *Pedro Paramo* are limited and defined by their circumstances. They possess a very rudimentary mentality, without any internal dimension. Each is obliged to follow a pattern of existence over which she has no control. Despite the absence of an alternative existence, each experiences guilt feelings. They live close to the earth and their lives are moved by elemental forces: hunger, violence, and love. They are passive women used by men. They accept their fate without resistance. They are stoic women who suffer quietly the anguish and desperation of an existence that offers no escape but death or insanity. These women share a willingness to die that is more the result of a disillusionment with life than of a hope for salvation. Some characters find more peace in death, but for most, even death holds no peace. "Death is not the summing up of all, but merely an agonized continuation of life; it is no longer a physical reality but tends to the metaphysical." [73]

One finds in Mexican literature, as in Mexican life, that woman by her essence has a weakness to overcome: She is born open and therefore passive. This, of course, could be said of women in general, but what makes this characteristic particularly Mexican is the identification of this weakness with "La Malinche," the personification of "La Chingada." This has kept women in an inferior condition for many years. The only woman who is free of this curse is the Virgin Mother, the Virgin of Guadalupe.

Women react in different ways to this "inherent" weakness. Some accept it passively, either with abject passivity or with the stoicism from which the myth of the long-suffering Mexican mother, "La Llorona," originated. Others lash back at individuals or at society (the "bad woman"); they are aggressive and thus become somehow closed and less "feminine."

Two criteria are used to judge women in literature: authenticity and unauthenticity. A woman is authentic when she uses her experiences to fulfill herself and to find her identity. The unauthentic woman hides herself behind a mask. She is the one who is always trying to be something that she is not, one who is only appearance or nothingness.

These virtues and defects recognize no ethnic or social-class barriers. Although they permeate all levels of society, they are seldom found in their purest forms. I have classified women in literature and in life, according to their dominant trait, but every woman presumably embodies all possible classifications to some extent.

These are the images of women found in some of the works of Octavio Paz, Carlos Fuentes, and Juan Rulfo. Would Mexican women agree with these images? For the time being that question remains unanswered.

NOTES

1. Julian Marias, *Modos de Vivir* (New York: Oxford University Press, 1964), p. 72.

2. Ibid., p. 73.

3. Octavio Paz, *The Labyrinth of Solitude*, tr. Lysander Kemp (New York: Grove Press, 1961), p. 35.

4. Ibid., p. 36.

5. Ibid., p. 38.

6. Carlos Monsivais, "Soñadora, Coqueta y Ardiente . . . ," *La Cultura en Mexico*, March 1973, p. iii.

7. Paz, *Labyrinth of Solitude*, pp. 65–66.

8. Ibid., p. 66.

9. Ibid., p. 76.

10. Ibid., p. 77.

11. Ibid., p. 79.

12. Ibid., p. 75.

13. Ibid., p. 79.

14. Ibid., p. 86.

15. Ibid., p. 39.

16. Ibid.

17. Evelyn P. Stevens, "Marianismo: The Other Face to Machismo in Latin America" (Paper presented at the Third LASA National Meeting, Austin, Texas, December 1971), p. 14.

18. Paz, *Labyrinth of Solitude*, pp. 85.

19. Luis Harss and Barbara Dohmann, *Into the Mainstream* (New York: Harper & Row, 1967), p. 286.

20. Paz, *Labyrinth of Solitude*, pp. 147–48.

21. Joseph Sommers, *After the Storm* (Albuquerque: University of New Mexico Press, 1968), p. 149.

22. Ibid., p. 119.

23. Ibid., p. 102.

24. Jo Ann Poole, "Mujeres en dos obras de Carlos Fuentes." Manuscript. The author gratefully acknowledges Ms. Poole's kind permission to read and use her as yet unpublished paper.

25. Carlos Fuentes, *Where the Air Is Clear* (New York: Farrar, Straus, 1960), p. 169.

26. Sommers, *After the Storm*, p. 145.

27. Fuentes, *Where the Air Is Clear*, p. 175.

28. Ibid., p. 177.

29. Ibid., p. 179.

30. POOLE, manuscript.

31. FUENTES, *Where the Air Is Clear*, p. 326.

32. Ibid., p. 333.

33. Ibid., p. 337.

34. Ibid., p. 273.

35. Ibid., p. 275.

36. POOLE, manuscript.

37. SOMMERS, *After the Storm*, p. 117.

38. FUENTES, *Where the Air Is Clear*, p. 124.

39. SOMMERS, *After the Storm*, p. 108.

40. FUENTES, *Where the Air Is Clear*, p. 261.

41. JUAN LOVELUCK, "Intención y Forma en *La Muerte de Artemio Cruz*," *Nueva Narrativa Hispanoamericana* 1 (January 1971): 114.

42. SOMMERS, *After the Storm*, p. 154.

43. CARLOS FUENTES, *The Death of Artemio Cruz*, tr. Sam Hileman (New York: Farrar, Straus, 1964).

44. Ibid., p. 76.

45. POOLE, manuscript.

46. FUENTES, *Death of Artemio Cruz*, p. 48.

47. Ibid., p. 49.

48. Ibid., pp. 107–8.

49. Ibid., p. 102.

50. Ibid., p. 145.

51. Ibid., p. 147.

52. Ibid., p. 152.

53. LOVELUCK, "Intención y Forma," p. 110.

54. CARLOS BLANCO AGUINAGA, "Presentación," p. 1.

55. GEORGE RONALD FREEMAN, *Paradise and Fall in Rulfo's Pedro Paramo* (Cuernavaca, Mexico: CIDOC, 1970), p. 1/6.

56. JUAN RULFO, *Pedro Paramo*, tr. Lysander Kemp (New York: Grove Press, 1959), p. 8.

57. Ibid., p. 28.

58. Ibid., pp. 49–50.

59. Ibid., p. 50.

60. Ibid., p. 55.

61. FREEMAN, *Paradise and Fall*, pp. 2/16, 2/17.

62. JOSÉ DE LA COLINA, "Susana San Juan y el mito femenino en Pedro Paramo," *Universidad de Mexico* 19, no. 8 (April 1965): 19.

63. FREEMAN, *Paradise and Fall*, p. 2/17.

64. RULFO, *Pedro Paramo*, p. 58.

65. Ibid., p. 64.

66. Harss and Dohmann, *Into the Mainstream*, p. 268.

67. Rulfo, *Pedro Paramo*, pp. 9–10.

68. Ibid., p. 99.

69. Ibid., pp. 80–81.

70. Colina, "Susana San Juan," p. 20.

71. Monsivais, "Notas sobre sexismo," p. iii.

72. Rulfo, *Pedro Paramo*, p. 122.

73. Thomas E. Lyon, "Orderly Observation to Symbolic Imagination," *Hispania* 54, no. 3 (September 1971): 450.

5

WOMEN
AND SOCIAL
INSTITUTIONS:
MALE
DOMINATION AND
FEMALE EXCLUSION

Women in Legal Perspective

Kathryn F. Clarenbach

The legal structure and processes are critical in maximizing social change.
To those in the women's movement, the central importance of law to changes in the status of women cannot be overemphasized. This article, then, is addressed to the general reader, containing, first, a rapid theoretical look at some facets of our legal structures and, second, a personal assessment of alternative means to achieve progress in improving the legal status of women. It is by no means intended as an exhaustive analysis of statutes and case law pertaining to the legal rights of women.

HISTORICAL BASIS

The legal inferiority of women dates from the Greeks, when women and slaves were both regarded as property. Some historians point out that in ancient Greece most women were slaves, and most slaves were women. Indeed, women slaves were in a worse position than their male counterparts; at least male slaves could be freed. Women remained chattel, that is, property. In fact, the word *manus*, "hand," comes from the Greek world where the giving of a hand in marriage literally meant passing the chattel from father to husband.[1]

Roman law modified this status slightly, regarding women as in perpetual tutelage, that is, a state of perpetual guardianship, or in other words, perpetual childhood. While women were not always considered property or slaves, they were thought to be incapable of caring for themselves; they needed the care of some adult male, often the woman's own son.

Many such concepts passed through canon law to English common law, and were in turn built into our American legal framework. For example, as the often quoted eighteenth-century English jurist Blackstone wrote, when a man and a woman marry they become one person in law, and that person is the man.[2] A century after Blackstone, though, another Englishman, John Stuart Mill wrote: "the principle which regulates the existing social relations between the two sexes—the legal subordination of one sex to the other—is wrong in itself, and now one of the chief hindrances to human improvement."[3] Today, once again a century since that writing, our country is on the brink of replacing that "hindrance" with a "principle of perfect equality, admitting no power or privilege on the one side, nor disability on the other."[4] That principle is embodied in the Equal Rights Amendment.

EQUAL RIGHTS AMENDMENT

Equality of rights under the law shall not be denied or abridged by the United States or by any state on account of sex.

If ratified by thirty-eight states, the Equal Rights Amendment will become the Twenty-seventh Amendment to the Constitution. At this writing, thirty-four states have ratified the amendment, regarded by many as the most comprehensive contemporary legal change affecting women—and thus, of course, men.

Versions of the amendment have been introduced in Congress yearly since 1923. The current version was finally passed overwhelmingly in March 1972. Its passage and the subsequent ratifications by state legislatures attest to the growing strength and persuasiveness of women's groups who have worked for the ERA. Delays in ratification and votes to rescind, however, are at the same time testimony to deep fears, lack of understanding, and acceptance of the status quo.

Once the ERA has been ratified, the states will have two years in which to conform their laws to its dictate of equality. The effect of the ERA has been hotly debated; its opponents argue that it would rob women of femininity, result in scandalous use of the same public rest rooms by both sexes, and subject women to the draft. In fact, responsible legal opinion states that the amendment would require the federal and state governments and branches thereof to treat men and women equally. The usual legal tests would be used to measure state action in regard to sex equality.[5] With respect to the rest room question, for example, rights of personal privacy would control so that separate facilities could be maintained. Possible draftability of women is unclear, as is the suggestion that they be required to participate in armed combat.

In this context, it is appropriate to make a note about our Constitution, its composition and its functioning. It was designed to serve as the fundamental law of the land, broad and general enough to cover many circumstances and many years. It is made current by interpretive court pronouncement and statute.[6] Thus, one of the great debates has been whether women could be accorded constitutional equality merely by Supreme Court interpretation of the Equal Protection clause of the Fourteenth Amendment, or whether a separate constitutional amendment would be required, or if not required, whether that choice would be preferable.

Under the Fourteenth Amendment, state action alleged to deny equal protection of the laws can be upheld under one of two standards.[7] Both standards are legal terms with very special meanings. What follows is an extremely abbreviated explanation. The first and usually employed test is whether the action being challenged has a "rational basis." Normally, if the state can say that its law or its action has a basis in reason, that law will not be found to violate the guarantee of equal protection. However, if (a) the interest affected by the state action is found by the Court to be a "fundamental interest," such as the right to procreation, the right to marital privacy, or the right to vote in a national general election; or if (b) that the class affected is a "suspect class," such as a racial classification, the government is required to meet the test of the "compelling state interest" in order for its action to withstand challenge. In other words, the state must have more than just a rational basis for its regulation in one of these latter two instances. The reason for acting must be compelling. And those who challenge the government therefore seek to show that they constitute a "suspect class," or that some fundamental interest has been affected because then the government has a harder case to uphold its action.

The Supreme Court has held race, alienage, and national origin to be definitely "suspect classes." It has never held sex classifications to be suspect, although in the recent case of *Frontiero* v. *Richardson* (1973) 411 U.S. 677, four justices indicated that they would so hold. But since a majority of the Court has never ruled sex a suspect class, governmental action challenged under the Equal Protection clause must merely meet the looser "rational basis" test to withstand attack.[8]

Despite that hopeful sign in *Frontiero*, of dubbing sex a "suspect class," the Court reaffirmed the rational basis standard in its 6–3 decision in *Kahn* v. *Shevin* (4/24/74) 42 Law Week 4591. There the Court held that a Florida tax statute was rationally based which allowed widows but not widowers a $500 property tax exemption; there was no sex-based discrimination against men, said the Court, because the intent of the statute was to cushion the loss to the burdened spouse—that is, make amends for disadvantages women suffer. That the statute was a tax law perhaps impelled the Court to invoke the lesser standard as well. This same test was used in *Geduldig* v. *Aiello* (6/18/74) 42 Law Week 4905 to uphold California's exclusion of normal pregnancy and childbirth from coverage under its disability insurance program. The Court reasoned that California was not rationally required to sacrifice a self-supporting insurance program or to make that program any more comprehensive than it was. Such reasoning came in the teeth of four years of concerted effort by women across the country to treat pregnancy and childbirth like any other medically related disability.[9] These two decisions do not bode well for the inclusion of sex as a suspect class. In view of these latest developments, a constitutional amendment forbidding governmental sex-based discrimination seems even more imperative.

LITIGATION AS A ROUTE TO EQUALITY

As suggested, women have gone to court to fight sex-based discrimination, and have done so in an increasingly organized fashion over the last five years. Case law is clearly one way to change the law, but it is a slow route. Class actions (lawsuits in which the same complaint of a large and similar group of people is litigated together) have proved to be useful tools because the coverage and impact is greater than in an individual suit; relief granted to the class is much weightier than to only one plaintiff. Recent decisions have made it harder to bring such suits, however. A lawsuit of any kind can take years from start to finish, and the cost often is phenomenal even when attorneys contribute their services. But the more serious disadvantage is that of jurisdictional complexities. Only a decision by the U.S. Supreme Court binds the entire nation. State court decisions are the law within that state only; federal court decisions hold for that particular federal district. (A decision in one jurisdiction is of course instructive although not binding in another.) One must not assume just because a court renders a decision that attitudes and practices will change immediately. School desegregation is a glaring example of the slow pace of social change in the wake of litigation—despite decisions by the Supreme Court and subsequent countless implementing statutes and enforcement actions.

Significant cases have been won, however, in federal and state courts alike by a variety of individual lawyers as well as by the National Women's Lawyers Association, the National Organization for Women, Women's Equity Action League, and Human Rights for Women. They have taken on such Goliaths as AT&T, Bell Telephone, American Newspaper Association, Colgate-Palmolive, Union Pacific Railways, and the federal government itself. The cases mentioned here are merely illustrative of the many gains made.

The decision interpreting Title VII of the 1964 Civil Rights Act in *Weeks* v. *Southern Bell Tel. & Tel. Co.* (1969) 408 F.2d 228 said that unless the employer had a good, factual reason to believe that "all or substantially all" women could not safely do a job (in that case lift a certain weight), he could not lawfully refuse to hire qualified women on that basis. Two years later the Supreme Court ruled in another Title VII case, *Griggs* v. *Duke Power Co.* (1971) 401 U.S. 424, that testing for employment must be job related, so that tests are a "reasonable measure of job performance." The impact of these decisions was to clear the way for more jobs for qualified women who theretofore had been unable to compete for positions. Recently, under both Title VII and the 1963 Equal Pay Act, women have won huge back-pay awards against Corning Glass, AT&T, and nine steel companies, among others.

Two of the most noted cases are of course the abortion cases, *Roe* v. *Wade* (1973) 410 U.S. 113 and *Doe* v. *Bolton* (1973) 410 U.S. 179. The decision in these companion cases said that during the first trimester of pregnancy an abortion decision is up to a woman and her doctor; during the second trimester the state has an interest in the health of the mother; and during the third trimester the state may have an interest in the health of a child. The rulings led to greatly liberalized abortion policies in many states, and in turn, brought in their wake increased litigation on numerous abortion-related rights. Just as in the instance of the Equal Rights Amendment, groups previously relatively uninvolved in the women's movement joined with women's groups to make the case for civil rights. Notable among such groups is the American Civil Liberties Union.

In the area of family law, forward-looking decisions combined with legislative changes have begun to move women in the direction of equal partnership in marriage and family management. In many states the marriage age for men and women has been equalized, as has the parental consent requirement. The requirements for dissolution of marriage are in many places more flexible and reasonable than previously. Spousal support after dissolution of marriage has begun to be awarded on the basis of economic need rather than as a punitive measure. Child custody is being awarded to both mothers and fathers according to the best interests of the children in light of the situations and capabilities of both parents.

STATUTES, REGULATIONS, GUIDELINES

Statutes which affect women's rights, that is, "the laws" as we usually think of them, constitute a developing area within our legal system where the women's movement has made itself felt. Although enactment of a statute and its implementation are certainly separate questions, several major pieces of federal legislation potentially could win women equal treatment.

Federal

The first of these to be passed was the Equal Pay Act of 1963, amended in 1972 to cover all employees. This provides for equal pay for women and men who do the same or comparable job. The Equal Pay Act is enforced by the Wage and Hour Division of the Employment Standards Administration of the Department of Labor.

Title VII of the 1964 Civil Rights Act prohibits sex discrimination in employment, including hiring, promotion, salaries, fringe benefits, training, and other conditions of employment. It has been amended, most recently by the Equal Employment Opportunity Act of 1972, so that it now covers most institutions with fifteen or more employees, including state and local governments and educational institutions. Title VII is enforced by the EEOC, the Equal Employment Opportunity Commission, which can investigate, conciliate, and file suit. The EEOC's Sex Discrimination Guidelines fill out the statutory proscriptions, such as advertising, discrimination against married women, maternity leave. Women's groups have been instrumental in drafting and reviewing these guidelines during the ten years since original passage of the act. They have as well been successful in narrowing the range of existing BFOQs (bona fide occupational qualifications) that serve as permissible grounds for discrimination under Title VII.

The 1968 Executive Order 11246 and its amendment 11375 were presidential directives having the force of law which prohibit sex discrimination in employment by federal government contractors and subcontractors. The OFCC, Office of Federal Contract Compliance, of the Department of Labor oversees enforcement of the Order, and has delegated to the Department of Health, Education, and Welfare (HEW) enforcement powers with respect to educational institutions that hold federal contracts. Revised Order 4 requires that federal nonconstruction contractors with fifty or more employees and a contract of $50,000 or more develop written affirmative action plans, including numerical goals and timetables based upon utilization analyses of women and minorities. The affirmitive action requirement has, as could be expected, unleashed a volley of protest and evasion maneuvers from employers, including institutions of higher education. It is instructive to note that since 1969 there have been well over 350 complaints against colleges and universities alone charging sex-based discrimination in employment.

Title IX of the Educational Amendments of 1972 of the Higher Education Act prohibits discrimination against students and employees (both current and prospective) on the basis of sex in many higher educational institutions receiving federal grants, loans, or contracts. (There are exemptions for religious and military schools; discrimination in admissions is prohibited in only particular schools.) The Office for Civil Rights of HEW has primary enforcement powers, but procedures are as yet unclear. Thus far, enforcement staff is far too limited. Proposed regulations under Title IX were issued only on June 20, 1974, by HEW Secretary Caspar Weinberger. These have met with severe criticism from women for their failure to deal adequately with the highly discriminatory area of college athletics. Regulations were finally published in the Federal Register, June 4, 1975. The effectiveness of Title IX continues to be in question.

A newer law which may eliminate some of the problems left by Title IX is the Equal Educational Opportunities Act of 1974. This act states that, "All children enrolled in public schools are entitled to equal educational opportunity without regard to race, color, sex, or national origin." Feminists should carefully scrutinize the administrative rule-making process by which interpretive and enforcement mechanisms are developed to make sure that the Equal Educational Opportunities Act does not suffer the fate of Title IX.

Other federal laws prohibiting sex discrimination in education include Title IV of the 1964 Civil Rights Act, which prohibits sex discrimination in school assignment; Titles VII and VIII of the Public Health Service Act, which prohibit sex discrimination in admission to federally funded health training programs; and Title IV of the Educational Amendments of 1972, which prohibits sex discrimination by lenders who use the Student Loan Marketing Association.

State

State statutes (plus administrative rulings, regulations, and opinions of attorneys general) vary widely from state to state. Many state laws are antiquated, only now being seriously reconsidered in light of the ERA. By 1974 ten states had enacted state equal rights amendments and others had begun to bring their codes into conformity with concepts of equal rights. It has been estimated that some 15,000 statutory provisions may have to be altered throughout the states to comply with the Equal Rights Amendment's command of equality for both sexes.[10]

It is not always the woman who is disadvantaged by sex-based laws. For example, the issue of "fathers' rights" is of current concern. In the cases of *Stanley* v. *Illinois* (1972) 405 U.S. 645 and the still-litigated case of *Rothstein* v. *Lutheran Social Services of Wisconsin and Upper Michigan* (1972) 405 U.S. 1051, *State ex rel. Lewis and Rothstein* v. *Lutheran Social Services of Wisconsin and Upper Michigan* (1973) 59 Wis. 2d 1, 207 N.W. 2d 826, questions were raised as to when unmarried fathers have rights in children, when children can be taken from their fathers, and what rights unwed parents have as against one another in children.

Women, though, seem to take the brunt of laws based upon nonbiological definitions of sex; these laws perpetuate double standards, promote women's dependency, and limit their personal autonomy. As mentioned previously, laws in the area of marriage and family are in flux. In addition to those noted, women have found demeaning restrictions on their ability to sign for children's drivers license permits and restrictions on use of their own names. The laws respecting property ownership and rights differ in the forty-two common-law states from those in the eight community-property states, but it is an open question which system reflects fewer concepts of sex equality. Consumer affairs and restrictions against granting women credit in their own right is another sector in which state laws or their absence have worked harshly against women. Finally, criminal laws have been attacked as blatantly discriminatory against women in such matters as rape, abortion, and differential sex-based sentencing.

State Protective Legislation

Other state laws, predominantly labor laws limiting the kinds of employment women may take, the hours they may work, and the conditions under which they may work—primarily weight-lifting restrictions—have long been matters of controversy. Promulgated under the guise of protection and benefit to women, these laws deprive women of responsibility for themselves and freedom to choose an occupation. (True protections such as mandatory meal periods, minimum-wage provisions, and requirements of proper lighting and transportation are not required for men in many states.)

There is some evidence that so-called protective state labor laws passed in the early 1900s were not entirely motivated by a desire to protect women. While many people believe that such laws were designed to control sweatshops, it appears that to some degree they were also the result of labor's fear that too many women were entering the labor force and were a competitive threat to male workers. To counteract competition for high-salaried jobs, legal restrictions on women's employment were enacted.[11]

Restrictive labor legislation has been attacked in state after state in the decade since passage of the federal Civil Rights Act in 1964. In 1971 the Ninth Circuit Court of Appeals decided in *Rosenfeld* v. *Southern Pacific Co.* 444 F. 2d 1219 that an employer could not defend against a charge of sex discrimination under Title VII by relying on its compliance with state protective labor legislation. Prevailing opinion is that with the advent of the ERA restrictive "protective" legislation will fall as discriminatory, and at the same time benign "protective" legislation will be extended to men as well.

Local Ordinances

Exciting legislative changes can be seen throughout the country on the local level, where women have made gains in public accommodations law, affirmative action in employment and housing discrimination. In addition, there have been successful legislative and case law assaults upon the bastion of restrictive licensing statutes, which, for example, forbid women from working in bars or fraternizing with male customers there. (Recently a federal court in Wisconsin ruled in *White* v. *Fleming* (5/7/74) 42 Law Week 2615 that such a city ordinance violated the Equal Protection clause of the Fourteenth Amendment.) Local governments may be easier for women to influence than state or national legislatures for several reasons: more women are involved in local government than at higher levels (which in itself is a result of sex discrimination and role stereotyping); the issues are more defined at the local level; there are fewer constituents and colleagues to influence. Local Human Rights Commissions are to be kept in mind in this respect.

THE TASK AHEAD

The challenge, then, for women is to understand the legal system in order to force the law to lead in the change of social practice and ideas, to set goals and to make requirements of people which they would otherwise avoid. Women can make great gains by actively participating in the legal process: by working for the ERA, by supporting feminist candidates and by running for office, by bringing suit (as plaintiffs and as attorneys) to challenge discriminatory laws.

Mention has already been made of the role of women's groups in passage of the ERA. In addition, women helped remove veteran Congressman Emanuel Celler of New York, arch foe of the ERA, who was defeated for reelection in 1972 by attorney Elizabeth Holtzman. And they participated in the successful opposition to Senate confirmation of Harrold Carswell to the U.S. Supreme Court when they joined with blacks and other progressives because of Judge Carswell's role in *Phillips* v. *Martin Marietta.*[12]

It can be hoped that more women themselves will be judges within the foreseeable future. Within the last several years the percentage of women in law schools has jumped dramatically, until some schools have 30–40 percent women students. This is indeed remarkable when one recalls that for many decades only 3 percent of the attorneys in this country have been women, and the number of women judges has been even more minuscule. Feminist law firms are appearing for the first time in most major metropolitan communities.

Along with greater numbers of women entering the legal profession, its literature too has recognized women and the importance of their legal status. Numerous law reviews have published symposium issues on the rights of women. *Hastings Law Journal* (1968, November 1972), *Drake Law Review* (vol. 20, no. 3, 1971), *New York Law Forum* (vol. 17, 1971), *Valparaiso University Law Review* (vol. 5, no. 2, 1971), *The Yale Law Journal* (vol. 80, no. 5, 1971), *Wisconsin Law Review* (vol. 1, no. 1, 1973), and *California Law Review* (vol. 61, no. 3, May 1973) are among those addressed to this subject.

Casebooks and law textbooks, too, have appeared. The first major casebook was published in 1974. This is *Sex-Based Discrimination* by Davidson, Ginsburg, and Kay (published by West Publishing Co. of Saint Paul, Minnesota). Other texts are in process at this writing. In an American Civil Liberties Union handbook series, Susan C. Ross published in 1973 *The Rights of Women.* Leo Kanowitz's *Women and the Law, the Unfinished Revolution* was first published in 1969.

Numerous law schools are now offering courses on sex-based discrimination, and the subject is being taught to undergraduates on some campuses. Many women's studies curricula incorporate some study of the legal aspects of women's status.

Congressional debate preparatory to passage of federal legislation to alleviate sex discrimination was instrumental in moving issues of the legal rights of women into the realm of serious public debate. Published proceedings of public hearings in Congress, which hearings themselves were well publicized and widely attended, have had broad distribution and constitute a vital part of the literature of the women's movement agenda. Three volumes were published in 1970 and 1971 on the Equal Rights Amendment. Two volumes entitled *Discrimination Against Women* report the hearings before the Special Subcommittee on Education of the House Committee on Education and Labor; those hearings were chaired by Representative Edith Green of Oregon in 1970. In 1973 Representative Martha Griffiths of Michigan chaired public hearings before the Joint Economic Committee on *Economic Problems of Women*. Three volumes of proceedings resulted.

Of late, women have been elected to public office in record numbers. Assistance has come from such organizations as the National Women's Political Caucus, the National Organization for Women, Women's Equity Action League, and the League of Women Voters. At this writing there are nineteen women in Congress. Those such as Bella Abzug, Yvonne Braithwaite Burke, Shirley Chisholm, Martha Griffiths, Edith Green, Elizabeth Holtzman, Barbara Jordan, and Patsy Mink took national leadership positions on significant questions. Their leadership and concerns cover the gamut, including affirmative action in employment, child care, education opportunity, military service, social security, credit, economic security for home-makers, welfare programs, health care, and taxation. The influence of this handful of women suggests the real potential for progress that true representation of women in Congress could achieve.

Both legal and political advances have been made, but the personal costs have been very high and the crucial problems are still ahead. Our laws are far from fair and our legislative structure is still massively masculist. Optimism must thus be tempered with a healthy pessimism coupled with a strong determination.

NOTES

1. H. MAINE, *Ancient Law* 135 (1905) and A. Gouldner, *Enter Plato* 10 (1965) cited by Jo Freeman in her article, "The Legal Basis of the Sexual Caste System," *Valparaiso University Law Review* 5, no. 2 (Symposium Issue 1971): 208.

2. SIR WILLIAM BLACKSTONE, *Commentaries on the Laws of England*, 1765.

3. JOHN STUART MILL, *The Subjugation of Women*, 1869.

4. Ibid.

5. "State action" is a legal term of art. It can sometimes include private actions with a sufficient connection with or similarity to state action.

6. Our Constitution differs from those of the USSR and Poland, for example, in this respect. The latter two, according to Nancy Reeves in *Womankind: Beyond the Stereotypes* (Chicago-New York: Aldine-Atherton, 1971), resemble in their specificity probable statutes or regulations under our system. Those Constitutions state explicitly how women shall and shall not be treated.

7. See note 5 for comment on "state action."

8. The California Supreme Court held sex a suspect class in *Sail'er Inn, Inc.* v. *Kirby* (1971) 5 Cal. 3d 1, 485 P. 2d 529, 95 Cal. Rptr. 329. This means only that in California—not throughout the nation—the higher standard obtains.

9. Note, however, that in *Cleveland Board of Education* v. *La Fleur* (1/21/74) 42 Law Week 4186, the Supreme Court held the school board's mandatory maternity leave policy for women teachers violative of the Due Process clause of the Fourteenth Amendment. The board's conclusive presumption that all pregnant women were incapable of teaching violated the right to decide to bear children. Note, however, that this decision did *not* rest on the Equal Protection clause.

10. In 1975 both Wisconsin and Washington brought all their state statutes into conformity with equal rights; other states have amended significant numbers of their laws. Other models for statutory changes are provided by the Proposed Uniform Acts and Model Codes drafted by the Commissioners on Uniform State Laws. Many family law revisions have been based upon the Uniform Acts.

11. Susan Deller Ross, Arthur Garfield Hays Civil Liberties Fellow, New York University Law School, "Sex Discrimination and 'Protective' Labor Legislation" (manuscript, 1972), p. 3: "Business observers of the early legislative period . . . allege that the motivation for 'protecting' child and female labor was more the protection and advancement of the male's status at work than a humanitarian attitude for the women and children in our society."

12. Carswell had heard the *Phillips* case in 1969 when he was a circuit judge in the Fifth Circuit and had voted with the majority against plaintiff, a mother with preschool children who had been denied employment for that reason. Eventually the Supreme Court ruled that women could not be denied employment on the grounds of "sex plus," that is, their having young children. *Phillips* v. *Martin Marietta Corporation* (1971) 400 U.S. 542.

Power, Patriarchy, and "Political Primitives"
Bonnie Cook Freeman

Political science might be described as the social science of the male power
structure, a science that excludes the world that women inhabit. As such,
political science exhibits a characteristic common to most of the social sciences and
humanities. Jessie Bernard has recently noted:

> From precursors like Hobbes, Locke, Rousseau, and even Adam Smith to recent times,
> one gets a picture of society as constituted entirely of men. "Man" does this, "men"
> believe that. Half of the human species is invisible. (Bernard 1973:782)

Because political scientists generally have devoted little attention to the
question of sex roles and their relationship to politics, a review of the image of
women in political science requires not only an investigation of those few studies
that have dealt with women, directly or indirectly, but also an exploration of the
discipline's assumptions about women, and its conceptions of what is "political."
Conventional attitudes toward women and a narrowly defined notion of politics
have led the academic student of politics to ignore women as either actors or
pawns.

In the first section of this chapter, I describe the predominant view of the
political role of women in the United States that is projected in survey research
studies. The second part focuses on political socialization research that to some
extent investigates sex differences in the development of political attitudes and
behavior. Next, I look at the female politico—what is and is not known about her?

241

Then I consider the male political scientist as a prisoner of time and place and examine the status of women within the discipline. Finally, I identify some questions and themes from the literature on women and point to areas in need of research.

THE IMAGE

Little research focuses directly on women because political scientists have perceived women as of little consequence to the political system. As a result, it is impossible to piece together more than a partial and ambiguous portrait of woman as a political person and of the political differences between males and females in the United States. The major conclusion from the sparse literature is that politics in the American culture is beyond the appropriate sphere of a woman's concern (Duverger 1953, Lane 1959, Milbrath 1964:45). This norm appears to be borne out in the political behavior of women, but serious and puzzling ambiguities exist in the data.

The Intensity of Political Involvement

A large number of studies show that women tend to vote proportionately less than men, although the ratio varies from election to election (Campbell et al. 1960, Milbrath 1965, Greenstein 1969, Costantini and Craik 1972). But voting is only one of the conventional forms of political activity. On other political dimensions as well, women are less active than men: They tend to express less interest in politics; indicate less information about issues, campaigns, and government; participate less often in political campaigns; and run for and hold office less often (Campbell et al. 1960, Milbrath 1965). College-educated women are likely to be more sophisticated in the way in which they think about political issues than women with high school or grade school educations. Yet, one study found that at each level of education, men were more advanced than women in their conceptualization of politics and fully 18 percent of college-educated women were described as exhibiting "no issue content" in their political evaluations (Campbell et al. 1960:491, Table 17-10).

Attitudes and the Direction of Political Participation

Political scientists have usually assumed that when women have opinions on public issues, they borrow them from their husbands (Lane 1959, Greenstein 1969). Yet, the differences between men and women on particular issues are of considerable significance. Summarizing the literature that emphasizes the less attractive features of women's political attitudes and behavior Costantini and Craik conclude:

> . . . *women voters are more provincial (in the sense of focusing upon local issues), more conservative in their stance on policy issues, more responsive to issues with moral overtones, more likely to personalize politics and to be more sensitive to the personality of politicians, less sophisticated in the level of concept formation and less comfortable with political conflict and contention. (1972:218)*

242   BONNIE COOK FREEMAN

On the other hand, women have some political opinions that might be considered preferable to those of men. For example, several studies have indicated that women tend to be more humanitarian and less supportive of the use of violence than men (Verba 1967, Rosenberg 1970, Lansing 1972, Steinem 1972:50). There is usually a large gap between men and women on the propriety of the use of military force or of governmental policies that might lead the country to war. Women, for example, are more likely than men to see our entry into World War II, Korea, and Vietnam as mistakes (Lansing 1972:8, Setlow and Steinem 1973). Furthermore, women tend to show greater opposition to universal military training, capital punishment, and the harsh punitive treatment of drug addicts. They favor gun control and support both conservation and consumer causes more often than their male counterparts (Rosenberg 1970, Lansing 1972, Setlow and Steinem 1973).

The Socioemotional Dimension

One concept that has been elevated to the position of a linchpin of democracy and the "civic culture" by some scholars is *political efficacy*—the feeling that one has control over one's fate and can to some extent shape his or her political future (Campbell et al. 1960). Not surprisingly, women tend to have lower scores on political efficacy measures than do men (Campbell et al. 1960, Milbrath 1965, Greenstein 1969). One line of reasoning advanced to explain this in part suggests that in the American culture women are not expected to exert power and control in the political arena, but rather to turn there for protection and guidance (Lane 1959).

Although women tend to accept the restricted role in politics assigned to them, they are said to make claims of authority on "moral" issues and to have a highly emotional and personal response to political stimuli—i.e., to see things in black and white, or either/or terms (Lane 1959:212). This more personal, emotional response is considered to represent women's less developed, immature conceptualization of the political realm (Easton and Dennis 1969), and their intolerance of any values other than their own (Lane 1959:213).

A Critique of the Image

One must begin an evaluation of the political scientist's description of the role of women in the political system by noting its brevity, its ambiguity, its shallowness, and its failure to answer important questions. For example, while it is clear from a number of reports that women participate less than men and in different ways, few students have systematically sought to discover *why* this is so. In a nominally democratic political system in which universal participation is theoretically expected, one would have anticipated more interest in such a notable anomaly as the pervasive absence of women from most levels of public decision making.

When political scientists have tried to explain the political behavior of women, they often have resorted to condescending and patronizing glibness. The result has been exercises in the conventional wisdom and folklore of sex-role behavior rather than incisive analysis. One of the most generally accepted propositions in the literature is that married women, on the whole, tend to vote like their husbands.* It

* The vote is a very rough indicator of attitudes and political tendencies—the result of a calculus

is obvious, first, that at least some part of this correlation may be the result of the influence of wives on their husbands' voting decisions. Quite apart from that, many variables that are supposed to affect the political attitudes of an individual—education, social class, social mobility, party identification, political generation, political socialization patterns, region of the country in which one resides, and so on—will be similar if not identical for both the husband and the wife. Therefore, one would expect a sizable convergence of attitudes between marital partners. In addition, it is reasonable to suspect that persons are attracted to one another, to some significant degree, by similarities in their attitudes and values. This, too, would lead to a correspondence in voting decisions. Finally, members of a family are likely to be exposed to the same political information via the press and communications media, as well as in personal conversations. For all these reasons, it is sensible to expect a very high correlation in voting preferences between husbands and wives.

Several studies report data which, if explored, might shed greater light on the nature of spouse voting. For example, one report indicates that the more education the woman has, the more likely she is to participate in politics but also to deviate from her husband's political predispositions (Campbell et al. 1960). In a study of 1962 Princeton graduates, 88 percent of the married men thought their wives had the same (generally conservative) attitudes that they held. When the women were questioned out of the company of their husbands, their political attitudes were found to be different from their husbands—they tended to be more liberal (Steinem 1972:49). None of the above findings or explanations requires one to assume that a woman is consciously or unconsciously deferring to the opinions of her husband as scholars have done (Milbrath 1965:54). Instead, the findings are mixed and seem to demand further investigation.

Another well-entrenched proposition about the behavior of women is that they are prone to fall for a handsome face in an election campaign (Converse and Dupeux, in Campbell 1966:316; Steinem 1970). This is thought to result from the largely irrational and "emotional" nature of the woman's relationship to politics and from her low comprehension of the issues at stake. One popular explanation of the massive popularity of Eisenhower among women was that he served as a warm and reassuring father figure for them. Yet, most men voted for Eisenhower as well (Campbell et al. 1960). In 1960 John F. Kennedy was credited with garnering more votes than he should have in a normal election because of his physical appeal to the ladies. Yet, recent analysis indicates that women voted disproportionately for Richard Nixon (hardly a sexually appealing figure) in 1960 (Setlow and Steinem 1973). In both 1964 and 1968 women were accused of being mesmerized by the personal qualities of Barry Goldwater and George Wallace. Yet, careful analysis indicates that females voted disproportionately for Lyndon Johnson in 1964 and Nixon and Hubert Humphrey in 1968 (Lansing 1972:7). The best that one can say about this proposition is that it is an oversimplification and that the data do not support it unambiguously.

Even when analysts discover some substantial differences between female and male behavior and attitudes, they are likely to interpret the position of woman as *less reasonable* and *less competent*. In the case of the proposition of the high

at a particular time. One would expect a higher correlation here between mates than one would expect on more specific issues.

personality content of women's vote decisions, one finds references to the gullibility of women, their easy acceptance of engineered images, their naive emphasis on the character and personal qualities of the candidate (Lane 1959; Campbell et al. 1960; Converse and Dupeux, in Campbell 1966). Yet when a candidate seems to attract large numbers of male adherents through the sheer force of his personality, we are likely to be treated to dissertations on "charisma" and "hot" and "cool" candidates (Levin 1966).

The analysis of female attitudes toward foreign policy is perhaps the best example of a tendency of political scientists to interpret women's opinions as unrealistic and immature. There is evidence to show that women have been more dovish than men in their attitudes toward the war in Southeast Asia (Verba 1967, Steinem 1972:50). Verba and his associates concluded that this was simply the result of lack of information and an inability to comprehend the complexities of the issues involved. Even when information level was controlled, however, women still indicated a more dovish stance—a finding not emphasized by the authors.

The propensity of women to inject moral considerations into political decisions has always been treated by political scientists with annoyance (e.g., Lane 1959:213). The mainstream of the discipline has attempted to rid itself of questions of right and wrong and to develop a hard, realistic, sophisticated approach to political matters (Crick 1962). Not only is an ethical approach thought to be embarrassing and naive, it may even be dangerous since it indicates a readiness to think in ideological terms of right and wrong and may thus lead to dogmatism and intolerance—the bane of the compromise and bargaining considered to be the essence of politics (Crick 1962, Lane 1959:213).

Scholarly interpretations of the political behavior of women often suffer from being bound by time and space. Most of the research on the subject was carried out during the 1950s. This may have distorted the results for several reasons. First, the Eisenhower years were a time of relative nonpartisanship, when candidates were not clearly differentiated in the public's mind and rather deliberate attempts were made to defuse or blunt the issues. (For some recent revisionist work on the importance of issue voting see Repass 1971, Pomper et al. 1972, Page and Brody 1972.) This may account for some of the apparent lack of precision and sophistication on the part of many women. Second, the 1950s were a time when the myth of the "feminine mystique" seems to have been especially pervasive (Friedan 1963). Against the powerful pressures to be either coy, seductive, and frivolous, or to be childbearing homebodies, apparently few women were able, or desired, to strike out into essentially male preserves such as politics and public careers.

It is fair to say that the political scientist's store of lore and wisdom on women was quite inadequate to predict or account for the striking developments in the late 1960s. The women's movement seems to have caught most scholars by surprise (J. Freeman 1973). There are no adequate explanations for the increased participation of women in the political system up until 1968 in voting and campaigning (Lansing 1972), the increased number of female candidates seeking and winning office, or the increased number of women's organizations registered as lobbyists in Washington* (Setlow and Steinem 1973). During this time the polls indicated a remarkable

* At the writing of Amundsen's book, *The Silenced Majority* (1971), there was only one registered women's lobby—NOW.

willingness on the part of women in general to vote for, or at least consider, the possibility of a female candidate for President—a significant change from the few women who would do so in 1959 (Lane 1959, Steinem 1972, Hartley 1972). Women's political life appears to be conditioned not only by the more general political climate of opinion in the country but also by the evolution of sex-role norms in the society. Rather than focus on the psychological or physiological properties that make politics inappropriate for women, scholars should attempt to specify the relationship between these factors and participation.

Another major difficulty of the literature on women is its tendency uncritically to lump all women in the same category. There is considerable research (some in political science—e.g., Matthews and Prothro 1966) suggesting extensive differences among women on such sociologically relevant variables as race, class, education, religion, ethnic group, and marital status, and their effects on their interests, values, and goals (Lane 1959, Campbell et al. 1960, Bernard 1971). The authors of *The American Voter* found that the greatest divergence between men and women in voting participation was in the lower socioeconomic levels of the society. On the one hand, women who have received advanced education tend to resemble more closely their male peers in their level of participation and their political efficacy. On the other hand, more highly educated women are more likely to deviate from their husband's political predispositions and hew their own political paths (Campbell et al. 1960, Steinem 1972). It is largely from this group that much of the current pressures (through conventional avenues) on the political system are being felt—that is, the largely middle-class and college-educated women who belong to and lead such organizations as the National Organization for Women, National Women's Political Caucus, Women's Equity Action League, Equal Rights Amendment groups, and so on (Lansing 1972).

While these women seem to have more personal resources to use on their own behalf, we have little political knowledge about their sisters in lower socioeconomic echelons. We do know that black women as a group, and women of the working class as a group, tend to vote less than their male peers. However, younger black women are voting more than their male peers (Lansing 1972), and women of the working class who work tend to vote more than their nonworking sisters of the same class but their votes are cast similarly to those of their male peers (Campbell et al. 1960). Many explanations are possible for this difference in behaviors, but none will be easily substantiated without further research that focuses on questions with more scope and depth than the very general indicator of the vote alone.

The few attempts on the part of political scientists to explain the generally lower rate of participation of women have been largely inadequate. One particularly bothersome tendency among political scientists is to attribute the phenomenon to certain attitudinal or psychological variables such as *political efficacy* (Campbell et al. 1960). This mode of explanation borders on the tautological. Political efficacy is defined as the feeling by a person that he or she "can cope with the complexities of politics and the belief that their participation carries some weight in the political process" (Campbell et al. 1960:490). Not surprisingly, political efficacy has been found to be closely related to voting turnout—one would expect that persons who believed that their vote was meaningless would be less likely to cast it than persons who thought it was very important. It seems clear, however, that lack of political efficacy is hardly a satisfactory explanation of decreased participation and is a variable itself in need of further explanation and justification.

A somewhat better attempt to explain women's lesser role in the political sphere has been made by Maurice Duverger, a French political sociologist (1953). He notes that women who fill the stereotypical role of wife and mother—a role that absorbs all their energies and isolates them from outside affairs, become psychologically dependent on their husbands to satisfy requirements outside the household. As she acquires no outside experience, a woman is expected to act like a minor in external matters, and her husband is expected to make independent decisions that will affect the entire family. Thus Duverger sympathetically but condescendingly concludes that "while women have legally ceased to be minors, they still have the mentality of minors in many fields and, particularly in politics, they usually accept paternalism on the part of men" (Duverger 1953:129).

Political science has ignored for the most part the normative dilemmas posed by the study of women in politics. The first is the existence of a double standard for men and women. While it is considered inappropriate for women to be active in politics, the democratic ideological norm that everyone should participate enjoys wide support. Had the group being excluded been male, one can anticipate much more concern on the part of academics. A second major conflict is that between our egalitarian democratic ideology and the actual treatment of women in our society. The existence of formally equal rights and lip service to equal standards does not erase the evidence of the pervasive and significant unequal treatment of women in the economic and social sphere. It is perhaps a measure of how well women have learned their lessons that they exhibit little feeling of power and mastery or interest in the political arena. The cultural lessons teaching passive response begin early in the female child's experiences.

THE POLITICAL SOCIALIZATION OF WOMEN

Although the area of socialization research probably affords one with the most knowledge about women in political science, most students of politics have conceived of political socialization in a very narrow sense. It has been defined as "the deliberate inculcation of political information, values and practices by instructional agents who have been formally charged with this responsibility" (Greenstein 1968:551). In addition to these conceptual limits, the political socialization literature has been largely atheoretical, has relied heavily on survey methods, and has attended only to explicitly recognized political variables. The consequence is a body of literature bound by the time periods in which the studies were conducted, the middle-class children interviewed, and the myopic political perspectives of those who determined the approaches used. While developmental psychologists (e.g., Maccoby 1966) have spent time examining theories of the development of sex differences, political scientists have been slow to attach themselves to the developmental process theories or to study sex differences.

In order to focus on sex differences in political socialization, in the following pages the concept of political socialization will be expanded to include not only explicitly political learning but also nominally nonpolitical learning that affects political behavior, such as the apprehension of politically relevant social attitudes, and the acquisition of politically relevant personality characteristics (Greenstein 1968:551). Therefore this discussion will emphasize the findings and concerns of some political socialization studies, the sex role socialization literature, and my own speculation about the effects on the young girl's personality of her status as a citizen in American society.

The chief agents of sex role socialization and political socialization include the family, the school, peer groups, and the media.

The Family as an Agent of Political Socialization

Because of its virtual monopoly of access to the small child, the family plays a primary role in the political socialization process (Dawson and Prewitt 1969:107–8). Hess and Torney believe the family exerts influence on the child through: (1) the transmission of valued attitudes; (2) the presentation of models for the child to emulate; and (3) the child's generalization of expectations formed from experience within the family to political objects (Hess and Torney 1967:110). The emphasis on the family as the primary agent for the transmission of cultural values has led many students to conclude that political socialization is a fundamentally conservative process (Dawson and Prewitt 1969:124). Research on the political similarities between parents and children shows a high correlation, but the studies examine only very gross kinds of political attitudes such as party identification (McClosky and Dahlgren 1959, Jennings and Niemi 1971).

Although little is known about the actual processes of socialization, studies indicate that the attitude that politics is not an appropriate concern within the female sex role develops early (Greenstein 1969, Iglitzin 1972). Greenstein suggests that it is probably a "subtle and complex process in which—through differential opportunities, rewards and punishments which vary by sex and by identification with one or the other parent—a sex identity is acquired" (Greenstein 1969:125). Some literature on sex-role learning suggests that a young female is encouraged to acquire personality traits counter to those thought proper for a citizen in a liberal democracy. The matrix of traits believed appropriate for a female child are:

> dependence, passivity, fragility, low pain tolerance, non-aggression, noncompetitiveness, inner orientation, interpersonal orientation, empathy, sensitivity, nurturance, subjectivity, intuitiveness, yieldingness, receptivity, inability to risk emotional liability, supportiveness. (Bardwick and Douvan 1971:147)

Jo Freeman has characterized the inculcation of such traits as the process of "interior colonization" (Freeman 1973). A person exhibiting these characteristics can be depicted as playing the role of a subject under the domination of a master. Recent empirical investigation has shown that women are somewhat more likely than men to acquire these traits (Broverman 1972).

In contrast to the characteristics believed appropriate for a girl, the young boy is encouraged to aspire to the following:

> independence, aggression, competitiveness, leadership, task orientation, outward orientation, assertiveness, innovation, self-discipline, stoicism, activity, objectivity, analytic-mindedness, courage, unsentimentality, rationality, confidence, and emotional control. (Bardwick and Douvan 1971:147)

These traits are largely those of persons in control of and responsible for themselves; moreover, they are considered characteristics of good citizens (Amundsen 1971:136). Although not specifically political variables, the development of these different personality traits in men and women lead to one group (men) having more personal political resources at hand to achieve their goals than the other group (women).

Little concern about this difference has been evidenced by political scientists. This is particularly striking when one observes that they have shown a great interest in developing the efficacy of the young male. A host of research projects have been dedicated to this concern alone. One finding is that perceived father inadequacies on the strength-power-potency dimension tend to be associated with feelings of low political efficacy among males. As Wolfenstein (1969:32) notes: "His father is the first model of power and authority, strength and rectitude, a model he [the son] seeks to emulate." Hence the attention given to father-absent families and the possible ill effects of the predominance of female teachers in the schools (Schultz 1969, Sexton 1969, and Langton 1969). No comparable concern has been voiced regarding the absence of strong female role models at home or in the schools for girls to emulate.

In our society adjustment to the demands of one's assigned sex role is highly valued. Those qualities associated with femininity are at once considered essential for the healthy development of the little girl and danger signs for one's general mental health (Broverman 1970). To be rewarded, the young female learns to fit the image of a "well-adjusted" young lady even if she continues to prefer to have been born male (Polk and Stein 1972).

Foremost, the young girl learns that it is inappropriate to want to be a male authority, or to be concerned about that arena of activity. Since girls are not encouraged to acquire political information in the same way as boys, they will not be motivated to obtain it (Greenstein 1969:114). As it is anticipated that most women will fill the role of mother, young girls are conditioned to inhabit private and personal realms while young men are urged to explore the wider environment beyond the home (Iglitzin 1972).

The aspirations of boys and girls begin to differ significantly at the end of elementary school. One study indicates that by fifth grade, boys and girls believe that men ought to be doctors, bosses, taxi drivers, mayors, factory workers, lawyers, college professors, and clerks; women ought to be cooks, teachers, artists, nurses, and house cleaners (Iglitzin 1972:5). When asked about their own career aspirations, boys express desires to become engineers, scientists, sportsmen, and pilots; girls say they wish to become teachers, artists, stewardesses, and nurses. Asked to describe their future lives, the girls gave extensive and detailed accounts of their housewifely routine. Even when they desired a career, "household chores seemed far more salient than the job" (Iglitzin 1972:8). The author concludes that the consequence of early learning is that these young children have developed remarkably distinct definitions of the proper roles for men and women in both home and community. In each sphere of activity, the children have learned that those positions of high power and status are rightfully monopolized by men (Iglitzin 1972:11).

In a study more specifically directed to aspirations for political office and support for the political system, Easton and Dennis found that by the end of eighth grade, the girls in their sample were less anxious to hold political positions than their male peers. In addition, while the boys became more and more "sophisticated" in their orientation to the political system, the girls stagnated at the level of "personalization"—that is, they tended to identify the government with the individual personalities (especially that of the President) who were in office. The boys, on the other hand, developed an institutional perspective that emphasized the political organs of government—the Congress or the Presidency—more than the particular men who happened to be in the positions at the time. Easton and Dennis considered the institutional orientation a more "mature" response than that of personalization, because institutions and roles are more influential than personalities (Easton and Dennis 1969:285). They conclude that girls are simply "political primitives" (Easton and Dennis 1969:339).

One may say several things about such a conclusion. It is important to ask what are the assumptions of these scholars and by what standards do they judge? For example, they seem to accept the male response as the norm and ridicule the girls for not making the grade. This is highly insensitive because it is possible that the male standard is itself inadequate and because there may be a number of extenuating factors that explain the gap between boys and girls without resorting to academic name-calling. Among professional political scientists there is considerable question as to the relative power of the Congress and the Presidency. Furthermore, a great deal of recent interest has been shown with respect to the impact of the President's personality on performance, and the "role vs. the man" debate is one of long standing with emphasis on either the role or the "man" being perfectly respectable (George and George 1964, Barber 1972). But even if one accepts the institutional perspective as a more advanced position than one which focuses on personalities, one is still left with the responsibility for making a serious attempt to explain the differences between the sexes.

The School and the Peer Group

While the school has been the place where interviews with children have been carried out, little research has been done on its effects on the general or more specifically political socialization of young women. Very brief scrutiny convinces one there is a near-total absence of female models in the history and government textbooks used in the schools. Yet, political scientists have indicated great surprise when women find it difficult to identify with such political authorities as a policeman, mayor, or President (all of whom are male models) or with male political authorities of the past (Hyman 1959, Greenstein 1969). Rather than treating this as the result of learning disabilities or lack of patriotism, political scientists should have examined the cultural barriers to young girls identifying with male political figures. Furthermore, they might have asked if the school may represent a *continuing exposure* to the notion that women are less valued by society than men.

The effects of peer groups and social climates on student attitudes and behavior are revealing. In a ground-breaking study of adolescents, Coleman (1961) found that girls consciously held down their grades even though they were brighter than boys. They followed the norm of being good but not brilliant. Peer pressures may result in a young intelligent female attempting to become increasingly feminine (i.e., to play dumb) and ultimately moving away from avenues of potential career success.

A great deal of serious academic scrutiny needs to be applied to the process of sex socialization. Such study would permit us to understand how the agents of socialization "channel women into lower occupational expectations and willingness to play a marginal role in the economic, political, and social aspects of society" (Iglitzin 1972:1).

As a result of the political socialization to which they have been exposed, women develop the personality qualities and political concepts of a lower-caste human being. Therefore it should be no surprise to find that when questioned, women rate as "political primitives." What is a surprise is: (1) the extent to which scholars of political socialization have placed such a premium on the adjustment of the child to the appropriate requirements of his or her political role in order to maintain the stability of the society (Easton and Dennis 1969); and (2) the fact that in the insidious circle of victimization, the traits inculcated into women are then used to ridicule them and to justify the failure to recruit them actively into positions of political leadership.

FEMALE POLITICOS

Female Politicos as Invisible Women

Students of politics tend to treat female activists as aberrations. They prefer to study only modal phenomena—either male politicians or the conventional political participation of men and women in general—and they ignore the occasional women who have held important offices or played prominent roles in politics.* This is an example of what Morton Kaplan (1964) calls "premature cloture"—the propensity to examine only the typical, average, or easy to explain, and to overlook the residuals, "errors," or deviations from what one expects.

Perhaps the best illustration of this oversight comes from leadership and community power studies. No matter what the definition of leadership, what the nature of the methodology used, or where the focus of attention, most studies paint a portrait of overwhelming male dominance in the United States (Bell 1961:34). As Wendell Bell notes, one is not sure whether "women's absence from the leadership structure either is so common that it is taken for granted or that their appearance as leaders is so rare that they are not considered as an important group for analysis" (Bell 1961:34). For example, Floyd Hunter (1959) used the reputational approach to produce a list of national "top leaders" that included only one woman—Oveta Culp Hobby. Women tend to be counted as members of the power structure more often at the community level than at the national level, but even there they have not attracted much scholarly attention (Bell 1961:34).

It is an open question whether women really so completely lack access to the higher echelons of political decision making or if the methods employed by students of community power operate systematically to remove women from their view.

---

* While exclusion from study is the general rule, and while there appear to be no major systematic attempts to examine the effects of sex on recruitment characteristics and behavioral patterns of political elites, there are some exceptions and these are rapidly multiplying (Werner 1966 and 1968, Lamson 1968, Jennings and Thomas 1968, Amundsen 1971, Bach 1971, Costantini and Craik 1972, Kirkpatrick 1973).

Both possibilities seem at least partially at work. One must also ask if those women who do find their way into positions of authority serve largely as symbolic ornamentation or tokens.*

Female Politicians as an Anomaly

If the majority of women are little attracted to political careers, it is because everything tends to turn them away from them; if they allow politics to remain essentially a man's business, it is because everything conduces to this belief, tradition, family life, education, religion, and literature. From birth, women are involved in a system which tends to make them think of themselves as feminine. The publicity which blazes around the few women who are outstandingly successful in "non-feminine" fields accentuates the fact that they are exceptions and the gulf which divides them from the normal woman's life. (Duverger 1953:129)

What about the women who enter the ranks of political leadership? What does it take in terms of background and personality for them to make their way in American politics? *For the most part we do not know.* So-called exceptional women who have run for office and won—Bella Abzug, Shirley Chisholm, Margaret Chase Smith, Edith Green—have been viewed as insignificant deviations from the rules of the game and not requiring explanation rather than as pioneers of a new trend for persons of their sex—despite the fact that they often have considered themselves in that light (Costantini and Craik 1972 are an excellent exception to this generalization).

In two separate research projects, women officeholders were asked to enumerate those factors which they believed operated to discourage women from seeking office or being fully effective once it was achieved. Some of the most important items were: (1) the attitude of men (particularly men in public life and one's husband) and the general reluctance to accept a woman as a public official; (2) the apathy of women in general to politics and to women in politics; (3) the antipathy of women toward the syndrome referred to as "politics"—conflict, misrepresentation, compromise, etc.; (4) the lack of the necessary "resources"—money, information, experience, knowledge, interest, encouragement; (5) the lack of time because of one's household responsibilities; (6) the lack of time in general; (7) the fear of defeat, ridicule, or making decisions; (8) the lack of self-confidence; (9) the tradition of the exclusion of women from politics, particularly if one is a young female; (10) the press of other commitments in the community (Bach 1971; study by the North Carolina Governor's Commission on the status of women, reported in Gruber 1968:237).

The Taking-on of Sex Roles Among Actives

Political socialization and institutionalized sex roles affect the women even within the elite stratum. In our culture woman's role outside the home is

---

* Many women who serve on otherwise all-male bodies deeply resent the suggestion that they are mere tokens, and I do not mean to denigrate their roles. But it is clear that whatever their subsequent influence and accomplishments, many women do function as tokens from the point of view of the men responsible for giving them the position.

subordinate to that of men. And as M. K. Jennings and N. Thomas (1968) note, "Even when females gain elite status, they are likely to be affected by sex-related contingencies in the channels (of mobility) utilized" (p. 479).

Most women active in politics who have any office or position are likely to be in local politics or to fill intraparty offices. By far the most common role is that of unpaid volunteer who works for a political party. According to Reeves, women volunteers "remain traditional hewers of wood and drawers of water: door bell ringers, raffle vendors, telephone recruiters, and stamp lickers" (Reeves 1971:76). In 1960 one source speculated that some 6 million women did some sort of volunteer work for their party (Gruberg 1968). According to Gruberg, "Women are often around as window dressing—forever seconding nominations, occupying figurehead offices, confined to the safe backwater of the women's auxiliary" (p. 50). Since men have a monopoly on the powerful decision-making positions, women can do little to help other women, and most have to rely on the support of a male sponsor to rise in the ranks of the party (Gruberg 1968:64–65).

When positions of power come open, men rush to fill the vacuum; when it is merely an honorary or symbolic position, it is more likely that they will offer it to a woman. It is important to note that men generally tend to prefer a certain type of female for such positions. They want women who are docile, agreeable, supportive, and selfless—persons who will not challenge the male claim to the monopoly of power (Gruberg 1968). It is unlikely that such women will recruit other women into the political system.

For most women who are active, politics tends to be more a "labor of love" where concern for the party, its candidates, and its programs assumes relatively greater importance than it does for men (Costantini and Craik 1972:235). Male leaders tend to be motivated more by self-serving considerations. It has been suggested by Costantini and Craik that participation for female elites in the party much resembles their participation in the family.

> The male party leader, like the husband, is more likely to specialize in the instrumental functions of the system involved (whether party or family)—that is, in those functions related to the external world. The female party leader, like the wife, tends to specialize in expressive functions of those concerned with "the 'internal' affairs of the system, the maintenance of integrative relations between (its) members" (Parsons and Bales 1955:47). In general, she is relegated to, or relegates herself to, a supportive role of more or less selfless service to her family or party, while the male partner or co-partyist pursues a career in the outside world. (Costantini and Craik 1972:235)

Women officeholders tend to have less influence and to be less active than their male peers in whatever political body they serve. In the state legislature women have been characterized as playing the role of "spectator"—a legislator without ambitions, political or otherwise (Barber 1965:25).

Until recently, most national congresswomen have fit a similar pattern. In fact, congresswomen so often gain office through appointment or election after the deaths of their congressmen husbands that the term "widow's mandate" has been coined to describe the phenomenon. By giving the office to the grieving widow, a political party can capitalize on the goodwill generated by the late husband and the public sympathy attendant upon his death (Amundsen 1971:68). Few women manage to win the ensuing election, however. Of the 65 congresswomen in American history, only 22 were or have been in office for four or more terms. Seven of the 10 female senators we have had served less than one year (Amundsen 1971).

Because of their short tenure and the requirements of the seniority system, women in Congress have had difficulty getting important committee posts. They have rarely made a legislative mark and have been distinguished only by being known as the "Lady Congresswoman," or "Sweetheart of the House" (Kirkpatrick 1973). On the whole women have been *outsiders*, excluded from the formal congressional leadership and unwelcome in the informal settings of barrooms and clubs where so much congressional "business" is conducted.

Politicians' Wives as Ornamental Satellites

One political role open to women is that of the politician's wife. Despite the myth that "behind every man is a woman who made him what he is" (Gruberg 1968:16), political wives have been largely ignored by students of politics and presumed to have little influence except in unusual circumstances such as the physical incapacity of their husbands, which gave both Edith Wilson and Eleanor Roosevelt unexpected powers. There seems to be an unwritten norm followed by most political wives that they should "be seen and not heard." Their functions are essentially social and they are not expected to discuss politics (Gruberg 1968:19). Of Pat Nixon it has been said:

> In China, she tastes soup in the hotel kitchen. In Russia, she visits schools and longs for a church to pray in. In the United States, she is admired for her wardrobe, and throughout the world she is known for how much she smiles and how little she says. (Ms. 1972:48)

While these women attract the attention of the press, we know more of what they wear, how they decorate, and which are their favorite recipes than we know about what they think or if they think at all. One presumes that the politician's wife does not think, or, at least, takes the same positions on political issues as her husband. If she differs, she never publicly indicates as much. This unarticulated norm of "me-tooism" tends to come into the open only in those rare circumstances when it is violated, as in the case of the controversial Eleanor Roosevelt. Abigail McCarthy (ex-wife of Senator Eugene McCarthy) has documented that a presidential candidate's wife is assigned a type of "bodyguard" to keep her from putting her foot in her mouth (McCarthy 1972:418). A more recent, alleged example is the assignment of a governmental agent to Martha Mitchell in an attempt to isolate her from the press. In this instance the agent apparently went so far as to drug her with an injection against her will.

The secondary role that political wives are expected to have as a matter of fact or habit suddenly becomes an issue of concern when a male is put in that same position. Fear that the male ego will be damaged, suspicion that the husband is the power behind the throne, or outright sympathy for the neglected spouse are the common response to those unusual cases where the shoe is on the other foot.

Evidence of a New Trend?

Recently some of the old norms have been called into question. While only a very few political scientists have done any analyses of the phenomena (Lansing 1972, Soule and McGrath 1972, J. Freeman 1973), there are some readily available indications that changes are taking place. The first is, quite obviously, the newly emergent, amorphous, unexplained Women's Movement that has politicized many women. A more specific manifestation of change was the 1972 Democratic National Convention. Due to the implementation of the McGovern-Fraser Commission recommendations to include at Democratic conventions groups previously excluded, the proportion of women delegates increased from 13 percent in 1968 to 40 percent in 1972 (Soule and McGrath 1973). While one might argue that the reforms alone were responsible for the increased participation of women, one must still explain why the female delegates differed so markedly from their predecessors. In earlier years the typical women delegates to a political convention were widows of important men with sizable bank accounts, and they were selected for their malleability (Gruberg 1968). But in 1972, one-third of the female delegates to the Democratic Convention were active in the women's movement and a majority of the delegates said that they had been affected by the movement (Soule and McGrath 1973). In addition, they were more liberal politically than the men at the convention. This women's bloc "constituted a politically distinct group with identifiable interests and issues, visible leaders, publicized meetings, press releases, and convention strategies" (Soule and McGrath 1973).*

Although it has by no means disappeared, the widow's mandate applies to fewer women active in politics today than in the past. In 1972 Shirley Chisholm campaigned "seriously" for the Presidency.** Although she did not receive as much publicity as Ms. Chisholm, Linda Jeness also ran for President on the Socialist Worker's party ticket (Burstein and Cimons 1973:84). For years the possibility of a woman President was the basis for humor and ridicule as exemplified by the "cute" idea expressed in the Hollywood movie *Kisses for My President* when the lady chief executive becomes pregnant while in office.

Another sign of changing attitudes and the emergence of a women's power bloc was the nomination of Frances "Sissy" Farenthold of Texas as a vice-presidential candidate for the Democratic party. With her main support coming from women, she received 420 delegate votes, second only to Senator Eagleton. Interestingly enough, when Eagleton withdrew, no one seems to have reconsidered her as a possible candidate (Steinem and Frapollo 1973).

Unlike many of their predecessors, women entering both the 91st and 92nd Congresses were more likely to be elected in their own right and not as surrogates of their late fathers or husbands. A few of these women have challenged the archaic formal and informal rules of Congress. A number have been reprimanded or otherwise harassed for their criticism of committee assignments, seniority rules, and other valued congressional "rules of the game." For example, Bella Abzug had her

---

* For a different interpretation of women's role at the 1972 Democratic Convention, see Germaine Greer, "McGovern, The Big Teaser" (*Harpers* 1972).

** She was not the first female candidate for the Presidency. This honor is reserved for Victoria Woodhull, who announced her candidacy in 1870. Her platform included advocacy of free love (Salper 1972:11).

seat reapportioned out of existence by the New York state legislature. When she announced for a neighboring post rather than retire "gracefully," a number of congressmen, hoping to prevent her return to Washington, actively dumped money into the campaign of the deathly ill William Ryan, and later, that of his widow (Nies 1973).

At the state level there were 20 percent more women elected to legislatures in 1972 than in 1970. Out of a total of 7700 state legislators nationwide, 425 were women in 1973, compared to only 350 from the previous election year. While the number of female candidates in 1972 increased significantly, they continued to suffer the usual difficulties of women being recruited to contest "no win" districts by local party officials eager to avoid charges of sex discrimination and being forced to manage inadequately funded campaigns.

Similar to innovators at the national level, female legislators at the state level appear to be developing a different style from that of a passive "spectator." In a recent study of effective women legislators, Jeanne Kirkpatrick found that her sample of women enjoyed active participation in campaigns and in the political activities of the legislature. They tended to adopt a strategy where they would be needed and respected. They did this by making themselves subject-matter experts.

These new developments may be harbingers of a new day for women in politics or they may be simply a temporary phenomenon. In either case they cannot be adequately understood without more serious and thoughtful analysis.

THE POLITICAL SCIENTIST AS A PRISONER OF PLACE AND TIME

The position of the observer affects his perception of the data under observation. While all people, lay persons and scholars, are predisposed to employ simplifications and polarities to reduce the confusion of reality to manageable proportions, the scholar's naiveté has the greater consequence since he as expert tends (1) to project distorted images as unassailable fact, and (2) treats his predispositions as verified conclusions. Because of these tendencies, *who* studies politics is particularly important: it affects (1) which questions will be asked, (2) what methods will be used, (3) the biases interwoven through perception into the process of research, and (4) the conclusions and interpretations reached.

Recruitment of Political Scientists

Political scientists are predominantly white middle-class males, and they recruit from a younger but basically similar population. Like other men in our society, political scientists probably tend to have conventional ideas about the nature of women, the functions they can and should perform in society, and their destiny in a man's world. Nor are the women who are recruited and self-selected into academic study, and particularly into the field of political science, themselves free from these assumptions about the nature of women.

A survey conducted by the American Political Science Association (APSA) Committee on the Status of Women (1969) shows that female participation in the discipline decreases proportionately the higher the academic status. Women constitute:

23.2% of undergraduate political science majors
17.5% of graduate students
14.7% of Ph.D. candidates
 8.7% of those who received Ph.D.s between 1960 and 1968
 8.6% of associate professors
  .1% of full professors (Jaquette 1971:530)

Many men use statistics such as these to argue that women simply are less committed to rigorous study (an opinion frequently voiced in the 1960s). A recent investigation reveals, however, that male faculty admit more discrimination against female graduate students than the females, themselves, perceive (Jaquette 1971:530). The males specified the discrimination occurred in graduate school admissions, the awarding of financial aid, admission to advanced degree candidacy, placement, and follow-up interest (WPSA Report, cited in Jaquette 1971:530). With reference to personal interaction, one study based on interviews with departmental chairmen indicated that when a male student expressed his intention to leave school, the chairman would try to persuade him to stay. On the other hand, if the student were female, the chairman would remain "neutral" (Ilchman and Rudolph 1971). Although discrimination occurs during academic preparation for the doctoral degree, it seems that the real brunt of sexism is felt at the point of seeking employment (Converse and Converse 1971).

Women as Faculty

Jane Jaquette reports from the findings of the APSA Survey that only 49.5 percent of the departments reported any female faculty at all; and that the distribution of women was skewed toward small institutions. Seventy-six percent of all women were teaching in departments with less than fifteen members (Jaquette 1971). In a survey done by the Western Political Science Association, 85 percent of the male professors reported that they had observed discrimination against women in job applications and 50 percent of them had observed discrimination against women in rank, promotion, tenure, and salary (Jaquette 1971). Eighty-five percent of female faculty has observed discrimination against women in job applications. While academics may be liberal on issues in the general political arena involving minorities and civil liberties, when it comes to their own backyards they exhibit conservative and even reactionary behavior (Faia 1974). From their interviews with departmental chairpersons, Ilchman and Rudolph (1971) found that few favor part-time jobs leading to tenure (an arrangement which might make it possible for husband-wife teams to obtain employment), 50 percent supported nepotism rules at the departmental level, and very few based any of their attitudes about female performance on real evidence.

Faced with various governmental and private demands to hire more women, many political scientists have resisted on the basis of arguments reminiscent of segregationists—that quotas are an abridgment of academic freedom and that they lead to the hiring of less-qualified instructors and a subsequent decline of the academic standards and reputation of an institution. Recently Judith Stiehm (1973) carried out a sample study of the comparative placement of men and women from the top political science graduate departments. She discovered that there were few differences in placement with the exception of a slight lead favoring male placement. Thus it would seem that the pressure for equal opportunity and the threats to withdraw government money from the universities have given women in academic political science access to employment in a market of decreasing demand, though it is not yet equal with that of the men.

Although in very recent years the American Political Science Association has approved a number of resolutions in favor of the recruitment of more women and an end to discrimination, one suspects that most political scientists are hoping that pressures for equity will be applied to someone else's department and that all this stir caused by the women's movement will, like so many dark clouds, pass quickly away so that things may return to normal.

Perhaps the greatest weakness of the political scientist in his attempt to describe and explain the political role of women is not simply his wrongheadedness, but rather his failure to probe beyond the conventional, superficial, and highly visible veneer of institutional politics. This error leads him to ignore many phenomena vital to an understanding of politics and to the developing of theory.

Even those who are currently engaged in research on women and politics tend to skim over: (1) the grass-roots organizing that is currently taking place among women who sometimes associate themselves with political views other than conventional democratic liberalism; (2) women who are in the organizing process without yet having banged their shoe on their Senator's door;* and (3) the coming to political awareness of gay women. The closure of mind that these omissions reflect can probably explain the political scientists' poor track record in predicting or explaining social movements and social change. It is always difficult to remove one's ideological and cultural blinders and look anew at one's own country, but to expect male political scientists to assess objectively the problem of women in America is probably to ask the impossible. The best solution is the active recruitment of large numbers of women into the discipline. Leaving that matter aside, however, several research strategies offer the possibility of shedding new light on this question.

One that I wish to mention here is a new emphasis on the micro-reality of political life. We should give more attention to the individual and small-group dimension of power wielding and sharing. Such an effort should greatly increase the student's ability to see the first, half-realized manifestations of social transformation. For example, women's consciousness-raising groups have been cited as having a great deal of impact at the micro-level in changing women's attitudes about themselves, their relations with men and women, and their goals for the future. When people begin to desire to change their life situations, they turn to those units that have the greatest impact on them—their families, their work places and unions, their communities.

It is the impression of many that the family is the strongest bulwark of male authority. If this is true, the fact that women of the younger generation are not

* "(b) between 1940 and 1969, membership in the American Association of University Women increased 148%; in the League of Women Voters, 208 percent. Between 1948 and 1969, membership in the National Secretaries Association increased 169 percent; and between 1954 and 1968, female membership in unions increased about a third" (Bernard 1972: 11; she took her information from Abbott L. Ferriss, *Indicators of Trends in the Status of American Women* [Russell Sage 1971: 404]).

turning to the family unit for fulfillment as much as they once did, and that there has been an increase in the number of households of unrelated individuals, may shed some light on the meaning and status of the family for our society and for its future (Bernard 1972:2). Women are forming the work force and labor unions at an increasing rate and have been involved in protests against their exclusion from positions of union leadership, their generally lower status of employment and pay, and the rejection of women's issues as bargaining demands.

As long as political scientists persist in the use of traditional concepts of politics and refuse to shift their priorities as to what is worthy of study, the literature on women is likely to remain in its "primitive" state. Outside the academic realm it is an open question whether politics will continue to be an exclusively male affair and whether women will remain the *what* of Harold Lasswell's famous definition of politics as "Who gets What, When, How" (Lasswell 1958).

REFERENCES

The entire issue of the *Annals*, January 1968.

ALMOND, GABRIEL A., AND VERBA, SIDNEY. *The Civic Culture.* Boston: Little, Brown, 1965.

ALTBACH, EDITH HOSHINO. *From Feminism to Liberation.* Cambridge, Mass.: Schenkman, 1971.

AMUNDSEN, KIRSTEN. *The Silenced Majority: Women and American Democracy.* Englewood Cliffs, N.J.: Prentice-Hall, 1971.

ANDREAS, CAROL. *Sex and Caste in America.* Englewood, Cliffs, N.J.: Prentice-Hall, 1971.

BACH, PATRICIA GORENCE. *Women in Public Life in Wisconsin.* Milwaukee: Alverno Research Center on Women, 1971.

BARBER, JAMES D. *The Lawmakers.* New Haven: Yale University Press, 1965.

BARBER, JAMES D. *The Presidential Character: Predicting Performance in the White House.* Englewood Cliffs, N.J.: Prentice-Hall, 1972.

BARDWICK, JUDITH M., AND DOUVAN, ELIZABETH. "Ambivalence: the Socialization of Women." In *Woman in Sexist Society*, edited by Vivian Gornick and Barbara Moran. New York: Basic Books, 1971.

BARRY, DONALD D., AND BOMMER, JAMES G. "Participation in APSA Annual Meetings, 1964–1969." *PS* 111 (Fall 1970): 629–40.

BELL, WENDELL. *Public Leadership.* San Francisco: Chandler, 1961.

BERNARD, JESSE. "Women and Marriage." *Women: Resource for a Changing World.* Cambridge, Mass.: Radcliffe Institute, 1972.

BERNARD, JESSE. "My Four Revolutions: An Autobiographical History of the ASA." *AJS* 78 (1973): 773–91.

BERNARD, JESSE. *Women and the Public Interest.* Chicago: Aldine/Atherton, 1971.

BIRD, C. *Born Female.* New York: David McKay, 1968.

BOND, J. R., AND VINACKE, W. E. "Coalitions in Mixed-Sex Triad." *Sociometry* 24 (1961): 61–75.

BONE, Hugh A. *Party Committees and National Politics.* Seattle: University of Washington Press, 1958.

BOYD, ROSEMARY. "Women and Politics in the U.S. and Canada." *Annals* (1968): 52–57.

BRECKENRIDGE, S. *Women in the Twentieth Century: A Study of Their Political, Social, and Economic Activities.* New York: McGraw-Hill, 1933.

BROVERMAN, INGE, et al. "Sex Role Stereotypes: A Current Appraisal." *Journal of Social Issues* 28 (1972): 59–78.

BROVERMAN, INGE, et al. "Sex Role Stereotypes and Clinical Judgments of Mental Health." *Journal of Consulting and Clinical Psychology* 34 (1970): 1–7.

BROWN, B. A.; EMERSON, T. I.; FALK, G.; AND FREEDMAN, A. E. "The Equal Rights Amendment: A Constitutional Basis for Equal Rights for Women." *Yale Law Journal* 80 (April 1971): 871–985.

BURSTEIN, PATRICIA, AND CIMONS, MARLENE. "Women Who Won." *Ms.* 1 (October 1973): 86.

CAMPBELL, ANGUS, et al. *The American Voter.* New York: Wiley, 1960.

CAMPBELL, ANGUS, et al. *Elections and the Political Order.* New York: Wiley, 1966.

CHESLER, PHYLLIS. "Are We a Threat to Each Other." *Ms.* 1 (October 1973): 86.

CHULENSKA, KAMILA. "Political Activity of Women in Eastern Europe." *Annals* 375 (January 1968): 67–71.

COLEMAN, JAMES. *Adolescent Society.* New York: Free Press, 1961.

COLLINS, RANDALL. "A Conflict Theory of Sexual Stratification." *Social Problems* 19 (Summer 1971): 3–22.

Constitutional Amendments to be Submitted to the Wisconsin Electorate on April 3, 1973. Informational Bulletin 73–1. Madison, Wis.: Legislative Reference Bureau at the State Capitol, 1973.

COSTANTINI, EDMOND, AND CRAIK, KENNETH H. "Women as Politicians." *Journal of Social Issues* 28 (1972): 217–36.

CRICK, BERNARD R. *In Defense of Politics.* Chicago: University of Chicago Press, 1962.

DAWSON, RICHARD E., AND PREWITT, KENNETH. *Political Socialization.* Boston: Little, Brown, 1969.

DREITZEL, HANS PETER, ed. *Family, Marriage, and the Struggle of the Sexes.* New York: Macmillan, 1972.

DUVERGER, M. *Political Role of Women.* Paris: UNESCO, 1953.

EASTON, DAVID, AND DENNIS, JACK. *Children in the Political System.* New York: McGraw-Hill, 1969.

FAIA, MICHAEL. "The Myth of the Liberal Professor." *Sociology of Education* 47 (Spring 1974): 171–202.

FASTEAU, BRENDA FEIGEN, AND LOBEL, BONNIE. "Rating the Candidates: Feminists Vote the Rascals In or Out." *New York* 4 (20 December 1971): 74.

FRASER, JOHN. "Orientations Toward Parents and Political Efficacy." *Western Political Quarterly* 25 (December 1972): 643–47.

FREEMAN, JO. "The Origins of the Women's Liberation Movement." *AJS* 78 (January 1973): 792–811.

FRIEDAN, BETTY. *The Feminine Mystique.* New York: Bantam, 1963.

GEBLEN, FRIEDA. "Women in Congress." *Trans-action* (October 1969): 37.

GEORGE, ALEXANDER L., AND GEORGE, JULIETTE. *Woodrow Wilson and Colonel House: A Personality Study.* New York: Dover, 1964.

GREENSTEIN, FRED I. "Political Socialization." In *International Encyclopedia of the Social Sciences*, edited by David L. Sills. New York: Macmillan and Free Press, 1968. Pp. 551–55.

GREENSTEIN, FRED I. *Children and Politics*. Revised ed. New Haven: Yale University Press, 1969.

GREER, GERMAINE. "McGovern, The Big Teaser." *Harpers* 254 (October 1972): 56.

GRUBERG, MARTIN. *Women in American Politics*. Oshkosh: Academia Press, 1968.

HAAVIO-MANNILA, ELENA. "Sex Role in Politics." In *Toward a Sociology of Women*, edited by Constantina Safilios Rothschild. Lexington, Mass.: Xerox College Publishing, 1972. Pp. 154–72.

HARTLEY, RUTH E. "Role Models and Role Outcomes." *Women: Resource for a Changing World*. Cambridge, Mass.: Radcliffe Institute, 1972.

HASTINGS, PHILIP K. "Hows and Howevers of the Woman Voter." *New York Times Magazine*, 12 June 1960, p. 14.

HELLER, AGNES. "On the Future of Relations between the Sexes?" *ISSJ* 21 (1969): 535–44.

HERSKAMEN, VERONICA STOLTE. "Sex Roles, Social Class and Political Consciousness." *Acta Sociologica* 14 (1971): 83–95.

HESS, ROBERT D., AND TORNEY, JUDITH V. *The Political Development of Attitudes in Children*. Garden City, N.Y.: Anchor, 1967.

HOLE, JUDITH, AND LEVINE, ELEN. *Rebirth of Feminism*. New York: Quadrangle, 1971.

HOLTER, HARRIET. "Sex Roles and Social Change." *Acta Sociologica* 14 (1971): 2–12.

HUNTER, FLOYD. *Top Leadership, U.S.A.* Chapel Hill: University of North Carolina Press, 1959.

HYMAN, HERBERT. *Political Socialization*. Glencoe, Ill.: Free Press, 1959.

"If Pat Nixon Were a Feminist." *Ms.* 1 (August 1972): 48.

IGLITZIN, LYNNE. "Political Education and Sexual Liberation." *Politics and Society* (Winter 1972).

IGLITZIN, LYNNE. "Sex Typing and Politicization in Children's Attitudes: Reflections on Studies Done and Undone." Paper prepared for delivery at the 1972 annual meeting of the American Political Science Association, Washington Hilton Hotel, Washington, D.C., 5–9 September 1972.

ILCHMAN, WARREN F., AND RUDOLPH, SUSANNE HOEBER. "Report on Interviews with a Panel of Political Science Department Chairmen." APSA Committee on the Status of Women in the Profession Report, 1971.

IRWIN, INEZ. *The Story of the Women's Party*. New York: Harcourt, Brace, 1921.

JAQUETTE, JANE. "The Status of Women in the Profession: Tokenism." *PS* 4 (Fall 1971): 530–32.

JENNINGS, M. K., AND THOMAS, N. "Men and Women in Party Elites: Social Roles and Political Resources." *Midwest Journal of Political Science* 12 (1968): 469–92.

JENNINGS, M. K., AND NIEMI, R. G. "The Division of Political Labor between Mothers and Fathers." *APSR* 56 (March 1971): 69–82.

KANOWITZ, L. "Law and the Married Woman." *St. Louis University Law Journal* 12 (1967): 3.

KANOWITZ, L. *Women and the Law*. Albuquerque: University of New Mexico Press, 1969.

KAPLAN, ABRAHAM. *Conduct of Inquiry: Methodology for Behavioral Sciences.* San Francisco: Chandler, 1964.

KEY, V. O. *Politics, Parties, and Pressure Groups.* 5th ed. New York: Crowell, 1964.

KIRKPATRICK, JEANNE JORDAN. "Women in Politics." Lecture delivered at the University of Wisconsin, Madison, Wis., Spring 1973.

KRUSCHKE, EARLE R. *Female Politicals and Apoliticals: Some Measurements and Comparisons.* Madison, Wis.: University of Wisconsin Press, 1963.

KUEHN, LUCILLE. "American Voluntarism: An Anti-History with Anti-Heroines." *Women: Resource for a Changing World.* Cambridge, Mass.: Radcliffe Institute, 1972.

LAMSON, PEGGY. *Few Are Chosen.* Boston: Houghton Mifflin, 1968.

LANE, R. E. *Political Life.* Glencoe, Ill.: Free Press, 1959.

LANGTON, KENNETH P. *Political Socialization.* New York: Oxford University Press, 1969.

LANSING, MARJORIE. "Women: The New Political Class." Manuscript, Ypsilanti, Mich., 1972.

LASSWELL, HAROLD D. *Politics: Who Gets What, When, How.* New York: Meridian Books, 1958.

LENSKI, GERHARD. *Power and Privilege.* New York: McGraw-Hill, 1966.

LEVIN, MURRAY BURTON. *Kennedy Campaigning: The System and Style as Practiced by Senator Edward Kennedy.* Boston: Beacon Press, 1966.

LIPSET, S. M. "The Politics of Academia." In *Perspectives on Campus Tensions*, edited by D. Nichols. (Washington, D.C.: American Council on Education, 1970). Pp. 85–118.

MCCARTHY, ABIGAIL. *Private Faces/Public Places.* Garden City, N.Y.: Doubleday, 1972.

MCCLOSKY, HERBERT, AND DAHLGREN, HAROLD E. "Primary Group Influence on Party Loyalty." *APSR* 53 (September 1959): 757–76.

MACCOBY, E., ed. *The Development of Sex Differences.* Stanford: Stanford University Press, 1966.

MANDLE, J. "Women's Liberation: Humanizing rather than Polarizing." *Annals of the American Academy of Political and Social Sciences* 397 (September 1971): 118–28.

MARCH, JAMES G. "Husband-Wife Interaction over Political Issues." *Public Opinion Quarterly* (Winter 1964): 468.

MATTHEWS, DONALD R., AND PROTHRO, JAMES W. *Negroes and the New Southern Politics.* New York: Harcourt, Brace, 1966.

MILBRATH, L. *Political Participation.* Chicago: Rand McNally, 1965.

MILLMAN, MARCIA. "Observations on Sex Role Research." *Journal of Marriage and the Family* 334 (November 1971): 772–76.

MITCHELL, JOYCE, AND STARR, RACHEL. "Aspirations, Achievement, and Professional Advancement in Political Science: The Prospect for Women in the West." In *Women in Political Science: Studies and Reports of the APSA Committee on the Status of Women in the Profession.* Washington, D.C.: American Political Science Association, 1971.

MITCHELL, JULIET. *Woman's Estate.* New York: Vintage, 1971.

MORGAN, ROBIN, ed. *Sisterhood Is Powerful.* New York: Vintage, 1970.

MURRAY, P., AND EASTWOOD, M. "Jane Crow and the Law: Sex Discrimination and Title VII." *George Washington Law Review* 34 (1965): 232.

NETTING, ROBERT. "Women's Weapons: The Politics of Domesticity among the Kafyar." *American Anthropologist* 71 (1969): 1037–45.

NIES, JUDITH. "The Abzug Race: A Lesson in Politics." *Ms.* 1 (February 1973): 76.

O'Neill, William. *Everyone Was Brave.* Chicago: Quadrangle, 1969.

Page, Benjamin I., and Brody, Richard A. "Policy, Voting, and the Electoral Process: The Vietnam War Issue." *APSR,* no. 3 (September 1972): 979–95.

Paxton, A. *Women in Congress.* Richmond: Dietz Press, 1945.

Polk, Barbara Bover, and Stein, Robert B. "Is the Grass Greener on the Other Side?" In *Toward a Sociology of Women,* edited by Constantina Safilios Rothschild. Lexington, Mass.: Xerox Publishing, 1972.

Pomper, Gerald M., et al. "Issue Voting." *APSR* 66 (June 1972): 415–70.

Reeves, Nancy. *Womankind.* Chicago: Aldine/Atherton, 1971.

Repass, David. "Issue Salience and Party Choice." *APSR* 65 (June 1971): 389–400.

Romer, K. T., and Secor, C., "The Time Is Here for Women's Lib." *Annals* 397 (September 1971): 129–39.

Rosenberg, Milton J.; Verba, Sidney; and Converse, Philip E. *Vietnam and the Silent Majority.* New York: Harper & Row, 1970.

Safilios-Rothschild, Constantina, ed. *Toward a Sociology of Women.* Lexington, Mass.: Xerox Publishing, 1972.

Salper, Roberta. *Female Liberation: History and Current Politics.* New York: Knopf, 1972.

Sanders, Marian K. *The Lady and the Vote.* Cambridge, Mass.: Riverside Press, 1956.

Schuck, Victoria. "'Femina Studens Rei Publicae': Notes on Her Professional Achievement." *PS* 3 (Fall 1970): 625.

Schuck, Victoria. "Women in Political Science: Some Preliminary Observations." *PS* 2 (Fall 1969): 642–53.

Schultz, David A. *Coming up Black.* Englewood Cliffs, N.J.: Prentice-Hall, 1969.

Scott, Anne Furor. *The Southern Lady, From Pedestal to Politics, 1830–1930.* Chicago: University of Chicago Press, 1970.

Setlow, Carolyn, and Steinem, Gloria. "Why Women Voted for Richard Nixon." *Ms.* 1 (March 1973): 66.

Sexton, Patricia Cayo. *The Feminized Male.* New York: Vintage, 1969.

Snyder, Eloise C. "Sex Role Differential and Juror Decisions." *Sociology and Social Research* 55 (July 1971): 442–48.

Soule, John W., and McGrath, Wilma E. "Rocking the Cradle or Rocking the Boat: Women at the 1972 Democratic National Convention." Manuscript.

Steinem, Gloria, and Frapollo, Elizabeth. "President Chisholm/Vice-President Farenthold." *Ms.* 1 (January 1973): 72.

Steinem, Gloria, and Frapollo, Elizabeth. "Women Voters Can't Be Trusted." *Ms.* 1 (July 1972): 47–51.

Stiehm, Judith. "To the Editor." *PS* 6 (Winter 1973): 84–85.

Time. Special Issue: The American Woman. 20 March 1972.

Tinker, Irene. "Nonacademic Professional Political Scientists." *American Behavioral Scientist* (December 1971): 206–12.

Turner, Ralph H. "Some Aspects of Women's Ambitions." *AJS* 10 (November 1964): 271–85.

Usegi, T. T., and Vinacke, W. E. "Strategy in a Feminine Game." *Sociometry* 26 (1963): 75–88.

VERBA, SIDNEY, et al. "Public Opinion and the War in Vietnam." *APSR* 61 (June 1967): 317–33.

VINACKE, W. E. "Sex Roles in a Three-Person Game." *Sociometry* 22 (1959).

WAHLKE, JOHN C.; HEINZ, EULAU; BUCHANAN, WILLIAM; AND FERGUSON, LEROY F. *The Legislative System: Explorations in Legislative Behavior.* New York: Wiley, 1962.

WATSON, GOODWIN. *Social Psychology: Issues and Insights.* Philadelphia: Lippincott, 1966.

WERNER, EMMY E. "Women in Congress: 1917–1964." *Western Political Quarterly* 19 (March 1966): 16–30.

WERNER, EMMY E. "Women in State Legislatures." *Western Political Quarterly* 21 (March 1968): 40–50.

WOLFENSTEIN, E. VICTOR. *Personality and Politics.* Belmont, Calif.: Dickenson, 1969.

WORTIS, HELEN, AND RABINOWITZ, CLARA. *The Women's Movement: Social and Psychological Perspectives.* New York: Wiley, 1972.

WRIGHT, DEREK. "A Sociological Portrait: Sex Differences," *New Society* 18 (October 1971).

YOUNG, L. M. *Understanding Politics.* New York: Pelligrini and Cudahy, 1950.

Women Who Work for Wages

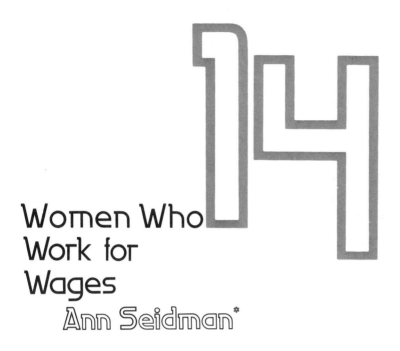

Ann Seidman[*]

Women who work get tired and even depressed by the unconscious (and not so unconscious) gibes and unspoken actions of their fellow workers, which added together express the attitude: "Oh, she's just a woman." "Don't give her jobs with responsibility; Don't encourage her to improve her status; She should stay home and do 'women's' work. . . ."

Far more serious than any psychological damage caused by this attitude is the fact that women are typically at the bottom of the employment ladder: their wages are about half those of men; their jobs are less secure; and, as a result, they and their children often suffer real poverty. This is even more likely to be true if they happen to be black.

This attitude, and the practices it perpetuates, has roots reaching far back into history. The initial division of labor in ancient times relegated women to tending homes, children, and food farms; men went out to hunt, defended the family, and helped with the physically heavy labor of clearing farms and building houses.[1] Social, political, and religious attitudes and institutions emerged over time to maintain this practical division of labor.

Today, technological conditions have dramatically developed, creating the objective conditions required to enable women to assume roles of complete equality with men in all fields. Much of the drudgery of housework has been

[*] I would like to express my sincere appreciation to Ms. Paddy Quick for her assistance in the collection of bibliographical materials for this brief paper.

replaced by factory-produced equipment and supplies; prepared foods, diaper cleaning services, house-cleaning and clothes-washing machinery have—for those who can afford them—sharply reduced the time needed to do household tasks. Likewise, technology has permitted a new division of labor in which much of the formerly heavy manual labor done by men is done by machines which both men and women can run.

Women today can do almost all the kinds of work that men do. In fact, half of all adult women now work outside the home. They constitute 38 percent of the national labor force. The problem is, the institutions and attitudes shaped in the past restrict their opportunities to the least skilled, most uninteresting jobs with the lowest pay. From the outset, girls are taught to lower their aspiration levels, to limit their occupational perspectives. Little girls are told to play with dolls, while boys are encouraged to play with blocks and trucks. And from school to job, ancient attitudes and institutions affect hiring, upgrading, and salaries of women at all levels. Black women, who suffer double discrimination because they are black as well as women, are affected most severely.

Given the fact that discrimination against women is embedded in attitudes and institutions that have emerged over thousands of years, its elimination requires a frontal attack on every level. This chapter seeks to present the facts of sex discrimination as it affects women who work, and to suggest some of the measures required to eliminate it.

WHY WOMEN WORK

It used to be a commonplace that women worked for "pin money"—and many uninformed persons still believe it. But the facts show that women work primarily to support themselves and their families. The U.S. Department of Labor has pointed out:

> *Decisions of individual women to seek employment outside the home are usually based on economic reasons. Most women in the labor force work because they or their families need the money they can earn—some work to raise family living standards above the level of poverty or deprivation; others, to help meet rising costs of food, education for the children, medical care, and the like. Relatively few women have the option of working solely for personal fulfillment.*[2]

In recent years, as prices have risen, spurred on by the war-inflated economy of the 1960s, more and more women—even married women with spouses present— have been forced to go to work to help support their families. Now, as unemployment mounts, increasing numbers of those who seek work have been forced into the ranks of the unemployed. This is reflected in figure 14.1.

Almost two-thirds of the women who work have absolutely no choice. They are either single, divorced, widowed, or married to men whose incomes are so low that if they did not work, the families would be living below poverty levels. Most of the remainder of women who work do so in order to earn a "little extra" for the family: perhaps better clothing, a car, a more comfortable home, a vacation at the seashore.

The profile of the average woman who works has changed considerably in the last half century as technology has changed and rising living costs have forced more and more women to leave their homes.

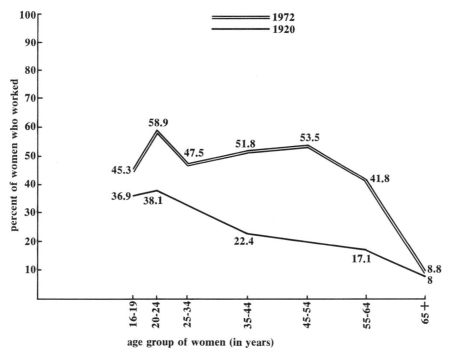

SOURCE: *U.S. Statistical Abstract, 1973* and *1951*.

Figure 14.1   Women Who Worked For Wages
In Each Age Group in 1920 Compared to 1972

TABLE 14.1   Profile of the Average Working Woman

1920	1970
28 years old Single	39 years old Married, living with husband
Most likely to be a factory worker. Large numbers in clerical, private household, farm work (i.e., limited choice)	Most likely to be a clerical worker; some service, factories, a few professionals (i.e., about 500 occupations), but 44% of nonwhite working women in private household or service work
Only one out of five 17-year-olds in the population had a high school education	A high school graduate, some college or post-secondary school education

SOURCE: U.S. Department of Labor, Women's Bureau, April 1970.

Faculty Rank	University of Wisconsin, Madison	Average for All Universities and Colleges
Professors	4.8	5.47
Associate Professors	6.8	10.4
Assistant Professors	11.5	14.8
Instructors	50.5	30.5

SOURCE: News release, University of Wisconsin, 22 March 1971.

The training and upgrading of women are limited at all levels of employment. This is true even in the universities, as table 14.2 indicates. The data show that the bulk of the women employed are held in low ranks. The Association of Faculty Women of the University of Wisconsin had in its files by 1972 a number of cases of women fully qualified for promotion to the rank of professor who had for more than a decade remained at levels of instructor or less.

Moreover, although women make up one-third of the entering graduate students at the University of Wisconsin, they constitute only 13 percent of those graduating with Ph.D.s. Is this because of inadequate counseling? Lack of adequate financial assistance? The continuing socialization of women that leads them to see their role primarily as housewives rather than as professionals? Lack of maternity and child-care facilities for women taking courses at the university? Or is it the lack of women at the professorial levels that convinces graduate students that there is no point in studying further to obtain more advanced placement?

These questions can be answered only by thorough studies, but the statistics clearly spell out why the U.S. Department of Health, Education, and Welfare declared in the spring of 1970 that a pattern of discrimination existed at the University of Wisconsin. The HEW report asserted that the university administration appeared willing to introduce measures to change the pattern, but the prevalence of hiring practices and attitudes—conscious and unconscious—tended to perpetuate it at departmental levels. If this is true in the universities, presumably the center of U.S. culture and learning, how much more probable is it that a discriminatory pattern affects women's incomes adversely at all levels of employment throughout the nation?

Table 14.3 suggests that, when wives join the paid labor force, they may contribute to a significantly increased family income. But women heads of families receive incomes that are only about half that of men family heads. A single woman's income is slightly more than half a single man's income. Black women's median incomes are about a third less than those of both black men's and white women's.

Not only are women's salaries lower than men's, but women tend to be among the last hired and the first fired. Hence they are the most affected by the unemployment characteristic of the current "stagflation."

Table 14.4 clearly illustrates that unemployment among female white workers was worse than among male white workers even in 1970. Unemployment has been significantly increased for both groups since then. Over 8 percent of all workers are

TABLE 14.3   Median Incomes of Men and Women, United States, 1971

Male Head	
Married, wife present	$10,990
Wife in paid labor force	12,853
Wife not in paid labor force	9,744
Other marital status	8,722
Female Head	5,114
Unrelated Individuals	
Male	4,627
Female	2,688

SOURCE: *U.S. Statistical Abstract, 1973* (Washington, D.C.: Government Printing Office, 1973), table 539.

currently jobless, according to official government statistics. It should be noted that trade unions argue that the real full-time unemployment is actually nearer 15 percent, but some workers, including a considerable number of women, have given up seeking employment and hence are excluded from official data. The 1973 data, shown in Table 14.4, indicates that those most affected by unemployment are members of black and other minority groups; already in that year, before the unemployment had reached the much higher 1975 rate, almost 8 percent of all blacks and other minorities were out of work, and over 9 percent of women in those groups were jobless.

Further breakdowns of the data show that younger workers, especially women, are most affected by unemployment. As early as April 1970, one out of four (24.9 percent) workers between the ages of 16 and 19 were unemployed. Almost one out of two (44 percent) women in this age bracket were jobless. Older women, too, once laid off find it more difficult than older men to obtain new jobs.[3] Not only their sex, but also their age is held against them. This poses a particularly serious problem for older women, since rising prices have rendered pensions and social security payments inadequate to cover living costs.

Many trade unions, particularly crafts unions, seem to have adopted attitudes and practices reflecting the general discriminatory pattern of society. Not

TABLE 14.4   Full-time Unemployment of U.S. Men and Women
as Percent of Total Unemployment, April 1973

Category of Workers	Percent of Total Unemployment in Each Category
All Workers	4.8
White	4.3
Male	5.7
Female	5.6
Blacks and Other Minority Races	
Male	7.9
Female	9.7

SOURCE: *U.S. Statistical Abstract, 1973*, table 317.

infrequently, they acquiesce and even support the exclusion of women from jobs and the denial of equal pay for equal work. Only about 13 percent of women wage and salary earners in private industry are in unions (compared to 31 percent of all male workers). The wages of women in trade unions tend to be about 25 to 50 percent higher than those of nonunion women. It seems somewhat shortsighted of unions not to organize women, however: As unemployment mounts, women become a potentially cheaper source of labor for employers seeking to reduce costs.

The overall effect of the discrimination against women workers in all areas of employment has been to force greater numbers of them, together with their children, into conditions of poverty. Families headed by women constitute only 14 percent of the population, but they make up almost half (44 percent) of the "poverty population" as defined by official U.S. Labor Department statistics. Black women are particularly seriously affected. Twenty-eight percent of all black families are headed by women; over half of them live in poverty. Elizabeth Wickenden, consultant on social policy to the National YWCA, has declared:

If the plight of the under-educated, unemployed, underpaid and undervalued Negro male is deserving of every social remedy we can bring to bear, the plight of the loyal but despised Negro mother is equally if not more so. . . . With her miserable earnings and niggardly assistance payments, she fends off as best she can both starvation and the harshest impact of community rejection for her children.[4]

TABLE 14.5   Households with Heads Under 65 Years Old
Living Below Poverty Level, 1968 and 1972 [a]

Category	Percent of Total Population in Each Category	
	1968	*1972*
White	9.2	9.9
Male	6.0	7.5
Female	26.8	38.0
Blacks and Other Races	29.3	30.9
Male	18.8	*n.a.*
Female	52.2	*n.a.*

[a] These statistics have not accounted specifically for increased costs of items on poverty budgets since 1964, so they probably constitute an understatement.
SOURCE: *U.S. Statistical Abstract, 1970*, table 500; *1973*, table 548.

The problems of double discrimination confronted by black women are compounded by the discrimination against black men, and vice versa, contributing to a vicious circle from generation to generation. Since the men's income is low, a higher proportion of black women must work than white women. As a result, given the inadequacy of child-care, health, housing and education facilities, family life suffers. The cumulative effect is that black children are deprived of equal opportunities at every stage of their lives.

THE NEED FOR A BROAD ATTACK AGAINST
SALARY AND JOB DISCRIMINATION

If, as hypothesized at the outset of this article, discrimination against women is embedded in attitudes and institutions shaped by historical conditions, then those attitudes and institutions must be fundamentally altered to end the prevailing pattern that relegates women to the lowest-paid and least secure kinds of employment—and forces tens of thousands of them and their children to live in conditions of poverty. It is now federal law that no firm receiving federal contracts may discriminate against women. Unfortunately, this law is as yet enforced only in a marginal way. Furthermore, the law needs to be extended to cover every type of employment. The facts should be exposed wherever discrimination exists. The community should be informed of the consequences of discriminatory patterns in terms of human suffering, as well as its incompatibility with the principles of equality of American democracy. Both men and women need to reevaluate the fact that the division of labor in the home should reflect the conditions of today's changed technology. As increasing numbers of women join the work force to help support their families, their husbands should join them in doing the housework on a share-and-share-alike basis, so that the women do not carry a double burden of housework and wage employment.

But more than that is needed. Those concerned with the problems of discrimination based on sex must work to achieve full peacetime employment in the entire society as the foundation for full equality. This is not the place to discuss the costs of the Vietnam war in terms of the 50,000 American youths and literally millions of Indochinese men, women, and children killed. But it cannot be overlooked that a war economy was a major factor laying the foundation of the current "stagflation" that affects every American and, because of discrimination, particularly women. The military for years consumed 10 percent of the nation's output. Negotiated war contracts, including vast sums for research and development, ensured that more and more U.S. taxpayer dollars were spent for automated machinery and equipment; less and less for jobs. Guaranteed prices for military output pushed up prices throughout the economy, cutting consumer purchasing power—thus increasing numbers of layoffs have taken place in consumer goods industries. Cutbacks in city, state, and national government programs to release tax dollars to pay for war meant less welfare, poorer education, greater despair in the ghettos, less public housing, inadequate medical care—all of which worsened the conditions in which mothers and children must live.

To end these conditions, America's national affluence needs to be redirected to meet the needs of the people, to ensure full employment and equitable pay for all as the basis for enabling women and children, as well as men, to obtain adequate food, education, health and housing. Our involvement in Vietnam has ended, yet billions of dollars are still proposed for military expenditures. Talk of reducing inflationary pressures is typically focused on cutting welfare programs.

As the congressional Black Caucus has emphasized, budget cuts in such areas as housing, health, and education will hurt most those who can least afford it. The Caucus members stressed the potential danger for women workers of particular cuts being considered: "[I]f day care funds are cut, thousands of working mothers will be forced to give up their jobs and go on welfare."[5]

Many young women are beginning to ask whether the political and economic system of the nation is capable of overcoming the problems of poverty amid plenty that have been especially burdensome for women and blacks.[6] Why, they ask, is it easier for a woman to become a doctor or an engineer or a scientist in a socialist country? How has it been possible for socialist countries to inscribe equal pay and working conditions as fundamental rights in their constitutions?

Economists have estimated that about 23 percent of all U.S. manufacturing profits are attributable to the payment of lower wages to women than to men.[7] Does the underlying cause of the persistence of economic discrimination against women lie in the domination of the political economy by private firms competing to maximize their profits by squeezing the wages of their employees?

It is not possible, in the short space available here, to even begin to answer these questions. It is a significant feature of the growing self-awareness of American women, however, that they are beginning to become conscious of the necessity to explore these issues in depth. Whatever the outcome of further studies, women are becoming increasingly aware that efforts to end discrimination against women in employment should be made part and parcel of national efforts to achieve a better society for all Americans. Such a society is technologically possible; what is needed is a broad united effort to make it a reality.

NOTES

1. Today in Africa, as a result of the imposition of practices and attitudes fostered by European colonial rule on top of the traditional division of labor, men tend to be the ones who produce cash crops or earn wages as an extension of their particular roles; even secretarial jobs are typically "men's" work, because it is a wage-earning occupation.

2. U.S. Department of Labor, Women's Bureau, *Why Women Work* (Washington, D.C.: Government Printing Office, 1970).

3. For statistics on higher unemployment rate among women than men, 45–64 years old, see *Bureau of Census, U.S. Statistical Abstract, 1973* (Washington, D.C.: U.S. Government Printing Office, 1973), p. 220.

4. "The Negro Family: Society's Victim or Scapegoat," *Discrimination Against Women, Hearings before Special Subcommittee on Education and Labor* (House of Representatives, 91st Cong., 1970).

5. CHARLES B. RANGEL, "Fight Inflation, Don't Step on Poor," *Boston Globe*, 17 August 1974.

6. E.g., JULIET MITCHELL, *Women's Estate* (New York: Vintage, 1973); SHEILA ROWBOTHAM, *Women Resistance and Revolution* (New York: Pantheon Books, 1972).

7. E. K. HUNT and H. J. SHERMAN, *Economics: An Introduction to Traditional and Radical Views* (New York: Harper & Row, 1972.)

BIBLIOGRAPHY

ABBOT, EDITH. *Women in Industry, A Study in American Economic History*. New York: Arno, 1960.

BAKER, ELIZABETH FAULKNER. *Technology and Women's Work*. New York: Columbia University Press, 1964.

CAIN, GLEN. *Married Women in the Labor Force: An Economic Analysis.* Chicago: University of Chicago Press, 1966.

FERRISS, ABBOTT L. *Indicators of Trends in the Status of American Women.* New York: Russell Sage Foundation, 1971.

GILMAN, CHARLOTTE P. *Women and Economics. A Study of the Economic Relations Between Men and Women as a Factor in Social Evolution,* edited by Carl N. Degler (New York, Harper & Row, 1970).

National Manpower Council. *Womanpower.* New York: Columbia University Press, 1957.

OPPENHEIMER, VALERIE KINCADE. *The Female Labour Force in the United States.* Berkeley: Institute of International Studies, University of California, 1970.

PINCHBECK, IVY. *Women Workers and the Industrial Revolution, 1759–1850.* London: George Rutledge & Sons, 1930.

SMUTS, ROBERT W. *Women and Work in America.* New York: Columbia University Press, 1959.

U.S. Department of Labor, Women's Bureau:
  Background Facts on Women Workers. 1970.
  Day Care Facts. May, 1970.
  Fact Sheet on the Earnings Gap. 1970.
  Facts About Women's Absenteeism and Labor Turnover. August 1969.
  1969 Handbook on Women Workers. 1969.
  Negro Women . . . in the Population and in the Labor Force. December 1967.
  Trends in the Educational Attainment of Women. October 1969.
  Women in Poverty—Jobs and the Need for Jobs. April 1968.
  Working Mothers and the Need for Child Care Services. June 1968.
  Working Wives—Their Contribution to Family Income. November 1968.

U.S. Department of Labor, *Monthly Labor Review.* "Sex and Equal Employment Rights" (August 1967). "Changes in the Labor Force Activity of Women" (June 1970). "Marital and Family Characteristics of the US Labor Force" (May 1970). "Working Women in Urban Poverty Neighborhoods" (June 1970).

WOMEN
AND THE QUEST
FOR EQUALITY:
CULTURAL
CHANGE AND SEX-
ROLE INNOVATION

The Ideal and the Reality: Women in Sweden
Ingrid Camerini

The intensive public debate about sex roles, carried on in Sweden since the beginning of the 1960s, received its impetus from an essay entitled "The Conditional Emancipation of Women" written by Eva Moberg and published in the anthology *Young Liberals* in 1961.[1] In this essay Moberg rejected the assumption that women have two roles, that of wife-mother and that of wage earner, a view held by Alva Myrdal and Viola Klein in *Women's Two Roles* published in 1956.[2] Moberg argued that men and women have the same human responsibilities. Both men and women must work to support themselves, and if they are married, they must share equally in the support and upbringing of their children as well as in the maintenance of the household.

Since hardly anyone in Sweden would dare to hold publicly the conservative view that a woman's place is in the home, the discussion during the 1960s was mainly between the moderates, who want women to give up their professional careers and stay home while their children are young; and the liberal-radicals who completely reject the housewife ideal, contending that equality between the sexes cannot be realized until women take up and continuously devote themselves to occupations outside the home and thereby become socially and economically independent. The moderate view tended to dominate the government commissions on family policy until the mid 1960s, but from the time of the 1968 report to the United Nations on *The Status of Women in Sweden*,[3] there has been a definite shift to the liberal-radical view by the same Social Democrat government.

Here it is spelled out that "the aim of a long-term program for women must be that every individual, irrespective of sex, shall have the same practical opportunities, not only for education and employment but also in principle the same responsibility for the upbringing of children and the upkeep of the home. Eventually to achieve complete equality in these rights and obligations, a radical change in deep-rooted traditions and attitudes must be brought about among both women and men, and active steps must be taken by the community to encourage a change in the roles played by both." [4]

Despite the fact that women in Sweden have had support from the top in their demands for equality, implementation of reforms has been a slow process. While granting that equality is a difficult goal to achieve, most men and women believe there will be a gradual change in their own attitudes and conduct. An active minority women's group maintains that reforms are meaningless and that only a socialist revolution can bring about equality between the sexes.

In these pages we shall look at some of the conditions in different fields prevailing in the life of women in today's Sweden.

THE FAMILY

The government's 1968 Report to the United Nations states: "The character of marriage as an institution for the support of women according to the western tradition has come to be an indirect obstacle to their emancipation in modern industrial society. Swedish opinion therefore has made a great point in stressing the independence of every individual both inside and outside marriage. Instead of one-sided emphasis on the function of motherhood, the importance of greater contact between father and children has been stressed. At the same time, the care and upbringing of children have come to be increasingly regarded as essential service to the community, which in principle ought to be paid for in cash in the same way as services to an employer. It has been felt that the social security of the parent who stays at home to take care of the children should be equivalent to that of the one who goes out to work." [5] Thus, on January 1, 1974, the earlier maternity benefits insurance was changed into a parenthood benefits insurance, which reimburses the husband for lost income should he stay home to care for the family while the wife gives birth. Parenthood insurance guarantees the family a certain income for six months when a new child is born. It also coordinates with health insurance, so that a parent who stays home to take care of a sick child receives the same reimbursement as if he or she had been sick.

In five years, between 1966 and 1971, the number of new marriages in Sweden went down by 35 percent and the number of children born out of wedlock increased from 15 to 21 percent. In order to overcome the reluctance of many people to marry, the government in 1973 enacted a new marriage law that makes it easier both to contract a marriage and to dissolve it. The legal age for marriage has been lowered to eighteen years. The religious ceremony is retained, but there is also a short and simple civil ceremony for those who so prefer. The judicial separation year has been abolished, but a six-month period of consideration for couples with children under the age of sixteen, or in cases where only one of the spouses wants a divorce, is to be maintained. No reasons have to be given to obtain a divorce, and infidelity is no longer considered by the court as a relevant factor.

In the 1950s when the birthrate was extremely low, a conscious family policy began to develop in Sweden. Every pregnant woman received free medical care before, during, and after childbirth. Since 1939 it has been illegal to dismiss a woman employee because of engagement or marriage. The law was extended in 1946 to include pregnancy and childbirth.

Since 1968 all families below a certain income receive housing allowances, graded according to the number of their children.

Most important for a family in which both parents are employed is the problem of finding adequate day-care services for their children. For younger children there are still not enough day nurseries, in spite of the demands of working parents. Although there has been a considerable increase of places in the day nurseries from 12,000 in 1965 to 52,000 in 1972, it has been estimated that in 1975 only 34 percent of demand will be met.[6] Some schoolchildren 7–12 years of age, 70 percent of whose mothers work, are able to spend their free days and afterschool time at supervised state-run leisure centers, where they can eat, play, and study. But since these centers are available to only one out of every twenty children who want them, plans are to keep the public grade schools open from 7 A.M. to 6 P.M.

It is obvious that child-care centers are essential in order to change sex roles and make possible the liberation of women, but they are equally important in the education of children. The Swedish view is that a child should be brought up with other children from different social levels and should meet adults other than its own parents. Another advantage of child-care centers is that boys and girls receive an identical upbringing, which means that the day nurseries could act as starting schools for a society without sex roles. It is felt that the task of bringing up young children belongs not only to women but also to men, and that not only mothers and fathers, but all adults, must share the responsibility for the children in society. Many women's groups are pressing for part-time jobs for both men and women who have young children and six-hour workdays for parents with children of school age. Other demands are for more and better housing services for families with children: restaurant service as an alternative or complement to the family cooking, maintenance service in the form of daily or weekly housecleaning, care of sick family members, laundry and shopping-center service—all available in the same building complex. Only a few such fully socialized complexes with integrated day nurseries and preschools exist in the suburbs of some cities in Sweden, but a government building committee is working on an expansion and improvement of this project, which is still in an experimental state and has so far been met with both negative and positive reactions.

EDUCATION

Apart from military academies, women have access to all schools and colleges in Sweden. All Swedish children start school at the age of seven and must complete nine years of the compulsory, coeducational comprehensive school which in its present form was established throughout the country in 1970. The National School Board has stated that "the school must work toward equality between men and women—in the family, on the labor market and in social life. It must study sex roles, stimulate the students to discuss and question the current situation."[7]

Teachers of social studies classes, where the sex-role question is predominately discussed, are asked to "stress to the students that men and women can do the same work both on the labor market and in the home and to stimulate the students to question the pattern of sex roles they meet in their surroundings." [8] But the textbooks in civics, used by teachers in the comprehensive school, are far from emancipated from traditional sex-role thinking, as shown in the report of an investigation of sex roles in textbooks undertaken by the Women's Committee of the Labor Market Board in 1968.[9] Although some of these books have now been revised to show that Sweden is on the way toward an egalitarian society, there is still the pressure of public opinion, advertising, and mass media, all traditional, conventional forces that the school must try to counterbalance.

After completing their nine years of compulsory education, nearly 90 percent of the students continue two or three years of further education in the integrated upper secondary school, where there are twenty-two lines of both academic and vocational training to choose from. Almost as many girls as boys continue their education in the secondary school, but they are extremely unevenly distributed among the different lines. The largest difference is found in the technology line, which in 1971 had only 7 percent girls. Most girls chose an education in nursing, social sciences, liberal arts, clothing manufacture, and clerical work.[10]

At the university level the same pattern prevails: In 1970 women overwhelmingly chose to pursue studies in the humanities and social sciences. Women constituted 65 percent of the student body in the humanities, 36 percent in the social sciences, 23 percent in the natural sciences, and 7 percent in engineering and technology. The school of pharmacy traditionally has a large number of women students for their lower degree (67 percent), and the school of dentistry is 37 percent women, of which many become dentists in the public school system. The school of medicine had 27 percent women in 1970.[11]

Looking at the tables of statistics for persons with university degrees in 1970, we find that women held 19 percent of all degrees in medicine, 30 percent in dentistry, 33 percent in pharmacy, 9 percent in theology, 11 percent in law, 57 percent in the humanities, 37 percent in social sciences, and 27 percent in the natural sciences. The prognosis for 1980 is that there will be a 5–10 percent increase in all these fields except natural science, where there will be a 2 percent decrease.[12]

Recognizing that the school so far has failed in its egalitarian efforts, the National School Board is now trying different remedies: special courses for teachers and parents on sex roles in society, attempts to attract more men to become preschool and grade school teachers by a quota system, and allocation of more money for adult education, preschools, and nursery schools. Starting in 1975 there will be a compulsory preschool for all six-year-olds.

But the fact remains that in spite of the nine-year comprehensive school, where boys and girls are taught the same subjects, including home economics, handicrafts, cooking, and child care, and where they have the same teachers, as soon as the students enter the differentiated high school, they choose their academic as well as vocational subjects according to well-established sex-role patterns, resulting in two sharply divided blocks: mostly female students in humanities and social studies, nursing, clerical, and other service-oriented fields—all usually taught by women— and mostly male students in mathematics and natural sciences, technology, and engineering—predominantly taught by men. It is obvious that girls are not being sufficiently stimulated to pursue studies leading to more skilled or nontraditional careers.

The blame, however, cannot be put solely on the school. The change in attitudes about sex roles must start in the home, and it has been suggested that perhaps the solution would be a compulsory school for parents, where they could be taught not to treat their sons and daughters differently. This is actually being done in adult education courses. Also, the news media must work for a changed attitude toward sex roles. *Dagens Nyheter*, the largest Swedish daily newspaper, has been the forerunner in the press in stimulating a public debate on sex roles. In film, Mai Zetterling has contributed with a sharp satire, *The Girls*, and Ingmar Bergman with a TV series on a modern marriage. During the 1973–74 season, Swedish television also presented a well-received series of programs on Swedish women in history and literature.

Women's Studies programs are being offered at the universities of Uppsala and Gothenburg. A great many books and dissertations have been published, all putting pressure on the government to act through legislation for reforms in the economic and social status of women.

THE LABOR MARKET

The industrial revolution came relatively late to Sweden, and it was not until the beginning of the 1930s that industry took the lead over agriculture. Today almost half the Swedish working population is engaged in industry, while the percentage occupied in agriculture has fallen to about 10 percent. The total Swedish labor force consisted in 1970 of 2.3 million men and 1.5 million women, or 86 percent of all men and 57 percent of all women.[13]

After the Second World War, Sweden proclaimed a full-employment policy, taking measures to forestall any recurrence of the mass unemployment of the 1930s. Apart from brief intervals of reduced labor demand during times of economic recession, Sweden has had full employment since the 1940s. The recession in 1971 caused an unemployment of 2.5 percent (2.4 percent for men and 2.8 for women).[14]

Full employment led married women to go into the labor market to an ever greater extent and widened their choice of occupation. Shortage of male labor in many branches of the Swedish industry and in the professions forced employers, particularly during the 1960s, to try to attract more female labor. While in 1930 less than 10 percent of married women were gainfully employed full or part time, there was an increase in 1950 to 15.6 percent, which was more than trebled during the 1960s to reach 55 percent in 1970. The estimate for 1985 is that 67 percent of all married women in Sweden will be gainfully employed on a full- or part-time basis.[15]

Because of the economic boom and the resulting shortage of male labor in the 1960s, women were able to enter fields of employment that once were reserved only for men. Women are now employed as bus drivers, subway train drivers, conductors, and taxi drivers in all the major cities. Certain sections of industry, where previously only men were found, now employ women exclusively. Although there have been these small changes, generally speaking there still exists one labor market for men and another for women in Sweden. It seems that the latest recession in the Swedish economy has put a stop to the tendency of equalization between male and female on the labor market, which had started to appear during the 1960s. Mining, manufacturing, building, and construction employ more than half of all working men, but only one-fifth of all women. In the teaching profession there are more women than men, but very few men are preschool or grade school teachers and very few women (less than 10 percent) are school principals or university professors. The medical profession is dominated by men, while with very few exceptions all nurses are female. Looking at the sex distribution among about 300 classified professions, one finds that 75 percent of the female labor force is concentrated in only 25 occupations.[16]

In 1962 Sweden ratified the International Labor Organization's convention on equal pay for equal work for both men and women and the prohibition against discrimination on grounds of sex; but still women do not get the same kind of work as men and are therefore paid less. In leading administrative posts in state service with the highest national salaries, only 2 percent are women, while in the lowest-paid posts 76 percent are women. Since there is no actual legislation affecting equal pay for men and women, the latter still average lower incomes than men in all occupations.[17]

To remedy the fact that 70–75 percent of the adult population in Sweden has had only six or seven years of formal schooling and most housewives have no vocational training, the Labor Board in 1968 started a program for training unemployed men and women in various occupations, with emphasis on those in greatest demand. The courses vary in length from three months to two years. Participants are trained free of charge and have their living expenses paid for during the time of training. In 1970 more than 50 percent of the trainees were women; despite efforts by government authorities to motivate them toward nontraditional occupations most of them chose traditional occupations such as nursing, clerical, and commercial work.[18]

Although there has been a large increase of female workers, there is still a large hidden unemployment among housewives who are not fully occupied in the home. A Swedish economist has recently estimated that Sweden's GNP would go up 25 percent if the unused labor potential of women were utilized fully, and an added 25 percent if sex discrimination and other barriers were abolished totally.[19] For Sweden to maintain its high standard of living, it is vital that its women work. The earlier attitude among some married men who still regard supporting a "housewife" as a mark of prestige is fortunately declining rapidly.

In the debate over whether married women should be gainfully employed or not, the moderates have maintained that every woman should have the freedom of choice, while the view of the liberal-radicals has been that there can be no equality as long as the wife and the children are solely supported by the husband and father. And if there should be a choice, that choice must also include men.

Under renewed pressure from feminist movement groups, the Swedish government in December 1972 established a committee on equality between men and women. Primarily concerned with labor-market problems of women, their first investigation dealt with part-time employment for both sexes. Asserting women's right to work and actually getting jobs, the delegation proposed a successive quota system, whereby women would get a 50 percent representation in all occupations with the exception of the military. The proposal was endorsed by parliament, and a pilot project was initiated in the fall of 1973. The women were offered a four-week introductory course, subsidized by the Labor Market Board, into such typical male jobs as lathe operators, milling machine workers, foundrymen, and engine fitters. The experiment turned out successfully for all parties concerned: the women themselves, their employers, their union, and their male colleagues—and as a result some women got better-paid jobs.

Proving the point that women can take on men's jobs, the experiment is now being carried on in several male-dominated industries located in small towns where there is a lack of other job opportunities for women.

POLITICS

Although women in Sweden were given suffrage in 1919, their political representation is still minimal: of 18 cabinet ministers in the government, only 2 are women; parliament has 20 percent women members, and local governments only 15.[20] The traditional attitude among both men and women in Sweden is that "politics is men's business." Thus women are less active in political parties. Because of the party custom of placing women candidates at the bottom of the ballot and thereby giving them a lesser chance to be elected, the proportion of women elected is lower than the proportion of women candidates.

Since all major Swedish political parties, except the Communists, have their own women's associations, most politically active women devote more time and energy to them than to the parties themselves.

Like the political parties, trade unions in Sweden are run by men. In the largest employees' organization, the Trade Union Confederation (LO), 30 percent of the members are women, but no women are on the board and only 3 percent are in its representative assembly. Even in member associations dominated by women, most leading positions are held by men.[21]

In all government-sponsored investigations, the committee members are overwhelmingly male. During the 1950–70 period in standing committees on problems concerning women, only three were chaired by women and had an average of 37 percent women members, while there were no women on committees on problems concerning men.

Since there is no legal barrier for women to enter politics, the feminist organizations are concentrating on changing the attitudes of women towards active participation in politics.

There is no equivalent in Sweden to the League of Women Voters in the United States. The most active political organization, apart from the political parties' women's associations, is the Fredrika Bremer Association with about 10,000 members. Founded in 1884, it is Sweden's oldest women's rights organization, carrying the name of the nineteenth-century Swedish writer and leader of the first feminist movement in Sweden, who in the 1850s demanded greater educational and legal equality for women. From the beginning a traditional liberal association, it later became more conservative, but is today quite radical in its demands for free legal abortion and a 50 percent representation of women in parliament.

Another very active feminist group was formed in 1968, the Marxist "Group 8." As the only militant feminist group in Sweden, they see women's liberation as a class struggle for both men and women in a capitalist society. They have been very influential in putting pressure on the government for reforms through the news media. One of their foremost demands has been for legalizing abortion; a demand that has been met by the government's proposal of a new abortion act presented to the parliament in Spring 1974, which came into force in January 1975. According to this new abortion act, prior to the thirteenth week of pregnancy, the question of abortion is decided by the woman herself; for abortion between the twelfth and eighteenth weeks, a special inquiry by a social worker would in principle be obligatory.[22]

Recently Sweden was nominated by the European business magazine *Vision* as the country in West Europe best prepared for the future. The publication had conducted a "Future Olympics" covering such fields as environment, democracy, and attitudes toward foreigners. Some three hundred experts voiced their opinions as to the achievements of West European countries in a total of fourteen fields. Of fourteen gold medals, Sweden gained eight, among these one for "equality between sexes."

It is true that Sweden can be proud of its legislation concerning equity for women, but it is equally true that these reforms must be regarded as only a beginning to the many reforms that are needed if Swedish women are to achieve equality with men in the labor market and in society in general.

Only through their own strong feminist movements, exerting pressure on an admittedly sympathetic government, can women in Sweden look forward to a future where they will share equally with men in the work and responsibilities of their society.

NOTES

1. Eva Moberg, *"Kvinnans villkorliga frigivning"* (The Conditional Emancipation of Women), in *Unga liberaler* (Young Liberals), Hans Hederberg, ed. (Stockholm, 1962); and Moberg, *Kvinnor och människor* (Women and People) (Stockholm, 1962).

2. Alva Myrdal and Viola Klein, *Women's Two Roles* (London, 1956).

3. *The Status of Women in Sweden. Report to the United Nations 1968* (Stockholm: Swedish Institute, 1968).

4. Ibid.

5. Ibid.

6. *Woman in Sweden in the Light of Statistics* (Stockholm, 1973).

7. *Läroplan för grundskolan* (Guidelines for the Comprehensive School) (Stockholm, 1969).

8. Ibid.

9. Ingrid Fredriksson, *Könsroller i läroböcker* (Sex Roles in Textbooks) (Stockholm, 1969).

10. *Status of Women in Sweden.*

11. Ibid.

12. Ibid.

13. Ibid.

14. Ibid.

15. Ibid.

16. Ibid.

17. Ibid.

18. Ibid.

19. Per Holmberg et al., *Kynne eller kön. Om könsroller i det moderna samhället.* (Temperament or Sex. Sex Roles in Modern Society) (Stockholm, 1966).

20. *Status of Women in Sweden.*

21. Ibid.

22. "Swedish Government Proposes New Abortions Act," Current Sweden, no. 27 (Swedish Institute, 1974).

BIBLIOGRAPHY

Books and pamphlets available in English.

Dahlström, Edmund, and Liljeström, Rita. *The Changing Role of Men and Women.* London, 1967.

Forsslund-Ljunghill, Lena. *The Comprehensive School in Sweden. The Nine-Year Compulsory School.* Stockholm: National Board of Education, 1971.

Forsslund-Ljunghill, Lena. *The Integrated Upper Secondary School. Three Schools in One.* Stockholm: National Board of Education, 1971.

Leijon, Anna-Greta. *Swedish Women—Swedish Men.* Stockholm: Swedish Institute, 1968.

Linnér, Birgitta, *Sex and Society in Sweden.* 2nd ed. New York, 1972.

Myrdal, Alva, and Klein, Viola. *Women's Two Roles.* 2nd ed. London, 1968.

Olsson—Stendahl. *The Emancipation of Women.* Stockholm, 1971. Textbook used in high schools in English and social studies.

Palme, Olof. "The Emancipation of Man." Address at the Women's National Democratic Club, Washington, D.C., 8 June 1970.

Paulston, Rolland G. *Educational Change in Sweden. Planning and Accepting the Comprehensive School Reforms.* New York: Teachers College Press, 1968.

The Status of Women in Sweden. Report to the United Nations 1968. Stockholm: Swedish Institute, 1968.

Towards Equality. The Alva Myrdal Report to the Swedish Social Democratic Party. Stockholm, 1971.

The Trade Unions and the Family. A Report by the LO Council for Family Questions. Stockholm, 1970.

Woman in Sweden in the Light of Statistics. Stockholm: Joint Female Labor Council, 1973.

16

Women in China: Problems of Sex Inequality and Socioeconomic Change
Kay Ann Johnson

WOMEN AND THE TRADITIONAL CHINESE FAMILY

In order to understand and evaluate the recent process of women's liberation in China, it is important to begin with some understanding of the roots of female oppression in the traditional Chinese family. Although the traditional Chinese family, and the norms and customs that defined the status of women within the family, varied geographically and with social class, it is nonetheless possible to make some generalizations about the traditions of the Han family in China.

Probably the safest generalization, which cuts across history, geography, and class in China, is that the status of women within the family was universally low. The subordination of women to men was inherent in the patrilineal and patrilocal nature of the family and the broader kinship system that allocated status and authority according to a hierarchy based on age and sex. Within this hierarchy of authority, women lacked rights of property ownership and management, and carried no independent decision-making authority in important matters affecting the family and clan. The status and power of women did, however, vary with different phases of their lives, and there were a few avenues for women to increase their family position. Most notably, women gained status through childbearing and with middle age, when they gained greater supervisory and religious functions in the home.

286

The most difficult and degrading phase of life was immediately after marriage. The arrangement of blind marriages by family heads, a custom that greatly enhanced the control of family elders over family life, was usually done without consulting their children. The young people usually never met or saw each other. Under this arrangement, the groom's family pays a "body price" to the bride's family, in effect buying the young woman as chattel and reimbursing her natal family for the expense of raising her. Marriage is not so much a contract between the couple as it is a contract between the families, transferring the woman to the husband's family for the purpose of bearing male heirs for the patrilineal family and performing necessary domestic work.

Thus the young woman enters an ongoing family as a stranger and an outsider. Physically severed from affectionate relations with her own family, she does not find the buffer of immediate affectionate ties with her husband to ease her initial transition. In fact, one function of the arranged marriage is to protect the filial bond between son and parents from being undermined by a strong conjugal bond that could threaten the patriarchal family hierarchy. The young wife, lacking status and the protection of affectionate ties, comes abruptly under the authority of her husband and in-laws. In day-to-day affairs she is supposed to be most directly under the authority and supervision of her mother-in-law, who organizes and controls the "women's work" within the household. Because the husband and his family have paid, often dearly, for the bride's services as a wife and daughter-in-law, they feel they have the right to regulate her labor and activities according to family needs.

Under this system divorce is almost impossible for an unhappy wife. Even if her husband dies, her in-laws, if they are still living, retain control over her. If she is allowed to leave the family and remarry, they will expect the new husband to pay them the "body price" they originally paid for her. Similarly, a divorce is unlikely to be granted by the husband or family unless the woman can buy back her freedom. Since the woman is totally dependent on the family economically, it is most unlikely she could meet the price. In some areas of China, remarriage of widows was not uncommon, although it was usually looked down upon.[1] Divorce for a woman was very rare, being sharply circumscribed by law and custom.

The brutalizing effect that this family system had on young women was a common theme of revolutionaries and progressive writers of the early twentieth century. These writers reflected on the physical and mental abuse suffered by young women and on their not infrequent resort to suicide as the only escape from intolerable circumstances. One of Mao Tse-tung's earliest articles concerned the suicide of a young bride in his home village. He asserted that her death, and the death of many others like her, was the inevitable result of the "iron net" cast around her by the old Chinese family system and the society that supported it.[2] The well-known writer Lu Hsün described this system as a "flesh-devouring" monster because of the physical and mental destruction it wrought on its own youth, and particularly on young women.[3]

One left-wing writer described the typical, almost routine, physical abuse suffered by the wife at the hands of husband and mother-in-law:

For women the old rule still holds good that as a daughter-in-law you have to put up with beating and abuse, but once you become a mother-in-law yourself you can beat and curse your daughter-in-law. If you don't you're failing to put up a good show of being a mother-in-law. The old rule for men in handling their wives is "a wife you've married is like a horse you've bought—you can ride them or flog them as you like." Any man who does not beat his wife is only proving that he is afraid of her.[4]

A woman begins to gain some status and respect in the family if and when she bears sons and if and when she develops a warm relationship with her husband which can partially shield her from arbitrary beatings and from her in-laws' authority. If a woman bears and raises a son to maturity and gets a wife for him, and a daughter-in-law for herself, she then gains the first real position of authority and control in her life. As a mother-in-law she gains household supervision over her son's new wife and her labor. As the passage quoted above suggests, the older woman, having suffered abuse under the authority of her mother-in-law, now assumes the same role over her young daughter-in-law. Even at this stage in life, with the greater status of age, she remains subordinate to her husband (and, theoretically, to his brothers) and, to a lesser extent, to her adult male children.

The control of women's lives by family males and elders was reinforced by the physical seclusion of women within the home—a seclusion that restricted their contact with nonfamily members and ensured economic dependence. A strict division of labor within the family was buttressed by traditional customs, norms, and superstitions that restricted proper women's work to manufacturing and processing materials for household consumption and other work that could be done near the home.[5] There were, however, important regional variations in the norms that restricted the physical movement and economic activities of women. In areas of southern China, women often participated in subsidiary agricultural work, such as weeding and transplanting, and helped during the busy harvest times. This productive, income-related activity probably improved the position of women in the home. Yet, even in these areas, women's activities were supposed to be closely supervised and controlled by family members, and women were generally barred by custom and superstition from many of the main productive activities. One survey taken in the 1930s showed that women performed only 13 percent of all agricultural labor, mostly in the form of secondary chores.[6]

Although it was important for all but the wealthiest women to learn a range of domestic skills, educational opportunities were generally denied to girls. Given the economic importance of the family unit, family resources were more profitably invested in sons than daughters. Daughters would leave their natal families permanently at marriage and were of little economic use to their original family and parents. The denial of education to women was also a natural outgrowth of the accepted sexual division of labor. Since women were barred from most occupations, they could find little use for an education. Sons, on the other hand, could gain official positions or enter various crafts and professions through educational achievement. And, unlike daughters, sons were permanent members of the family and had lifelong obligations to work to support their parents.

Thus, the general economic and social restrictions placed on women made them wholly dependent beings, reinforcing their subordination to men and family authority. The practice of footbinding, which crippled and partially immobilized women for life, symbolized this overall crippling of women's spirit and lives. (It is significant that in the South, where women were allowed to participate more actively in economic activity, footbinding was much less prevalent than in the

North. In the South the practice tended to be limited to leisured women of the upper classes.)

The hierarchy of status and norms governing the proper roles and behavior of women assume, to a large extent, the "ideal," multigenerational stem or joint family. In fact, such families were in the minority, especially among the poor.[7] Predictably, family size and complexity were directly correlated with wealth and status,[8] and conformity to traditional and Confucian norms was more easily maintained by the wealthy landowning classes. Because of high mortality rates, famine, war, and disruptions of the rural economy in the nineteenth and twentieth centuries, many poor peasants were incapable of raising and maintaining the "ideal" large families. For many peasants, poverty greatly weakened, and often destroyed, family life, making conformity to accepted norms impossible. Sometimes the sons of the poor could not even raise a "bride price" or afford to feed an extra mouth, and could not marry at all. Thus, despite widely accepted norms that confined women to the home, economic necessity often forced poorer women out of accepted family roles to obtain food.

But it should not be inferred that less conformity to social norms among the poor necessarily meant that poorer women were more "liberated" or suffered less under male supremacy. Some poor women who were compelled by poverty to engage in income-related work no doubt did gain greater independence and power in family affairs.[9] But poverty also frequently compounded the suffering and humiliation of women which resulted from their subordinate status. Even in economically compelling situations where the alternative might be starvation, ingrained taboos and lack of experience might make it extremely difficult for women to take the necessary steps to fend for themselves. When the poor aspired to maintain the "proper" socialized values, the inability to do so painfully affected poor women's self-esteem and community respect.

This point is well illustrated by the testimony of a poor young peasant woman in North China at the turn of the century. Her unreliable opium-smoking husband rarely brought home food for her and her baby daughter. Finally, facing starvation, she was tormented over what she should or could do:

> A woman could not go out of the court. If a woman went out to service the neighbors all laughed. They said "So and so's wife has gone out to service." Or they say "So and so's daughter has gone out to service." I didn't know enough even to beg. So I sat at home and starved. I was so hungry one day that I took a brick, pounded it to bits, and ate it. It made me feel better.
>
> How could I know what to do? We women knew nothing but to comb our hair and bind our feet and wait at home for our men. When my mother had been hungry she had sat at home and waited for my father to bring her food, so when I was hungry I waited at home for my husband to bring me food.[10]

In order to survive, the most poverty-stricken families were sometimes forced to sell their infant children, especially daughters, since they held less promise of being able to contribute to the economic future of the family. Husbands might have to sell wives as servants or concubines to those who could afford them. In the worst circumstances, infanticide was practiced, mostly against baby girls. The generally reported high ratios of males to females in the population throughout China (as high as 156 to 100 in one Shensi county in 1829) can probably be explained partially by the practice of female infanticide and higher mortality among young women in general resulting from low status and neglect.[11] This strongly suggests the disproportionate toll that poverty took on women. Incidents such as female infanticide, the selling of wives and infant daughters as concubines or slaves, and depriving women of equal access to scarce family food supplies frequently emerge in the social literature of the revolutionary period as illustrations of a brutal and sick feudal society—a society in which women especially were the victims, regardless of class.[12]

REFORM OF MARRIAGE AND THE FAMILY

The family system was seen by many as intimately tied to those social norms and economic structures that defined this sick society. The fact that the family system and its norms pervaded nearly all aspects of local Chinese society[13] made it a necessary target for any movement which hoped to bring about fundamental social change. From the very beginning, the movement for revolutionary change in China had to relate to family reform and the small but growing women's movement for sex equality.

The introduction of Western ideas of democracy and equality greatly influenced the early twentieth century May Fourth generation of progressive youth. This youth movement enlisted growing numbers of educated urban women who demanded equal economic and political rights. Both left-wing Nationalists and Communists sought to enlist the support of women and supported the principle of sex equality. The Nationalist government's constitution and laws promised to improve women's political and economic rights. But during Nationalist rule the practical effect of these reforms, and the women's movement itself, remained confined to a small segment of urban intellectuals with little or no effect on the vast rural areas. Significantly, an independent, meaningful women's movement never really developed in the rural areas due to the particular kind of overwhelming female oppression and the social isolation of women from one another. The only political force in China that was willing and able to carry out family reforms was the Communist party, which brought marriage reform and women's property rights to the remote liberated areas and, after 1949, to the whole country.

Two of the early major reforms undertaken by the new Communist government were land reform and the new Marriage Law. Both these reforms affected the nature of the traditional family and the status of women.

The Marriage Law of 1950 was aimed at directly subverting the authoritarian age and sex hierarchy of the family by abolishing the system of arranged "buying and selling" marriage, prohibiting child betrothal, concubinage, polygamy, and interference in the remarriage of widows. The law also gives women the right independently to sue for divorce. The marriage contract is one between two freely consenting adults, at a minimum age of eighteen for women and twenty for men, and "no third party shall be allowed to interfere." [14]

The abolition of arranged marriages obviously weakens the control of parents over their children. Marriage by free choice of the couple strengthens the conjugal relationship and potentially makes this relationship the core of a new family, equaling or superseding the relationship between parents and son. This, ideally, increases the status and position of the young bride, since she no longer enters an ongoing family as a stranger and outsider. From the outset, she can lay claim to her own volition in choosing her mate and entering his family. This new, more equal position gives the young woman some leverage to gain greater control and respect from family members. Coupling this with the right of divorce further increases this leverage, for the woman can now legally choose to leave her husband and in-laws if she finds her treatment unbearable. An account of the early days of implementation of the new law in a northern village indicates that some women were able to take advantage of this new leverage to gain better treatment in their homes.[15]

But for women to take meaningful advantage of their new legal rights in marriage and divorce, they had to have some basis of economic independence outside the family. Land reform, which distributed land equally to every individual man and woman, was necessary to give fuller meaning to family reform. Women were also given formal rights to shared household property. Chinese Marxists have always emphasized the need for women to gain economic independence to achieve true equality. Owning land and family property in their own name was seen as essential to begin the process of liberating women.

Land ownership gave real bite to the right of divorce since it made it more economically feasible for women to make such a choice. Nevertheless, the inexperience, lack of necessary skills, and persistent taboos against women participating in certain kinds of labor made it difficult for all but the most determined women to assert their independence from husband and family. It had a more general psychological effect, however. Many women felt their bargaining power had been enhanced, which gave them greater confidence and self-esteem. One peasant woman expressed this sense of new status and self-respect:

> Our husbands regard us as some sort of dogs who keep the house. We even despise ourselves. But that is because for a thousand years it has been, "The men go to the hsien [county] and women go the yuan [courtyard]." We were criticized if we even stepped out the door. After we get our share [of land] we will be masters of our own fate.[16]

Another woman said:

> Always before when we quarrelled my husband said, "Get out of my house." Now I can give it right back to him. I can say, "Get out of my house yourself!"[17]

It was necessary to invest a great deal of organizational and political energy to popularize and actually carry out these new reforms in the villages. In addition to mobilizing the new government and party apparatus, women themselves had to be organized to help overcome resistance. For the most part, local women had no previous experience in organizing themselves, and setting up local women's associations was crucial to the initial success of family reform. These women's organizations were to help oversee the implementation of the Marriage Law and new property rights, to educate and raise the political consciousness of women, and to mobilize women to take part in land reform and village political life. Most important, the women's organizations provided an essential base of physical and psychological support outside the home that women could rely on for help in asserting their new rights.

Probably the most crucial and difficult task of these early organizations was to break down the psychology of deference, fear, and fatalism that kept women passive, mystified, and incredulous about any possibility of altering their "fate" through collective political action. To this end, women were encouraged to come to meetings to "speak bitterness" and to report gross mistreatment so that the women's association could take collective action to "reform" or chastise the culprit. Predictably, the initial efforts to bring women out of the home to attend meetings often met resistance by men and in-laws who could intimidate women with threats and beatings to keep them at home. Women organizers investigated and attempted to bring pressure on family members who obstructed the right of women to go to meetings. Occasionally a public "show of force" by the women's association against a few reluctant men was a necessary and effective means of breaking down such barriers to organizing women. The worst husbands and fathers-in-law might be forcibly brought to public meetings for mass criticism and even beatings by angry women taking their long-sought revenge. Such incidents often had an explosive, catalytic effect on the participants, showing women for the first time that they could stand up to men, that they need not passively accept their abuse and inferior status, that they could, under the system of the new people's government, "turn over" *(fanshen)*.[18] These women's organizations thus served to create pressure for changing the most personal relationships that oppressed women by politically mobilizing women for collective action and by politicizing family relationships. The way in which a man treated his wife was no longer a "private matter" but a public political issue.

Between 1950 and 1953, the nationwide effort to popularize the new Marriage Law also broadly mobilized the joint organizational and political energies of the trade unions, youth organizations, the mass media, and Communist party branches at all levels. The courts were moved to action as large numbers of matrimonial and divorce cases were brought for litigation. The overwhelming majority of divorce suits in rural areas were brought by women,[19] indicating the practical effect of women standing up to take advantage of new freedoms.

Though there were many important legal, psychological, and practical effects from this early period of intense pressure to transform the family and status of women, it was far from an unqualified success by the time the campaign began to subside after 1953. There were many problems of implementation, and local resistance to such radical changes was evidently widespread.

The liberation of women was theoretically considered an important and necessary concomitant of general political and economic transformation of society, and in many areas the mobilization of women did add important support to the new political and economic order. However, in many ways the struggle for women's equality seemed to complicate, and even threaten the success of, reorganizing political power in the villages. The assertion of new rights for women threatened the economic and psychological prerogatives of all men, regardless of class. It thereby created a political cleavage between the sexes that cut across class lines and categories that formed the basis for the consolidation of the peasants' new power.

Men who had fought against the Japanese, Nationalists, and landlords to bring the Communist party and peasant associations to power were now being asked by their political allies to give up much of the engrained, traditional, socialized basis of their "manhood." Many men who had struggled for a radical transformation of political and property relations in the villages nonetheless accepted reactionary, traditional views about the "proper" subordination of women to men. For some men, having to give up such views was particularly ironic. Many of the poorest peasants had been unable to afford marriage or to raise and keep their families intact. Their poverty had thus denied them the dignity of being a complete man. Land reform and the new society promised economic and social benefits that could reunite separated families and allow those previously unable to, to start a family of their own. Now, as this vision was within reach, these men, allies of the revolution, were being pressured to make painful adjustments which undermined their concept of a man's rightful authority within his own family.[20]

The predominantly male central leadership was not unresponsive to such sentiments. As early as 1948, a Central Committee directive indicated that the organization of women was to be carefully managed by the party so that it would not endanger land reform.[21] In other words, the most militant manifestations of the women's struggle against male oppression were to be contained so as not to alienate peasant men and detract from the struggle against the landlords. At the same time the directive indicated that in some areas the family reforms were being completely ignored by local cadres, and this too should be remedied. However, it was probably much easier for the party to contain historically more disadvantaged women than to quickly gain cooperation from recalcitrant male comrades.

Furthermore, the tensions and conflicts engendered were not simply between oppressed women and their male overlords. There were also inherent tensions and conflicts among the women themselves, particularly between the young daughters and daughters-in-law and the older mothers and mothers-in-law. Part of this was due to the greater difficulty that older women had in accepting new ideas so late in life.[22] This conservative-progressive split between old and young was reinforced by the fact that traditional norms inflicted the greatest stress on young women, and this stress eased somewhat with age. But this split was more than a natural generational gap over new ideas. The mothers-in-law, in particular, experienced many of the demands for change put forward by younger women as a real threat to their interests and basic needs—their emotional and economic security in old age. These demands also threatened the mother-in-law's single privilege of commanding the labor of her daughter-in-law so as to lighten her own workload as she grew older.

As an illustration of this conflict, one perceptive observer, William Hinton, recounts an incident he witnessed at a village meeting. One man was criticized at some length for siding more with his wife than his mother in family affairs. He was accused of not being a proper "filial son." This criticism hardly seemed in line with the spirit of the new marriage reforms which aimed at strengthening the bonds between husband and wife and ending the worst oppression that fell on young wives who had always occupied the lowest rung in the family hierarchy. Hinton explains this apparent contradiction:

> When I thought it over, I realized that it was the older women who had "mounted the horse," and with millenniums of tradition on their side, no one dared contradict them.

They saw in the new equality which gave a daughter-in-law the right to challenge her mother-in-law a threat to the only security they had ever known: filial obedience from their sons and absolute command over their son's wives. Bought, sold, beaten, and oppressed as they had always been, they traditionally had but one chance for power, one opportunity for revenge, one possibility for prestige, and that was as a mother to a grown son, as mistress to a daughter-in-law. Now, it would appear, even this was threatened. Young women no longer obeyed. Sons sided with their wives. Old women might well pass out of life as girl babies came into it, unwanted, neglected, and quickly forgotten when gone. Unable to comprehend the many-sided security which the land reform and the new property laws were bringing in their wake, many older women were fearful lest reforms destroy the one traditional prop, the one long-awaited support of their old age.

Old Lady Wang felt this keenly because her only son was soon to marry. She herself had handpicked the girl and had tried to choose a compliant one. But still she feared that new ideas might transform even this young bride. What would happen then?[23]

As Hinton implies, the key to resolving this conflict in favor of the young and future generations of Chinese women lay in making the older generation feel that new social and economic forms offered them a new, dependable source of security and dignity, that they need not fear an old age of poverty and neglect, and that they need not rely on particularistic control of younger and weaker family members. In the future people would be guaranteed economic and social security by the community and state. In other words, the rights of guaranteed social welfare must supplant reliance on the family in order that the particularistic, selfish, and oppressive relationships of the family be transformed into broader community identities and more humane personal relationships. This transformation has not yet been brought about. The problems encountered are not only the force of old habits, but factors related to general economic underdevelopment and the persistently low level of socialized community services and welfare which such an economy can support, particularly in the countryside. Top-level political awareness and choices about economic and social development and organization also influence the degree and speed of family reform and women's emancipation. These political and economic policy choices sometimes conflict with and sometimes reinforce the needs of women's emancipation. After 1953, this complex of factors created temporarily insurmountable obstacles for the women's movement for equal status in the home and the economy.

Probably the greatest single obstacle arose from the potential for serious disruptions, even backlash, as a result of the local resistance inherent in the types of conflicts already discussed. While there was great local variation in the success and intensity of the early campaign for women's rights and family reform,[24] in some areas the conflicts and tensions apparently brought fellow villagers to the brink of covert sexual warfare. Not only were men sometimes violently beaten by organized women, but there is some indication that the rate of suicide, torture, and murder of women increased alarmingly during the early 1950s. That these deaths were connected to the struggles to transform the family is indicated by one Communist writer who claimed that most of the deaths were of progressive young women who were active in the struggle for women's rights and against the old family institution.[25] It seems safe to infer that many of these women were victims of a backlash by men and elders against the unprecedented rebellion of women in those areas where they were not adequately protected by the new women's organizations and local party branch. Such violent and uncontrolled confrontations, even if limited to a minority of villages, indicated the potential for disruption and discord created by the national campaign to enforce the Marriage Law. Many local cadres were probably relieved when the intensity of the movement was allowed to subside after 1953 so that they could turn their energies more fully to other economic and political priorities and restore stability.

Other problems encountered in the implementation of the reforms involved the nature and responsiveness of the apparatus expected to carry them out. Local courts were not always dependable in enforcing the new law, finding it difficult to break with traditional legal views that discriminated against women. Traditional views were also deeply rooted in the local, predominantly male party organizations and village administrations which sometimes showed reluctance to carry out central directives that challenged their male supremacy and prerogatives. Repeated press criticism and directives issued by central authorities indicated concern over the persistent problems in getting local organs to respond effectively to their legal and political responsibilities.[26]

Where such problems existed, it created an atmosphere in which activist women could not be certain of local support. This situation, no doubt, dampened enthusiasm and made women wary of going "too far." Given the thorough and widespread nature of centuries of female oppression, oppression that kept women isolated from one another and from meaningful community life, oppression that made them almost wholly dependent beings within the narrow circle of the family, it was impossible for women to take the necessary psychological, political, and organizational steps to liberate themselves without external encouragement, dependable support, and ultimately, protection. Even when such support was supplied by the top leadership, local party, and courts, the process was difficult and sometimes brutal for men and women.

The concern at upper policy-making levels over minimizing the potential for further domestic disruption and local strife at the outset of the First Five-Year Plan seemed to sanction an end to the intense political and legal attack on the family and female subordination. After land reform, urgent priorities focused on increasing production, nationalization, and collectivization of agriculture. Under such circumstances, the costs of the struggle against the old family institution, in terms of increased tension and the local political energy that was being detracted from more urgent and basic needs, seemed too great. Moreover, many rationalized at this time that proper socioeconomic conditions did not yet exist for more complete reform.

WOMEN IN THE ECONOMY

In light of the problems of local resistance to ideological pressure, of economic priorities of the central leadership, and of the apparent conviction that change of the family institution is ultimately dependent on transformation of broader social and economic forces, the policy of a political and ideological frontal attack on the family shifted to a more exclusive emphasis on changing the economic position of women by gradually bringing them into the productive labor force in industry and agriculture.

Therefore, in the mid-1950s it was emphasized that "real equality between men and women can only be realized in the process of the socialist transformation of the entire society." [27] Through this process, women play an increasing role in the collective economy. Particularly in the countryside, eliminating the family as the primary unit of ownership, production, and labor organization through collectivization helps break down the strict division of labor within the confines of the family. Labor can be organized on a broader, more rational basis, and women can then be encouraged to work outside the home to earn wages from the collective or state. By earning wages and contributing labor to the economy, women presumably gain higher status in the community and greater independence and power within the family. Bringing women into the economy as a means of gaining greater sexual equality is particularly important in a society where the ruling ideology places the greatest value on productive social labor and service to the collective; and where old norms, as well as new ones, reinforce the low valuation of domestic household labor as compared to income-producing labor.

Yet during the mid-1950s and the initial collectivization of agriculture, the level and pattern of both urban and rural development, coupled with the scarcity of welfare and social services, made it extremely difficult for women to move out of the home and into the economy. At least until 1958, there continued to be serious economic and organizational obstacles to going beyond ideological exhortation and legal reform for women's rights.

During the First Five-Year Plan, which emphasized the development of capital-intensive heavy industry, the creation of new jobs was not equal to the large numbers of people seeking nonagricultural employment.[28] Under these circumstances it was impossible to bring large numbers of young women and previously unemployed housewives into the urban economy. Women suffered a further disadvantage in competing with unemployed men for those new jobs that were available, due to norms regulating "women's place" that mitigated against hiring women in heavy industry. Women were more equitably represented in some light industry and handicraft production, but these sectors grew much more slowly under the First Five-Year Plan. The percentage increase of women workers and employees during this period, therefore, was very small, rising from 11.7 percent in 1952 to 13.4 percent by the end of 1957.[29]

Factors contributing to differential and discriminatory employment patterns for women were many. They ranged from those internal, socialized attitudes that created difficulty for women to leave the home and labeled certain kinds of work as inappropriate for women, to blatant discrimination in hiring practices. Factory managers and administrators often refused to hire qualified women because, it was argued, women were inherently less efficient than men. Under labor-insurance guarantees, factories and offices had to pay women during maternity leave; nursery services needed to be set up. Even concern over women's presumably "special" problems during menstruation made them seem less efficient and reliable workers. In short, hiring women increased operating costs and was "uneconomical." [30] Young educated women might even be denied jobs if they had future plans for marriage or childbearing.[31] Since there was a surplus of unemployed male labor competing for scarce jobs, it was doubly difficult to eliminate such practices in hiring. Given priorities for increasing heavy industrial production and pressure on factory management to meet new quotas within a set budget, adequate pressure from the top was not forthcoming, despite complaints by top women leaders.

As unemployment grew in late 1957 and early 1958, it was even suggested in such authoritative organs as the Women's Association journal *Women of China* that some employed women should return to housework so that men could fill their jobs.[32] So, while telling women in the early 1950s that the road to their full emancipation required participation in productive labor, for most urban women the obstacles to doing so were insurmountable. There was some attempt to reconcile this obvious conflict by rationalizing that women's domestic labor can indirectly be considered "productive social labor" in that it serves and encourages husbands and children who are socially productive. In other words, by being a good "socialist family woman," women can contribute to socialist construction without appreciably changing their traditional roles. Such an argument, however, seems to beg the question of creating the prerequisites for raising the status of women. It ties their possibilities for social worth to the role they play in maintaining the still largely patriarchal family unit. Thus, women remain socially and economically dependent on, and hence controlled by, men, in-laws, and childbearing functions.

Despite the serious consequences for women, some policy makers were apparently arguing that, at this stage of early industrial development, full employment for men should be given priority over the political and social goal of liberating women. This argument is similar to one that has arisen in debates over the proper role of women in economic development in many other developing countries. Many economists have argued that at early stages of development, when unemployment and labor utilization problems commonly arise, women should not be encouraged to change their traditional roles. According to this argument, because of rural-urban migration patterns and population increases, new, more socially equal roles for women within the economy cannot be accommodated. While heavy and time-consuming traditional housework continues to be necessary or useful, it is "counterproductive" to add women to the labor force while men remain unemployed. Women seeking new jobs outside the family simply contribute to labor discontent and greater unemployment among men by creating an even larger pool of surplus labor. Therefore, during early development, employing male breadwinners should be given top priority and policies furthering women's equality should await a later stage of economic development.[33] This line of reasoning has further ramifications detrimental to women: it encourages educational policies that give priority to males and perpetuates differential socialization of females to prepare them for traditional, subordinate roles. The inescapable conclusion of this argument is that women's emancipation—politically, socially, and economically—is a threat to economic development.

Others, however, have pointed out that it is not necessarily correct to assume that early large-scale unemployment due to rural-urban migration is initially unavoidable. The rural labor problem is usually not one where a sizable percentage of the population suffers from total year-round unemployment and consequent destitution. Rather, it is more often a problem of "functional" seasonal unemployment or underemployment. Many men who seek better jobs in the cities can return to at least subsistence-level living in the villages. Further, economic policies that emphasize developing more labor-intensive agriculture and diversification could provide fuller year-round rural employment, which would slow or prevent migration. By doing so, industrial economic development in the towns and cities could then benefit from mobilizing women into new jobs.[34] It can even be argued that it is more economically efficient to bring urban women into the industrial labor force because it provides new labor for development without proportionally increasing the size of the urban population. Rapid urban population growth, compared to general population growth, places a much greater burden on public investment budgets in terms of house, light, water, sanitation, schools, hospitals, etc.[35] Rural populations, on the other hand, can be more adequately self-reliant in dealing with some of these needs. Yet, because economic development is so often thought to be synonymous with industrial development, because of private and foreign investment patterns, and because of the frequent urban biases of political and economic elites, employment opportunities in agriculture have often been overlooked and public investment in agriculture neglected. In China, too, the early pattern of industrial development began to give rise to these problems.

Although the extreme economic arguments against women's liberation never officially gained ascendancy in China, the First Five-Year Plan did not deal adequately with urban/rural labor utilization. It therefore led to economic policies that indirectly conflicted with avowed social-political goals of sex equality. Later, during the Great Leap Forward and again during the Cultural Revolution, Maoist politics and policies challenged these policies, arguing that progress in ideological, social goals, and progress in economic development can be made to reinforce, not conflict with each other.

In the pre-1958 period, however, rural women, like urban women, encountered serious obstacles to doing productive work outside the home. In addition to the persistent norms and attitudes that made it difficult for women to leave the home, the nature of the agricultural economy, and the lack of organized social services for women, kept women confined to domestic work most of the time.

In many areas, the rural economy, like the urban economy, could not in its present state absorb much new labor except for periodic busy seasons. Seasonal underemployment was widespread even for men.[36] Even after initial collectivization, the scope of the rural economy did not change appreciably to accommodate underemployment and seasonal fluctuation. This was due in part to the lack of capital investment in agriculture under the First Five-Year Plan.[37] In addition, the organization of labor and resources in the early cooperatives was not rationalized enough to take advantage of the pool of underutilized labor.[38]

Another factor inhibiting women's participation in the rural economy was the heavy burden of domestic work. In the countryside the burden of household and family responsibilities was, and continues to be, much greater than in the urban areas. The rural family traditionally has manufactured most of its own consumer goods. Throughout the mid-1950s and to a lesser extent in the 1960s, the manufacturing of household goods was not socially organized on a large scale and continued to be done on an individual basis within each family. This redundant labor consumed almost the full time of one or more females per family. Making clothes, shoes, and bedding; processing and preserving foodstuffs; taking care of children, the elderly, or the sick; cleaning house and preparing meals—all without the benefit of time-saving conveniences—was the individual responsibility of the women within each household. Such heavy, and unpaid, work left most women with little time to join the wage-earning collective work of the production teams. For the most part, the traditional division of labor that kept women tied to the home, maintaining their dependence and lower status in the family, was not altered greatly. Further changes in the organization of work and village life were needed. Simply removing the family as the primary unit of ownership and production by socializing the means of production was not enough. And as long as there was no labor shortage in most areas, there was little economic pressure to liberate women collectively from housework and mobilize them into the economy.

The ambitious policies of the Great Leap Forward and commune movement were meant to deal simultaneously with urban and rural unemployment and underemployment. This was to be done at a time when the rate of capital formation alone could not meet these needs. Therefore, these policies emphasized the rapid expansion of labor-intensive enterprises and projects, attempting to turn China's huge population and surplus labor problem into an immediate asset. Human capital became a major source of investment for rapid development.

These policies dealt in two ways with the obstacles hindering the liberation of women. First, by dealing with unemployment through reorganizing and mobilizing labor, new jobs were created and large numbers of women were organized to take part in work. Second, since many women were prevented from working by the burden of domestic work, community welfare and social services were organized to socialize some of the redundant household labor. In urban areas, small-scale labor-intensive factories were set up as "satellite" factories to large industrial enterprises and as "street industries" operating within residential areas. These factories relied on waste material from large industries, locally available capital, low-level indigenous technology, and the intensive labor of the previously unemployed, particularly women. By 1960, 85 percent of 4 million new workers in these enterprises were women.[39]

Although in 1958 the absolute numbers of women employed in industrial and office work more than doubled,[40] the female share of the nonagricultural labor force increased only 1 percent. By 1959, their percentage had increased by another 3 percent, putting the total percentage of the nonagricultural female labor force occupied by women at 18.8 percent.[41] One reason for this relatively small increase is that women were prevented from taking equal advantage of the large number of new jobs opened in heavy industry where norms concerning proper women's work inhibited female employment. The Great Leap policies, it seems, did not attack norms that operated against women's participation in certain types of work so much as it created new jobs in areas that women could enter more easily.

At the same time, the rural economy was diversified and intensified by the establishment of small, commune-run industries, water conservancy, afforestation, and construction projects, and increased sideline production in fisheries and animal husbandry. This created a demand for more labor and thus led to the mobilization of underutilized labor including large numbers of women. The bulk of the several hundred million people mobilized for water conservation and afforestration projects between 1958 and 1960 were women.[42]

In order to free women for these new jobs, many household tasks were collectivized. Nurseries and kindergartens were rapidly set up in the villages and urban centers. Urban canteens and commune-run dining halls were also set up to rid women of time-consuming food processing and cooking chores. Other services such as laundries, weaving and sewing cooperatives, shoe making and repair shops were organized in many areas to reduce further the need for individual women's work within the family. Not only did these socialized services greatly reduce the need for women to stay at home, they also created a large number of income-earning jobs filled almost exclusively by women who staffed the nurseries, dining halls, and shops. More than half of the 10 million workers in the commune dining halls were women, and almost all of the 6 to 7 million workers in commune nurseries were women.[43]

Thus, in many areas the mobilization of women did not break down norms concerning the type of work appropriate for women. Rather, it involved taking traditionally defined, unpaid, redundant female labor out of private homes and collectivizing it. It thereby becomes socially "productive" labor for which women usually receive income. This both raises the status of such work and contributes to the economic independence and authority of women within their own families.

The importance of economic independence as a central factor contributing to the emancipation of women has been, and continues to be, much emphasized by the Chinese:

> In the old society, women were generally regarded as men's dependents, no matter how hard they worked at home. The profession of housewife did not pay. Apart from political and social discrimination against women, the economic dependence of women was the source of men's superiority complex and their undisputed authority as head of the family. Under such circumstances, notwithstanding all talk to the contrary, inequality between men and women existed in fact so long as women had to depend on men for their support. . . .
>
> Liberation brought political and social discrimination against women to an end [sic]. But the problem of economic dependence of women took a long time to solve, with the result that women were usually at a disadvantage in public life. This unfortunate state of affairs changes rapidly when women stand on their own feet economically and become equal partners with men in supporting the family. In this way the status of women is raised. . . . Thus women acquire an increasing sense of their economic independence and the old practice of the male head of the family bossing around the home is on the way out.[44]

According to this view, socializing housework and giving women wage-earning jobs outside the home will inevitably revolutionize the old patriarchal family relations. The socioeconomic changes brought on by the Great Leap policies were, indeed, intimately related to the emancipation of women and the transformation of the family system. Such socioeconomic developments are portrayed as the key, at times the only, way to further sex equality. Only during the Cultural Revolution is it suggested that a return to direct ideological and political attack on male chauvinist and "feudal" patriarchal attitudes is necessary before further socioeconomic change can benefit women fully. This latter approach implies a more militant, politically activist approach to the problem. It points to the existence of special normative and ideological problems operating against sex equality that are not easily swept away by changes in the socioeconomic realm and that in fact stop women from taking part fully in those changes.

As mentioned, the employment policies of the Great Leap period did not aim specifically at destroying a sexually defined division of labor beyond the point of socializing women's work. The main objective was to get women out of the home and into the economy where their labor could be used more rationally and productively. In fact, sex-typing in jobs was actually encouraged in some areas and was considered "natural." At a women's conference held in Peking in November 1958, Tsai Ch'ang, chairman of the National Women's Federation of China

> *called on women to take a yet more active part in cultural, educational, medical and public health work as well as in welfare and other social services. She said women should gradually replace men in all such work that was specifically suitable for women so as to attain a more reasonable distribution of social labor force.*[45]

As a transitional step, this sexual division of labor can make it psychologically easier for women to enter the labor force and can help shield women from job competition with relatively advantaged and more experienced men. Furthermore, from the point of view of national decision makers, it may seem more "rational," "efficient," and less disruptive to channel women into jobs to which previous socialization has best suited them. Thus, child care, elementary and secondary teaching, nurturant jobs in public health and medicine, community services and many handicrafts are considered particularly suitable to the temperament and "special responsibilities" of women. Only a few have seriously questioned the permanent, long-range legitimacy of this pattern, which assumes innate female characteristics that are relevant to employment patterns. Nevertheless, legitimizing sex-typing serves to rationalize, institutionalize discriminatory attitudes and authority structures that limit women's access to jobs in many areas of the economy. It also helps perpetuate a "natural" division of labor and authority within the family. In particular, such attitudes justify and reinforce the continuing low representation of women in more prestigious and higher-paying modern and heavy industrial sectors. For the most part, those areas where women work in large numbers are lower-status and lower-paying jobs.

Regardless of how one evaluates the patterns of female recruitment, the Great Leap period did significantly increase the participation of women in the economy and mobilize them into broader social roles outside the family. Unfortunately, the serious economic difficulties that followed this period, resulting in part from unusually bad weather and problems in policy implementation, caused a setback in the mobilization of women during the 1960s. Nurseries, mess halls, and other services were scaled down or abolished. The massive water conservancy and other special projects that had employed so many women were halted. Many street industries run mainly by and for housewives were consolidated or closed. The result was that women were laid off in large numbers in the early 1960s. Although general unemployment also rose, not surprisingly women were affected disproportionately by the recession. Thus, many women returned to the home and full-time household duties.

In the mid 1960s the official view of the prospects for women's equality was more pessimistic than in 1958. While serious inequities were recognized, it was implied that economic circumstances would allow little alteration in the situation:

> *Concerning the status of women, marital status and family relationships, survivals of old ideas and viewpoints still remain.*

On top of this, the extent of women's participation in social labor, viewed either from the number of persons employed or from the role they have played, still suffers a certain limitation although it is the correct proportion in relation to the present stage of development of our national economy. *As a result of this limitation, there is still a difference in fact though not in law for women in the enjoyment of equal rights with men both in society and in the home. This difference will gradually disappear following the further development of production. That is to say, to do away completely with the old survivals in marriage and family relationships, it is necessary to create the more mature socio-economic and ideological conditions this requires.*[46] *[Emphasis added.]*

The insistence that liberation could be furthered, at this point, only through increased economic development and "more mature socioeconomic conditions" discouraged women from politically organizing to oppose the "old survivals in marriage and family relationships" as they had been encouraged to do in the early 1950s. The official view apparently was used to shield authorities from criticism for not moving to remedy the low representation of women in industry and political organizations. Although general economic recovery during this period did reopen jobs gradually, little concerted effort was made on the economic and political front for women again until the Cultural Revolution when, in addition to general political mobilization of women, many Great Leap innovations were reemphasized on a smaller scale and in a more orderly manner. Until this time, the problems and contradictions facing women in the 1960s were similar to the pre-1958 period. Women were told that the only road to liberation was through participation in productive social labor; yet the problems of heavy domestic work and scarcity of jobs made it very difficult for women to work.

Coincident with the return of many women to home life, and the absence of political agitation for women's rights, there was a reemergence in popular literature of the legitimacy of certain traditional kinship relations, though in reformed guise. One analyst found that the fictional literature of the 1962–66 period, in contrast to previous periods, stressed the value of filial obligations, respect for older generations and for patriarchal authority within the family.[47] Elders are depicted as having a legitimate, if sometimes misguided, interest in the marriages of their children and, particularly, in the acquisition of a daughter-in-law. These stories continue to portray the conflict between a liberated woman's obligations to her work in a socialist society and her duties to her family and household. But the mother is now shown as more home oriented and the father, more dominant compared to earlier literature.

Articles appearing in the youth and women's journals during this time confirm this interpretation of the fictional literature. In 1962, the *Chinese Youth Journal* carried several articles on the filial obligations of children to parents. One of these articles was written in response to a letter from a mother-in-law who was distressed by a daughter-in-law's attempt to interfere in the son's filial obligations to his parents—specifically his obligation to live with and support them.[48] Although the surface issue was one of financial support, the underlying problem is the tension engendered by a rebellious daughter-in-law who seeks greater independence from traditional norms and thus threatens the control and security of her in-laws. The editor's response to this letter supported the mother-in-law's position, saying that a daughter-in-law is obligated to support parents-in-law and should not "instigate" her husband to ignore his responsibilities by leaving his mother's household to set up a separate one with his wife.° While adult children in general are obligated by law to support elderly parents, it is asserted that there is a special obligation of sons and daughters-in-law to support the husband's elders. Significantly, the editor points to the moral force of tradition as the mainstay of this duty and asserts that in a socialist society this duty is even greater. What is most important to remember is that "it has always been a traditional practice in our country for a son and his wife to support his parents."

The individual rebellion and defiance of young wives, once encouraged as a means of politicizing and transforming the family, is now depicted as selfish, disruptive, and counter to broader "socialist duties." (Compare this also with the militant slogans of the Cultural Revolution: "Rebellion is justified," "Dare to struggle," and the call to attack the "Four Olds"—old customs, old habits, old culture, and old ideas.) It was thus difficult for women to use the ideology of sex equality directly to attack the authority of traditional relations within the family.

The persistence and qualified sanctioning of traditional family patterns points to the continued importance of the family as an essential provider of welfare and social security. Significantly, filial obligations were emphasized during a period of economic recession when state and community welfare services were especially taxed. In the transitional Chinese economy, these welfare services, particularly in rural areas, continue to be inadequate: old age and hardship security requires major responsibility from family and kin whenever possible. Only 1 or 2 percent of the average commune's income is invested in general welfare funds. Therefore, the level of support for a needy individual is usually quite low. Moreover, commune welfare services take the form of "public assistance" rather than the fixed and guaranteed "social security" system found in state industries and offices.[49] Commune welfare is usually administered on an individual basis after a local investigation to determine the cause and level of "special hardship" and to determine whether the problem can be handled by immediate relatives. There seems to be some of the same social stigma attached to this process of receiving aid as there might be to receiving "charity." This makes it psychologically a less attractive form of support than that afforded by children. Under such circumstances, parents continue to seek old-age security through their relations with adult children. Thus traditional filial relations continue to have vital economic significance. If young women rebel against old customs that subordinate them to husbands and in-laws, the strength of those traditional obligations that guarantee support are threatened.

Particularly revealing is the editor's statement in the *Chinese Youth Journal*: "Sons and daughters-in-law care for parents and society is responsible for those with no sons and daughters-in-law." [50] The prestige and economic value of having many sons in traditional China has often been noted. The religious incentives for bearing many sons have largely been removed by the disintegration of clan

---

° Although the questions of financial support for the husband's parents and living together with them are two separate issues, it is significant that the editor does not point out the distinction. It is thus indirectly implied that the daughter-in-law's obligations include living in her in-law's household if this is possible. Living together also has the practical effect of strengthening and ensuring the financial obligations of sons and daughters-in-law.

organizations since 1949.[51] So have some of the economic incentives, such as the ability of the family patriarch to invest the labor of many sons to increase family property and social class.[52] But as long as state or commune support is psychologically and materially insufficient, the traditional preference for sons over daughters is still reinforced. The Chinese leadership, including Mao Tse-tung, has frequently commented on the continued preference for male children among the peasantry.[53] Since daughters continue to be temporary members of their natal families, moving away to join their husband's family at marriage, they still do not fulfill the social and economic security needs as well as sons do. Even though more and more women are likely to become economically capable of support, maternal kinship ties and obligations in this respect are traditionally weaker than paternal ties.

The persistence of these traditional patterns continues to influence the differential socialization of sons and daughters since the family may continue to prefer to "invest" in a son's income-related skills and education. A daughter is more apt to be encouraged to leave school early to help at home where she learns domestic skills.[54] The reluctance of villages, as well as families, to invest scarce resources in the educational and political development of girls also continues to be a problem. The frequent custom of girls marrying outside their natal village leads local leaders to feel they are apt to "lose" their investment if they cultivate the skills and leadership abilities of young girls instead of boys. An article appearing in *People's Daily* as recently as 1971 complained about the existence of this view among party cadres on the question of giving special training to women:

> [Some] people said: "No matter how well we train them, they [young women] will be taken away one day." This is a result of viewing the matter from the standpoint of only one village or one brigade without considering the interest of the revolutionary cause as a whole. As long as we can train outstanding female Party members, they will help make the Party strong even when they are married away to another village. How can we say "it does not pay"?[55]

The article noted that the common expectation that young women will become housewives after marriage also contributes to discriminatory attitudes about training young women. Significantly, this article implies that this real "practical problem," arising out of concrete socioeconomic conditions, can be appreciably alleviated through correct "ideological and political work." However, "ideological and political work" was hardly emphasized in the 1960s until the Cultural Revolution. Rather, the "need for more mature socioeconomic conditions" was emphasized as a prerequisite for furthering sex equality.

Relieving women of heavy household work and mobilizing them into the economy will not necessarily, nor quickly, destroy accepted customs and stubborn, social norms that significantly differentiate the life patterns of males and females through marriage and patriliny. Nor does collectivizing broader areas of work and social services inevitably destroy public and private views that uphold sexual stereotyping. Such problems are deeply rooted in patterns of village and family life in which they are accepted as "natural" and politically "neutral." In many ways the development of sexual equality directly threatens the political and economic power of men who have controlled village and family life. The problem, then, is not simply one of "cultural adaptation" to economic role changes, but it is also one which requires a fundamental redistribution of power at all levels of society. As such it is a distinctly "political" issue.

WOMEN IN POLITICS

In both urban and rural China since 1949, women's political participation has been generally low. Those capable and determined individual women who were able to hurdle the initial obstacles to women's participation have been encouraged and promoted to high-level political positions in line with the leaders' commitment to sex equality. But women as a group have attained only a small percentage of middle- and upper-level leadership posts. The campaign to popularize the Marriage Law did increase significantly the percentage of women cadres from 8 percent in 1951 to 14.6 percent in 1955. At the higher levels of leadership their percentage declined, however, from 6 percent to under 3 percent, during this same period.[56] In 1956, only 10 percent of the membership of the Communist party were women.[57] These figures probably did not change appreciably before the Cultural Revolution.

In general, women hold a relatively larger proportion of leadership posts at local levels and their percentage declines at progressively higher levels. At the top, only 13 of 170 Communist party Central Committee members are women today. In 1965, it was reported that 25 percent of the production team (lowest rural unit) cadres in Kwangtung province were women. But in the commune-level organizations, probably only 5 percent were women.[58] In urban areas these percentages are generally higher, especially at lower levels. Over 30 percent of all cadres in Peking in 1963 were women.[59] Since women are heavily represented in the local neighborhood organizations (sometimes as high as 50 to 80 percent), the percentages here, too, are sharply lower above these local levels of leadership.

Many of the same obstacles that have hindered women's economic participation also stop their political participation. Heavy housework and family responsibilities make the extra time required by political and organizational work difficult. Even in routine mass political activities, such as all-village meetings, women often are unable to participate because they are expected to stay home to take care of children and the household while the men attend the meetings.[60]

As mentioned, because of this accepted sexual division of labor within the family, local party branches are hesitant to recruit and train young women.[61] Furthermore, parents, husbands, and in-laws often discourage young women from political work because it causes them to neglect family responsibilities and, contrary to old norms of "proper" behavior, it brings them into contact with men outside the family. The kind of behavior and social contact required of a political cadre may, some families feel, compromise a woman's reputation, causing a loss of face within the community.[62] One woman cadre in North China complained that most of the older women in her village think it "indecent and immoral and shocking that young people talk with each other," and "they scold their daughters and daughters-in-law and granddaughters for not observing decent behavior."[63] These attitudes are often a more serious obstacle to political activity than to participation in collective work outside the home. In rural work, women are usually organized to work in women's brigades or to do "women's work" together. But in political work, women may have to work with young men. Rural women activists complain that it is often difficult for younger women to ignore the pressure and influence of the older women because they must live and work together.[64]

Women cadres who are undeterred by such pressures must sometimes endure rumors about their moral and sexual behavior.[65] Old superstitions that stigmatize women are also used to keep women out of important positions usually reserved for men:

> When the brigade Party branch committee was re-organized and I was elected secretary, these class enemies spread rumors and superstition about me. "With a woman at the head the trees won't grow," they said. And, "A woman in the leadership will bring bad luck." They reinforced their rumors by compiling a list of "crimes" I was supposed to have committed in order to disqualify me from the post.[66]

Such attitudes obviously discourage women from seeking political posts and make it even more difficult to overcome the sexist division of housework and family responsibilities. It takes an unusually self-confident and capable woman to overcome these handicaps and pressures in order to become involved permanently in politics.

For several reasons, urban women have experienced greater ease in taking up political activity than their rural counterparts, at least at the lowest local level. First, attitudes about acceptable female behavior and old superstitions are probably less prevalent in more modern urban settings. Young married women are less subject to conservative pressures from relatives and in-laws because, in the urban living setting, they are less likely to live or work together. Compared to rural women, young urban women have more peer group and nonfamilial contact.[67] Second, urban women have greater access to social services and goods such as day-care centers, laundries, canteens, preprocessed foods, and a wide range of consumer goods that women must still manufacture in many rural households. Urban husbands also seem somewhat more willing to "help out around the house" occasionally.[68]

Probably the most significant factor related to greater local political participation of urban women occurs because residential areas are organizationally, and often geographically, separate from major production units. In rural areas, the composition and functions of the commune, brigade, and team leadership groups reflect the greater integration of rural living with the work setting. In this situation, women compete with the most active working men for political posts (except for positions in the women's association, of course). Therefore, women who participate in collective production only part time or not at all rarely gain access to such positions. In urban areas, residential leadership groups take responsibility for the wide range of social problems and activities not directly related to the activities of state factories and offices. Women who are not employed full-time outside the home play an important, often predominant, role in these community organizations.

Residents committees were set up in the early 1950s to provide organization for aspects of urban living that fall outside the scope of the major enterprises and to provide organization for the otherwise unorganized—the elderly, disabled, retired workers, housewives, and other family dependents.

The tasks of these residents committees originally included such things as neighborhood public security, fire prevention, and street sanitation; organizing public education programs such as political study groups and literacy classes; carrying out welfare work and investigation of special needs; organizing community services such as day care; arbitration of local disputes; and mobilization of residents to participate in periodic national political campaigns.[69] During the 1958–60 Great Leap period, when small neighborhood factories and socialized household services were established, production-related activities within the neighborhoods increased. The organization and mobilization of labor for these activities increased the scope of residents organizations. During the years of economic retrenchment in the early 1960s, many of these production and service facilities were scaled down or closed. During this period, the residential organizations seemed to lose political vitality as well. The Cultural Revolution revitalized these local organizations and again increased their scope. Residents committees now help run neighborhood schools and the rapidly growing neighborhood health clinics. Increasing the number and size of neighborhood factories, or "housewife" factories, is again emphasized, and residential nursery services have been enlarged.

Most of the neighborhood political work, and many of the community-run services such as health clinics and the smaller nursery stations, are undertaken by unpaid volunteer workers, drawing heavily on unemployed women and retired workers. Such work carries political responsibility and prestige within the community and provides women with accessible avenues for entering community social and political life. But this kind of work does not fulfill the often mentioned requirement of economic independence for women within the family. The small neighborhood factories and many of the service-related workshops (for tailoring, laundering, repairing, etc.) provide wages, although they are low compared to the wages of regular industrial and office workers. As these small-scale enterprises increase, more and more women will be able to gain a source of independent income and access to the leadership posts within these enterprises.

In contrast to local leadership in residential organizations, leadership groups in state-run factories and offices show underrepresentation of women similar to rural political organizations. Women's representation in political and administrative groups in factories is usually far below the percentage of women in the factories' total labor force. One visitor to China who investigated 35 industrial enterprises in the late 1960s estimated that 25 percent of the workers and employees in China's "major industrial cities" were women. (The percentage for all urban areas is probably lower.)[70] Yet, he reported that women comprised only 8 to 15 percent of the middle- and top-level leadership. He found no women directors of industry. Women were better represented at the lower levels of factory leadership.[71] My own observations in the summer of 1971 confirm this pattern. Even in those types of light industrial factories where women often constitute the majority of workers, such as textiles, food processing, and some kinds of handicrafts, women usually comprise only a small percentage of the leadership in these units. In one Sian textile factory, 60 percent of the 3350 workers were women in 1971. Yet only 20 percent of the leadership in the newly reconstituted (post-Cultural Revolution) Party Committee and Revolutionary Committee were women. In an embroidery handicraft factory in Suchow, over 80 percent of the 1400 workers were women, while 35 percent and 40 percent of the Revolutionary Committee and Party Committee, respectively, were women. The heads of these committees and the factory were men. In both these factories, the percentage of women leaders was said to reflect an increase from pre-Cultural Revolution levels.

Women who work in state-run industries enjoy advantages and access to services that other women often do not have. They usually have access to conveniently located, full-time, inexpensive infant and child-care services. (Rural women and women working in the neighborhood factories and organizations may have access to local day care, but it is often a makeshift arrangement, or limited to certain hours of the day or available only during busy seasons.) State workers also have access to minimal-cost dining services and canteens for all meals and, in some factories, for their families if they wish to avoid preparing meals at home. They receive high wages compared to peasants and other nonagricultural workers, and they get guaranteed retirement benefits. Their relatively high incomes, usually in addition to a husband's income, afford them access to many household consumer goods and services that other women may have to spend much time making or doing themselves. In other words, these advantaged working women have the material means to solve many of those "practical obstacles" that hinder women's emancipation. In addition, they have gained a large measure of economic independence from and equality with their husbands. Yet, as the figures on factory leadership suggest, even those economically liberated women who have been mobilized into the mainstream of the nation's economic life still encounter systematic discrimination against their full and equal participation and representation in political life.

It is one thing to assert that the nation lacks the socioeconomic conditions necessary fully to liberate housewives and part-time rural female laborers. But it needs to be recognized that even for those women who have largely solved the present contradiction between domestic labor and collective labor, this has not been enough to gain them true sexual equality. Subtle attitudes that characterize women as better suited to particular kinds of work, that characterize their temperaments and "special duties" as specific to their sex, help to perpetuate the notion of women as followers and men as leaders. Thus, women have been unable to gain their share of political representation where they have had to compete with men for these positions. The accepted functional division of labor within the economy also spills over into political organizations. Women who gain political posts often do so specifically in the capacity of advising on and implementing policies concerning special women's welfare work, such as helping with day-care needs or maternity problems. In other words, they are recruited to serve as women leaders of women. While this is obviously an area where women are needed, when this recruitment pattern is viewed together with the overall low percentage of women participating in leadership groups, it further underlies the extent to which other more general leadership concerns are dominated by men. Moreover, recent press criticism indicates that, in general, this political work concerning specifically women's problems has been treated by party cadres as less important and less prestigious than other types of leadership work. Women's political functions, like many of their economic ones, tend to be both separate and unequal.

In light of the centuries of total exclusion of women from political activity of all kinds, special, widespread, and long-term efforts to give women political education, leadership skills, and experience seems necessary to promote women's political equality. Traditionally, the exclusion of women from political and decision-making activity was even greater than their exclusion from economic activity. This pattern seems to continue in the factories and communes, with families and the community more readily accepting women in productive work than in decision-making roles. A recent article pointed out the existence of this pattern:

Some people do not believe in the revolutionary consciousness of the broad masses of working women. They think that while women may participate in productive labor, politics is certainly not for them. This viewpoint is not a Marxist one. . . .

As Lenin pointed out, "Our task is to turn politics into something in which every working woman can participate." Those ideas and practices that regard women as incapable of engaging in politics and exclude them from proletarian politics are all wrong.[72]

This article, written in 1971, implies that a successful policy toward the problem of sex equality must give greater emphasis to mobilizing women politically, while attacking male supremacist attitudes. Yet, the predominant policy toward the woman problem from 1954 to the Cultural Revolution emphasized, almost exclusively, the need for women to engage in the collective economy to gain full equality. It was more or less assumed that little else needed to be done, or, alternatively, could be done, to destroy the "ideological vestiges" of feudal patriarchy, male chauvinism, and female subordination in the family and community. An accepted division of labor based on sexual stereotypes and restrictive norms defining "appropriate women's work" within the collective economy escaped serious scrutiny and criticism. The important thing was to get women out of the restricted circle of the family, to transfer their labor into the collective economy.

At the same time, this policy tended to neglect the political education and mobilization of women for many years. Women failed to gain the political skills, understanding, and self-confidence necessary to assert themselves effectively when they were in situations competing with more advantaged men.

CULTURAL REVOLUTION AND AFTER

The Cultural Revolution represented, among other things, an attempt to promote revolutionary political and social goals, such as sex equality, by directly revolutionizing the "superstructure" of society. The "voluntarist" Maoist assumptions that led to the notion of cultural revolution opened the way for mass mobilization to further revolutionary political goals and to attack entrenched bureaucratic and political interests that obstructed such action. As noted, in the early and mid-1960s as the economy was just pulling out of a recession, it was suggested that little more could be done to further the social and political goals of sex equality or to destroy old ideas and habits concerning women without a further development of socioeconomic conditions. The Maoist assumptions of the Cultural Revolution suggested that through the use of mass political action and revolutionary ideology such revolutionary goals could be, indeed must be, furthered at the current stage of socioeconomic development. The key to furthering revolutionary goals, and thus the transformation of society as a whole, lay in "putting politics in command," in transforming people's way of thinking and ideological consciousness.

The Cultural Revolution affected women through the general political mobilization of the population, including working women and housewives, for political action, political study, and mass criticism of established structures of authority. Women were encouraged to organize in order to criticize and question the power structure in their places of work, their communities, and their families.

In some factories, militant women accused the leadership in the trade unions, women's associations, party branches, and management of revisionist and feudal thinking on the question of women. Such revisionist thinking was said to manifest itself in the theory that "women are backward and useless," that women lack political consciousness, that women should therefore be "combatants not commanders." These attitudes led the leadership to neglect the training of women cadres, impeded the political education and activity of women, and dampened their enthusiasm.

Women were also encouraged to form political study groups in their neighborhoods in order to discover and repudiate the "Four Olds" (old ideas, old culture, old customs, old habits) in their families and communities. Criticism by women of their family's undemocratic authority structure and of their treatment by parents, husbands, and in-laws was encouraged by articles in the press such as the following:

> Over thousands of years our family relations have been that son obeys what his father says and wife obeys what her husband says. Now we must rebel against this idea. . . . We should make a complete change in this. . . . It should no longer be a matter of who is supposed to speak and who is supposed to obey in a family but a matter of whose words are in line with Mao Tse-tung's Thought.[73]

In line with the Cultural Revolution's more radical approach toward women's roles, the journal of the Women's Association, *Women of China*, was attacked for past editorial policies and for trying to resist the policies of the Cultural Revolution.[74] The chief editor, Tung Pien, was accused of slighting women's potential political role and emphasizing women's "natural duties" to nurture children and care for a family. She thereby encouraged women to become "intoxicated with the small heaven of motherhood." She was said to have echoed "modern revisionist" theories of "mother love" and "feminine tenderness" and reactionary and feudalistic conceptions such as "respecting men but denigrating women and demanding obedience at the three levels (obedience to father, son, and husband)." [75] As noted, some of the writing that appeared in journals and short stories between 1962 and 1966 did in fact subtly reinforce traditional notions of patriarchal authority, patrilineal obligations, and, hence, the subordination of women. Though the criticism leveled at Tung Pien was somewhat overdrawn, the women's journal had for many years emphasized the special responsibilities of women in reproduction, raising and socializing youth, and in household economy.[76] In contrast to this, during the Cultural Revolution women were portrayed primarily as participants in revolutionary politics.

Thus the Cultural Revolution, more than previous periods, placed emphasis on the need to mobilize women to participate in politics as well as production. Not only were barriers to women's rights of participation attacked, but intense normative pressure was generated to impress upon women that they had an obligation to devote themselves more fully to social and political responsibilities outside the home. Red Guards and the mass media widely propagated norms of behavior that stressed that the individual's role and responsibilities to the collective should take precedence over more narrow and individualistic family roles and responsibilities.

But the high level of political participation fostered during the Cultural Revolution could not be maintained for long. The general mass mobilization tapered off in the late 1960s. Though it had left its mark throughout Chinese society, it had not, of course, solved social and political problems, including the many problems that hindered sex equality. It did, however, leave in its wake several more permanent political and socioeconomic improvements in addition to the less tangible effects of ideological radicalization.

In line with the new ideological emphasis on women's political participation, the top leadership took measures to ensure the institutionalization of a higher level of female participation in leadership groups. In the later stages of the Cultural Revolution, when new leadership groups were being set up and when party committees were being reconstituted, Mao Tse-tung directed that a "reasonable percentage" of women should be included in all new party leadership groups. When new committees submitted their membership to higher levels for approval, they were supposed to be rejected if they did not contain women. The actual size of the quotas set up was to be "appropriate to local circumstances." They were usually modest, flexible, and varied geographically and according to level of leadership. Nevertheless, they seem to have led to a definite overall increase in female representation.

In one rural Kwangtung commune that I visited in 1971 the improvement was quite modest. Three of 21 members of the commune Party Committee were women, and 2 of the 25 members of the Revolutionary Committee were women. Two of these women apparently gained their position as a result of the Cultural Revolution directive.[77] One commune near Shanghai, however, had a minimum guideline of 25 percent for top leadership groups. In fact the commune's Revolutionary Committee was 30 percent women and the vice-chairman was a woman. Many of the brigades and teams had even higher percentages.[78] The quota levels in this commune were comparable to those set for the urban districts of Shanghai. In another part of the country, in the northeast, a brigade visited in 1962 and again in 1969 also showed improvement. In 1962 only 1 of 12 brigade management committee members were women. In 1969, 3 of the 11 members of the new Revolutionary Committee were women.[79]

There has also been a revitalization of organizations and policies that directly and indirectly benefit women. Commune and neighborhoods have been encouraged to expand social services such as crèches, cooperative sewing shops, and food-processing facilities to aid women with household duties. There have been renewed efforts to deal with underemployed and unemployed housewives. The economic policies coming out of the Cultural Revolution again stress decentralization of light industry and the creation of small, self-reliant agri-industries in rural areas. These enterprises promote a fuller utilization of the locally available surplus and seasonal labor, including women. In the cities, there has been a new emphasis on creating and expanding small-scale neighborhood factories that employ housewives. For example, in Nanking in 1972, there were 500 such neighborhood enterprises employing 20,000 people, 75 percent of whom were women. Women served as directors in 300 of the 500 factories. It was reported that the total output value of neighborhood industries in Nanking was 43 times that of 1965.[80] These figures obviously indicate a policy of rapid expansion.

The expansion of this type of industry is significant because these factories provide women who otherwise would not find full-time wage-earning employment with the opportunity to do useful work outside the home. The wages are usually sufficient to increase family income noticeably and, therefore, create an incentive for women to rearrange family duties so they can work. Also, employment in some of these neighborhood factories is somewhat more flexible than in state factories so that women may be able, in special circumstances, to maneuver employment around heavy family demands. It should be noted, however, that this "flexibility" may simply encourage a situation where family women are expected to take up a job without decreasing their family burdens or changing the sexist division of labor within the home.

In spite of the fact that these neighborhood enterprises are in many ways an innovative and practical way to deal with women's employment in an undercapitalized economy, they are not, from the standpoint of sex equality, an adequate substitute for increasing the proportion of women recruited into the main industrial sectors. The "housewife factories" lack the status of other industries because they are engaged in production of subsidiary importance to the economy, frequently using discarded industrial equipment and wastes as their main source of capital. As indigenous, self-reliant undertakings that receive no state investment, the level of technology, working conditions, wage scale, and welfare benefits are necessarily far below the standards of state-run enterprises. A few of these "housewife factories" have been able to develop successfully into fairly mechanized, modern enterprises with increased wages, improved working conditions, and welfare services.[81] But for the most part the neighborhood industries constitute a second-class employment sector in which women predominate. At the same time, there is little evidence that the proportion of women in state industry has increased significantly since the Great Leap or that it will increase in the near future. Men continue to enjoy priority in recruitment into most modern sectors of the economy. Although occasional stories appear in the press about determined women who defy public opinion and expectations and successfully take up "men's tasks," [82] little effort has been made to alter significantly the basic patterns of recruitment.

After the height of the Cultural Revolution passed, concern for women's political participation and education also seemed to subside, and a more exclusive emphasis on productive work for women reemerged. Party branches again gave women's political work low priority. Interviews with several women leaders in 1971 revealed some current thinking on the issue of sex equality.[83] Many urban women cadres maintained that, as a result of the Cultural Revolution, women and men were now basically equal. Presumably, because the Cultural Revolution had been so effective in exposing and isolating serious revisionist thinking on women's equality, there was no longer need for special women's groups or special party work concerning the recruitment and training of women. In the factories, the women's association groups, like the trade unions, had been disbanded during the Cultural Revolution because of alleged political conservatism and their overemphasis on the special welfare privileges of state-employed workers. It was maintained now that working women did not need special representation for their welfare interests because they enjoyed full labor-insurance guarantees. Nor did they need special channels of representation for their political interests since these interests were the same as fellow men workers. The Revolutionary Committees and Party Committees within each factory represented the political interests of the working class, including women. The continued low representation of women on these committees was therefore not an urgent problem, but one that would naturally correct itself with time. The militant criticism and mobilization of the Cultural Revolution had apparently given way to efforts to achieve political conciliation and stability by depoliticizing grievances and conflicts. The problem of sex equality no longer seemed a salient political issue.

But current views on the nature of the problem of sex equality and how best to deal with it are not uniform. In late 1971, several articles appeared that again stressed the urgency of the problem and pointed out that too many party members do not take the issue seriously enough and resist efforts to promote sex equality. These articles asserted that remaining problems were not only serious ones, but that they involved issues central to the continuation of the revolution. One article argued that the central problem was the failure to recognize widespread male supremacist attitudes that still blocked the economic and political progress of women.[84]

One article, which appeared in the party's theoretical journal, *Red Flag*, recognized that practical difficulties such as insufficient socialized domestic services still exist. But it was stressed that these problems should not be used as an excuse to slow the progress of women's liberation, to subordinate women to housework, or to exclude them from political leadership.

> *Perhaps some comrades say: "A home must be run by somebody. This is a practical problem." . . . As long as we have the correct idea of supporting women to participate in the three great revolutionary movements, we will be able to think out ways to solve these practical problems, patriarchal ideas, vigorously promoting the "four olds" of the exploiting class, spreading the "theory that women are backward" and the "theory that women are useless," and stirring up the evil of pre-arranged marriages in order to disrupt the women's liberation movement. Within the ranks of the people, there still are present mistaken ideas of various sorts which belittle women and impede the coming into play of women's revolutionary strength. For this reason, to make a success of women's work is a serious class struggle as well as a battle for changing customs. We must not lose sight of this. As for the destructive activities of the class enemies, we should resolutely strike at them. As regards the various "four old" viewpoints that belittle women as promoted by the exploiting class, we should eliminate their influence through revolutionary mass criticism. . . . Party committees at various levels should put women's work on the order of the day and grasp it seriously and properly as an important task of struggle-criticism-transformation.*
>
> *We must continue to carry out Chairman Mao's proletarian revolutionary line, "wage a resolute struggle against the concepts of belittling the women's movement," and completely get rid of the old idea of having high regard for man and belittling women.[85]*

This emphasis probably represents a "radical" minority view within the party. The criticisms it and subsequent articles raise indicate that among party cadres there is resistance to implementing a special policy to train more women and to giving high priority to the issue of sex equality.

In contrast to this "radical" view, other women leaders have expressed the view that the use of frontal tactics to change the views of family members and men are disruptive and counterproductive. Lu Yu-lan, a prominent women's leader, implicitly argued for a somewhat different approach when she wrote:

> A current wrong idea is that women win their freedom by seizing control in the family and this wrong idea leads to a lot of fruitless quarrelling among husband, wife and in-laws . . . disrupted family harmony and failed to win public sympathy and achieve its aim. . . . Women began taking a broader view, to understand that to achieve their own emancipation they must look at things in terms of the entire society, to see the family as a basic social unit, as changing with the transformation of society as a whole. It was realized that after women take their position in society, changes in family relations will follow, and men and women can be equal.[86]

Again the emphasis is being placed on relying on broader socioeconomic changes to change family relations and women's status. During land reform and the campaign to enforce the Marriage Law, the political tactic of politicizing the personal grievances of women within the family was used to mobilize women and bring about political change. In this way, political struggle was brought into the private structure of family relationships in order to liberate women for political participation and productive work. The Cultural Revolution created a similar politicization of private attitudes and relations in order to raise political consciousness and release new energies for social and economic change. Some apparently felt that the ensuing tensions and fractionalizing in interpersonal relations caused too much disruption. When production was endangered, many leaders sought to restore stability through conciliation of various social groups and the depoliticization of interpersonal relations and grievances. Thus, Lu Yu-lan asserts that struggle within the family is counterproductive and fails to win support for women. Instead, she suggests that women should put more exclusive emphasis on taking up work and increasing their contribution to socialist construction. As a result of this participation, the family authority structure and attitudes that discriminate against women will be transformed.

But this approach tends to mask the still widespread existence of discriminatory attitudes and ignores the independent role that such culturally defined attitudes and norms can play in obstructing the progress of sex equality. Simply urging women to take a fuller part in production does not necessarily deal with the continuing existence of contradictory values and expectations imposed on women by family members and men, which make it difficult for women to achieve sex equality. For family members not only continue to expect women to respond to special obligations in ways that take up a greater proportion of their time, but they also impose norms regarding "proper" behavior and appropriate "women's work" that make it difficult for women to interact equally with men even after they take up productive work. The special emphasis on ideological reform among family members and men, as put forward by the "radicals" on the women's question, might help women resolve these tensions in favor of greater and more equal social participation by easing the pressure of traditional and proprietary family norms and obligations. From this perspective, some disruption of "family harmony" may be a necessary by-product of liberating women. It requires a reordering of family roles and a lessening of family control over the economic, social, and political activities of women. In contrast to this, the insistence that men and women are now "basically equal," that the Cultural Revolution swept away most of the remaining barriers, that equality will automatically accrue to women as they take up productive work, intentionally obscures the need to take special political action to further sex equality.

Recently, those concerned with the continuing inequality between the sexes seem to have received some top-level support for renewing a more politically activist approach. This effort apparently includes encouraging a more critical appraisal of current problems, and rebuilding and strengthening special women's organizations at all levels.[87] As mentioned, in 1971 such organizations were still inoperative in urban factories, and the dominant view seemed to be they were "no longer necessary." At the national level, too, attempts are underway to reconstitute the Women's Federation.

To date, progress for women has been fairly dependent on a general leadership commitment to the ideology of sex equality, prodded on by the small number of high-level women leaders. But the leadership has also been able quietly to shelve women's demands when these have not coincided with other interests and priorities. The initial militance of oppressed women in many areas during the family reform campaign indicated that many keenly perceived their inferior status and suffering. The issues raised by some women during the Cultural Revolution illustrated a continuing base of unfulfilled aspirations and perceived tensions. But women are a politically and culturally disadvantaged group with a unique history of social isolation. They have generally lacked the experience, awareness, and independent social resources necessary to turn their force into a consistent organized political force capable of compelling greater sensitivity to women's particular cultural and social handicaps. Without this organized power, women's groups have been unable to sustain their demands when these have met with resistance from stronger groups.

For the most part, various leadership groups have tended to view the liberation of women as primarily an economic problem and only secondarily a political and ideological problem. Thus policies have usually failed to deal directly with cultural barriers and traditional sexist attitudes. While women leaders might be more sensitive to these problems, they are a tiny minority among the top circles. Furthermore, many top women have in a sense been coopted by virtue of their past experiences and their individual success. For this small percentage of talented, educated, politically active women, most of whom have personal knowledge of the wretched female past, the new system has worked well. They are a symbolic testimonial that "women are liberated." Such radical symbolic changes may actually help to mask the fact that, for most women, real changes have been far less substantial.

However, the Cultural Revolution may have accelerated the creation of a new generation of young women leaders. These women, without personal knowledge of the wretched female oppression of the past, may be more conscious of the persistence of serious discrimination of the present. Like the Red Guards who, taking their elder's socialist ideal seriously, became critically aware of the elitist nature of established institutions before their elders in authority, young educated women may be more likely to take the propagated ideals of sex equality to demand more complete equality in politics, family life, and work. What is certain is that the struggle to make families, jobs, and opportunities equal has only begun. Liberation will be won only through protracted struggles—struggles that persistently raise issues of sex inequality to the level of political saliency and that overcome the ever present tendency to shelve these issues and mask continued inegalitarian practices and values.

NOTES

1. For example, see JAN MYRDAL, *Report from a Chinese Village* (New York: Signet, 1965), pp. 235, 241.

2. STUART SCHRAM, *The Political Thought of Mao Tse-tung* (rev. ed.; New York: Praeger, 1969), pp. 334–37.

3. For examples of writing that portray the brutal circumstances of women under the traditional family system, see PA CHIN, *The Family* (Peking: Foreign Languages Press, 1958); JOU SHIH, "Slave's Mother," CHAO SHU-LI, "Meng Xiang-ying Stands Up," LU HSÜN, "New Year's Sacrifice," in *Modern Chinese Short Stories*, tr. W. J. F. Jenner (London: Oxford University Press, 1970). One of the most poignant autobiographical stories recorded is "Gold Flower's Story," as told to author JACK BELDEN in *China Shakes the World* (New York: Monthly Review Press, 1970), pp. 275–307.

4. CHAO SHU-LI, in Jenner, *Short Stories*, p. 121.

5. C. K. YANG, *The Chinese Family in Communist Revolution* (Cambridge, Mass.: MIT Press, 1959), p. 139.

6. JOHN L. BUCK, *Land Utilization in China* (New York: Paragon Book, 1964), p. 292.

7. IRENE TAEUBER, "The Families of Chinese Farmers," in *Family and Kinship in Chinese Society*, ed. Maurice Freedman (Stanford: Stanford University Press, 1970), pp. 81–85.

8. Ibid., p. 3.

9. Mao Tse-tung makes this point in his "Report of an Investigation into the Peasant Movement in Hunan," in *Selected Works of Mao Tse-tung* (Peking: Foreign Languages Press, 1965), 1:44–47. In the original report, he also makes the point that poor peasant women enjoyed greater sexual freedom, although this was later deleted from the text. See SCHRAM, *Thought of Mao Tse-tung*, p. 258.

10. IDA PRUITT, *A Daughter of Han: The Autobiography of a Chinese Working Woman* (Stanford: Stanford University Press, 1967), p. 55.

11. HOU CHI-MING, "Man-power, Employment and Unemployment," in *Economic Trends in Communist China*, ed. Alexander Eckstein et al. (Chicago: Aldine, 1968), pp. 336–38. Underenumeration of females in population registration is also thought to contribute to the high sex ratios reported.

12. For an illustration of the special burdens imposed by poverty on women, see JOU SHIH, "Slave's Mother" in Jenner, *Short Stories*.

13. YANG, *Chinese Family*, p. 138.

14. Text of "The Marriage Law of the People's Republic of China, 1950" appears in ibid., pp. 221–26.

15. WILLIAM HINTON, *Fanshen* (New York: Random House, 1968), p. 159.

16. Ibid., p. 397.

17. Ibid.

18. For one account of these meetings and the psychological effect on women and their relationships with men, see BELDEN, *China Shakes the World*, pp. 288–307.

19. YANG, *Chinese Family*, pp. 69–71.

20. For example, see HINTON, *Fanshen*, p. 159.

21. See ISABEL and DAVID CROOK, *The First Years of Yangyi Commune* (London: Routledge & Kegan Paul, 1966), p. 241.

22. For example, see MYRDAL, *Chinese Village*, p. 252.

23. HINTON, *Fanshen*, pp. 353–54.

24. The village visited by Jan Myrdal, for example, appeared to little women's organizational work until 1955–56. See MYRDAL, *Chinese Village*, pp. 252, 255.

25. CH'EN YU-T'UNG, "Liquidation of the Old Legal View as a Condition for Thorough Implementation of the Marriage Law," *Hsin Chung-kuo Fu-nu* (New Chinese Women), no. 9 (September 1952): 7–8, cited in YANG, *Chinese Family*, pp. 81, 109. Also see YANG, pp. 107–10.

26. YANG, *Chinese Family*, pp. 36–39, 78–82.

27. MAO TSE-TUNG, *Socialist Upsurge in the Countryside*, vol. I (Peking, 1956), quoted in *Peking Review*, no. 11 (1964): 19.

28. JOHN PHILIP EMERSON, "Employment in Mainland China: Problems and Prospects," in *An Economic Profile of Mainland China* (New York: Praeger, 1968), p. 433.

29. Ibid., p. 433.

30. YANG, *Chinese Family*, p. 151.

31. Ibid.

32. AN TZU-WEN, "A Correct Approach to the Problem of Retirement of Women Cadres," *Chung-kuo Fu-nü* (Women of China), no. 2 (1 February 1958): 14–18.

33. ESTER BOSERUP, *Women's Role in Economic Development* (London: Allen & Unwin, 1970), pp. 194–96.

34. Ibid., pp. 196–200.

35. Ibid., pp. 206–7.

36. HOU, "Manpower," pp. 378–79.

37. Ibid., p. 377.

38. See FRANZ SCHURMANN, *Ideology and Organization in Communist China* (rev. ed.; Berkeley: University of California Press, 1968), pp. 469–74. Also see *Peking Review*, no. 10 (8 March 1960): 7.

39. EMERSON, "Employment," p. 435. Also see JOHN P. EMERSON, *Sex, Age and Level of Skill of Non-agricultural Labor Force of Mainland China* (Washington, D.C.: Foreign Demographic Analysis Division, Bureau of Census, 1965).

40. YANG, *Chinese Family*, p. 152.

41. EMERSON, "Employment," p. 433.

42. Ibid., p. 434. Also see HOU, "Manpower," p. 380.

43. EMERSON, "Employment."

44. YANG KAN-LING, "Family Life—the New Way," *Peking Review*, 18 November 1958, pp. 9–10.

45. *Peking Review*, 9 December 1958, p. 13.

46. YANG LIU, "Reform of Marriage and Family Systems in China," *Peking Review*, 13 March 1964, p. 19.

47. CHIN AI-LI, "Family Relations in Modern Chinese Fiction," in Freedman, *Family and Kinship*, pp. 87–120.

48. "Is a Daughter-in-law Obliged to Support Her Father-in-law and Mother-in-law?" *Chung-kuo Ch'ing-nien Pao* (Chinese Youth Journal), 12 May 1962, tr. *Selections from China Mainland Magazines*, no. 2756 (15 May 1962): 15.

49. For a discussion of "public assistance" and "social security" for workers, see JOYCE KALLGREN, "Social Welfare and China's Industrial workers," in *Chinese Communist Politics in Action*, ed. A. Doak Barnett (Seattle: University of Washington Press, 1969), pp. 540–73.

50. "Is a Daughter-in-law Obliged?"

51. JANET SALAFF, "Institutionalized Motivation for Fertility Limitation in China," *Population Studies* 26, no. 2 (July 1972): 243.

52. Ibid., p. 239.

53. EDGAR SNOW, *The Long Revolution* (New York: Random House, 1971), p. 44.

54. MYRDAL, *Chinese Village*, pp. 245–46.

55. "Pay Attention to the Development of Female Party Members," *Jen-min Jih-pao* (People's Daily), 13 September 1971, tr. *Current Background*, November 1971, pp. 9–10.

56. SALAFF, "Institutionalized Motivation," p. 256.

57. Ibid., p. 252.

58. Ibid., p. 257.

59. Ibid.

60. JAN MYRDAL and GUN KESSLE, *China: The Revolution Continued* (New York: Vintage, 1970), p. 134. Committee of Concerned Asian Scholars, *China! Inside the People's Republic* (New York: Bantam, 1972), p. 162.

61. "Development of Female Cadre Members."

62. JANET SALAFF, "The Role of the Family in Health Care" in *Medicine and Public Health in the People's Republic of China*, ed. Joseph R. Quinn (Washington, D.C.: U.S. Department of Health, Education, and Welfare, 1972), p. 40.

63. MYRDAL, *Chinese Village*, p. 252.

64. Interview with woman cadre, July 1971.

65. SALAFF, "Institutionalized Motivation," p. 252.

66. LU YU-LAN, "A Liberated Woman Speaks," in *New Women in New China* (Peking: Foreign Languages Press, 1972), p. 12.

67. SALAFF, "Institutionalized Motivation," p. 252.

68. Interviews, July 1971. Urban men usually acknowledge that they *ought* to share some household responsibilities. But most men and women readily admitted that the major responsibilities were still primarily looked after by women.

69. For a more detailed description of the early residents groups, see SCHURMANN, *Organization and Ideology*, pp. 274–80.

70. SALAFF, "Institutionalized Motivation," pp. 255–56.

71. BARRY RICHMAN, *Industrial Society in Communist China* (New York: Random House, 1969), pp. 304–5, 396.

72. "Bring the Role of Women into Full Play in Revolution and Construction," *Hung-ch'i* (Red Flag), no. 10, 1 September 1971, tr. *Selections from China Mainland Magazines*, October 1971, pp. 73–78.

73. Translated and cited by Salaff in JANET SALAFF and JUDITH MERKLE, "Women in Revolution: The Lessons of the Soviet Union and China," *Socialist Revolution* 1, no. 4 (July–August 1970).

74. *Great Cultural Revolution in China*, p. 181.

75. SALAFF and MERKLE, "Women in Revolution."

76. Ibid.

77. Interview, July 1971.

78. Interview, July 1971.

79. MYRDAL and KESSLE, *China*, p. 134.

80. *Peking Review*, 23 March 1973, p. 23.

81. *New Women in New China* (Peking: Foreign Languages Press, 1972), pp. 55–61.

82. YIN YI-PING, "Half the Population," in *The Seeds and Other Stories* (Peking: Foreign Languages Press, 1972), pp. 27–36.

83. The following account is derived from interviews and discussions with a number of middle- and upper-level women cadres in Shanghai and Sian, July 1971.

84. "Bring the Role of Women into Full Play."

85. Ibid., p. 78.

86. LU YU-LAN, "Liberated Woman," pp. 7–8.

87. See for example, "Working Women are a Great Revolutionary Force," *Jen-min Jih-pao* (People's Daily), 8 March 1973, tr. *Peking Review*, 16 March 1973.

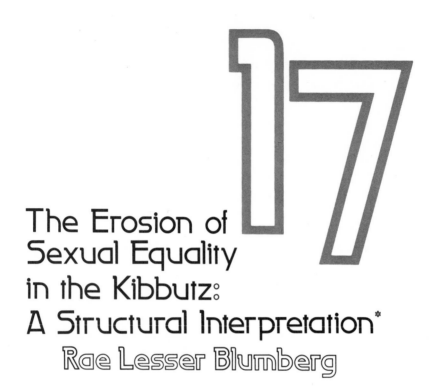

The Erosion of Sexual Equality in the Kibbutz: A Structural Interpretation*
Rae Lesser Blumberg

The Israeli kibbutz is perhaps best known in economic development circles as a living experiment in socialism that has proved a continuing economic miracle with respect to productivity. The first kibbutz was founded in 1909; today there are 233 of them, encompassing somewhat under 4 percent of the population of Israel. All but 17 of the kibbutzim are organized into three major federations varying largely in the purity of their socialist ideology. Nevertheless, all were founded upon, and remain faithful to, a collectivist economic system; all are characterized by a devotion to maximizing production for the kibbutz and the glories of work for the individual.

Not only are all means of production collectively owned, the service economy is collectivized as well. With few and minor exceptions, all children are raised in children's houses, meals are eaten communally, laundry is handled collectively, and private property of all sorts is minimized. Thus, economic equality has in fact been achieved with respect to distribution. But—and this is very important for the argument I present here concerning the erosion of women's position in the kibbutz—the kibbutz prestige system has always been organized to accord

* This article is based on "Women of the Kibbutz: Retreat from Sexual Equality" (Paper presented at the meetings of the Society for Applied Anthropology, Tucson, 1973). Two more detailed subsequent papers on this topic, framed in terms of a theory of structural factors affecting the status of women, are Blumberg 1974a and 1976a. The comments and criticisms of Haim Barkai, Pauline B. Bart, Dorit Padan-Eisenstark, Menacham Rosner, and Robert F. Winch are gratefully acknowledged.

320

maximum status to "productive"—i.e., capital creating—activities, as opposed to "service"—capital consuming—[1] activities. Moreover, within branches of productive activity, Spiro (1963:17) has gone so far as to suggest that those yielding the highest rate of return are deemed most important, and that the economic importance of the branch generalizes to the social importance of the person who works in that branch. Nonetheless, ideology remains officially egalitarian in all spheres—economic, social, and political.

Against this background must be seen the gradual but unrelenting emergence of the "problem of the woman"—testimony that for one group, reality has been increasingly falling short of the promised egalitarian millennium in matters economic, social, and political.

All major authorities (e.g., Spiro 1963, Rosner 1967, Rabin 1970, Talmon 1972, Gerson 1972) agree on the existence of two stages with respect to the status of women in the kibbutz:

Stage 1: In their early pioneering phase, the kibbutzim had little sexual division of labor and were characterized by a strongly egalitarian ideology with respect to sexual status. Not only did women drive tractors and work beside the men in the fields, but the service sector was absolutely minimal and more or less shared by both sexes.[2] During this stage, births were very rare.

Stage 2: Over time, the kibbutzim have gradually developed a highly sex-differentiated division of labor in which men do well-esteemed productive and managerial work, while women are overwhelmingly engaged in the service activities encompassing their traditional domestic role: cooking, washing, sewing, child care, etc. These service activities are of low prestige and—barring child care—generally considered drudgework. The "problem of the woman" consists in two major facts: (1) significant numbers of women are vocally unhappy with this state of affairs; and (2) some of the most dissatisfied women have pushed in a direction viewed by ideological purists as subversive to kibbutz collectivist ideals: They have been pressing for increased *private, familial* responsibilities. These demands have ranged from eating some meals alone with their families in their rooms to having their children sleep regularly in their quarters.

What I find most surprising in this literature is the paucity of analysis as to how the kibbutzim passed from Stage 1 to Stage 2. Perhaps this is understandable in view of the fact that most of these authorities view the passage as perhaps regrettable but nevertheless inevitable. They differ in the reasons cited, but tend to see the "drift of women back to their traditional roles and occupations" as largely *initiated by the women themselves.* The explanations tend to emphasize physical and psychological reasons for the "drift" of women into service occupations.

First, the physical reasons. Spiro and Talmon, for example, both mention that women could not completely replace men in certain agricultural tasks because the work was too hard—or too far away from the nurseries. Accordingly, Talmon suggests, it was considered "a waste to allow [women] to work in agriculture and at the same time assign able-bodied men to services" (p. 19).

Second, the psychological reasons. These abound in great numbers in the literature. They range from the maternal drives posited by the Freudians. Included also is the idea that group pressures from other women to spend more and more time with the children that led them to seek service jobs located closer to the nurseries (Shomgar, in interview with author, 1972), to the ingrained psychological habits resulting from centuries of oppression (Gerson 1972).

Third, the practical reasons. A corollary set of reasons involves the "naturalness" or "convenience" cited in having *women* be the ones to undertake service tasks that became inevitable once both affluence and children arrived.

In sum, these explanations concentrate on factors that "pull" women into service occupations. For the most part, women are viewed as the initiators of this response.

In the tentative explanation of the emergence of an unequal sexual division of labor which I attempt to develop in this paper, I try to turn the frame of reference upside down. In contrast to the above explanations, I propose a "push" explanation that emphasizes women being eased out, by forces over which they had little control, from productive to service activities. Furthermore, I propose, given the nature of the kibbutz as a social and productive system, this switch was accompanied by a slide into second-class citizenship, in what I characterize as an accelerating "positive feedback"[3] process.

Actually, several factors I mention in my proposed preliminary model of the process were mentioned by three of the major authors reviewed. But the authors in question never pursued the implications of these particular factors to seek an explanation not linked with the "manifest destiny" of women as to why an unequal sexual division of labor emerged in the kibbutz. The three authors and factors are:

1. Talmon. Her explanation focuses on the "convenience" of having women do service work, as opposed to the "waste" of having men do it. However, she also notes (as I too argue) that "sex differentiation in the occupational sphere was kept at a minimum as long as women were young and had few children, and as long as all efforts were concentrated in production and the standard of living was low." Even more relevant for my argument is the stress she places on the great expansion of the kibbutz service sector under the joint impact of a higher birthrate and a rising standard of living. She notes: "Nonproductive work now requires about 50 percent of all workers and absorbs most of the women, who usually number less than half of the kibbutz population" (p. 19).

2. Spiro. He sees reproduction and agricultural production as incompatible. Hence, as the birthrate increased, "more and more women were forced to leave the 'productive' branches of the economy and enter its 'service' branches." He goes on to make the important point: "But as they left the 'productive' branches, it was *necessary* that their *places* be *filled,* and they were *filled by men*" (1963:225, emphasis added). I shall be concerned with who these replacement males are.

3. Rabin. Citing an idea quite popular in this literature Rabin sees the early absence of a sexual division of labor in the kibbutz caused by the pathological zeal of the women to overidentify with male activities (i.e., agricultural production and political participation) in order to achieve equality[4]— He notes: "There was no attempt in the opposite direction—for *males* to assume the roles and functions that have been traditionally labeled as *feminine*" (1970:304, emphasis added).

Before going into my proposed explanation of the emergence of unequal sexual differentiation in the kibbutz, let me refer briefly to the model on which my explanation is ultimately based. This is one involving the nature of societal development that springs from my research on the relationship between societal complexity and familial complexity (see, e.g., Blumberg 1970; Blumberg and Winch

1972, 1973). My work in these areas has taught me that: (1) victims typically are blamed for situations caused by structural variables (e.g., the poor peasant is condemned for his failure to adopt agricultural innovations, and his lack of such alleged requirements for success as "need for achievement" ("nAch"), when the agricultural innovation in question requires credit to buy fertilizer for which he is not eligible, and involves a danger of variable yield which he cannot risk in his position on the far edge of subsistence); and (2) in general, technological, economic, and population factors are more likely to initiate changes in social organization and ideology than vice versa.

This second notion is shared by many non-Marxian as well as Marxian evolutionary theories. For example, Lenski (1970) argues that if the elements of sociocultural systems which can initiate social change are categorized as technological, social organizational, and ideological, the most important and frequent "autogenous source of change" is technology. Marxians also consider the technological component of the "mode of production" (see below) as the leading element in long-run social change. Supporting evidence comes from studies of both preliterate societies and contemporary developing and industrialized ones. With respect to preindustrial societies, see Gouldner and Peterson (1962) and Sheils (1969); with respect to contemporary nations, see Berry (1960), Schnore (1961), Adelman and Morris (1967), and Sawyer (1967). All have found that the most important factor in accounting for the level of development is a technological-economic one. Moreover, our work (e.g., Blumberg and Winch 1973) supports this as well. We have found that subsistence technology explains a significant proportion of variance in familial organization in a large sample of preindustrial societies.

Figure 17.1 presents a schematic representation of the paradigm concerning the primary sources of social change with respect to family organization which guided the Blumberg and Winch 1973 study. It is presented here because the top four boxes—1A through 3—are conceived as the primary locus of *most* changes in social organization and ideology over the great sweep of human existence. Moreover, these same four boxes will be invoked in the present attempt at a structural explanation of why sexual equality eroded in the Israeli kibbutz. Three of these four boxes (1A, 2, and 3) collectively refer to a society's "mode of production"; box 1B involves the environmental and demographic matrix in which the mode of production is located.

The *mode of production* is concerned not only with the techno-economic system by which the society supports itself, but also with who controls the means and benefits of production. In fact, most definitions of the mode of production (see, e.g., Edwards et al., 1972:50) divide it into two principal components: (1) the *"forces of production,"* which encompass the technology, equipment, and work organization involved; and (2) the *"social relations of production,"* which tell us about the extent to which the society produces a surplus and who controls both the factors and fruits of production. In Figure 17.1, the social relations of production are shown in box 3, while boxes 1A and 2 present what I have conceptualized as the two main aspects of the forces of production: first (and ultimately the most influential), the techno-economic base (Box 1A, *Subsistence Technology*), and second, the *nature* and *division of labor* of the work involved (Box 2).

It is important to note that even though Box 1A, *Subsistence Technology*, is accorded somewhat more weight over the long run, it is considered to be in reciprocal interaction with 1B, *Environmental and Demographic Potentialities and Constraints*. In terms of the raw impact of the environment, this factor is undoubtedly more important in very simple societies with a low level of technology. Nevertheless, if the demographic structure and population pressures with respect to environment and labor force are taken into account, this box is of major importance in accounting for social change at any level of societal complexity. (For example, Boserup 1965 has marshaled impressive evidence that population pressure is the driving force in causing agricultural societies to increase the intensity of cultivation.)

Tied into these are what may be phrased "first order economic consequences." On the one hand, we have Box 2, *Nature of Work and Division of Labor*, which we conceptualize as including *both* the occupational and sexual division of labor, as well as the units and organization of labor. Thus, one of the main questions concerning the division of labor is that of the sexual division of labor, or more to the point, the contribution of women to subsistence in a given society. It is known that different subsistence bases typically involve greater or lesser female participation. Specifically, analysis of the 1170 preindustrial societies included in Murdock's 1967 Ethnographic Atlas shows, for example, the hunting, herding, or fishing of large species as male activities; whereas gathering or shifting hoe agriculture typically are performed by a predominantly female labor force. Conversely, an agrarian mode of production (plow agriculture on permanent fields) involves the switch to a male primary labor force. And, as will be stressed below, an agrarian base was the one chosen by the kibbutz.

The next box is 3, *Surplus and Control of Means of Production*. Once the means of generating a consistent surplus are at hand in a given society, how that surplus is concentrated, and how this affects access to the means and fruits of production, become perhaps the immediate determinants of life chances for the majority in the society.

Since Boxes 2 and 3 too are seen in reciprocal interaction, it would be conceivable to lump Boxes 1A through 3 in figure 17.1 into a single cluster incorporating what we may title (following Marvin Harris's 1968 argument) the "techno-economic-ecological" complex. Less awkwardly, it could be termed the *subsistence environment* impinging on a group. Thus, "subsistence environment" is a conceptualization attempting to integrate recent sociological and anthropological evolutionist approaches (e.g., Lenski 1966, 1970; Duncan 1964; Goldschmidt 1959; Harris 1968; see also Childe 1950, 1951; Steward 1955; White 1949, 1959) with Marxian and demographically oriented (e.g., Boserup 1965, Harner 1970) formulations. In sum, I interpret the evidence as indicating that this "subsistence environment" complex more frequently generates change in the social organizational and ideological systems of a society than vice versa, and that the root explanatory variables of both familial organization and the status of women are incorporated within this rubric.

I shall now attempt a tentative explanation of the erosion of the status of women in the kibbutz in terms of the major variables involved in this model of "subsistence environment," i.e., the combination of mode of production and environment/population constraints.

We must begin by recalling that the kibbutz began with an agrarian subsistence technological base—one that would seem to make it an uphill struggle to

Figure 17.1   Tentative Model of Determinants of Familial Organization[a]

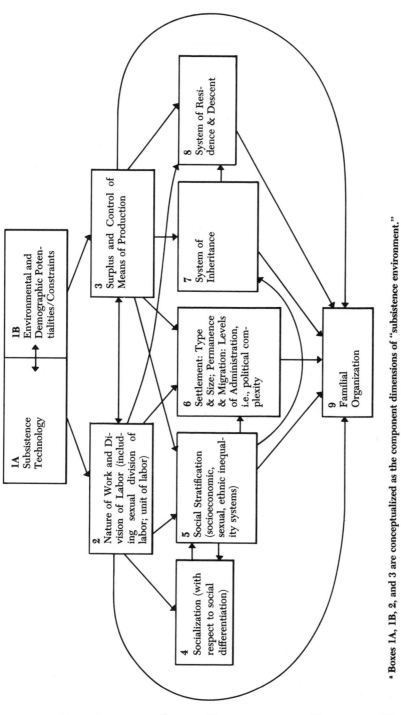

[a] Boxes 1A, 1B, 2, and 3 are conceptualized as the component dimensions of "subsistence environment."

implement and maintain sexual equality, given that in other societies practicing it: (1) women are almost never important contributors to production; and (2) women are almost always severely subjugated (see, e.g., Michaelson and Goldschmidt 1971).

Furthermore, the kibbutz founders chose *socialism* as their system for the economic and social relations of production. A number of implications follow from their version of socialism in addition to the fact that neither men nor women control an independent "piece of the action." In the context of the kibbutz these implications include the greater importance attributed to "productive" as opposed to "service" activities; and the fact that from the start the kibbutz has been economically rational, and has striven to maximize production within the constraints imposed by its socialist ideology and available resources. This stress on economic growth has further emphasized the higher evaluation of productive activities that boost what may be termed "GKP"—Gross Kibbutz Product.

One other point derived from the founders' socialist ideology must be mentioned, since it has demographic consequences which, I shall argue, affected the status of women in the kibbutz. This is the notion that the kibbutz's labor must be "self labor"—not that of hired workers. Accordingly, it is not surprising that the kibbutz encouraged immigration from the start. In the beginning, it saw itself as a revolutionary vanguard and was committed also to expanding the size of this vanguard.

Although it has remained an island in a nonsocialist society, in general the kibbutz has managed to live up to its founding principles quite well—except in the area of de facto (vs. de jure) sexual equality. Let us turn now to how, when, and why women's status declined.

My tentative historical sequence of the retreat from sexual equality in the kibbutz involves five arbitrary phases: (1) the revolutionary, pioneering phase; (2) institutionalization; (3) growth (and immigration); (4) the downward spiral of women's status; and (5) recent trends (including industrialization).

THE "REVOLUTIONARY," PIONEERING STAGE

This stage involves the struggle to achieve economic survival and encompasses the preproduction phases of clearing and preparing the land, as well as the first production phase. Ideology was sometimes almost literally the main nourishing force, and all hands were needed for the enormous labor demands required at this stage. Accordingly, all women tended to participate in "productive activities." Moreover, the service sector was very small, with catch-as-catch-can allocation of clothing and laundry, and the common pot for much of the food. These tasks were shared by both sexes, although, as noted, certain authorities emphasize that this was done less than equally in many kibbutzim. Demographically, at this stage women comprised only 20–35 percent of the membership, according to Talmon (1972:9), and children were rare.

INSTITUTIONALIZATION

Once the kibbutz "turned the corner on survival," it may be hypothesized that most energy still had to be devoted to subsistence. However, goals of efficiency presumably gained in impact as the first tide of revolutionary fervor receded. This would involve attempts to maximize—and reinvest—surplus. The mechanisms for stimulating output were increased technological inputs and capital investments; an additional result would be the beginning of a decrease in required labor intensity per unit of production. Descriptive materials on the kibbutz indicate that births began to occur around this point. Apparently, the slight increase in economic well-being and the slight drop in labor requirements permitted the temporary release from full-time production of women during the period surrounding childbirth—and the *permanent* release of a few women to care for the babies. Ironically, for all their egalitarian ideology, kibbutzim never assigned men to infant care (see, e.g., Gerson, Talmon). Furthermore, the presence of children placed additional demands militating for an expansion in the service sector because the high value placed on children in the kibbutz meant more of an investment in nutrition, laundry, and nurseries—not just in child care.

GROWTH

At this stage, the kibbutz grew in all areas. Production increased, spurred by maximum use of available capitalization and technological inputs; and the size of the service sector rose precipitously, as the standard of living was permitted to rise and more and more children were born. Moreover, at this stage, immigration to the kibbutzim constituted an important factor in their growth. By this time, the kibbutz had slid from its pioneering "revolutionary" phase into a second "economic" phase (see, e.g., Talmon), in which efficiency—particularly economic efficiency—came to yield relatively greater rewards than ideology. What was to prove crucial for the fate of the women in the kibbutz was the continuing influx of a labor force that may well have been viewed as more efficient. Young, childless, predominantly *male* immigrants were arriving, attracted to the kibbutz for ideological reasons.

It is my hypothesis that the handling of the new immigrants provided the key choice-point with respect to the continuation of a sexually egalitarian division of labor in the kibbutz. From an ideological standpoint, the immigrants had to be received with open arms: as noted, the early kibbutzim believed themselves to be a revolutionary vanguard and were committed to growth. Moreover, and more importantly, the immigrants provided the kibbutz with a way to minimize the ideologically abhorrent use of outside hired labor. Even though many pioneer-era kibbutzim at this point in their growth were suffering from the effects of the Depression, it appears that the service sector was continuing its inexorable process of expansion, and the kibbutzniks were eager as ever to encourage growth in production.

Who would be sent to the expanding service sector, and who would be sent to the fields? At this point, the kibbutz *could* have preserved the still relatively egalitarian sexual division of labor and status by enforcing a strict *seniority* principle in the assignment of the high-prestige agricultural production activities— a principle already being followed in the allocation of other scarce goods such as newly constructed housing. Presumably, this would have meant assigning the new arrivals to the unglamorous service tasks such as laundry and kitchen. This would have freed most of the young pioneer mothers to return to productive tasks. The immigrants went overwhelmingly to the fields, however, and more and more of the young mothers ended up in domestic and child-care services. What happened and why?

For one thing, Barkai (1971) has found that the attempts of the kibbutzim to increase production tended to lead them to further emphasis on agrarian production of dry (cereal) crops and animal husbandry. An important reason for the ever-growing emphasis on these *macho* activities springs from the kibbutz bookkeeping system. As orthodox socialists, the kibbutzniks believe in the "labor theory of value": that of the factors of production (labor, land, capital), only labor results in added value. So they designed an internal accounting system that ignores the prices of land and capital and calculates only how much *labor* is needed to produce the output of each branch of agricultural activity. This is called the "income per labor day" approach, according to Barkai, who criticizes it as unrealistic. Yet, it seems to have influenced kibbutz decisions on the sorts of farming activities to be pursued. Moreover, it has turned out to be an obstacle to female participation in production. We have noted previously that the empirical evidence of the 1170 societies of the Ethnographic Atlas shows plow agrarian pursuits to be a predominantly male preserve, while women tend to be the main labor force in hoe horticulture. As it happens agrarian cultivation involves large fields and uses considerable land but relatively little labor. Conversely, horticultural production is the opposite: higher labor inputs on smaller plots. So the activities which tend to have female labor forces worldwide look bad in the kibbutz accounting ledgers, in comparison with the *macho* agrarian crops.

What seems to have happened is that the "female farming" horticultural activities were militated against, at least in part, by accounting procedures; whereas the alternative, the agrarian activities, seemed to militate against female participation. Concerning the latter, the *distance* to the far-flung cereal-crops fields is often mentioned as an inconvenience factor hindering kibbutz women in agrarian work once they became mothers. They were and are expected to visit their children for breastfeeding or affection at least once during the work day—an inconvenient and tiring round trip from the fields. (This trip is minimized for those doing horticultural activities, which tend to be located much closer to the center of the kibbutz where the nurseries, and adult eating, laundering, and living facilities are found.) Additionally, plow agriculture may involve more of a need for physical strength than horticultural cultivation—and so women have tended to be perceived as being at a physical disadvantage for field crops work.

There is evidence that kibbutz women became concerned quite early in the game about the emphasis on agrarian activities and the concomitant danger of their being squeezed out of production: A large 1966 conference on the problems of women voiced their fears (see Viteles, 1967 for the proceedings). Moreover, the women at the conference explicitly requested more emphasis on horticultural-type vegetable and tree crops, at which they claimed to feel themselves at no disadvantage to males.

Perhaps without the continuing arrival of the immigrants, and given the kibbutz's reluctance to use outside hired labor, it might have heeded the women's requests and ultimately would have achieved a mix of production activities that included more of those favored by the women. But the immigrants did arrive, and as a minimum eliminated any incipient pressure on the kibbutz to reduce its emphasis on the "glamor" agrarian field crops. According to Padan-Eisenstark (1963b), enough women disliked working in these field activities to cause them not to insist on strict seniority in production when the immigrants arrived. Padan-Eisenstark argues that perhaps these women resented that their choice was so narrow—participation in an economic base that included few congenial activities or relegation to the domestic services from which they had presumably been liberated. However, she believes that a number of women did tend to view the service sector as the "lesser of two evils." It should be pointed out that about half the workers in services are occupied in the well-esteemed "childhood education" sector consisting of the children's houses and their classrooms. But from the start the remaining service tasks (kitchen, laundry, etc.) have been viewed as mere drudgework, and it is to these activities that the "lesser of two evils" notion would presumably apply.

I, however, prefer to emphasize the other side of the coin. With the immigrants being viewed as a more desirable, efficient labor force in the kibbutz's main "glamor" sector, "lesser of two evils" interpretations may emphasize justification after the fact on the part of many of the women. Other factors as well militated for sending the immigrants to the fields and creating a de facto situation where more and more of the young pioneer *mothers* were replaced in production.

These other factors revolved around two foci: On the one hand, the service sector had become institutionalized and a necessity to the economy that must continue to be staffed, regardless of the labor demands of production. On the other hand, the commitment of the immigrants could well be viewed as conditional. After all, the immigrants overwhelmingly consisted of young males who were overeducated to be peasants were it not for their strong ideological commitments. Moreover, the ideology that attracted the immigrants emphasized the vision of pioneering it out on the tractors of revolution with one's comrades (as opposed to perhaps an initial three-year stint of laundry and pots and pans under a strong seniority system). The immigrants began with few personal ties in the kibbutz that might keep them there, as contrasted with the tremendous emotional and physical investment of the young pioneer mothers. It may therefore be inferred that the pioneer mothers would be less likely to leave if assigned the least-rewarding service tasks. All of the above, coupled with the perception of the male as more efficient in agrarian production, resulted in quite a powerful "push" toward both sending the immigrants to the fields and making the service sector "women's work." And from that point on, I propose, it was all downhill for the kibbutz women.

THE DOWNWARD SPIRAL OF WOMEN'S STATUS

At this point, I would like to suggest, a "positive feedback" process began. "Positive feedback" is the systems theory concept Flannery (1971) invokes to account for the emergence of agriculture among hunting and gathering groups. An initially small, temporary, or insignificant change sets off other, continually intensifying, escalating changes, until "you can't go home again." (Note: In the emergence of agriculture hypothesis, genetic changes in the plants, increasing population density, the rescheduling of the group's annual food procurement cycle, and the consequent impact on the ecological balance of the area ultimately—over hundreds and hundreds of years—made a return to hunting and gathering unprofitable and probably impossible. Flannery's hypothesis thus provides the *mechanism* for the gradual shift to agriculture, but Meyers [1971] has criticized his theory as incomplete in that it doesn't explain *why* the groups in question picked up on these changes. Meyers posits *population pressure,* either due to in-migration [Binford 1971], or internal growth [Meyers] as the force that made it advantageous for the affected groups to intensify subsistence efficiency by pushing agriculture [and accelerating the positive feedback]. My use of "positive feedback" as the mechanism of the erosion of sexual equality is somewhat analogous, but I do not argue that the process is irreversible insofar as the women of the kibbutz are concerned. In fact, in the next section of this paper I discuss changes in the techno-economic and demographic base of the kibbutz that may initiate a "new shuffle of the deck" vis-à-vis the status of its women.)

The "positive feedback" argument with respect to the kibbutz stems from my positing that women began to enter the low-valued service tasks just as an alternate source of labor appeared. This labor supply made it possible to replace them in production—thereby freezing them into a sector due to undergo enormous and continued expansion as the standard of living—and the birthrate—in the kibbutz rose. The situation today is such that the service jobs typically account for more than 50 percent of the labor force, and around 90 percent of the women (see, e.g., Viteles 1967, Spiro 1963). It is a moot point whether the services would have become so labor-swollen if there had remained production branches where the kibbutz women could have been employed in large numbers.

This segregation of the women in the service sector was accompanied by secondary consequences that reduced their status and level of political participation as a group, in an accelerating downward slide. Basically, I propose that two sets of factors accelerated this "positive feedback": on the one hand, the vicious circle stemming from women working in activities which are lowly esteemed; and on the other, the attempts by the dissatisfied women to make the best of a bad situation.

1. *The vicious circle: helping the victims blame themselves.* As noted, the service sector has always been held in low esteem for a combination of reasons that include an ideology stressing the importance of production, a feeling that services drain scarce kibbutz resources (vs. contributing to capital), and the intrinsically drudgework nature of most of its nonchild-related jobs. Women, like everyone else, are valued on the basis of the perceived value of their occupational branch. Thus, those women working in services other than childhood education were low valued—both by those working in other activities (i.e., predominantly men), and by *themselves.* These feelings of inferiority as a function of work assignment emerge quite clearly in Rosner's empirical findings (1967). Moreover, in historical terms, as women shrank as a percentage of the productive labor force, they began to lose their voice in the important decision making of the kibbutz. For one thing, women became less prominent participators in the "town meeting" direct democracy of the kibbutz. But, more importantly, as women's role in production declined, they all but disappeared from the economic committees in which real power in the kibbutz has almost from the first resided. Women today are fully represented only

on the committees related to consumer services and childhood education (e.g., see Rabin 1970).

In sum, men thus came to control not just the economically productive occupations, but the managerial functions as well, while women in service jobs or even service-related committees came to be looked upon as less than equal partners by both the men and themselves. (Kibbutz admiration, however, continues to be given to those few of their sisters who hang on in production or kibbutz office; the official ideology continues to proclaim sexual equality.)

This loss in self-esteem, male evaluation, and real power, I argue, made the perpetuation and increase of women in low-evaluated service jobs even more likely and "natural."

2. *The push for domestic responsibilities for women further erodes their status.* Women fed up with a job involving "cleaning, *or* cooking, *or* sewing, *or* washing, *or* taking care of children all day long" (Spiro 1963:229) began to advocate that they be given increased participation in the pleasures of their own family's domestic concerns—from occasional family meals to highly controversial demands of having their children sleep in their parents' quarters rather than the children's house.

Although supported by many men, this movement did *not* extend to those women who worked in productive activities or held kibbutz office, according to Talmon (1972:111). This led her to conclude that women's dissatisfaction with their (service) work was the primary reason for their dissatisfaction with the kibbutz communalization of family arrangements. Simultaneously with the push for increased private, familial responsibilities came a call for lowering the occupational work hours of married women so as to make up for the additional hours they now had to devote to domestic responsibilities with their families. This push was noticeably less successful than that for increased domestic familism. Nevertheless, given the kibbutz attitude toward work, this probably resulted in further erosion of women's status. My own data from 1972 indicate that managers of productive branches in particular used this as self-evident proof of the lesser value of women to the kibbutz and as further justification for their reluctance to give "real" productive jobs to women who would lose hours each day attending to family concerns (interview with Leshem, 1972).

RECENT TRENDS (INCLUDING INDUSTRIALIZATION)

Let us now examine a number of trends affecting the kibbutzim that may have consequences for the present sexual division of labor and the actual status of women. In keeping with the conceptual approach of this paper, I shall concentrate on trends that affect the variables constituting the kibbutz "subsistence environment" (Boxes 1A–3 in figure 17.1).

First and foremost is the "industrial revolution" that is coming to the kibbutz. Beginning in the 1950s, and accelerating greatly in the last decade, has been a move to industry that seems even more of a production miracle than the original agrarian base. Since I take the position that it has been the agrarian mode of production—plus the arrival of the immigrants—that underlies the inability of the kibbutzim to maintain sexual equality, a major shift in the subsistence base must be viewed as having great potential consequences for the women of the kibbutz. Initially, many kibbutzim were attracted to setting up some industry as a solution to the problems of the aging pioneer generation, especially the men who had become too old for fieldwork.[5] However, industry seems to be affecting women as well. Even though women are almost everywhere around 10 percent of the kibbutz agricultural labor force (see, e.g., Viteles 1967:333, 336; Spiro 1963:225), Leviatan (1972) notes that women are about *30 percent* of the labor force in kibbutz industry. Some reasons *why* women are gaining a substantial place in industrial production are considered below. Here, it is enough to note that kibbutz industry is proving even more profitable than agriculture. For many kibbutzim, industrial enterprises already contribute proportionately even more to "GKP" than the former agrarian "glamor" sector focused around field crops. As women become more represented in a high-productivity area of the kibbutz economy, then, their participation in related committees and office *might* be expected to increase, with the generalized advantages to their status that this should entail.

Several additional factors involving changes in the techno-economic base also should be mentioned. For one thing, some kibbutzim have been.experimenting with service activities that *do* contribute to "GKP." According to Rosner (1972 interview with author), these range from providing computer software assistance to setting up research institutes for (outside) clients. He also notes that women are well-represented in these new activities.

Even in agriculture, a technologically advanced new productive activity may provide opportunities for women. One such example is the introduction of "hothouse crops." These involve horticultural production of highly perishable items such as certain fruits and even flowers, which can be flown to Europe during the winter. Apparently, women have been able to get in on this new production branch from the start. Significantly, the head of the inter-kibbutz–Hebrew University advanced training institute for kibbutz production managers and general managers has found that an increasing number of the very few females sent by their kibbutzim to their most elite training institution come from the new production branch of "hothouse crops" (Sharon, 1972 interview). In fact, the percentage of women enrolled at the institute in mid-1972 amounted to 6 percent of 220 students, i.e., 14 women. According to Sharon, only 2 of the 14 are studying general management. The others are scattered across the three-year production manager curriculum, and almost all come from the few non-field crop agricultural branches in which female participation never was eliminated: for example, poultry, dairy, and now the new hothouse crops.

Changes are also starting to take place in the service sector. At last, perhaps because of the additional demands for labor posed by industry, and/or the arrival of sufficient affluence, investment *is* taking place in the "drudgework" (and labor intensive) services such as laundry, kitchen, dining hall, and so on. This is not only an answer to years of goading from dissatisfied women, but is also having the consequences of reducing labor intensity in the services and introducing occasional males in the mechanized sectors of these services. Per Leshem (1972 interview), a few males have entered as technicians—for example, to service the new equipment in an automatic laundry. Since these services still are not viewed as contributing to the economy, all this would seem to do is decrease the pressure that service slots be filled by women and increase their availability for industry and other new, capital-creating activities.

The above discussion has centered on changes affecting the subsistence base and distribution of the labor force, i.e., the factors treated in Boxes 1A and 2 of Figure 17.1. No substantial changes are anticipated with respect to the kibbutz handling of its socialist relations of production (Box 3). However, new trends have emerged affecting the size and nature of the potential labor force. It is to these demographic factors (see Box 1B) that we now turn.

First, even though immigration to Israel has continued over the last couple of decades, little of that immigration has been attracted to the kibbutz. (The kibbutzim are now primarily dependent on internal rates of population growth to maintain their numbers. Apparently, kibbutz birthrates have been above replacement rate for a long time.) Instead of a stream of ideologically committed immigrants to handle the labor requirements of agrarian production, the kibbutzim of late have been attracting a new source of *temporary* labor: youth groups and students from the developed countries who come to visit and work in the kibbutzim for brief periods, especially in the summer. Accordingly, at these periods kibbutzim have many temporary voluntary workers to help in the least desirable service tasks, as well as in seasonal fieldwork.

On the other hand, kibbutz reluctance to use outside labor—especially hired labor—continues strong, and is causing somewhat of a crisis because of the labor requirements of industry. Kibbutzim *have* been making somewhat greater use of hired labor in industry (even though as a proportion of total labor force, Barkai 1971 notes that hired labor has barely risen from its long-maintained 8 percent level), and self-criticism has been great. Unless such schemes as joint ownership with a non-kibbutz group are accepted as ideologically permissible justifications for large hired labor forces, kibbutzim will be looking for ways to free additional workers from within their membership to work in kibbutz industry. Kibbutz industry itself is clearly here to stay. Given the drying up of immigration to the kibbutz and the total unacceptability of child labor, that leaves only kibbutz adults. With so many kibbutz men working in agricultural production branches where labor intensivity is already minimal, the solution is to reduce labor intensivity in the remaining branches. And that means primarily services, and primarily women workers, who will be freed for industry.

A final demographic constraint on kibbutz sexual division of labor must be mentioned: the male battle deaths resulting from two high-casualty wars between 1967 and 1973. Because kibbutz males are more likely to be engaged in actual ground or air combat than other Israeli men, their losses have been even higher, proportionately. One likely consequence of this tragic aftermath of war, then, could be a more intensive use of female members in all labor-short areas of production.

So much for the components of "subsistence environment." Are there other possible sources of change in the position of women in the kibbutz?

On the one hand, the recent resurgence of a worldwide women's movement (which was totally lacking both in the kibbutz and elsewhere in the days of the erosion of kibbutz women's position) could have consequences for the kibbutz. Whether or not kibbutz women organize on their own behalf, the "movement" itself could provide impetus and ideological backing for changes in the sexual division of labor and status of women along the new lines suggested above. Naturally, if kibbutz women organize, these changes might be faster and farther-reaching. Whether they will in the face of recent war and strong perceived threats to national security (which have had the effect on Israel as elsewhere of muting domestic discord "for the duration") is problematic. At any rate, no one has yet written of the emergence of "consciousness-raising rap groups" among the women of the kibbutzim.

An even less likely development, in my opinion, is the "greening" of the kibbutz under conditions of ever increasing affluence. There *has* been an increasing stress on "self-actualization," particularly among the youth, but in conjunction with an increased emphasis on education and professional training as a basis of prestige. So, while it may be that one no longer need be a tractor-driving cereal crop branch manager to be a kibbutz culture hero, I would argue that the kibbutz is unlikely to accept the notion that everyone's work has equal value. For a generation this latter attitude has been periodically and vainly pushed by kibbutz leaders as a solution to the "problem of the woman" for the last generation (Viteles 1967).

CONCLUSIONS

Thus, my suggested explanation of the erosion of sexual equality in the kibbutz has focused not around psychological or physiological factors but around structural ones that I propose to be the predominant wellsprings of *most* major social changes. I have presented four components of what I term "subsistence environment" (1. subsistence technology; 2. environmental constraints, including demographic factors; 3. nature of work and division of labor; and 4. surplus, capital, and relation to means of production). And I have suggested that the major variables responsible for the decline in women's position in the kibbutz can be subsumed under these dimensions of "subsistence environment." Moreover, in the preceding section on possible trends, I have once again concentrated on these same variables: changes in technological inputs and subsistence activity mix (e.g., industrialization) in the kibbutz economy, resulting changes in labor-force requirements, the arrival of outside workers (but now temporary volunteers as opposed to the ideologically oriented permanent immigrants who figured in the erosion of women's position), changes in the service sector, etc.

Nevertheless, although this paper *orients* itself around the components of "subsistence environment," it is beyond its scope to try to weave them into a systematic theory. (The task of developing a paradigm of structural factors affecting the power and position of women cross-societally is undertaken in Blumberg 1974b, and utilized in Blumberg 1976b. I am presently testing the paradigm with a 61-society pilot sample; felicitously, the results to date support the hypotheses.)

But systematically developed or not, the factors presented in this paper do seem to indicate the outlines of a plausible structural alernative to the extant literature explaining what happened to the women of the kibbutz in psychobiological terms. The extant interpretation in the literature shares with this one the conclusion that the kibbutz ideology of sexual equality proved insufficient, despite good intentions, to save either the best-regarded jobs or the high status of the women. The explanations differ as to why this is so.

My structural interpretation takes off from the mode of production chosen by the kibbutz founders: agrarian socialism. Their choice of agrarian production committed them to a techno-economic base that has proven hostile ground for female equality almost anywhere and everywhere. In part, this has been because of agrarian production's relative incompatibility with baby-care responsibilities, especially breastfeeding (see, e.g., Brown 1970 and Murdock and Provost 1973 for further consideration of this point). Kibbutz socialism committed them, among other things, to absorb immigrants, shun hired labor, and extol sexual equality. But the (mostly male) kibbutz pioneers did not work out the contradictions in their ideology and practice. For example, their internal accounting system stacked the deck against the kinds of farm work the women preferred, but there is no evidence that this was considered.[6] Nor did they seem to examine critically their culturally tinged commitments to low-rating the value of domestic and child related service work—or having women be the ones to take over *all* tasks related to small children.

Given this set of circumstances relating to the kibbutz's chosen mode of production, it appears that the retreat from sexual equality was sparked by a demographic factor: the young, childless, mostly male stream of immigrants which flowed into the early kibbutz. This made it possible for the kibbutz to devote ever more attention to the childcare-incompatible agrarian field crops, which the women disliked. In this way, females were slowly eased out of what came to be virtually the only "productive" jobs around, and into the domestic and childcare jobs that were virtually the only remaining spheres open to them.

Obviously, further research is needed. But as a minimum, my suggested interpretation would seem to make it difficult to continue to attribute the fate of the kibbutz women to a unilateral and deterministic view that, due to the intrinsic nature of human females, "Laundry is Destiny."

NOTES

1. Since the sources consulted break down the kibbutz economy into "productive" vs. "service" sectors, I continue this practice throughout the paper—although recognizing that many economists are unhappy with such a simple dichotomy (e.g., BARKAI, private communication with author, 1973).

2. Sources differ in their emphasis on the degree of initial equality in the pioneer kibbutz's nascent service sector, with BARKAI, PADAN-EISENSTARK, and ROSNER, in 1973 communications with the author, asserting that women did more of the "domestic" services even from the start.

3. This is a cybernetic term for a process in which an initially small, perhaps even accidental change in a system causes ever increasing reverberations. They can be good or bad—"positive" feedback is a deviance amplification process, as opposed to "negative" feedback, which is a self-regulating, or homeostatic, process. "Positive feedback" is further discussed below. See also FLANNERY 1971, MARUYAMA 1963.

4. A fourth authority is relevant at this point: PADAN-EISENSTARK. In 1973 discussions with the author she emphasized two points. First, in the agrarian mode of production chosen by the (mostly male) kibbutz founders, women never have achieved equality anywhere in the world. And second, the kind of fieldwork involved in agrarian production was not viewed favorably by many women who wanted to work in "production activities" but

not those required by the kibbutz's agrarian economic base. Accordingly, they reluctantly opted for "service" as the "lesser of two evils" when given the choice. PADAN-EISENSTARK's first point is especially relevant for the argument I present.

5. TALMON presents clear evidence that both sexes agree it's harder for a woman than a man to grow old in the kibbutz; and older women tend to be even less happy than their younger sisters. This apparently runs counter to her cyclic theory of productive labor for the young girl, service and child-care for the early child-rearing years, and then opportunities for increased "social participation." Moreover, data on female representation in the kibbutz political structure, for example (see SPIRO 1963, RABIN 1970, and references summarized in RABIN), show women underrepresented, apparently regardless of age, in all but service-related committees. Furthermore, it appears that as women age, their work assignments tend to slip from the relatively well-esteemed childhood education sector to the "lower depths" of kitchen, laundry, and so on. See BART 1969, 1971 for discussions of middle-aged women in other cultural contexts.

6. Actually, the evidence on the early days of the kibbutz tends to be mainly impressionistic, anecdotal, spotty, and/or partisan (see, e.g., LEON, 1964 for this latter quality). Recent trends are better documented.

REFERENCES

ADELMAN, IRMA, AND MORRIS, CYNTHIA TAFT. *Society, Politics, and Economic Development.* Baltimore, Md.: Johns Hopkins University Press, 1967.

ANONYMOUS. *Statistical Data on the Kibbutz Population as of 30 September 1970.* Tel Aviv: Central Control Commission of Agricultural Workers' Cooperatives (Hebrew), 1970.

BARKAI, HAIM. "The Kibbutz: An Experiment in Microsocialism." Research report No. 34. Jerusalem: Hebrew University of Jerusalem, 1971.

BARKAI, HAIM. Interview and communication with author. January–September 1973.

BART, PAULINE B. "Depression in Middle-aged Women." In *Woman in Sexist Society*, edited by Vivian Gornick and Barbara K. Moran. New York: Basic Books, 1971. Pp. 163–86.

BART, PAULINE B. "Middle Age: The Turns of the Social Ferris Wheel." *Sociological Symposium* 1 (Fall 1969).

BERRY, BRIAN. "An Inductive Approach to the Regionalization of Economic Development." In *Essays on Geography and Economic Development*, edited by Norton S. Ginsburg. Chicago: University of Chicago Press, 1960. Pp. 78–107.

BINFORD, LEWIS R. "Post-pleistocene Adaptations." In *Prehistoric Agriculture*, edited by Stuart Struever. Garden City, N.Y.: Natural History Press, 1971.

BLUMBERG, RAE LESSER. "Societal Complexity and Familial Complexity: Inter- and Intrasocietal Correlates of Family Structure, Functionality and Influence." Ph.D. dissertation, Northwestern University, 1970.

BLUMBERG, RAE LESSER. "Women of the Kibbutz: Retreat from Sexual Equality." Paper read at the meetings of the Society for Applied Anthropology, Tucson, 1973.

BLUMBERG, RAE LESSER. "From Liberation to Laundry: a Structural Interpretation of the Retreat from Sexual Equality in the Israeli Kibbutz." Paper read at the meetings of the American Political Science Association, Chicago, 1974a.

BLUMBERG, RAE LESSER. "Structural Factors Affecting Women's Status: a Crosssocietal

Paradigm." Paper read at the meetings of the International Sociological Association, Toronto, 1974b.

BLUMBERG, RAE LESSER. "Kibbutz Women: From the Fields of Revolution to the Laundries of Discontent." In *Women in the World: a Comparative Study*, edited by Lynne Iglitzin and Ruth Ross. Santa Barbara: ABC Clio, 1976a (in press).

BLUMBERG, RAE LESSER. *Stratification: Socioeconomic and Sexual Inequality*. Dubuque: Wm. C. Brown, 1976b (in press).

BLUMBERG, RAE LESSER, AND WINCH, ROBERT F. "The Rise and Fall of the Complex Family: Some Implications for an Evolutionary Theory of Societal Development." Paper read at the meetings of the American Sociological Association, New York, 1973.

BOSERUP, ESTER. *The Conditions of Agricultural Growth: The Economics of Agrarian Change Under Population Pressure*. Chicago: Aldine, 1965.

BROWN, JUDITH K. "A Note on the Division of Labor by Sex." *American Anthropologist* 72 (1970): 1074–78.

BUBER, M. *Paths in Utopia*. Boston: Beacon Press, 1958.

CHILDE, V. G. "The Urban Revolution." *Town Planning Review* 21 (1950): 3–17.

CHILDE, V. G. *Man Makes Himself*. New York: Mentor, 1951.

DE BEAUVOIR, SIMONE. *The Second Sex*. New York: Knopf, 1952.

DUNCAN, OTIS DUDLEY. "Social Organization and the Ecosystem." In *Handbook of Modern Sociology*, edited by Robert E. L. Faris, Chicago: Rand-McNally, 1964. Pp. 36–82.

EDWARDS, R. C.; REICH, M.; AND WEISSKOPF, T. E. *The Capitalist System*. Englewood Cliffs, N.J.: Prentice-Hall, 1971.

FINE, KEITHA SAPSIN. "Worker Participation in Israel." In *Workers Control*, edited by Gerry Hunnius et al. New York: Vintage, 1973. Pp. 225–65.

FLANNERY, KENT V. "Archeological Systems Theory and Early Mesoamerica." In *Prehistoric Agriculture*, edited by Stuart Struever. Garden City, N.Y.: Natural History Press, 1971. Pp. 80–100.

GERSON, MENACHEM. "Lesson from the Kibbutz: A Cautionary Tale." In *The Future of the Family*, edited by Louise Kapp Howe. New York: Simon & Schuster, 1972. Pp. 326–38.

GOLDSCHMIDT, WALTER. *Man's Way: A Preface to the Understanding of Human Society*. New York: Holt, 1959.

GOULDNER, ALVIN W., AND PETERSON, RICHARD A. *Notes on Technology and the Moral Order*. Indianapolis: Bobbs-Merrill, 1962.

HARNER, M. J. "Population Pressures and the Social Evolution of Agriculturalists." *Southwest Journal of Anthropology* 26 (1970): 67–86.

HARRIS, MARVIN. *The Rise of Anthropological Theory*. New York: Crowell, 1968.

KANOVSKY, E. *The Economy of the Israeli Kibbutz*. Harvard Middle Eastern Monographs 13. Cambridge, Mass.: Harvard University Press, 1966.

LENSKI, GERHARD E. *Power and Privilege: A Theory of Social Stratification*. New York: McGraw-Hill, 1966.

LENSKI, GERHARD E. *Human Societies*. New York: McGraw-Hill, 1970.

LEON, DAN. *The Kibbutz*. Tel Aviv: Israel Horizons, 1964.

LESHEM, E. Interview with author, Jerusalem, June 1972.

LEVIATAN, URI. "The Industrial Process in the Israeli Kibbutzim: Problems and Their Solution." Paper presented at the International Conference on Trends in Industrial and Labor Relations, Tel Aviv, 1972.

MARUYUMA, MAGORAH. "The Second Cybernetics: Deviation Amplifying Mutual Causal Processes." *American Scientist* 51 (1963): 164–79.

MEDNICK, MARTHA SHUCH. "Women and the Communal Experience: The Case of the Kibbutz." Paper read at the meetings of the American Psychological Association, Montreal, 1973.

MEYERS, J. THOMAS. "The Origin of Agriculture: An Evaluation of Three Hypotheses." In *Prehistoric Agriculture*, edited by Stuart Struever. Garden City, N.Y.: Natural History Press, 1971. Pp. 101–21.

MICHAELSON, EVALYN JACOBSON, AND GOLDSCHMIDT, WALTER. "Female Roles and Male Dominance among Peasants." *Southwestern Journal of Anthropology* 27: 330–352.

MURDOCK, GEORGE PETER. "Ethnographic Atlas: A Summary." *Ethnology* 6 (1967): 109–256.

MURDOCK, GEORGE P., AND PROVOST, CATERINA. "Factors in the Division of Labor by Sex: A Cross-cultural Analysis." *Ethnology* 12 (1973): 203–25.

PADAN-EISENSTARK, DORIT. "Are Israeli Women Really Equal? Trends and Patterns of Israeli Women's Labor Force Participation: A Comparative Analysis." *Journal of Marriage and the Family* (1973a): 538–45.

PADAN-EISENSTARK, DORIT. Interview with author, Madison, Wisconsin, October 1973b.

RABIN, A. I. "The Sexes: Ideology and Reality in the Israeli Kibbutz." In *Sex Roles in Changing Society*, edited by G. H. Seward and R. C. Williamson. New York: Random House, 1970. Pp. 285–307.

RABIN, A. I. *Kibbutz Studies*. Ann Arbor: Michigan State University Press, 1971.

ROSNER, MENACHEM. Personal communication with author, August 1973.

ROSNER, MENACHEM. Interview with author, Netanyah, Israel, June 1972a.

ROSNER, MENACHEM. "Worker Participation in Decision Making in Kibbutz Industry." Paper presented at the International Conference on Trends in Industrial and Labor Relations, Ruppin Institute, Kibbutz Management Center, Tel Aviv, 1972b.

ROSNER, MENACHEM. "Women in the Kibbutz: Changing Status and Concepts." *Asian and African Studies* 3 (1967): 35–68.

ROSNER, MENACHEM. *The Kibbutz as a Way of Life in Modern Society*. Givat Haviva, Israel: Center for Social Research on the Kibbutz, n.d.

SAWYER, JACK. "Dimensions of Nations: Size, Wealth and Politics," *American Journal of Sociology*, 73 (1967): 145–72.

SCHNORE, LEO. "The Statistical Measurement of Urbanization and Economic Development." *Land Economics* 37 (1961): 228–45.

SHAFER, JOSEPH. *The Reflection of Children's Sleeping Arrangements in the Social Structure of the Kibbutz*. Tel Aviv: Ichud, 1967.

SHAPIRO, REUVEN. "There Is a Chance for the Woman in Active Femininity." *Hedim* 75 (1963): 31–41.

SHARON, ARYEH. Interview with author, Rehovot, Israel, July 1972.

SHEILS, HOWARD DEAN. "Agricultural Technology and Societal Evolution." Ph.D. dissertation, University of Wisconsin, 1969.

SHOMGAR, LEAH. Interview with author, Jerusalem, June 1972.

SHUR, SHIMON. *Kibbutz Bibliography*. Jerusalem: Council for Higher Education of the Federation of Kibbutz Movement, 1971.

SPIRO, MELFORD E. *Kibbutz: Venture in Utopia*. New York: Schocken Books, 1963.

SPIRO, MELFORD E. *Children of the Kibbutz*. New York: Schocken Books, 1965.

STEWARD, JULIAN H. *Theory of Culture Change: The Methodology of Multilinear Evolution*. Urbana: University of Illinois Press, 1955.

TALMON, YONINA. *Family and Community in the Kibbutz*. Cambridge, Mass.: Harvard University Press, 1972.

VITELES, HARRY. *Book Two: The Evolution of the Kibbutz Movement, of A History of the Cooperative Movement in Israel: A Source Book in Seven Volumes*. London: Vallentine-Mitchell, 1967.

WEINTRAUB, DOV; LISSAK, M.; AND AZMON, Y. *Moshava, Kibbutz and Moshav*. Ithaca: Cornell University Press, 1969.

WHITE, LESLIE A. *The Science of Culture: A Study of Man and Civilization*. New York: Grove, 1949.

WHITE, LESLIE A. *The Evolution of Culture*. New York: McGraw-Hill, 1959.

WINCH, ROBERT F. *The Modern Family*. 3rd ed. New York: Holt, Rinehart & Winston, 1971.

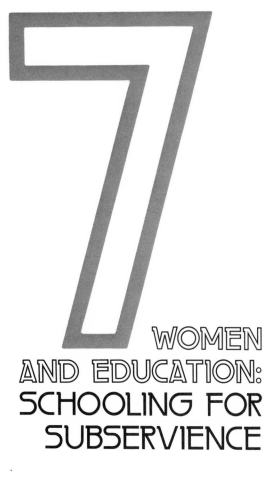

7

WOMEN AND EDUCATION: SCHOOLING FOR SUBSERVIENCE

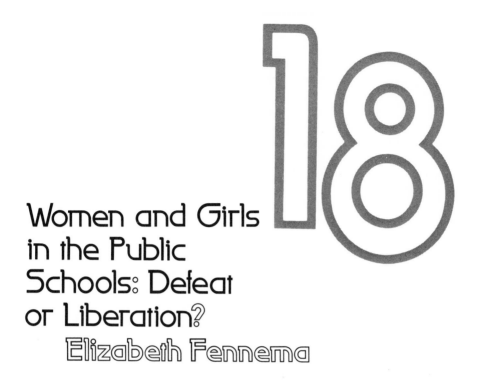

Women and Girls in the Public Schools: Defeat or Liberation?
Elizabeth Fennema

For many years the various governing agencies of the public schools of the United States have assumed that they practiced nondiscriminatory treatment of the sexes. Education was one profession into which women were welcomed, and for years women have dominated the field—in numbers at least. If any discrimination in the treatment of boys and girls did slip into the schools, it was definitely believed to be in the girls' favor. In support of the schools' bias in favor of girls, reading specialists have cited many studies which show that girls learn to read better than boys. Psychologists have also discoursed at great length concerning the behavior problems of boys. According to these psychologists, the boys' behavior problems are caused by the predominant number of women teachers in the lower grades. Girls do not have these same behavior problems because they have teachers, i.e., women, who understand the female sex. Therefore, boys are discriminated against because they do not have male teachers who understand the male sex.

But do schools treat both sexes equally? Are women able to occupy the same professional positions as men? Are girls and boys given an equal chance to develop their cognitive abilities in the public schools? This chapter attempts to answer these questions.

THE PROFESSIONAL ROLE OF WOMEN IN THE SCHOOLS

Women held a predominant role in instruction in 1955 and continue to do so. In 1955, 88 percent of elementary teachers were women, as were 54 percent of secondary teachers. In 1970, 85 percent of elementary teachers and 50 percent of secondary teachers were women (Anon 1971). There are fewer women teachers proportionately at the secondary level than at the elementary level, but there are many more elementary teachers than secondary teachers. This makes the total number of women in public school teaching much larger than the number of men. Do women really dominate the field? Numbers do not necessarily mean that women are the powerful sex in the schools. To answer the question of which sex—if any—dominates, other roles than teaching must be examined.

Several important professional positions other than teaching exist in the public schools and theoretically can be held by men or women. A superintendent is usually the highest-paid and most powerful professional in a school system. In June 1971, Gregg and Knezevich (1971) reported that 1 percent of American superintendents were women. There were none in school systems with enrollments of more than 25,000, three in school systems enrolling 3000–24,999 pupils, and four in school systems enrolling 300–2999. Smaller systems (less than 300 pupils) had slightly more women superintendents. Not only was the number of women superintendents pitifully small in 1971, but there were even fewer in 1972. In 1972, in school systems with more than 300 pupils there were only two women superintendents (Anon 1972b). Women obviously do not hold this high position of authority—and the chances of their doing so appear to be deteriorating.

The superintendent delegates responsibility to various other people, the most common of whom are building principals, who are aided and abetted by various other administrators. These administrators hold positions of authority and power because of their responsibilities, which encompass the hiring and firing of teachers, the assignment of children to classes, important decisions of what should be taught, how schools are organized, etc. These administrators often work with teacher groups in arriving at various decisions, but the power remains with the administrators. The sex of these administrators is predominantly male.

Statewide studies in California, Kentucky, Colorado, and Oklahoma were conducted between 1950 and 1956 to determine the ratio of men to women occupying positions as principals. The female/male ratio varied from two/three to three/four with men in all cases predominant. Not only did women hold fewer principalships than men, but Burns (1964) found a marked decline in the proportion of women principals from 1950 to 1960. In 1972 it was reported (Anon 1972b) that the ratio of men/women principals is five/one so the number of women in administrative positions is declining sharply. There is some evidence that women are more apt to occupy positions in various roles that have less power in administration such as library coordinators or supervisors.

An examination of the data shows clearly that opportunity for the powerful professional positions is not equal for men and women and that such opportunity seems to be declining. Women are most apt to occupy an elementary school teacher's role, the lowest-ranking professional position offered by the public schools. At the secondary level, where teachers occupy a position of higher status than at the elementary level, there are proportionately fewer women. At higher power and status positions, i.e., administrators, there are still fewer women.

Why does this situation exist? Are women less capable in power positions than men? Data indicate that this is not true. Gross and Trask (1964) in a study of elementary school principals in cities of over 50,000 found higher pupil learning and higher professional performance in schools with women principals. Although there are personality differences between male and female principals, these differences are not related to their effectiveness as principals. Women do not do a poorer job and are not less capable as educational administrators than are men.

For an answer to the question of why women have occupied primarily low-ranking positions in the field of education where they have dominated in numbers for decades, one must turn to society at large. Society forms people, both men and women, within large inherent limits and makes them to a large extent what they are. This in turn determines what roles they play in life and in the schools. As Mead says, "Standardized personality differences between the sexes is of this order, cultural creations to which each generation, male or female is trained to conform" (Mead 1949). Women occupy their present positions in the public schools because society has trained both women and men to believe that the women are not as capable as men of holding high-power positions.

Educators (both men and women) have long believed that women are not as professional as men. In 1956 Myron Lieberman stated in his book *Education as a Profession*, "The predominance of women in teaching is one of the most important and most neglected facts about American education. Under present conditions it must be regarded as one of the two or three most important obstacles to the professionalization of education" (pp. 241–42). Although the statement is almost two decades old, this belief seemingly has not changed much. In November 1971, R. E. Gross of Stanford University School of Education said at a national meeting: "Teachers, the majority of whom are women, tend to be conventional, cautious and conservative and studies have shown that this is another reason why the educational establishment is slow to change" (*Wisconsin State Journal*, 28 November 1971). In 1971, women were still seen as a factor that keeps the profession of education from growing.

Another reason that women do not occupy higher-status, power positions is that they do not wish to be principals and administrators. Studies have shown that women teachers do not aspire to higher positions; many are quite content to remain as teachers (Gross and Trask 1964; Burns 1964). Women are trained to accept a sexual identity that corresponds to what society says is an appropriate sexual standard, and the female sexual standard has not included power positions. Nevertheless, women can assume equal or even more dominant roles than men in the public schools when both women and men perceive women as capable of performing well in a variety of roles and when society as a whole accepts a female sexual standard that includes authority positions. Lieberman (1956) said that "education will not become a leading profession unless either the proportion of men to women is drastically increased or there occurs a cultural revolution concerning the role of the woman in American society" (p. 242). Perhaps the beginning of that cultural revolution is being felt now.

Society forces children from a very young age to develop a sexual identity in accord with an accepted sexual standard. The school is only one of many social agencies that play a part in developing sexual identity; the schools' role is not unique. However, the school has been entrusted with one aspect of development explicitly: the development of the intellectual abilities of children. Because of this unique role of the school, only that aspect of sexual identity and its development relative to intellectual functioning are discussed here.

THE INTELLECTUAL ABILITIES OF GIRLS

There is no evidence concerning which sex measures higher on tests of general intelligence or inherent mental ability because the authors of such tests have deliberately made them neuter tests. Any item that discriminated between the sexes was eliminated. One trend related to IQ is important to the issue. In several longitudinal studies, persons have been tested and retested on various instruments. While these studies were done to find out the stability of IQ within one person over a period of years, the trend is clearly evident that over the years of development, boys improve more in IQ (or lose less) than girls (Maccoby 1966: 26). Something causes boys to improve their intellectual ability more than girls improve theirs. Girls do not fulfill their intellectual functioning after completion of the public schools. In a follow-up study of gifted children, no relationship was found between level of occupational achievement and IQ for girls, but a substantial relationship was found for boys (Terman and Oden 1947). The intellectual ability of a girl does not play a major role in deciding her life's work.

Although achievement in various academic and intellectual tasks is not as highly correlated with sex as are "aggression" or "dependency," several interesting trends can be found. In general the literature supports the idea that girls in grades K–4 typically outperform boys on academic achievement in general (Kagan 1964). Gradually throughout development girls' overall performances decline so that by late adolescence boys perform better on tests of academic achievement. Girls often begin to be underachievers at onset of puberty, while the opposite is true of boys. Girls tend to do somewhat better in the so-called soft subjects: English, spelling, writing, and art; while boys tend to do better in mathematics reasoning, history, geography, and science (Tyler 1969).

Up to about fourth grade, girls are clearly superior to boys in reading, and reading specialists as a group believe that schools discriminate in favor of girls. After about fourth grade this marked difference in reading ability begins to disappear; thereafter, no difference in reading ability is evidenced (Heilman 1967:401–4).

Reading skills comprise a subset of a much larger set of skills that are usually placed together under the rubric of verbal ability. Included are low-level cognitive skills (spelling, punctuation, and talkativeness) as well as considerably higher-level skills (comprehension of complex written text, quick understanding of complex logical relations expressed in verbal terms, and verbal creativity of the sort measured by Guilford's tests of divergent thinking). On this entire set of skills females tend to be superior to males (Maccoby and Jacklin 1972).

Boys and girls enter kindergarten knowing about the same amount of mathematics. In early elementary school no differences in mathematics learning are evident. As children reach puberty, differences in mathematics achievement do not always appear but, if significant, they are more apt to be in the boys' favor when higher-level cognitive tasks are being measured and in the girls' favor when lower-level cognitive tasks are being measured (Fennema 1973).

Data on problem solving and analytic ability are somewhat ambiguous. Kagan (1964) states, "It appears that degree of involvement in most academic problems is greater for adolescent and adult males than for females. . . . By late adolescence and adulthood, the typical female feels inadequate when faced with most problems requiring analysis and reasoning" (pp. 156–57), while a male is more analytic, and exercises a higher degree of autonomy and persistence. This ability appears to be more dominant in males as early as preschool and lasts into adulthood. Sherman (1967) disagrees with Kagan that males are more analytic than females. She argues that analytic differences which have been evidenced are a result of females' inferior development of spatial ability. This is a persuasive argument as she demonstrates that analytic tests with a spatial component show significant differences in favor of boys while analytic tests that do not have spatial components show no significant differences between males and females. Males have evidenced consistently better spatial ability than females.

Although sex differences in academic achievement are not as great as has long been assumed, one would have to conclude that males overall tend to improve their academic performance as they progress through school while female performance tends to decline. Explaining the cause of such complex behavior is hazardous, but one hypothesis appears plausible.

The school reflects the sex-role standard of the society that supports it, and how a person behaves in intellectual areas is partly determined by the sex-role standard of the school one attends. For example, boys in the United States are infamous for low achievement in reading in the first three grades of elementary school. This long has been attributed to the fact that boys are "not as ready" physiologically to read as are girls, and the early difference in beginning reading is caused by an inherent factor within boys and girls. However, Johnson (1973–74) reported that young boys in other cultures, specifically England and Nigeria, actually achieve at a higher rate than young girls. Evidently ability to learn to read at a young age is not only physiologically determined, as has been assumed in the United States, but is also affected by the environment of the learner. This evidence supports the belief that the culture has a marked influence on how one behaves intellectually. If the sex-role standard says that it is not "male" to read well, then the chances are that a boy won't read well. Conversely, if the sex-role standard says it isn't "feminine" to achieve, then the chances are good that a girl won't achieve.

There may be several partial explanations for boys' increasingly better performance in academic achievement of various kinds. Certainly one aspect of high achievement is competitiveness. This is a male-approved trait and one that is consistently practiced. It is not appropriate for females. Girls are conditioned to believe that they should not compete if they want to have an accepted sexual identity. Developing and maintaining a sexual identity becomes increasingly important as girls enter puberty, and this is when girls often become underachievers. These two concurrent happenings lend credence to the belief that girls' beliefs about sexual identity are related to their achievement in traditional school subjects.

Although Clark (1967) offers evidence that the closure of the gap between elementary school boys and girls in performance on academic achievement tests results from a deceleration in girls' achievement rather than an acceleration by the boys, one confounding factor must be considered when considering the relationship between sexual identity and academic achievement in secondary school students. More teen-age boys than teen-age girls drop out of school. Probably the boys who drop out are those who achieve at the lower end of the scale. As a result, the sample of boys from which data is collected becomes more homogeneous, and the boys' achievement appears more favorable when compared to the heterogeneous sample of girls.

Girls are conditioned to believe that they are not as capable intellectually as boys as shown by studies dealing with boys' and girls' beliefs about their intellectual abilities. The self-concept of girls called upon to do intellectual tasks is not high. Crandall, Katkovsky, and Preston (1962) asked some children if they thought they could do a selected task. The brighter the boy, the better he expected to do on it ($r = .62$). This is a reasonable finding because bright children have been able to solve many problems. However, the brighter the girl, the less well she expected to do ($r = -.41$). When these same children were asked why they could solve some of the problems, the brighter boys more often believed it was because of their own efforts; brighter girls believed that chance led to the solution. If a girl, even when she measures high on IQ tests, has so little confidence in her own ability to solve problems that she has to believe in chance to solve problems, her perception of her own abilities is obviously inadequate. Other studies have indicated that boys are more likely to rise to intellectual challenge while girls retreat (Maccoby 1966:33), and that as girls move from fourth to sixth grade their self-concepts decrease markedly. This trend is probably tied to the fact that girls become underachievers with the onset of puberty. Related to this idea is the girls' image of their contributions. In a test of creativity (Torrance 1963), children were asked who contributed the best ideas. Both boys and girls thought that boys did, when in fact the rater found no difference in the quality of the contributions. Clark (1967) offers evidence that girls do not show superior achievement in arithmetic and science simply because they feel that girls should not show superior achievement in those areas.

Minuchin (1966) offers direct evidence that schools affect the developing sexual identity of learners. This study described four schools ranging from traditional to modern (basically on an authoritarian–freedom dimension). After watching and analyzing behavior in these schools over a period of time, they concluded that each school influenced sex-role standards. In schools near the freedom end of the continuum that minimized sexual differences, the differences between the traits manifested by boys and girls softened, and in some cases seemed to disappear. The conclusion is inescapable that the schools girls attend influence the development of intellectual capacities in a negative way at least partly by reinforcing the idea that females are and should be less capable intellectually.

The schools reinforce one's idea of how one should behave intellectually in relation to one's sex in at least two important ways: (1) by providing adult sexual models that one may pattern intellectual behavior on, and (2) by these adult models explicitly reinforcing certain kinds of intellectual behavior. What do the schools provide in the way of models and do they indeed reinforce sex-related intellectual behavior?

Teachers are the most important models provided by schools. Each sex selects models of the same sex so women teachers serve as models and probably effect markedly the sexual identity of the girls with whom they interact. As mentioned, the women in schools occupy the lower-ranking positions in power and authority. One might safely assume that girls who are using these women as models might well accept as part of their sexual identity the belief that their role should be a subservient one. Teachers specialize in subject areas when they teach in junior high and high schools. Although no data were found, it appears that there are proportionately fewer women mathematics or science teachers than men. These subjects are also regarded as the difficult ones with higher-status intellectual content. Since women don't teach these, do girls assume that women are less capable intellectually?

Another model provided for girls are females portrayed in texts and other books given them to read. The role of women in books is one that feminists have been analyzing for some time, and many summaries are available (see Howe 1971). One problem with some of these analyses is that they have not used carefully constructed categories. However, there is no reason to doubt the veracity of their conclusions since both impressionistic and exhaustive studies produce similar findings. Certainly there is much evidence that texts and other children's books provide girls with models predominantly playing the stereotyped roles that females have been thought to hold for years. Women are portrayed as mothers, nurses, or teachers; they are not the adventurers or problem solvers but occupy the nurturant role that some people feel is proper for women. Although more data must be collected before coming to any conclusion about the effect of seeing such stereotyped unrealistic portrayals upon the developing sexual identity of girls, it seems safe to say that it narrows one's perspectives, ambitions, and beliefs in a female's abilities.

Learners add to their sexual identity those traits that are reinforced. Part of the reason for girls functioning intellectually in certain areas at a lower level than boys is because people are reinforcing the beliefs that it is better if they don't function well. Teachers reinforce learners in the school, and girls may be controlled more by teachers than are boys (Kagan 1964). Traits such as gentleness, attractiveness, or any nurturant characteristic are often fostered in the female. Many of these traits receive reinforcement from *outside* the individual, e.g., one is gentle to someone else and in so doing receives the reward of a smile. Boys, on the other hand, receive rewards more from themselves, e.g., power at sports. The reward comes from the ball going through the basket, not necessarily from someone saying anything. Boys also regard the school, particularly at an early age, as basically feminine. In various studies, when asked the sex of school-related objects—desks, blackboard, etc.—both boys and girls think of them predominantly as feminine. However, there is no evidence that boys will allow female teachers and the school to mold their behavior as much as girls will. Certainly this is reflected in the ratio of behavior problems as boys are much more apt to exhibit learning and behavior disorders than are girls (Bentzen 1966). In fact, the development of girls' intellectual ability may be more influenced by teachers because girls apparently are conditioned to respond more to external reinforcement and because boys may resist reinforcement by people of the opposite sex.

Not only is intellectual development of boys and girls affected, but treatment of boys and girls by teachers is different. Although schools believe and accept as right the idea that both sexes should be treated not only equally but identically, there is evidence that this belief is erroneous. Teachers in one study were asked if they treated boys and girls the same (Sears and Feldman 1966). In general they thought that their goals of instruction for both sexes were identical and that both sexes were treated the same. This appeared to be a very well done study, but if the findings really reflect the beliefs of teachers, then teachers are guilty of flagrant blindness. Meyer and Thompson (1956) report a study in which three sixth-grade classrooms were observed for thirty hours per classroom. Teacher-pupil interactions were analyzed as to blame-praise contacts. The boys received significantly more blame contacts than did girls and also more praise contacts than girls. In other words, the teachers were actually interacting with boys much more often than they were with girls. In the study reported by Sears and Feldman (1966), teachers were asked to describe incidents in which they rewarded creative behavior: 224 incidents were reported, 172 of them mentioning the sex of the child. Seventy-four percent were boys. Teachers reward boys more for creative behavior.

Obviously, teachers do not treat boys and girls alike. Boys are rewarded for male appropriate behavior and girls for female appropriate behavior as perceived by the teacher. In general, the more intellectual traits are perceived as male, so boys are rewarded. Nonintellectual traits are seen as female. As a result, schools are inhibiting the intellectual development of girls. This is a severe indictment of the schools of the United States.

An encouraging trend may be emerging. There is some evidence that sex differences in intellectual functioning may be diminishing (Jacklin and Maccoby 1972). Several recent studies have shown little or no significant differences in areas in which differences were once presumably well documented. Certainly data such as these lend evidence to the belief that boys and girls function intellectually as they do because society and the schools expect the sexes to perform differently in intellectual areas. As sex-role standards have evidenced change, intellectual performance is also evidencing change. These data should encourage teachers to hold the same expectations for both boys and girls and to erase the differential treatment given to the sexes.

WHAT MUST BE DONE IN EDUCATION

The most important thing to be done in education is to change the opportunities that girls are given to develop their intellectual abilities. Girls must be trained to believe that to be intellectual is not to be unfeminine. This will be done only when teachers are retrained so that in all intellectual tasks, boys and girls are treated identically and both sexes have equal opportunity to develop their intellectual abilities. Schools and their personnel believe that boys and girls must have equal rights in intellectual development, but teachers must be helped to find ways of implementing this belief. They must be made aware of the implicit assumptions that affect how they treat the sexes and must be helped to practice that equality of treatment that will permit each child, regardless of sex, to develop his or her own ability to the utmost.

For female teachers, there are at least two specifics which, if immediately acted upon, would make it easier for women who, at this time, have the double responsibility of a family and a profession. Maternity leaves should be available without penalty. Progress is being made in this area. In January 1972 a federal court judge in Richmond, Virginia, ruled that a teacher's dismissal from her teaching job because of her pregnancy was unconstitutional (Anon 1972a). The petitioning teacher, Mrs. Susan Cohen, became the first of the nation's educators to challenge and win the right to be pregnant and continue teaching in her classroom beyond the fifth month of pregnancy. This ruling influenced a series of court cases and will directly or indirectly affect nearly 70 percent of the women educators in the nation's public schools. Certainly teachers must not be penalized for pregnancy, and maternity leaves must be liberalized.

Although part-time jobs in professional education are practically unheard of, there is no professional reason why women in half-time positions should not be a real asset to schools. The contribution of two half-time good teachers is no less and may, for a variety of reasons, even be greater than the contribution of one full-time teacher. The principal's responsibilities could be divided easily among two people. Part-time jobs, which have the same status and power as full-time jobs, should be available to women.

Both these specific changes should be a goal of those concerned with the role of women in education. However, what is of primary importance is a change in the belief of men and women concerning the abilities of women. Before women can be treated equally professionally, they must begin to aspire to holding principals' positions and higher administrative roles, and those in power must see that women are placed in a variety of roles in the schools. Only when women are given the opportunity to demonstrate their proficiency and to reject their subservient role in the schools will the schools be able to fulfill their prime function: to help all learners, regardless of sex, to develop their intellectual abilities to the limit.

REFERENCES

ANON. *National Education Association Research Bulletin* 49, no. 2 (May 1971): 47.

ANON. "School Supervisor: News and Comment for Elementary School Leaders." *Teacher* 89, no. 6 (January 1972a): 31.

ANON. *Updating School Board Policies* 3, no. 2 (February 1972b). Data acquired from Research Division, NEA; AASA; and NSBA.

BENTZEN, F. "Sex Ratios in Learning and Behavior Disorders." *National Elementary Principal* 46, no. 2 (November 1966): 13–17.

BURNS, DOROTHY M. "Women in Educational Administration: A Study of Leadership in California Public Schools." Ph.D. dissertation, University of Oregon, 1964.

CLARK, E. T. "Sex Differences in the Perception of Academic Achievement among Elementary School Children." *Journal of Psychology* 67 (November 1967): 244–56.

CRANDALL, V. J.; KATKOVSKY, W.; AND PRESTON, A. "Motivational and Ability Determinants of Young Children's Intellectual Achievement Behaviors." *Child Development* 33 (1962): 643–61.

FENNEMA, ELIZABETH. "Mathematics Learning and the Sexes: A Review." *Journal for Research in Mathematics Education* 5, no. 3 (May 1974): 126–39.

GREGG, R. T., AND KNEZEVICH, S. J. "The Superintendent: What Makes Him What He Is." *American School Board Journal* 158, no. 12 (June 1971): 12–17.

GROSS, N., AND TRASK, A. E. "Men and Women as Elementary School Principals." Cooperative Research Project 853. Part 2. USOE and Harvard University, 1964.

HEILMAN, A. W. *Principles and Practices of Teaching Reading.* Columbus, Ohio: Charles E. Merrill, 1967.

HOWE, F. "Sexual Stereotypes Start Early." *Saturday Review*, 16 October 1971, p. 76.

JACKLIN, C. N., AND MACCOBY, E. E. "Sex Differences in Intellectual Abilities: A Reassessment and a Look at Some New Explanations." Paper presented at the annual meeting of the American Educational Research Association, Chicago, 1972.

JOHNSON, D. D. "Sex Differences in Reading Across Cultures." *Reading Research Quarterly* 9, no. 1 (1973–74): 67–86.

KAGAN, J. "Acquisition and Significance of Sex Typing and Sex Role Identity." In *Review of Child Development Research*, edited by M. L. Hoffman and L. Hoffman. Vol. I. New York: Russell Sage Foundation, 1964.

LIEBERMAN, MYRON. *Education as a Profession.* Englewood Cliffs, N.J.: Prentice-Hall, 1956.

MACCOBY, E. E. "Sex Differences in Intellectual Functioning." In *The Development of Sex Differences.* Stanford: Stanford University Press, 1966. Pp. 25–55.

MACCOBY, E. E., AND JACKLIN, C. N. "Sex Differences in Intellectual Functioning." In *Assessment in a Pluralistic Society, Proceedings of the 1972 Invitational Conference on Testing Problems.* Princeton, N.J.: Educational Testing Service, 1972. Pp. 37–55.

MEAD, MARGARET. *Male and Female.* New York: William Morrow, 1949. Pp. 190–91.

MEYER, W. J., AND THOMPSON, G. G. "Sex Differences in the Distribution of Teacher Approval and Disapproval among Sixth-grade Children. *Journal of Educational Psychology* 47, no. 7 (November 1956): 385–96.

MINUCHIN, P. P. "Sex Differences in Children: Research Findings in an Educational Context." *National Elementary Principal* 46, no. 2 (November 1966): 45–48.

SEARS, P. S., AND FELDMAN, D. H. "Teacher Interactions with Boys and Girls." *National Elementary Principal* 46, no. 2 (November 1966): 30–35.

SHERMAN, J. "Problem of Sex Differences in Space Perception and Aspects of Intellectual Functioning." *Psychological Review* 4 (1967): 290–99.

TERMAN, L. M., AND ODEN, M. H. *The Gifted Child Grows Up.* Stanford: Stanford University Press, 1947.

TORRANCE, E. P. "Changing Reactions of Preadolescent Girls to Tasks Requiring Creative Scientific Thinking." *Journal of Genetic Psychology* 102 (1963): 217–23.

TYLER, L. E. "Sex Differences." In *Encyclopedia of Educational Research*, edited by R. L. Ebel. New York: Macmillan, 1969. Pp. 1217–21.

Wisconsin State Journal, 28 November 1971.

19

Women and Higher Education: Voices from the Sexual Siberia

Karen Merritt

In their 1958 study of *The Academic Marketplace*, Theodore Caplow and
Reece J. McGee made the following two statements that summed up the
status of women as professionals in academia. "Women tend to be discriminated
against in the academic profession not because they have low prestige, but because
they are outside the prestige system entirely and for this reason are of no use to a
department in future recruitment."[1] And, "Women scholars are not taken seriously
and cannot look forward to a normal professional career. [Bias against women] is
not peculiar to the academic world, but it does blight prospects of female
scholars."[2] By and large this is still an accurate assessment of the situation.

One starting point to provide a background for the situation Caplow and
McGee found in the late 1950s is a survey of higher education for women in the
United States. In this chapter, through a review of the literature, I summarize how
women got into higher education in the first place, since that was a major battle
fought by feminists of the last century; then I concentrate on the common problems
faced by women who have wished to enter college teaching and research careers.

Many of the old proscriptions and assumptions concerning higher education and
women make amusing historical anecdotes, but a large number of difficulties faced
by women in the nineteenth century have been faced by women in this century and
are faced by women today.[3] At the outset of the nineteenth century, the education
that existed for girls was primarily limited to private instruction for the wealthy in
the so-called accomplishments, such as French, embroidery, and the playing of a
musical instrument. Any number of objections were raised against educating

women's minds. Women would contract brain fever or their childbearing apparatus would be damaged; even if this latter calamity did not occur, ladies who wanted education were enemies of marriage and the family; hence, the entire future of the race would be endangered. Subjects taught to men were too hard for women; since there were no women geniuses, what was the point of educating them at all? In a letter, Sarah Grimké, the early-nineteenth-century women's rights advocate, recalled one masculine opinion: "Chemistry enough to keep the pot boiling and geography enough to know the location of different rooms in her house is learning sufficient for a woman."

In general, the women who pioneered advanced education for women came from families that stimulated them to learn. A characteristic of the background of these women is a good-humored relationship between an instructive father and a precocious daughter, very often an only child. Often these women who discovered that, without suffering brain fever or any other predicted horror, learning was quite pleasant, felt that intellectual pursuit was something others of their sex deserved as much as they did. Although some of the pioneers in women's education subscribed to Rousseau's dictum that the whole education of women ought to be relative to men, the schools and programs they developed made strides in the direction of providing as demanding a curriculum for women as was available to men.

Two ongoing goals of early education liberationists inspired Emma Willard in efforts that led to the founding of a "female seminary" in 1821. She was concerned that financial aid be extended to women so that not only the wealthiest among them might receive an education. She was also concerned that the state of teacher education be improved. At this early date, women were already beginning to enter teaching, the only profession open to them at that point and for many decades afterward. Willard herself had paid a Middlebury College student to educate her after hours in things he had been learning during the day in school. Part of her effort was aimed at persuading the New York state legislature in 1819 to fund the education of girls. She failed, but she founded her seminary in which she offered for the first time an education analogous to that which young men at the time might receive. In her pleas to the New York legislators, she made it clear that her plans were not seditious: "I would not be understood to insinuate that we women are not in particular situations to yield obedience to the other sex. Whenever one class of human beings derives from the other the benefits of support and protection, they must pay its equivalent, obedience. Neither would I be understood to mean that our sex should not seek to make themselves agreeable to the other." [4] Her ideal curriculum for a female seminary still stressed "the accomplishments," domestic chores, the ornamental studies in which she included drawing and painting, music, and "the grace of motion." She included with these religious and moral studies. Her innovation occurred when she recommended in her curriculum "natural philosophy"—the kind of studies young men of the time were receiving.

The first education available on the basis of equality to both men and women originated at Oberlin, which opened as a seminary in 1833. Its founders stated as a part of the purpose of the college "the elevation of the female character bringing within the reach of this misjudged and neglected sex all the instructional privileges which hitherto have unreasonably distinguished the leading sex from theirs." Nevertheless, the first young women at Oberlin could not be exposed to too much elevation at once! They were limited to a shortened version of the men's course;

even after 1837, when the first woman was allowed to enter the so-called full course with men, the shortened ladies' version continued to be offered. Further concern for their welfare led to the assignment of special duties to women at Oberlin. One history of Oberlin records the institution's concern for women as the mothers of the race; hence, they were expected to wash the male students' clothes, care for them, serve them at tables, and listen to their orations while remaining silent in public assemblages. The Oberlin coeds were being prepared for intelligent motherhood and a properly subservient wifehood.

Mount Holyoke, founded as a seminary by Mary Lyon in 1857, continued to train women in the "accomplishments" of French and music; and for practical purposes, to defray the expenses of the seminary, women were also required to perform domestic chores. But the core activities were purely academic, and the admissions policy was innovative for the time. Only girls of sixteen years and over were admitted, and they were chosen according to their maturity and the promise they showed for intellectual growth.

The first effort to bridge the gap of quality between men's and women's colleges came when Vassar opened in 1865. Its preparatory department helped girls who had poor academic backgrounds. Such girls made up the majority of those participating in advanced education at this time. Preparatory education made it possible for the girls to enter the rigorous core curriculum offered by the school. The measure of Vassar's first success was taken by Frances Albert in a report she made in the November 1895 issue of *Forum* on the 1082 women who had graduated between 1862 and 1894. Virtually everyone who has dealt with statistics on women in higher education has reflected her first concern, to explain how many of these highly educated women had been married. Of the group at large, 38 percent had been married. She pointed out in addition that the statistics for 1867–70 showed that 63 percent of the graduates were married. Professionally, 37.6 percent had become teachers, and 18.3 percent were lifetime teachers. Among the distinguished alumnae were professors and instructors of Vassar, Smith, Wellesley, and a number of other schools. Ellen Swallow Richards, who graduated in the class of 1869, became MIT's first female instructor and achieved a bachelor of arts degree at the school, partly through what she described as her ingratiating way with the faculty members—binding up Professor A's sore thumb, for instance, and mending Professor B's suspenders. Of the 1082 Vassar graduates, 118 had completed or were pursuing advanced professional degrees. There were 59 published writers, among whom one had written an article demonstrating that higher education was decidedly *not* injurious to the health of young women!

As early as the opening of Vassar, though, talented women found the going uphill even at a college founded for women. One of the outstanding members of the first Vassar faculty of 22 women and 8 men was Maria Mitchell, an eminent astronomer, who became the first of her sex to be admitted to a number of professional organizations and discovered a comet that was subsequently named after her. Her complaint against the male president and the male board of trustees was that they favored men for higher academic jobs and committee appointments and that they resisted equalizing salaries for men and women on the faculty, charges that have an unhappily modern ring.

Major innovations in women's education marked the founding of other "seven sisters" schools. Smith, which opened in 1875, had a first class of fourteen women, for the fledgling college admitted women only if they could pass the entrance examination for Harvard University. Unlike Vassar, Smith had no preparatory department. In 1882 the Society for the Collegiate Instruction of Women recognized officially the fact that women able to pass entrance examinations had been receiving instruction from Harvard professors since 1879. This so-called Harvard Annex, eventually to become Radcliffe College, also granted degrees to qualified women. To Bryn Mawr, founded in 1885, went the distinction of offering the first graduate program to women. Bryn Mawr president M. Carrie Thomas, who was one of the first women to hold a doctorate in America and who fostered graduate education at Bryn Mawr, made the following assessment of higher education for women in 1908. Looking back over the first century that higher education had been available to women, she said:

> *I think I can best tell you in a concrete way what has been accomplished in women's education by describing to you the condition of affairs which I found in 1884. Women were teaching in Wellesley, Mt. Holyoke and Smith without even the elementary training of a college course behind them. . . . When I protested to the president of the most advanced college for women in regard to this lack of training, he told me that . . . there was an intuitive something in ladies of birth and position that enabled them to do without college training and to make on the whole better professors for women college students than if they had themselves been to college. Everyone I consulted prophesied disaster if we carried out our plan of appointing to our professorships young unmarried men of high scientific promise. They said: in the first place, such men will not consent to teach women in a women's college; in the second place, if they should consent, their unmarried students will distract their minds; and in the third place, if by chance they should be able to teach coherently, then surely such will be the charm of their bachelor estate that girl students will compete with each other for proposals out of the classroom rather than for marks in the classroom . . . Unmarried men are now teaching at all colleges for women. The experience of Bryn Mawr has proved that men of the highest scholarly reputations are not only willing to accept positions in a college for women but they decline to resign them except for the most tempting posts in colleges for men.*

She continued with an incisive analysis of the needs of higher education of women, which retains a timely sound:

> *I am astounded to see the efforts which have been made in the past few years, and perhaps never more persistently than during the past year to persuade, I might almost say to compel, those in charge of women's education to riddle the college curriculum of women with hygiene, and sanitary drainage, and domestic science and all the rest of the so-called practical studies. The argument is a specious one at first sight and seems reasonable. It is urged that college courses for women should be less varied than for men and should fit them primarily for the two great vocations of women: marriage or teaching, the training of children at home or in the schoolroom. Nothing could be more disastrous for women, or for men, than specialized education for women as a sex. It has been wholly overlooked that any form of specialized education which differs from men's education, will tend to unfit women in less than a generation to teach their own boys at home, as well as, of course, other boys in the schoolroom. . . . Sanitary and domestic science are not among the great disciplinary studies. The place for such studies are after the college course, not during it. They belong with law . . . engineering, architecture and agriculture in the professional*

school, not in the college. And for college women who may be teachers as well as for those who may be mothers, any form of special education is highly objectionable. If the education of women is directed mainly, or exclusively, toward the profession of teaching, such specialized training will drive women who must support themselves into the teaching profession without regard to their special qualifications for teaching. . . . If women are to support themselves, even as generally as they do now, they must be trained so as to find ready admission into the professions and into different kinds of business activity. The education must be at least as varied, and open to modification, as men's education.[5]

Nineteenth-century pioneers like Carrie Thomas achieved brilliantly in making first-rate higher education increasingly available to women. By 1880 women constituted one-third of all those enrolled in higher education, though it is important to realize that women's education then and now tended to be inferior to men's in the single-sex colleges.[6] Many problems came with success. Mitchell's complaints against the trustees at Vassar have been cited. Thomas's assessment of the state of women's education implied that many problems existed, particularly in the continuing pressure to direct women only to particular fields considered suitable to their situation in life. In spite of recent breakthroughs in the employment of women, a nagging complaint among women graduates reflects a complaint made at the end of the last century, that women are overprepared to do the sort of jobs readily open to them. To paraphrase Caroline Bird in *Born Female*, Ivy League graduates are still put in management training programs, the graduates of the "seven sisters" are still put in the secretarial pool. The chief complaint of well-to-do and well-educated nineteenth-century women was that unless they were going to teach, nothing but marriage or idle spinsterhood remained open to them.

The peaking of women's movement in higher education came in the decades from 1920 to 1940. By this time, creditable percentages of women were receiving bachelor's and advanced degrees, and women had made their own contribution to the university curriculum via the home economics movement. The 1930s depression in part, but particularly the so-called flight back to the home after World War II, negatively affected the proportion of women in college and in the academic profession.

The proportion of advanced degrees granted to women is an excellent gauge of the degree of acceptability for women who wish to make their careers through and in higher education. The percentage of doctorates granted to women in 1900 was 6 percent, in 1920 was 15 percent, and in the 1930s peaked at 15–16 percent. In 1950, the percentage had dropped to 10 percent, and by 1968 it had climbed back to 13 percent. The figures for the percentage of women who received master's degrees and were hired on academic staffs show the same trends. In 1920, 47.3 percent of all college students were women. By 1950, only 30.2 percent of all college students were women. More recently, women have been better than 40 percent of all enrollees in college, though percentages are still short of the 1920 high.

What had been happening to women in higher education was not brought under close study until the 1960s when it became clear that needed job power could be, but was not, supplied by women. Jessie Bernard constructed the first important statistically based profile of women in higher education in 1964, a study followed in 1969 by Helen Astin's major analysis of women who received their Ph.Ds in 1957 and 1958. Astin's study remains the best and most often quoted survey of academic women, but Jessie Bernard's insights and conclusions are worth reviewing.

It is a sign of Jessie Bernard's mild-mannered approach to the subject that she was able to say, without consciousness of irony, in the preface to *Academic Women*[7] that in "40 years in academia I have never been so far as I know, subjected to professional discrimination by colleagues because of my sex, although I was once chased out of the sacred precincts of the faculty club at a great university when I inadvertently stepped across the invisible line." She soft-pedaled discrimination to such an extent, in fact, that Dean Ben Euwema, under whom she worked, felt called upon to supply a rather less sanguine assessment of the true situation in academia.

Of interest is Bernard's effort to show the extent to which women had accepted without overt complaint lower positions and salaries, lifelong professional existence on the fringes, and marriage as an ideal that overshadowed the career of the academic woman. Bernard's profile of academic women revealed characteristics shared widely by the class of faculty member Caplow and McGee described as "outside the prestige system entirely." She found that women more often than men were directed by external forces to enter academia. Of faculty women questioned in a Minnesota study, 60 percent said that they had chosen academic careers solely because college jobs had been offered to them. Only 32 percent of the men questioned had made such a response. Bernard found that women who held doctorates tended to come from wealthier and better-educated backgrounds than did men with doctorates. Generally, these women were brighter in terms of test knowledge than their male counterparts, generally they were older, and generally they worked at lower status institutions than the men who had received degrees from the same universities from which the women had graduated. In their careers, they were more likely to receive low pay, and they were more likely to be held at the low rank than men of equivalent productivity and qualifications. She pointed out the role anomaly women faced, and still frequently face, in academia: faculty women found themselves classified as a group with faculty wives in social settings.

Of all writers on the subject of academic women, Bernard is one of the few to speak at length about the "fringe benefit" status of so many women, women in particular who were married to faculty members and thus geographically limited in where they might pursue professions. Very frequently, such women have become financial assets to the university in that they will teach lower-level courses or fill any number of staff positions for a fraction of the pay that men with comparable training and credentials would receive. They are essentially on the fringe of the academic profession though not a part of it, seldom in tenured faculty positions. They are a fringe benefit the university receives when hiring the husband in that they can provide highly skilled cut-rate labor. Though affirmative action pressure has made minimal inroads into this problem area, it remains a major one, particularly outside the large urban centers.

Helen Astin's study of the women who received Ph.D.s in 1957 and 1958, *The Woman Doctorate in America*,[8] has been both enlightening and heartening to feminists seeking an answer to the critics' charge that advanced degrees are wasted on women: they will only marry, have children, and drop out of professional life altogether. Astin contacted 1653 women representing 86 percent of all women who were granted doctorates in 1957 and 1958. She found that eight years after receiving their doctorates, after a span of time which would allow them to be married and have young children, 81 percent were employed full time, 10 percent part time, a grand total of 91 percent of all women doctorates at work, double the employment rate of women at large. Astin countered the complaint lodged against women that they hurt their careers because of long gaps during which they bear and rear children. The contemporary national pattern of women's work showed women entering the job market in their early twenties, dropping out for about ten years, then reentering after their children were in school. Among Astin's employed respondents, 79 percent answered that they had never interrupted their careers, and among the 18 percent who had, the usual time ran between eleven and fifteen months. In short, the Astin study supported the hypothesis that the more education the woman receives, the more likely she is to remain in the work force.

Astin's profile of academic women depicted a somewhat more vigorous, independent woman than did Bernard's. The process of selection by which they survived was a severe one, for of all women who received B.A.s in the period of Astin's study, only about 1 percent completed Ph.D.s, versus a little better than 10 percent of comparable men. One-quarter of the mothers of these women worked, over 70 percent in the professions and in business and managerial occupations. Doctorate-holding women tended to take longer to finish their degrees than men, and on the average were 4.5 years older than the men who received Ph.D.s in 1957 and 1958. In fact, only 7 percent of the respondents reported beginning their doctorate studies immediately after the B.A. and finishing in four years. The average lapse between B.A. and Ph.D. was twelve years, with women in sciences finishing youngest and women in education finishing oldest as a rule.

Since 70 percent of the working respondents were employed in colleges and universities, and 10 percent were in junior colleges and school systems, Astin's questions concentrated on various aspects of the life of a professional academic. As was true of academic women in the nineteenth century, the marriage rate was lower for these women; a little more than 50 percent of them were or had been married, versus 94 percent of women of comparable age in the United States at large and 81 percent of the B.A.s questioned in another study. Women holding doctorates also tended to have families smaller than the national average; one-quarter of the married respondents were childless. Women tended to be older when they married, and frequently married men with doctorates or professional degrees.

The youngest women in the sample were the most mobile, followed by married women, with a considerable difference! Very often that mobility was conditioned by the husband's career rather than by choice. Still, these women were more likely than any comparable group to be at their first jobs, single women were more likely than married women to be working in general, and married women in large cities of 100,000 people or more were more likely to be working than those in smaller cities. Women with young children and with husbands who earned the highest incomes were least likely to be working, while women who married during graduate school or who had graduate assistantships were more likely to be working.

On the whole, women were less productive than men in terms of publication and research and showed a different attitude toward their work, one that reflected less strain over occupational success. One-third of the respondents said they had entered advanced education because "it was fun," while many indicated that continued education was intrinsically rewarding. Women identified their professional emphases in the following way: on the average, about 50 percent of their time was spent on teaching; about 25 percent on research; and about 25 percent on administration, service to clients, and other professionally related duties. In contrast, in a 1965 study, men in higher education recorded that on the average they devoted 31 percent of their time to teaching, 41 percent to research, 20 percent to administration, and 8 percent to other activities.

A key to these statistics is the fact that women are more often employed at the college or junior college level than at the university level. In fact, the research production levels for university women and *comparable* men were not found to be significantly different. Astin found that 75 percent of her respondents had published at least one article, 13 percent had published eleven or more, and the average was between three and four. The third of Astin's sample who had received special honors were generally the most productive in research.

Astin particularly noted that complaints of discrimination came not from women who could be accused of a "sour grapes" attitude, but rather from the highest achievers among the women. Thirty-three percent of the respondents felt that discrimination against their sex had adversely affected their career; 25 percent reported prejudice encountered in hiring, 40 percent in salary, 33 percent in tenure and promotion, and 33 percent in assignment of administrative chores. In general, too, married women discovered that they made less money than single women did. Among these women, most frequently reported obstacles to their careers, besides discrimination, were the lack of suitable child-care and household help, the mobility of their husbands, and husbands' antagonism.

Nevertheless, Astin's conclusions were promising. Over 50 percent of the sample held the rank of full or associate professor, and the median salary was significant. An interesting sidelight was the fact that women in junior colleges and school systems seemed to be earning more than women in universities. The autobiographical portraits that Astin solicited showed, despite discrimination, happy, active women in a variety of academic fields.

The effect of subsequent studies of academic women has been to refine a number of Bernard's and Astin's observations. The attrition rate for women has remained higher than for men since the early 1950s. Ann Sutherland Harris sought to account for this fact by reference to factors other than marriage and family. She found broad implications in the studies done by Rosenthal and Jacobson that demonstrated the extent to which teachers' or experimenters' expectations of subjects' success are likely to predestine that success. She summarized studies in which randomly selected students scored higher on IQ tests after a year in which teachers expected them to bloom as compared to control-group students who were not expected to bloom; in fact, rats seemed to be able to run mazes better when experimenters believed they were exceptionally bright rats. What would be the effect on a woman of comments such as: "You're so cute, I can't see you as a professor of anything." "Why don't you find a rich husband and give all this up?" "I know you're competent and your thesis adviser knows you're competent. The question in our minds is, are you really serious about what you're doing?" [9] Alice Rossi has told a story of a friend who worked as a research assistant during her second pregnancy, did her graduate work while her children were preschoolers, finished the analysis of her data in the summer prior to her first full-time teaching job with the expectation of writing her thesis in the following summer, introduced children to their new school, arranged for household help, and prepared her first year's lectures. Nevertheless, her chairman let her go after the first year, his excuse being that he did not think she would finish her thesis. Several young men at the same institution, whose theses were far from done, were retained.[10]

The expectations that women will do less well or are less competent than men have been demonstrated in a variety of studies. A particularly poignant study, which reveals the assumptions some women make about themselves and by implication other women, was conducted at Connecticut College for Women and shows the extent to which women tend to disparage the achievements of other women. An identical article was presented, one as John McKay's work, the other as Joan McKay's, to different groups of sophomores. The group that thought the article was John's work called it impressive; those who thought it was Joan's work thought it was poor.[11] Further studies have concluded that women have no trouble valuing proven success achieved by women or men, but may disparage women who are struggling to succeed. In short, the victims have taken on the assumptions of the victimizers.

The following study goes a step further to show how lower expectations about women or a lower estimate of their work can lead to discrimination. Lawrence Simpson focused on hiring practices of six Pennsylvania schools as they affect women. He collected 234 responses from hiring agents, generally department chairmen and deans, to questionnaires containing identical résumés for job applicants, identical except that the sex of the fictional candidates varied. He found that all other things being equal, men were preferred to women by those who hire and that the fewer women there were in the field, the less likely the woman was to be hired. A superior woman would be hired over an average man, but sex rather than qualifications clearly was the chief consideration. It is interesting also, in view of the Connecticut College study, that women respondents to this questionnaire selected more female candidates than did the men.[12]

The institutional preference for men as teachers and administrators has in recent years been a major source of criticism against the "seven sisters" and several other eastern women's colleges. Recently women presidents of Bryn Mawr, Vassar, and Sarah Lawrence have been succeeded by men. The curricula of these colleges in which so much hope was invested in the last century tend now to be strongest in service-oriented departments, the decorative arts, the humanities—the so-called women's fields—and weakest in the so-called masculine subjects, mathematics and physical science. In general, the educational quality of these colleges has been rated below that of men's colleges.[13]

In general, too, the attitude toward women in higher education can still be summed up by the statement Kingman Brewster made to Yale women irate over the tokenism at Yale: "We are all for women, but Yale must produce a thousand male leaders a year." The level of society's initial expectation of women remains characteristically low. A woman entering college today may still be directed toward "women's subjects," and if she perseveres through a doctoral program with the aim of entering academia, she may still be hired only if she is better than the men with whom she competes. Equal-opportunity laws to the contrary, she may still be paid less than men of comparable achievements. Chances are that she will advance more slowly through the ranks than men of equal achievements, be limited in committee participation, and all but excluded from the highest ranks of administration.

To what extent has this profile changed or is it changing as a result of the feminist revival and new women's rights laws of recent years? The Civil Rights Act of 1964, supplemented by recent executive orders and laws, specifically make discrimination in employment due to race or sex illegal in institutions of higher education. In a painstakingly slow process, the Department of Health, Education, and Welfare has, at the instigation of the Women's Equity Action League, been investigating charges of discrimination made against some of the most prestigious schools in the United States. In the past three years, the University of Michigan was required, over its objections, to submit an affirmative action program to HEW and live by it. Columbia was temporarily deprived of government funds because its proposed programs were not satisfactory. More positive responses came from the University of Oregon, which announced that half of all new hires would be women, and the University of Texas, which stated its commitment to hiring 100 percent women.

Nevertheless, gains made by women on the faculties, particularly of the large universities with strong academic reputations, have been extremely small, in spite of affirmative action programs. Overall increases in the proportion of women on the faculty have amounted to little more than a percentage point or two, in spite of many individual cases of women, held for years in nontenure track, low-paying lectureships and other adjunct roles, who have been moved to status and pay levels more representative of their qualifications and experience. In the matter of equalizing salary levels, too, though some gains have been made, nationally compiled statistics still show a substantial gap between male and female salary averages.

Part of the reason for the minimal progress has been the nationwide trend of falling enrollments matched with a severe inflationary impact on the buying power of colleges and universities. This has led to a small but vocal backlash which claims that bright young men can no longer find jobs; they are blocked by women and minority-group members. Feminists respond angrily that bright young women have been prevented for decades from taking university positions, to the consequent harm of the curriculum and instruction of students, women and men both. The prestigious Carnegie Commission has managed to come out on both sides of the issue in its publications; on the one hand, by several strong exhortations that universities must be prepared to see women assume their rightful place as students and faculty; and on the other, by claiming that affirmative action harms the quality of the university. This conflict will not be resolved soon.

Women as students are beginning to benefit from new laws that guarantee the right to equality of opportunity in higher education. Title IX of the 1972 Education Amendments to the Higher Education Act render illegal acts of discrimination based on sex in any educational activities carried on by institutions of higher education that receive federal aid. In matters of admission, counseling, financial aids, access to courses, and other educational activities, even in such touchy areas as intercollegiate athletics, equity for women is now mandated by law.

In the subtle matter of attitudes, too, there are signs of slow but significant changes. Vassar girls of the mid-1950s said they wanted marriage with or without a career; by the mid-1960s, graduates of Vassar preferred careers, with or without marriage. The growing acceptance of the new curricular area of Women's Studies shows a recognition of the fact that university studies have been one-sided in making male personality and achievements the standard of measurement for too long. At the 1971 convention of the Modern Language Association, the membership heard its president make these comments:

> *There are similar lessons to be learned from the writing and curriculum planning of the women's movement. The objective of female studies is not simply to create one more department or another interdisciplinary grab bag, but to change the consciousness of women. And more. Changing consciousness is seen as part of the struggle to transform male-dominated institutions, and to humanize relationships between the sexes. Consequently, feminist literary criticism has profoundly challenged the notion of literature as a self-enclosed field with a set of autonomous rules. Here the concern of criticism is with what literature does to people's heads; how it serves to fix sexual stereotypes; how it twists the consciousness of women—and how this can be changed. The feminist critique challenges us to change the canon of literature, to radically shift our valuations of that canon, and to remember that in the classroom we are men and women affecting the thoughts and feelings of other men and women. In short, feminists do not regard literary study as an activity apart from the general concerns of feminism.[14]*

What actual changes such shifting emphases and new awarenesses will create, in the context of the changing status of women in higher education as faculty and students, is one of the most interesting questions of the 1970s.

NOTES

1. Garden City, N.Y.: Anchor Books, 1965, p. 95.

2. Ibid., p. 194.

3. The bulk of the historical development narrative that follows is condensed from ELEANOR FLEXNER's *Century of Struggle* (New York: Atheneum, 1970).

4. Quoted in AILEEN S. KRADITOR, *Up from the Pedestal* (Chicago: Quadrangle Books, 1968), pp. 81–82.

5. Quoted in ibid., pp. 92–96.

6. See Doris Pullen's article in MARY LOU THOMPSON's *Voices of the New Feminism* (Boston: Beacon Press, 1970).

7. University Park, Penn.: Pennsylvania State University Press, 1964.

8. New York, 1969.

9. "The Second Sex in Academe," *AAUP Bulletin* (September 1970): 283–95.

10. "Discrimination and Demography Restrict Opportunities for Academic Women," *College and University Business* (February 1970): 74–78.

11. Philip Goldberg, "Are Women Prejudiced Against Women?" *Trans-action* (April 1968): 28–30.

12. "A Myth Is Better than a Miss," *College and University Business* (February 1970): 72–73.

13. PULLEN, in THOMPSON, *New Feminism.*

14. LOUIS KAMPF, "It's Alright, Ma (I'm only Bleeding): Literature and Language in the Academy," *PMLA* (May 1972): 377–83.

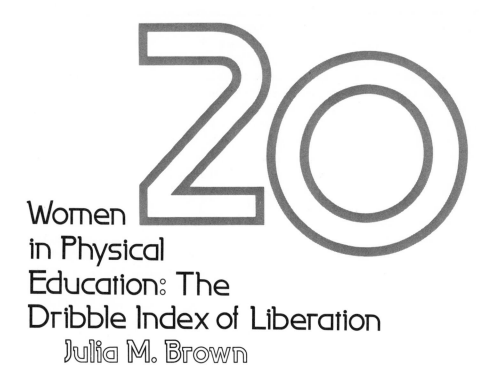

Women in Physical Education: The Dribble Index of Liberation
Julia M. Brown

BASKETBALL: HISTORICAL REFLECTIONS

In 1891 the game of basketball was invented and widely adopted by YMCA schools as an indoor winter sport for men. The game held great appeal for the players as it was easily learned, involved teamwork and strategy, and stimulated interest and excitement as players attempted to put a soccer ball into a vertical target. It was not long before girls were also playing the game *using the same rules as the men*. The five players on a team could run anywhere on the court, bounce the ball any number of times, and snatch the ball from an opponent's hands. Noting that these rules produced a rough and physical game when played by girls, Senda Berenson, who first introduced the game to women at Smith College, made several modifications. Primarily, players were not permitted to steal the ball from an opponent. This led to standing and waiting with the ball until a teammate could get free. Therefore, a three-second rule was created to force the player to pass within that time. Then the players discovered they could bounce the ball every three seconds and thus keep possession. In order to promote teamwork and to eliminate the possibility of one player dominating the ball, no more than three bounces were permitted. To protect against excessive fatigue and further against dominance by the best player, the court was divided into three sections, and two girls on the six-player team were restricted to each area.[1]

Within a short time, these rules became official for women, and changed as attitudes themselves changed. In 1914, two rule changes limited a player to one bounce and permitted small courts to be divided into two instead of three sections. In 1938, two areas became official for all courts. In 1949, girls were allowed two bounces. In the early 1950s, the unlimited dribble was tried on an experimental basis but rejected as being too strenuous. In 1961, three bounces were once again permitted. In 1962, two of the players on a team were allowed to rove or play the entire court. A player was also permitted to steal the ball from an opponent. Finally, the end of the 1960s saw a return to the five-player team, an unlimited dribble, and freedom to move into any area of the court.[2]

Underlying this brief outline of major rule changes are the attitudes of women leaders in physical education toward the participation of girls and women in competitive sports. This picture suggests a concern for the well-being of the participant. It shows a response to fears that the stress of sports competition gave rise to psychological and physiological states harmful to a female. It illustrates a strong desire on the part of women to be independent of men's organizations and to control their own sports. It serves as a point of departure in the examination of the philosophy of women physical educators as they struggled for an image of respectability in a world of physical activity and athletics dominated by men. The struggle has been reaction to both the classic image of woman as a delicate and physically inept creature and the stereotype of the muscular, mannish female athlete. Sensitivity to both these pictures has influenced the direction of physical education programs for girls and women.

LEADERSHIP

The organization that assumes the leadership role in women's sports is the Division for Girls and Women's Sports (DGWS), a nonprofit educational association made up of women members of the parent organization, the American Alliance for Health, Physical Education and Recreation. These women are professional leaders in schools, colleges, communities, industrial plants, military service, private and public clubs, and agencies. This group has the responsibility for making rules for competitive sports for women, establishing policy, setting standards, training and rating officials, and formulating desirable practices for the conduct of women's programs. The currently stated purpose is "to foster the development of sports programs for the enrichment of the life of the participant."[3] Underlying the purpose of the organization since its beginnings in the early 1900s has been the attempt to identify what is "healthful" and what is "desirable" in the conduct of sports programs for women. Frequently incorporated into the philosophical statement has been the often repeated expression, "*a sport for every girl and every girl in sport.*"[4] Basic concerns throughout the years have included: ensuring broad participation, providing health safeguards, maintaining a spirit of amateurism, and seeking independence from the control of men.

SEPARATE AND UNEQUAL

The value of light exercise for girls and women has long been recognized by women educators. As early as the 1850s, the finishing-school girl and the college woman were generally offered a program of light calisthenics, rhythmic exercise, and, later, dancing,[5] all activities considered both healthful and appropriate for "young ladies."

Sports activities were not a part of school programs until the latter part of the century when they began to flourish in women's colleges. Vassar was among the first to offer riding and Wellesley to offer rowing. Sports clubs sprang up to further the interest in such sports as tennis and fencing. As participation grew, it became apparent that women were not as delicate as commonly thought, and the woman in sport grew in acceptance by society.

Although participation in sport was gaining in popularity with college women, formal sports *competition* for women was virtually nonexistent. In January 1892, a woman writer for the *Atlantic Monthly* stated that "the part which athletics plays in college life for men has no answering equivalent in college life for women."[6]

Two years later, Senda Berenson of Smith College introduced the game of basketball, and it was basketball which, within a decade of its origin, marked the beginning of competition for women in colleges throughout the United States. In fact, in many instances, the women organized teams and competed on an intercollegiate level before the men did. Smith College played Bryn Mawr, Radcliffe played Mount Holyoke, Barnard played Syracuse, Ripon played Oshkosh Normal, and Stanford played California.[7]

The original game of basketball was considered by Berenson to be too rough and too strenuous for ladies, and she quickly modified the rules to eliminate snatching the ball and to restrict the running area. Not all playing groups knew about these modifications, and at least five different versions of the game were played. Club teams were coached largely by men who used men's rules and men officials. There was a strong need for some standardization. The first *Official Basketball Guide for Women* was published in the Spaulding Athletic Library Series in 1901. In 1905, the Women's Basketball Committee was formed. The organization of this committee represented the first attempt by women to control sports, particularly competitive sports, for women. Its formation also initiated questions and controversy concerning healthful and desirable aspects of athletics for women. Was the men's game of basketball really too rough for ladies to play? Did the unrestricted use of the full court lead to the "glorification" of one player? Was it physiologically unsound for females to play the whole court? Was the acceptance of men's rules a symbol of male domination?

Basketball grew in popularity, intercollegiate competition for women grew in popularity, and professional women in physical education grew more cautious. They did not want to imitate the undesirable aspects they saw in men's athletic programs. Said Berenson in 1901, "The greatest element of evil in the spirit of athletics in this country is the idea that one must win at any cost—that defeat is an unspeakable disgrace."[8] Said Lucille Eaton Hill, director of physical training at Wellesley College, "We hear constantly of the '*abuse* of men's athletics,' we should hear nothing but the '*use* of women's athletics.'" She further stated, "We must avoid the evils which are so apparent to thoughtful people in the conduct of athletics for men."[9] Hill also recommended that if the proper leadership and facilities were not available, interscholastic matches should not be permitted.[10] There were not enough women leaders to teach and organize the matches, and men stepped in to fill the demand. Men coaches were strongly criticized for exposing the girls on their teams to "severe" training techniques and "rigorous" playing conditions. Critics argued that women players were being subjected to exploitation and commercialism.

The women leaders, with denunciations of the men's programs, began to formulate a philosophy for the conduct of their own programs. Hill stated that sports should contribute the "greatest good to the greatest number; not the greatest good to the smallest number," [11] as was the case in basketball. She reported a statement made by Dean Briggs of Wellesley in his commencement address, "Fiercely competitive athletics have their dangers for men, but they develop manly strength. For women their dangers are greater, and the qualities they tend to develop are not womanly." [12] Interschool games in basketball were criticized by others as being unfeminine and both psychologically and physiologically unsound for girls. As early as 1904, a woman officer of the Wisconsin Physical Education Society concurred with the Midwest Conference of Deans of Women who had passed a resolution opposing intercollegiate athletic competition for women.[13]

Philosophical roots were thus set down. It is not surprising that with the organization of the forerunner of the DGWS in 1917, the following principles were proposed: An athletic program for girls should consist of no interschool competition; it should be directed by a woman; and it should not be an imitation of men's athletics. It should be "sport for sport's sake" and there should be "a sport for every girl, and every girl in a sport." [14]

The influence of this position was widespread. A 1923 survey[15] of fifty colleges revealed that only eleven permitted intercollegiate competition for women. Ninety-three percent of the women physical education teachers surveyed were opposed to its conduct. The reasons were reiterated from the past. Such programs led to: excessive commercialism, a "win at all costs" philosophy, a neglect of the exercise needs of the majority, betting, a spirit of professionalism, and potential physiological harm. In a 1930 survey,[16] less than half of 1 percent of the girls in the sampled schools were in intercollegiate competition.

Outside the schools, there was increasing control by men over women's athletics. In 1915, the Amateur Athletic Union began to sanction athletic and swimming events for women and to keep records. In the 1920s and 1930s, a variety of national championships were sponsored by the AAU. The teams were largely coached by men, and events were officiated by men using men's rules and standards. Women from the United States began to compete in the Olympics in swimming in 1920.

It became evident that some leadership was necessary to coordinate the many sports organizations and to control practices involving women. Under the direction of Mrs. Herbert Hoover, the Women's Division of the National Amateur Athletic Federation was formed; and with the help of prominent professional leaders of college programs for women, the purposes were formulated. The division was to promote broad participation in sports and to discourage highly specialized intense competition.[17] Their platform was influential and served as a model for similar statements by a number of physical education organizations.

In 1928, the United States sent a women's track team to participate in the Olympics. The next year, the Women's Division of the NAAF went "on record as disapproving of competition for girls and women in the Olympic Games." [18] The reasons offered were: (1) preparation entails specialized training of a few girls; (2) participation offers opportunity for exploitation; and (3) there might be possible overstrain in preparation for or during performance at the games. The division requested permission from the Olympic Committee to put on a festival for women concurrent with the next Olympic games to be held in Los Angeles in 1932. The plan was to have singing, dancing, mass sports and games, luncheons, conferences, demonstrations, and other activities that would promote the idea of "play for play's sake." The idea was not accepted by the Olympic Committee, but the position taken clearly reinforced sexism in athletics, and for the next thirty years, seriously curtailed sports opportunities for the highly skilled woman.

The first alternative to intercollegiate competition was the *playday*, which had its origin in the 1920s. This was primarily an interschool social affair in which women could participate on teams that lacked any school identity. The emphasis was on the sociability during the tea that followed the games. A school might be allowed to play an informal impromptu game with another school afterward if there were no preliminary practices, no announcement of scores, and no basketball.[19]

Later the sports day form of competition was introduced. This was also a social event in which the school group participated as a team composed of players who had demonstrated interest in the sport and willingness to play on that occasion. The team did not have the advantage of a training and conditioning program nor any coaching as a team. They often had greater interest than skill.

Still later, telegraphic meets were added to the list of acceptable forms of competition. This offered the opportunity for a girl in an individual sport to test herself against other top-level performers but avoided the face-to-face competitive situation.

These forms of competition dominated physical education programs for women through the 1940s. There were criticisms from students who sought opportunities with outside agencies because the schools were not filling the needs of the skilled players. There were bitter criticisms of those states and those schools where interschool programs did exist. After World War II this attitude began to be more widely challenged. Women had proved themselves quite capable of enduring long hours in defense plants and were eager for new physical challenges. There was renewed interest in seeking greater opportunities for competition provided it was conducted in accord with standards established by DGWS regarding health, participation, leadership, and publicity. By 1955, half the physical educators surveyed favored intercollegiate team sports for women, and 70 percent favored intercollegiate competition in individual sports.[20]

Others, however, reacted to the growing interschool programs with resolutions of opposition or of caution. The DGWS Standards of 1958 stated that if an institution assumes responsibility for sponsoring any type of intercollege event, the following principles should apply. College women shall not participate (1) as part of men's intercollegiate teams, (2) in touch football or similar exhibitions, (3) with or against men in contact sports.[21]

It was clear that practices were changing, and with them attitudes of women in physical education. Unfortunately, years of minimal use of athletic space by women had firmly established the pattern of giving men's and boys' programs priority of time, facilities, coaching, and financing. Enthusiastic teachers of women's physical education began to donate their time in the interest of providing greater opportunities for skilled girls. They pleaded with school administrators for practice time in the gyms, the pools, or on the tracks, in the early morning or in the evening hours. They invented ways, such as bake sales and candy peddling, to raise money to fund their teams. They faced humiliation when they were forced out of the practice areas by men coaches and male athletes.[22] Less persistent teachers gave in when they met strong opposition from men or other women who still did not agree that women should participate in interschool competition. Other teachers were content to conduct the physical education classes and intramurals for the masses. Programs remained largely separate and unequal.

The basketball rules changes of the 1960s reflected the growing interest in *cooperating* with men's athletics. The DGWS, influenced by the AAU Basketball Committee, took measures to revise the game to be more similar to that played by the men. The unrestricted use of the full court, a five-player team, an unlimited dribble, and permissive snatching of the ball created a faster, more exciting game than it had been since the turn of the century. Pressure for these changes came not only from players who wanted greater physical and mental challenge, but also from a desire to keep pace with at least six other groups that were making basketball rules attractive to the players, and from interest in producing qualified players to compete with international teams who were already playing the full-court faster game.[23]

Not only did women physical educators concern themselves with the game of basketball in the early 1960s, but a small group of leaders devoted their efforts to increasing high-level competition in the interest of better representation in the Olympic Games, particularly in track and gymnastics. Few women had ever learned even the basic skills of these activities, and fewer knew how to teach or coach them on a more advanced level. The Women's Board of the United States Olympic Development Committee conceived an idea that would both expand the opportunities for sports participation by women and increase the depth of experience of present participants.[24] The plan was to sponsor in cooperation with the DGWS a series of national institutes on girls' sports. State representatives would be invited to attend a five-day training session and then conduct similar training sessions in their own states. In November 1963, the first institute was held.

IMAGES AND ATTITUDES

"Strenuous exercise is harmful." During the 1850s and '60s, walking a mile or two at a moderate pace was considered a great deal of exercise for young ladies. Society hardly entertained the idea that women could participate in sports. The female was of a delicate nature and strenuous activity was harmful, particularly to the reproductive organs. During the menstrual period, a woman was advised to *"Do less than usual. . . . Over-exertion is a most fruitful cause of disease. Long walks, shopping, dancing, riding, hard work whether for pleasure or profit, should be avoided to the utmost."* [25]

As women became increasingly interested in sports, they began to participate in archery, croquet, lawn tennis, golf, and swimming. These were sports that capitalized not so much on physical prowess as on coordination and the use of the intellect. Nevertheless, certain modifications were advised. The ladies were to stand still while playing tennis, hang on to the coattails of their escorts while ice skating, and keep the head of the golf club below the shoulders while swinging.[26] It was a generally held belief that ladies should not perspire. They might merely "glow."

Modern-day evidence of the lingering effects of this attitude can be seen in the presentation of requests to be excused from physical education classes during the menstrual period and in the admonitions of some parents, teachers, and doctors to "take it easy" and "don't overdo." Females have long been considered the "weaker sex."

Much of the adverse attitude toward women in athletics has been related to the biological nature of the female. There have been numerous attempts, particularly on the part of the medical profession, to show that strenuous activity, particularly during adolescence, was harmful to the reproductive function and a cause of menstrual problems. The outcomes of most of the studies provided more evidence to suggest beneficial effects of activity rather than harmful effects. The accumulated findings of research during the last twenty years dispel the myth that women are unable to withstand the physiological demands of participation in strenuous sports or the psychological stress of competition.

Erdelyi's[27] findings in an extensive study of 729 Hungarian female athletes revealed that strenuous training and competition did not adversely affect the onset of menarche or the menstrual function itself. Extensive physiological studies conducted on Swedish girl champion swimmers and former champions who participated in a rigorous training program revealed no injuries or gynecological abnormalities.[28] Very active synchronized swimmers had *less* trouble with dysmenorrhea than a nonswimming control group.[29] A survey of the women athletes in the Tokyo Olympics indicated that menstrual changes were well within normal limits as a result of training and competition.[30] The diving women of Korea and Japan engage in daily deep diving even during their menstrual periods, and surveys have indicated their cycles to be quite regular. Indeed, they dive up to the day of delivery of their children.[31]

No evidence can support the belief that girls should not engage in jumping activities. Thomas[32] points out that the uterus essentially floats free in a protective pool of pelvic viscera with no air spaces around it. Any normal force, such as an external blow or the landing from a jump, would be dissipated by the external surface before being transmitted to the internal organs; anatomically, the uterus is well protected against potential shock or stress of vigorous activity.

There is more positive than negative evidence to suggest the significant value of activity for women in relation to their childbearing function. The female Hungarian athletes had shorter labor, and the need for Caesarean section was 50 percent less than for a control group.[33] Exercise programs have been shown to benefit those suffering from dysmenorrhea. The benefits of a postpartum exercise program for sedentary patients who experience back pain after delivery have been reported.[34] Athletes apparently have fewer complications in pregnancies and deliveries, possibly because of strong abdominal muscles, overall fitness, and the ability to relax in the face of pain and discomfort.

Contrary to the popular notion that strenuous activity is harmful to the growing girl, studies reveal that there is little difference in the physical work capacity between boys and girls between seven and thirteen years of age.[35] Girls and boys in elementary school are on an equal basis in the performance of motor skills. There are only slight average differences in muscle mass and in stature. However, the adolescent growth spurt begins earlier in females, and full stature is attained about three years ahead of males. Recent record-breaking performances of young girls in swimming and track tend to support the belief held by many exercise physiologists that adolescent girls are at their physiological peak and are socially and psychologically ready for disciplined physical training.[36]

Research findings have helped to illustrate the beneficial physiological effects of female participation in sport. In 1964, an American Medical Association Committee on Medical Aspects of Sports asserted the benefits of exercise for females as well as males and expressed its concern about the inadequate opportunities for the greater part of the female population to engage in suitable and regular physical activity.[37]

"The female athlete is unfeminine." The female competitor has always been less accepted than the woman in recreational sport. The era of the female competitor began in earnest with the introduction of men's basketball, which became immensely popular with girls in schools, colleges, and clubs. Competition between groups became widespread and intense. Undoubtedly, some of these performers were rather strong, big, and muscular. Some had even taken men as their models; they dressed like men, tried to play like men, and even swore like men. There were cases of exploitation and commercialism. Rice[38] reported an instance in which the sponsoring agency of a ladies' basketball game had the players parade in the streets in their bathing suits to generate interest in their upcoming game. The stereotypical female sports figure became impressed in the mind of the public. It was an image from which most women, particularly most women physical educators, wanted to disassociate themselves. It could be said that this image gave rise to the attitude that sports are unfeminine.

Newspaper sportswriters (all men) helped to perpetuate the image of the unfeminine female athlete. In reporting the accomplishments of one of the women shot putters in an Olympic game, the writer stated, "All the genius of the Renaissance which worked to form an image of woman considered as an object of leisure and repose is shattered by the panting strides or hefty image of women who look like woodsmen such as those carved on bas-relief." [39]

Athletes themselves became concerned about their image and went to great lengths to appear feminine. Fashion began to make the sports pages when Gussie Moran was photographed on the tennis court in lace panties. Later, the Texas track club became noted for their glamorous hairdos. The news reporting of the 1965 International Track Meet in New York was full of feminine fashion and the exuberance of the athletes. It focused attention on the fact that pretty girls all over the world were enjoying track and field events, except in the United States where there was a noticeable lack of depth in participation.[40]

A changing image was also reflected by the sportswriters. "Stereotype Doesn't Fit" was the headline penned by Standaert in late 1971 for the *Wisconsin State Journal*. In reporting Kay Lunda's inclusion on the U.S. speed skating team for the 1972 Winter Olympics, he stated, "After all, female athletes, especially those in such a strenuous and demanding activity, are supposed to be tomboyish, slightly conceited, and decidedly unfeminine—a sort of roller derby girl on skates." [41] He goes on to say that Kay is "a dramatic departure from that unfair generality." This reporter, in addition to reporting the accomplishment of a sports figure, was publicizing his own revelation of sex-typing in athletics.

As women have received greater opportunities for proving themselves in competition, for winning greater sums of money, and for receiving greater news coverage and publicity, public recognition has increased. News items include less about masculinity-femininity characteristics or what the performer is wearing and more about her performance. Indeed, in some cases there is even a trace of admiration. When Stonger of the Associated Press reported the election of the female athlete of the year, he described Olga Korbut as "the Soviet Union's littlest soldier who won three gold medals, a silver medal, and the hearts of the world at the Munich Olympics." [42]

"Girls Lack Motivation." Despite the fact that physical education for women has operated for nearly eighty years on the principle of promoting broad participation, relatively few women assume a life style that includes physical activity on a regular basis. Playgrounds and community recreation centers are used primarily by men and boys. Few girls play "catch" in the back yard or shoot baskets over the garage door. Fathers despair of teaching their little girls to throw a ball, and mothers discourage their daughters from playing "tomboy" games. Commercial enterprises appeal to the female vanity with their "slimnastics" and "figure fun" programs. Golf courses sponsor "ladies days" and sports clubs reduce the membership fees for women.

Studies conducted in the 1960s of participation patterns of girls in schools and colleges indicate a drop in interest in sports between ninth and twelfth grades. Sheriff[43] discussed some of the findings. The reasons offered by the girls themselves reflected cultural rather than biological influences. High school girls reported their lack of participation due to nonparticipation by friends, pressure of studies, lack of participation in physical education, and feeling of inadequacy in sports. Major factors influencing the participation of college women were listed as lack of time due to studies and other interests, and lack of participating companions. These reasons suggested the position of sports participation in the female personal hierarchy of values.

Other reasons offered for lack of participation have included inadequate facilities, insufficient staff, communication problems, lack of previous experience, lack of organization, and need for skill instruction. These reasons suggest that little incentive has been offered to girls to participate. Time, money, and effort in the male-dominated administrative structure of the schools have been spent on the programs for the boys.

Sheriff[44] also discussed several studies conducted in the late 1960s which indicated that the attitude of the general public toward women in sports competition was less favorable than that of either the spectators or the players. Teen-age boys were the most critical of women in sports. Teen-age girls reported a belief that female sports competitors tend to assume masculine mannerisms and attitudes. It is still evident that, unlike her male counterpart, the social status of the high school or college girl hardly depends on success in athletics.

Some sports are appropriate. Some sports have almost always been acceptable for women: swimming, diving, figure skating, golf, archery, bowling, and skiing. Metheny[45] identified the characteristics of these activities as the manipulation of a fairly light object, or projection of the body in aesthetically pleasing patterns, or use of a manufactured device to increase velocity and/or maneuverability. These sports are not dependent upon great power or strength.

Face-to-face competitive sports such as tennis, badminton, and volleyball have been acceptable because of a spatial barrier that prevents body contact with the opponent. As a rule, women do not oppose men in these competitions unless both teams are mixed.

Field hockey, brought to the United States from England in 1901 by a woman, caught the interest of girls in many private schools and colleges in the East at the same time that basketball was becoming so popular. An interesting note is that this game was a great deal more strenuous and rougher than basketball, yet no attempt was made to modify the rules, other than to shorten the time periods from thirty to twenty-five or twenty minutes. The game was introduced by a woman, and played almost exclusively by women. Few men in the United States appeared interested in playing the game although it is considered a men's sport elsewhere in the world and is played exclusively by men in the Olympic Games.

There are still some sports considered inappropriate for women: wrestling, boxing, weight lifting, hammer throw, pole vault, high hurdles, water polo, football, and ice hockey. In the 1950s the list would have included judo, shot-put, discus, javelin, low hurdles, long jump, gymnastics, free exercise, and long races. Touch football has been a recreation sport for women for a number of years; water polo is undergoing experimentation as a game for women; and ice hockey is generating enough interest among girls that they are requesting ice time for team practice and play.

Attitudes do change. As women continued to assert their rights in various aspects of our society, the woman in sport was an object of a changing public attitude. Metheny[46] suggests the game of tennis as an interesting illustration of the changing status of women. Not until women had gained some equality with their husbands did they play the game at all, and then only with the same sex. When mixed doubles began to be played, the woman was positioned at the net in a supportive role while the man played the baseline to cover up the mistakes of his partner. Present-day style is to play side by side for mutual advantage. Metheny's example can be updated. Although mixed doubles play has long been acceptable, it was not until the early 1970s that it became even tolerable for women to compete officially in tennis against men. As a result of lawsuits or threatened legal actions, high school girls in at least eight states may now try out for the boys' varsity tennis teams. In the world of professional tennis, the barrier was broken in 1973 when Bobby Riggs at age fifty-five challenged and beat Margaret Court for a $10,000 purse. The match, the participants, and the sponsors were strongly criticized in the press.[47] The match between Bobby Riggs and Billy Jean King, 1973 champion at Wimbledon, guaranteed the winner at least $200,000, and the loser $100,000, one of the largest purses offered athletes for a single performance. Another sign of the growing equality of the female competition in tennis was the July 1973 announcement that prize money at Forest Hills would be equal for men and women.

Images and attitudes have changed and are continuing to change. During the past 120 years, society has rejected, tolerated, accepted, and in some recent instances, appreciated the woman in sport.

SEPARATE AND EQUAL

As in the early 1900s, women in physical education are once again struggling with the questions associated with rapidly expanding opportunities for women in sport. Some of the same circumstances exist once again. Women want greater challenge in sport. They want better opportunities for participating in recreational sport. They want equal opportunity in a sports world dominated by men. Law suits, threats, demands, play-ins, swim-ins, and shower-ins have illustrated dramatically how much women want to be a part of that world. School administrators have been slow to curtail a successful athletic program for boys by giving up practice space for girls. In many cases, girls are joining men's programs and receiving their coaching from men. Skilled women want to be a part of men's intercollegiate programs and to be subsidized to an equal extent. The situation presses women in physical education to answer many of the same old questions with new information and attitudes.

Can women play the same sports as men? Klafs and Lyon[48] in *The Female Athlete* summarize the anthropometric, physiological, and psychological status of the woman in sport. Medical evidence has pointed up the value of exercise in the physical development of both men and women. Women, as well as men, enjoy taking risks. Women, as well as men, can tolerate the stress of competition. Women respond in the same way, although not to the same degree, to training and conditioning techniques. Women are capable of creditable performances in endurance events. There is no difference between the sexes in motor learning until strength becomes a factor in the learning task. With specific training, women can learn to overcome the mechanical disadvantages associated with anatomical differences. It would appear that women could play *most* of the same sports played by men.

A question arises, however, in relation to female participation in contact sports. Here, the male, with his larger muscle mass and consequent greater strength, has greater natural protection against injury. Muscle tissue serves as a cushion in the absorption of shock. Muscular strength is necessary to develop counterforces to particular stresses. Females have a lighter bone density and less rugged ligamentous support at the joints. The female thus assumes a greater degree of risk of injury in sports that permit physical contact or involve great speed where physical contact may occur.

The school program must be concerned with risk and accordingly sponsor those activities for both girls and boys that minimize chance of injury. Part of the task of physical education should be to help a student realize his or her own capacity in relation to the demands of a sport.

Can women play the same sports with men? There is no question that most mature men have greater strength, size, and speed than most mature women. In sports where these attributes are important to success, the woman will be at a distinct disadvantage if the competition is between the sexes. The top men will beat the top women. However, these characteristics vary so greatly within the sexes that, unquestionably, some women will perform better than some men. Some women can outplay men in tennis, badminton, squash, volleyball, basketball, etc. The cultural attitude has far outweighed the physical reasons why men and women do not compete against each other in noncontact sports. Implications of this suggest that skill-level classifications rather than sex might well become part of the learning process. Graded competitions would give more skilled women opportunities for competition on their own level.

Girls and boys in elementary school are on an equal basis in performance of motor skills. There are only slight average differences in muscle mass and in stature. There appears to be little physiological evidence to suggest any separation of the sexes in sports during this age period. Traditionally, as the sex role becomes increasingly differentiated, boys and girls have been introduced to the sports "appropriate" to their sex. Children might be better served if, during this part of the school program, they were taught a variety of skills basic to a number of different kinds of sports.

During the adolescent years, growth differences become marked. The growth spurt begins earlier in females and full stature is attained about three years ahead of males. During this period, many girls are able to outperform many boys of the same age. It is probably at this point that girls and boys should be separated in the contact sports and differentiated according to skill level for ·instruction in other sports. As in the earlier grades, there is probably no reason why boys and girls should not learn and practice basic sports skills together.

Can women meet the male standard? After the adolescent growth spurt, there are obvious sex differences that can affect performance in sports. Males generally end up larger in weight, height, and other external measurements. The male, at about age eighteen, has broader shoulders, deeper chest, and longer legs and forearms. When comparing averages, this skeletal difference may affect performance. The broader hips and relatively narrow shoulders of the female produce a lower center of gravity to make it more difficult to overcome inertial mass and gain speed quickly. Men, in general, might thus have the advantage in runs, jumps, and some forms of gymnastics. On the other hand, the lower center of gravity of the female produces greater stability, and women would thus have the advantage in balance activities. A difference in angle formed by the upper and lower arm and length of upper limbs may have implications for throwing activities. Pelvic bone and cartilage formation, the angle between the hip and upper leg, and joint distensions may provide the female some drawback in running and jumping. The female is anatomically more adapted than the male to activities demanding flexibility.

The biological differences between the sexes imply that most universal records will be set by men, but the differences will probably vary with respect to the type of activity. Typically, top women athletes attain 75 to 90 percent of the results achieved by men in events that require strength, speed, and endurance. The percentage differential is narrowed in the longer running and swimming events. Recent performances of women in competition have shown marked improvement. The women are shattering more records for their events than are the men over the same period of time.[49]

Where physical attributes are important to performance, there should continue to be two standards, one for women and one for men. Where skill depends on manual dexterity and strategy, there might possibly be but one standard.

Should school teams be integrated? A rapidly developing pattern in school athletics is to permit girls to try out for the boys' teams. This answers the demand for "equal opportunity" to compete for the school in a very superficial way. Complete integration implies that there would be one top team, composed of the best players in that school. Because of natural endowment, in most instances, more boys than girls will make that top team. In many instances, no girls at all will make that team. This scheme would appear to enhance the opportunity for the exceptional girl to compete on a higher level, but in effect, it will drastically reduce opportunities for better-than-average skilled girls. Funds that might be distributed equally to a girls' and a boys' team would be allocated to one team which, in all probability, would be male dominated.

A two-team system based on sex appears to be the most equitable in providing opportunities in the school system. There appears to be no reason why some coaching and training sessions should not be integrated. Equal status should be accorded both teams. Basic team membership should be *restricted* by sex. Where women are permitted to try out for the men's teams, men should be allowed to try out for the women's teams. The result would again be male dominance.

The time-honored principle of broad participation should be maintained. Money must be allocated in terms of a broad-based pyramidal program, the pinnacle being the integrated top team of the institution only after the foundation has been established.

Should women's programs follow the same patterns as the men's? Interschool competition for girls on the high school level could generally follow the same pattern as that established for the boys. Traditionally, women physical educators have been concerned with high standards of leadership, health, travel, and publicity, and if these are maintained, what is good for the boys should be good for the girls.

Men's intercollegiate athletic programs in the larger universities have many aspects of professionalism and big business. The organization becomes obligated to the paying spectator because its existence depends on gate receipts. In order to put on a performance that will be attractive to the customer, it is necessary to scout for the best talent available. The task is to entice the boy to come to the particular university with the promise of a scholarship and certain other fringe benefits. The next task is to keep the boy in condition, generally happy, and eligible scholastically. An added incentive is the promise of a professional career if he plays well in college. Before women demand to be a part of this, the pattern ought to be reviewed in its entirety with respect to its place in higher education, the vast expenditures of money for so few students, and the allocation of time to the business aspects. Other patterns ought to be investigated that will provide competition for the highly skilled girl and not be out of proportion financially with other university activities.

Should women maintain control over women's programs? At present, few women have experience in coaching, managing, training, and conditioning. Few women have been appointed to administrative posts in departments of athletics or coed physical education. Women need to get this kind of experience before they can compete successfully with men for these positions. Maintaining separate but cooperative programs should give women both responsibility and the assistance they need to learn the job. More important, girls and women who wish to participate in sport need role models. They need to associate with women who know sport, who know competition, and who hold high standards for the conduct of these programs.

The changes in the game of women's basketball since before the turn of the century reflect the concern of women in physical education with defining what is healthful and what is desirable for women in sport. These concerns have been in response to beliefs about the physical capacities of females, the sociocultural image of the woman in sport, and the general public attitude toward the female competitor. Early women leaders saw the need to establish control over their own programs in order to govern practices. Objections to highly competitive situations and determination to avoid the pitfalls of commercialism and exploitation seen in men's athletics widened the gap between men's and women's programs. Ironically, this basic philosophical position served to restrict opportunities for female participation in sport.

Numerous conferences on competition prompted a review of the former position and practices. Without relinquishing the principle of broad participation, more attention was given to the needs of the highly skilled girl. Workshops and institutes were designed to increase participation and depth of experience. Emphasis on "equal rights" led to changes of DGWS policies regarding forms of competition, gate receipts, coaching by men, participation on men's teams, and scholarships. A regulatory body (Association for Intercollegiate Athletics for Women) was established to govern intercollegiate competition for women. Over two hundred colleges took a charter membership in this organization. Seven national tournaments were conducted in its first year.

Increasing opportunities for women's competition have raised again some sixty-year-old questions which debate and argument have not yet settled. It is clear that girls and women must be given as much chance to engage in sports as boys and men. What is not clear is whether tradition will be overturned and the emerging pattern will be identical to that of the men, or whether strong philosophical ties with the past will prevail and women will continue to develop their own programs—separate but cooperative and equal.

NOTES

1. RONALD A. SMITH, "The Rise of Basketball for Women in Colleges." 1970. Mimeographed. Pp. 2–4.

2. Ibid., pp. 12–14.

3. Division for Girls and Women's Sports, *Outing Activities and Winter Sports Guide, July 1973–July 1975* (Washington, D.C.: AAHPER, 1973), p. 5. This statement is found in all current DGWS *Guides*.

4. DGWS, *Guides* from 1966 to 1972.

5. ELLEN W. GERBER, "The Changing Female Image: A Brief Commentary on Sport Competition for Women," *Journal of Health, Physical Education and Recreation* (October 1971): 59–61.

6. ANNIE P. CALL, "The Greatest Need of College Girls," *Atlantic Monthly* 69 (January 1892): 102.

7. SMITH, "Basketball for Women," pp. 6–7.

8. SENDA BERENSON, *Basketball for Women* (New York: American Sports Publishing Co., 1901), p. 20.

9. LUCILLE EATON HILL, ed., *Athletics and Out-Door Sports for Women* (New York: Grosset & Dunlap, 1903), p. 5.

10. Ibid., p. 12.

11. Ibid., p. 5.

12. Ibid., p. 6.

13. Reported by SMITH, "Basketball for Women," p. 7.

14. Ibid., p. 8.

15. MABEL LEE, "The Case for and against Intercollegiate Athletics for Women and the Situation as It Stands Today," *Mind and Body* 30 (November 1923): 246–55.

16. MABEL LEE, "The Case for and against Intercollegiate Athletics for Women and the Situation since 1923," *Research Quarterly* (May 1931): 93–127.

17. ALICE ALLENE SEFTON, *The Women's Division National Amateur Athletic Federation* (Stanford: Stanford University Press, 1941), pp. 10–11.

18. Ibid., p. 82.

19. LEE, "Intercollegiate Athletics Since 1923," pp. 104–6.

20. NAOMI LEYHE, "Attitudes of Women Members of the American Association for Health, Physical Education, and Recreation Toward Competition in Sports for Girls and Women" (Ph.D. dissertation, Indiana University, 1955), p. 270.

21. Division for Girls and Women's Sports, *Standards in Sports for Girls and Women* (Washington, D.C.: AAHPER, 1958), p. 49.

22. BILL GILBERT and NANCY WILLIAMSON, "Women Are Getting a Raw Deal," *Sports Illustrated*, 28 May 1973, pp. 88–98.

23. SMITH, "Basketball for Women," p. 14.

24. SARA STAFF JERNIGAN, "The Institute Challenge," *Proceedings of First National Institute on Girls Sports* (Washington, D.C.: AAHPER, 1965), pp. 3–4.

25. GEORGE H. NAPHEYS, *The Physical Life of Woman: Advice to the Maiden, Wife and Mother* (Philadelphia: David McKay, 1893), p. 61.

26. Reported by GERBER, "Changing Female Image," p. 59.

27. GYULA ERDELYI, "Gynecological Survey of Female Athletes," *Journal of Sports Medicine and Physical Fitness* 2 (1962): 174–79.

28. PER-OLAF ASTRAND et al., "Girl Swimmers with Special Reference to Respiratory and Circulatory Adaptation and Gynecological and Psychiatric Aspects," *Acta Paediatrica Scandinavica*, Supplementum 147 (1963).

29. THERESA ANDERSON, "Swimming and Exercise during Menstruation," *Journal of Health, Physical Education and Recreation* 36 (October 1965): 66–68.

30. E. ZAHARIEVA, "Survey of Sportswomen at the Tokyo Olympics," *Journal of Sports Medicine and Physical Fitness* 5 (1965): 215–19.

31. SUK KI HONG and HERMAN ROHN. "The Diving Women of Korea and Japan," *Scientific American* 216 (May 1967): 34–43.

32. CLAYTON L. THOMAS, "The Female Sports Participant: Some Physiological Questions," in *DGWS Research Reports: Women in Sports* (Washington, D.C.: AAHPER, 1971), pp. 37–44.

33. ERDELYI, "Gynecological Survey."

34. EVALYN GENDEL, "Pregnancy, Fitness, and Sports," in *American Medical Association Proceedings of the Seventh National Conference on the Medical Aspects of Sports* (Chicago: The Association, 1967).

35. J. H. WILMORE and P. O. SIGERSETH. "Physical Work Capacity of Young Girls, 7–13 Years of Age," *Journal of Applied Physiology* 22 (May 1967): 923–28.

36. CARL E. KLAFS and M. JOAN LYON, *The Female Athlete* (St. Louis: C. V. Mosby, 1973), p. 52.

37. AMA Committee on Medical Aspects of Sports, Statement report, *Journal of Health, Physical Education and Recreation*, November–December 1964.

38. EMMETT A. RICE, JOHN L. HUTCHINSON, and MABEL LEE, *A Brief History of Physical Education* (5th ed.; New York: Ronald Press, 1969), p. 279.

39. Report by MARIE-THERESE EYQUEM, "Women and the Olympic Games," in *Proceedings, Fourth International Congress on Physical Education and Sports for Girls and Women, August 6–12, 1961* (Washington, D.C.: ICPESGW, 1962), p. 127.

40. DONNA MAE MILLER and KATHRYN R. E. RUSSELL, *Sport: A Contemporary View* (Philadelphia: Lea & Febiger, 1971), p. 130.

41. JEFF STANDAERT, "Stereotype Doesn't Fit," *Wisconsin State Journal*, 22 December 1971, p. 2.

42. KAROL STONGER, "Soviet Gymnast Named Female Athlete of Year," *Wisconsin State Journal*, 18 January 1973, p. 1.

43. MARIE SHERIFF, "Girls Compete???" *DGWS Research Reports: Women in Sports* (Washington, D.C.: AAHPER, 1971).

44. Ibid.

45. ELEANOR METHENY, "Symbolic Forms of Movement: The Feminine Image in Sports," in *Connotations of Movement in Sport and Dance* (Dubuque, Iowa: William C. Brown, 1965), pp. 43–56.

46. Ibid., p. 54.

47. MARK SHAPIRO, "Court, Riggs Will Prove Little," *Wisconsin State Journal*, 8 May 1973, p. 4.

48. KLAFS and LYON, *Female Athlete*, pp. 23–77.

49. Ibid., pp. 48–50.

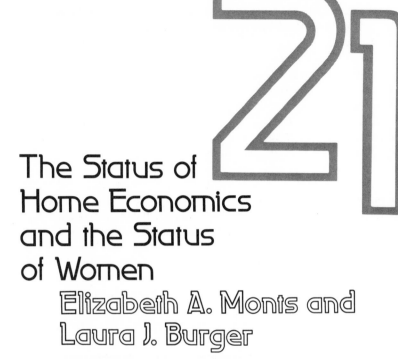

The Status of Home Economics and the Status of Women
Elizabeth A. Monts and Laura J. Burger

The relationship between the status of women and the status of home economics, a profession predominated by women and designed for both male and female clientele, can best be understood by comparing the evolution of home economics and its status as a profession with changes in the status of women.

Noticeable intellectual changes that supported special concerns of women began after 1780 and continued into the 1800s. The ideas of natural rights, humanitarianism, rationality of human beings, and the realization of the utility of higher education, all provided a new perspective on the nature of human existence (McGrath 1968:8). Concurrently, as the number of women attending academies and female seminaries increased, educational leaders were pressured to give some thought to what should be the nature of education for women. Two positions were taken: first, that education for women should be no different than education for men; and second, that education for women should provide for the particular educational "needs" of women.

If an educational program was to be designed for women's particular needs, what were women doing? What was their status at that time—what were their needs? Historically, the primary involvement of women within society was that of being a wife and mother. A married woman derived her status from that of her husband, and if the woman was single, her status was identified with the status of her father.

From 1819 through 1829, Emma Hart Willard and Catherine Beecher, both prominent in women's education, advocated learning in the traditional subjects, but in addition emphasized the scientific practical training for women's duties in the home. This latter portion of education included the teaching of chemistry, philosophy, and economics from the domestic point of view (Ferrar 1964:4). One of the strongest supporters of this emphasis on the home was Edward Yowmans, a chemist in the first half of the nineteenth century who deplored the unsanitary aspects of food preparation.

The Morrill Land Grant Act in 1862 promoted "the liberal and practical education of the industrial classes in the several pursuits and professions in life" (Ferrar 1964:6) and established the land-grant colleges. Within these institutions home economics (domestic science) received its first impetus as a scientifically based area of study. Initial growth took place in the Midwest, with eastern schools clinging to the traditional pattern in which the educational needs of women were not viewed as different from the educational needs of men.

During 1880–90 home economics, then termed domestic science, was introduced into the public secondary schools. The demand for teachers led to an increase in the number of training schools. As could be expected, the focus was on skill training in those activities in the home which consumed most of women's time, such as food preparation, clothing care and construction, laundering, home nursing, and sanitation.

It was from a lack of social, economic, and political concern for the quality of family life that in 1899 a group of persons interested in education for the home held a conference at Lake Placid, New York. This meeting was initiated by Ellen H. Richards, a sanitary chemist from MIT. The disciplines of chemistry, biology, physics, bacteriology, economics, sanitary science, hygiene, domestic science, psychology, and sociology were represented by nine women and one man. The term "home economics" was selected as the name for this new field of study. This organizing group encouraged recognition of home economics as a separate and distinct area of study, whose main concern was the economic and sociological study of the home. From this beginning, home economics was given a broad vision and perceived as appropriate for both men and women.

Quotes taken from these early conferences illustrate that the underlying philosophy of home economics focused on the following:

—*Utilization of modern science to improve home life*
—*Study of humanities to improve home life*
—*Research in order to add to the sum of reliable information*
—*Use of all resources to make home and family life effective parts of the social fabric*
—*Constant emphasis upon the ultimate purpose of controlling the material things and making natural and social forces do our bidding*
—*Provision of an opportunity for creativeness and self-expression in home living*

and that by definition

Home Economics in its most comprehensive sense is the study of laws, conditions, principles and ideals which are concerned on the one hand with man's immediate environment and on the other hand with his nature as a social being, and is the study specifically of the relation between those two factors.

In a narrow sense the study is given to the study of the empirical sciences with a special reference to the practical problems of housework, cooking, etc. (Ferrar 1964:12)

As a result of these early conferences the national organization, American Home Economics Association, was founded in 1908. By this time most land-grant colleges had departments of home economics and the field was recognized by the National Education Association as an academic area appropriate to institutions of higher education.

The establishment in 1912 of a U.S. Children's Bureau gave impetus to the inclusion of child development within the area of home economics. In 1914, 1917, and 1919 federal legislation linked agriculture and home economics together and gave public support and funds to extension, secondary education, and teacher-education programs. The focus was on rural families, which in some ways deterred the development of home economics. Also, legislation may have created an overdependence on agriculture as well as developing a false sense of security that federal funding and accompanying recognition would continue forever. Historically, these legislative acts were a primary force in the rapid extension of home economics programs at the college level and promotion of research in the field.

No special recognition was given to women as women, other than as a member of the family unit, until 1960–62, when the department of home economics at the University of Kansas established an interdisciplinary course called Woman in Contemporary Culture. This was the beginning of interdisciplinary research in home economics with other departments. This trend has continued but has never been realized fully. Today, courses within home economics that might be considered appropriate for a Women's Studies program are very limited.

In summary, home economics can be said to be an applied service field that has evolved from changing forces within our society and focuses on all aspects of the family unit—housing, nutrition, food, child development, human relationships, clothing, textiles, management, decision making, health, safety, self-expression, and consumer economics. The study of these various facets of the field is found at all levels, preschool through adult education. The content deals with principles, concepts, and constructs of cognitive nature with limited emphasis today upon motor skills. The exercise of forceful leadership in support of women in the sense of women's liberation has been lacking.

Research laboratories, classrooms, and extension services are the vehicles for developing and extending home economics content to individuals within the family. This mission has been pursued on a national and an international basis. Throughout its short history, home economics has experienced all the growing pains in establishing itself and identifying what it is.

What is the present status of home economics? Within the academic society, one view of home economics is that it is narrow in scope, has no body of knowledge of its own, and no central purpose. The counter argument is that new knowledge has been synthesized from several disciplines and applied to one of the basic institutions of our society, the family. Another view regarding the present status of home economics is that it has become so fragmented that it would be better to reposition the various fragments within the basic disciplines. For example, the study of family relationships could come within anthropology or sociology. This creates problems because the study of the family as a fully functioning unit within society requires background in economics, biology, psychology, nutrition, housing, etc. Another position is that there is a unified core to home economics and that specialized areas are supportive of and develop from this core.

Within the profession, a similar divergence in points of view can be found. Even the name, home economics, creates a problem—does the name identify the mission? Recent suggestions for name changes reveal this dilemma.

There are additional problems relating to the current status of home economics. Status levels can be found within the profession. Home economics has its caste system even as other professions. Researchers have more prestige than teachers. Areas such as food, nutritional science, are more closely allied to the pure discipline and may deemphasize the area of teacher education. When academicians look at all the academic areas of study, home economics is frequently thought of as near the bottom of the list.

Given the present societal conditions, in what direction should home economics move? Has home economics been fully cognizant of social transformations? How should home economics be organized? All these questions have not yet been answered satisfactorily.

An intensive study of home economics in higher education was completed in 1968. Its conclusion was that "it is a wiser social policy to help and to encourage home economics to adapt to new social needs than to abandon or dismember it as a field of study or to shift its elements to the American system of higher education. Hence, we advocate improving the practice of home economics and extending its beneficial influence to other phases of American life. But delay will be pernicious. Rapid alteration and adaptation are imperative" (McGrath 1968:83–84). A task force of administrators in home economics has defined the following major mission goals for research in home economics:

1. To improve the conditions contributing to man's psychological and social development

2. To improve the conditions contributing to man's physiological health and development

3. To improve the physical components of man's near environment

4. To improve consumer competence and family resource use

5. To improve the quality and availability of community services which enrich family life (National Goals and Guidelines 1970:7)

With this background on the evolution and status of home economics, let us return to examining the profession as it has related to the evolving status of women. Early movements for the emancipation of women began about the same time as home economics emerged. The profession has since become involved in the status of families, which is broader than, but includes, the status of women. From its beginnings at the Lake Placid Conference in 1899, home economics was visualized neither as limited to women nor an attempt to support the restriction of women to one mode of living within American society. From the beginning, men have been members of the field at the professional level, particularly in areas of child development, related art, textiles, housing, family relationships, nutrition, and foods. At the present time, however, male membership constitutes less than 5 percent of the total number of professional home economists.

Throughout the past seventy years, home economics has been encouraging women to utilize their intellectual capabilities beyond the immediate home environment, to act in the community as responsible citizens. The home was viewed as an equally shared responsibility of all members of the family unit. The profession has been involved in federal and state legislation directed toward improving the quality of family life. In 1924 it endorsed the passage of child labor laws. It has currently supported consumer legislation in the areas of housing, clothing and textiles, food and child care.

Particular emphasis is given today to the multiple roles of men and women as homemakers and wage earners. The 1968 Vocational Education Amendment provided federal funds for programs designed to prepare young men and women in occupations related to home economics. Students are exposed to numerous career opportunities, and marriage is not perceived as the ultimate goal for women. In 1971, 42 percent of all women of working age, sixteen years old and over, were gainfully employed (Simpson 1971:60). We do not ignore that women will increasingly be employed outside the home.

Home economics has demonstrated limited yet continuous support, directly and indirectly, for enhancing the status of women. This action has been realized through improving the quality of living for the family unit. The profession has, however, not taken full advantage of political and social forces to exercise the necessary leadership for achieving its goals and becoming a recognized force in improving our society. The following illustration is a case in point. In 1940, amid the surge of patriotism surrounding the war effort in which many women became involved,

> It was very evident that the membership wished to place the services of the Association at the disposal of the government, though the situation had not then developed sufficiently to make specific proposals.

The following was sent to President Roosevelt:

> Whereas the home is the first line for national defense and the center of influence in the development of the democratic way of life, and whereas home economics is concerned with the best use of time, material, and human resources with the family; therefore, resolved that the American Home Economics Association, assembled in annual convention in Cleveland, pledge its support to national defense and urge the President of the United States to utilize the services of its members. (Editorial, Journal of Home Economics 1940:464)

In 1971, somewhat firmer though conservative examples of leadership were taken on the following societal issues:

Abortion: *It was resolved "that the American Home Economics Association support the repeal of laws restricting or prohibiting abortions performed by a duly licensed physician."*

Status of Women: *It was resolved (a) that the American Home Economics Association support both governmental and private efforts to eliminate discrimination on the basis of sex and marital status in educational systems, industry, and government, and (b) to support the equal rights amendment now pending before Congress and (c) that the individual state associations support the establishment and the continuation of commissions on the status of women at the state and national levels.*

Some areas in which home economics has not exercised decisive leadership are: (a) recognizing and actively changing those concepts of home economics that have reinforced class, sex, and value stereotyping; and (b) assuming an active political role in initiating change.

Hopefully, the profession will be more sensitive to the direction of social change and become a cohesive profession exercising leadership in improving those aspects of society that impinge on each and every member of the family.

The development of the status of home economics and of women in general has been similar in that each group has accepted a role given by others. Not until recently has a vigorous attempt been made to be decisive about role image. Both home economists and women in general have usually coped with society by adjustment rather than initiative. In addition, the profession and the women's movement have paralleled in time sequence but had infrequent and brief contacts until recently. Hopefully, in the future the scope will be widened to provide a strong and dedicated mutual support.

REFERENCES

BUDEWIG, CAROLINE, et al. *The Field of Home Economics—What It Is.* AHEA, 1964.

"Council Meetings." *Journal of Home Economics* 16, no. 9 (September 1924): 525.

Editorial. *Journal of Home Economics* 32, no. 7 (September 1940): 464.

FERRAR, BARBARA M. *The History of Home Economics Education in America and Its Implications for Liberal Education.* Ann Arbor: Michigan State University, 1964.

McGRATH, EARL J., AND JOHNSON, JACK T., *The Changing Mission of Home Economics.* New York: Columbia University, Teachers College Press, 1968.

National Goals and Guidelines for Research in Home Economics. Ann Arbor: Michigan State University, 1970.

"Resolutions from the 1971 Annual Meeting." *Journal of Home Economics* 63, no. 6 (September 1971): 473.

SIMPSON, ELIZABETH. "The New Womanhood: Education for Viable Alternatives." In *The Courage to Change*, edited by Roman C. Pucinski and Sharlene P. Hirsch. Englewood Cliffs, N.J.: Prentice-Hall, 1971. Pp. 59–81.